Cisco Networking Academy Program

CCNP 4: Network Troubleshooting Companion Guide

Wayne Lewis, Ph.D.

Cisco Networking Academy Program

Cisco Press

800 East 96th Street

Indianapolis, Indiana 46240 USA

www.ciscopress.com

Cisco Networking Academy Program

CCNP 4: Network Troubleshooting Companion Guide

Cisco Systems, Inc.

Cisco Networking Academy Program

Copyright © 2005 Cisco Systems, Inc.

Published by:
Cisco Press
800 East 96th Street
Indianapolis, Indiana 46240 USA

Printed in the United States of America 2 3 4 5 6 7 8 9 0

Second Printing   January 2005

Library of Congress Cataloging-in-Publication Number: 2003114386

ISBN: 1-58713-141-2

Trademark Acknowledgments

All terms mentioned in this book that are known to be trademarks or service marks have been appropriately capitalized. Cisco Press or Cisco Systems, Inc. cannot attest to the accuracy of this information. Use of a term in this book should not be regarded as affecting the validity of any trademark or service mark.

Warning and Disclaimer

This book is designed to provide information about the Cisco Networking Academy Program CCNP 4: Network Troubleshooting course. Every effort has been made to make this book as complete and accurate as possible, but no warranty or fitness is implied.

The information is provided on an "as is" basis. The author, Cisco Press, and Cisco Systems, Inc. shall have neither liability nor responsibility to any person or entity with respect to any loss or damages arising from the information contained in this book or from the use of the disks or programs that may accompany it.

The opinions expressed in this book belong to the author and are not necessarily those of Cisco Systems, Inc.

This book is part of the Cisco Networking Academy® Program series from Cisco Press. The products in this series support and complement the Cisco Networking Academy Program curriculum. If you are using this book outside the Networking Academy program, then you are not preparing with a Cisco trained and authorized Networking Academy provider.

For information on the Cisco Networking Academy Program or to locate a Networking Academy, please visit www.cisco.com/edu.

Corporate and Government Sales

Cisco Press offers excellent discounts on this book when ordered in quantity for bulk purchases or special sales.

For more information please contact:

U.S. Corporate and Government Sales   1-800-382-3419 corpsales@pearsontechgroup.com

For sales outside the U.S. please contact:

International Sales international@pearsoned.com

Feedback Information

At Cisco Press, our goal is to create in-depth technical books of the highest quality and value. Each book is crafted with care and precision, undergoing rigorous development that involves the unique expertise of members of the professional technical community.

Reader feedback is a natural continuation of this process. If you have any comments on how we could improve the quality of this book, or otherwise alter it to better suit your needs, you can contact us through e-mail at feedback@ciscopress.com. Please be sure to include the book title and ISBN in your message.

We greatly appreciate your assistance.

Publisher	John Wait
Editor-in-Chief	John Kane
Executive Editor	Mary Beth Ray
Cisco Representative	Anthony Wolfenden
Cisco Press Program Manager	Sonia Torres Chavez
Production Manager	Patrick Kanouse
Development Editor	Allison Beaumont Johnson
Project Editor	Marc Fowler
Copy Editor	Gayle Johnson
Technical Editors	Troy Nakagawa, David Planchard, Rob Rummel
Cover Designer	Louisa Adair
Compositor	Octal Publishing, Inc.
Indexer	Larry Sweazy

CISCO SYSTEMS

Corporate Headquarters
Cisco Systems, Inc.
170 West Tasman Drive
San Jose, CA 95134-1706
USA
www.cisco.com
Tel: 408 526-4000
    800 553-NETS (6387)
Fax: 408 526-4100

European Headquarters
Cisco Systems International BV
Haarlerbergpark
Haarlerbergweg 13-19
1101 CH Amsterdam
The Netherlands
www-europe.cisco.com
Tel: 31 0 20 357 1000
Fax: 31 0 20 357 1100

Americas Headquarters
Cisco Systems, Inc.
170 West Tasman Drive
San Jose, CA 95134-1706
USA
www.cisco.com
Tel: 408 526-7660
Fax: 408 527-0883

Asia Pacific Headquarters
Cisco Systems, Inc.
Capital Tower
168 Robinson Road
#22-01 to #29-01
Singapore 068912
www.cisco.com
Tel: +65 6317 7777
Fax: +65 6317 7799

Cisco Systems has more than 200 offices in the following countries and regions. Addresses, phone numbers, and fax numbers are listed on the **Cisco.com Web site at www.cisco.com/go/offices.**

Argentina • Australia • Austria • Belgium • Brazil • Bulgaria • Canada • Chile • China PRC • Colombia • Costa Rica • Croatia • Czech Republic • Denmark • Dubai, UAE • Finland • France • Germany • Greece • Hong Kong SAR • Hungary • India • Indonesia • Ireland • Israel • Italy • Japan • Korea • Luxembourg • Malaysia • Mexico • The Netherlands • New Zealand • Norway • Peru • Philippines • Poland • Portugal • Puerto Rico • Romania • Russia • Saudi Arabia • Scotland • Singapore • Slovakia • Slovenia • South Africa • Spain • Sweden • Switzerland • Taiwan • Thailand • Turkey • Ukraine • United Kingdom • United States • Venezuela • Vietnam • Zimbabwe

About the Author

Wayne Lewis is the Cisco Academy Manager for the Pacific Center for Advanced Technology Training, based at Honolulu Community College. Since 1998, he has taught routing and switching, remote access, troubleshooting, network security, and wireless networking to instructors from universities, colleges, and high schools in Australia, Canada, Central America, China, Hong Kong, Indonesia, Japan, Mexico, Singapore, South America, Taiwan, and the United States, both onsite and at HCC. Before teaching computer networking, he began teaching math at age 20 at Wichita State University, followed by the University of Hawaii and HCC. He received a Ph.D. in math from the University of Hawaii in 1992. He works as a contractor for Cisco Systems, developing curriculum for the Academy program. He enjoys surfing the North Shore of Oahu when he's not distracted by work.

About the Technical Reviewers

Troy Nakagawa, CCIE No. 4132, is a Senior Systems Engineer for Cisco Systems. He focuses on enterprise customers to develop advanced solutions. He has five years of voice experience as a telecommunications technician, has completed a telecommunications apprenticeship program, and has an FCC General Radiotelephone Operator License. He has two years of mainframe experience as an operations analyst and eight years of Cisco experience as a systems engineer working for Cisco Systems.

David Planchard is the Vice President of Technology at D&M Education in Hopkinton, Massachusetts. He has a bachelor of science degree in mechanical engineering from Northeastern University and a master of science from WPI. He holds the Cisco certifications of CCNA, CCAI, and CCNP in advanced routing. He holds five U.S. patents and one international patent. He has written and published numerous technical papers and seven books on networking and 3D SolidWorks modeling. He teaches Cisco certification classes at Cisco Systems Inc. in Boxbough, Massachusetts.

Rob Rummel, CCIE No. 9012, is a presales engineer at Envision Networked Solutions in Hawaii. His focus is on designing converged voice, video, and data solutions and providing engineering support to account executives in the presales process. He has more than 15 years of networking and telecommunications experience. He has a diverse background, ranging from serving eight years in the Navy to operating a satellite teleport.

Overview

Table of Contents

Cisco Systems Networking Icon Legend

Cisco Systems, Inc. uses a standardized set of icons to represent devices in network topology illustrations. The following icon legend shows the most commonly used icons you will encounter throughout this book.

Command Syntax Conventions

The conventions used to present command syntax in this book are the same conventions used in the Cisco IOS software Command Reference. The Command Reference describes these conventions as follows:

- **Bold** indicates commands and keywords that are entered exactly as shown.
- *Italic* indicates arguments for which you supply values.
- Vertical bars (|) separate alternative, mutually exclusive elements.
- Square brackets ([ ]) indicate an optional element.
- Braces ({ }) indicate a required choice.
- Braces within brackets ([{ }]) indicate a required choice within an optional element.

Introduction

This Companion Guide is designed as a desk reference to supplement your classroom and laboratory experience with version 3.0 of the CCNP 4 course in the Cisco Networking Academy Program.

CCNP 4: Network Troubleshooting Version 3.0 is the last of four courses leading to the Cisco Certified Network Professional certification. The goal of CCNP 4 is to provide you with hands-on experience in troubleshooting suboptimal performance in a converged network. The content is an integral part of any approach to obtaining the technical proficiency of Cisco Certified Network Professional (CCNP). CCNP 4 deepens your technical ability rather than introducing new baseline technology.

While taking the course, use this Companion Guide to help you prepare for the Cisco Internetwork Troubleshooting 642-831 CIT exam, which is one of the required exams to obtain the CCNP certification.

This Book's Goal

The goal of this book is to build on the concepts you learned while studying for the BSCI, BCRAN, and BCMSN exams and to teach you the troubleshooting tools successfully implemented by network engineers in modern internetworks. The topics are designed to prepare you to pass the Cisco Internetwork Troubleshooting exam (642-831 CIT).

The Cisco Internetwork Troubleshooting exam is a qualifying exam for the CCNP certification. The 642-831 CIT exam tests materials covered under the new Cisco Internetwork Troubleshooting course and exam objectives. The exam certifies that the successful candidate has the knowledge and skills necessary to troubleshoot suboptimal performance in a converged network environment. The exam covers establishing a baseline, determining an effective troubleshooting strategy, resolving problems at the physical and data-link layers, resolving problems at the network layer, and resolving problems at the transport and application layers.

The key methodologies used in this book are to help you discover the exam topics you need to review in more depth, to help you fully understand and remember those details, and to help you prove to yourself that you have retained your knowledge of those topics. This book does not try to help you pass by memorization; it helps you truly learn and understand the topics. This book focuses on introducing techniques and technology for implementing troubleshooting solutions. To fully benefit from this book, you should be familiar with general networking terms and concepts and should have basic knowledge of the following:

- Cisco router operation and configuration
- TCP/IP operation and configuration

- Routing protocols such as RIPv1, RIPv2, OSPF, IS-IS, IGRP, EIGRP, and BGP

- Remote-access networks, including ISDN and Frame Relay

- Building and maintaining a multilayer campus switched infrastructure

This Book's Audience

This book has a few different audiences. First, it is intended for students who are interested in network troubleshooting. In particular, it is targeted toward students in the Cisco Networking Academy Program CCNP 4: Network Troubleshooting course. In the classroom, this book serves as a supplement to the online curriculum. This book is also appropriate for corporate training, faculty and staff, and general users.

This book is useful for network administrators who are responsible for implementing and troubleshooting Cisco routers in enterprise networks. Furthermore, it is valuable for anyone who is interested in learning advanced network troubleshooting techniques and passing the Cisco Internetwork Troubleshooting exam (CIT 642-831).

This Book's Features

Many of this book's features help facilitate a full understanding of the topics covered in this book:

- **Objectives**—Each chapter starts with a list of objectives that you should have mastered by the end of the chapter. The objectives reference the key concepts covered in the chapter.

- **Figures, examples, tables, and scenarios**—This book contains figures, examples, and tables that help explain theories, concepts, commands, and setup sequences that reinforce concepts and help you visualize the content covered in the chapter. In addition, the specific scenarios provide real-life situations that detail the problem and its solution.

- **Chapter summaries**—At the end of each chapter is a summary of the concepts covered in the chapter. It provides a synopsis of the chapter and serves as a study aid.

- **Key terms**—Each chapter includes a list of defined key terms that are covered in the chapter. The key terms appear in color throughout the chapter where they are used in context. The definitions of these terms serve as a study aid. In addition, the key terms reinforce the concepts introduced in the chapter and help you understand the chapter material before you move on to new concepts.

- **Check Your Understanding questions and answers**—Review questions, presented at the end of each chapter, serve as a self-assessment tool. They reinforce the concepts introduced in the chapter and help test your understanding before you move on to a new chapter. An answer key to all the questions is provided in Appendix A, "Check Your Understanding Answer Key."

- **Certification exam practice questions**—To further assess your understanding, you will find on the companion CD-ROM a test bank of questions exclusive to Cisco Press that covers the full range of exam topics published by Cisco Systems for the CCNP CIT 642-831 exam. The robust test engine is powered by Boson Software, Inc.

- **Skill-building activities**—Throughout the book are references to additional skill-building activities to connect theory with practice. You can easily spot these activities by the following icon:

Lab Activity

The collection of lab activities developed for the course can be found in the *Cisco Networking Academy Program CCNP 4: Network Troubleshooting Lab Companion.*

How This Book Is Organized

Although you could read this book cover to cover, it is designed to be flexible and to allow you to easily move between chapters and sections of chapters to cover just the material you need to work with more. If you do intend to read all the chapters, the order in which they are presented is the ideal sequence. This book also contains two appendixes. The following list summarizes the topics of this book's elements:

- **Chapter 1, "Documenting and Baselining the Network"**—To effectively trouble-shoot a network, you must first establish a baseline. The baseline information will be included in the network documentation. This chapter discusses the basic requirements of establishing a baseline and creating a coherent set of network documentation.

- **Chapter 2, "Troubleshooting Methodologies and Tools"**—Troubleshooting net-works is more important than ever. As time goes on, services continue to be added to networks. With each added service come more variables. This adds to the complexity of the network troubleshooting as well as the network itself. Organizations increasingly depend on network administrators and network engineers who have strong trouble-shooting skills.

  Troubleshooting begins by looking at a methodology that breaks the process of trouble-shooting into manageable pieces. This permits a systematic approach, minimizes con-fusion, and cuts down on time otherwise wasted with trial-and-error troubleshooting.

Network engineers, administrators, and support personnel realize that troubleshooting is the process that takes the greatest percentage of their time. This chapter presents efficient troubleshooting techniques to help you shorten your overall troubleshooting time when working in a production environment.

- **Chapter 3, "Troubleshooting at the Physical Layer"**—Problems that occur at Layer 1 are distinctly different from problems that occur at higher layers. The physical layer is the only layer with physically tangible properties such as wires, cards, and antennas. In this chapter, identifiable characteristics and commands are used to isolate and correct problems at the physical layer.

- **Chapter 4, "Layer 2 Troubleshooting"**—Troubleshooting Layer 2 problems can be a challenging process. Although data link protocols are usually quite simple, the configuration and operation of these protocols is critical to creating a functional, well-tuned network.

  This chapter explores the following Layer 2 protocols and technologies and outlines troubleshooting strategies for and common problems with each:

  - Switching protocols and switched technologies
  - ISDN
  - Frame Relay
  - PPP

- **Chapter 5, "Layer 3 Troubleshooting"**—This chapter focuses on the most common troubleshooting issues related to static routing and dynamic routing. Troubleshooting dynamic routing protocols is supplemented by exploring issues common to most routing protocols. Considerable detail is afforded to the analysis of troubleshooting issues specific to the individual routing protocols RIPv1, RIPv2, IGRP, EIGRP, OSPF, IS-IS, and BGP. This chapter also analyzes troubleshooting issues pertaining to route redistribution.

- **Chapter 6, "Layer 4 Troubleshooting"**—This chapter covers the operation of various transport-layer networking technologies used on routers and hosts, including

  - TCP
  - UDP
  - NetBIOS
  - NAT
  - Extended access lists

  This chapter also discusses tools and methodologies you can use to help you troubleshoot transport-layer networking issues.

- **Chapter 7, "Layer 1–7 Troubleshooting"**—The primary responsibility of the upper layers of the OSI model is to provide services such as e-mail, file transfer, and data transport. Application layer problems result when data is not delivered to the destination or when network performance degrades to a level where productivity is affected.

  The same general troubleshooting process used to isolate problems at the lower layers can be used to isolate problems at the application layer. The ideas are the same, but the technological focus shifts to include things such as refused or timed-out connections, access lists, and DNS issues. Specifically, this chapter explores troubleshooting Telnet, HTTP, e-mail, FTP, DHCP, NTP, Syslog, and DNS.

- **Appendix A, "Check Your Understanding Answer Key"**—This appendix provides the answers to the quizzes that appear at the end of each chapter.

- **Appendix B, "Catalyst OS Troubleshooting"**—This appendix provides information on troubleshooting common issues on the Catalyst 6000/6500 series switches running in hybrid mode: CatOS on the Supervisor Engine and IOS on the Multilayer Switch Feature Card (MSFC).

- **Glossary of Key Terms**—Provides a compiled list of all the key terms that appear throughout the book.

About the CD-ROM

The CD-ROM included with this book contains a test engine by Boson Software, Inc. with a total of 200 multiple choice, drag and drop, and fill in the blank practice exam questions that are exclusive to Cisco Press. The questions cover the full range of exam topics published by Cisco Systems for the CCNP CIT 642-831 exam. Boson Software, Inc. is a software and training company specializing in test preparation and hands-on skills acquisition product development. Boson was among the first software vendors to support Cisco certifications, and is now an authorized Cisco Learning Partner as well as Premier Reseller. Additional Boson practice tests, simulation products, and other study aids are available at www.boson.com <http://www.boson.com>.

Objectives

After completing this chapter, you will be able to perform tasks related to the following:

- Know the purpose of and methodology for network baselining
- Be familiar with the elements of network configuration documentation
- Be familiar with the elements of a topology diagram
- Be familiar with the elements of an end-system configuration table
- Be familiar with the elements of an end-system topology table

Chapter 1

Documenting and Baselining the Network

A network *baseline* is a collection of data used to determine where opportunities exist for optimizing the network environment. A network baseline is used to decide whether to make recommendations to add bandwidth or introduce quality of service (QoS) to enhance services. To effectively troubleshoot a network, a baseline must first be established. The baseline information is included in the network documentation. This chapter discusses the basic requirements for establishing a baseline and creating a coherent set of network documentation.

Some of the biggest challenges facing the IT world are the expenses incurred as a result of network outages. The negative impact of these expenses makes it a high priority of network professionals to be able to diagnose and correct a network problem as efficiently as possible. To assist in accomplishing this, a baseline must be established to provide a snapshot of the configuration of a network while it is performing at an acceptable level. Using baseline information as a standard reduces the time that a troubleshooter needs to spend learning about the network's structure and configuration. It also helps troubleshooters know when they have reached the goal of returning the network to its baseline level. Without a baseline, troubleshooters have to guess and estimate whether they have reached their goal. Troubleshooting in this manner is haphazard and inefficient.

Network Baselining

When networks are first designed and installed, user requirements are gathered, analyzed, and translated into a network topology that satisfies the user requirements. The user requirements may be further extended into network performance goals such as bandwidth utilization, network latency and delay, and collision and error thresholds. To validate and document that the goals were achieved, specialized network monitoring and data collection are required. The process of collecting data to be used as a reference for future decision-making and troubleshooting is called *baselining*. The interpretation of the collected data is called *baseline analysis*, or performance analysis.

Network Baselining Overview

Baselining allows you to discover the network's true performance and operation in terms of the policies that have been defined. You can identify performance trends and faults by comparing future performance metrics to the baseline metrics.

After you identify data of interest for a policy, baselining gives you a snapshot of the current state of variables throughout the network. Establishing a baseline for a network provides answers to the following questions:

- How does the network perform day to day?
- Which areas are underutilized or overutilized?
- What errors are occurring most?
- What thresholds should be set for the devices that need to be monitored?
- Can the network deliver the identified policies?
- What are acceptable network errors?

The purpose of conducting a network baseline is to measure the initial performance and availability of critical network devices and links to compare them to future performance. The baseline allows a network administrator to determine the difference between abnormal behavior and proper network performance. It also provides insight into whether the current network design can deliver the required policies.

The task of baselining can best be accomplished in large, complex networks, using sophisticated network management software with integrated remote monitoring network devices. In simpler networks, these data collection tasks might require a combination of hand collection of data, augmented with simple network protocol inspectors such as Fluke Protocol Expert or other shareware utilities that can be downloaded from the Internet at sites such as http://www.statscout.com. Ethereal is a protocol analyzer you can download from www.ethereal.com. Sniffer is a commercial product for protocol analysis—see http://www.networkassociates.com/us/products/sniffer/home.asp. Selected examples of tools that may be used for baselining are discussed in Chapter 2, "Troubleshooting Methodologies and Tools"; outputs for one of these tools are illustrated in Figures 1-1, 1-2, and 1-3. In Figure 1-3, the colors represent different protocols active on the network.

Figure 1-1 Protocol Analyzers Can Display Network Utilization

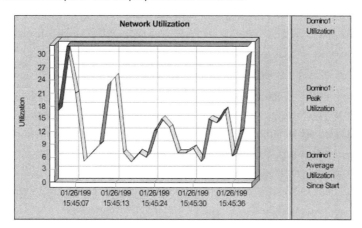

Figure 1-2 Protocol Analyzers Can Display Ethernet Statistics as a Function of MAC Addresses

Nodename/ Address	Total # Bytes	Total # Frames	Avg Size	Min Frame	Max Frame
00000AAA.0000C0931C95	4085530	9043	451	64	1092
00000AAA.00AA003EF4A0	3903568	40581	96	66	498
198.85.45.254	999236	2889	345	64	550
0000AAA1.02000000BADC	833189	10309	80	64	1082
00000AAA.0080E5700FB3	381322	2067	184	66	498
00000AAA.0000C0736CB8	268409	1290	208	66	544
00000AAA.00AA005942F5	271338	1506	180	66	498
00000AAA.02000000BADC	266826	1481	180	66	498
00000AAA.00AA005944E0	258637	1447	178	66	498
00000AAA.02000000BADB	257485	1447	177	66	498
0000DDD1.02000000BADB	203744	2042	99	64	570
00022AAA.0080E5700FB3	197853	937	211	98	501
08022AAA.00AA003EF4A0	179533	790	225	98	501

Station Statistics - LAN:D1

Figure 1-3 Protocol Analyzers Can Display Protocol Distribution as a Pie Chart

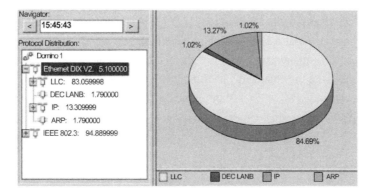

The collected data reveals the true nature of congestion or potential congestion in a network. It also might reveal underutilized areas in the network. Analysis after an initial baseline tends to reveal hidden problems and quite often can lead to network redesign efforts based on quality and capacity observations. Another reason for conducting a baseline is that no two networks operate or behave the same way.

Without a baseline, no standard exists to measure the optimum nature of network traffic and congestion levels. Establishing an initial baseline or conducting a performance monitoring analysis by collecting current data and comparing it to the baseline requires sufficient time to accurately reflect network performance. Network management software or protocol inspectors and sniffers might run continuously over the course of the data collection process. Manual collection by way of **show** commands on individual network devices is extremely time-consuming and should be limited to mission-critical network devices.

The following sections describe the general methodology for defining, collecting, and reporting a network performance baseline. This entails the collection of key performance data from the ports and devices considered to be mission-critical. The baseline is a vital preliminary step in determining the network's personality. It also simplifies the setting of effective thresholds.

The following are steps to building and using a baseline:

- Planning for the first baseline
- Identifying devices and ports of interest
- Determining the baseline's duration
- Using the baseline data
- Identifying undesired network behavior
- Identifying thresholds
- Predicting long-term performance and capacity trends
- Verifying policies

Planning for the First Baseline

When conducting the initial baseline, start by selecting a few variables that represent the defined policies. If too many data points are selected, the amount of data can be overwhelming, making analysis of the collected data difficult. Hence, start out simple, and fine-tune along the way. Generally, some good starting measures are interface utilization, shown in Figure 1-4, and CPU utilization, shown in Figure 1-5.

Figure 1-4 Interface Utilization Should Be Recorded in a Baseline

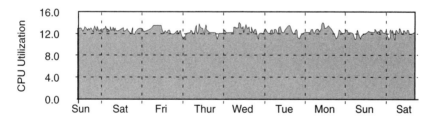

Figure 1-5 CPU Utilization Should Be Recorded in a Baseline

Weekly Graph (30-Minute Average)

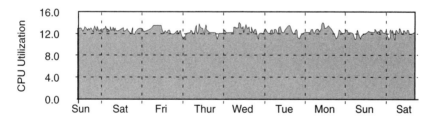

Max 1 min. Load: 14% Average 1 min. Load: 12% Current 1 min. Load: 12%
Max 5 min. Load: 14% Average 5 min. Load: 12% Current 5 min. Load: 13%

Collect data for a day or two before starting the actual baseline study to determine whether the right data is being gathered from the right devices. After recording a couple of days' worth of data, graph the collected data in different ways to better show where the network needs improvement. Slicing through the data in different ways can reveal interesting and sometimes surprising observations.

Pick the top few reports that are relevant, and study them to determine whether you need more information to understand a particular pattern or trend. Then, fine-tune the data to be collected, and begin the actual baseline study.

Baseline analysis of the network should be conducted on a regular basis. Perform an annual analysis of the entire network, or baseline different sections of the network on a rotating basis. You must conduct analysis regularly to understand how the network is affected by growth and other changes. In some cases, recurring baselines will replace the previous baselines, and in other cases, the recurring baselines will be equally relevant for continued analysis and troubleshooting. In any case, all baselines should be recorded as part of the network documentation.

Gathering the information in a consistent manner and analyzing the data allows informed design decisions and expedites fault isolation.

Identifying Devices and Ports of Interest

As part of planning a baseline, you must identify the devices and ports of interest. Figure 1-6 shows devices detected by the Fluke Network Inspector software. Ports of interest include network device ports that connect to other network devices, servers, key users, and anything else considered critical to the operation. If you narrow the ports polled, the reports will be clearer, and network and device management load will be minimized. Remember that an interface on a router or switch can be a virtual interface (see Figure 1-7), such as a switch virtual interface (SVI).

After the ports have been identified, you must ensure that processes are in place either to keep that connection from being changed or to generate a report informing the network administrator that a change has occurred. Without this assurance, reports will become inaccurate. A report might indicate that a backbone port on a particular device is performing fine, when in fact, the device connected to that port is not a router, but a PC, because of an undocumented change.

One method to track the ports of interest is to use the port description fields on devices to indicate what is connected. If backbone Router A is connected to Catalyst 6509 switch port 1/1 on the main campus, the port description on switch port 1/1 should be configured for the device (Router A) on the other end. The port description can then be used to add clarity to the reports created from the baseline and to monitor performance. Carefully worded port descriptions are a huge time saver.

Figure 1-6 Network Management Software Can Be Used to Compile a Database of Devices on the Network

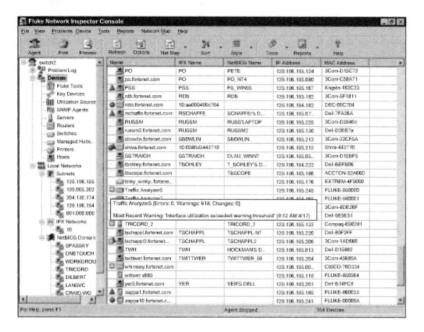

Figure 1-7 Ports of Interest Include Virtual Interfaces, Such as Switch Virtual Interfaces

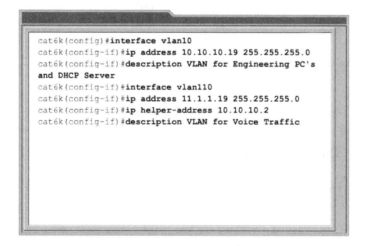

```
cat6k(config)#interface vlan10
cat6k(config-if)#ip address 10.10.10.19 255.255.255.0
cat6k(config-if)#description VLAN for Engineering PC's
and DHCP Server
cat6k(config-if)#interface vlan110
cat6k(config-if)#ip address 11.1.1.19 255.255.255.0
cat6k(config-if)#ip helper-address 10.10.10.2
cat6k(config-if)#description VLAN for Voice Traffic
```

Determining the Duration of the Baseline

It is important that the length of time and the baseline information being gathered are sufficient to establish a typical picture of the network. This period should be at least seven days so that you can capture any daily or weekly trends. Weekly trends are just as important as daily or hourly trends.

For example, suppose the engineers in Building 7 run a massive backup and software refresh on Sundays at 2 P.M. on all 200 of their workstations. Because the backup server is in Building 9, the push and backup saturate the corporate backbone. If the baseline were performed only Monday through Friday, the saturation would be missed.

A baseline needs to last no more than six weeks unless specific long-term trends need to be measured. Generally, a two-to-four-week baseline is adequate.

Examples of baselines for CPU utilization over various intervals of time can be provided by the Multi-Router Traffic Grapher (MRTG), as shown in Figures 1-8 to 1-11. This tool can be found at http://www.mrtg.hdl.com/mrtg.html.

Figure 1-8 MRTG Can Display in Terms of 5-Minute Averages

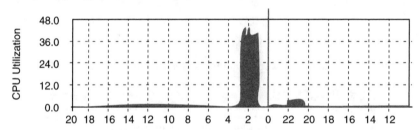

Daily Graph (5-Minute Average)

Max Load: 46% Average Load: 3% Current Load: 1%

Figure 1-9 MRTG Can Display in Terms of 30-Minute Averages

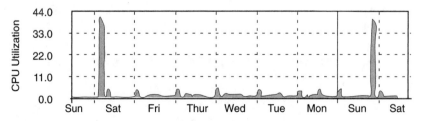

Weekly Graph (30-Minute Average)

Max Load: 43% Average Load: 2% Current Load: 1%

Figure 1-10 MRTG Can Display in Terms of 2-Hour Averages

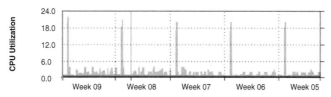

Monthly Graph (2-Hour Average)

Max Load: **43%**   Average Load: **2%**   Current Load: **1%**

Figure 1-11 MRTG Can Display in Terms of 1-Day Averages

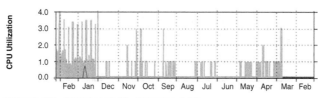

Yearly Graph (1-Day Average)

Max Load: **43%**   Average Load: **0%**   Current Load: **1%**

It is recommended that you not perform baseline measurement during times of unique traffic patterns. For example, it would not be beneficial to perform the baseline over a holiday or during December if most of the company is on vacation.

Using the Baseline Data

This is where all the attention to detail when collecting baseline information pays off. Policies have been defined, including variables that measure the policies. Also, data has been collected from critical devices and connections for a period of time. By performing baseline tests on the network, you can better understand the capacity and QoS a network delivers. Now it is time to analyze the snapshot.

You can use the data in the following ways to learn more about the network:

- Identifying undesired network behavior
- Identifying thresholds for fault and performance monitoring
- Predicting long-term performance and capacity trends
- Verifying policies

Identifying Undesired Network Behavior

An immediate benefit of baselining the network is the objective identification of undesired network behavior. By generating reports that identify the most-used lines, you can readily identify areas of the network that are either experiencing problems or that are prime candidates for failure, as shown in Figure 1-12.

Figure 1-12 Per-Port Bandwidth Utilization Statistics Are Very Useful for Troubleshooting

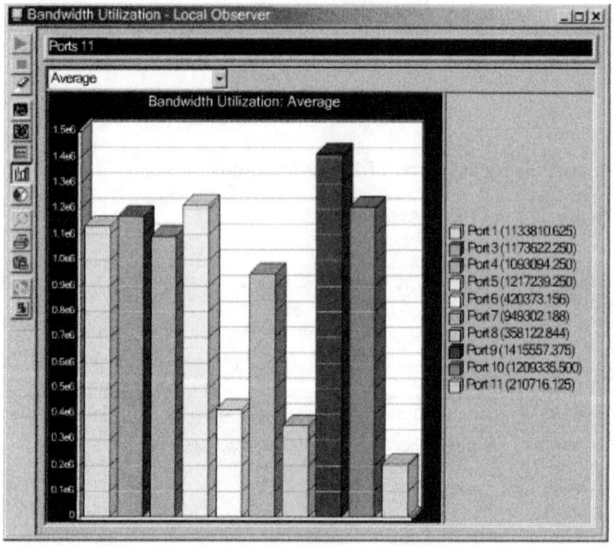

At the same time, underused areas of the network can be identified. Where redundancy is involved, you might discover that traffic is routing almost entirely over only one of the redundant connections. This might be undesirable, because the bandwidth could be almost doubled in a properly configured network with load sharing.

The identification of undesired network behavior might lead to a network redesign or a change in network policy. You also might discover that a device is configured incorrectly.

Identifying Thresholds

Efficient troubleshooting requires setting *thresholds* that reflect different warning levels, as shown in Figure 1-13. Arriving at the appropriate thresholds for each of the network policies requires a baseline analysis. Thresholds are set according to network policies resulting from a baseline analysis. In the figure, the Expert Thresholds tab lists utilization and packet counts.

Figure 1-13 Thresholds Are Set According to Network Policies Resulting from a Baseline Analysis

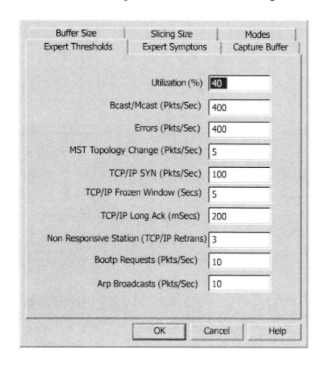

Initially, most network administrators consult the network device documentation or vendor technical support for a set of recommended or default thresholds. Generally, the answer received is "It depends—the thresholds vary according to individual networks."

Unfortunately, the nature of distributed networking makes the process of identifying or predicting a fault somewhat of an art form. Vendors who develop performance and fault tools might provide a set of defaults. Generally you must fine-tune these default settings to meet the needs of individual networks.

The baseline analysis provides the data to study performance and fault patterns over a period of time. From this data, you can determine the appropriate thresholds as they apply to network policies.

Predicting Long-Term Performance and Capacity Trends

As part of the planning cycle for the network, you must study network growth over a period of time. This study will help you understand how the network might continue to grow and will provide data that might help you obtain funds for network expansion.

As stated earlier, baseline studies should be scheduled on a regular basis. By comparing the data from each baseline, you can isolate long-term growth trends.

These types of reports tend to be reported in terms of total bandwidth or total capacity for each link, for each device, and for the network as a whole, as shown in Figure 1-14.

Figure 1-14 Total Bandwidth Utilization Is Used to Predict Long-Term Network Growth

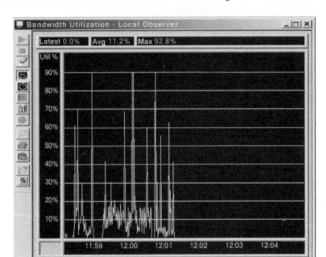

Network growth tends to occur in large bursts. Monitoring the hardware components is just one aspect of maintaining the network's performance. The network administrator must also coordinate the use and upgrade of software applications, adjusting the network configuration accordingly.

Verifying Policies

Determining whether a policy can be achieved in the network is a good use of a network baseline. By reporting the data in terms of the defined policies, you can determine whether the network is adhering to or violating a policy, and to what degree adherence or violations are occurring.

Figure 1-15 displays a sample network policy. A network policy often specifies the consequences of policy violations.

Figure 1-15 A Network Policy Often Specifies the Consequences of Policy Violations

MSCNS Netwok Policy Statement

The MSCNS network consists of over 500 manageable network devices and contains more than 10,000 network nodes. It contains public domain space on WUSTL.EDU and also private space on WUCON.WUSTL.EDU. It is complex in nature, utilizing the latest technologies in routing, switching and security. Managing this network requires staff trained in these areas, equipping them with the proper management tools, and paying strict attention to the details. There can be many things that degrade the performance of the network: security exploits, excessive utilization, and improper configuration of network devices, are just a few. MSCNS strives to control as many of the variables as possible and, in attempting to do so, has instituted the following policy.

MSCNS prohibits the attachment of any network device, to include routers, switches, repeaters, wireless access-points, and firewalls to any point of the network that MSCNS manages. These devices if configured improperly will degrade network performance, pose security threats, and, in some cases, cause the network to become unstable. We ask that departments who choose MSCNS as their network service provider do not build a network infrastructure using the above devices on top of the MSCNS network. Experience has shown that we can not provide the level of service required if we allow these devices to be put on the network and managed by personnel other than MSCNS. In addition to the network instabilities that can occur, the manpower needed to isolate problems to these errant devices is large and MSCNS is not staffed accordingly. Experience has shown that trouble calls received due to these devices causes MSCNS to spend many exhaustive hours in pursuit of a problem that originates from a source that is not under our administrative control. Inevitably, MSCNS is involved in solving a problem that is not associated with its administrative domain at the expense of the goals and objective set by its staff. To devote resources to solving these types of problems would degrade the level of service that we provide.

If the data reflects a policy violation, the issue must be resolved:

- How serious is the violation?
- How often does it occur?
- How long does it last?
- Is the source of the violation an incorrect configuration?

Either the policy must be redefined based on what the network currently delivers, or a network redesign might be required.

If the study reveals the need for a network redesign, you can use data from the baseline analysis objectively to justify the need for new equipment or service purchases.

Network Configuration Documentation

When troubleshooting a network, a troubleshooter uses a baseline to efficiently diagnose and correct network problems. A network's baseline information is captured in documentation such as network configuration tables and topology diagrams. This section discusses the creation of relevant and accurate network documentation as a troubleshooting tool for returning an underperforming, or failing, network to an acceptable condition. The information contained in this section assumes a worst-case scenario in which the network administrator is almost completely unfamiliar with a network and needs to create documentation from scratch.

Network Configuration Documentation Overview

Useful network documentation facilitates more effective troubleshooting, thereby saving you time and effort. When the network configuration is failing or underperforming, a network configuration table provides a saved configuration that should perform at an acceptable level. Network documentation also eliminates the time-consuming and error-prone process of creating a network configuration from scratch.

Network configuration documentation should include elements that provide a logical diagram of the network and detailed information about each component. The troubleshooter should find this information in a single location, either hard copy or on the network at a protected Web site. At a minimum, network documentation should include the following details:

- Network configuration tables
- Network topology diagrams

Note that it is now common practice to compile network documentation on a Web site, as shown in Figure 1-16.

Figure 1-16 It Is Useful to Maintain Network Documentation on a Secure Web site

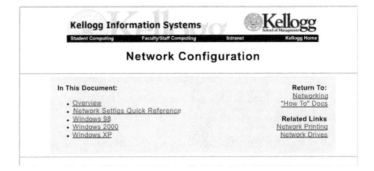

Identifying the Components of a Network Configuration Table

A *network configuration table* contains accurate, up-to-date records of the hardware and software used in a network. The network configuration table should provide the troubleshooter with all the information necessary to identify and correct the network fault.

When a network configuration table is created for troubleshooting, the contents vary, depending on the type of device that is documented. A minimum amount of data should be included for all components:

- The type of device and model designation
- The device network host name

- The device's location (building, floor, room, rack, and panel)
- If it is a modular device, include all the module types and in which module slot they are located
- Data-link layer addresses
- Network layer addresses
- Any additional important information about the device's physical aspects

Because of the complex nature of most networks, a great deal of information could be recorded. For simplicity and efficiency, network configuration tables should group information based on the layers of the OSI networking model, as shown in Table 1-1. Tools such as CiscoWorks can also be used to track the information just listed, as well as IOS versions on the network.

Network documentation varies depending on its purpose and the types of devices that are being documented. A configuration table constructed for budgetary purposes might include the serial number, date of purchase, cost, vendor, and warranty expiration date. These items would not benefit a troubleshooter and should be maintained in separate tables.

Table 1-1 Information in a Network Configuration Table

Category	Data
Device configuration	Device name
	CPU type
	Quantity of Flash installed
	IOS version and feature set
Physical layer	CPU type
	Flash memory
	DRAM
	MAC addresses
	Media types
	Speed
	Duplex
	Trunk or access status
	Interface/port identifier

continues

Table 1-1 Information in a Network Configuration Table (Continued)

Category	Data
Data-link layer	Device name
	Device model
	MAC addresses
	Duplex
	Port identifier
	STP state
	PortFast state
	EtherChannel
Network layer	IP address
	Secondary IP address
	Subnet mask
	Routing protocols
	Access lists
	VLANs
	Neighboring devices
	Interface names
	Username/password

Configuration table contents also vary depending on the features implemented on the devices. The Router ID is an important piece of information to record about a router running OSPF. However, the Router ID would not be recorded if only EIGRP were running.

Table 1-2 displays an example of a network configuration table for a router. Table 1-3 documents an example of a network configuration table for a switch.

Table 1-2 Sample Network Configuration Table for a Router

Device Name, Model	Interface Name	MAC Address	IP Address/ Subnet Mask	IP Routing Protocol(s)	Location Information	IOS Version
Etna, Cisco 1760V	Fa0/0	0007.8580.a159	10.2.3.1/16	EIGRP 10		
	Fa0/1	0007.8580.a160	10.0.1.1/16	EIGRP 10		
	S0/1	—	192.168.34.1/24	OSPF		
	S1/1	—	172.18.1.1/16	EIGRP 10		
Vesuvius, Cisco 2611XM	S0/1	—	192.168.34.2/24	OSPF		
	S1/1	—	172.18.1.1/16	EIGRP 10		

Table 1-3 Sample Network Configuration Table for a Switch

Catalyst Name, Model, Management IP Address	Port Name	Speed	Duplex	STP State	Port- Fast	Trunk Status	Ether- Channel	VLANs	Key	Location Information	IOS Version
Burlington, WS-3550-24-SMI, 10.3.2.33/27	Fa0/1	10	Full	Fwd	No	On	1	1			
	Fa0/2	100	Full	Block	No	Off	1	1			
	Fa0/3	100	Half	Fwd	Yes	Off		4			
	Fa0/4	100	Auto	Fwd	No	On	L2	1			

continues

Table 1-3 Sample Network Configuration Table for a Switch (Continued)

Catalyst Name, Model, Management IP Address	Port Name	Speed	Duplex	STP State	Port-Fast	Trunk Status	Ether-Channel	VLANs	Key	Location Information	IOS Version
Burlington, WS-3550-24-SMI, 10.3.2.33/27 (*Continued*)	Fa0/5	100	Auto	Fwd	No	On	L2	1			
	Fa0/6	100	Auto	Fwd	No	On	L2	1			
	Fa0/7	100	Auto	Fwd	No	On	L2	1			
	Fa0/8								Not connected		
	Fa0/9								Not connected		
	Fa0/10								Not connected		
	Fa0/11								Not connected		
	Fa0/12								Not connected		

Identifying the Components of a Topology Diagram

A *topology diagram* is a graphical representation of a network. It illustrates how each device in a network is connected while also detailing the aspects of its logical architecture. Topology diagrams share many of the same components as their network configuration table counterparts.

Each network device should be represented on the diagram with consistent notation or a graphical symbol. Also, each logical and physical connection should be represented using a simple line or some other appropriate symbol. At a minimum, most topology diagrams include illustrations of all devices and how they are connected.

Many topologies also include network cloud symbols. A labeled cloud symbol often represents entities that are either outside the network's autonomous control or outside the scope of the topology diagram. The cloud symbols are placeholders signifying that a network, or collection of networks, exists. It is not particularly relevant to the diagram to know anything specific about those networks.

Although the components of a topology diagram can be restricted to a particular layer of the TCP/IP model, most often they are a combination of the most important components of several logical layers. For example, you might include the important components of the network layer of the TCP/IP model—IP addresses, subnet masks, and routing protocols (as shown in Table 1-4).

Table 1-4 Components of a Topology Diagram

Layer	Components
Physical layer	Device name Media types
Data-link layer	MAC addresses
Network layer	IP address Subnet mask Interface names Routing protocols

Some topologies are informal hand-drawn sketches, and others are more elaborate, using detailed symbols, multiple colors, and different views. The latter are typically created using graphics applications that vary in functionality. Whereas some applications can be used to manually create a network diagram, others can automatically create and maintain a topology of an existing network.

Figure 1-17 is an example of a topology diagram including the device name, interface name, IP address, and routing protocols. Figure 1-18 is an example of a topology diagram including the device name, interface name, and IP address.

Figure 1-17 A Topology Diagram Typically Includes Device Names and Interface Names

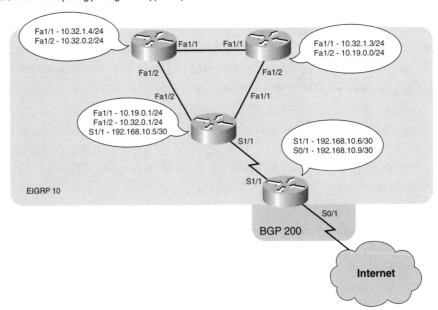

Discovering Network Configuration Information

The following steps outline the procedure for discovering the network configuration of a router or multilayer switch:

Step 1 View the device's name and model, as well as the version of its operating system. Enter **show version**.

Step 2 Determine active interfaces and their addresses. Enter **show ip interfaces**.

Step 3 View a brief summary of the interfaces on the device, including the IP address, interface name, media type, status of the configuration, and physical and data-link operational status. Enter **show ip interfaces brief**.

Figure 1-18 A Topology Table Can Include IP Addresses and Media Types

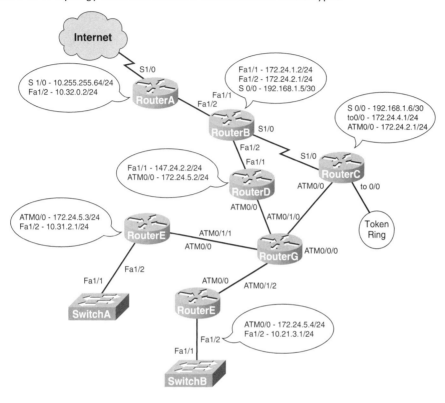

Step 4   View the MAC address for any interface or port.

Enter **show ip interface** {**interface-name**} for each interface, or enter **show interfaces** to see a list of all interfaces at once.

Step 5   View a summary of both the IP and non-IP routing protocols enabled for the device.

Enter **show ip protocols**.

Step 6   View details about the device's spanning-tree status.

Depending on the IOS version, enter **show spanning-tree** or **show spantree**.

Step 7   View a list of directly connected Cisco devices.

Enter **show cdp neighbors**.

Step 8   View details about any connected devices, such as IP address and capabilities.

Enter **show cdp entry** {*device id*}.

The following steps outline the procedure for discovering the network configuration of a Layer 2 switch:

Step 1   View the device's name and model, as well as the version of the operating system that the device is running.

Enter **show version**.

Step 2   Determine active ports and their addresses.

Enter **show interfaces description**.

Step 3   View a summary of the ports on the device, including port names, port status, duplex, and speed.

Enter **show interfaces status**.

Step 4   View a summary of the device's EtherChannel configuration.

Enter **show etherchannel summary**.

Step 5   View a summary of the trunk status of any ports that are in trunking mode.

Enter **show interfaces trunk**.

Step 6   View details about the device's spanning-tree status.

Depending on the IOS version, enter **show spanning-tree** or **show spantree**.

Step 7   View a list of directly connected Cisco devices.

Enter **show cdp neighbors**.

Step 8   View details about any connected devices, such as IP address and capabilities.

Enter **show cdp entry** {*entry name*}.

All of this information can be displayed using the command **show tech-support**. However, the output from this command generates a lot more information than you actually need.

Describing the Process of Creating Network Documentation

For the process of creating network documentation, it is recommended that the network configuration table and topology diagram be created together. Figure 1-19 shows a flow chart for creating network documentation. Table 1-5 lists the steps for creating network documentation. It is beneficial to create one type of document first, depending on your specific needs and the amount of documentation already available.

Figure 1-19 Creating Network Documentation Includes Compiling the Network Configuration Table and Topology Diagram

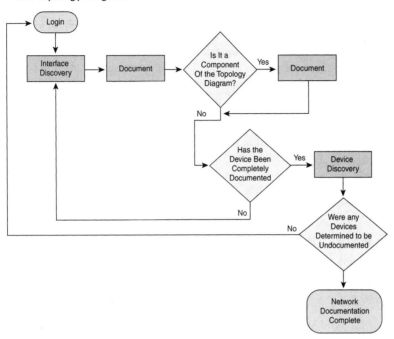

Table 1-5 Steps for Creating Network Documentation

Stage	Description
Stage 1: Log In	To start, log in to an undocumented device.
Stage 2: Interface Discovery	Discover relevant information about the device. Relevant information is determined by the components of your network configuration table.
Stage 3: Document	Document the information you discover about the device on the network configuration table. If the information you document is also a component of the topology diagram, proceed to Stage 4. If all the relevant information about the device has been documented, skip Stage 4 and move on to Stage 5.

continues

Table 1-5 Steps for Creating Network Documentation (Continued)

Stage	Description
Stage 4: Diagram	Transfer any information about the device from the network configuration table that corresponds to the components of your topology diagram. As soon as the information has been transferred, if all relevant information about the device has been documented, move on to Stage 5. Otherwise, return to Stage 2.
Stage 5: Device Discovery	Determine if any devices that neighbor the device you are logged in to are undocumented. If you determine that new neighboring devices exist, return to Stage 1. Otherwise, if no new neighboring devices exist, the network documentation is complete.

Creating Network Documentation

Good network configuration documentation allows rapid discovery of specific information about network devices. Here are some guidelines for creating effective network documentation:

- Know which end-systems are part of the domain to determine the scope of the end-system network documentation.
- Collect only data that is relevant to the objective, and provide sufficient detail for those relative pieces. Extra layers of information will only make the documentation more difficult to use.
- Use consistent terminology, abbreviations, and style.
- Make the documents orderly and easy to understand.
- Use templates, and keep a library of symbols and graphic icons that can be reused.
- Store the network documentation in a location where it is readily available on the job. A copy of the documentation should also be kept in a secure off-site location.
- Modify the network documentation as conditions and devices in the network change.

Here are some guidelines for creating network documentation:

- Know the objective
- Be consistent
- Keep the documents accessible
- Maintain the documentation!

A standardized process should be implemented for handling changes to network documentation. Factors in this process that need to be accounted for include reporting network changes, maintaining version control, and assigning responsibility for modifying and distributing updated documents.

Network Documentation Example

Last year, documentation of the network for a branch of the corporation was completed. One year later, troubleshooters still use the network documentation to successfully troubleshoot network problems. The following is a list of reasons that the documentation process was successful:

- Network segments and devices were identified within the domain of responsibility.
- The purpose for creating the documentation was determined.
- The most experienced network employees were queried to learn what information would be the most useful to meet their needs.
- Consistent symbols and terminology were used to represent the data in both graphical and tabular form.
- Logical locations were designated to store copies of the documentation, and indexing permitted networking personnel to easily find the needed data. A sign-out sheet was implemented so that copies of the network documentation could be accounted for.
- A reporting system was instituted so that employees could relay information about changing conditions in the network to a central location. When a change in network conditions took place, employees knew whom to notify. That person promptly modified, dated, and distributed the updated documentation to the designated locations.

 Lab 1.2.6   Network Baseline Discovery

In this lab exercise, you establish the baseline for the network's configuration and operation. You complete the following tasks: determine network topology and device configurations, complete network configuration tables, and update the base network diagram for your workgroup to include data-link layer switch features and network layer addressing.

End-System Configuration Documentation

Network documentation can be a valuable troubleshooting tool. However, a network is incomplete without end-systems. An incorrectly configured end-system can have a negative impact on a network's overall performance. This section discusses the creation of configuration documentation for the purposes of troubleshooting end-systems connected to a network. The information contained in this section assumes a scenario in which network devices have already been documented but the network administrator is unfamiliar with the configuration. Therefore, the end-system portion of the network documentation needs to be created from scratch.

Identifying the Components of an End-System Network Configuration Table

End-system devices such as servers, network management consoles, and desktop workstations play a large role in how a network operates and, therefore, should not be ignored. Maintaining relevant documentation about the configuration of end-systems provides a complete picture of the network and allows intelligent decisions about any modifications or upgrades that end-systems might require. Including end-system network configuration information in the baseline helps you troubleshoot problems in a timely and efficient manner.

An *end-system network configuration table* is baseline documentation that shows accurate records of the hardware and software used in end-systems, as shown in Table 1-6.

When creating an end-system network configuration table for troubleshooting, you should document the following:

- Device name (purpose)
- Operating system/version
- IP address or DHCP server used
- Subnet mask
- Default gateway, DNS server, and WINS server addresses
- Any high-bandwidth network applications that the end-system runs

An end-system network configuration table will contain different components based on its use. Some tables are used administratively for inventory. Some simply list the physical location of the device and perhaps a note about when it needs to be backed up. Others are used as a troubleshooting tool.

An end-system network configuration table used for troubleshooting typically varies, depending on the device being recorded. There are many different types of end-systems and, therefore, quite a bit of information can be recorded. To simplify things, it can be helpful to divide the recorded information into categories based on the relationship the component has with the layers of the TCP/IP model. It is important to find out what the most useful pieces of information are for troubleshooting particular end-systems. See Table 1-7.

Table 1-6 End-System Network Configuration Table

Device Name (Purpose)	Operating System/ Version	IP Address/ Subnet Mask	Default Gateway Address	DNS Server Address	WINS Server Address	High-Bandwidth Applications	Network Applications

Table 1-7 Information for Troubleshooting End-Systems

Layer	Data
Physical layer	CPU type
	Flash memory
	DRAM
	Media types
	Speed
	Duplex
	Trunk or access status
Data-link layer	Device name
	Device model
	MAC addresses
	Duplex
	Port identifier
	STP state
	PortFast state
	EtherChannel
Network layer	IP address
	Secondary IP address
	Subnet mask
	Routing protocols
	Access lists
	VLANs
	Neighboring devices
	Interface names
	Username/password

Recording network applications that are available on an end-system is also useful information to include in an end-system network configuration table. Additionally, record any high-bandwidth network applications that are running on the end-system, because they can have a significant impact on network performance. Examples of high-bandwidth applications are streaming video such as QuickTime and multicast applications such as IP/TV.

Table 1-8 provides an example of an end-system configuration table using the following categories to document a device's network-related properties:

- Device name (purpose)
- Operating system/version
- IP address/subnet mask
- Default gateway address
- DNS server address
- WINS server address
- High-bandwidth applications
- Network applications

Identifying the Components of an End-System Topology Diagram

An *end-system topology diagram*, shown in Figure 1-20, is a graphical representation of selected tabular data gathered in the end-system network configuration table. Topologies should illustrate how end-systems are both physically and logically connected to the network. Because end-systems are frequently added to existing network diagrams, topology diagrams that include end-systems often include components of network device configurations.

Table 1-8 Sample End-System Configuration Table

Device Name (Purpose)	Operating System/ Version	IP Address/ Subnet Mask	Default Gateway Address	DNS Server Address	WINS Server Address	High-Bandwidth Applications	Network Applications
Server1 (file server)	Windows 2003	10.32.6.1/24	10.32.6.1/24	10.32.6.100	10.32.6.100	—	—
DNS01 (DNS server)	Windows 2003	10.22.1.2/24	10.22.1.1/24	10.32.17.10	10.22.1.100	—	—
TermA (admin terminal)	UNIX	10.22.2.2/24	10.22.2.1/24	10.100.17.10	—	—	—
DB01 (e-commerce Database)	UNIX	10.32.3.4/24	10.32.3.1/24	10.100.17.10	—	—	—
Server2 (Web/FTP server)	UNIX	10.32.4.4/24	10.32.4.2/24	10.100.17.10	—	—	—

Figure 1-20 An End-System Topology Diagram Graphically Represents the Information in the End-System Network Configuration Table

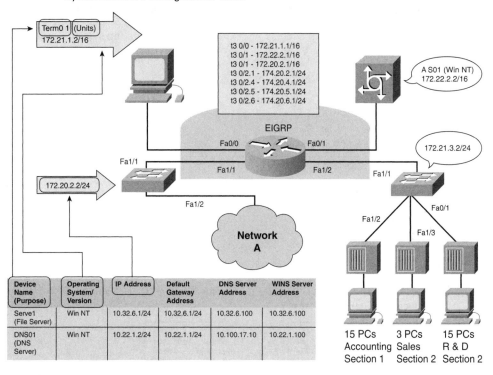

Device Name (Purpose)	Operating System/ Version	IP Address	Default Gateway Address	DNS Server Address	WINS Server Address
Serve1 (File Server)	Win NT	10.32.6.1/24	10.32.6.1/24	10.32.6.100	10.32.6.100
DNS01 (DNS Server)	Win NT	10.22.1.2/24	10.22.1.1/24	10.100.17.10	10.22.1.100

Like the network devices in a topology diagram, end-systems in a network topology do not typically include every component of the end-system network configuration table. Minimally, the end-systems on a topology diagram should include the name, an illustration of the device, and how it is connected to the network.

Like an end-system network configuration table, the components of a topology diagram that include end-systems can have different components, depending on the types of end-systems in the network. These components can also be categorized according to logical TCP/IP layers. See Table 1-9.

A topology diagram that includes end-systems will differ depending on its focus. A topology that is focused on the end-systems rather than the configuration of network devices might represent the network components as a network cloud symbol with the details of the end-systems connected to it. On the other hand, all the details of the network device configuration might be included on the same diagram as the end-systems.

Table 1-9 Components of an End-System Topology Diagram by TCP/IP Layer

Network Interface Layer	Internet Layer	Application Layer
Physical location	IP address	Operating system/version
	Subnet mask	Operating system/viewer
	Device name	
	Device purpose	
	VLANs	
	Interface names	

Figure 1-21 provides an example including the following components related to end-systems:

- Device name and purpose
- Operating system
- IP address

Figure 1-21 An End-System Topology Diagram Commonly Includes Device Name, Device Function, and IP Addresses

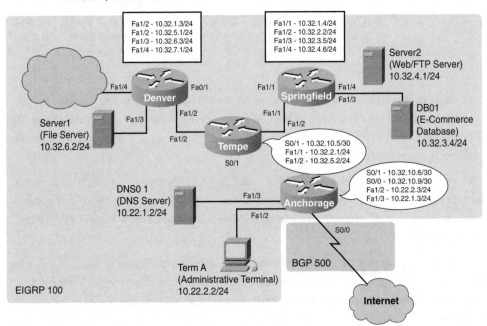

Identifying Commands and Applications Used to Discover Information about End-System Configurations

Table 1-10 shows general commands that a troubleshooter uses to gather information about an end-system's network configuration. These commands are considered general because they can be applied on end-systems running the most common operating systems.

Table 1-10 Standard Windows Troubleshooting Commands

Command	Description
arp -a	Displays the current mappings of IP addresses to MAC addresses.
ping	Sends echo request packets to an address and awaits replies. The argument can be a host name or IP address for the target system.
route print	Displays the current contents of the IP routing table.
telnet	Used to gain terminal access to devices on a network. A successful connection also indicates that the TCP/IP protocol stack is functioning and that the end-system supports all seven layers.

Table 1-11 shows commands that a troubleshooter uses on an end-system running a Windows operating system to gather information about the end-system's network configuration.

Table 1-11 More Windows Troubleshooting Commands

Command	Description
ipconfig /all	Displays IP information for hosts running Microsoft Windows 2000, XP, and 2003.
tracert	Determines the path taken to a destination by sending ICMP echo request messages with varying Time-to-Live (TTL) values. The argument is either a host name or IP address.
winipcfg	Displays IP information for hosts running Windows 9x and Me.

Table 1-12 shows commands that a troubleshooter uses on an end-system running the UNIX or Mac OS X operating system to gather information about an end-system's network configuration.

Table 1-12 UNIX and Mac OS X Troubleshooting Commands

Command	Description
ifconfig -a	Displays IP information for UNIX and Mac OS X hosts.
traceroute	Identifies the path a packet takes through the network. The destination argument is a host name or IP address of the target system.

Discovering End-System Configuration Information

The following steps outline the procedure for discovering an end-system's network configuration:

NOTE

On a Windows end-system, you can access information about the operating system and hardware by choosing **Start > Settings > Control Panel** and then double-clicking the **Systems** icon. On a Mac running Mac OS X, click the **Apple** icon and choose **About This Mac**.

NOTE

To access a command line on a Windows end-system, choose **Start > MS-DOS** or **Start > Command Prompt**. The command-line Terminal utility on Mac OS X can be found in the Utilities folder located in the Applications directory.

Step 1   View information about the device's operating system and hardware.

Step 2   Access a command line.

Step 3   View detailed information about a device's TCP/IP settings. You do this by entering the **ipconfig /all** or **winipcfg** command in a Windows command prompt or by entering **ifconfig -a** in a UNIX or Mac OS X command line. The important information to record includes IP address/subnet mask, default gateway address, and any DNS or WINS server addresses. When viewing the information returned from **ipconfig /all**, it is helpful to note if a device's IP address is static or if it has been temporarily assigned through DHCP.

Step 4   Display any active routes by entering the **route print** command in the command line.

Step 5   View Address Resolution Protocol (ARP) information by entering the **arp -a** command.

Step 6   Check connectivity to remote devices by attempting to **ping** a device across a link.

Step 7   View the route that is used to connect to a remote address such as the default gateway. To accomplish this, enter **tracert {ip-address | hostname}** in a Windows command prompt or enter **traceroute {ip-address | hostname}** on a UNIX or Mac OS X command line.

Step 8   Check that TCP is available and functioning on the end-system by entering the **telnet {ip-address | hostname}** command.

Creating End-System Network Configuration Documentation

Good end-system network configuration documentation allows rapid discovery of specific information about end-systems. Here are some guidelines for creating effective end-system network configuration documentation:

- Know which end-systems are part of the domain to determine the scope of the end-system network documentation.
- Collect only data that is relevant to the objective, and provide sufficient detail for those relative pieces. Extra layers of information will only make the documentation more difficult to use.
- Use consistent terminology, abbreviations, and style.
- Try to make the documents orderly and easy to understand.
- Use templates, and keep a library of symbols and graphic icons.
- Store the network documentation in a location where it is readily available on the job. A copy of the documentation should be kept in a secure location off-site.
- Maintain the documentation!
- Modify the network documentation as conditions and devices in the network change.

Here's a condensed version of these guidelines:

- Determine the scope.
- Know the objective.
- Be consistent.
- Keep the documents accessible.
- Maintain the documentation!

A process should be implemented for handling changes to the network documentation. Factors in this process that need to be accounted for are reporting network changes, maintaining version control, and assigning responsibility for modifying and distributing updated documents.

Example: Creating End-System Network Configuration Documentation

A network technician's primary job function might be to maintain and troubleshoot network servers and desktops. The team already does a respectable job of fixing problems but has been asked to create documentation of the network end-systems to expedite troubleshooting efforts and cut down on costs. The company currently has configuration tables and topology diagrams of the network configuration without end-systems.

A month later, the network support staff has been using the end-system documentation for troubleshooting. Estimates have determined that the time that the department spends troubleshooting end-systems in the past month has dropped considerably. The documentation was a success for the following reasons:

- The scope of the documentation was determined accurately because of familiarity with the end-systems on the network.
- The appropriate types and amounts of information for each documented end-system were recorded.
- Standardized symbols and terminology consistent with the existing network documentation were used.
- Documentation was kept current by implementing a system for employees to report changes and by updating the documentation in a timely manner.
- The documentation was stored in convenient and clearly marked locations close to each administrative terminal.

 Lab 1.3.5 End-System Baseline Discovery

In this lab exercise, you establish the baseline for the configuration and operation of the end-systems in the network. You complete the following tasks: determine end-system network configuration, determine end-system connectivity, and complete end-system network configuration tables.

Summary

This chapter explained that a network baseline is required for effective troubleshooting. Devices and key interfaces should be baselined to provide a reference for subsequent analysis. The thresholds for these devices and interfaces should be documented.

The need for network documentation consisting of a network configuration table and topology diagram was emphasized. The components of a network configuration table and topology diagram can be categorized by the logical layers that they are associated with in the TCP/IP model. Following established procedures, a troubleshooter can gather relevant configuration information about routers and switches. Performing the five stages in the process of creating network documentation allows a troubleshooter to create a network configuration table and topology diagram. The following guidelines make it easy for a troubleshooter to create useful and effective network configuration documentation.

End-system documentation consists of a configuration table and end-to-end topology diagram. The components of an end-system configuration table and topology diagram can be split into physical and logical categories. Following established procedures, a troubleshooter can gather relevant configuration information about a variety of end-systems. Several commands and applications are available for discovering configuration information about end-systems. Good end-system configuration documentation allows rapid discovery of specific information about end-systems.

The next chapter expands on internetwork troubleshooting by exploring troubleshooting methodologies and tools.

Key Terms

baseline   A collection of data used to determine where opportunities exist for optimizing the network environment. A network baseline is used to decide whether to make recommendations to add bandwidth or introduce quality of service to enhance services.

baseline analysis   The interpretation of the data collected in a baseline.

baselining   The process of collecting data to be used as a reference for future decision-making and troubleshooting.

end-system network configuration table   Baseline documentation that shows accurate records of the hardware and software used in end-systems.

end-system topology diagram   A graphical representation of selected tabular data gathered in the end-system network configuration table.

network configuration table   A table including accurate, up-to-date records of the hardware and software used in a network. The network configuration table should provide the troubleshooter with all the information necessary to identify and correct the network fault.

threshold   A measure that indicates a warning level, such as collisions and errors.

topology diagram   A graphical representation of a network. A topology diagram illustrates how each device in a network is connected, while also detailing the aspects of its logical architecture.

Check Your Understanding

Use the following review questions to test your understanding of the concepts covered in this chapter. Answers are listed in Appendix A, "Check Your Understanding Answer Key."

1. _____ allows for discovery of the true performance and operation of the network in terms of the policies that have been defined. It also allows for a snapshot of the current state of variables throughout the network.

   A. Performance monitoring

   B. Fault isolation

   C. Baselining

   D. Troubleshooting

2. How often should baseline analysis of the network be conducted?

   A. Once

   B. Weekly

   C. Monthly

   D. On a regular basis

3. In planning a baseline, which of the following should be identified? Choose all that apply.

   A. QoS

   B. Boundaries

   C. Devices

   D. Ports of interest

4. Which of the following are two qualifications for the duration of the baseline?

   A. 1 day

   B. No more than 6 weeks

   C. 1 year

   D. At least 7 days

5. Baseline information is recorded in what types of documentation? Choose all that apply.

   A. Network management databases

   B. QoS databases

   C. Network configuration tables

   D. Topology diagrams

6. What is normally included in a network configuration table? Choose all that apply.

   A. Device name

   B. Data-link layer addresses

   C. Network layer addresses

   D. Applications

7. What is normally included in a topology diagram? Choose all that apply.

   A. Device names

   B. Routing protocols

   C. IP addresses

   D. Media types

8. Guidelines for creating network documentation include which of the following? Choose all that apply.

   A. Knowing the objective

   B. Being consistent

   C. Keeping the documents accessible

   D. Maintaining the documentation

9. What is normally included in an end-system configuration table? Choose all that apply.

   A. DNS server

   B. IP address

   C. Operating system

   D. Device name

10. What is normally included in an end-system topology diagram? Choose all that apply.

   A. Port speed

   B. How devices are connected to the network

   C. IP address

   D. Device name and function

Objectives

After completing this chapter, you will be able to perform tasks related to the following:

- List the stages of the general troubleshooting process
- Be familiar with the bottom-up, top-down, and divide-and-conquer troubleshooting approaches
- Know how to select an effective troubleshooting approach based on a specific situation
- Be familiar with the process of gathering symptoms from a network
- Be familiar with the guidelines for gathering symptoms from a user
- Be familiar with the process of gathering symptoms from an end-system
- Understand basic network management concepts and the tools used for network management
- Be familiar with the five conceptual areas of network management in the ISO network management model

Chapter 2

Troubleshooting Methodologies and Tools

Troubleshooting networks is more important than ever. As time goes on, services continue to be added to networks. With each added service comes more variables. This adds to the complexity of network troubleshooting as well as the network itself. Organizations increasingly depend on network administrators and network engineers to have strong troubleshooting skills.

Troubleshooting begins by looking at a methodology that breaks the troubleshooting process into manageable pieces. This permits a systematic approach, minimizes confusion, and cuts down on time otherwise wasted with trial-and-error troubleshooting.

Network engineers, administrators, and support personnel realize that troubleshooting is a process that takes the greatest percentage of their time. One of the primary goals of this chapter is to present efficient troubleshooting techniques to shorten overall troubleshooting time when working in a production environment.

Two extreme approaches to troubleshooting almost always result in disappointment, delay, or failure. On one extreme is the theorist, or rocket scientist, approach. On the other is the practical, or caveman, approach. Because both of these approaches are extremes, the better approach is somewhere in the middle using elements of both.

The rocket scientist analyzes and reanalyzes the situation until he or she identifies the root cause of the problem and corrects it with surgical precision. This sometimes requires taking a high-end protocol analyzer and collecting a huge sample, possibly megabytes, of the network traffic, while the problem is present. The sample is then inspected in minute detail. Although this process is fairly reliable, few companies can afford to have their networks down for the hours, or days, it can take for this exhaustive analysis.

The caveman's first instinct is to start swapping cards, cables, hardware, and software until miraculously the network begins operating again. This does not mean that the network is working properly—just that it is operating. Unfortunately, the troubleshooting section in some manuals actually recommends caveman-style procedures as a way to avoid providing more technical information. Although this approach might achieve a change in symptoms faster, it is not very reliable, and the root cause of the problem might still be present. In fact, the parts used for swapping might include marginal or failed parts swapped out during prior troubleshooting episodes. The caveman approach is also known as shotgun troubleshooting.

Analyze the network as a whole rather than in a piecemeal fashion. One technician following a logical sequence will almost always be more successful than a gang of technicians, each with their own theories and troubleshooting methods.

Using a Layered Architectural Model to Describe Data Flow

Logical networking models separate network functionality into modular layers. These modular layers are applied to the physical network to isolate network problems and even create divisions of labor. For example, if the symptoms of a communications problem suggest a physical connection problem, the telephone company service person can focus on troubleshooting the T1 circuit that operates at the physical layer. The repair person does not have to know anything about TCP/IP, which operates at the network and transport layers, and does not have to attempt to make changes to devices operating outside of the realm of the suspected logical layer. The repair person can concentrate on the physical circuit. If it functions properly, either the repair person or a different specialist looks at areas in another layer that could be causing the problem.

Encapsulating Data

The Open Systems Interconnection (OSI) model provides a common language for network engineers. Having looked at using a systematic approach, documentation, and network architectures, you can see that the OSI model is pervasive in troubleshooting networks. This model allows troubleshooting to be described in a structured fashion. Problems are typically described in terms of a given OSI model layer. At this stage, it is assumed that you are very familiar with this model. Taking a quick look at the OSI model will help clarify its role in troubleshooting methodology.

The OSI reference model describes how information from a software application in one computer moves through a network medium to a software application in another computer. The

OSI reference model is a conceptual model composed of seven layers, each specifying particular network functions (see Figure 2-1). With this technique, one transition is guaranteed for each bit cycle, or bit time. The model was developed by the International Organization for Standardization (ISO) in 1984, and it is now considered the primary architectural model for intercomputer communications. The OSI model divides the tasks involved with moving information between networked computers into seven smaller, more manageable task groups. A task or group of tasks is then assigned to each of the seven OSI layers. Each layer is reasonably self-contained so that the tasks assigned to each layer can be implemented independently. This enables the solutions offered by one layer to be updated without adversely affecting the other layers.

Figure 2-1 The OSI Model Is Used, Among Other Things, to Provide a Framework for Organized Troubleshooting

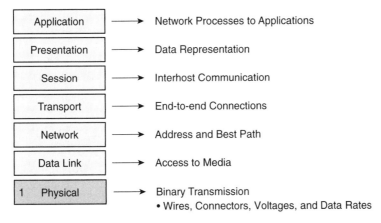

The OSI model provides a logical framework and a common language used by network engineers to articulate network scenarios. The Layer 1 to 7 terminology is so common that most engineers do not think twice about it any more.

The upper layers (5 to 7) of the OSI model deal with application issues and generally are implemented only in software. The application layer is closest to the end user. Both users and application layer processes interact with software applications that contain a communications component.

The lower layers (1 to 4) of the OSI model handle data-transport issues. The physical layer and data-link layer are implemented in hardware and software. The other lower layers generally are implemented only in software. The physical layer is closest to the physical network medium, such as the network cabling, and is responsible for actually placing information on the medium.

When data is sent from an application in one host to an application in a second host, the network software on the source host takes the data from the application and converts it as needed for transmission over a physical network. The process involves the following:

- Converting data into segments
- Encapsulating segments with header information that includes logical network addressing information—also the process of converting segments into packets
- Encapsulating packets with a header, including physical addressing information, and converting packets into frames
- Encoding frames into bits

Figure 2-2 illustrates the process.

Figure 2-2 Segments, Packets, Frames, and Bits Are the Respective Means of Communicating Information at the Transport, Network, Data-Link, and Physical Layers

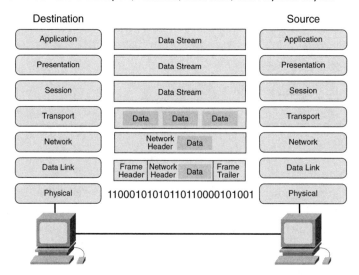

The data is now ready for travel over the physical medium as bits. The encapsulation process as a whole represents the initial stage in transferring data between two end-systems, as shown in Figure 2-3.

Figure 2-3 As Data Is Sent Between End-Systems, the Encapsulation Process Takes Place

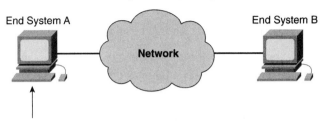

This involves:
- Converting data into segments.
- Encapsulating segments with a header that includes network addressing information and converting segments into packets.
- Encapsulating packets with a header that includes physical addressing information and converting packets into frames.
- Converting frames into bits.

Bits on the Physical Medium

The Ethernet receiver derives the clock rate from the incoming data stream. Using a direct signal encoding of 0 volts for a logic 0 value and 5 volts for a logic 1 value could lead to timing problems. Specifically, a long string of 1s or 0s could cause the receiver to lose synchronization with the data. Furthermore, the recipient would be unable to determine the difference between an idle sender (0 voltage) and a string of 0s (again, 0 voltage).

The solution for this dilemma is found in the Ethernet encoding scheme. Rather than transmitting the logic level directly, Manchester encoding is used. With this technique, one transition is guaranteed for each bit cycle, as shown in Figure 2-4.

Figure 2-4 Manchester Encoding Is Used to Transmit 0s and 1s at the Physical Layer on Ethernet Media

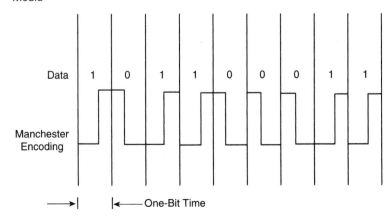

With a Manchester-encoded signal, a binary 1 is represented by a change of amplitude from a low to a high during the middle of a bit time. Conversely, a binary 0 is represented by a change of amplitude from a high to a low during the middle of a bit time.

However, the trade-off for this synchronization technique is that twice the signaling bandwidth is required, because there must be two pulses for every bit transmitted. As a result, 10-Mbps Ethernet actually works with a 20-MHz serial data signal.

Table 2-1 describes the stages of encapsulation and decapsulation.

Table 2-1 Encapsulation and Decapsulation

Stage	Description
Stage 1	End-system A takes data from an application and converts it as needed for transmission over a physical network. This involves the following steps: ■ Converting data into segments ■ Encapsulating segments with a header that includes network addressing information and converting segments into packets ■ Encapsulating packets with a header that includes physical addressing information and converting packets into frames ■ Converting frames into bits
Stage 2	Data passes over the physical medium as bits.
Stage 3	When data reaches a network device, the device removes data control information as needed. Layer 2 devices such as switches and bridges read physical addressing information and forward frames to an interface. Routers, firewalls, and multilayer switches read network addressing information and forward packets to an interface. Stages 2 and 3 alternate until the data flows through all devices that are necessary to reach the interface of the target end-system.
Stage 4	The interface of end-system B receives the data from the physical medium, removes the data control information, and converts the data as needed for use with the target application.

Data moving through the physical layer medium from the source to the destination is the end product of the encapsulation process.

Network Devices Utilize Control Information

Layer 2 network devices use the control information in a frame to assess where a frame is physically destined for on a local network segment. The physical address, or Media Access

Control (MAC) address, of the destination network adapter, or interface, is read so that the proper decision on switching to an appropriate port can be made. In addition to addressing information, the Layer 2 device can check on the frame's validity by recalculating the frame check sequence (FCS) and matching it with the FCS included as part of the encapsulation process at the data-link layer.

Layer 3 network devices are responsible for determining logical paths between networks through an internetwork. Layer 3 devices read the networking address of a destination contained in packets' control information and then forward the packets to an appropriate interface. Layer 3 addressing is hierarchical so that intermediate devices need only know which network the destination device is a member of to deliver the packet to the correct location.

Data flow alternates between the physical medium, which is Stage 2 of data flow, and Layer 2 and 3 devices, representing the third stage in the flow of data from a source to a target end-system.

Decapsulation

When an end-system's interface receives data from the physical medium, frames must be extracted from the bit stream so that the end-system can verify that the frame's destination physical address equals its own. When the physical address is verified, the packet is decapsulated from the frame control information, and the packet's logical control information is examined. Data is further decapsulated from packets as needed for use with the target application.

This represents the fourth stage in the layered model of data flow. Data returned to the original sender goes through the same process:

Stage 1—Encapsulation

Stage 2—Transmission over the physical medium

Stage 3—Network devices using control information to deliver data to the appropriate end-system

Stage 4—Decapsulation of data as needed for use with the target application

OSI Model Versus TCP/IP Model

Similar to the OSI networking model, the TCP/IP networking model divides the networking architecture into modular layers. Figure 2-5 shows how the TCP/IP networking model maps to the layers of the OSI networking model. It is this close mapping that allows the TCP/IP suite of protocols to successfully communicate with so many networking technologies.

Figure 2-5 The OSI Model and the TCP/IP Model Are Both Used Frequently to Articulate Information About Computer Networks

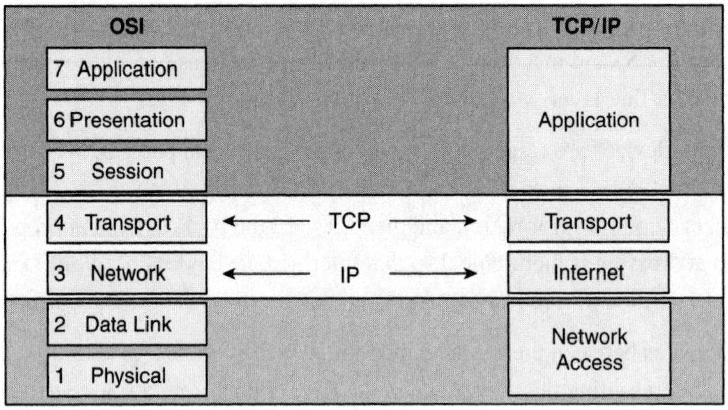

The TCP/IP network access layer corresponds to the OSI physical and data-link layers. The network access layer communicates directly with the network medium and provides an interface between the network's architecture and the Internet layer.

The TCP/IP Internet layer relates to the OSI network layer. The Internet layer of the TCP/IP protocol model is responsible for placing messages in a fixed format that allows devices to handle them.

The transport layers of TCP/IP and OSI directly correspond in function. The transport layer is responsible for exchanging packets between devices on a TCP/IP network.

The application layer in the TCP/IP suite actually combines the functions of the OSI model's session, presentation, and application layers. The application layer provides communication between applications such as FTP, HTTP, and SMTP on separate hosts.

Position of Network Devices in Layered Model

Being able to identify which layers pertain to a networking device lets a troubleshooter minimize a problem's complexity by dividing the problem into manageable parts, as shown in Table 2-2.

For instance, knowing that Layer 3 issues are of no importance to a switch, aside from multilayer switches, defines the boundaries of a task as Layer 1 and Layer 2. Given that there is still plenty to consider at only these two layers, this simple knowledge can prevent the wasting of time troubleshooting irrelevant possibilities and can significantly reduce the amount of time spent attempting to correct a problem. However, it is still important to note that there are network applications that are part of these devices that move into Layers 4 to 7.

Table 2-2 Devices and OSI Layers

Device	OSI Layers That Are Possible Troubleshooting Targets
Router	Physical, data-link, network
Firewall	Physical, data-link, network
Multilayer switch	Physical, data-link, network
Layer 2 switch	Physical, data-link
Hub	Physical, data-link
End-system	All layers

Troubleshooting Approaches

In general, troubleshooting involves gathering symptoms, isolating the problem, and correcting the problem. This section discusses various methods of implementing this general approach, including the bottom-up, top-down, and divide-and-conquer approaches.

General Troubleshooting Process

The steps of the general troubleshooting process are as follows:

Step 1   Gather symptoms.

Step 2   Isolate the problem.

Step 3   Correct the problem.

These steps are not mutually exclusive. At any point in the process, you might need to return to previous steps. For instance, you might need to gather more symptoms while isolating a problem. Additionally, when attempting to correct a problem, you might create another unidentified problem. As a result, you would need to gather the symptoms, isolate the new problem, and correct it. Figure 2-6 outlines the process.

A troubleshooting policy should be established for each stage. A policy gives you a consistent manner in which to perform each stage. Part of the policy should include documenting every important piece of information.

Figure 2-6 The General Troubleshooting Process is to Gather Symptoms, Isolate the Problem, and Correct the Problem

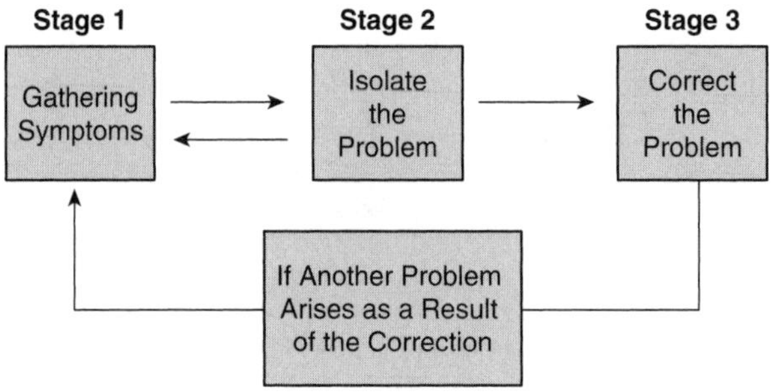

Step 1: Gather Symptoms

To perform the "Gather Symptoms" stage of the general troubleshooting process, the trouble-shooter gathers and documents symptoms from the network, end-systems, or users. In addition, the troubleshooter determines what network components have been affected and how the network's functionality has changed compared to the baseline. Symptoms might include alerts from the network management system, console messages, and user complaints.

While gathering symptoms, you should ask questions as a method of localizing the problem to a smaller range of possibilities. However, the problem is not truly isolated until a single problem or set of related problems is identified. One question to always ask is what has changed relative to before the problem occurred.

Step 2: Isolate the Problem

To perform the "Isolate the Problem" stage of the general troubleshooting process, the trou-bleshooter identifies the characteristics of problems at the logical layers of the network so that the most likely cause can be selected. At this stage, the troubleshooter might gather and document more symptoms, depending on the problem characteristics that are identified.

Step 3: Correct the Problem

To perform the "Correct the Problem" stage, the troubleshooter corrects an identified problem by implementing, testing, and documenting a solution. If the troubleshooter determines that the corrective action has created another problem, the attempted solution is documented, the changes are removed, and the troubleshooter returns to gathering symptoms and isolating the problem.

Bottom-Up

When applying a bottom-up approach to troubleshooting a networking problem, you start the examination with the network's physical components. You then work up through the layers of the OSI model until you identify the problem's cause, as shown in Figure 2-7. This is a good approach to use when you suspect the problem is physical. Most networking problems reside at the lower levels, so implementing the bottom-up approach often produces results. If Layer 1 is broken, every layer above it will not function.

Figure 2-7 The Bottom-Up Troubleshooting Approach Generally Is the Most Effective Method

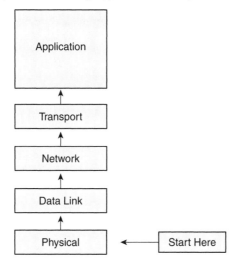

The downside of selecting this approach is that you must check every device and interface on the network until you find the possible cause of the problem. You must document each conclusion and possibility. The challenge is to determine which devices to start with.

In many cases, you can find problems within the first four layers by entering a **ping** or **traceroute** command. If the connection is successful, the cause is likely at the application level. Otherwise, a closer look at the lower levels is needed to locate the problem.

Verify that Internet Control Message Protocol (ICMP) echo request and echo reply are enabled on the network so that commands such as **ping** and **traceroute** will work. This action should include authorization from the network administrator and documentation of that authorization. If **ping** has been disabled on the network, it is a result of the implementation of policy. Document in a station log or your personal work log that **ping**, or any command that was initially disabled, was enabled for network testing and subsequently was disabled. This is important in case an unauthorized intrusion into the network occurs while you are trouble-shooting the network. If they are disabled, the failure of the **ping** or **traceroute** commands can easily be mistaken for a loss of connectivity. It is common for echo requests and echo replies to be blocked by a firewall.

Top-Down

When applying a top-down approach to troubleshooting a networking problem, you examine the end-user application first. Then you work down from the upper layers of the OSI model until you identify the cause of the problem, as shown in Figure 2-8. When you select this approach, you test an end-system's applications before tackling the more specific networking pieces. You would most likely select this approach for simpler problems or when you think the problem is with a piece of software.

Figure 2-8 The Top-Down Approach Generally Is Used When Software Is Suspected to Be the Cause of the Problem

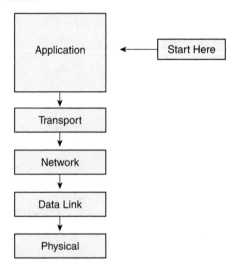

The disadvantage of selecting this approach is that you must check every network application until you find the possible cause of the problem. You must document each conclusion and possibility. Like the bottom-up approach, the challenge is to determine which application to start with.

Divide and Conquer

When the divide-and-conquer approach is applied to troubleshooting a networking problem, a layer is selected and tested in both directions from the starting layer. The divide-and-conquer approach is initiated at a particular layer, as shown in Figure 2-9. Which layer you choose is based on your experience level and the symptoms you gathered about the problem. After you identify the direction of the problem, your troubleshooting follows that direction until the cause of the problem is found.

Figure 2-9 The Divide-and-Conquer Approach Begins at the Transport, Network, or Data-Link Layer

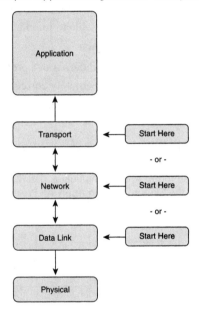

If you can verify that a layer is functioning, it is typically a safe assumption that the layers below it are functioning as well. If a layer is not functioning properly, gather symptoms of the problem at that layer, and work downward to lower layers.

Guidelines for Selecting an Approach

When you select an effective troubleshooting approach to solve a network problem, you usually resolve the problem in a quicker, more cost-effective manner.

Consider the following when selecting an effective troubleshooting approach:

- **Determine the scope of the problem**—A troubleshooting approach is often selected based on its complexity. A bottom-up approach typically works better for complex problems. Using a bottom-up approach for a simple problem might be overkill and inefficient. Typically, if symptoms come from users, a top-down approach is used. If symptoms come from the network, a bottom-up approach usually is more effective.

- **Apply previous experiences**—If a particular problem has been experienced previously, the troubleshooter might know of a way to shorten the troubleshooting process. A less-experienced troubleshooter will likely implement a bottom-up approach, whereas a skilled troubleshooter might be able to jump into a problem at a different layer using the divide-and-conquer approach.

- **Analyze the symptoms**—The more you know about a problem, the better the chance it can be solved. It might be possible to immediately correct a problem simply by analyzing the symptoms. Many times it is useful to recreate the problem in a controlled environment, such as a lab.

Figure 2-10 summarizes the guidelines for selecting an approach.

Figure 2-10 Selecting a Troubleshooting Approach Involves Determining the Scope of the Problem, Analyzing the Symptoms, and Applying Previous Experiences

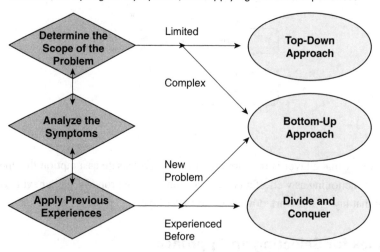

Example Utilizing the Divide-and-Conquer Approach

Two IP routers have been identified in a network. They have connectivity but are not exchanging routing information. Before attempting to solve the problem, you need to select a troubleshooting approach. You've seen similar symptoms before, which points to a likely protocol issue. Because the routers have connectivity between them, it is not likely to be a problem at the physical or data-link layer. Based on your past experience, you decide to use the divide-and-conquer approach. You begin testing the TCP/IP-related functions at the network layer.

Gathering Symptoms

Troubleshooting requires the network engineer to gather symptoms related to the problem. Depending on the particular situation, the following symptoms should be documented: network problems, end-user hardware problems, end-user software problems, and answers to questions asked of end users.

Gathering Symptoms for a Network Problem

The following are the stages of gathering symptoms for a network problem:

Stage 1—You analyze symptoms gathered from the trouble ticket, users, or end-systems affected by the problem to define the problem.

Stage 2—If the problem is in your system, you must move on to Stage 3. If the problem is outside your control, you must contact an administrator for the external system before gathering additional network symptoms.

Stage 3—You determine if the problem is at the network's core, distribution, or access layer. At the identified layer, analyze the symptoms and use your knowledge of the network topology to determine which piece or pieces of equipment are the most likely cause.

Stage 4—Using a layered troubleshooting approach, you gather hardware and software symptoms from the suspect devices. You start with the most likely possibility, and use your knowledge and experience to determine if the problem is more likely a hardware or software configuration problem.

Stage 5—Document any hardware or software symptoms. If the problem can be solved using the documented symptoms, you solve the problem and document the solution. If you can't solve the problem, you begin the isolating phase of the general troubleshooting process. You should review any changes that have occurred during the process of gathering symptoms.

Figure 2-11 maps out the process of gathering symptoms. Table 2-3 shows the commands most commonly used for troubleshooting on a Cisco router.

Figure 2-11 Gathering Symptoms Is Conveniently Broken Down into a Five-Step Process

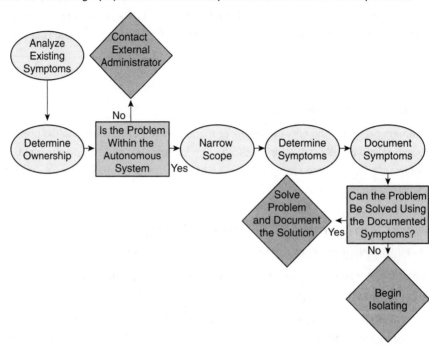

Table 2-3 ping, telnet, and traceroute

Command	Description
ping {*host* I *ip-address*}	Sends an echo request packet to an address and then waits for a reply. The *host* I *ip-address* variable is the IP alias or IP address of the target system.
traceroute {*destination*}	Identifies the path a packet takes through the networks. The destination variable is the host name or IP address of the target system.
telnet {*host* I *ip-address*}	Connects to an IP address using the Telnet application.
show ip interface brief	Summarizes the status of all interfaces on a device.
show ip route	Displays the current state of the IP routing table.
show running-config interface	Displays the contents of the currently running configuration file.

Table 2-3 ping, **telnet**, and **traceroute** (Continued)

Command	Description
[no] debug ?	Displays a list of options for enabling or disabling debugging events on a device.
show protocols	Displays the configured protocols and shows the global and interface-specific status of any configured Layer 3 protocol.

Be conservative with the use of the **debug** command on a network. It generates enough console message traffic that the performance of a network device can be noticeably affected. Be sure to disable debugging when its capabilities are no longer needed.

Gathering Symptoms from an End User: Hardware

When gathering symptoms for perceived hardware problems, a troubleshooter should physically inspect or ask for physical inspection of the devices using the senses of hearing, sight, smell, and touch. Physical symptoms might be related, but not limited, to the following:

- Electromagnetic interference (EMI) from radio and television transmitters, or the introduction to the area of portable devices that create EMI
- Indicator lights of a NIC or networking device
- Cable connections, the crimping of connectors, and the physical state of connection sockets
- Incorrect seating of modules and cards
- Burning smells from insulating material that has melted, or of burned-out components
- Overheating caused by cooling fan malfunction

Gathering Symptoms from an End User: Software

When gathering symptoms for probable software configuration problems, a troubleshooter should start at the last known point where the network functioned correctly. If an end-user station can successfully ping the gateway but not the DNS server on another network segment, an entire set of potential problems associated with the physical layer at the user site can be eliminated. Effective questioning techniques can discover this type of information without requiring a trip to the end-user location. You can use the commands shown in Table 2-4 to check the status of various devices and to determine which configuration aspects to inspect.

Table 2-4 End-System Troubleshooting Commands

Command	Description
ping {*host* I *ip-address*}	Sends an echo request packet to an address and then waits for a reply. The *host* I *ip-address* variable is the IP alias or IP address of the target system.
telnet {*host* I *ip-address*}	Connects to an IP address or host name using the Telnet application.
Windows: **tracert** {*destination*} Mac/UNIX: **traceroute** {*destination*}	Identifies the path a packet takes through the network. The *destination* variable is the host name or IP address of the target system.
Windows: **ipconfig /all** Mac/UNIX: **ifconfig -a**	Displays information about an end-system's IP configuration.

The troubleshooter should use effective questioning techniques to document the symptoms of a problem:

- Ask questions that are pertinent to the problem.
- Use each question as a means to either eliminate or discover possible problems.
- Speak at a technical level that the user can understand.
- Ask the user when the problem was first noticed.
- Ask the user to recreate the problem if possible.
- Determine the sequence of events that took place before the problem happened.
- Match the symptoms the user describes with common problem causes.

Questions to Ask an End User

When asking an end user questions, it is important to follow a specific sequence so that you can gain the knowledge necessary to attain a solution. Some rules of thumb are given in Table 2-5.

Table 2-5 Interviewing End Users

Question Criteria	Questions to the End User
Ask questions that are pertinent to the problem.	When did the user first notice the problem?
Use questions to either eliminate or discover possible problems.	Can the user re-create the problem?
Speak at a technical level the user can understand.	What sequence of events took place before the problem happened?
Match user symptoms with common problem causes.	

Here's a typical format for interviewing end users concerning their problems:

- What doesn't work?
- What does work?
- Are the things that do and don't work related?
- Has the thing that doesn't work ever worked?
- When was the problem first noticed?
- What has changed since the last time it did work?
- Has anything unusual happened since the last time it worked?
- When exactly does the problem occur?
- Can the problem be reproduced? If so, how?

Flow Charts for Gathering Network and End-System Symptoms

A four-step process is recommended for gathering end-system symptoms of a problem, as shown in Figure 2-12.

Step 1   **Interview the user**—If possible, a troubleshooter gathers initial symptoms from the user and uses these symptoms as a basis for additional troubleshooting.

Step 2   **Analyze symptoms**—A troubleshooter gets a description of the problem by analyzing any gathered symptoms from the user.

Step 3 **Determine symptoms**—Using a layered troubleshooting approach, a trouble-shooter gathers hardware and software symptoms from the end-system, starting with the most likely cause. The troubleshooter should rely on previous experience, if possible, to decide if the problem is more likely a hardware or software problem.

Step 4 **Document symptoms**—Document any hardware and software symptoms. If the problem can be solved using the documented symptoms, a troubleshooter solves the problem and documents the solution. If the problem cannot be solved at this point, the isolating phase of the general troubleshooting process is initiated.

Figure 2-12 A Four-Step Process Is Recommended for Gathering End-System Symptoms of a Problem

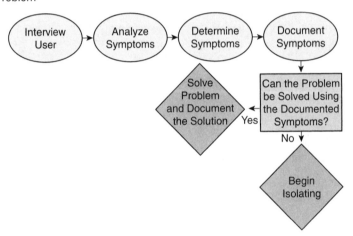

 Lab 2.3.5 Gathering Symptoms

In this lab exercise, the class is given a simple problem situation reported by the user. They must decide what questions to ask the user and what tools to use to completely document the symptoms of the problem. The class uses the troubleshooting checklist and Cisco IOS commands to work through a troubleshooting scenario. You define the problem by questioning users and using Cisco IOS tools.

Network Management Tools

Network management can range from a solitary network consultant monitoring network activity with a simple protocol analyzer to the use of a distributed database with auto polling of network devices. Network management can even include the use of high-end workstations generating real-time graphical views of network topology changes and traffic. In general, network management is a service that employs a variety of tools, applications, and devices to assist network managers in monitoring and maintaining networks. The following sections discuss some of these tools.

Network Management System Frameworks

Most network management architectures use the same basic structure and set of relationships. End stations, or managed devices, such as computer systems and other network devices, run software that lets them send alerts when they recognize problems. An example is when one or more users determine that thresholds have been exceeded.

Upon receiving these alerts, management entities are programmed to react by executing an action or group of actions. This includes operator notification, event logging, system shutdown, and automatic attempts at system repair.

Management entities can also poll end stations to check the values of certain variables. Polling can be automatic or user-initiated, but agents in the managed devices respond to all polls. Agents are software modules that first compile information about the managed devices in which they reside and then store this information in a management database. Finally, agents provide information proactively or reactively to management entities within network management systems (NMSs) via a network management protocol. Well-known network management protocols include Simple Network Management Protocol (SNMP) and Common Management Information Protocol (CMIP). Management proxies are entities that provide management information on behalf of other entities. Figure 2-13 shows a common network management architecture.

Figure 2-13 Network Management Systems Typically Involve a Sophisticated Network Management Software Package That Relies on SNMP to Communicate with Network Devices

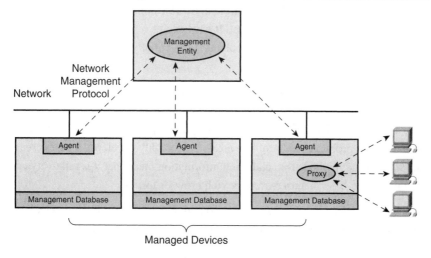

The ISO has contributed a great deal to network standardization. The organization's network management model is the primary means of understanding the major functions of NMSs. This model consists of five conceptual areas:

- **Performance management**—The goal is to measure and provide various aspects of network performance to maintain internetwork performance at an acceptable level. Examples of performance variables include network throughput, user response times, and line utilization.
- **Configuration management**—The goal is to monitor network and system configuration information so that the effects on network operation of various versions of hardware and software elements can be tracked and managed.
- **Accounting management**—The goal is to measure network utilization parameters so that individual or group use of the network can be regulated appropriately. Such regulation minimizes network problems because network resources can be apportioned based on resource capacities. It also maximizes the fairness of network access among users.
- **Fault management**—The goal is to detect, log, notify users of, and, if possible, automatically fix network problems to keep the network running effectively. Because faults can cause downtime or unacceptable network degradation, fault management is perhaps the most widely implemented of the ISO network management elements.
- **Security management**—The goals are to control access to network resources to prevent the network from being sabotaged or unintentionally brought down and to prevent sensitive information from being accessed by unauthorized users. A security management subsystem can monitor users logging on to a network resource and deny access to those who enter inappropriate access codes.

Knowledge-Base Tools

Knowledge-bases are an invaluable tool for the network troubleshooter. The most visible example of a knowledge-base is the Internet. It has become a very valuable tool for many individuals seeking answers to specific problems. It potentially represents a vast pool of experience-based information.

A *knowledge-base* is often a database of empirical information on a specific technical area. It consists of real solutions to problems encountered on a single occasion or numerous occasions. The art in knowledge-base tools is in identifying keywords or phrases that are associated with particular problems and problem areas. With highly developed Internet search engines, standardized methods for cataloging information mean that it is relatively easy to present a knowledge-base in a user-friendly Web browser format.

The Cisco Systems Web site at http://www.cisco.com incorporates a free knowledge-base tool on Cisco-related hardware and software. This site represents an invaluable troubleshooting resource for Cisco customers, support staff, and design personnel. It contains trouble-shooting procedures, implementation guides, and the original white papers on all aspects of data networking technology.

Knowledge-bases can also exist in customized form for specific technology areas. These knowledge-bases might be highly lucrative products for non-open-system architectures. Such a knowledge-base is shown in Figure 2-14.

Figure 2-14 Cisco.com Includes an Array of Knowledge-Bases, Such as the Cisco VPN Solution Center

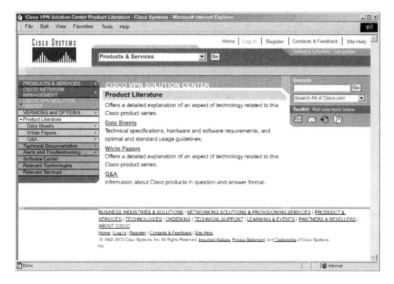

Performance Measurement and Reporting Tools

Cisco has developed numerous tools to manage and model network traffic flows. Each of the management tools described in this section has a distinct purpose.

The Cisco Security Device Manager (SDM) is a Web-based device management tool supported on Cisco 830, 1700, 2600XM, 3600, and 3700 series routers and 7204VXR, 7206XVR, and 7301 series routers. Network engineers use SDM for faster and easier deployment of Cisco routers for both WAN access and security features.

The Cisco Cluster Management Suite (CMS) software is Web-based network management software embedded in Catalyst fixed-configuration switches designed for midsize enterprise and branch office networks. The software reduces the time it takes to deploy and configure multiple switches by simplifying repetitive and time-consuming network management tasks and providing monitoring and troubleshooting tools. CMS is embedded in Catalyst 2900XL,

3500XL, 2950, and 3550 switches. It can manage a mix of all these plus the Catalyst 1900/2820 switches in a single interface.

CiscoWorks is the Cisco flagship network management product line. It delivers device-level monitoring, configuration, and fault management tools. The CiscoView device management software provides dynamic status, statistics, and configuration information for switched products.

CiscoWorks2000 includes the VPN/Security Management Solution (VMS). VMS is an integral part of the Cisco SAFE blueprint for network security. It combines web-based tools for configuring, monitoring, and troubleshooting enterprise virtual private networks (VPNs), firewalls, and network and host-based intrusion detection systems (IDSs). VMS delivers the industry's first robust and scalable foundation and feature set that addresses the needs of small and large-scale VPN and security deployments.

The CiscoView Software graphically displays a physical view of Cisco devices, allowing network managers to monitor remote devices without actually physically checking them. This tool provides monitoring functions and offers basic troubleshooting. The CiscoView Software, pictured for a particular 2950 switch in Figure 2-15, can be integrated with the following network management platforms:

- Sun Microsystems SunNet Manager
- Hewlett-Packard OpenView
- IBM NetView for AIX

Figure 2-15 CiscoView Permits Easy Management of Certain Catalyst Switches

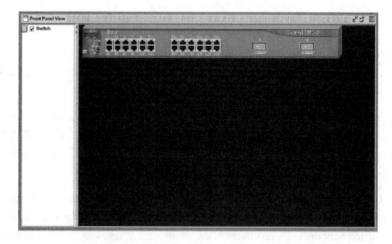

The CiscoWorks2000 product line offers a set of solutions designed to assist in managing an enterprise network. These solutions focus on three key areas in the network:

- LAN (see Figure 2-16)
- WAN
- Service-level management

Figure 2-16 CiscoWorks2000 Includes a LAN Management Solution

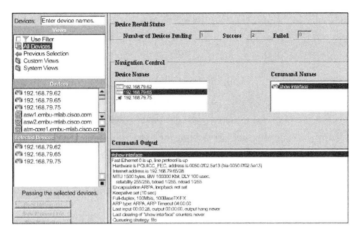

Although most CiscoWorks2000 offerings can be grouped into three areas, advanced packages are also available. For example, CiscoWorks Blue is designed for managing a consolidated Systems Network Architecture (SNA) and an IP network. Three CiscoWorks Blue packages are available:

- CiscoWorks Blue Internetwork Status Monitor (ISM) provides mainframe operators with full visibility of a Cisco router network from a single mainframe console.
- CiscoWorks Blue Maps provides dynamic views showing the state of the SNA protocols as they relate to the routed network.
- CiscoWorks Blue SNA View provides an easy-to-use Web interface that takes whatever information an end user can provide and quickly highlights the probable cause of an SNA problem.

Another advanced package is the Cisco Netsys Baseliner, a simulation-based planning and problem-solving tool for network managers, analysts, and designers. It allows offline test

NOTE

Netsys Baseliner and CiscoWorks Blue are designated as "end-of-life" (EOL) by Cisco and are no longer sold or supported.

configurations and changes before committing them to a live network. Netsys Baseliner lets a network administrator do the following:

- Test configurations and changes offline before committing them to the live network. Cisco Netsys Baseliner for Windows NT creates a model of the network and checks for more than 100 common yet difficult-to-isolate configuration problems.

- Graphically view the network as configured, not as planned or discovered. Baseliner shows you the big picture instantly, allowing you to visually navigate the network and gain a complete understanding of how it works.

- Proactively monitor configuration changes. When problems occur, recent configuration changes are often to blame.

With a general move toward fully switched networks and the impetus to include voice traffic within the data network, a greater level of accountability for traffic traveling on Ethernet networks is required than has previously been the case. Additionally, because of the time-sensitive and possibly financially sensitive nature of voice over IP (VoIP) traffic and the breaking up of the switched domain into VLANs, it is desirable to monitor and record the statistics and flows of data from individual VLANs or ports in the network to judge the impact of each on performance.

The Cisco Network Analysis Module (NAM), shown in Figure 2-17, allows a network administrator to do all of this. You also can manipulate the network performance information captured to get a real-time analysis of network performance and advance warning of bottlenecks or failures within a network. The NAM is a module for a Catalyst 6500 series chassis that contains hard drive storage to record information captured from a switched network from a number of Switch Port Analyzer (SPAN) sessions implemented on Cisco switches.

NAMs give network managers visibility into all layers of network traffic by providing application-level Remote Monitoring (RMON) functions based on RMON2 and other advanced Management Information Bases (MIBs). NAMs add to the built-in Remote Monitoring features in Catalyst 6500 series switches and Cisco 7600 series routers that provide port-level traffic statistics at the MAC or data-link layer. The NAMs provide intelligence to analyze traffic flows for applications, hosts, conversations, and network-based services such as quality of service (QoS) VoIP.

You also can access the NAM via a web-based browser, as shown in Figure 2-18, to find interactive information and reports on network performance and statistics based on the information captured.

Figure 2-17 The NAM Is Used in Catalyst 6500 Switches to Enhance Network Management

Figure 2-18 The Web Interface for the NAM Eases Configuration and Data Compilation

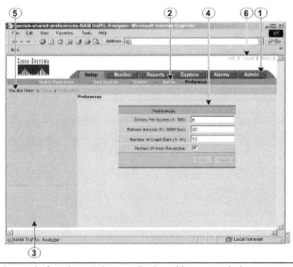

1) Tabs for accessing main functions; tabs are displayed in every window
2) Options associated with each tab; functions change in each tab depending on context
3) Where applicable, contents of functions related to the current context
4) Content area where graphs, tables, dialog boxes, charts, and instruction boxes are displayed
5) Context line that shows path to the current function
6) Toolbar to access global functions

Event and Fault Management Tools

Protocol analyzers, pair testers, and frequency-based field certification testers are classes of event and fault management tools.

Event Management Tools

A protocol analyzer decodes the various protocol layers in a recorded frame and presents them as readable abbreviations or summaries, detailing which layer is involved, such as physical, data-link, and so forth. In addition, it displays what function each byte or set of bytes serves.

Most protocol analyzers can filter traffic that meets certain criteria so that, for example, all traffic to and from a particular device can be captured.

Time-Stamped Capturing of Data

Time-stamped capturing of data performs the following tasks:

- Presents protocol layers in an easily readable form.
- Generates frames and transmits them onto the network.
- Incorporates an *expert system*, in which the analyzer uses a set of rules. These rules are combined with information about the network configuration and operation and are used to diagnose, solve, or offer potential solutions to network problems.

An example of a protocol inspector is the Fluke Optiview, shown in Figure 2-19.

Figure 2-19 Fluke Optiview Protocol Expert Is an Excellent Protocol Analyzer

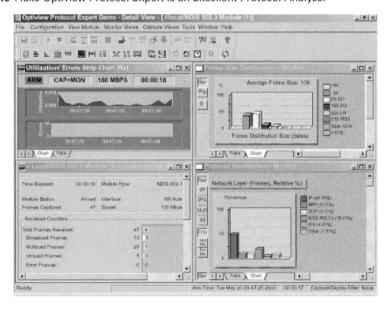

Fault management tools include pair testers and frequency-based certification testers.

Pair Testers

This category of tester is distinguished from a continuity tester by its ability to detect a split pair. A split pair is the simplest problem related to frequency that plagues network cable. It should be a minimum entry point for a network cable tester. If a cable passes the split pair test, it has a good chance of passing a basic Category 5 certification test. The Fluke 620 LAN Cablemeter, shown in Figure 2-20, is a simple but effective pair tester.

Figure 2-20 The Fluke 620 Is Used to Certify Category 5 Cables

Frequency-Based Field Certification Testers (Cable Analyzers)

The first generation of field certification testers usually offered selections for Category 5 cable types with a maximum frequency rating of 10 or 20 MHz. The second generation of field certification testers became available in late 1995 and offered 100 MHz testing. This generation of testers could certify Category 5 cable but not Category 5e cable (both 100 MHz). The third generation of field certification testers became available in late 1997 and offered testing to Category 6 speeds or higher. Unfortunately, the size of the tester has been increasing with each new generation. Many additional electronics are required to perform the growing suite of tests at ever-greater accuracy levels. One cable analyzer is shown in Figure 2-21.

Figure 2-21 The Fluke DSP-4300 Is a Sophisticated Cable Analyzer Used to Certify Category 5 and 6 Cable as Well as Fiber-Optic Cable

Policy Management Tools

Several policy management tools are available, with security policy management becoming ever more relevant for today's networks. This section introduces these policy management tools.

The Need for Policy-Based Security

Complex security technologies are necessary to protect highly available mission-critical networks from corruption and intrusion. Of particular interest in the past few years has been protecting geographically dispersed enterprise networks, which use a combination of public and private WAN lines to connect remote and branch offices to major centers. Intranets, extranets, Internet connections, WANs, and LANs each have unique security requirements. Many companies want to extend their mission-critical applications to remote offices by way of an intranet, or want to communicate directly with industry partners, suppliers, and key customers through extranets. These technologies allow organizations to securely conduct business in today's open environments.

Yet with all of the advanced capabilities of today's applications, it is surprising to find that the task of securing the complex networks that support them is still done by hand. Administrators often use detailed command-line interfaces (CLIs) to configure network devices one at a time across distributed enterprises. What's more, when policies change, implementation takes time.

Scaling Networks and Maintaining Security

In very large networks, scalability issues can make security deployment quite expensive and can lead to misconfigured systems and inconsistent policy enforcement. No centralized, coordinated mechanism exists to implement a consistent policy throughout the network, verify that it is installed and functioning properly, change it easily as required, or detect attacks, mistakes, and misuse within the network. A policy management solution must be scalable and must integrate network security.

Cisco Policy Management Solution

Cisco believes that administrators should be able to define, deploy, and enforce a security policy without requiring network administrators to work one-by-one across dozens (or hundreds or thousands) of devices. The Cisco Policy Management Solution provides end-to-end security policy management by placing a layer of intelligence between the administrator and the network itself. This layer provides translation between the intuitive policies developed to support business processes and the implementation of those policies in network devices.

The Cisco Policy Management Solution provides sophisticated tools that can analyze, interpret, configure, and monitor the state of security policy with browser-based user interfaces.

Examples of the Cisco Policy Management solution are

- Cisco VPN Solution Center Software, shown in Figure 2-22
- CiscoWorks VPN/Security Management Solution
- Cisco Secure User Registration Tool

Figure 2-22 The Cisco VPN Solution Center Is Part of the Integrated Cisco Policy Management Solution

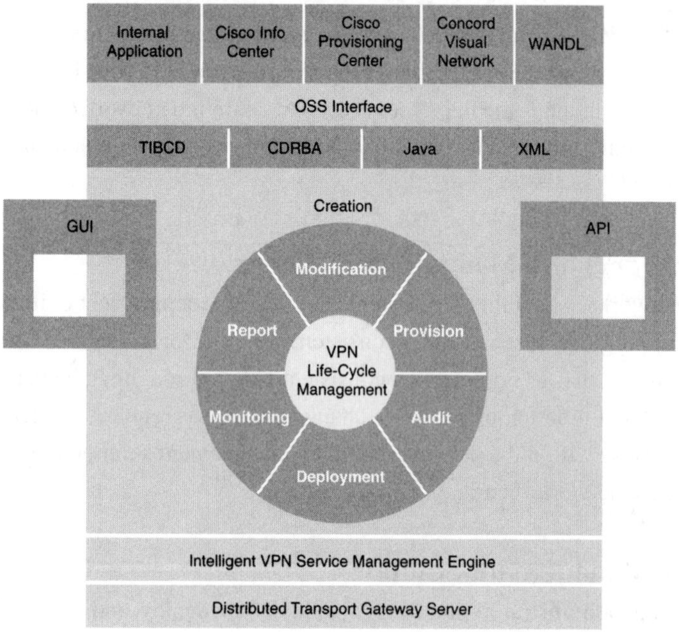

Summary

You should be able to list the stages of encapsulated data flow process. You also should be able to compare the logical layers of the OSI and TCP/IP networking models, and identify the logical layers used by devices on a network.

You should understand the following:

- The stages of the general troubleshooting process
- The bottom-up troubleshooting approach
- The top-down troubleshooting approach
- The divide-and-conquer troubleshooting approach
- How to select an effective troubleshooting approach based on a specific situation
- The process of gathering symptoms from a network
- Guidelines for gathering symptoms from a user
- The process of gathering symptoms from an end-system

Figure 2-23 summarizes the troubleshooting process.

Figure 2-23 The Troubleshooting Process Should Not Be Overly Complicated; Three Basic Steps Do the Job

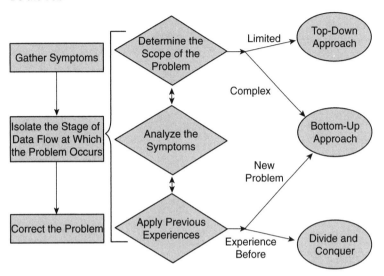

Key Terms

expert system   A system that uses a set of rules, combined with information about network configuration and operation, to diagnose, solve, or offer potential solutions to network problems.

knowledge-base   A database collection of empirical information on a specific technical area. It includes real solutions to common problems encountered.

Check Your Understanding

Use the following review questions to test your understanding of the concepts covered in this chapter. Answers are listed in Appendix A, "Check Your Understanding Answer Key."

1. Encapsulation at the transport layer involves what?

    A. Bits

    B. Packets

    C. Segments

    D. Frames

2. What are the three stages of the general troubleshooting process? Choose all that apply.

    A. Documenting the problem

    B. Correcting the problem

    C. Gathering symptoms

    D. Isolating the problem

3. What is the correct order for the three stages from Question 2?

    A. D, A, B

    B. C, D, B

    C. C, D, A

    D. C, A, B

4. What troubleshooting approach is recommended for complicated problems?

    A. Top-down

    B. Replacement

    C. Bottom-up

    D. Divide-and-conquer

5. What might be a suspected problem when using the top-down troubleshooting approach?

    A. Connectivity problem

    B. Hardware issue

    C. Software issue

    D. Physical fault

6. What troubleshooting approach is generally recommended for a new problem?

    A. Replacement

    B. Divide-and-conquer

    C. Bottom-up

    D. Top-down

7. What is often helpful when employing the divide-and-conquer approach to trouble-shooting?

    A. Network configuration diagram

    B. Sophisticated network management tool

    C. Past troubleshooting experience

    D. Topology diagram

8. What are the five stages of gathering symptoms for a network problem, in order?

    A. Analyze existing symptoms, determine ownership, narrow the scope, determine symptoms, document symptoms

    B. Narrow the scope, analyze existing symptoms, determine ownership, determine symptoms, document symptoms

    C. Analyze existing symptoms, narrow the scope, determine ownership, determine symptoms, document symptoms

    D. Determine ownership, analyze existing symptoms, narrow the scope, determine symptoms, document symptoms

9. What are the five stages of gathering end-system symptoms, in order?

    A. Determine symptoms, document symptoms, analyze symptoms, interview the user

    B. Determine symptoms, interview the user, analyze symptoms, document symptoms

    C. Analyze symptoms, interview the user, determine symptoms, document symptoms

    D. Interview the user, analyze symptoms, determine symptoms, document symptoms

10. Which type of network management has the goal of detecting, logging, and notifying users of network problems to keep the network running effectively?

    A. Performance management

    B. Configuration management

    C. Accounting management

    D. Fault management

Objectives

After completing this chapter, you will be able to perform tasks related to the following:

- Identify the characteristics of a physical layer failure problem
- Identify the characteristics of a physical layer optimization problem
- Identify end-system commands and applications that gather physical layer component information
- Identify the Cisco commands and applications that gather physical layer component information
- Recognize possible causes of common physical layer problems
- Isolate a problem at the physical layer
- Implement physical layer solutions

Chapter 3

Troubleshooting at the Physical Layer

The physical layer transmits bits from one computer to another and regulates the transmission of a stream of bits over the physical medium. This layer defines how the cable or antenna is attached to the network adapter and what transmission technique is used to send data over the medium.

Repeaters, hubs, multiplexers, and network interface cards (NICs) operate at the physical layer. A NIC is primarily a Layer 2 device, but it also operates at the physical layer of the Open System Interconnection (OSI) model. A NIC performs Media Access Control (MAC) sublayer functions, but it also encodes bits and sends them out on the medium. Repeaters, hubs, and multiplexers have no interest in higher-layer functions. They simply regenerate and propagate received bit streams to outgoing ports.

Failures and suboptimal conditions at the physical layer do not merely inconvenience users. Networks that experience these kinds of conditions usually come to a grinding halt. Because the upper layers of the OSI model depend on the physical layer to function, a network technician must be able to effectively isolate and correct problems at this layer.

Problems that occur at Layer 1 are distinctly different from problems that occur at higher layers. The physical layer is the only layer with physically tangible properties such as wires, cards, and antennas. This chapter describes identifiable characteristics and commands that help you isolate problems at the physical layer.

Characteristics of Physical Layer Failure Problems

Physical layer failures can be characterized by critical and noncritical characteristics. Critical characteristics include connectivity and upper-layer component operations. Noncritical characteristics include equipment indicators, power failures, and console messages.

Critical Characteristics—Connectivity

Whenever a physical layer failure occurs, a loss of connectivity is experienced. A user or group of users affected by the problem usually calls the help desk, complaining that they have lost their network connection. Less astute users might complain only that a specific service or application is not working. If a technician can log in to one of the affected devices and start gathering information, it is evident that no component above the physical layer is operating. A physical layer problem could also include someone unplugging a PC or switch.

Unlike network failures, all cable failures are approached in approximately the same manner, whether the link is newly installed or has failed during operation. There are many instances in which a poor-quality link has been in service, but because of the operating environment and influences, it has stopped working. These influences include visible damage to the cable, new electrical noise sources near the cable, or accidental movement of the cables.

Most networks have converted from coaxial cable to Category 5 or Category 5e unshielded twisted-pair (UTP) links, as shown in Figure 3-1. However, a surprising amount of coaxial cable still exists in legacy network segments. Fiber-optic cable is approaching a price point where it will rival Category 6 UTP in overall cost. The overall cost of a fiber-optic cable installation includes materials, labor, and network adapters. All of these items have become less expensive in recent years. Each cable type has different installation and maintenance issues.

Critical Characteristics—Upper Layer Component Operation

With the exception of Layer 1, each layer of the OSI model depends on the layer below it for communication to work. In the event of a Layer 1 connectivity problem, no component above the physical layer will be operational. For example, name resolutions, Address Resolution Protocol (ARP) requests, and Dynamic Host Configuration Protocol (DHCP) requests all rely on Layer 1 for connectivity. See Figure 3-2.

Figure 3-1 The Vast Majority of Switch Ports Are Dedicated to Category 5 and 6 UTP Cable
　　　　　　Installations

Figure 3-2 A Problem at the Physical Layer Translates into Problems at All OSI Layers

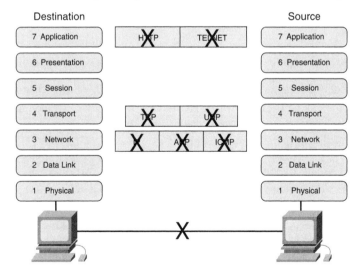

An example of upper-layer protocol failure would be a corporate user attempting to access a file server from a workstation. Depending on the location of the fault, the following types of communication components might fail:

- All pings to external devices would time out.
- The user would not be able to Telnet into any other device.
- The user would not be able to access network drives.
- E-mail messages would not be sent or received, and there might be an undeliverable message to this effect when you attempt to send.
- "Page cannot be displayed" messages occur when you attempt to gain intranet or Internet access.

Noncritical Characteristics—Equipment Indicators

The light emitting diodes (LEDs) on a device can give feedback for diagnosing the device's operational status. When the equipment has a physical problem, the LEDs of the failing device are usually off, flashing, or a different color than usual.

Most LED link lights are now controlled by software, so they are no longer reliable as a sole indicator of connectivity. If the link light is illuminated, it might or might not mean that a valid link is present. If the port is faulty, it might be possible to disconnect the cable and still see the link light illuminated. If the link light is off, however, it is still a fairly good indication that no link is present. For devices using multispeed interfaces such as 10/100 and 10/100/ 1000 NICs, it is not uncommon to see link lights at one end of a failing link, but not at the other.

If a 10BASE-T device is connected to a switch that is "hard-set" or only capable of 100BASE-TX, the link LED on the 10BASE-T device often shows that the link is active, but the network card fails to communicate. The 100BASE-TX switch does not show a link, and the 100BASE-TX Ethernet segment is unaffected.

If a 100BASE-TX-only station is connected to a shared-medium 10BASE-T hub, it does not show a link. The workstation causes somewhere between 33 percent and 100 percent collisions on the 10BASE-T collision domain. The 10BASE-T hub shows the link, and if it has status LEDs, it usually also shows constant utilization and/or collisions with those status LEDs. To troubleshoot mismatched speeds, a more thorough examination than just looking at the link-state LED is needed.

If a cable fault is the cause of link failure, an autonegotiating 10/100 device might successfully negotiate a link to 100BASE-TX, but it might not be able to subsequently establish and maintain signaling synchronization. This causes the link light to blink on and off as the Ethernet chipset repeatedly negotiates a connection speed and then fails to link. If the cable fault is not severe, the link might come up and operate very poorly for a short time before the link fails and is again renegotiated. If the affected port is a parallel uplink between switches, this fault can cause spanning-tree problems and loss of logical connectivity across a broadcast domain.

Noncritical Characteristics—Power Failures

A major category of physical layer problems you might encounter are power related. If power is not supplied to each network device within specific tolerances, a loss of service or damage to the unit might occur. If the power fluctuates above the design specifications for that device, either the device will have insufficient power to function, or it might be damaged. These fluctuations could include the following:

- **Power failure**—A power failure is characterized by a loss of power. Incoming power is subject to blackouts, which are complete power outages, often caused by downed power lines or electrical failures.

- **Power spike**—A power spike is a short burst of excessive power, usually lasting less than 1/60 of a second. Unprotected electronic equipment is vulnerable to this sudden, potentially massive increase in voltage. Power spikes are similar in nature to power surges, which can last as long as several seconds.

- **Brownouts**—Brownouts are inline power reductions of 10 percent or more. They are usually caused by utility company problems or a sudden drain of electricity from a particular part of the power grid.

- **Dirty power**—Dirty power is caused by electrical circuits experiencing transients and noise. Transients are brief high-speed electrical fluctuations caused by lightning or improper grounding. *Noise* is electromagnetic or radio frequency interference in the power signal caused by disruption from the external power grid or by feedback from local mechanical devices, such as printers and copiers.

Redundant power supplies are the norm for chassis-based Catalyst switches (see Figure 3-3). UPS installations are critical for dealing with power issues. In places such as hospitals or military installations, it is necessary to have generators in place in case of emergency.

Figure 3-3 Power Supplies in a Catalyst 6513 Can Be Both AC-Input, Both DC-Input, or One AC-Input and One DC-Input

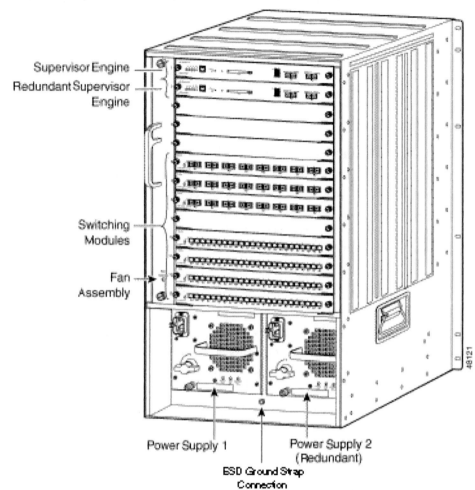

Many network devices, such as IP phones, are powered over Ethernet. Power over Ethernet is specified in IEEE 802.3af, delivering 48 volts of AC power over UTP cable (Category 3, 5, 5e, or 6). This means that it is more important than ever to protect Ethernet switches and inline power patch panels from power fluctuations.

Noncritical Characteristics—Console Messages

With a physical layer failure problem, sometimes a problem is discovered when a device shows console messages indicating that an interface is not functioning. For instance, the

show interfaces command for a failing interface might show one of the following (see Example 3-1):

- "interface is down, line protocol is down" (FastEthernet)
- "initialized, down state" (Token Ring)

Example 3-1 *When the IOS Declares the Interface to Be Down, You Know You Have Some Troubleshooting to Do*

```
RTA#show interfaces fastEthernet 0/0
FastEthernet0/0 is administratively down, line protocol is down
  Hardware is AmdFE, address is 0004.c136.66e0 (bia 0004.c136.66e0)
  Internet address is 10.30.18.41/24
<output omitted>
```

You can spoof an unattached Ethernet LAN interface to an "interface is up, line protocol is up" state by issuing the **no keepalive** command. Therefore, this command should not be used in a live network as a substitute for testing at the physical layer.

Table 3-1 lists possible problems that can cause the line status or line protocol to be down.

Table 3-1 Ethernet or Serial Interface "line protocol is down"

Interface Type	Interface Status	Line Protocol	Possible Cause
Any	Administratively Down	Down	Interface is shut down.
Fast Ethernet	Down	Down	Interface has a hardware problem.
Fast Ethernet	Up	Down	Interface does not have Layer 1 connectivity to the hub, switch, or other device.
Serial	Down	Down	Interface does not have Layer 1 connectivity to the telco.
Serial	Up	Down	Encapsulations are mismatched.
Serial (HDLC)	Up	Down	Interface has Layer 1 connectivity to the telco but does not have Layer 2 connectivity to the remote router.

continues

Table 3-1 Ethernet or Serial Interface "line protocol is down" (Continued)

Interface Type	Interface Status	Line Protocol	Possible Cause
Serial (PPP)	Up	Down	PPP authentication is unsuccessful.
Serial (Frame)	Up	Down	Interface has Layer 1 connectivity to the telco but does not have Layer 2 connectivity to the frame switch.

In a Frame Relay environment, troubleshooting is not so simple. For example, if the circuit goes down on one side of the *nonbroadcast multiaccess (NBMA) network*, but the connection to the local loop on the other side is functional and configured on a physical interface, the interface for that device still shows as administratively up and line protocol up. The connection of the remote router to the local switch is still up, even though the circuit with its partner is down.

If the connection is configured with subinterfaces on both ends, a loss of connectivity on either side causes both subinterfaces to go down.

Characteristics of Physical Layer Optimization Problems

Physical layer optimization problems are harder to troubleshoot than physical layer failures. A baseline is important for isolating physical layer optimization problems. Problems might result from exceeding cable design limits or poor-quality cabling or connections. These issues and their symptoms are described in this section.

Performance Lower Than Baseline

If there is a problem with suboptimal operation at the physical layer, the network is operational, but performance is consistently or intermittently lower than the level specified in the baseline.

If performance is unsatisfactory all the time, the problem is probably related to a poor configuration, inadequate capacity somewhere, or some other systemic problem. If performance varies and is not always unsatisfactory, the problem is probably related to an error condition or is being affected by traffic from other sources:

- Unstable routing because of a marginal port or link somewhere beyond the broadcast domain, possibly the result of a bad cable
- Excessive traffic across a low-speed LAN or WAN link, possibly causing traffic to be discarded or buffer capacity to be exceeded
- Overloaded server or service

A physical layer optimization problem occurs when the connection's physical properties are substandard, causing data to be transferred at a rate that is constantly less than the rate of data flow established in the baseline.

A number of factors can be involved in decreasing the rate at which data is transmitted across media. Major causes of networks performing below baseline are as follows:

- Exceeding the design limits of the media in terms of cabling distance or network devices
- Large collision domains in shared media networks such as CSMA/CD Ethernet
- *Electromagnetic interference (EMI)* effects
- Faulty media or hardware

Exceeding Cable Design Limits, Poor-Quality Cabling, and Connections

Attenuation and return loss are common symptoms of problems with exceeding cable design limits, poor-quality cabling, or connections.

Attenuation

A common issue of exceeding the design limits of a media type is the *attenuation* of the bit stream transmitted along the medium. Attenuation depends on the medium over which the traffic is being transmitted. Attenuation might occur to such an extent that the receiving device cannot always successfully distinguish the component bits of the stream from each other. This ends in a garbled transmission and results in a request from the receiving device for retransmission of the missed traffic by the sender.

Each network medium is rated for a specific distance. Category 5 media have a maximum rated cabling distance of 100 meters. Beyond that distance, the signal must be regenerated, or it might degenerate and be unreadable by the receiving end. To get an accurate measurement of a cable's length, use a cable tester.

A far more common source of attenuation is a very poor connection resulting from a loose cable or dirty or oxidized contacts. One bad patch cable can easily cause an entire link to fail. Another source of this fault is using the wrong category of cable, such as using Category 3 cable for a link being tested to Category 5e limits.

Return Loss

Return loss is a measure of all reflections that are caused by the impedance mismatches at all locations along the link. It indicates how well the characteristic impedance of the cable matches its rated impedance over a range of frequencies. The characteristic impedance of links tends to vary from higher values at low frequencies to lower values at higher frequencies. Return loss is expressed in decibels.

The termination resistance at both ends of the link must be equal to the link's characteristic impedance to avoid reflections. A good match between characteristic impedance and termination resistance in the end equipment provides for a good transfer of power to and from the link and minimizes reflections. Return loss results vary significantly with frequency.

One small source of return loss is variations in the value of the characteristic impedance along the cable. This might be caused by slight untwisting or separation of wires in the pairs or variations in the wire's metal and the insulation's uniformity. Another source of return loss is reflections from inside the installed link, mainly from connectors. Mismatches predominantly occur at locations where connectors are present. The main impact of return loss is not on loss of signal strength but rather the introduction of signal jitter, the variation in delay over time from point to point. Jitter is of special concern for time-sensitive traffic such as voice over IP (VoIP). Excessive jitter seriously degrades call quality. Signal reflections truly cause loss of signal strength, but generally this loss, because of return loss, does not create a significant problem.

Return loss is of particular concern in the implementation of Gigabit Ethernet.

Noise

Local EMI is commonly called noise. Four types of noise are most significant to data networks:

- Impulse noise—voltage fluctuations or current spikes induced on the cabling
- Random (white) noise distributed over the frequency spectrum
- Alien *crosstalk*
- Near-end crosstalk (NEXT)

The default threshold level for the detection and registration of impulse noise is 270 millivolts (mV) (determined by the 10BASE-T specification in the IEEE 802.3i standard). For high-speed network applications such as 1000BASE-T (Gigabit Ethernet), the recommended threshold value for impulse noise detection is 30 or 40 mV.

Random noise can be generated by many sources, including wireless communications, such as FM radio stations, police radio, building security, avionics for automated landing, and many more. A spectrum analyzer is needed to determine the frequency characteristics and magnitude of the noise signals picked up by the cabling links. This laboratory-type device can identify the frequencies of the signals (noise) on the link as well as the relative magnitude of the signals at the different frequencies.

Alien crosstalk is noise induced by other cables in the same pathway. It is detected the same way that random noise is. Anytime a UTP link is tested in a bundle of cables in which some links are active, chances are very good that the tester will detect alien crosstalk, especially when the traffic is 100BASE-T. The tester reports the "external noise detected" message. Typically, this alien crosstalk does not affect the network traffic's reliability.

Excessive crosstalk is usually reported in the NEXT test results on cable-testing devices. NEXT can originate either inside or outside the link. Crosstalk originating nearest the transmission source is usually the loudest and has the greatest amplitude or leaks into the measured pair. To minimize crosstalk, ensure that the cable, at each termination point, is left untwisted for no more than the allowed 13 mm (0.5 inch). Crosstalk becomes correspondingly worse as more cable is untwisted.

The crosstalk occurring outside the link is actually crosstalk from other adjacent cables or noise from a variety of sources. Noise sources include nearby electric cables and devices, usually with high current loads. These can include large electric motors, elevators, photocopiers, coffee makers, fans, heaters, welders, compressors, fluorescent lights, and so on. Another, less obvious source is radiated emissions from transmitters. This includes TVs, radios, microwaves, cell phone towers, handheld radios, and anything else that includes a transmitter more powerful than a cell phone.

Collisions

Collision domain problems affect the local medium and disrupt communications to Layer 2 or Layer 3 infrastructure devices, local servers, or services. They typically result from the following problems:

- Bad cables
- Marginal or intermittent workstation NICs
- Marginal or intermittent ports on hubs or switches
- Errors or excessive traffic on the local collision domain
- Duplex mismatches (probably the most common problem)
- Electrical noise and other environmental disruptions

Collisions are normally a more significant problem on shared media than on switch ports. Increasing the number of collision domains (by getting rid of hubs) solves most of the problems involving collision domains. Average collision counts on shared media should generally be less than 5 percent, but that number is conservative. Be sure that judgments are based on the average and not a peak or spike in collisions.

If the average utilization is high (sustained peaks greater than 60 percent for shared media and greater than 80 to 90 percent for switched links), and collision counts are acceptable (an average of less than 5 percent for shared media and less than 1 percent for switched links), the network might simply be saturated. Too many stations might be transmitting within this collision domain, or the network architecture might need optimizing for shorter distances between distant stations.

Physical layer or Layer 1 network devices act to increase the span of a collision domain, effectively increasing the scope of a potential problem from bad to worse. Layer 1 devices such as repeaters and hubs act to regenerate signals and, therefore, increase the maximum distance over which a network can operate. Hubs additionally act to increase the size of the collision domain. They contain from four to 48 ports for station connectivity. A hub regenerates any signal received and resends it out all active ports.

Be very careful when troubleshooting collision problems, because the obvious answer is usually wrong. The addresses found in collision fragments belong to stations that transmitted legally. Stations that send enough of the current frame to have a source address in a collision fragment usually start transmitting first, although that depends in part on the monitoring point within the collision domain. Most of the stations that collide with those legally transmitted frames also operate legally. They do not "hear" anything on the wire, so they begin transmitting. If a station has gone "deaf" and is stepping on other transmissions because it does not hear them, it will probably never be discovered, because its frame collides with another transmission and its data is always corrupted. Troubleshoot the presence of too many collisions, but don't examine the fragments closely. Using the corrupted data from collision fragments will just cause you frustration.

Late Collisions

A late collision is counted when a collision is detected by a device after it has sent the 512th bit of its frame. No more than a few late collisions should ever occur in any environment. If a device is incrementing a collision counter, further investigation is needed as a significant problem is occurring. If the number of late collisions is occurring at a steady rate, you might notice performance degradation.

Any of the following conditions might cause late collisions:

- Incorrect configuration
- Duplex mismatch (one host operating at half duplex while another host is operating at full duplex)
- Faulty cabling
- Faulty hub or shared media device
- Faulty NIC or switch port
- Excessive network traffic beyond the limitations of the shared media hub or switch port

The old theory that a late collision is the result of a too-long cable is challenged by calculating the delay introduced by the cable only. Although delay introduced by the cable is a factor, it is much more likely that other factors such as cable impedance mismatches, signal attenuation along the cable, too many repeaters, and marginal interfaces result in situations in which a shortened cable eliminates late collisions. Table 3-2 lists some of the possible causes.

NOTE

Collisions and late collisions should never occur on any router, switch, or NIC port operating at full duplex. Some Cisco Catalyst switches, such as the Catalyst 6500, disable ports on excessive late collisions, even when operating at half duplex.

Table 3-2 Causes of Late Collisions with Half-Duplex Ethernet

Cause	Error Type				
	Late Collision	Short Frame	Jabber	FCS	Ghost
Bad software drivers	•	•	•	•	
Faulty/marginal NIC	•	•	•	•	•
Transceiver fault	•		•	•	•
Repeater fault	•		•	•	•
Too many repeaters	•			•	
Coax taps too close	•			•	•
Illegal hardware configuration	•		•	•	•
Cable too long	•			•	
Cable fault	•		•	•	•
Termination	•		•	•	•
Bad grounding	•		•	•	•
Induced noise	•		•	•	•
Duplex mismatch	•			•	

Other Data Transmission Issues

Some other data transmission issues that cause physical layer optimization problems are short frames, jabber, and ghosts.

Short Frames

The most likely cause of a short frame is a faulty card or an improperly configured or corrupt NIC driver file.

Jabber

Jabber is often defined as the condition in which a network device continually transmits random, meaningless data onto the network. Table 3-3 lists possible causes. IEEE 802.3, found at http://www.ieee802.org/3/, defines jabber as a data packet whose length exceeds the standard. These packets are called long frames. Cyclically lock out the port, and then check later to see if it is OK. The standard says that after the jabber timer expires (20,000 to 50,000 bit times), the hub should close the port for a while before reopening it to see if the attached device has stopped transmitting. If jabber is again detected, the port might be closed for another cycle. This might continue forever.

Table 3-3 Causes of Errors with Full-Duplex Ethernet

	Error Type					
Cause	**Collision Fragment**	**Short Frame**	**Jabber**	**FCS**[*]	**Dropped Link**	**Alignment**
Bad software drivers		•	•	•		
Faulty/marginal NIC	•	•	•	•	•	•
Duplex mismatch	•			•		•
Cable too long				•	•	
Cable fault			•	•	•	•
Induced noise			•	•	•	•

[*]   FCS errors are likely to include late collision.

In general, jabber is not a common occurrence. The most likely causes of jabber are a faulty NIC and/or faulty or corrupt NIC driver files, bad cabling, and grounding problems.

Ghosts

Ghosts are easily created by a variety of causes on coaxial Ethernet. They also might be caused by something as simple as installing a second crossover cable between two hubs on half-duplex 10BASE-T. The parallel path sometimes causes very strange symptoms. The hub does one of the following:

- Locks out one port, sometimes requiring a power cycle or Simple Network Management Protocol (SNMP) management intervention to reopen it. Fortunately, this is the most common result.
- Allows the error to continue uninterrupted. This is not permitted by the standard.

The error level often fluctuates between very little and the available bandwidth for no apparent reason. In addition to ghosts, this second crossover cable fault usually produces collisions, late collisions, and frame check sequence (FCS) errors.

Resources

If network resources are operating at or near maximum capacity, this can cause physical layer problems. In some instances of suboptimal network performance, data might flow at expected rates, but it starts and stops unexpectedly. In other instances the data flows continuously, but at an undesirable rate.

Poor performance might be caused by the same conditions that prevent a connection from being established in the first place, or from the same conditions that cause connections to drop. Some common causes of slow or poor performance are as follows:

- Network resources operating at maximum capacity
- Recent changes on the problem server or station
- Viruses on the user station

The following procedures assume that the connection was operating properly before the problem and that the following have already been checked:

- Nothing has been changed recently on the problem station or on the server or service that might have caused this problem, such as reconfiguring or adding new software or hardware.
- Potential station memory allocation problems and software conflicts on the station have been eliminated by unloading all but the minimum software required to operate a test application across the network. For this test, disable any virus checking or security software, but re-enable it immediately after the test.
- The user's station has been tested for viruses. You also have looked for applications that are consuming disproportionate amounts of the microprocessor resources or that are hanging the system long enough to exceed connection timers.

The most common reasons for slow or poor performance include overloaded or underpowered servers, unsuitable switch or router configurations, traffic congestion on a low-capacity link, and chronic frame loss.

Utilization

A component might be operating suboptimally at the physical layer because it is being used at a higher average than it is configured to operate. When you troubleshoot this type of problem, it will become evident that resources for the device are operating at or near maximum capacity and that the number of interface errors is increasing. Gathering symptoms reveals excessive runts, late collisions, or an increase in the number of buffer failures. The output from a **ping** or **traceroute** command results in excessive packet loss or latency.

How Much Utilization Is OK?

Shared Ethernet networks are believed to suffer from throughput problems when average traffic loads approach a maximum average capacity level of 40 percent. This percentage is actually conservative. Higher average percentages are certainly possible. The classic solution to excessive traffic is to microsegment LANs by installing switches. This solution works well until the amount of broadcast traffic grows too large. Because bridges and switches always forward all broadcast traffic to all ports, even infrequent broadcasts from each station eventually become too numerous when the station count for the broadcast domain goes up.

If a single station is connected to a half-duplex switch port, acceptable utilization is best learned by monitoring switch port statistics. There will be some level of collisions, but because that link has only two devices (the switch and the station), the utilization level should be capable of averaging quite high. The switch probably will periodically report excessive collision errors, resulting from the Ethernet capture effect. This problem is not terribly significant overall and results in a slight reduction in performance. If the link is allowed to negotiate to full duplex instead of half, the connection should be able to approach theoretical limits for full-line-rate Ethernet. This depends on the processing power of the attached station. The current generation of switches is quite capable of sustaining line-rate traffic at the minimum frame size.

Another problem can occur when access to servers or services is reached through a single switch uplink path. Unless the bandwidth of the uplink path is bigger than the total of simultaneous station requests, the uplink itself becomes a bottleneck. This scenario arises when a network is designed with all servers collected in a server farm, separated from the virtual LANs (VLANs) they serve.

Network bottlenecks or congestion typically manifest themselves to users with the following symptoms:

- Highly variable response times
- Network timeouts or server disconnects
- Inability to establish network connections
- Slower application loading and/or running

Even when network resources are on the same LAN segment as the users, you still must examine the network architecture to see if bottlenecks exist. If too much traffic is required to pass through an inadequate aggregation path, a potentially useful architecture design is defeated. To prevent this, the network administrator should limit intersegment traffic by carefully considering which nodes should attach to each segment. This process involves an investment of time and might need to be repeated regularly on extremely dynamic networks. Monitor uplink paths as a part of routine maintenance to detect impending saturation of any one path.

Quality of service (QoS) technologies are also available for prioritizing traffic (such as low-latency queuing [LLQ] for voice traffic), congestion avoidance (such as Weighted Random Early Detection [WRED]), and rate limiting (such as committed access rate [CAR]).

Console Messages

All error messages begin with a percent sign and are displayed in the following format:

`%FACILITY-SEVERITY-MNEMONIC: Message-text`

FACILITY is a code consisting of two or more uppercase letters that indicates the facility to which the message refers. A facility might be a hardware device, a protocol, or a module of the system software. Table 3-4 lists the codes for some of the system facilities.

Table 3-4 System Facility Codes

Code	Facility
AAA	TACACS+ authentication, authorization, and accounting security
ALIGN	Memory optimization in the Reduced Instruction Set Computer (RISC) processor
ARAP	Apple Remote Access Protocol
IP	Internet Protocol

continues

Table 3-4 System Facility Codes (Continued)

Code	Facility
IPMCAST	Gigabit switch router line card IP multicast
IP-SNMP	Simple Network Management Protocol specific to IP
IPX	Internetwork Packet Exchange protocol
LSS	LightStream Switching Subsystem
PIM	Protocol-Independent Multicast
RIP	IP Routing Information Protocol
SMF	Software MAC Filter
SNMP	Simple Network Management Protocol
SNMP_MGR	SNMP proxy
TACACS	Terminal Access Controller Access Control System
TBRIDGE	Transparent bridging
TCP	Transmission Control Protocol

SEVERITY is a single-digit code from 0 to 7 that reflects the condition's severity: the lower the number, the more serious the situation. Table 3-5 lists the severity levels.

Table 3-5 Severity Levels

Severity Level	Severity Type	Description
0	Emergency	System unusable
1	Alert	Immediate action is needed
2	Critical	Critical condition
3	Error	Error condition
4	Warning	Warning condition
5	Notification	Normal but significant condition
6	Informational	Informational message only
7	Debugging	Appears during debugging only

MNEMONIC is a code consisting of uppercase letters that uniquely identifies the message.

Message-text is a text string describing the condition. This portion of the message sometimes contains detailed information about the event being reported, including terminal port numbers, network addresses, or addresses that correspond to locations in the system memory address space. Because the information in these variable fields changes from message to message, it is represented in Table 3-6 by short strings enclosed in square brackets ([ ]). For example, a decimal number is represented as [dec]. Table 3-6 is a complete list of the kinds of variable fields and the information contained in them.

Table 3-6 Representations of Variable Fields in Error Message Text

Representation	Type of Information
[dec]	Decimal number
[hex]	Hexadecimal number
[char]	Single character
[chars]	Character string
[sci_notation]	Scientific notation
[node]	Address or node name
[atalk_address]	AppleTalk address
[atalk_net]	AppleTalk network, either 600 or 600-601
[enet]	Ethernet address (for example, 0000.FRED.00C0)
[inet]	Internet address (for example, 12.128.2.16)
[t-line]	Terminal line number in octal (or decimal if the decimal-TTY service is enabled)
[v-name]	VINES name or number (hex or decimal)

Here's a sample error message:

```
Error message: %HELLO-2-NORDB: Redistributed IGRP without rdb
```

In this message, HELLO is the facility, 2 is the severity, and NORDB is the mnemonic. This message indicates that an internal software error has occurred. The corrective action in this case is to contact technical support for assistance.

Here's another sample error message:

```
Error message: %IP-4-DUPADDR Duplicate address [inet] on [chars], sourced by [enet]
```

This error message indicates that two systems are using an identical IP address and that it should be changed on one of the two systems.

Windows and Cisco Commands for Physical Layer Information Gathering

Microsoft Windows operating systems, UNIX operating systems, and Macintosh operating systems all have useful commands for troubleshooting physical layer problems.

End-System Commands—Common Commands

To gather information on a physical layer problem, it is important to be familiar with end-station commands that exist for this purpose. Interrogating devices at the periphery of the network is a good idea when end systems are experiencing connectivity problems.

A number of commands are common to popular operating platforms such as Windows, UNIX, and Mac OS. You can use these to ascertain whether an end station is achieving connectivity with the network.

The **ping** {*host* | *ip-address*} command is used to verify connectivity between hosts by sending an Internet Control Message Protocol (ICMP) echo request to the target IP address. If all host unreachable results are returned to the sending station, this indicates that the station does not have connectivity to the network. It is typical to ping a LAN segment's directly attached router interface and then ping progressively further into the network to establish the point at which loss of connectivity occurs.

A **traceroute** utility can be used on end systems to test connectivity to a destination device. It lets a user map the route taken on the way to the destination.

ARP utilities can be used on end systems to view Layer 2 to Layer 3 mappings.

End-System Commands—Windows Only

For Windows end systems, the user often queries a network connection at the MS-DOS command prompt. By entering commands at the DOS command prompt, or by using the Run window on the Start menu, a user can establish whether a connection is present with other network devices. The path that data takes to reach the destination also can be determined. It can be used to verify multiple links and also the reliability of any connection. Some Windows end-system commands are described in Table 3-7.

Table 3-7 ipconfig, tracert, and winipcfg

Command	Description
ipconfig /all	Displays IP information for hosts running Windows NT/2000/XP.
tracert [*destination*]	Verifies connectivity to a destination device for Windows hosts. The destination variable is the IP alias or IP address of the target system.
winipcfg	Displays information for hosts running Windows 9x or Me.

The **ipconfig /all** command is a simple way to check connectivity on a Windows NT/2000/XP system. It identifies the host MAC address, DNS, DHCP, NT, and WINS servers that the host is attached to if it has physical connectivity.

The **tracert** command can be used to test connectivity to a destination device. It lets a user map the route taken on the way to the destination.

The **winipcfg** command is used in older versions of Windows, from 9x up to Me. As the name suggests, **winipcfg** shows the Windows IP configuration information.

arp -a is a very useful interrogatory command, because it establishes whether a LAN segment has Layer 2 and Layer 3 connectivity. The ARP table is flushed and renewed periodically. If this command does not return a list of MAC addresses and associated IP addresses, the loss of connectivity is very likely to be at the physical layer. This also is the case if the MAC address corresponding to the attached router interface is not present. Although peer machines are still present in an ARP table, the link to the router interface or the interface itself is likely to be the problem.

End-System Commands—UNIX/Mac OS

For UNIX or Mac OS end systems, the user often queries the status of the network connection by using run mode to execute network connectivity queries. By entering commands, a user can establish whether a connection is present with other network devices, the path that data takes to reach the target, and the reliability of any connection. Table 3-8 lists a couple of UNIX troubleshooting commands.

Table 3-8 ifconfig -a and traceroute

Command	Description
ifconfig -a	Displays IP information for Mac OS X and UNIX hosts.
traceroute [*destination*]	Identifies the path a packet takes through the network. The *destination* variable is the IP alias or IP address of the target system.

The **ifconfig -a** command performs the same function that the **ipconfig** command performs for Windows NT/2000/XP systems. It lists the IP address information for Mac OS X and UNIX hosts.

The **traceroute** command can be used to show the path a packet takes through the network. It is useful to identify at what point a link is broken, or suboptimal, in the network.

Common Cisco IOS Commands

A variety of commands exist under the Cisco IOS to gather information on connectivity problems, as shown in Table 3-9. When a router experiences an absence or intermittent loss of connectivity to other network components, the device can be interrogated for statistics collected on a port or interface. Additionally, networking processes can be monitored in real time to determine at what point in the sequence connectivity is lost. When numerous routes to a desired destination exist, and the destination is suffering intermittent or total loss of connectivity, you can collect information on the point at which the break occurs.

Table 3-9 Common Cisco IOS Commands

Command	Description
clear counters	Resets the counters for statistics that are accumulated for an interface or port.
debug {*options*}	Shows detailed information about a connection's operation.
diag [*slot*]	Tests components of a line card.
ping {*host* | *ip-address*}	(User or extended) Verifies and diagnoses connectivity between hosts.
traceroute {*host* | *ip-address*}	Diagnoses the connection route between hosts.
undebug all	Disables all enabled debugging applications.

Cisco IOS show Commands

IOS **show** commands, shown in Table 3-10, represent the most complete set of tools in the IOS armory for collecting information on network outages. A very wide range of parameters can be examined individually or in combination with other related parameters. Individual components in a router or switch can be examined from a number of different angles. Use the **show** commands to gain insight into likely causes of loss of network connectivity.

Table 3-10 Cisco IOS **show** Commands

Command	Description
show arp	Displays the contents of the ARP cache.
show buffers	Displays statistics of the memory buffer pool for a device.
show cdp neighbors	Displays the device type, IP address, and Cisco IOS version.
show context	Displays information stored in nonvolatile RAM (NVRAM) when an exception occurs.
show controllers	Displays controller statistics, and verifies that a cable is properly connected. Data terminal equipment/data communications equipment (DTE/DCE) status of a serial interface can also be verified.
show diag [*slot*]	Diagnoses information about the components of a line card.
show diagbus [*slot*]	Diagnoses the controller, interface processor, and port adapters associated with a specified slot.
show environment	Displays information about the power supplies and the temperature inside the device.
show interfaces	Displays the operational status of an interface as well as the amount and type of traffic being sent and received.
show ip interface [*brief*]	Displays a summary of the status of all interfaces on a device.
show logging	Verifies the type of messages that generate logging output.
show mac-address-table [*module/port*]	Displays the MAC counters for traffic passing through a port, such as received frames, transmit frames, out-lost, and in-lost.
show memory	Displays the contents of the RAM memory for the device.

continues

Table 3-10 Cisco IOS **show** Commands (Continued)

Command	Description
show module	Displays a summary of the status of modules on a Catalyst switch.
show port {*module/port*}	Displays a detailed description of a specific port.
show port status	Displays a summary of the status of all ports on a Catalyst switch.
show processes cpu	Displays CPU utilization statistics.
show processes memory	Displays a list of all processes running on the system.
show running-config	Displays the current configuration, including keepalive settings.
show stacks	Displays the processor stacks on a router. Requires a stack decoder to analyze the output.
show tech-support	Provides general information about a device that can be useful for reporting problems to the Cisco Technical Assistance Center (TAC).
show version	Verifies that Cisco IOS recognizes all installed hardware components.

Not all of the commands listed are available on some versions of Cisco operating systems. To determine which commands are available for use with particular devices, consult the online documentation for Cisco devices at http://www.cisco.com/univercd/home/home.htm.

 Lab 3.1.1 Applying a Logical Layered Model to a Physical Network

In this lab exercise, you use various Cisco IOS commands and a protocol analyzer to map the layers in the OSI model to the encapsulated data flow in the classroom network. You complete the following tasks: Develop a logical diagram for data link layer and network layer functionality in the core, noting which MACs relate to which ports; map traffic flows for ping, Telnet, and HTTP traffic from the workgroup PCs; and capture and analyze background traffic.

Identifying Physical Layer Problems

Identifying physical layer problems means looking for power-related issues, cable faults, hardware failures, sources of collisions, sources of external interference, configuration errors, and causes of CPU overload.

Power-Related

Power-related issues are the most fundamental reason for network failure. The main AC power flows into either an external or internal AC-to-DC transformer module within a device. The transformer provides correctly modulated DC current, which powers device circuits, connectors, ports, and the blowers used for device cooling.

If a power-related issue is suspected, a physical inspection of the power module is often carried out. You can use the flow chart shown in Figure 3-4 to help troubleshoot power-related problems.

Initially, with the power switch on, does the blower operate?

- If it does, the AC input checks out.
- If it doesn't, suspect the AC input, AC source, router circuit breaker, or power supply cable.

With the power switch on and system LEDs lit, do the fans operate?

- If not, suspect the fans.

Does the system shut down after being on a short time?

- Suspect an environmentally induced shutdown.
- Check the environmental site requirements in the device documentation, and ensure that the chassis intake and exhaust vents are clear.
- Suspect a power supply failure. Have other devices in the area powered down?

The system partially boots, but LEDs do not light.

- Suspect a 5-volt power supply failure.
- Check the UPS devices.

Figure 3-4 With Power-Related Problems, It Is Important to Check That the Fans Are Operating

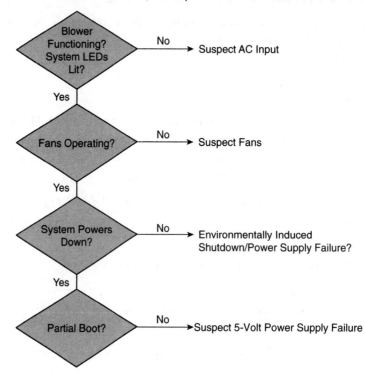

Distribution- and core-layer Cisco devices are generally modular in nature. This approach can follow through for these units' power supplies. Often parallel and backup power supplies exist in the chassis to balance the power load and to provide uninterrupted operation in the event of failure of a single or multiple online power modules.

To help isolate a power subsystem problem, follow these steps:

Step 1 Check whether the power supply LED labeled GOOD is off or if the LED labeled FAIL is on.

Step 2 If the LED labeled GOOD is off or if the LED labeled FAIL is on, follow these steps:

a. Ensure that the power supply is flush with the back of the chassis.

b. Unplug the power cord, loosen and reinstall the power supply, tighten the captive installation screws, and then plug in the power cord.

Step 3   If the LED labeled GOOD remains off, there might be a problem with the AC source or the power cable. Connect the power cord to another power source if one is available.

Step 4   If the LED labeled GOOD fails to light after the power supply is connected to a new power source, replace the power cord.

If this unit has more than one power cord, repeat the steps for each power supply.

Cabling Faults—Cat5

You can correct many problems by simply reseating cables that have become partially disconnected. When performing a physical inspection, look for damaged cables, improper cable types, and poorly crimped registered jack-45s (RJ-45s). Suspect drop cables should be subjected to a simple cable test and exchanged with a known-good cable. Do not assume that just because a cable is new, just out of the package, that it will work. Test it first. You should also test cables made on-site before attempting to troubleshoot with them. Anyone can have a bad day and miswire the termination. Also test for simple cable faults such as shorts, opens, and split pairs.

Determine whether a station connected by UTP or fiber is successfully linking to the network at the MAC layer. Use the command **ipconfig /all** for Windows NT/2000/XP/2003-based systems and **ifconfig -a** for UNIX/Mac OS platforms. Test UTP for voltage levels and the presence and polarity of link pulses. Many new switches and some NICs have auto-sensing ports that compensate for polarity faults on a copper cable. Moving a station from a newer switch that compensates for some types of cable faults to an older hub or switch might make you think the older device is at fault, when in fact, the newer switch is compensating for a pre-existing cable fault.

Copper links between one hub and another, between two switches, or between two PCs require crossover connections. Stations are connected to Layer 1 or 2 devices with cables that are not crossed over, often called straight-through cables (see Figure 3-5). Check for crossover cables or hub and switch ports that are configured as a crossover with a simple button press. Many new switches, as well as all 1000BASE-T links, can compensate for crossover cables used instead of straight cables. Some simple hubs use a single connection internally to service a crossover port and an adjacent normal port. Only one of them might be used for RJ-45 jacks. This configuration is usually indicated beside the jacks for the shared port.

Figure 3-5 Straight-Through Cables Align the Individual Wires in a One-to-One Fashion on
Opposite Connectors

Split-pair cables operate either poorly or not at all, depending on the Ethernet speed used, the
length of the split segment, and how far it is located from either end. The farther the split is
from a transmitter, the less effect it has because of signal attenuation. If the split is short, such
as a patch cable, and it is located midway between the two ends of a long run, 10BASE-T
might operate mostly error-free. Even a short split cable anywhere along a 1000BASE-T link
will likely disrupt traffic and might even prevent the link from coming up.

Cabling Faults—Fiber and Coax

Cabling faults for coaxial cable and fiber-optic cable are described in this section. Coaxial
cable is no longer deployed for Ethernet networks but is still used with cable TV installations.

Coaxial Cable

Coaxial cabling, shown in Figure 3-6, runs from a bus topology. Each station NIC acts as an
intermediary connector for the run, linking devices in the LAN in one continuous run. Thin
Ethernet (10BASE2) can contain 30 hosts in a LAN segment. Breaks in the cable can be difficult to locate because all stations form a continuous segment, with no microsegmentation
occurring.

Problems with coaxial cable often occur at the connectors. When the center conductor on the
coaxial cable end is not straight and of the correct length, a good connection is not achieved.

Figure 3-6 Coaxial Cable Is Used with Cable TV Installations

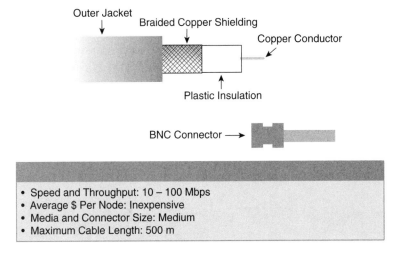

- Speed and Throughput: 10 – 100 Mbps
- Average $ Per Node: Inexpensive
- Media and Connector Size: Medium
- Maximum Cable Length: 500 m

When the center conductor is not straight or is not the correct length, cut the coaxial cable behind the connector end, and pull back the insulation. Make sure that the newly exposed center conductor is straight. Before replacing the new cable connector end, check the cable's general condition. Make sure that the new cable conductor end is securely crimped to the cable. The center connector should extend 3.2 mm (1/8 inch) beyond the end of the connector.

Check that the coaxial cable end is securely screwed onto the F-connector at the back of the cable access router. Hand-tighten the connector, making sure that it is finger-tight, and then give it a 1/6 turn.

The connection of a host NIC to 10BASE2 cabling is usually via a BNC connector. Some buildings use a special type of connector in place of the more common BNC to try to prevent problems that arise when users disconnect or reconnect their equipment. Without the special connector, a person unplugging equipment could cause a break in the transmission medium, inhibiting communication between other users. The end of each segment of cable must be terminated with a 50-ohm BNC terminator.

Thick Ethernet (10BASE5) cabling runs use thick coaxial cable to form a bus topology. A maximum of 100 transceivers can be used for host connection to the bus. Thick Ethernet cabling is difficult to install because of its weight and large diameter of 0.5 inch. It is unacceptable to bend 10BASE5 cabling. There are also constraints on how tightly the cabling run can be curved. Thick Ethernet was primarily used for LAN backbone connections. It was uncommon to find it used to connect end stations to the LAN.

Fiber-Optic Cable

All fiber links are crossed over. The connectors are always the same on stations and infrastructure equipment, so the TX output is connected to the RX input through careful attention to the cable polarity. Check fiber for swapped RX/TX connections when polarized or small form factor multifiber connectors are not used. Someone might have reconnected the cable incorrectly after disconnecting it for some reason. Figure 3-7 illustrates fiber-optic cable.

Figure 3-7 Fiber-Optic Cable Installations Are Growing for Both the LAN and WAN. Fiber-Optic Cable to the House Is Becoming Fairly Common in Japan.

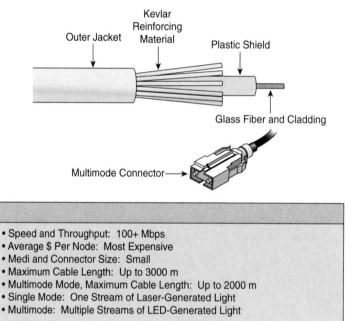

- Speed and Throughput: 100+ Mbps
- Average $ Per Node: Most Expensive
- Medi and Connector Size: Small
- Maximum Cable Length: Up to 3000 m
- Multimode Mode, Maximum Cable Length: Up to 2000 m
- Single Mode: One Stream of Laser-Generated Light
- Multimode: Multiple Streams of LED-Generated Light

If a spare fiber-optic cable does not have dust covers, it should be considered suspect even if it tested good yesterday. Clean all fiber-optic cables before attaching them as routine procedure.

If a fiber power test fails, inspect and clean all connections on the link. While walking the cable run route, watch for excessively tight bends and over-tightened cable ties that cause microbends.

Test fiber for power level and link indicator LEDs.

Hardware

When Layer 1 or Layer 2 hardware components fail, a system experiences a sudden loss of physical connectivity. Various occurrences in frames transported over shared-access media indicate a faulty NIC or interface in Layer 1 through 3 equipment. A NIC is shown in Figure 3-8.

Figure 3-8 It Is Expected That Auto Negotiating 10/100/1000 Mbps NICs Will Enjoy Almost Complete Market Share by 2005. A 10 Gbps Intel NIC Is Shown Here.

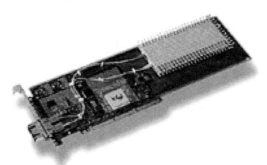

Check for link lights at both the station and hub or switch end. However, because of increased software control, the presence of a link light is not a guarantee that the port works. The absence of a link light is still a fairly reliable indication of a problem.

Disconnect the problem station or the station identified as the source of the frames with errors from the network. Attach a monitoring tool in its place. Be sure to use the original cable of the problem station at this time, not a known-good cable.

Also test from the network side back toward the suspect station. Use a spare cable to attach the test tool to the station, and watch the power-up process. If you're unfamiliar with low-level operating system commands, you often must cold-start the station to get it to speak on the network. After a station has completed the initial boot-up process, it might not speak on the network again without these special commands. Observe the link process and the protocols that the station is sending. Ensure that the station is communicating, because many problems relate to station configurations not recognizing or attempting to use the network adapter. Look for signal strength and other physical layer parameters.

Not all network adapter faults are exhibited during testing. If the fault appears to be intermittent, it might be appropriate to replace the network adapter and driver software as part of the diagnostic process. If that solves the problem, try exchanging just the network adapter to see if the fault was associated with the network adapter or driver software. If the network adapter was inexpensive, it might be more expedient to simply discard the suspect adapter if the user later reports that the problem has been resolved by replacing it.

Some portable PC network adapter cards ship with a special power-saving feature enabled. This feature causes the NIC to listen for link pulse, but it does not transmit anything (including link pulse) until it hears a signal on the receive circuit. To conserve power, the entire transmit circuit in the NIC is shut down until the receive circuit indicates that a transmission is warranted. This feature has been known to cause link problems with some other network devices. Try disabling this feature in the NIC's software configuration, or use a test tool to see what signals the NIC offers.

Collision-Based Problems—Shared Media

Excessive collisions are most often caused by a problem with the physical media, such as missing or incorrect terminators, impedance discontinuities (bad connectors, cable stubs, crushed cables, and so on), and bad network interface cards.

There are several things to watch for in relation to collisions:

- Does the detected collision level track approximately with the utilization level?

  If changes in utilization and collision levels track together reasonably closely, too many stations might be transmitting on the collision domain, assuming that a collision problem even exists.

- Are there spikes of detected collisions that do not follow the utilization level?

  If there are spikes of detected collisions that are significantly different from the general fluctuation in utilization, the collisions might often be traced back to a single source. It might be a bad cable to a single station, a bad uplink cable on a hub or a port on a hub, or a link that is exposed to external electrical noise. Over time, you might isolate the problem station by monitoring the traffic sources at the same time the collision level bursts higher. Note which station(s) are transmitting at the time when spikes of collisions are detected. If the problem seems to relate to transmissions from a single station, troubleshoot that suspect link. If the problem seems to relate to transmissions from multiple stations, compare that information against the functional network diagram to see if there is a common path between those stations and the rest of the collision domain. The single station could be an uplink from the collision domain to a switch, and the functional diagram should reveal that all the other stations are beyond that link. One or more stations set to full duplex within a collision domain also causes this sort of collision problem, as well as other errors.

- Do collisions occur when there is no apparent utilization to cause them?

  If abnormal numbers of collisions take place when there is little or no utilization to cause them, suspect a noise source near a cable or hub. Use divide-and-conquer troubleshooting to isolate the location of the fault, adding traffic to the network from the monitoring tool while troubleshooting. This sort of fault usually must be diagnosed after-hours because portions of the collision domain are disconnected from the network during troubleshooting.

- Are there approximately 33 percent or 100 percent collisions?

  If the level of collisions is either 33 percent or 100 percent, a 100-Mbps station might be attempting to connect to a 10-Mbps segment. This collision level results from a station transmitting an MLT-3 encoded 100-Mbps signal to the 10-Mbps hub. The 10-Mbps hub turns on the link-state LED and forwards its best interpretation of the MLT-3 signal as Manchester-encoded data. The 100-Mbps end cannot establish synchronization and, thus, does not turn on the link-state LED or forward any received traffic to the MAC layer. The reverse situation does not result in a problem. If a 10-Mbps station attempts to insert into a 100-Mbps-only hub, that station does not achieve MLT-3 synchronization, and the hub does not turn on the link-state LED or attempt to interpret and forward the Manchester-encoded signal.

To track down the source of collisions, it is often necessary to have traffic on the network. Use a traffic generator to add a small amount of traffic while monitoring. A safe, insignificant level of traffic is 100 frames per second, 100-byte frames, which is still sufficient to sensitize nearby faults and allow them to be located. Be sure that the destination MAC address for generated traffic will not affect other parts of the network during troubleshooting. Using a destination address within the collision domain prevents the traffic from crossing bridged connections and disrupting other users. Do not make up a nonexistent destination MAC address, because it will flood to all parts of the broadcast domain. If the generated level of traffic is very low, the destination address could be set to that of the tool or station generating the traffic without disrupting its operation.

Some media-related problems are traffic level-dependent. Try gradually raising the traffic level to more than 50 percent while watching the error and collision levels. Many monitoring tools offer LED indicators for both, which makes it much easier to vary the traffic level while watching for resulting errors or elevated collision levels. Be careful when doing this, because it can easily saturate the network. Solving collision-related problems can be very tricky, because the measurements are largely dependent on the observation point. Results might vary between two observation points separated by only a few feet on the same cable. Carry out tests at multiple locations, and watch for changes in the nature of the problem.

If collisions get worse in direct proportion to the level of traffic, if the number of collisions approaches 100 percent, or if there is no good traffic at all, the cable system might have failed.

For UTP cable, test the entire cable path between the hub and the station connection. Substitute a known-good patch cable before testing, because patch cables are the most likely source of the problem.

For coaxial cable, try a DC continuity test. You should see about 25 ohms if both terminators are present and testing occurs from a BNC T connection, or 50 ohms if you're testing from an end.

For fiber-optic cable, check to see if the connections are fully seated and clean. A loose or dirty connection can result in the receiver's misinterpreting input signals as a result of poor signal quality. This can cause other errors in addition to collisions.

External Interference

One of the most notable causes of EMI is lightning. When electrical disturbances occur in the environment, they affect radio and television broadcast signals. This often results in crackling and popping sounds in speakers or bright flashes on the screen. Common occurrences in a building utility system, such as main power lines near data cables, cabling that run passing elevator installations, or other features that use electrical motors, can cause interference as well. Loose connections, damaged or aging equipment, and dusty insulators are a few of the conditions causing electrical noise from the outside world.

Noise

On any line, even in the absence of a data signal, random fluctuations of the line voltage and current occur. This effect is known as line noise level, or simply background noise. One benefit of fiber-optic cabling is that it is unaffected by noise. This noise has three main causes:

- Crosstalk
- Impulse noise
- Thermal noise (not discussed here)

Crosstalk

Crosstalk noise occurs when a signal on one line is picked up by adjacent lines as a small noise signal. Particularly troublesome is NEXT, caused when a strong transmitter output signal interferes with a much weaker incoming receiver signal.

Impulse Noise

Impulse noise is caused by external activity or equipment and generally takes the form of electrical impulses on the line. These impulses can cause large signal distortion for their duration and can bring down the entire network whenever they occur.

Proper common-mode line terminations, shown in Table 3-11, must be used for the unused Category 5 UTP cable pairs 4/5 and 7/8. Common-mode termination reduces the contributions to EMI and susceptibility to common-mode sources. Wire pairs 4/5 and 7/8 are actively terminated in the RJ-45 100BASE-TX port circuitry in the FE-TX port adapter.

Table 3-11 Common-Mode Line Terminations

Pin	Signal Name	Description
1	tpe0	Transmit data +
2	tpe1	Transmit data –
3	tpe2	Transmit data +
4	Common mode determination	Termination
5	Common mode determination	Termination
6	tpe3	Receive data –
7	Common mode determination	Termination
8	Common mode determination	Termination

Configuration Script Errors

Many things can be misconfigured on an interface to cause it to go down. This causes a loss of connectivity with attached network segments. Changing an interface's subnet to a different one from the directly attached network segment is an obvious way to shut down their connection, but this is not a physical layer problem.

If a LAN segment has multiple links to the network core, modifying the bandwidth parameter in a routing protocol can also cause a router to favor alternative routes over the local link, resulting in suboptimal network performance.

Other misconfigurations that are directly related to the physical layer include

- Serial links reconfigured as asynchronous instead of synchronous
- Incorrect clock rate
- Incorrect clock source
- Interface shutdown
- Keepalive mismatch

Switchport duplex configuration mismatches can cause collisions or port shutdown to occur. Although the current state of auto negotiation can often negate this type of problem, at least one of the attached devices needs to be capable of link speed and duplex negotiation.

CPU Overload

The following list describes common symptoms of high CPU utilization. If you notice any of these symptoms, follow the troubleshooting steps described next to alleviate the problem:

- High percentages in the **show processes cpu** command output
- Input queue drops
- Slow performance
- Services on the router fail to respond—for instance:
  - Slow response in Telnet or being unable to Telnet to the router
  - Slow or no response to ping
  - Router does not send routing updates

The output of the **show processes cpu** command from a Cisco device can be used by Output Interpreter to display potential issues and fixes.

The **show processes cpu** command, shown in Example 3-2, can be used to check if CPU utilization is high because of interrupts. If it is not, check which process is loading the CPU.

Example 3-2 *CPU Utilization Can Be Viewed on a Cisco Router, Similar to What You Would See on a UNIX or Windows Server*

```
router-5#show processes cpu
CPU utilization for five seconds: 1%/0%; one minute: 0%; five minutes: 0%
 PID Runtime(ms)   Invoked     uSecs   5Sec    1Min   5Min TTY Process
   1          0         1         0  0.00%   0.00%  0.00%   0 Chunk Manager
   2       1180    736669         1  0.00%   0.00%  0.00%   0 Load Meter
   3        128        77      1662  0.98%   0.18%  0.04%   0 Exec
   5    1676424    484049      3463  0.00%   0.03%  0.00%   0 Check heaps
   6         12        12      1000  0.00%   0.00%  0.00%   0 Pool Manager
   7          0         2         0  0.00%   0.00%  0.00%   0 Timers
   8          0         2         0  0.00%   0.00%  0.00%   0 Serial Backgroun
   9      62732    817228        76  0.00%   0.00%  0.00%   0 ALARM_TRIGGER_SC
  10          0    122777         0  0.00%   0.00%  0.00%   0 Environmental mo
  11      11968     95216       125  0.00%   0.00%  0.00%   0 ARP Input
  12       1308    204313         6  0.00%   0.00%  0.00%   0 HC Counter Timer
  13          0         3         0  0.00%   0.00%  0.00%   0 DDR Timers
  14          0         2         0  0.00%   0.00%  0.00%   0 Dialer event
  15          8         3      2666  0.00%   0.00%  0.00%   0 Entity MIB API
  16          0         1         0  0.00%   0.00%  0.00%   0 SERIAL A'detect
  17          4         1      4000  0.00%   0.00%  0.00%   0 Critical Bkgnd
```

Example 3-2 *CPU Utilization Can Be Viewed on a Cisco Router, Similar to What You Would See on a UNIX or Windows Server (Continued)*

```
 18     17644     491025       35  0.00%  0.00%  0.00%   0 Net Background
 19         4         18      222  0.00%  0.00%  0.00%   0 Logger
 20       104    3683241        0  0.00%  0.00%  0.00%   0 TTY Background
 21       496    4086243        0  0.00%  0.00%  0.00%   0 Per-Second Jobs
 22         4          2     2000  0.00%  0.00%  0.00%   0 Hawkeye Background
```

The main cause of CPU interrupts is the fast switching of traffic. Interrupts are also generated any time a character is output from a router's console or auxiliary ports. However, Universal Asynchronous Receiver/Transmitters (UARTs) are slow compared to a router's processing speed, so it is unlikely that console or auxiliary interrupts can cause high CPU utilization on the router.

There are several reasons for high CPU utilization because of interrupts:

- Voice ports are configured on the router. Even if there is no traffic, software continues to monitor channel associated signaling (CAS).
- The router has active Asynchronous Transfer Mode (ATM) interfaces. The ATM interfaces continually send out null cells (per ATM standards) and continue to use CPU resources.
- An inappropriate switching path is configured on the router.
- The CPU is performing memory alignment corrections. If %ALIGN-3-CORRECT messages are logged, the high CPU utilization is caused by memory alignment corrections, which indicates bugs in the version of the Cisco IOS used.

If the router is overloaded with traffic, the **show interfaces** and **show interfaces switching** commands provide information about which interfaces are overloaded, as shown in Example 3-3.

Example 3-3 *Overloaded Interfaces Can Be Identified with the* **show interfaces** *Command*

```
Kingston#show interfaces
FastEthernet0/0 is up, line protocol is up
  Hardware is AmdFE, address is 0004.c136.66e0 (bia 0004.c136.66e0)
  Internet address is 10.30.18.41/24
  MTU 1500 bytes, BW 100000 Kbit, DLY 100 usec,
     reliability 255/255, txload 1/255, rxload 1/255
  Encapsulation ARPA, loopback not set
  Keepalive set (10 sec)
```

continues

Example 3-3 *Overloaded Interfaces Can Be Identified with the* **show interfaces** *Command (Continued)*

```
  Full-duplex, 100Mb/s, 100BaseTX/FX
  ARP type: ARPA, ARP Timeout 04:00:00
  Last input 00:00:00, output 00:00:04, output hang never
  Last clearing of "show interface" counters never
  Input queue: 0/75/0/0 (size/max/drops/flushes); Total output drops: 0
  Queueing strategy: fifo
  Output queue: 0/40 (size/max)
  5 minute input rate 3000 bits/sec, 0 packets/sec
  5 minute output rate 0 bits/sec, 0 packets/sec
     598824 packets input, 299773434 bytes
     Received 598824 broadcasts, 0 runts, 0 giants, 0 throttles
     0 input errors, 0 CRC, 0 frame, 0 overrun, 0 ignored
     0 watchdog
     0 input packets with dribble condition detected
     173373 packets output, 85673841 bytes, 0 underruns
     0 output errors, 0 collisions, 1 interface resets
     0 babbles, 0 late collision, 0 deferred
     0 lost carrier, 0 no carrier
     0 output buffer failures, 0 output buffers swapped out
<output omitted>
```

Output from the **show interfaces** command can be used to examine the load and number of throttles on interfaces. Throttles are a good indication of an overloaded router. They show how many times the receiver on the port has been disabled, possibly because of buffer or processor overload. Together with high CPU utilization on an interrupt level, throttles indicate that the router is overloaded with traffic.

Output from the **show interfaces** switching command can be used to see what kind of traffic, protocol, and switching path are going through the overloaded interface. If some interfaces are too overloaded with traffic, consider redesigning the traffic flow in the network or upgrading the hardware.

A single device might be generating packets at an extremely high rate and overloading the router. In this case you can isolate the device's MAC address by adding the **ip accounting mac-address {input | output}** interface configuration command to the configuration of the overloaded interface. The **show interfaces [type number] mac-accounting** or **show interfaces mac** commands display the collected information. As soon as the source device's MAC address is found, you can find the corresponding IP address by checking the output of the **show arp** privileged EXEC command.

A last possibility is that there might be a bug in the Cisco IOS software version running on the device. After you've followed all the previous steps in this list, check the Bug Navigator (registered customers only) for a bug that reports similar symptoms in a similar environment.

Isolating Physical Layer Problems

Isolating physical layer problems requires using an effective and systematic technique. A network engineer needs to know what tools to use before a problem occurs. In particular, you should be able to isolate bad cabling, incorrect cabling, and physical interface problems. Operational statistics help you isolate physical layer problems.

Methodology

To isolate networking problems that occur at the physical layer, use the effective and systematic technique shown in Figure 3-9 to reach a successful outcome.

Figure 3-9 Four Steps Are Typically Involved in Isolating Problems at the Physical Layer

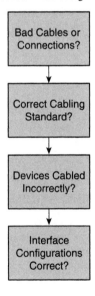

To isolate problems at the physical layer, do the following:

- Check for bad cables or connections.
- Verify that the cable from the source interface is properly connected and is in good condition. When you doubt a cable's integrity, swap it with a known working cable.

- If you doubt that the connection is good, remove the cable, physically inspect both the cable and the interface, and then reseat the cable. Use a cable tester with a suspect wall jack to ensure that the jack is properly wired. A glowing link light also indicates a successful connection.

- Check that the correct cabling standard is adhered to throughout the network.

- Verify that the proper cable is being used. A crossover cable might be required for direct connections between some devices.

- Ensure that the cable is correctly wired.

- Check to make sure that all cables are connected to their correct ports or interfaces. Make sure that any cross-connects are properly patched to the correct location.

- Verify proper interface configurations.

- Check that all switch or hub ports are set in the correct VLAN or collision domain and that spanning-tree, speed, and duplex settings are correctly configured. Confirm that any active ports or interfaces are not shut down.

- Check operational statistics and data error rates.

- Use Cisco **show** commands to check for statistics such as collisions, input, and output errors. The characteristics of these statistics vary depending on the protocols used on the network.

Tools for the Job

There are two primary categories of physical layer analyzer products:

- Cable testers
- Handheld network testers (hybrid)

Other common tools that are used for troubleshooting at OSI Layers 2 to 7 are protocol analyzer and network management tools. Figure 3-10 illustrates the various tools.

Cable testers are used as much for maintenance as they are for new installations.

Handheld network analyzers were created to bridge the skills gap between the senior network support staff and the help desk staff. They generally include the most commonly used features from the other testing tool categories but do not eliminate the need for these other categories. The focus is to validate or troubleshoot end-to-end connectivity up through OSI Layer 3.

In the interest of restoring network service as quickly as possible, this category is best used as a first-in tool when a problem is reported. Although they often can help locate and eliminate the source of a network problem, they can be just as effective in quickly eliminating many possible sources of the problem so that the other tools and staff might be deployed more effectively.

Figure 3-10 Network Testing Tools Are Generally Categorized as Cable Testers or Handhelds

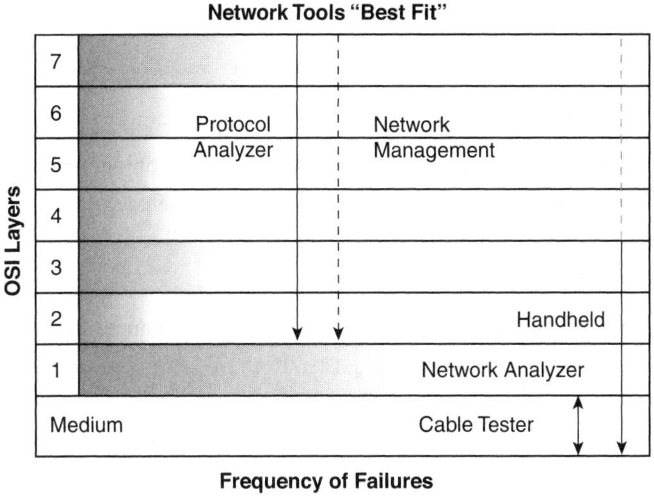

Network Tools "Best Fit"

Bad Cabling

Before troubleshooting a failing cable, verify the tester configuration. This step is critical to obtaining accurate test results, because testers capable of Category 5e and higher performance use a wide selection of cable interface adapters and might have somewhat complicated test configurations. At a minimum, verify that the correct test specification and link type have been selected. Also, the test standards have evolved sufficiently that the requirements for a particular test, such as ISO Class D, might no longer be the same as what is loaded in the tester's software. Check the Web site of the tester's manufacturer for new tester software two or three times per year.

Most wire map failures occur at cable terminations, either at the RJ-45 (plug or jack) or at an intermediate cross-connect or patch panel. Faults at the RJ-45 can usually be seen by checking the wire colors carefully against T568A or T568B pinout colors or by checking the RJ-45 plug for wires that did not seat fully to the end of the connector when it was crimped.

Another source of RJ-45-related problems is how well the connector was crimped.

Delay

TIA/EIA-568-B permits up to 498 nanoseconds (ns) of propagation delay for the permanent link and up to 555 ns of propagation delay for the channel link for all categories. It is unlikely that this parameter could fail without other parameters failing as well. Failing propagation delay suggests an inappropriate or bad cable in the link.

Check the cable's overall length. Inspect it closely to see if the correct type of cable was installed. If this is the only parameter that failed, you probably need to replace the cable link.

Delay Skew

Delay skew occurs as a result of different wire pairs within a cable being insulated with different materials. This can occur if there is an industry supply problem for a favored insulating material. In this case, the critical RX and TX pairs might be coated with the favored insulative materials, and the pairs not used in TIA/EIA-568-A or TIA/EIA-568-B standards are coated using suboptimal insulative materials.

TIA/EIA-568-B permits up to 44 ns of delay skew for the permanent link and up to 50 ns of delay skew for the channel link for all categories. Both of these numbers are quite generous. It is fairly difficult to fail delay skew if good materials were used in the link. A delay skew failure is possible if wire pairs in a single cable have different insulative material on some pairs. A failure is also possible if various lengths of twisted-wire pairs were used as a patch cable or jumper at a connection point.

Varying the lengths of pairs at any point along the link probably indicates bad workmanship, because individual pairs should never be used for networking applications. This situation should cause other parameters to fail too.

Inspect the connection points in the link. If the workmanship appears reasonable, you might have little choice but to replace the entire cable run. Test a sample of the new cable before installing it to be sure that the materials are not causing the problem.

Figure 3-11 shows a list of common cabling errors.

Cabling Incorrect

Check for wires that were not fully seated in the crimping process. Also check to see if the correct type of RJ-45 was used, stranded or solid-wire pins. This is difficult after the end has been crimped. Using the wrong style of pin might cause intermittent connections after a period of time, although the cable usually works immediately after it is made. Figure 3-11 lists likely causes of cable test failures.

If a nonproprietary terminator with a nonstandard pinning is used, the connection might look the same, but the internal wiring could be off.

Check the standard used. There have been notable cases in which large campus sites have been wired by two different groups of contractors. If the cabling process is not coordinated correctly, different contractors might use different wiring standards in their cabling. This would result in incompatible wiring schemes in the two halves of what was meant to be a single network.

Figure 3-11 Common Cabling Errors Include Poorly Terminated Cables

Open	Short	Reversed Pair	Crossed Pair	Split Pair	Length or Length Mismatch	Delay Skew	Insertion Loss	NEXT or PSN TXT	Return Loss	ELF EXT or PSE LFE XT	Description
•									•		Cut, broken or otherwise abused cable
•	•										Damaged RJ-45 plug or jack
			•								Mixed T56A and T56B color codes on same cable
						•					Different insulation material on some pairs
				•				•			Split Pair
								•	•		Poor workmanship at cable junction or connector
								•	•		Improper wiring at cable junction or connector
								•	•		Improper, poor quality, or Telco rated RJ45 coupler
								•	•		Bad, or poor quality patch cord(s)
									•		Mixed use of 100 ohm and non-100 ohm cable
•					•					•	Cable is too long or NVP is set incorrectly
								•	•	•	Untwisted or poorly twisted cable (includes too low of a cable rating, such as Category 3 instead of Category 5e
								•			Cable ties too tightly fastened along cable
								•			Poorly matched plug and jack (usually Category 5e or higher rated links, especially Category 6 or Class e)
								•		•	External noise source near cable
								•	•	•	Poor quality RJ-45 jack or coupler (includes too low of a plug or jack rating, such as Category 3 instead of Category 5e)

Cabling length is also a major issue. Cabling guidelines are constructed to take into account factors such as propagation delay and signal attenuation, which are related to the length of the cable used.

- Do not install long cables. Make all runs as short as possible, certainly no longer than is permitted by the media access protocol being used. For example, never install UTP runs longer than 100 meters.

- Whether building cables on site or buying premade cables, be sure to test them with a reliable cable tester before using them, especially if you're already in troubleshooting mode.

You also must take into account other issues, such as grounding and the ability to exclude internal and external noise from interfering with data transmission. UTP is not the correct cable type to be laid near strong sources of external EMI, such as elevator cavities, power lines, radio, microwaves, television signals, and transmission stations. In these types of environments where redirection of the data cables cannot occur, either shielded Category 5 or fiber-optic cable must be considered as a replacement.

More dangerous is where each end of the cabling runs has a different electrical potential. The terminating device might become live and be capable of discharging significant voltage to other attached equipment, or even personnel. In this case, fiber-optic cable should be used instead of UTP or shielded twisted-pair (STP), because it does not carry an electronic signal. It uses nonelectrically conductive material that transmits modulated light signals instead.

Interface Configuration

Before you examine the interface configurations on network devices, it is important to discount the physical causes:

- Verify cable connectivity.
- Verify that the power supply is on and running.
- Verify the router LED status. If all LEDs are down, the problem most likely is an issue with the device's power supply or with incorrectly seated modules in a modular router or switch.

When examining interfaces on a Layer 2 switching device, do the following:

- Start by looking for duplex and speed mismatches. Hard-coding the speed and duplex on permanent connections, such as between switches and routers, is a good practice.

- Ensure that the correct VLAN encapsulation method has been applied if the port is a trunking port and that the port has been designated for trunking rather than access.

- Ensure that individual ports have been assigned to the EtherChannel group for trunking ports combined to form an EtherChannel.

- Ensure that the port has not been accidentally assigned an IP address. On 3550 and 6500 series switches, the **no switchport** command with an IP address specified converts the switch port to a routing port.
- Look under port configuration to make sure the port has not been assigned as an RSPAN reflector port.

When examining a Layer 3 device, do the following:

- Ensure that the IP addressing on both sides of the link is within the same subnet, as shown in Figure 3-12.
- Ensure that the interface is not administratively shut down.
- Ensure that serial ports designated as DCE end are assigned the correct clock rate for the link.

Figure 3-12 Inconsistent Subnet Masks Is a Common Interface Configuration Error

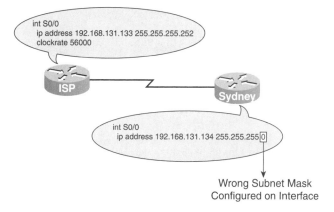

Console Not Responding

Console problems occur when the router becomes unresponsive to input at the console port. If the console is not responsive, a high-priority process is preventing the console driver from responding to input. If traffic is still flowing through the device, try disconnecting network interfaces, and see if the router starts responding. Many times the router thinks it is doing something too important to service executive sessions. The **scheduler interval** or **scheduler allocate** command can be used to allocate enough CPU process time to system tasks, such as console access, in case the CPU gets flooded.

Another possibility is that one of the device interfaces might be down. Several events can cause this, such as a wrong configuration command or a hardware failure of the interface or the cable. If some interfaces appear down when you use the **show interfaces** command, try to find out what caused this.

Operational Statistics

A variety of end-station and network device commands can be used to gather operational statistics on a network or on specific component links and devices. These commands were explored earlier in this chapter.

The **show tech-support** Cisco IOS command is often requested by Cisco TAC support staff when you're troubleshooting a problem. This command provides detailed operational statistics, as shown in Example 3-4.

Example 3-4 *The* **show tech-support** *Command Provides Exhaustive Operational Statistics for Troubleshooting*

```
SanJose1#show tech-support


----------------- show version ------------------


Cisco Internetwork Operating System Software
IOS (tm) C2600 Software (C2600-JK9O3S-M), Version 12.2(23), RELEASE SOFTWARE
  (fc2)
Copyright (c) 1986-2004 by cisco Systems, Inc.
Compiled Wed 28-Jan-04 17:48 by kellmill
Image text-base: 0x8000808C, data-base: 0x81602CE4


ROM: System Bootstrap, Version 11.3(2)XA4, RELEASE SOFTWARE (fc1)


SanJose1 uptime is 6 weeks, 5 days, 8 hours, 17 minutes
System returned to ROM by reload
System image file is "flash:c2600-jk9o3s-mz.122-23.bin"




This product contains cryptographic features and is subject to United
States and local country laws governing import, export, transfer and
use. Delivery of Cisco cryptographic products does not imply
third-party authority to import, export, distribute or use encryption.
Importers, exporters, distributors and users are responsible for
compliance with U.S. and local country laws. By using this product you
agree to comply with applicable laws and regulations. If you are unable
to comply with U.S. and local laws, return this product immediately.
```

Example 3-4 *The* **show tech-support** *Command Provides Exhaustive Operational Statistics for Troubleshooting (Continued)*

```
A summary of U.S. laws governing Cisco cryptographic products may be found at:
http://www.cisco.com/wwl/export/crypto/tool/stqrg.html

If you require further assistance please contact us by sending email to
export@cisco.com.

cisco 2621 (MPC860) processor (revision 0x102) with 59392K/6144K bytes of memory.
Processor board ID JAD045257N4 (1209607925)
M860 processor: part number 0, mask 49
Bridging software.
X.25 software, Version 3.0.0.
SuperLAT software (copyright 1990 by Meridian Technology Corp).
TN3270 Emulation software.
2 FastEthernet/IEEE 802.3 interface(s)
2 Serial(sync/async) network interface(s)
32K bytes of non-volatile configuration memory.
16384K bytes of processor board System flash (Read/Write)

Configuration register is 0x2102


------------------ show running-config ------------------


Building configuration...

Current configuration : 639 bytes
!
version 12.2
service timestamps debug uptime
service timestamps log uptime
no service password-encryption
!
hostname SanJose1
```

continues

Example 3-4 *The* **show tech-support** *Command Provides Exhaustive Operational Statistics for Troubleshooting (Continued)*

```
!
memory-size iomem 10
ip subnet-zero
!
ip audit notify log
ip audit po max-events 100
!
call rsvp-sync
!
interface FastEthernet0/0
 ip address 10.30.18.41 255.255.255.0
 duplex auto
 speed auto
!
interface Serial0/0
 no ip address
 shutdown
 no fair-queue
!
interface FastEthernet0/1
 no ip address
 shutdown
 duplex auto
 speed auto
!
interface Serial0/1
 no ip address
 shutdown
!
ip classless
ip http server
!
```

Example 3-4 *The* **show tech-support** *Command Provides Exhaustive Operational Statistics for Troubleshooting (Continued)*

```
dial-peer cor custom
!
line con 0
line aux 0
line vty 0 4
!
end




----------------- show stacks -----------------
<output omitted>
```

Operational statistics can also be gained from centrally located network analysis software or even dedicated hardware. SNMP can be used to get each SNMP-capable network device to report back to a central monitoring host that is loaded with software to interpret input from network devices. Similarly, the Network Analysis Module (NAM), designed for Cisco 6500 series devices, can become the nerve center for analyzing network functionality. The NAM stores operational statistics collected using remote VLAN and port-centric or local VLAN Switchport Analyzer sessions for each Cisco switching component of the network. The data can then be compared to historical data. Increasing the level of data capture occurring on network operational statistics, a troubleshooter can gain valuable intelligence on a network. This data can be used to isolate network problems and also to identify under-resourced or overused links and components within the network.

Implementing Physical Layer Solutions

A doctor would not be considered successful unless he or she could follow-up his or her diagnosis of a patient's problem with a successful solution. The same idea applies to network troubleshooters. Isolating a problem is a big step in troubleshooting, but the process is considered incomplete until the problem is solved and the network is returned to its baseline state. Figure 3-13 outlines the methodology for solving a physical layer problem.

Figure 3-13 It Is Useful to Have a Formal Methodology for Solving a Physical Layer Problem

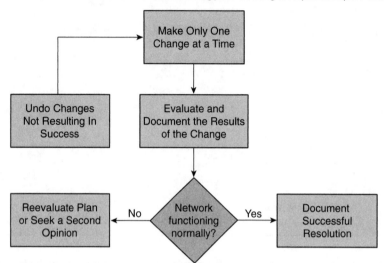

Solving Common Problems—Methodology

Do the following to correct an isolated problem at the physical layer:

1. Make initial configuration changes.

2. If the correction requires more than one change, make only one change at a time.

3. Evaluate and document the results of each change made.

4. If you follow the problem-solving steps and the results are unsuccessful, immediately undo the changes. If the problem is intermittent, you might need to wait to see if the problem occurs again before evaluating the effect of any changes.

5. Stop making changes when the original problem appears to be solved.

6. Verify that the changes made actually fixed the problem without introducing any new problems.

7. Return the network to the baseline operation. No new or old symptoms should be present. If the problem is not solved, undo all the changes made. If you discover new or additional problems during troubleshooting and problem correction, step back and modify the correction plan.

8. If necessary, get input from outside resources.

9. If none of the attempts to correct the problem are successful, take the problem to another person. This might be a coworker, consultant, or the Cisco TAC. On rare occasions you might need to perform a core dump, which creates output that a specialist at Cisco Systems can analyze.

10. As soon as the problem is resolved, document the solution.

Also, if possible, recreate the problem in a controlled environment so that the production network need not be further disrupted.

ARP Commands

The IP network layer protocol uses ARP to map IP network addresses to the hardware addresses used by the data-link protocol. ARP operates below the network layer as a part of the OSI data link layer and is used when IP is used over the Internet.

The MAC address is a data link layer address and depends on the interface card that is used. IP operates at the network layer and is not concerned with the nodes' IP addresses. ARP therefore is used to translate between the two types of addresses. The ARP client and server processes operate on all computers using IP over the Internet. These processes are normally implemented as part of the software driver that drives the NIC.

An end station constructs an Address Resolution Table when it is connected to a network and attempting to communicate with devices on its LAN segment. To reduce the number of address resolution requests, a client normally caches resolved addresses for a (short) period of time. The ARP cache has a finite size. It would become full of incomplete and obsolete entries for computers that are not in use if it were allowed to grow without check. Therefore, the ARP cache is periodically flushed of all entries. This deletes unused entries and frees space in the cache. It also removes any unsuccessful attempts to contact hosts that are not currently running.

The **arp** command, described in Table 3-12, can be used on an end station to verify that the device is actually communicating with other devices on its LAN segment. The presence of an ARP table indicates that the end station has at least been connected to the network in the very recent past.

Table 3-12 ARP Commands

Command	Description
arp -s *ip-address mac-address*	Adds an entry to an ARP table.
arp -d *ip-address*	Deletes an entry from an ARP table. Note that **arp -d *** deletes all host entries.

Solving Common Problems—Windows and UNIX/Mac OS End-System Commands

On Windows 2000 and XP systems, you can use the **ipconfig** command to establish whether a NIC has successfully bound to the required IP address. Figure 3-14 shows the various **ipconfig** options. Sometimes a NIC does not release an old IP address. Using the **ipconfig /release** command option forces the NIC to release the currently held address. Following with the **ipconfig /renew** command causes the NIC to attempt to bind to an address supplied by a DHCP server or to a manually configured IP address.

Figure 3-14 The **ipconfig** Command Is Extremely Useful in the Windows Environment

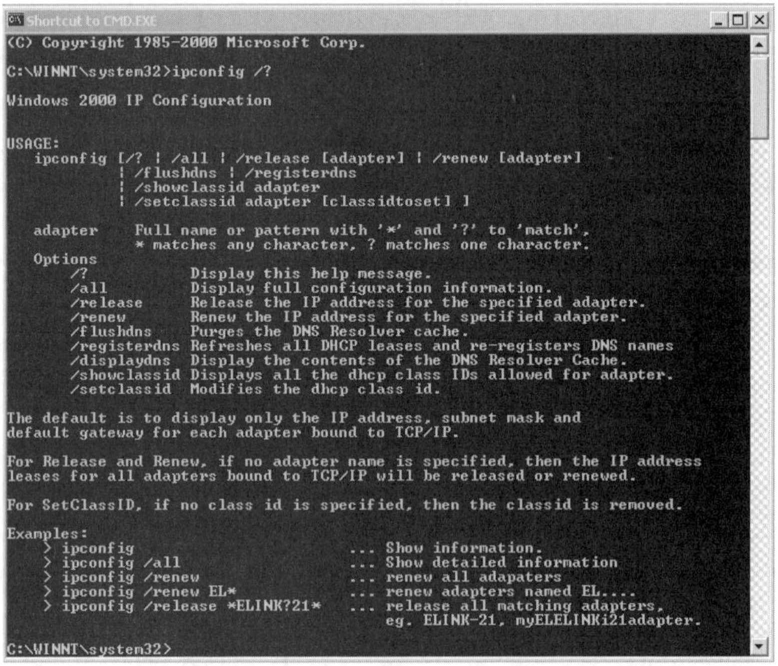

```
Shortcut to CMD.EXE
(C) Copyright 1985-2000 Microsoft Corp.

C:\WINNT\system32>ipconfig /?

Windows 2000 IP Configuration

USAGE:
   ipconfig [/? | /all | /release [adapter] | /renew [adapter]
            | /flushdns | /registerdns
            | /showclassid adapter
            | /setclassid adapter [classidtoset] ]

   adapter    Full name or pattern with '*' and '?' to 'match',
              * matches any character, ? matches one character.
   Options
       /?           Display this help message.
       /all         Display full configuration information.
       /release     Release the IP address for the specified adapter.
       /renew       Renew the IP address for the specified adapter.
       /flushdns    Purges the DNS Resolver cache.
       /registerdns Refreshes all DHCP leases and re-registers DNS names
       /displaydns  Display the contents of the DNS Resolver Cache.
       /showclassid Displays all the dhcp class IDs allowed for adapter.
       /setclassid  Modifies the dhcp class id.

The default is to display only the IP address, subnet mask and
default gateway for each adapter bound to TCP/IP.

For Release and Renew, if no adapter name is specified, then the IP address
leases for all adapters bound to TCP/IP will be released or renewed.

For SetClassID, if no class id is specified, then the classid is removed.

Examples:
    > ipconfig                       ... Show information.
    > ipconfig /all                  ... Show detailed information
    > ipconfig /renew                ... renew all adapaters
    > ipconfig /renew EL*            ... renew adapters named EL....
    > ipconfig /release *ELINK?21*   ... release all matching adapters,
                                         eg. ELINK-21, myELELINKi21adapter.

C:\WINNT\system32>
```

For UNIX and Mac OS X end systems, you can use the **ifconfig -a** command to establish if a NIC has bound to the correct IP address.

Solving Common Problems—Cisco IOS Commands

Interface configuration is a common source of physical layer problems. If an interface configuration does not match the corresponding configuration of a port on an attached device, the interface status will be either

- interface is down, line protocol is down
- interface is up, line protocol is down

Commonly on serial interfaces, lack of physical connectivity occurs because the interface at the clocking end has not been set with a clock rate, or it has been set incorrectly. Also, the **no shutdown** command must be applied to the interface; otherwise, it will remain in an administratively down state, which means that it has effectively been turned off.

On serial connections using Frame Relay or ISDN-equivalent encapsulation, protocols must be set at both sides of the link. High-Level Data Link Control (HDLC) has many implementations, with different vendors creating different HDLC versions that most often are proprietary and incompatible with each other. Cisco has developed its own implementation of HDLC. Among Cisco devices this is fine. However, if a Cisco device is connected via a serial link to another vendor's equipment, it is usual to implement the Internet Engineering Task Force (IETF) HDLC on both devices. This version of HDLC is often used between dissimilar equipment because it is a common second choice when a proprietary version of HDLC does not suffice.

Table 3-13 lists some common IOS interface mode commands.

Table 3-13 Cisco IOS Commands Involving Physical Interfaces

Command	Description
clock rate {*value*}	Supplies clocking on DCE interfaces.
configure terminal	Enters global configuration mode.
copy running-config startup-config	Copies the current configuration into NVRAM as the newest startup configuration file.
disable	Exits privileged mode.
enable	Enters privileged mode.
encapsulation {*options*}	Specifies an encapsulation type on serial WAN interfaces.
exit	Moves up to the next level in configuration mode.
interface {*type*} {*slot/number*}	Accesses a particular interface while in global configuration mode.
no shutdown	Administratively activates an interface.
shutdown	Administratively deactivates an interface.

Redundancy

When installing or maintaining a network, it is important to have contingencies in place to counter physical layer problems. Table 3-14 lists common physical problems and resolutions. The presence of an Uninterruptible Power Supply (UPS), surge protectors, or line filters can protect a network from short-term power interruptions, brownouts, and power spikes.

Table 3-14 Common Physical Layer Problems

Physical Problem	Resolution
Power-related	Install UPS, surge protection, or line filters.
Failing hardware components	Test and replace any failing components.
Incorrect cabling	Test and replace any incorrect cables.
External electromagnetic interference	Remove the interfering external source, move the equipment, or use optical cables.
Running configuration script is misconfigured	Replace with a working configuration stored in backup.
Framing and clocking issues	Use the correct CSU/DSU settings or replace the CSU/DSU.

You should have replacement units on hand for core layer hardware. It is a good idea to install modular hardware wherever possible. That way, the failure of a single module does not result in the entire device's being taken offline. Having replacement modules in store is also cost-effective. In the event of component failure, the modules can be interchangeably used in a variety of compliant chassis.

When changes are made to device or network configurations, backup copies of the previous functional configurations should be on hand in the event of network failure resulting from these changes. This minimizes network failure duration, and troubleshooting can occur independent of the network.

Having additional cabling and testers on hand is also highly recommended. On network installation, it is important to protect backbone cabling from damage by running it through wall, floor, or roof cavities. In the event of damage to patch cables or backbone cabling, it is essential that replacement cable be on hand to shorten outage duration.

The dual-core network design with redundant uplinks from access layer to distribution layer and from distribution layer to core layer and running STP and HSRP within each switch block ensures reliable failover when any one device fails.

Solving Common Problems—Support Resources

Online resources represent an invaluable tool for the network troubleshooter. The Internet has become a very valuable corporate tool for those seeking answers on specific technical problems. It also potentially represents a vast pool of experience-based information.

The Cisco systems Web site (http://www.cisco.com), shown in Figure 3-15, incorporates customer support, press-release information, and a free knowledge-base tool on all things Cisco. This site represents an invaluable resource for Cisco customers, support staff, and network administration, troubleshooting, and design personnel in general. It contains troubleshooting and implementation advice and the original white papers on all aspects of data networking technology.

Figure 3-15 The Primary Resource for Troubleshooting Cisco-Related Issues Is Found at http://www.cisco.com

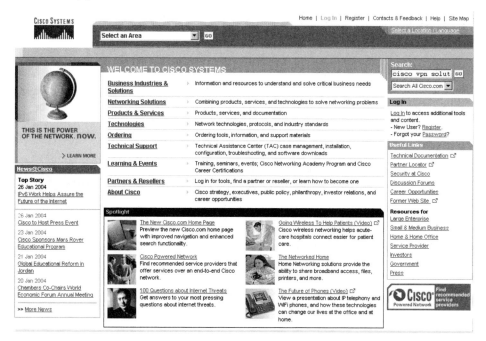

Here are some other highly useful resource sites:

- Microsoft Web site: http://www.microsoft.com
- Apple Web site: http://www.apple.com
- Sun Web site: http://www.sun.com
- Linux Web site: http://www.linux.org
- Protocols in general: http://www.protocols.com

Vendor Web sites also contain a wealth of information and support resources. Here are some computer vendors:

- http://www.dell.com
- http://www.gateway.com
- http://www.ibm.com
- http://www.toshiba.com

Summary

This chapter explored the following topics:

- Characteristics of physical layer problems
- Characteristics of physical layer optimization problems
- End-system and Cisco commands and applications for gathering information about physical layer components
- Common physical layer problems
- Guidelines for isolating problems at the physical layer
- End-system and Cisco commands and applications for configuring physical layer components
- Common physical layer problem resolutions
- Support resources for troubleshooting physical layer components
- A procedure for correcting physical layer problems

Figure 3-16 summarizes the physical layer issues addressed in this chapter.

Figure 3-16 Physical Layer Problems Include Hardware Faults and Media Issues

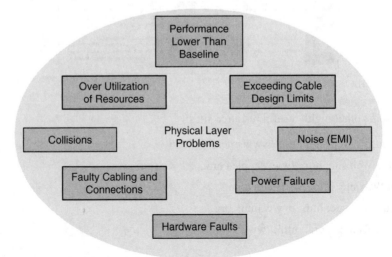

Key Terms

attenuation   Loss of communication signal energy.

crosstalk   Interfering energy transferred from one circuit to another.

electromagnetic interference (EMI)   Interference by electromagnetic signals that can cause reduced data integrity and increased error rates on transmission channels.

jabber   A condition in which a network device continually transmits random, meaningless data onto the network.

noise   Undesirable communications channel signals. Random noise can be generated by many sources, including wireless communications such as FM radio stations, police radio, building security, avionics for automated landing, and many more.

nonbroadcast multiaccess (NBMA) network   A multiaccess network that does not support broadcasting (such as Frame Relay) or in which broadcasting is not feasible (for example, an SMDS broadcast group).

return loss   A measure of all reflections that are caused by the impedance mismatches at all locations along the link. It indicates how well the characteristic impedance of the cable matches its rated impedance over a range of frequencies.

Check Your Understanding

Use the following review questions to test your understanding of the concepts covered in this chapter. Answers are listed in Appendix A, "Check Your Understanding Answer Key."

1. Failure at the physical layer translates into failure at which of the following OSI layers? Choose all that apply.

   A. Network

   B. Transport

   C. Data link

   D. Application

2. Power fluctuations are manifested in which of the following ways? Choose all that apply.

   A. Power failure

   B. Power spike

   C. Brownout

   D. Dirty power

3. If **show interfaces** output indicates "interface is up, line protocol is down" on a serial link, what are some possible causes? Choose all that apply.

   A. Encapsulation mismatch

   B. Layer 1 connectivity to the telco, but no Layer 2 connectivity to the remote router

   C. The interface does not have Layer 1 connectivity to the telco

   D. PPP authentication was unsuccessful

4. Which of the following might be factors in decreasing the rate at which data is transmitted across the medium? Choose all that apply.

   A. Faulty medium or hardware

   B. Large collision domains

   C. EMI effects

   D. Exceeding the medium's design limits

5. What issue arises from exceeding the design limits of a particular medium?

   A. NEXT

   B. Return loss

   C. Attenuation

   D. FEXT

6. What term represents a measure of all reflections caused by impedance mismatches along a physical path?

   A. Return loss

   B. Noise quotient

   C. Cumulative impedance

   D. Attenuation

7. A late collision occurs when a collision is detected by a device after it has sent the _____ bit of its frame.

   A. 1st

   B. 128th

   C. 512th

   D. 1512th

8. Shared Ethernet networks are believed to suffer from throughput problems when average traffic loads approach a maximum average capacity of _____ percent.

    A. 40

    B. 50

    C. 60

    D. 70

9. Error messages with Cisco IOS are displayed as what?

    A. #FACILITY-MNEMONIC-SEVERITY: Message-text

    B. &FACILITY-MNEMONIC-SEVERITY: Message-text

    C. $FACILITY-SEVERITY-MNEMONIC: Message-text

    D. %FACILITY-SEVERITY-MNEMONIC: Message-text

10. Which IOS command is used to determine if high CPU utilization is a problem on a router?

    A. **show interfaces**

    B. **show controllers**

    C. **show buffers**

    D. **show processes cpu**

Objectives

After completing this chapter, you will be able to perform tasks related to the following:

- Be familiar with the most common types of data-link layer problems
- Identify and resolve Layer 2-to-Layer 3 mapping problems
- Know the commands used for Layer 2 troubleshooting on Windows and UNIX operating systems
- Understand how to effectively use the **show cdp neighbors** command
- Troubleshoot switch flooding and STP loops
- Be familiar with the **show** and **debug** commands commonly used to troubleshoot ISDN, Frame Relay, and T1 links
- Troubleshoot PAP and CHAP authentication
- Troubleshoot split horizon and routing update issues in an NBMA environment

Chapter 4

Layer 2 Troubleshooting

Troubleshooting Layer 2 problems can be a challenging process. Although data-link protocols are usually quite simple, the configuration and operation of these protocols is critical to creating a functional, well-tuned network.

This chapter explores the following Layer 2 protocols and technologies and outlines trouble-shooting strategies and common problems for each of them:

- Switches and switched technologies
- PPP
- ISDN
- Frame Relay

The interaction of Layer 3 protocols with various Layer 2 protocols is often the source of network problems. Specific examples and troubleshooting techniques for routed and routing protocols in various Layer 2 environments are also examined.

Characteristics of Data-Link Layer Problems

Framing errors, encapsulation errors, and Layer 2-to-Layer 3 mapping errors are common errors relating to the data-link layer. This section explores these errors as well as causes of networks functioning at less than the baseline level.

Data-Link Layer Problems Overview

Data-link layer problems have common symptoms that help you identify Layer 2 issues. Recognizing these symptoms helps you narrow down the possible causes of a problem. Before examining the individual protocols and their unique characteristics, it is helpful to know the symptoms that are associated with data-link layer problems in general. Here are some of the possible causes of Layer 2 issues:

- No functionality or connectivity at the network layer or above
- The network is not operating at baseline performance levels, either consistently or intermittently
- Encapsulation errors
- Address resolution errors
- Framing errors, excessive *cyclic redundancy check (CRC)* errors, or frame check sequence (FCS) errors
- Large quantities of broadcast traffic
- A MAC address is cycling between ports
- Console messages
- System log file messages
- Management system alarms

No Component Above the Data-Link Layer Is Functional

Because each layer of the OSI model encapsulates the layer above it, any failure of a Layer 2 protocol on a link prevents the valid exchange of Layer 3 to Layer 7 information. Some Layer 2 problems can stop the exchange of frames across a link, and others only cause network performance to degrade.

Consider the simple Layer 2 problem illustrated in Figure 4-1.

A leased-line WAN link is misconfigured such that the router at one end of the link is configured using Frame Relay as the encapsulation type and the router at the other end is using High-Level Data Link Control (HDLC) as the encapsulation type. Obviously, HDLC frames received by the Frame Relay interface are meaningless to the router. Therefore, no information can be exchanged at Layer 2. In a Cisco environment this could be confirmed using the **show cdp neighbors** command. If no information is received about a neighbor when CDP is enabled, this is a very good indication that Layer 2 frames are not being received. Because Layer 2 is not functioning, a Layer 3 test such as ping would also fail. Layer 4 Transmission Control Protocol (TCP) services would also fail, which might be indicated by a Border Gateway Protocol (BGP) router's failure to peer with neighboring routers. All applications that require the services of lower layers of the OSI model are affected.

Figure 4-1 An Encapsulation Mismatch Prevents Layer 3 Connectivity

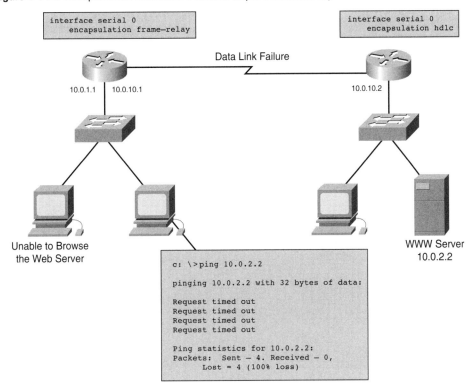

Although this is a simple concept, it underpins one of the fastest ways to narrow down a problem. Network faults are often first indicated by the failure of Layer 7 applications that require network connectivity. The troubleshooter's first instinct is to test connectivity at lower layers to attempt to isolate the failure at a specific OSI model layer or layers.

The network layer **ping** command is the most convenient method of testing connectivity. If a **ping** is successful, the lower layers can be eliminated as possible sources of the problem. However, if the pings fail, even intermittently, the next step is to find the boundary of the Layer 3 problem. In other words, how far does the ping work? See Figures 4-2 and 4-3.

Figure 4-2 A Ping to the Default Gateway Is Successful

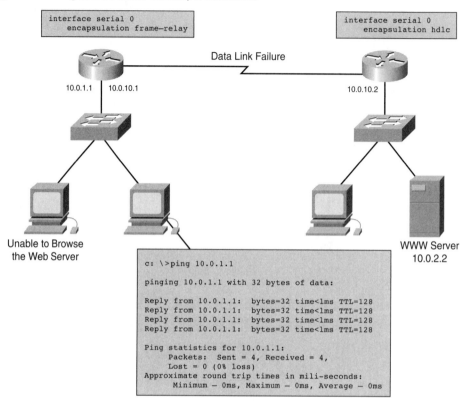

```
c: \>ping 10.0.1.1

pinging 10.0.1.1 with 32 bytes of data:

Reply from 10.0.1.1:  bytes=32 time<1ms TTL=128
Reply from 10.0.1.1:  bytes=32 time<1ms TTL=128
Reply from 10.0.1.1:  bytes=32 time<1ms TTL=128
Reply from 10.0.1.1:  bytes=32 time<1ms TTL=128

Ping statistics for 10.0.1.1:
    Packets:  Sent = 4, Received = 4,
    Lost = 0 (0% loss)
Approximate round trip times in mili-seconds:
    Minimum — 0ms, Maximum — 0ms, Average — 0ms
```

After examining the router's Layer 3 configuration, you can confirm the Layer 2 operation at the edge of this boundary. In a Cisco environment this is likely to involve the **show cdp neighbors** command. You can also examine the output of the **show interfaces** command to determine the status of the line protocol, as shown in Example 4-1.

In most instances Layer 2 problems are not difficult to troubleshoot because they are confined to communications between directly connected devices. Also, Layer 2 protocols tend to be less complex than Layer 3 protocols. The troubleshooting process is enhanced by the ability to drill down through the OSI model to determine if Layer 2 issues exist.

Figure 4-3 The Ping Fails Because of Encapsulation Mismatch

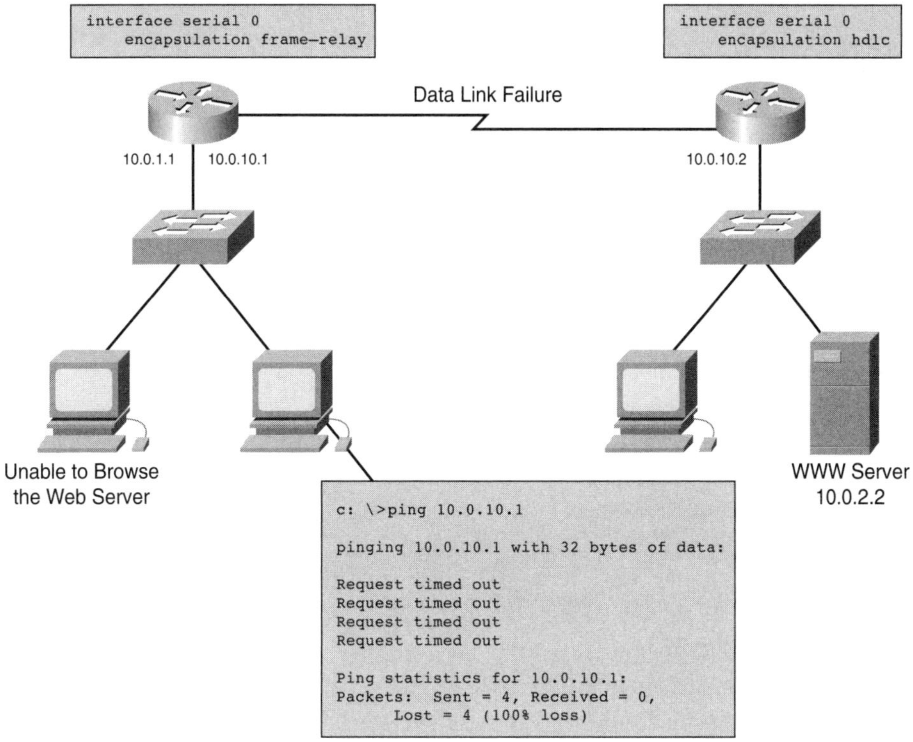

Example 4-1 *The **show interfaces** Command Displays the Status of the Line Protocol*

```
Router#show interfaces serial 0
Serial0 is up, line protocol is down
  Hardware is HD64570
  Internet address is 10.0.10.1/24
  MTU 1500 bytes, BW 1544 Kbit, DLY 20000 usec,
     reliability 255/255, txload 1/255, rxload 1/255
  Encapsulation FRAME-RELAY, loopback not set
  Keepalive set (10 sec)
  LMI enq sent  5, LMI stat recvd 0, LMI upd recvd 0, DTE
    LMI down
```

continues

Example 4-1 *The* **show interfaces** *Command Displays the Status of the Line Protocol (Continued)*

```
      LMI enq recvd 0, LMI stat sent  0, LMI upd sent  0
      LMI DLCI 1023  LMI type is CISCO  frame relay DTE
      Broadcast queue 0/64, broadcasts sent/dropped 0/0,
        interface broadcasts 0
      Last input 00:01:04, output 00:00:04, output hang never
      Last clearing of "show interface" counters 00:00:54
      Input queue: 0/75/12/0 (size/max/drops/flushes); Total
        output drops: 0
      Queueing strategy: fifo
      Output queue :0/40 (size/max)
      5 minute input rate 0 bits/sec, 0 packets/sec
      5 minute output rate 0 bits/sec, 0 packets/sec
         12 packets input, 676 bytes, 0 no buffer
         Received 0 broadcasts, 0 runts, 0 giants, 0
           throttles
         0 input errors, 0 CRC, 0 frame, 0 overrun, 0
           ignored, 0 abort
         8 packets output, 105 bytes, 0 underruns
         0 output errors, 0 collisions, 0 interface resets
         0 output buffer failures, 0 output buffers swapped
           out
         6 carrier transitions
         DCD=up  DSR=up  DTR=up  RTS=up  CTS=up
```

The Network Is Functional, But Operating at Less Than the Baseline Level

Although complete data-link layer failures are relatively easy to identify and rectify, it is much more difficult to isolate problems caused by suboptimal Layer 2 operations. The fact that some, or all, frames do actually reach their destination can make it difficult to determine the problem's boundaries and focus on the devices or links causing the problem. Two distinct types of suboptimal Layer 2 operation can occur in a network:

- Frames take an illogical path to their destination, but they do arrive, as pictured in Figure 4-4.
- Some frames are dropped.

Figure 4-4 Suboptimal Traffic Flow at Layer 2 Can Result from Misconfiguration

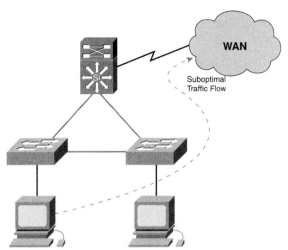

Although these are very different problems that can be caused by Layer 2 or Layer 1 faults or design issues, they share some similar symptoms:

■ Network delays

■ Lack of throughput

■ Poor network application performance

It is important to remember that the loss of some frames can be tolerated by many applications, because TCP retransmits the lost segment. For delay-sensitive traffic such as voice, video, or IBM's *Systems Network Architecture (SNA)*, suboptimal levels of performance can actually bring the application to a halt.

An example of a problem that causes frames to take an illogical path through the network is a poorly designed Layer 2 spanning-tree topology. In this case, the network might experience high bandwidth utilization on links that should not have that level of traffic. Problems that cause frames to actually be dropped can be identified through error counter statistics and console error messages that appear on the switch or router. In an Ethernet environment, an extended or continuous **ping** also reveals if any frames are being dropped, as shown in Example 4-2.

Example 4-2 *A Continuous Ping Reveals Intermittent Dropped Frames*

```
C:>ping 10.0.10.1 -t
pinging 10.0.10.1 with 32 bytes of data:


Reply from 10.0.10.1: bytes=32 time=573ms TTL=245
Reply from 10.0.10.1: bytes=32 time=562ms TTL=245
Request timed out.
Reply from 10.0.10.1: bytes=32 time=890ms TTL=245
Request timed out.
Request timed out.
Reply from 10.0.10.1: bytes=32 time=680ms TTL=245
Reply from 10.0.10.1: bytes=32 time=573ms TTL=245
Reply from 10.0.10.1: bytes=32 time=815ms TTL=245
Reply from 10.0.10.1: bytes=32 time=563ms TTL=245


Ping statistics for 10.0.10.1 :
    Packets: Sent = 10, Received = 7, Lost = 3  (30% loss),
Approximate round trip times in milli-seconds:
    Minimum = 555ms, Maximum = 890ms, Average = 677ms
Control-C
^C
C:>
```

Some Layer 2 protocols, such as X.25, have their own retransmission mechanisms that ensure that dropped frames are retransmitted. In this case, it can be difficult to determine if frames are being dropped. Variations in round-trip times for **ping** replies can indicate a problem, but to be certain that frames are being lost or corrupted, you must examine the error counters on the interface.

Framing Errors

The data-link layer uses standardized frame formats and physical addressing to establish communication within a broadcast domain. If devices disagree on the frame format, communication fails.

Problems with the frame format usually translate to encapsulation incompatibilities between nodes. Actual framing errors occur when a frame does not end on an 8-bit byte boundary for one of the following reasons:

- Noisy serial line.

- Improperly designed cable—This could be caused by serial cable that is too long, or the cable from the *CSU* or *DSU* to the router is not shielded.

- The CSU line clock is incorrectly configured—For example, the clock on one of the CSUs might be configured for local clocking. Clocking problems are the most common problem. Normally it is preferable to have one master clock with all the interfaces synchronizing to it.

- Ones-density problem on a T1 link—This is caused by incorrect framing or a coding specification.

All these problems cause a receiver to have difficulty establishing where one frame ends and another frame starts. When the interface can recognize this condition, the **show interfaces** command reveals an incrementing frame error count, as shown in Example 4-3.

Example 4-3 *Input Errors Are Revealed by the* **show interfaces** *Command*

```
RouterA#show interfaces serial 0
serial is down, line protocol is down
    Hardware is HD64570
    Description: First serial in network 1
    Internet address is 131.108.156.98/28
    MTU 1500 bytes, BW 1544 Kbit, DLY 20000 usec,
      rely 255/255, load 1/255
    Encapsulation HDLC, loopback not set,
      keepalive set (10 sec)
    Last input never, output never, output hang
      never
    Last clearing of "show interface" counters
      never
    Input queue: 0/75/301 (size/max/drops); Total
      output drops: 5762
    Queueing strategy: weighted fair
```

continues

Example 4-3 *Input Errors Are Revealed by the* **show interfaces** *Command (Continued)*

```
     Output queue: 0/1000/64/345 (size/max
      total/threshold/drops)
       Conversations 0/0/256 (active/max active/max
       total)
       Reserved Conversations 0/0 (allocated/max
       allocated)
     5 minute input rate 0 bits/sec, 0 packets/sec
     5 minute output rate 0 bits/sec, 0 packets/sec
       0 packets input, 0 bytes, 0 no buffer
       Received 757 broadcasts, 0 runts, 0 giants,
       0 throttles
       146124 input errors, 87243 CRC, 5887 frame,
       0 overrun, 0 ignored, 3 abort
       5298824 packets output, 765689898 bytes, 0
       underruns
       0 output errors, 0 collisions, 2941
       interface resets
       0 output buffer failures, 0 output buffers
       swapped out
       2 carrier transitions
       DCD=up DSR=up DTR=down RTS=down CTS=up
RouterA>
```

These problems are critical, because they cause the communications protocol itself to fail, or frames are incorrectly addressed and fail to reach their destination.

At times the framing problems might be minor and the interface might not recognize that a framing error has occurred. However, a misread bit results in the Layer 2 frame's having an invalid CRC. This error also is seen as an incrementing error count with the **show interfaces** command. In this case, the CRC error count increments.

Depending on the severity of the framing problem, the interface might be able to interpret some of the frames. Too many invalid frames might prevent valid keepalives from being exchanged, causing the **show interfaces** command to report the following:

```
Interface is up, line protocol is down
```

In summary, the following are all symptoms of a framing or related clocking problem:

- Frame errors
- CRC errors
- Interface and/or line protocol down

Encapsulation Errors

Whereas framing errors result in communication problems because an interface has trouble recognizing the bit positions, an encapsulation error occurs because the bits placed in a particular field by the sender are not what the receiver expects to see. This condition occurs when the encapsulation at one end of a WAN link is different from the encapsulation in use at the far end. If the protocol is one that expects to see appropriately formatted keepalives or correctly structured negotiation frames, such as Point-to-Point Protocol (PPP), it is likely that the interface will enter the following state:

```
Interface is up, line protocol is down
```

However, if the Layer 2 protocol is a broadcast medium such as Ethernet, keepalives are not exchanged between data terminal equipment (DTE) devices, and the interface remains in this state:

```
Interface is up, line protocol is up
```

This is true even if incompatible Ethernet encapsulation types are being used. Fortunately, in an IP environment it is rare to change the Ethernet encapsulation type to anything other than the default Advanced Research Projects Agency (ARPA). Example 4-4 shows how to identify the current encapsulation setting for an interface. Ethernet encapsulation type mismatches are most likely to occur in an Internetwork Packet Exchange (IPX) environment where the default Ethernet encapsulation has changed over the years with different versions of Novell's NetWare server operating system.

Example 4-4 *The IOS Makes It Easy to Check the Encapsulation Setting for an Interface*

```
Router#show interfaces
Ethernet 0 is up, line protocol is down
Hardware is MCI Ethernet, address is 0000.0c00.750c (bia 0000.0c00.750c)
Internet address is 131.108.28.8, subnet mask is 255.255.255.0
MTU 1500 bytes, BW 10000 Kbit, DLY 100000 usec, rely 255/255, load 1/255
Encapsulation ARPA, loopback not set, keepalive set (10 sec)
ARP type: ARPA, ARP Timeout 4:00:00
Last input 0:00:00, output 0:00:00, output hang never
```

continues

Example 4-4 *The IOS Makes It Easy to Check the Encapsulation Setting for an Interface (Continued)*

```
Last clearing of "show interface" counters 0:00:00
Output queue 0/40, 0 drops; input queue 0/75, 0 drops
Five minute input rate 0 bits/sec, 0 packets/sec
  Five minute output rate 2000 bits/sec, 4 packets/sec
1127576 packets input, 447251251 bytes, 0 no buffer
Received 354125 broadcasts, 0 runts, 0 giants, 57186* throttles
0 input errors, 0 CRC, 0 frame, 0 overrun, 0 ignored, 0 abort
5332142 packets output, 496316039 bytes, 0 underruns
0 output errors, 432 collisions, 0 interface resets, 0 restarts
```

In the case of Ethernet, there are no telltale signs that Ethernet encapsulation mismatches exist, because the interface simply ignores encapsulation types for which it is not configured.

You should adopt the following guidelines when troubleshooting Ethernet problems:

- In an IP environment, treat any Ethernet encapsulation other than ARPA as very suspicious.
- In an IPX environment, check the encapsulations in use on the servers, because this is a common misconfiguration on the router.

Layer 2-to-Layer 3 Address Mapping Errors

When a Layer 3 packet is to be forwarded to a next-hop address, the packet is encapsulated within a frame, and a Layer 2 destination address is applied to the frame.

Precisely how this Layer 2 address is determined depends on the Layer 2 protocol being used. For a point-to-point protocol such as PPP or HDLC, there are only two devices on each link. These protocols have no need to specifically address the far-end device, because the frame has only one possible recipient. In the case of PPP, the frame always contains the all-1s broadcast address and, therefore, is intended for any device at the far end of the link. Because of the nature of point-to-point protocols, it is unlikely that a Layer 2-to-Layer 3 address mapping error will occur.

In topologies such as point-to-multipoint, Frame Relay, or broadcast Ethernet, it is essential that an appropriate Layer 2 destination address be given to the frame. This ensures its arrival at the correct destination. To achieve this, the network device must match a destination Layer 3 (IP) address with the correct Layer 2 address. Two mechanisms can be used:

- Static maps
- Dynamic maps (ARP)

When using static maps, an incorrect map is a common mistake. In an Ethernet environment, this can easily occur when a network interface card (NIC) is replaced, because the NIC determines the MAC address. In a Frame Relay environment, it is possible for data-link connection identifiers (DLCIs) to be incorrectly assigned by the telco. In either case, simple configuration errors can result in a mismatch of Layer 2 and Layer 3 addressing information.

Common Layer 2-to-Layer 3 mappings include

- ARP (IP-to-MAC address)
- Inverse ARP (data-link connection identifier (DLCI) to IP address)
- Frame Relay map (IP address to DLCI)

In a dynamic environment, the mapping of Layer 2 and Layer 3 information can fail for the following reasons:

- Devices might not respond to ARP or Inverse-ARP requests because this has been specifically configured, as with the command **no frame-relay inverse-arp**.
- The Layer 2 or 3 information that is cached might have physically changed. A router caches MAC addresses for 14400 seconds, or 4 hours, by default.
- Invalid ARP replies are received, which could be because of misconfiguration or as part of a denial of service (DoS) or man-in-the-middle security attack.

With the exception of a man-in-the-middle attack, all of these problems result in similar failure characteristics:

- No Layer 3 communications between directly connected devices.
- Layer 2 communications appear OK.
- Appropriate debugs or console messages might indicate encapsulation failures when a Layer 2 address is required but can't be obtained.
- Careful inspection of ARP caches reveals no Layer 2 address or an incorrect Layer 2 address.

Here are some useful commands for troubleshooting suspected Layer 2-to-Layer 3 mapping problems:

- **show arp**—Examines the ARP cache, as shown in Example 4-5 and Table 4-1.
- **show cdp neighbor detail**—Determines neighbors' IP addresses.
- **clear arp-cache**—Forces relearning of MAC addresses when a NIC has been changed.
- **show frame-relay map**—Determines DLCI-to-IP address mapping, as shown in Example 4-6 and Table 4-2.

Example 4-5 *The ARP Cache Can Be Viewed with the* **show arp** *Command*

```
Router#show arp
Protocol  Address              Age (min)  Hardware Addr   Type   Interface
Internet  131.108.42.112       120        0000.a710.4baf  ARPA   Ethernet3
<output omitted>
```

Table 4-1 show arp Field Descriptions

Field	Description
Protocol	The type of network address this entry includes.
Address	The network address that is mapped to the MAC address in this entry.
Age (min)	The interval (in minutes) since this entry was entered into the table, rather than the interval since the entry was last used. (The timeout value is 4 hours.)
Hardware Addr	The MAC address mapped to the network address in this entry.
Type	The encapsulation type the Cisco IOS software is using for the network address in this entry. Possible values include ARPA SNAP ETLK (EtherTalk) SMDS
Interface	The interface associated with this network address.

Example 4-6 *The IP-to-DLCI Mappings Can Be Viewed with the* **show frame-relay map** *Command*

```
Router#show frame-relay map
Serial 1 (administratively down): ip 131.108.177.177
DLCI 177 (0xB1,0x2c10), static,
Broadcast,
CISCO
TCP/IP Header Compression (inherited), passive (inherited)
```

Table 4-2 show frame-relay map Field Descriptions

Field	Description
Serial 1 (administratively down)	Identifies a Frame Relay interface and its status (up or down).
ip 131.108.177.177	Destination IP address.
DLCI 177 (0xB1, 0x2C10)	A DLCI that identifies the logical connection being used to reach this interface. This value is displayed in three ways: its decimal value (177), its hexadecimal value (0xB1), and its value as it would appear on the wire (0x2C10).
static	Indicates whether this is a static or dynamic entry.
CISCO	Indicates the encapsulation type for this map, either CISCO or IETF.
TCP/IP Header Compression (inherited), passive (inherited)	Indicates whether the TCP/IP header compression characteristics were inherited from the interface or were explicitly configured for the IP map.

Critical Characteristics—No Network Layer Connectivity

Total failure of Layer 2 always results in a loss of network layer connectivity, because the Layer 2 frames are required to encapsulate and transmit packets. Layer 2 failures include

- Framing errors
- Layer 2-to-Layer 3 addressing problems
- Encapsulation mismatches

Regardless of the cause of the Layer 2 problem, the Layer 3 symptom is the same—a loss of connectivity. This can reveal itself in a number of ways:

- Inability to ping across a failing data-link
- Routing protocols reporting the link as being down or inaccessible
- Routing protocols reporting configured neighbors as unreachable, as shown in Example 4-7.
- Console messages

Example 4-7 *EIGRP Conveniently Displays Neighbor Reachability*

```
Orlando#
Dec 16 21:14:24: %LINEPROTO-5-UPDOWN: Line protocol on
Interface Serial1/0, changed state to down
Dec 16 21:13:24 %DUAL-5-NBRCHANGE: IP-EIGRP 101: Neighbor
172.21.177.1 (Serial1/0)is down: interface down
Orlando#
```

These symptoms are similar to those experienced when Layer 3 fails. It is necessary for the troubleshooter to distinguish between a Layer 2 failure and a Layer 3 failure. To specifically test Layer 2 connectivity, check that CDP is enabled on both devices, and then use the **show cdp neighbors** command. If two neighboring devices can see each other using the **show cdp neighbors** command, but it is impossible to **ping** between the devices, there are two explanations. The problem might be with Layer 2-to-Layer 3 addressing, or it is, in fact, a Layer 3 problem.

Upper Layer Component Operation

A failure at the data-link layer has a profound effect on the layers above it.

A failure at the data-link layer can be either total or intermittent. A total failure at the data-link layer prevents communication at higher layers. However, the effects of intermittent errors at the data-link layer depend on the particular Layer 2 protocol in use. If the Layer 2 protocol is designed to implement reliable communications such as X.25, it might be difficult to identify Layer 2 problems from the behavior of the upper layers. This is because the Layer 2 protocol simply retransmits any lost frames. If frames are lost frequently, application network performance might be sluggish, or application timeouts might occur.

For Layer 2 protocols that can be classified as best-effort delivery, such as Ethernet, the loss of a frame immediately translates into the loss of a packet and, in the case of TCP, a segment. In this case, it is TCP's responsibility to retransmit lost segments. Again, if the frame losses are intermittent, the effects on the application might be that it runs sluggishly, or the loss of performance might not be noticeable at all. However, TCP statistics should show evidence of the segment loss and retransmissions.

Table 4-3 outlines the symptoms that might be experienced at each of the layers of the TCP model when an intermittent or total Layer 2 failure occurs.

Although these characteristics give some indication that a Layer 2 problem exists, it is inconclusive until the devices attached to the nonfunctional data-link are examined. Performing a **traceroute** or **tracert** command immediately identifies the failing link, allowing the devices at each end of the link to be checked for appropriate Layer 2-to-Layer 3 mapping operations.

Table 4-3 Frame Loss Symptoms at Layers 3 to 7

Layers	Symptoms with Intermittent Loss of Frames	Symptoms with Total Loss of Frames
2 and 3 (encapsulation)	Debugging IOS devices reveals occasional encapsulation failures or the inability to associate a Layer 2 frame with a Layer 3 interface.	Debugging IOS devices reveals that encapsulation fails for all packets, or the Layer 2 frames cannot be associated with a Layer 3 interface.
3 (network)	In an Ethernet environment, packet statistics show that packets are being lost. On point-to-point links, it might be possible to identify that the number of packets being sent across a link is greater than the number received at the other end. Extended continuous pings reveal packet loss. For reliable protocols such as X.25, the loss of frames might not be noticeable or might show up as increased round trip times for pings.	No network layer communication is possible. All pings time out.
4 (TCP)	TCP statistics show evidence of retransmission that might be detectable as being above baseline. Remember that TCP uses segment loss as a mechanism to control congestion, so retransmissions can be a feature of an otherwise healthy network.	No TCP sessions are established. All time out.
5 to 7 (application)	Varying levels of network application performance degradation. This can vary from unnoticeable to unbearable, depending on the percentage of frame loss being experienced.	Applications are unable to establish communications across the network.

Table 4-3 summarizes the effects of data-link layer problems on the other layers. Use these characteristics to help determine whether a problem being experienced could be a Layer 2 failure.

Critical Characteristics—Console Messages

In some instances, a router recognizes that a Layer 2 problem has occurred and sends alert messages to the console. Typically, a router does this when it detects a problem with interpreting incoming frames (encapsulation or framing problems) or when keepalives are expected but do not arrive. The most common console message that indicates a Layer 2 problem is **line protocol down**, as shown in Example 4-8.

Example 4-8 *The IOS Reports Via the Console That a Line Protocol Has Gone Down, Provided That Console Logging Is Enabled*

```
Line Protocol State Change to Down 00:01:32:
%LINEPROTO-5-UPDOWN: Line protocol on Interface Serial0,
changed state to down
```

Lab 4.1.1   Isolating Physical and Data-Link Layer Problems

In this lab exercise, you are given a problem situation escalated to Level 2, Engineering. You analyze user feedback and end-system data and use Cisco commands and applications to isolate the specific cause of any problem. You use a troubleshooting methodology and Cisco commands to isolate the specific causes of any network problems.

End-System Commands for Gathering Data-Link Layer Information

Several popular network operating systems (NOSs), such as Windows 2003 Server, Red Hat Linux, Mac OS X, and Solaris, are used in corporate networking. These operating systems have a variety of troubleshooting commands available. The most common end-system commands are detailed in this section, as well as useful Cisco IOS commands for gathering Layer 2 information.

Common End-System Commands

The following commands are basic tools for Layer 2 troubleshooting and are implemented on Windows, UNIX, and Mac OS X operating systems:

- **ping**
- **arp -a**

Table 4-4 describes these commands.

Table 4-4 Instances of **ping** and **arp** Are Available on Each NOS

Command	Description
ping {*host* | *ip-address*}	Sends an echo request packet to an address and then waits for a reply. The *host* | *ip-address* variable is the IP alias or IP address of the target system.
arp -a	Displays the current mappings of the IP address to the MAC address in the ARP table.

Although **ping** operates as part of the IP suite of protocols, it is useful for troubleshooting Layer 2, because it is a means of establishing the fault's boundaries. The continuous **ping** is also a useful method of generating test frames and observing error counters.

The **arp -a** command is useful for verifying that the ARP process is functioning correctly and is not being overridden by static entries configured on a workstation or router.

Microsoft Windows End-System Commands

The commands displayed in Table 4-5, available in the Microsoft Windows environment, are useful in gathering basic Layer 2 information from host systems:

- **winipcfg**
- **ipconfig /all**
- **tracert**
- **netstat -r**
- **netstat -n**
- **arp -a**

Table 4-5 Microsoft's NOSs Provide an Array of Layer 2 Troubleshooting Commands

Command	Description
ipconfig /all	Displays IP information for hosts running Windows NT/2000/XP/2003.
tracert [*destination*]	Verifies connectivity to a destination device for Windows hosts. The *destination* variable is the IP alias or IP address of the target system.
winipcfg	Displays IP information for hosts running Windows 9x and Me.
netstat -r	Displays the routing table.
netstat -n	Displays the status of all connected devices and links without querying a DNS server.

winipcfg can be run from the command prompt or the Run window. It is a quick way of determining the MAC address of a Windows 9x- or Me-based PC, as shown in Figure 4-5.

Figure 4-5 winipcfg Is Used on Windows 9x and Me

Later versions of the Microsoft Windows operating system, such as Windows 2000, XP, and 2003, use the **ipconfig /all** command from the command prompt to obtain more detailed information, as shown in Figure 4-6.

Figure 4-6 ipconfig is Used on Windows 2000, XP, and 2003

```
Shortcut to CMD.EXE                                                    _|□|×|
C:\WINNT\system32>ipconfig/all

Windows 2000 IP Configuration

        Host Name . . . . . . . . . . . . : walewis-w2k
        Primary DNS Suffix  . . . . . . . : amer.cisco.com
        Node Type . . . . . . . . . . . . : Hybrid
        IP Routing Enabled. . . . . . . . : No
        WINS Proxy Enabled. . . . . . . . : No
        DNS Suffix Search List. . . . . . : cisco.com
                                            cisco.com

Ethernet adapter 80211b Connection:

        Connection-specific DNS Suffix  . : hawaii.rr.com
        Description . . . . . . . . . . . : Cisco Systems 340 Series PCMCIA Wireless LAN Adapter
        Physical Address. . . . . . . . . : 00-40-96-34-70-21
        DHCP Enabled. . . . . . . . . . . : Yes
        Autoconfiguration Enabled . . . . : Yes
        IP Address. . . . . . . . . . . . : 192.168.1.100
        Subnet Mask . . . . . . . . . . . : 255.255.255.0
        Default Gateway . . . . . . . . . : 192.168.1.1
        DHCP Server . . . . . . . . . . . : 192.168.1.1
        DNS Servers . . . . . . . . . . . : 171.68.226.120
                                            171.70.168.183
        Primary WINS Server . . . . . . . : 171.69.2.87
        Secondary WINS Server . . . . . . : 171.68.235.228
        Lease Obtained. . . . . . . . . . : Thursday, January 29, 2004 2:25:51 PM
        Lease Expires . . . . . . . . . . : Friday, January 30, 2004 2:25:51 PM

Ethernet adapter Ethernet Connection:

        Media State . . . . . . . . . . . : Cable Disconnected
        Description . . . . . . . . . . . : Intel(R) PRO/100 VE Network Connection
        Physical Address. . . . . . . . . : 00-09-6B-02-A2-BC

C:\WINNT\system32>
```

Although **tracert** is a Layer 3 tool that displays the path packets take to get to a destination, it is also a quick way to find where a Layer 2 failure has occurred. The **tracert** command is similar to the Cisco IOS **traceroute** command.

netstat -r also provides MAC address information, as shown in Figure 4-7. **netstat -r** has the added benefit of displaying the host's routing table, which can help you make sense of multi-homed workstations. **netstat -n** displays addresses and port numbers in numerical form.

Figure 4-7 netstat Can Be Used to View the Routing Table

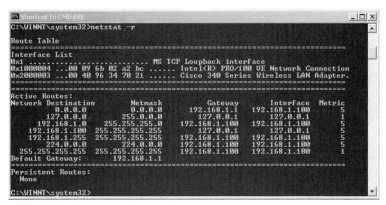

arp -a is similar to the Cisco IOS **show arp** command. It displays the ARP table of MAC-to-IP addresses for a device.

UNIX/Mac Operating System End-System Commands

The **ifconfig -a** and **traceroute** commands are available on most UNIX variants, including Mac OS X. They are described in Table 4-6.

Table 4-6 UNIX NOS Troubleshooting Commands

Command	Description
ifconfig -a	Displays IP information.
traceroute	Identifies the path that a packet takes through the network.

General Cisco IOS Commands

The Cisco IOS has a rich set of **show** and **debug** commands for troubleshooting Layer 2 problems. Use the commands listed in Table 4-7 as a guide when troubleshooting Layer 2 problems.

In addition to the **ping**, **trace**, and **debug** commands, the IOS **clear counters** command lets the network engineer make use of the output of the **show interfaces** command for troubleshooting various interface frame counts.

Table 4-7 Common IOS Troubleshooting Commands

Command	Description
ping {*host* | *ip-address*}	Sends an echo request packet to an address and waits for a reply.
trace [*destination*]	Identifies the path a packet takes through the network.
[un]debug	Displays a list of options for enabling or disabling debugging events on a device.

Cisco IOS show Commands

A wealth of information can be gathered from Layer 2 Cisco IOS **show** commands. The two main challenges troubleshooters face when using **show** commands are choosing the right command to obtain the desired information and correctly interpreting the command output. Table 4-8 lists pertinent **show** commands.

Table 4-8 Common IOS **show** Commands for Troubleshooting

Command	Description
show arp	Shows the contents of the ARP cache.
show buffers	Shows statistics on the memory buffer pool for a device.
show cdp neighbors	Shows the device type, IP address, and Cisco IOS version.
show context	Shows information stored in nonvolatile RAM (NVRAM) when an exception occurs.
show controllers	Shows controller statistics and verifies that a cable is properly detected. DTE/DCE status of a serial interface can also be verified.
show diag [*slot*]	Diagnoses information about the components of a line card. Not applicable to all Cisco hardware.
show interfaces	Shows the operational status of an interface as well as the amount and type of traffic being sent and received.
show ip interfaces brief	Shows a summary of the status of all interfaces on a device.
show logging	Verifies the types of messages that generate logging output.

Table 4-8 Common IOS **show** Commands for Troubleshooting (Continued)

Command	Description
show mac address-table {*module/port*}	Shows the MAC counters for traffic passing through a port, such as received frames, transmitted frames, out-lost, and in-lost.
show memory	Shows the contents of the RAM memory for the device.
show module	Shows a summary of the status of modules on a Catalyst switch.
show port {*module/port*}	Shows a detailed description of a specific port.
show port status	Shows a summary of the status of all ports on a Catalyst switch.
show processes cpu	Shows CPU utilization statistics.
show processes memory	Shows a list of all processes running on the system.
show running-configuration	Shows the current configuration, including keepalive settings.
show stacks	Shows the processor stacks on a router. Requires a stack decoder to analyze the output.
show tech-support	Provides general information about a device that can be useful for reporting problems to the Cisco Technical Assistance Center (TAC).
show version	Verifies that Cisco IOS recognizes all installed hardware components.

The show cdp neighbors Command

The **show cdp neighbors** command is one of the quickest ways to verify Layer 2 connectivity between two directly connected Cisco devices. However, CDP is often turned off to limit bandwidth usage or to enhance network security. Furthermore, most non-Cisco devices do not speak CDP. Before relying on the **show cdp neighbors** command, verify that the device at the other end of the data-link is configured to allow CDP. On a Cisco device running IOS, use the global configuration command **cdp run** to enable CDP on that device:

```
Router(config)#cdp run
```

Use the interface configuration command **cdp enable** to allow CDP on a particular interface if it has been specifically disabled:

```
Router(config-if)#cdp enable
```

An example of the output produced by the **show cdp neighbors** command is shown in Example 4-9. Appending the **detail** keyword to this command provides more detailed output on the neighbors, including basic IP address information.

Example 4-9 *The* **show cdp neighbors** *IOS Command Is Extremely Useful for Identifying Layer 2 and Layer 3 Information for Connected Cisco Devices*

```
Router#show cdp neighbors
Capability Codes: R - Router, T - Trans Bridge, B - Source Route Bridge
S - Switch, H - Host, I - IGMP, r - Repeater
Device ID      Local Intrfce      Holtme      Capability      Platform      Port ID
lab-7206            Eth 0           157            R             7206VXR      Fas 0/0/0
```

 Lab 4.1.2   Correcting Problems at the Physical and Data-Link Layers

In this lab exercise, you correct the problems isolated in Lab 4.1.1 using various Cisco commands to correct network problems. The steps include

- Implementing a troubleshooting plan
- Verifying that the data flow in the network matches your network baseline

Troubleshooting Switched Ethernet Networks

Troubleshooting Layer 2 might involve LANs or WANs. This section describes what to look for when troubleshooting LANs. Techniques for troubleshooting LANs include STP, broadcasts, flooding, Virtual Terminal Protocol (VTP), and EtherChannel.

Troubleshooting the Spanning Tree Protocol

Spanning Tree Protocol (STP) is designed to allow a logical loop-free network in a switched network featuring redundant links. This is achieved by strategically blocking some ports from forwarding data. STP is a straightforward protocol that has been in use for many years.

STP is likely to fail when there is a problem with the exchange of Bridge Protocol Data Units (BPDUs). The key parameters for STP operation are the HELLO time and the MAX AGE time. The HELLO time determines how often BPDUs are sent. The MAX AGE time determines how long a port waits since the last BPDU was heard before deciding that a link is no longer connected to a switch and is therefore no longer part of a loop.

Symptoms of STP failure and consequent switching loops include the following:

- Unusually high backplane utilization caused by forwarding frames at line speed.

- Rapid address relearning, because the loop allows a switch to see the same source address entering on multiple ports.

- Rapidly incrementing frame counters on the affected ports as they receive frames at line speed.

- Extremely poor link performance, high latency on **ping** replies, and TCP timeouts as this traffic has to compete with broadcast frames caught in the loop.

- Broadcast storms in a Layer 2 domain. Because broadcasts are perpetuated by a loop, their effect is felt throughout the switched network.

Any network problem that prevents BPDUs from being received within the MAX AGE time causes an STP topology recalculation. Ports that need to be blocked are placed in a forwarding state, and a switching loop occurs.

A switching loop is more serious than a routing loop because, unlike low-end routers, even a modest switch can forward broadcast frames at the full line speed. This can fully saturate a link and further prevent BPDUs from being exchanged. Thus, the loop is maintained.

How is it possible for the switch to stop receiving BPDUs while the port is up? The most obvious answer is that the STP has been turned off. Another common cause is the unidirectional link. A link is considered unidirectional when

- Links are up on both sides of the connection.
- The local side does not receive packets sent by the remote side.
- The remote side receives packets sent by the local side.

Consider the scenario shown in Figure 4-8, in which the arrows indicate the flow of STP BPDUs.

Figure 4-8 BPDU Flow for STP

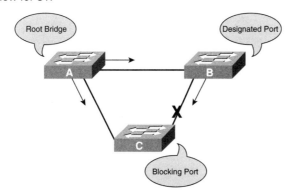

During normal operation, bridge B is designated on the link B–C. Bridge B sends BPDUs to C, which is blocking the port. The port is blocked while C sees BPDUs from B on that link.

Consider what happens if the link B–C fails in the direction of C, as illustrated in Figure 4-9. C stops receiving traffic from B, but B still receives traffic from C.

Figure 4-9 Unidirectional Failure of BPDU Flow

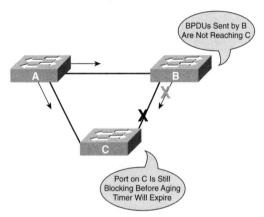

C stops receiving BPDUs on the link B–C and ages the information received with the last BPDU. This takes up to 20 seconds, depending on the MAX AGE STP timer. As soon as the STP information is aged out on the port, it transitions from blocking state to listening, learning, and eventually forwarding STP state. This creates a forwarding loop, because no blocking port exists in the triangle A–B–C. Packets cycle along the path (B still receives packets from C), taking more and more bandwidth until the links are filled up completely, bringing down the network.

Troubleshooting STP Loops

As soon as an STP loop has been identified, it is important to isolate the reason behind the loop. One of the first things to check is if STP is running on each of the switches. A switch should have STP disabled only if it is not part of a physically looped topology. Unless there is a very good reason for turning off STP, every switch should have it enabled.

The IOS command to verify STP operation is **show spanning-tree**, illustrated in Example 4-10.

Example 4-10 *The* **show spanning-tree** *Command Displays Spanning-Tree Information for Each VLAN*

```
Switch#show spanning-tree


VLAN0001
  Spanning tree enabled protocol ieee
  Root ID    Priority    32769
             Address     0007.84f9.f680
             Cost        19
             Port        15 (FastEthernet0/15)
             Hello Time   2 sec  Max Age 20 sec  Forward Delay 15 sec


  Bridge ID  Priority    32769  (priority 32768 sys-id-ext 1)
             Address     000a.4122.3780
             Hello Time   2 sec  Max Age 20 sec  Forward Delay 15 sec
             Aging Time 300
<output omitted>
```

It is clear from the output of the **show spanning-tree** command if STP is not running, as shown in Example 4-11.

Example 4-11 *Spanning Tree Is Enabled by Default, But if It Is Manually Disabled,* **show spanning-tree** *Output Is Empty*

```
Switch#show spanning-tree
```

No spanning-tree instances exist. It is important to remember that spanning tree operates on a per-VLAN basis by default on Cisco devices (PVST/PVST+) and that executing a **show spanning-tree** command reports on VLAN 1 only. Use the **show spanning-tree** [**vlan** *ID*] command to verify STP operations for other VLANs.

If STP is not operating, it can be enabled using the **spanning-tree vlan** *ID* command.

Preventing STP Loops

To detect unidirectional links before the forwarding loop is created, Cisco designed and implemented the UDLD protocol.

UDLD is a Layer 2 protocol that works with Layer 1 mechanisms to determine a link's physical status. At Layer 1, autonegotiation takes care of physical signaling and fault detection. UDLD performs tasks that autonegotiation cannot perform, such as detecting the identities of neighbors and shutting down misconnected ports. When UDLD is enabled, it works with autonegotiation to prevent physical and logical unidirectional connections from forming and causing other protocols to malfunction.

UDLD works by exchanging protocol packets between the neighboring devices. For UDLD to work, both devices on the link must support UDLD and have it enabled on respective ports.

Each switch port configured for UDLD sends UDLD protocol packets containing the port's own device/port ID and the neighbor's device/port IDs seen by UDLD on that port. Neighboring ports should see their own device/port ID (echo) in the packets received from the other side.

If the port does not see its own device/port ID in the incoming UDLD packets for a specific duration of time, the link is considered unidirectional. This echo algorithm allows the detection of several issues:

- The link is up on both sides, but packets are received by only one side
- Wiring mistakes, when receive and transmit fibers are not connected to the same port on the remote side

As soon as UDLD detects the unidirectional link, the respective port is disabled and the following message appears on the console:

```
UDLD-3-DISABLE: Unidirectional link detected on port 1/2. Port disabled
```

Port shutdown by UDLD remains disabled until it is manually reenabled or until errdisable timeout expires if configured.

The following commands allow you to configure UDLD on Catalyst switches running Cisco IOS. By default, UDLD is disabled. First, you need to enable UDLD globally by issuing the following command:

```
Switch(config)#udld enable
```

By default, this command enables UDLD on all interfaces.

You can enable UDLD on a specific interface by issuing the following command:

```
Switch(config-if)#udld enable
```

The **interface** command overrides the global configuration command. UDLD can be verified with the following command:

```
Switch#show udld interface
```

Example 4-12 shows an example of the output produced.

Example 4-12 *The* **show udld** *Command Displays Useful UDLD Information for an Interface*

```
Switch#show udld f0/1


Interface Fa0/1

---

Port enable administrative configuration setting: Enabled

Port enable operational state: Enabled

Current bidirectional state: Unknown

Current operational state: Advertisement

Message interval: 7

Time out interval: 5

No neighbor cache information stored
```

Should it be necessary to override the UDLD configuration on individual interfaces, this can be accomplished from interface configuration mode:

```
Switch(config)#interface fastethernet 0/12
Switch(config-if)#udld enable
```

In an environment that supports UDLD, enabling this functionality has the potential to prevent STP loops and the resulting loss of network connectivity. Cisco recommends that UDLD should be enabled wherever possible. One case in which a unidirectional fault can happen is when a TX fiber link from a pair is accidentally cut.

Troubleshooting Incorrect STP Root Configuration

Switches have become the basic building block of even the simplest networks. They form a seamless replacement for hubs and come with STP enabled by default. Link redundancy can be implemented without any switch configuration being necessary. In fact, it is possible to construct a highly redundant switched network, as shown in Figure 4-10, without ever having heard of STP.

Figure 4-10 STP Can Prevent Propagated Ethernet Frames from Bringing Down the Network

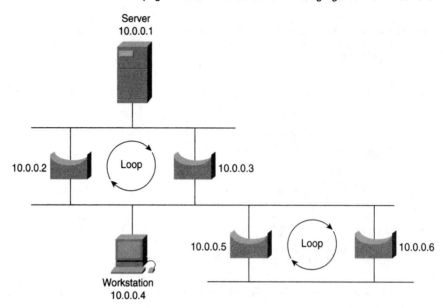

Poorly configured Layer 2 designs usually result from a lack of knowledge of STP or a misunderstanding of its operation.

Examine the switched network topology shown in Figure 4-11. At first glance, it appears to be an efficient design. A few pings to devices in the network reveal full connectivity. However, upon closer inspection, the traffic flow in this topology reveals suboptimal traffic patterns. To really analyze the network topology, you must look at the spanning-tree states of each of the ports. In Figure 4-12, it is apparent that the network has unfortunately chosen the Marketing department switch as the STP root.

Spanning tree has placed the Data Center port leading to the Telephone Sales Center in a blocking state. Consequently, the majority of traffic must take the longest path to the Data Center. With the Data Center at one end of the Spanning Tree, the link between the switch in Reception and the Data Center must carry the organization's entire traffic load.

Figure 4-11 Suboptimal Traffic Flow

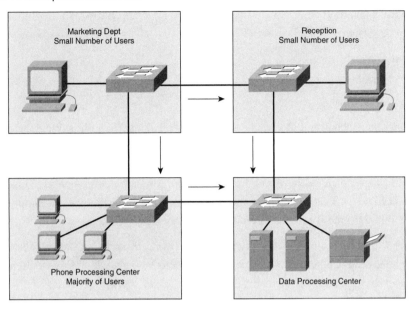

Figure 4-12 Improperly Placed Spanning-Tree Root

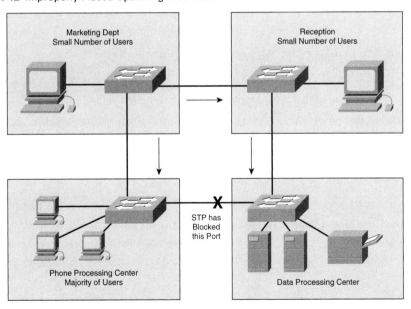

The symptoms of suboptimal Layer 2 design are usually those of congestion and often are noticed only when traffic levels increase. In the worst case, the following are symptoms of poor Layer 2 design:

- Lost packets
- High latency
- Poor throughput

Troubleshooting suboptimal Layer 2 design can be a challenge. Traditional tools, such as traceroute, operate at Layer 3 and reveal nothing about the Layer 2 topology. It is a common error to overlook Layer 2 as the culprit and incorrectly troubleshoot the higher layers when faced with congestion caused by poor Layer 2 design. Another common mistake made by inexperienced network administrators and engineers is to assume that there is simply a lack of bandwidth; thus, the solution chosen is a link bandwidth upgrade.

Consider the network administrator's view of the network. If complaints are received from the Telephone Sales Center that network performance is lacking, which link would he or she recommend be upgraded? Instinctively, the inexperienced administrator orders the 100 Mbps between the Telephone Sales Center and the Data Center to be upgraded to Gigabit Ethernet. Embarrassingly, the upgrade has no effect on the network's performance.

The correct course of action is to set the Data Center switch as the STP root. It is possible that an upgrade to the link is still required, but at least the full benefits of the upgrade are now realized.

When considering a Layer 2 topology and STP, keep in mind the following:

- By default, the STP root is the switch with the lowest MAC address.
- The switch from which the majority of traffic is centered should be the STP root.
- Switches that provide access ports for server farms or the Internet gateway should be given consideration as the STP root. Often this is the distribution layer switch.
- The physical topology can be misleading. You must determine which ports are blocking to trace the traffic path through the network.

Tools exist that allow the mapping of the Layer 2 topology. When you deal with large, complex networks, or if you work regularly with unfamiliar networks, these tools can be of great benefit. For simpler, familiar networks, simply documenting the STP states in the LAN is sufficient, as shown in Table 4-9.

Table 4-9 Layer 2 Documentation Should Include the Interfaces' STP States

Catalyst Name, Model, Management IP Address	Port Name	Speed	Duplex	STP State (Fwd/Block)	PortFast (Yes/No)	Trunk Status	EtherChannel (L2 or L3)	VLANs
Burlington, WS C3550-24-SMI, 10.3.2.33/27								
	fa0/1	10	Full	Fwd	No	On	—	—
	fa0/2	100	Full	Block	No	Off	—	—
	fa0/3	100	Half	Fwd	Yes	Off	—	4
	fa0/4	100	Auto	Fwd	No	On	L2	—
	fa0/5	100	Auto	Fwd	No	On	L2	—
	fa0/6	100	Auto	Fwd	No	On	L2	—
	fa0/7	100	Auto	Fwd	No	On	L2	—

Troubleshooting Ethernet Broadcast Traffic

One of the key performance benefits of a switch is its ability to keep local traffic local while still allowing any two devices to communicate. Switches can do this because switching decisions are based on the destination MAC address. Assuming that VLANs are not in use, there are three instances in which a switch cannot forward a frame to a single interface and instead floods the frame out all the ports. These situations occur when the destination MAC address is

- The Ethernet broadcast address
- A multicast address and the switch is not multicast-aware
- A MAC address that is unknown to the switch

In each case, the behavior is required for normal network operation. However, excessive broadcasts result in one or both of the following problems:

- Increased congestion
- Poor host performance caused by each host's having to examine all broadcast packets

The number of broadcasts present in a network can be determined using most protocol analyzers. As an alternative, the information can be determined using the **show interfaces** command on an IOS-based switch or router, as shown in Example 4-13. It can be difficult to judge whether the number of broadcasts present is excessive. There are no rules as to what is normal. It really depends on the applications and upper-layer protocols being used. The IP protocol uses broadcasts extensively to address multiple hosts, ARP, and routing updates. It is not unusual to find that up to 30 percent of traffic is made up of broadcasts. When you encounter a situation where it appears that network performance might be degraded because of excessive broadcasts, it is helpful if the network documentation baselines normal broadcast levels so that you can make a comparison.

Example 4-13 *Ethernet Broadcast Counts Are Displayed with the* **show interfaces** *Command*

```
Switch#show interfaces fa0/1
FastEthernet0/1 is up, line protocol is up
  Hardware is Fast Ethernet, address is 000a.4122.3781 (bia 000a.4122.3781)
  MTU 1500 bytes, BW 100000 Kbit, DLY 100 usec,
     reliability 255/255, txload 1/255, rxload 1/255
  Encapsulation ARPA, loopback not set
  Keepalive set (10 sec)
  Full-duplex, 100Mb/s
  input flow-control is off, output flow-control is off
  ARP type: ARPA, ARP Timeout 04:00:00
  Last input 00:00:13, output 00:00:01, output hang never
```

Example 4-13 *Ethernet Broadcast Counts Are Displayed with the* **show interfaces** *Command (Continued)*

```
Last clearing of "show interface" counters never
Input queue: 0/75/0/0 (size/max/drops/flushes); Total output drops: 0
Queueing strategy: fifo
Output queue :0/40 (size/max)
5 minute input rate 0 bits/sec, 0 packets/sec
5 minute output rate 0 bits/sec, 0 packets/sec
   169902 packets input, 16278748 bytes, 0 no buffer
   Received 95713 broadcasts, 0 runts, 0 giants, 0 throttles
   0 input errors, 0 CRC, 0 frame, 0 overrun, 0 ignored
   0 watchdog, 95536 multicast, 0 pause input
   0 input packets with dribble condition detected
   683657 packets output, 55690789 bytes, 0 underruns
   0 output errors, 0 collisions, 1 interface resets
   0 babbles, 0 late collision, 0 deferred
   0 lost carrier, 0 no carrier, 0 PAUSE output
   0 output buffer failures, 0 output buffers swapped out
```

Where you observe excessive broadcasts, it is important to identify the source of the broadcasts so that appropriate steps can be taken. When analyzing traffic, keep in mind that switches respond to broadcast frames, whereas traffic analyzers are usually more concerned about Layer 3 packets. Generally this is not a problem, because a broadcast packet is carried by a broadcast frame, but different tools report broadcasts differently, depending on whether they have a Layer 2 or Layer 3 focus.

Generally, excessive broadcasts result from one of the following situations:

- Poorly programmed or configured applications
- Very large Layer 2 broadcast domains
- Underlying network problems such as STP loops or route flapping

Using a protocol analyzer, you can readily ascertain the problem's source. Each of these situations dictates a different solution.

Some applications, such as Symantec's Ghost server and streaming video servers, use broadcast and multicast traffic. This is an attempt to reduce the number of streams of traffic sent, thereby minimizing bandwidth usage and improving performance. Although it might be possible to reconfigure the application so that it does not use multicasts or broadcasts, often this introduces other problems. If the network requires applications that are heavy producers of broadcast and multicast traffic, consider the following techniques to reduce the impact on other devices in the network:

- Create a separate VLAN for devices and hosts that are broadcast-intensive.
- Configure switches to be multicast-aware.
- Consider using scheduling for distribution services, such as Ghost, so that broadcast traffic can be limited to off-peak times.

Very large Layer 2 broadcast domains can sometimes occur where the hosts themselves do not generate much traffic and their perceived network needs are not great. It is tempting in these situations to avoid the expense of a Layer 3 hierarchy and simply adopt a flat, switched structure. Unfortunately, modern operating systems use broadcasts extensively to discover network services and other hosts. Very large, lightly loaded Layer 2 networks quickly find that the majority of their traffic is made up of broadcasts. Laptop users who complain that their computer runs applications faster when they are not connected to the network indicates that there might be excessive broadcasts. The solution is to use a proven hierarchical network structure using routers to break up the broadcast domains.

Many routing protocols, notably distance vector, use broadcasts. Link-state routing protocols such as OSPF use multicasts. These mechanisms are required for exchanging routing updates. Network instability that results in routes being added to and removed from routing tables can generate significant amounts of broadcast traffic.

Troubleshooting Ethernet Switch Flooding

LAN switches use forwarding tables, called Content-Addressable Memory (CAM), to direct traffic to specific ports based on the VLAN number and the frame's destination MAC address. When no entry corresponds to the frame's destination MAC address in the incoming VLAN, the unicast frame is sent to all forwarding ports in the respective VLAN. This is called flooding. Limited flooding is part of the normal switching process. However, there are situations in which continuous flooding can cause adverse performance effects on the network.

Note that Catalyst switches, including the Catalyst 2900 XL, 3500 XL, 2950, 3550, 4000, 5000, and 6000, maintain Layer 2 forwarding tables for each VLAN.

Low-bandwidth links can become saturated with large amounts of flooded traffic. When this happens, network performance degrades, occasionally causing a loss of connectivity.

In Figure 4-13, Server S1 in VLAN 1 is running a bulk data transfer backup to server S2 in VLAN 2. Server S1 has its default gateway pointing to router A's VLAN 1 interface. Server S2 has its default gateway pointing to router B's VLAN 2 interface.

Figure 4-13 *Unnecessary Flooding Because of Asymmetric Routing*

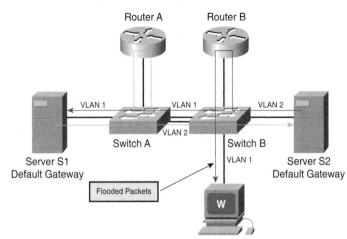

Packets from S1 to S2 follow this path:

S1-VLAN 1→Switch A→Router A→VLAN 2→Switch B→VLAN 2→S2 (orange line)

Packets from S2 to S1 follow this path:

S2-VLAN 2→Switch B→Router B→VLAN 1→Switch A→flooded to VLAN 1→S1 (red line)

Note that with such an arrangement, switch A does not "see" traffic from the S2 MAC address in VLAN 2. This is because the source MAC address is rewritten by Router B, and the packet only arrives in VLAN 1. This means that every time switch A needs to send the packet to the S2 MAC address, the packet is flooded to VLAN 2. The same situation occurs with the S1 MAC address on Switch B.

This behavior is called asymmetric routing. Packets follow different paths depending on the direction. Asymmetric routing is one of the two most common causes of flooding.

Returning to the preceding example, all packets contained in the data transfer between the two servers are flooded to all ports on Switch A that belong to VLAN 2 and all ports on Switch B that are members of VLAN 1. Any workstation attached to one of these ports (in this example, Workstation W) receives all packets of the conversation between S1 and S2. Suppose the server backup takes 50 Mbps of bandwidth, which saturates 10-Mbps links. The result for the PCs is either a complete connectivity outage or significant performance degradation.

This flooding is caused by asymmetric routing and might stop when server S1 sends a broadcast packet such as Address Resolution Protocol (ARP). Switch A floods this packet to VLAN 1, and switch B receives and learns S1's MAC address. Because the switch does not receive traffic constantly, this forwarding entry eventually ages out, and flooding resumes. The same process applies to S2.

There are different approaches to limit the flooding caused by asymmetric routing. The approach is normally to bring the router's ARP timeout and the switches' forwarding table-aging time close to each other. This causes the ARP packets to be broadcast. Relearning must occur before the L2 forwarding table entry ages out.

A typical scenario in which this kind of issue might be observed is when redundant Layer 3 switches, such as a Catalyst 6500 with Mutilayer Switch Feature Card (MSFC), are configured to load-balance with Hot Standby Router Protocol (HSRP). In this case, one switch is active for even-numbered VLANs, and the other one is active for odd-numbered VLANs.

Another common issue caused by flooding is STP Topology Change Notification (TCN). TCN is designed to correct forwarding tables after the forwarding topology has changed. This is necessary to avoid a connectivity outage, because after a topology change, some destinations previously accessible via particular ports might become accessible via different ports. TCN operates by shortening the forwarding table aging time such that if the address is not relearned, it ages out, and flooding occurs.

TCNs are triggered by a port that is transitioning to or from the forwarding state. After the TCN and even if the particular destination MAC address has aged out, flooding should not happen. If it does occur, it is brief in most cases because the address is relearned. However, an issue might arise if TCNs are occurring repeatedly with short intervals. The switches constantly fast-age their forwarding tables so that flooding is nearly constant.

Whenever a port on switch goes down or up, the STP state transitions to or from the forwarding state. If a port is flapping, it causes repetitive TCNs that can lead to flooding.

Ports with the STP portfast feature enabled do not cause TCNs when going to or from the forwarding state. Configuring portfast on all end-device ports such as printers, PCs, servers, and so on should limit TCNs to a low number.

Another possible cause of flooding can be overflow of the switch forwarding table. In this case, new addresses cannot be learned, and packets destined for such addresses are flooded. When space becomes available in the forwarding table, new addresses can then be learned. This is possible but rare, because most modern switches have large-enough forwarding tables to accommodate MAC addresses for most designs.

Forwarding table exhaustion can also be caused by an attack on the network in which one host starts generating frames, each sourced with a different MAC address. This ties up all the forwarding table resources. As soon as the forwarding tables become saturated, other traffic is flooded, because new learning cannot occur. You can detect this kind of attack by examining the switch forwarding table. Most of the MAC addresses point to the same port or group of ports. You can prevent such attacks by limiting the number of MAC addresses learned on untrusted ports by using the port security feature.

Macof, a popular tool for launching this type of attack, can generate 155,000 MAC entries on a switch per minute. The switch sees this traffic and thinks that the MAC address from the packet the attacker sent is a valid port and adds an entry. The goal is to flood the switch with traffic by filling the CAM table with false entries. Once flooded, the switch broadcasts traffic without a CAM entry out its local VLAN, allowing the attacker to see traffic he or she wouldn't ordinarily see. Flooding is easy, even with big tables and high-end switches.

The following configuration enables the port security feature on an interface and then specifies that the interface can have no more than 50 MAC addresses associated with it:

```
Switch(config)#interface fastethernet 0/1
Switch(config-if)#switchport port-security
Switch(config-if)#switchport port-security maximum 50
```

The maximum number of MAC addresses that can be associated with an interface when port security is active is 132.

In extremely rare cases, port VLAN information might be programmed incorrectly, and the port might forward packets unexpectedly for the wrong VLAN. Such incorrect programming might result in packets from one VLAN being seen incorrectly on another VLAN.

A misplaced cable or VLAN assignment can lead to unicast frames crossing VLAN boundaries. Under normal conditions, the switch should maintain VLAN boundaries, and a router such as an MSFC should route only those packets with source and destination IP addresses on different IP networks. If multicasts also cross VLAN boundaries, there is a good chance that spanning-tree BPDUs are being flooded; therefore, the STP tree of the two VLANs has merged. To validate this hypothesis, capture the **show spanning-tree** [**vlan** *id*] command for the two VLANs. Although the same physical switch might serve as the root for two VLANs, it uses unique root bridge IDs for each VLAN. If the output displays the same root bridge ID for both VLANs, the two VLANs are bridged somewhere in the network.

To isolate the cause of the problem, follow these steps:

Step 1   Select a PC on VLAN A.

Step 2   Select a PC on VLAN B.

Step 3   Assign the PC on VLAN B to an IP address on VLAN 2. This step effectively removes the router from the fault domain. If **ping** is successful between the devices, there is strong evidence to support a bridged connection, likely accidental, between the two VLANs.

At this point, the next steps are to trace the path of the packet between the two hosts. Capture the **show mac-address-table** command for both hosts. Is the MAC being learned on one VLAN or two? What are the source ports?

Unfortunately, there is no special command to detect flooding on the switches. You might detect flooding by capturing a trace of packets seen on a workstation during the time of slow-down or outage. Normally, unicast packets not involving the workstation should not be seen repeatedly on the port. If this is happening, flooding probably is occurring. Packet traces might look different when flooding has various causes. This would be a good time to reference the baseline in the documentation pertaining to the affected devices to see what the normal traffic load is.

With asymmetric routing, there are likely to be packets to specific MAC addresses that will not stop flooding after the destination replies. With TCNs, the flooding includes many different addresses but should eventually stop, and then start again.

With Layer 2 forwarding table overflow, the same kind of flooding might be visible as with asymmetric routing. The difference is that there will likely be a large number of strange packets, or normal packets in abnormal quantities with a different source MAC address.

Troubleshooting VTP Misconfiguration

VLANs allow switched networks to be broken into Layer 2 broadcast domains. The VLAN Trunking Protocol (VTP) is a Layer 2 protocol that ensures VLAN consistency within a VTP domain. In practice, this means that if a VLAN is created on one switch in a network, that same VLAN is propagated to all switches in the VTP domain. A failure of the VTP protocol prevents switches from agreeing on the VLAN configuration within a network. This might cause communications between switches to fail or might result in entire VLANs being deleted.

The first indication of a VTP problem often occurs when a VLAN is created on a switch but fails to propagate to all other switches within the domain. When this occurs, the first thing to check is the VTP mode. Each switch can be placed in one of the following VTP modes:

- Server
- Client
- Transparent

Changes to the VLAN configuration within a VTP domain can only be made on a switch that is in VTP server mode. Furthermore, VLAN information is propagated only to switches in a

VTP mode of server or client that are in the same VTP domain. You can verify the VTP mode and domain using the **show vtp status** command, as shown in Example 4-14.

Example 4-14 *The* **show vtp status** *Command Lists the VTP Domain Name and Configuration Revision Number*

```
Switch#show vtp status
VTP Version                   : 2
Configuration Revision        : 0
Maximum VLANs supported locally : 1005
Number of existing VLANs      : 9
VTP Operating Mode            : Transparent
VTP Domain Name               : kiki
VTP Pruning Mode              : Disabled
VTP V2 Mode                   : Enabled
VTP Traps Generation          : Disabled
MD5 digest                    : 0x9A 0xCF 0x9D 0x22 0xC7 0x11 0xEB 0x2B
Configuration last modified by 0.0.0.0 at 3-1-93 18:03:09
```

This problem occurs when there is a large switched network where all switches are part of the same VTP domain, and another switch is added to the network.

Assume that this switch has been used previously and already has an appropriate VTP domain name entered. The switch is configured as a VTP client and then is connected to the rest of the network. The instant the trunk link is brought up to the rest of the network, the whole network goes down. What could have happened?

The most likely explanation is that the configuration revision number of the inserted switch was higher than the configuration revision of the VTP domain. Therefore, the recently introduced switch with minimal VLAN information has erased all VLANs through the VTP domain.

This situation happens whether the switch is a VTP client or a VTP server. A VTP client can erase VLAN information on a VTP server. This is evident when many of the ports in the network go into inactive state and are assigned to a nonexistent VLAN.

Quickly reconfigure all the VLANs on one of the VTP servers. Always make sure that the configuration revision of all switches inserted into the VTP domain is lower than the configuration revision of the switches already in the VTP domain.

One popular opinion now is that VTP is not worth the trouble. With Layer 3 switching speeds approximating that of Layer 2 switching, and with campus-wide VLANs replaced with local VLANs, it makes sense to configure all the switches in VTP transparent mode.

Troubleshooting EtherChannel

Fast EtherChannel allows multiple physical Fast Ethernet links to be combined into one logical channel. This allows load sharing of traffic among the links in the channel as well as redundancy if one or more links in the channel fails. Fast EtherChannel can be used to interconnect LAN switches, routers, servers, and clients via unshielded twisted-pair (UTP) wiring or single-mode and multimode fiber. The Fast EtherChannel, Gigabit EtherChannel, Port Channel, Channel, and Port Group all refer to Ethernet. The information given in this chapter applies to all of these EtherChannels.

From the STP point of view, an EtherChannel is seen as a single port. This presents a danger of creating forwarding loops if channeling ports are not consistent on both sides of the channel.

For example, if switch A has two separate links and switch B considers those same links part of the channel, switch B sends a broadcast or unknown unicast packet. That packet is forwarded back to switch B, as shown in Figure 4-14. This causes packet duplication and changes the forwarding table on switch B to point in the wrong direction.

Figure 4-14 Misconfigured EtherChannel

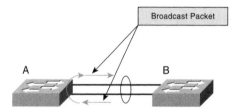

Symptoms associated with misconfigured EtherChannels include

- Loss of connectivity because of switching loops
- Increased backplane utilization might be noticed from the LEDs on a normally lightly loaded switch
- Console messages reporting that ports are rapidly relearning MAC addresses
- Interfaces might be automatically placed in an ErrDisable state

When configuring EtherChannel, ensure that both sides of the link are configured correctly. Ports do not form an EtherChannel unless they are configured identically in terms of speed, duplex, native VLAN trunk, and so on.

The goal of EtherChannel is to distribute traffic over several physical links to enhance performance and availability. One area that is often not considered when configuring EtherChannel is how EtherChannel determines the physical link over which the frame is sent.

The following summarizes the default behavior for EtherChannel in a switched and routed environment:

- Switches allocate links based on Layer 2 addresses.
- Routers allocate links based on Layer 3 addresses.
- Switches allocate links based on source address.
- Routers allocate links based on destination address.

Strictly speaking, this summary is true only of lower-end switches and routers such as the 2500, 2600, and 2950. Higher-end routers and switches might take into account all of these factors, as well as TCP port numbers when making a link forwarding decision.

Assuming that the routers and switches in the network are using these defaults, load balancing works well in typical topologies. In these situations, the switch sees many source MAC addresses, and the router sees many destination IP addresses. This allows traffic to be effectively spread across the available links.

However, consider the situation shown in Figure 4-15. The top switch forwards traffic across the EtherChannel based on the source MAC address. In this instance there is only one source MAC address—the MAC address on the router. Consequently, traffic flowing from the router to the PCs uses only a single Ethernet link.

Figure 4-15 EtherChannel Frame Distribution

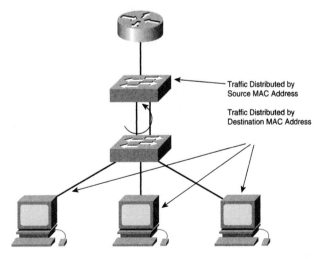

The solution is to configure the top switch to allocate links based on the destination MAC address using the **port-channel load-balance** {**dst-mac** | **src-mac**} global configuration command:

```
switch(config)#port-channel load-balance dst-mac
```

Table 4-10 explains how to configure frame distribution with EtherChannel.

Table 4-10 The **load-balance** Keyword Permits Specification of the Frame Distribution Method

Step	Command	Description
1	**configure terminal**	Enter global configuration mode.
2		Configure an EtherChannel load-balancing method. The default is **-mac**. Select one of these keywords to determine the load distribution method:
		■ **dst-mac**—Load distribution is based on the destination host MAC address of the incoming packet. Packets to the same destination are sent on the same port, but packets to different destinations are sent on different ports in the channel.
		■ **mac**—Load distribution is based on the source MAC address of the incoming packet. Packets from different hosts use different ports in the channel, but packets from the same host use the same port in the channel.
		■ If the link partner to the switch is a physical learner, set the load distribution method to one of these:
		■ If the **channel-group** interface configuration command is set to **auto** or **desirable**, the switch automatically uses the load distribution method based on the source MAC address, regardless of the configured load distribution method.
		■ If the **channel-group** interface configuration command is set to **on**, set the load distribution method based on the source MAC address by using the **port-channel load-balance -mac** global configuration command.
3	**end**	Return to privileged EXEC mode.
4	**show etherchannel load-balance**	Verify your entries.
5	**copy running-config start-up config**	(Optional) Save your entries in the configuration file.

Wherever possible and whenever supported by the network device, use a mechanism for distributing traffic that takes into account many addresses when determining which link to use.

If the switches or routers support only minimal addresses for making the distribution decision, take particular care to consider the Layer 2 data flow destined for, or sourced from, single nodes such as routers, servers, and storage area network (SAN) devices.

Troubleshooting ISDN

It is common to have to troubleshoot ISDN at Layer 2. Some of the common problems include T1 PRI framing errors, ISDN switch type, local loop communication, and dialer configurations.

T1 Framing Errors

When an interface receives a frame, the receiving party must be able to locate several parts—the start of the frame, the components in the frame, and the end of the frame. These low-level activities rely on the receiver's being able to extract clocking information from the signal and recognize the difference between a 1 and a 0. Where these essential elements break down, framing errors occur.

Framing errors are most likely to occur where different frame and encoding formats are used and where equipment from different vendors is expected to work together. This situation is likely to occur where corporate networks link to those provided by telcos. Although this section concentrates on T1 connections such as the ISDN primary rate services, the principles are broadly applicable to other Layer 2 technologies.

In Example 4-15, the **show controllers t1** command provides the following information that you can use to determine whether framing errors are occurring:

- Statistics about the T1 link. If a slot and port number are specified, statistics for each 15-minute period are displayed.
- Information to troubleshoot physical layer and data-link layer problems.
- Local or remote alarm information, if any, on the T1 line.

Example 4-15 *The Framing, Line Code, and Clock Source Can Be Viewed with the* **show controllers t1** *Command*

```
Router#show controllers t1


T1 4/1 is up.
  No alarms detected.
```

continues

Example 4-15 *The Framing, Line Code, and Clock Source Can Be Viewed with the* **show controllers t1**
Command (Continued)

```
Framing is ESF, Line Code is AMI, Clock Source is line
Data in current interval (0 seconds elapsed):
    0 Line Code Violations, 0 Path Code Violations, 0 Slip Secs, 0 Fr Loss Secs,
    0 Line Err Secs, 0 Degraded Mins, 0 Errored Secs, 0 Bursty Err Secs,
    0 Severely Err Secs, 0 Unavail Secs
Total Data (last 79 15 minute intervals):
    0 Line Code Violations, 0 Path Code Violations, 0 Slip Secs, 0 Fr Loss Secs,
    0 Line Err Secs, 0 Degraded Mins, 0 Errored Secs, 0 Bursty Err Secs,
    0 Severely Err Secs, 0 Unavail Secs
```

Use the **show controllers** command to verify if alarms or errors are displayed by the controller,
as shown in Example 4-16. To determine if the framing, line coding, and slip seconds error
counters are increasing, use the **show controllers t1** command repeatedly. Note the values of
the counters for the current interval.

Example 4-16 *Alarms and Errors Can Be Seen with the* **show controllers t1** *Command*

```
Router#show controllers t1
T1 1/0/0:1 is up.
No alarms detected.
Framing is ESF, Line Code is AMI, Clock Source is Line.
Data in current interval (770 seconds elapsed):
5 Line Code Violations, 8 Path Code Violations
0 Slip Secs, 0 Fr Loss Secs, 7 Line Err Secs, 0 Degraded Mins
0 Errored Secs, 0 Bursty Err Secs, 0 Severely Err Secs, 7 Unavail Secs
Total Data (last 81 15 minute intervals):
7 Line Code Violations, 4 Path Code Violations,
6 Slip Secs, 20 Fr Loss Secs, 2 Line Err Secs, 0 Degraded Mins,
0 Errored Secs, 0 Bursty Err Secs, 0 Severely Err Secs, 2 Unavail Secs
T1 1/0/1:5 is down.
Transmitter is sending remote alarm.
Receiver has loss of frame.
Framing is SF, Line Code is AMI, Clock Source is Line.
Data in current interval (770 seconds elapsed):
50 Line Code Violations, 5 Path Code Violations
```

Example 4-16 *Alarms and Errors Can Be Seen with the* **show controllers t1** *Command (Continued)*

```
0 Slip Secs, 7 Fr Loss Secs, 7 Line Err Secs, 0 Degraded Mins
0 Errored Secs, 0 Bursty Err Secs, 0 Severely Err Secs, 7 Unavail Secs
Total Data (last 81 15 minute intervals):
27 Line Code Violations, 22 Path Code Violations,
0 Slip Secs, 13 Fr Loss Secs, 13 Line Err Secs, 0 Degraded Mins,
0 Errored Secs, 0 Bursty Err Secs, 0 Severely Err Secs, 13 Unavail Secs
Router#
```

As a first step when troubleshooting a suspected framing problem, ask the telco or service provider to provide details on the required framing and line coding settings. It is common to use binary 8-zero substitution (B8ZS) line coding with Extended Super Frame (ESF) and alternate mark inversion (AMI) line coding with superframe (SF).

If slip secs are present on the T1 line (in the **show controllers t1** output), there is a clocking problem. The customer premises equipment (CPE) needs to synchronize to the clocking from the T1 provider. To correct this problem, ensure that the clocking source is provided by the telco, and then review the output from the **show controllers t1** command to ensure that Clock Source is Line.

Set both the primary and secondary T1 clock source from controller configuration mode:

```
Router(config-controller)#clock source line primary
Router(config-controller)#clock source line secondary 1
```

Ensure that the T1s that were specified as the primary and secondary are both active and stable.

Ensure that the framing format configured on the port matches the line's framing format. Look for the statement "Framing is {ESF|SF}" in the **show controllers t1** output.

To change the framing format, use the **framing** {**sf** | **esf**} command in controller configuration mode:

```
Router(config-controller)#framing esf
```

Change the line build-out using the **cablelength long** or **cablelength short** command.

Contact the service provider and consult the Cisco website documentation for details on build-out settings. Basically, this command changes the signal levels used by the T1 interface to allow for losses experienced because of the distance between the WAN connection and the telco office.

Line codes are a method of encoding data such that there are regular transitions between 1s and 0s. This is necessary in a digital environment because the 1s and 0s are represented by the presence or absence of a signal. Long sequences of 1s or 0s make it difficult for the controller

NOTE

If multiple T1s are coming into an access server, only one can be the primary source. The other T1s derive the clock from the primary source. If there are multiple T1s, ensure that the T1 line designated as the primary clock source is configured correctly. A second T1 line can also be configured that provides clocking in case the primary source goes down. To do this, use the **clock source line secondary** command from controller configuration mode.

to know just how many 1s or 0s are occurring. Figure 4-16 shows an incoming signal with regular transitions that is easy to interpret. However, the long sequence of 0s makes it more difficult. In fact, the longer the sequence, the more accurate the clocks must be, and the more susceptible to errors the controller will be.

Figure 4-16 Frequent Transitions Between 0 and 1 Are Critical for T1

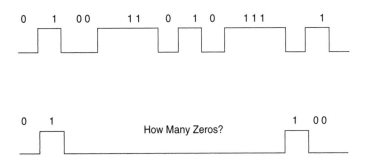

To avoid the difficulties associated with long sequences of 1s and 0s, line coding algorithms are used to ensure that regular 1-to-0 and 0-to-1 transitions occur.

Ensure that the line coding configured on the port matches the line coding of the line. Look for the statement "Line Code is {B8ZS|AMI}" in the **show controllers t1** output.

B8ZS stands for binary 8-zero substitution. This means that continuous sequences of 0s are replaced with a special B8ZS code that includes transitions. B8ZS is used with alternate mark inversion (AMI), which encodes 1s alternately as positive and negative voltages and is more compatible with transformers and older cabling technologies used by telcos in the local loop. See Figure 4-17.

To change the line coding, use the **linecode {ami | b8zs}** command in controller configuration mode. For example:

```
Router(config-controller)#linecode b8zs
```

Aside from the necessity of correct encoding, the actual line voltage levels also need to be within certain limits. The signal level diminishes as the length of the local loop increases. This variation can be compensated for with the **cablelength long** or **cablelength short** command.

Path code violations are frame synchronization errors when superframes are in use, and CRC errors for Extended Superframes. Path code violations and line code violations typically are present simultaneously.

Figure 4-17 Line Code Specifies Encoding Technique

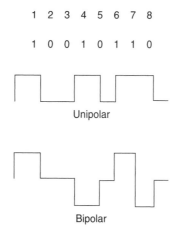

Troubleshooting ISDN Primary Rate Switch Types

To communicate correctly, a router must be told what type of ISDN switching equipment the telco uses. Depending on the combination of telco equipment and the ISDN switch type configuration, a variety of symptoms are possible. It is usually quickest to simply make a careful check using the **show running-config** command and verify that **isdn switch-type** and **pri-group timeslots** are configured correctly. To specify the central office switch type on the ISDN interface, use the **isdn switch-type** global configuration command. Options for this command include

- **primary-5ess**
- **primary-dms100**
- **primary-ni**

Contact the service provider for the correct values to use.

Do the following to configure the **isdn switch-type** and **pri-group** commands:

```
Router#configure terminal
Router(config)#isdn switch-type primary-5ess
Router(config)#controller t1 0
Router(config-controller)#pri-group timeslots 1-24
```

Troubleshooting ISDN BRI-to-Telco Communications

ISDN problems generally fall into one of the following categories:

- Communication problems between the router and the telco's ISDN switch
- Logical configuration problems with dialers
- Problems with the number being called

A divide-and-conquer approach is the best way to troubleshoot ISDN. The **show isdn status** command quickly determines whether the router is communicating correctly with the telco's ISDN switch. If there is a problem in this regard, the **show isdn status** command often provides helpful diagnostic information.

In particular, Layer 1 should be active, Layer 2 should have MULTIPLE_FRAME_ESTAB-LISHED, and service profile identifiers (SPIDs) should be valid, as shown in Example 4-17.

Example 4-17 *The* **show isdn status** *Command Displays Whether the Configured SPIDs Are Valid*

```
Router#show isdn status
The current ISDN Switchtype = basic-ni1
ISDN BRI0 interface
Layer 1 Status:
ACTIVE
Layer 2 Status:
TEI = 109, State = MULTIPLE_FRAME_ESTABLISHED
TEI = 110, State = MULTIPLE_FRAME_ESTABLISHED
Spid Status:
TEI 109, ces = 1, state = 8(established)
spid1 configured, spid1 sent, spid1 valid
Endpoint ID Info: epsf = 0, usid = 1, tid = 1
TEI 110, ces = 2, state = 8(established)
spid2 configured, spid2 sent, spid2 valid
Endpoint ID Info: epsf = 0, usid = 3, tid = 1
Layer 3 Status:
0 Active Layer 3 Call(s)
Activated dsl 0 CCBs = 0
Total Allocated ISDN CCBs = 0
```

If Layer 1 is deactivated, as shown in Example 4-18, troubleshoot the following physical layer problems:

- Physical cabling
- Interface is activated (no shutdown)
- ISDN switch type

Example 4-18 *Deactivated Layer 2 Status with ISDN BRI Normally Indicates a Cabling Problem or Invalid Switch Type*

```
Router#show isdn status
Global ISDN Switchtype = basic-ni
ISDN BRI0 interface dsl 0, interface ISDN Switchtype = basic-ni
Layer 1 Status:
DEACTIVATED
Layer 2 Status:
Layer 2 NOT Activated
Spid Status:
TEI Not Assigned, ces = 1, state = 3(await establishment)
spid1 configured, spid1 NOT sent, spid1 NOT valid
TEI Not Assigned, ces = 2, state = 1(terminal down)
spid2 configured, spid2 NOT sent, spid2 NOT valid
Layer 3 Status:
0 Active Layer 3 Call(s)
Activated dsl 0 CCBs = 0
The Free Channel Mask: 0x80000003
Total Allocated ISDN CCBs = 0
```

Like primary rate interfaces, basic rate interfaces must be told what type of ISDN switching equipment the telco uses. The configured ISDN switch type can also be determined with the **show isdn status** command, as shown in Example 4-19.

Example 4-19 **show isdn status** *Displays the Configured ISDN Switch Type*

```
Router#show isdn status
**** No Global ISDN Switchtype currently defined ****
ISDN BRI0 interface
dsl 0, interface ISDN Switchtype = none
Layer 1 Status:
ACTIVE
Layer 2 Status:
Layer 2 NOT Activated
Layer 3 Status:
0 Active Layer 3 Call(s)
Activated dsl 0 CCBs = 0
The Free Channel Mask: 0x80000003
Total Allocated ISDN CCBs = 0
```

In Example 4-19, no switch type has been configured. A misconfigured switch type can result in either Layer 1 or Layer 1/2 status "NOT Activated." In early versions of the Cisco IOS, the switch type was configured from global configuration, and a router could be used with only one ISDN switch type service. Later versions of the IOS allowed the switch type to be specified at an interface level, removing this constraint.

If Layer 1 is functioning but Layer 2 is inactive, check the ISDN switch type, as shown in Example 4-20.

Example 4-20 *The ISDN Switch Type Can Be the Cause of a Situation in Which Layer 1 Is Active, But Layer 2 is Inactive*

```
Router#show isdn status
Global ISDN Switchtype = basic-ni
ISDN BRI0 interface
dsl 0, interface ISDN Switchtype = basic-ni
Layer 1 Status:
ACTIVE
Layer 2 Status:
Layer 2 NOT Activated
Spid Status:
TEI Not Assigned, ces = 1, state = 3(await establishment)
spid1 configured, spid1 NOT sent, spid1 NOT valid
TEI Not Assigned, ces = 2, state = 1(terminal down)
spid2 configured, spid2 NOT sent, spid2 NOT valid
Layer 3 Status:
TWAIT timer active
0 Active Layer 3 Call(s)
Activated dsl 0 CCBs = 0
The Free Channel Mask: 0x80000003
Total Allocated ISDN CCBs = 0
```

If SPID1 or SPID2 is invalid, carefully check the configured SPIDs and verify these with the telco. See Example 4-21. It might be necessary to shut down the BRI and then reactivate it or reboot the router to force SPID negotiation after the configuration is changed. Some versions of the IOS have a known bug that reports an invalid SPID even though the configured value is correct. As long as the BRI can make calls, this "cosmetic" bug should not be reason for concern.

Example 4-21 *Incorrect SPIDs Is a Common Configuration Error with ISDN BRI*

```
Router#show isdn status
Global ISDN Switchtype = basic-ni
ISDN BRI0 interface
dsl 0, interface ISDN Switchtype = basic-ni
Layer 1 Status:
ACTIVE
Layer 2 Status:
Layer 2 NOT Activated
Spid Status:
TEI Not Assigned, ces = 1, state = 3(await establishment)
spid1 configured, spid1 NOT sent, spid1 NOT valid
TEI Not Assigned, ces = 2, state = 1(terminal down)
spid2 configured, spid2 NOT sent, spid2 NOT valid
Layer 3 Status:
TWAIT timer active
0 Active Layer 3 Call(s)
Activated dsl 0 CCBs = 0
The Free Channel Mask: 0x80000003
Total Allocated ISDN CCBs = 0
```

In certain parts of the world, notably Europe, telco ISDN switches might deactivate Layer 1
or 2 when there are no active calls. Hence, when there are no active calls, **show isdn status**
indicates that Layers 1 and 2 are down. But when a call occurs, Layers 1 and 2 are brought
up. Make a test BRI call to verify whether the BRI is functioning. If the call succeeds, no further ISDN troubleshooting is required.

```
Layer 3 Status:
TWAIT timer active
0 Active Layer 3 Call(s)
Activated dsl 0 CCBs = 0
The Free Channel Mask: 0x80000003
Total Allocated ISDN CCBs = 0
```

Reboot the ISDN router by cycling the power. When the router comes up, the BRI interface
will be unable to establish a call for a random period of time. Executing the **show isdn status**
command reveals that the TWAIT timer is active. This is a feature that prevents a telco's ISDN
switch from being overloaded after a major power outage is restored, and multiple ISDN devices
simultaneously try to establish a connection.

You can clear the timer by manually shutting down the BRI interface and reactivating it.

You can change the delayed behavior using the **isdn twait-disable** interface configuration command.

The **debug isdn q921** command can also be used to troubleshoot Layer 2 ISDN issues. Sample output for this command is shown in Example 4-22. This command shows the Layer 2 exchanges between the router and the telco's ISDN switch. However, the **show isdn status** command normally is of more use, because it effectively decodes the Q921 messages and displays them in a more understandable format.

Example 4-22 *The* **debug isdn q921** *Command Displays TEI and SAPI Assignments*

```
*Mar  1 01:33:48.559: ISDN BR0: TX -> RRp sapi = 0  tei = 96 NR = 0
*Mar  1 01:33:48.579: ISDN BR0: RX <- RRf sapi = 0  tei = 96  NR = 0
*Mar  1 01:34:18.347: ISDN BR0: TX -> RRp sapi = 0  tei = 96 NR = 0
*Mar  1 01:34:18.367: ISDN BR0: RX <- RRf sapi = 0  tei = 96  NR = 0
```

Troubleshooting ISDN BRI Dialer Problems

Assuming that the **show isdn status** command, shown in Example 4-23, indicates that communication between the router and the telco's switch is performing correctly, the next step is to ensure that the router is actually dialing the far end.

Example 4-23 *The* **show isdn status** *Command Is Normally Used to Verify Layer 1 and 2 Connectivity Between the Router and the ISDN Switch*

```
Router#show isdn status
The current ISDN Switchtype = basic-ni1
ISDN BRI0 interface
Layer 1 Status:
ACTIVE
Layer 2 Status:
TEI = 109, State = MULTIPLE_FRAME_ESTABLISHED
TEI = 110, State = MULTIPLE_FRAME_ESTABLISHED
Spid Status:
TEI 109, ces = 1, state = 8(established)
spid1 configured, spid1 sent, spid1 valid
Endpoint ID Info: epsf = 0, usid = 1, tid = 1
TEI 110, ces = 2, state = 8(established)
spid2 configured, spid2 sent, spid2 valid
Endpoint ID Info: epsf = 0, usid = 3, tid = 1
Layer 3 Status:
```

Example 4-23 *The* **show isdn status** *Command Is Normally Used to Verify Layer 1 and 2 Connectivity Between the Router and the ISDN Switch (Continued)*

```
0 Active Layer 3 Call(s)
Activated dsl 0 CCBs = 0
Total Allocated ISDN CCBs = 0
```

The most effective way to troubleshoot dialing is to use the **debug dialer** command and then try to establish a call to the remote site, as shown in Example 4-24. A common symptom is that the **debug dialer** command reveals no dialer activity. This almost always points to one of the following:

- Interesting traffic has not been defined or is incorrect.
- No dialer map is present, or the IP address is incorrect.
- The router has no route to the IP address being pinged.

Example 4-24 *The* **debug dialer** *Command Is Used to Troubleshoot Problems with Dialed Calls After Layer 1 and 2 Connectivity Has Been Established Between the Router and the ISDN Switch*

```
Router#debug dialer

4d22: BR0/0 DDR: Dialing cause ip (s-5.5.5.1, d-5.5.5.2)
4d22h: BR0/0 DDR: Attempting to dial 5554000
4d22h: %LINK-3-UPDOWN: Interface BR0/0:1, changed state
  to up.
4d22h: BR0/0:1 DDR: dialer protocol up.
4d22h: %LINEPROTO-5-UPDOWN: Line protocol on Interface
  BRI0/0:1, changed state to up.
```

If the **debug dialer** or **debug dialer events** command reveals no dialer activity, use the **show running-config** command to verify that the following commands are present and are configured with the appropriate parameters:

- Dialer list
- Dialer map
- Appropriate routing protocol or static route such that the next-hop IP address matches the dialer map

Assuming that the router is actually attempting to dial, Table 4-11 lists a number of possible error messages and their causes.

Table 4-11 The Output of the **debug dialer** Command Is Easy to Interpret Relative to Most **debug** Commands

Error Message	Description
Dialer0: Already *xxx* call(s) in progress on Dialer, dialing not allowed	The number of calls in progress (*xxx*) has exceeded the maximum number of calls set on the interface.
Dialer0: No free dialer - starting fast idle timer	All the lines in the interface or rotary group are busy, and a packet is waiting to be sent to the destination.
BRIO: rotary group to *xxx* overloaded (*yyy*)	The number dialer (*xxx*) has exceeded the load set on the interface (*yyy*).
BRIO: authenticated host *xxx* with no matching dialer profile	No dialer profile matches *xxx*, the remote host's CHAP name or remote name.
BRIO: authenticated host *xxx* with no matching dialer map	No dialer map matches *xxx*, the remote host's CHAP name or remote name.
BRIO: Can't place call, verify configuration	You have not set the dialer string or dialer pool on an interface.
Serial 0: Dialer result = *xxxxxxxxx*	Displays the result returned from the V.25bis dialer. It is useful in debugging if calls are failing. On some hardware platforms, this message cannot be displayed because of hardware limitations. Possible values for the *xxxxxxxxx* variable depend on the V.25bis device with which the router is communicating.
7Serial 0: No dialer string defined. Dialing cannot occur.	A packet is received that should cause a call to be placed. However, no dialer string is configured, so dialing cannot occur. This message usually indicates a configuration problem.
Serial 0: Attempting to dial *xxxxxxxxx*	A packet has been received that passes the dial-on-demand access lists. That packet causes phone number *xxxxxxxxx* to be dialed.
Serial 0: Unable to dial *xxxxxxxxx*	For some reason the phone call to *xxxxxxxxx* cannot be placed. This failure might be caused by lack of memory, full output queues, or other problems.

Table 4-11 The Output of the **debug dialer** Command Is Easy to Interpret Relative to Most **debug** Commands (Continued)

Error Message	Description
Serial 0: disconnecting call	The router hangs up a call.
Serial 0: idle timeout Serial 0: re-enable timeout Serial 0: wait for carrier timeout	One of these three messages is displayed when a dialer timer expires. These messages are mostly informational, but are useful for debugging a disconnected call or call failure.

If dialing occurs but connectivity fails, there are several possible causes:

- The remote ISDN service line is busy
- Incorrect or missing ISDN phone number
- Incorrect encapsulation
- Incorrect authentication parameters

The first two problems keep a call from being established, and the last two establish the call only to have it terminated because of Layer 2 errors. To help determine which of these problems is being experienced, try to ping the remote site. If the line protocol fails to change to an up state, even briefly, it is likely that the ISDN call itself is failing. If the line comes up and then goes down, it is more likely that configuration incompatibilities are terminating the call shortly after it is established.

If the line protocol goes up and down several times, once for every echo request, an authentication failure would be a strong suspect. For more information on troubleshooting PPP authentication, refer to the "Troubleshooting PPP Authentication PAP" section. Authentication problems have this characteristic because a failed authentication attempt immediately terminates the call. This occurs so quickly that the next ping packet can reinitiate a new call. In contrast, misconfigured parameters such as encapsulation terminate the call only after several keepalives have been missed.

Debugging ISDN Call Setup Failures

If it appears that the router is attempting to dial but calls are not getting through, the problem can be investigated further using the **debug isdn q931** command. This command provides information on the ISDN call status as reported to the router by the telco's ISDN switch. A simple test is to execute **debug isdn q931** on both routers to determine whether the far-end router is actually receiving the call. Look for any q931 debug output. Further explicit information about the call failure is provided in the debug messages. Although the debug output reports the basic reasons for a disconnect, more detailed information might be required.

```
Aug 13 18:23:14.734: ISDN BR0: RX <- RELEASE_COMP pd = 8 callref = 0x86
Aug 13 18:23:14.742: Cause i = 0x829C - Invalid number format (incomplete number)
```

The first most significant byte after 0x indicates where in the circuit path the disconnected cause code was generated. In this example, 82 indicates that the call was disconnected from the local telco switch. The following list defines the cause code origination points to help you figure out where the call was disconnected. The ISDN cause code origination points indicate where the code was generated and why a call was disconnected.

- **80**—From the router
- **81**—From the private network near the local user (possibly a local private branch exchange [PBX])
- **82**—From the public network near the local user (local telco switch)
- **83**—From the transit network (in the ISDN cloud)
- **84**—From the public network near the remote user (remote telco switch)
- **85**—From the private network near the remote user (possibly a remote PBX)
- **87**—From the international network
- **8A**—From a network beyond the internetworking point

In the example, the next byte that follows the cause code origination point byte, 9C, is the disconnect cause code. It is significant in troubleshooting. Use the disconnect cause code file to associate a disconnect cause code (in hex) and the cause description to determine the disconnect reason. For the **debug isdn q931** command output, drop the highest bit of the cause value before using this table. For example, a cause value of 0x90 becomes 0x10.

Troubleshooting Frame Relay

Frame Relay is still widely used for WAN traffic but is slowly being replaced by higher-bandwidth options. This section discusses the common problems that occur with Frame Relay circuits and provides a step-by-step approach to solving problems with Frame Relay connections.

Steps for Troubleshooting Frame Relay

When Frame Relay is properly provisioned by the service provider, the installation of a Frame Relay network using Cisco routers is usually a trouble-free task involving minimal configuration. However, if problems arise in the Frame Relay network, proven techniques can be applied to isolate and solve them. As shown in Figure 4-18, troubleshooting Frame Relay network issues can be broken into four easy steps:

Step 1   Verify the physical connection between the CSU/DSU and the router.

Step 2   Verify that the router and Frame Relay provider are properly exchanging Local Management Interface (LMI) information.

Step 3   Verify that the permanent virtual circuit (PVC) status is active.

Step 4   Verify that the Frame Relay encapsulation matches on both routers.

Figure 4-18 Troubleshooting Frame Relay

Numerous diagnostic tools are available for these tasks. However, most Frame Relay problems can be diagnosed by using the following simple commands:

- **show interfaces**
- **show frame-relay lmi**
- **show frame-relay pvc**
- **show frame-relay map**
- **debug frame-relay lmi**
- **debug frame-relay events**
- **debug frame-relay packet**

The show frame-relay lmi Command

The **show frame-relay lmi** command is invaluable for determining the status of the link between the router and the Frame Relay switch. Examine the output from item A in Figure 4-19 to determine the locally configured LMI type.

Figure 4-19 show frame-relay lmi Command

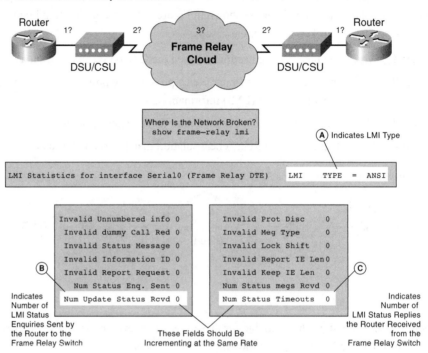

An incrementing "Num Status Enq. Sent" and "Num Status msgs Rcvd" indicates that successful router-to-Frame Relay switch communications are occurring, as shown in Example 4-25.

Example 4-25 *The* **show frame-relay lmi** *Command Is Useful for Troubleshooting Connections Between the Router and the Frame Relay Switch*

```
Router1#show frame-relay lmi
LMI Statistics for interface Serial0 (Frame Relay DCE) LMI TYPE = CISCO
    Invalid Unnumbered info 0          Invalid Prot Disc 0
    Invalid dummy Call Ref 0           Invalid Msg Type 0
    Invalid Status Message 0           Invalid Lock Shift 0
    Invalid Information ID 0           Invalid Report IE Len 0
    Invalid Report Request 0          Invalid Keep IE Len 0
    Num Status Enq. Rcvd 72            Num Status msgs Sent 71
    Num Update Status Sent 3           Num St Enq. Timeouts 4
Router1#
```

If the router is sending status messages but not receiving them, check the physical layer between the router and the Frame Relay switch. Ensure that the LMI encapsulation used by the router and the Frame Relay switch are the same. By default, the LMI type used by the IOS is set to Cisco.

The show frame-relay pvc Command

Use the **show frame-relay pvc** command to verify the PVC status and end-to-end Layer 2 connectivity of the routers. An active PVC is illustrated in Figure 4-20.

Figure 4-20 **show frame-relay pvc** Command

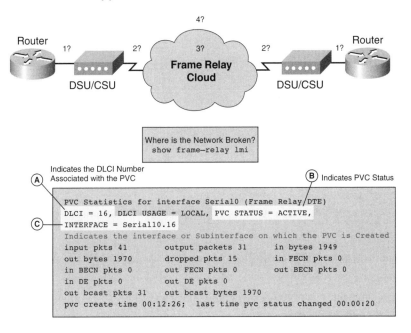

The three likely PVC status messages are

■ Active

■ Inactive

■ Deleted

Understanding a PVC's status will quickly focus your troubleshooting efforts.

A Frame Relay PVC status of "active" indicates Frame Relay end-to-end connectivity at Layer 2 and is associated with a working Frame Relay circuit. If the status is "active" and problems are occurring, attention should be given to Layer 3 issues such as mapping IP addresses to DLCIs and telco DLCI allocations.

Note that in Example 4-26 PVC 30 is active. This indicates end-to-end connectivity. PVC 21 is still inactive, which indicates a problem.

Example 4-26 *An Inactive PVC Might Be the Result of an Incorrectly Configured DLCI*

```
Router#show frame-relay pvc
PVC Statistics for interface Serial0 (Frame Relay DTE)
DLCI = 21, DLCI USAGE = LOCAL, PVC STATUS = INACTIVE, INTERFACE = Serial0.1
  input pkts 0            output pkts 0           in bytes 0
  out bytes 0             dropped pkts 0          in FECN pkts 0
  in BECN pkts 0          out FECN pkts 0         out BECN pkts 0
  in DE pkts 0            out DE pkts 0
  out bcast pkts 0          out bcast bytes 0
  pvc create time 00:00:26, last time pvc status changed 00:00:05

DLCI = 30, DLCI USAGE = LOCAL, PVC STATUS = ACTIVE, INTERFACE = Serial0.2
  input pkts 6            output pkts 1           in bytes 1770
  out bytes 276          dropped pkts 3          in FECN pkts 0
  in BECN pkts 0          out FECN pkts 0         out BECN pkts 0
  in DE pkts 0            out DE pkts 0
  out bcast pkts 1          out bcast bytes 276
  pvc create time 00:00:27, last time pvc status changed 00:00:17
```

A PVC status of "inactive" suggests that the router recognizes the DLCI configured on its interface as being present on the Frame Relay switch, but the PVC associated with the DLCI cannot communicate end-to-end. Usually this indicates that the router on the far side of the PVC is not configured correctly.

A Frame Relay status of "deleted," as shown in Example 4-27, indicates that the Frame Relay switch is not reporting the DLCI configured on the serial interface.

Example 4-27 *A Deleted PVC Means That the Problem Lies in the Local Loop*

```
Router#show frame-relay pvc
PVC Statistics for interface Serial0 (Frame Relay DTE)

DLCI = 20, DLCI USAGE = LOCAL, PVC STATUS = DELETED, INTERFACE = Serial0.1
  input pkts 0            output pkts 0           in bytes 0
  out bytes 0             dropped pkts 0          in FECN pkts 0
  in BECN pkts 0          out FECN pkts 0         out BECN pkts 0
```

Example 4-27 *A Deleted PVC Means That the Problem Lies in the Local Loop (Continued)*

```
    in DE pkts 0              out DE pkts 0
    pvc create time 00:00:19, last time pvc status changed 00:00:18


DLCI = 41, DLCI USAGE = LOCAL, PVC STATUS = DELETED, INTERFACE = Serial0.2
    input pkts 0             output pkts 0            in bytes 0
    out bytes 0              dropped pkts 0           in FECN pkts 0
    in BECN pkts 0           out FECN pkts 0          out BECN pkts 0
    in DE pkts 0             out DE pkts 0
    pvc create time 00:00:20, last time pvc status changed 00:00:19
```

Suggested troubleshooting steps are

- Check that the physical layer is up.
- Verify a working LMI with the **show frame-relay lmi** command.

If these steps indicate that the router is communicating successfully with the Frame Relay switch, the "deleted" status indicates that the Frame Relay switch is not reporting the DLCI as being available. Therefore, the router interprets that the telco has "deleted" it. The most likely cause of this problem is a misconfigured DLCI on either the router or at the telco.

Frame Relay Encapsulation Type

If none of the previous steps have solved the Frame Relay issue, the problem might be related to Frame Relay encapsulation. Cisco routers default to Cisco Frame Relay encapsulation, which is valid only between other Cisco routers that are using Cisco Frame Relay encapsulation. If connecting to a third-party router, the Frame Relay encapsulation must be changed from **cisco** to **ietf**. To configure **ietf** Frame Relay encapsulation, replace the **encapsulation frame-relay** command with **encapsulation frame-relay ietf**.

Troubleshooting Frame Relay Using the Line Status

Further information on the status of Frame Relay can be determined from the **show interface** command. There are four common line status conditions:

- Interface is down, line protocol is down
- Interface is up, line protocol is down
- Interface is up, line protocol is up
- Interface is administratively down

The output "serial0/0 is down, line protocol is down" indicates a problem with the CSU/DSU or the serial line. Troubleshoot the problem with a loopback test by following these steps:

Step 1   Set the serial line encapsulation to HDLC and keepalive to 10 seconds. The commands to accomplish this are the interface configuration commands **encapsulation hdlc** and **keepalive 10**.

Step 2   Place the CSU/DSU or modem in local loop mode. Look for a "line protocol is up (looped)" message. If the line protocol comes, this suggests that the problem is occurring beyond the local CSU/DSU. If the status line does not change states, look for a problem in the router, connecting cable, CSU/DSU, or modem. In most cases, the problem is with the CSU/DSU or modem.

Step 3   Ping your own IP address with the CSU/DSU or modem looped. There should not be any misses. An extended ping of 0x0000 is helpful in resolving line problems because a T1 or E1 derives clock from data and requires a transition every 8 bits. B8ZS ensures synchronization. A heavy 0 data pattern helps to determine if the transitions are appropriately forced on the trunk. A heavy 1s pattern is used to appropriately simulate a high 0 load in case there is a pair of data inverters in the path. The alternating pattern (0x5555) represents a "typical" data pattern. If pings fail or if there are cyclic redundancy check (CRC) errors, a bit error rate tester (BERT) with an appropriate analyzer from the telco is needed.

When testing is complete, change the encapsulation back to Frame Relay.

The output "serial0/0 is up, line protocol is down" means that the router is getting a carrier signal from the CSU/DSU or modem, but Layer 2 communication has failed. Troubleshoot the problem using the following steps:

Step 1   Check to make sure that the Frame Relay provider has activated its port. Verify that the router and telco LMI settings match. Generally, the Frame Relay switch ignores the DTE unless it sees the correct LMI.

Step 2   Check to make sure that the Cisco router is transmitting data. You most likely need to check the line integrity using loop tests at various locations, beginning with the local CSU and working your way out until you get to the provider's Frame Relay switch. See the preceding steps for how to perform a loopback test.

Unless keepalives have been turned off, the output **serial0/0 is up, line protocol is up** means that the router is talking with the provider's Frame Relay switch. The router should indicate a successful exchange of two-way traffic on the serial interface, with no CRC errors.

The output **serial0/0 is down, line protocol is up** is not possible.

Keepalives are necessary in Frame Relay because they are the mechanism that the router uses to "learn" which DLCIs the provider has provisioned. To watch the exchange, you can use the **debug frame-relay lmi** command in almost all situations. This command generates very few messages but can provide answers to questions such as these:

- Is the Cisco router talking to the local Frame Relay switch?
- Is the router getting full LMI status messages for the subscribed permanent virtual circuits (PVCs) from the Frame Relay provider?
- Are the DLCIs correct?

Example 4-28 shows sample **debug frame-relay lmi** output from a successful connection.

Example 4-28 *The Best Way to Determine What DLCIs Are Being Advertised by the Frame Relay Switch Is the* **debug frame-relay lmi** *Command*

```
*Mar  1 01:17:58.763: Serial0(out): StEnq, myseq 92, yourseen 64, DTE up
*Mar  1 01:17:58.763:  datagramstart = 0x20007C, datagramsize = 14
*Mar  1 01:17:58.763:  FR encap = 0x0001030800 75 95 01 01 01 03 02 5C 40
*Mar  1 01:17:58.767:
*Mar  1 01:17:58.815: Serial0(in): Status, myseq 92
*Mar  1 01:17:58.815: RT IE 1, length 1, type 1
*Mar  1 01:17:58.815: KA IE 3, length 2, yourseq 65, myseq 92
*Mar  1 01:18:08.763: Serial0(out): StEnq, myseq 93, yourseen 65, DTE up
*Mar  1 01:18:08.763:  datagramstart = 0x20007C, datagramsize = 14
*Mar  1 01:18:08.763:  FR encap = 0x0001030800 75 95 01 01 01 03 02 5D 41
*Mar  1 01:18:08.767:
*Mar  1 01:18:08.815: Serial0(in): Status, myseq 93
*Mar  1 01:18:08.815: RT IE 1, length 1, type 1
*Mar  1 01:18:08.815: KA IE 3, length 2, yourseq 66, myseq 93
*Mar  1 01:18:18.763: Serial0(out): StEnq, myseq 94, yourseen 66, DTE up
*Mar  1 01:18:18.763:  datagramstart = 0x20007C, datagramsize = 14
*Mar  1 01:18:18.763:  FR encap = 0x0001030800 75 95 01 01 00 03 02 5E 42
*Mar  1 01:18:18.767:
*Mar  1 01:18:18.815: Serial0(in): Status, myseq 94
*Mar  1 01:18:18.815: RT IE 1, length 1, type 0
*Mar  1 01:18:18.819: KA IE 3, length 2, yourseq 67, myseq 94
*Mar  1 01:18:18.819: PVC IE 0x7 , length 0x3 , dlci 980, status 0x2
```

Notice the status of DLCI 980 in the output. The possible values of the status field are explained in Table 4-12.

Table 4-12 The Possible Values of the Status Field Include 0x0 (Added/Inactive) and 0x2 (Added/Active)

Status Field	Description
0x0	Added/inactive. The switch has this DLCI programmed, but for some reason (such as the other end of the PVC is down), it is unusable.
0x2	Added/active. The Frame Relay switch has the DLCI, and everything is operational. You can start sending it traffic with this DLCI in the header.
0x3	A combination of an active status (0x2) and the RNR (or r-bit) that is sent (0x1). This means that the switch (or a particular queue on the switch) for this PVC is backed up, and you stop transmitting in case frames are spilled.
0x4	Deleted. The Frame Relay switch doesn't have this DLCI programmed for the router. But it was programmed at some point in the past. This could also be caused by the DLCIs being reversed on the router, or by the PVC being deleted by the telco in the Frame Relay cloud. Configuring a DLCI (that the switch doesn't have) shows up as a 0x4.
0x8	New/Inactive
0x0a	New/Active

Ping the Local IP Address with Multipoint Frame Relay

A ping performed on the local IP address on a multipoint Frame Relay interface, as shown in Figure 4-21, does not work. This is because Frame Relay multipoint physical and subinterfaces are nonbroadcast. Recall that Ethernet and point-to-point interfaces such as HDLC and Frame Relay point-to-point subinterfaces are broadcast. Because multipoint interfaces can have multiple destinations, the router must have a mapping for every destination. The router does not have any Layer 3-to-Layer 2 mapping for its own address and does not know how to encapsulate the packet. An encapsulation failure results.

Furthermore, **ping** is unsuccessful from one spoke to another in a hub-and-spoke configuration. This is because there is no mapping for the local IP address, and none were learned by way of Inverse ARP. But if a static map is configured with the **frame-relay map** command for the local IP address or one for the remote spoke to use the local DLCI, **ping** is successful.

Figure 4-21 Ping to the Local Multipoint Frame Relay Interface

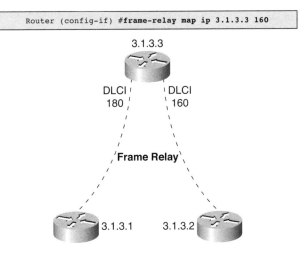

Before you add the static Frame Relay map, the result of pinging a local interface is as follows:

```
Router#ping 3.1.3.3
Type escape sequence to abort.
Sending 5, 100-byte ICMP Echos to 3.1.3.3, timeout is 2 seconds:
.....
Success rate is 0 percent (0/5)
```

To permit the pinging of local Frame Relay interfaces, you must add the following static map command:

```
Router#configure terminal
Enter configuration commands, one per line. End with CNTL/Z.
Router(config)#interface serial 0/1
Router (config-if)#frame-relay map ip 3.1.3.3 160
```

This can be verified using the **show frame-relay map** command:

```
Router#show frame-relay map
Serial0/1 (up): ip 3.1.3.1 dlci 180(0xA0,0x2800), dynamic, broadcast, status
  defined, active
Serial0/1 (up): ip 3.1.3.2 dlci 160(0xA0,0x2800), static, CISCO, status defined,
  active
Serial0/1 (up): ip 3.1.3.3 dlci 160(0xA0,0x2800), static, CISCO, status defined,
  active
```

It now is possible to ping the local interface:

```
Router#ping 3.1.3.3
Type escape sequence to abort.
Sending 5, 100-byte ICMP Echos to 3.1.3.3, timeout is 2 seconds:
!!!!!
Success rate is 100 percent (5/5), round-trip min/avg/max = 64/68/76 ms
```

Here is the running configuration file for Serial 0/1:

```
interface Serial0/1
ip address 3.1.3.3 255.255.255.0
no ip directed-broadcast
encapsulation frame-relay
frame-relay map ip 3.1.3.2 160
frame-relay map ip 3.1.3.3 160
frame-relay interface-dlci 160
!
```

Reconfiguring a Subinterface

After a specific type of subinterface has been created, it cannot be changed without a reload. For example, **subinterface serial0.2 multipoint** cannot be changed to **subinterface serial0.2 point-to-point**. To make a change, either reload the router or create another subinterface. This is how the Frame Relay code works in the Cisco IOS software. See Example 4-29.

Example 4-29 *A Reload Is Required to Change a Multipoint Frame Relay Subinterface to a Point-to-Point Subinterface, and Vice Versa*

```
r1(config)#interface s0/1.1 multipoint
r1(config-subif)#
3w6d:%LINEPROTO-5-UPDOWN: Line protocol on Interface
 Serial0/1, changed state to down
r1(config-subif)#exit
r1(config)#interface s0/1.1 point-to-point
% Warning: cannot change link type
r1(config-subif)#exit
r1(config)#no interface s0/1.1
% Not all config may be removed and may reappear after
 reactivating the sub-interface
r1(config)#end
r1#show interface
<output omitted>
Serial0/1.1 is deleted, line protocol is down
 Hardware is PowerQUICC Serial
 MTU 1500 bytes, BW 1544 Kbit, DLY 20000 usec,
    reliability 255/255, txload 1/255, rxload 1/255
 Encapsulation FRAME-RELAY
```

PPP and Layer 2 Considerations for Routed and Routing Protocols

PPP is typically used on ISDN B channels, as well as on dedicated leased lines. PPP relies on Link Control Protocol (LCP) for link negotiation. Many PPP problems can be traced to incompatible LCP parameters. This section discusses PPP problems and solutions as well as troubleshooting common issues relating to nonbroadcast multiaccess (NBMA) networks and maximum transmission unit (MTU) settings.

Link Control Protocol

PPP has become the protocol of choice for dialup, leased lines, and many other point-to-point WAN applications. The reasons for its popularity include multiprotocol support, multilink, address negotiation, and compression.

The PPP protocol is broken into the Layer 2 component LCP and a Layer 3 component called Network Control Protocol (NCP).

The PPP LCP provides a method of establishing, configuring, maintaining, and terminating the point-to-point connection. LCP goes through four distinct phases.

First, link establishment and configuration negotiation occur. Before any network layer datagrams such as IP can be exchanged, LCP must open the connection and negotiate configuration parameters. This phase is complete when a configuration-acknowledgment frame has been both sent and received.

This is followed by link quality determination. LCP allows an optional link quality determination phase following the link-establishment and configuration-negotiation phase. In this phase, the link is tested to determine whether the link quality is sufficient to bring up network layer protocols. This phase is optional. LCP can delay transmission of network layer protocol information until this phase is complete.

At this point, network layer protocol configuration negotiation occurs. After LCP has finished the link quality determination phase, network layer protocols can be configured separately by the appropriate NCP and can be brought up and taken down at any time. If LCP closes the link, it informs the network layer protocols so that the protocols can take appropriate action.

Finally, link termination occurs. LCP can terminate the link at any time. This usually is done at the request of a user, but it can happen because of a physical event such as the loss of carrier or the expiration of an idle-period timer.

Most of the problems that occur with PPP involve link negotiation. Typically the problems can be classified as follows:

- Authentication
- Incorrect encapsulation at the far end
- Conflicting PPP parameters

The first step in troubleshooting a PPP problem is to check that the appropriate encapsulation is in use with the **show interfaces serial** command, as shown in Example 4-30.

Example 4-30 *PPP Encapsulation Can Be Verified with the* **show interfaces** *Command*

```
prat#show interfaces serial 0
Serial0 is up, line protocol is up
  Hardware is HD64570
  Internet address is 5.0.2.1/24
  MTU 1500 bytes, BW 1544 Kbit, DLY 20000 usec,
     reliability 255/255, txload 1/255, rxload 1/255
  Encapsulation PPP, loopback not set
  Keepalive set (10 sec)
  LCP Open
  Open: IPCP
  Last input 00:00:05, output 00:00:05, output hang never
  Last clearing of "show interface" counters 00:09:58
  Input queue: 0/75/0/0 (size/max/drops/flushes); Total output drops: 0
  Queueing strategy: weighted fair
  Output queue: 0/1000/64/0 (size/max total/threshold/drops)
     Conversations  0/1/256 (active/max active/max total)
     Reserved Conversations 0/0 (allocated/max allocated)
     Available Bandwidth 1158 kilobits/sec
  5 minute input rate 0 bits/sec, 1 packets/sec
  5 minute output rate 0 bits/sec, 0 packets/sec
     122 packets input, 2824 bytes, 0 no buffer
     Received 0 broadcasts, 0 runts, 0 giants, 0 throttles
     0 input errors, 0 CRC, 0 frame, 0 overrun, 0 ignored, 0 abort
     132 packets output, 2964 bytes, 0 underruns
     0 output errors, 0 collisions, 2 interface resets
     0 output buffer failures, 0 output buffers swapped out
     6 carrier transitions
     DCD=up  DSR=up  DTR=up  RTS=up  CTS=up
prat#
```

Assuming that the correct encapsulation is in use, the next step is to confirm that the LCP negotiations have succeeded by checking the output for LCP Open. Finally, the Layer 3 component can be verified by checking for Open:IPCP or whatever other Layer 3 protocol is expected.

If one of these elements appears incorrect, obtain a detailed debug of the negotiation process using the command **debug ppp negotiation**. Example 4-31 displays in graphic detail each step in a successful PPP link establishment.

Example 4-31 *The* **debug ppp negotiation** *Command Is the Most Useful Debugging Command for PPP Link Establishment*

```
maui-soho-01#debug ppp negotiation
PPP protocol negotiation debugging is on
maui-soho-01#
*Mar  1 00:06:36.645: %LINK-3-UPDOWN: Interface BRI0:1, changed state to up
! -- Physical Layer (BRI Interface) is up. Only now can PPP negotiation begin
*Mar  1 00:06:36.661: BR0:1 PPP: Treating connection as a callin
*Mar  1 00:06:36.665: BR0:1 PPP: Phase is ESTABLISHING, Passive Open [0 sess, 0
  load]
! -- PPP Phase is ESTABLISHING. LCP negotiation will now occur
*Mar  1 00:06:36.669: BR0:1 LCP: State is Listen
*Mar  1 00:06:37.034: BR0:1 LCP: I CONFREQ [Listen] id 7 len 17
! -- Incoming CONFREQ. ID field is 7
*Mar  1 00:06:37.038: BR0:1 LCP:    AuthProto PAP (0x0304C023)
*Mar  1 00:06:37.042: BR0:1 LCP:    MagicNumber 0x507A214D (0x0506507A214D)
*Mar  1 00:06:37.046: BR0:1 LCP:    Callback 0  (0x0D0300)
! -- The peer has requested:
! -- Option: Authentication Protocol, Value: PAP
! -- Option: MagicNumber (used to detect loopbacks and is always sent)
! -- Option: Callback, Value: 0 (for PPP Callback; MS Callback is 6)
*Mar  1 00:06:37.054: BR0:1 LCP: O CONFREQ [Listen] id 4 len 15
! -- An outgoing CONFREQ, with parameters it wishes the peer to do
! -- Note that the ID Field is 4, so is not related to the previous CONFREQ
! -- message
*Mar  1 00:06:37.058: BR0:1 LCP:    AuthProto CHAP (0x0305C22305)
*Mar  1 00:06:37.062: BR0:1 LCP:    MagicNumber 0x1081E7E1 (0x05061081E7E1)
! -- This router is requesting:
! -- Option: Authentication Protocol, Value: CHAP
! -- Option: MagicNumber (used to detect loopbacks and is always sent)
```

continues

Example 4-31 *The* **debug ppp negotiation** *Command Is the Most Useful Debugging Command for PPP*
Link Establishment (Continued)

```
*Mar  1 00:06:37.066: BR0:1 LCP: O CONFREJ [Listen] id 7 len 7

! -- Outgoing CONFREJ for message with Field ID 7

! -- This is the response to the CONFREQ received first

*Mar  1 00:06:37.070: BR0:1 LCP:    Callback 0  (0x0D0300)

! -- The option that this router rejects is Callback

! -- If the router wanted to do MS Callback rather than PPP Callback it

! -- would have sent a CONFNAK instead

*Mar  1 00:06:37.098: BR0:1 LCP: I CONFACK [REQsent] id 4 len 15

! -- Incoming CONFACK for message with Field ID 4

*Mar  1 00:06:37.102: BR0:1 LCP:    AuthProto CHAP (0x0305C22305)

*Mar  1 00:06:37.106: BR0:1 LCP:    MagicNumber 0x1081E7E1 (0x05061081E7E1)

! -- The peer can support all requested parameters

*Mar  1 00:06:37.114: BR0:1 LCP: I CONFREQ [ACKrcvd] id 8 len 14

! -- Incoming CONFREQ. ID field is 8

! -- This is a new CONFREQ from the peer in response to the CONFREJ id:7

*Mar  1 00:06:37.117: BR0:1 LCP:    AuthProto PAP (0x0304C023)

*Mar  1 00:06:37.121: BR0:1 LCP:    MagicNumber 0x507A214D (0x0506507A214D)

! -- The peer has requested:

! -- Option: Authentication Protocol, Value: PAP

! -- Option: MagicNumber (used to detect loopbacks and is always sent)

*Mar  1 00:06:37.125: BR0:1 LCP: O CONFNAK [ACKrcvd] id 8 len 9

! -- Outgoing CONFNACK for message with Field ID 8

*Mar  1 00:06:37.129: BR0:1 LCP:    AuthProto CHAP (0x0305C22305)

! -- This router recognizes the option Authentication Protocol

! -- but does not accept the value PAP. In the CONFNAK message, it suggests CHAP

! -- instead

*Mar  1 00:06:37.165: BR0:1 LCP: I CONFREQ [ACKrcvd] id 9 len 15

! -- Incoming CONFREQ with Field ID 9

*Mar  1 00:06:37.169: BR0:1 LCP:    AuthProto CHAP (0x0305C22305)

*Mar  1 00:06:37.173: BR0:1 LCP:    MagicNumber 0x507A214D (0x0506507A214D)

! -- CHAP authentication is requested

*Mar  1 00:06:37.177: BR0:1 LCP: O CONFACK [ACKrcvd] id 9 len 15

! -- Outgoing CONFACK for message with Field ID 9

*Mar  1 00:06:37.181: BR0:1 LCP:    AuthProto CHAP (0x0305C22305)

*Mar  1 00:06:37.185: BR0:1 LCP:    MagicNumber 0x507A214D (0x0506507A214D)
```

Example 4-31 *The* **debug ppp negotiation** *Command Is the Most Useful Debugging Command for PPP
Link Establishment (Continued)*

```
*Mar  1 00:06:37.189: BR0:1 LCP: State is Open
! -- LCP state goes to Open
*Mar  1 00:06:37.193: BR0:1 PPP: Phase is AUTHENTICATING, by both [0 sess, 0 load]
! -- PPP Phase is AUTHENTICATING. PPP Authentication occurs now
! -- Two-way authentication will be performed (indicated by the both keyword)
*Mar  1 00:06:37.201: BR0:1 CHAP: O CHALLENGE id 4 len 33 from "maui-soho-01"
! -- Outgoing CHAP Challenge.
! -- In LCP we had agreed upon CHAP as the authentication protocol
*Mar  1 00:06:37.225: BR0:1 CHAP: I CHALLENGE id 3 len 33 from "maui-soho-03"
! -- Incoming Challenge from peer
*Mar  1 00:06:37.229: BR0:1 CHAP: Waiting for peer to authenticate first
*Mar  1 00:06:37.237: BR0:1 CHAP: I RESPONSE id 4 len 33 from "maui-soho-03"
! -- Incoming response from peer
*Mar  1 00:06:37.244: BR0:1 CHAP: O SUCCESS id 4 len 4
! -- This router has successfully authenticated the peer.
*Mar  1 00:06:37.248: BR0:1 CHAP: Processing saved Challenge, id 3
*Mar  1 00:06:37.260: BR0:1 CHAP: O RESPONSE id 3 len 33 from "maui-soho-01"
*Mar  1 00:06:37.292: BR0:1 CHAP: I SUCCESS id 3 len 4
```

One of the most likely problems with bringing up a link is an authentication failure. This is covered in the next sections.

Troubleshooting PPP Authentication PAP

PPP currently supports two authentication protocols: Password Authentication Protocol (PAP) and Challenge Handshake Authentication Protocol (CHAP). Both are specified in RFC 1334 and are supported on synchronous and asynchronous interfaces.

PAP provides a simple method for a remote node to establish its identity using a two-way handshake. After the PPP link establishment phase is complete, a username and password pair is repeatedly sent by the remote node across the link (in clear text) until authentication is acknowledged or until the connection is terminated.

PAP is an insecure authentication protocol. Passwords are sent across the link in clear text, and there is no protection from playback or trail-and-error attacks. Another important consideration is that the remote node is in control of the frequency and timing of the login attempts.

Despite its shortcomings, PAP might be used in the following environments:

- A large installed base of client applications that do not support CHAP
- Incompatibilities between different vendor implementations of CHAP
- Situations in which a plaintext password must be available to simulate a login at the remote host

As with most types of authentication, PAP supports bidirectional (two-way) and unidirectional (one way) authentication. With unidirectional authentication, only the side receiving the call authenticates the remote side (client). The remote client does not authenticate the server.

With bidirectional authentication, each side independently sends an Authenticate-Request (AUTH-REQ) and receives either an Authenticate-Acknowledge (AUTH-ACK) or Authenticate-Not Acknowledged (AUTH-NAK). These can be seen with the **debug ppp authentication** command, as shown in Example 4-32.

Example 4-32 *The* **debug ppp authentication** *Command Is Indispensable for Troubleshooting PPP Authentication Problems*

```
*Mar  6 19:18:53.322: BR0:1 PAP: O AUTH-REQ id 7 len 18 from "PAPUSER"

! --- Outgoing PAP AUTH-REQ. We are sending out our
! --- username (PAPUSER) and password to the NAS.
! --- The NAS will verify that the username/password
! --- is correct.

*Mar  6 19:18:53.441: BR0:1 PAP: I AUTH-ACK id 7 Len 5

! --- Incoming AUTH-ACK.
! --- The NAS verified the username and password and
! --- responded with an AUTH-ACK.
! --- One-way authentication is complete at this point.

*Mar  6 19:18:53.445: BR0:1 PAP: I AUTH-REQ id 1 Len 14
from "NAS"

! --- Incoming AUTH-REQ from the NAS. This means we now
! --- verify the identity of the NAS.
```

Example 4-32 *The* **debug ppp authentication** *Command Is Indispensable for Troubleshooting PPP Authentication Problems (Continued)*

```
*Mar  6 19:18:53.453: BR0:1 PAP: Authenticating peer NAS


! --- Performing a lookup for the username (NAS) and
! --- password.


*Mar  6 19:18:53.457: BR0:1 PAP: O AUTH-ACK id 1 Len 5


! --- Outgoing AUTH-ACK.
! --- We have verified the username/password of the NAS
! --- and responded with an AUTH-ACK.
! --- Two-way authentication is complete.
```

In the debug output, the authentication is bidirectional. However, if unidirectional authentication had been configured, only the first two debug lines would be shown.

Use the global configuration command **username** *username* **password** *password* to match a remote host. The local router uses this username and password to authenticate the PPP peer. When the peer sends its PAP username and password, the local router checks whether that username and password are configured locally. If there is a match, the peer is authenticated.

The function of the username command for PAP is different from its function for CHAP. With CHAP, this username and password are used to generate the response to the challenge, but PAP only uses it to verify that an incoming username and password are valid.

For one-way authentication, this command is required only on the called router. For two-way authentication, this command is necessary on both sides.

Use the global configuration command **ppp pap sent-username** *username* **password** *password* to enable outbound PAP authentication. The local router uses the username and password specified by the **ppp pap sent-username** command to authenticate itself to a remote device. The other router must have this same username and password configured using the **username** command just described. This is illustrated in Example 4-33.

Example 4-33 *PAP Authentication Configuration Is Unfortunately Quite Different from CHAP Authentication Configuration*

```
! --- Note: Only the relevant sections of the 1
! --- configuration are shown.
```

continues

Example 4-33 *PAP Authentication Configuration Is Unfortunately Quite Different from CHAP Authentication Configuration (Continued)*

```
Calling Side (Client) Configuration
interface BRI0

! --- BRI interface for the dialout.

 ip address negotiated
 encapsulation ppp

! --- Use PPP encapsulation. This command is a required
! --- for PAP.

 dialer string 3785555 class 56k

! --- Number to dial for the outgoing connection.

 dialer-group 1
 isdn switch-type basic-ni
 isdn spid1 51299611110101 9961111
 isdn spid2 51299622220101 9962222
 ppp authentication pap callin

! --- Use PAP authentication for incoming calls.
! --- The callin keyword has made this a one-way
! --- authentication scenario.
! --- This router (client) will not request that the
! --- peer (server) authenticate itself back to the
! --- client.

 ppp pap sent-username PAPUSER password 7 <deleted>

! --- Permit outbound authentication of this router
! --- (client) to the peer.
! --- Send a PAP AUTH-REQ packet to the peer with the
! --- username PAPUSER and password.
! --- The peer must have the username PAPUSER and
```

Example 4-33 *PAP Authentication Configuration Is Unfortunately Quite Different from CHAP Authentication Configuration (Continued)*

```
! --- password configured on it.
Receiving Side (Server) Configuration
username PAPUSER password 0 cisco

! --- Username PAPUSER is the same as the one sent by
! --- the client.
! --- Upon receiving the AUTH-REQ packet from the
! --- client, we will verify that the username and
! --- password match the one configured here.

interface Serial0:23

! --- This is the D channel for the PRI on the access
! --- server receiving the call.

 ip unnumbered Ethernet0
 no ip directed-broadcast
 encapsulation ppp

! --- Use PPP encapsulation. This command is required
! --- for PAP.

 dialer-group 1
 isdn switch-type primary-ni
 isdn incoming-voice modem
 peer default ip address pool default
 fair-queue 64 256 0
 ppp authentication pap

! --- Use PAP authentication for incoming calls.
! --- This router (server) will request that the peer
! --- authenticate itself to us.
! --- Note: the callin option is not used as this router
! --- is not initiating the call.
```

If one-way authentication is used, the command is only necessary on the router initiating the call. For two-way authentication, this command must be configured on both sides.

To debug a PPP PAP issue, use the **debug ppp negotiation** and **debug ppp authentication** commands. Two main issues must be considered:

- Do both sides agree that PAP is the method of authentication?
- If so, does the PAP authentication succeed?

Refer to the debugs in Examples 4-34 and 4-35 for an annotated, successful debug from the client and server side.

Example 4-34 *The Calling Side of a One-Way PAP Authentication Process Has PPP Authentication Debugging Enabled*

```
maui-soho-01#show debug
PPP:
  PPP authentication debugging is on
  PPP protocol negotiation debugging is on
maui-soho-01#ping 172.22.53.144
Type escape sequence to abort.
Sending 5, 100-byte ICMP Echos to 172.22.53.144, timeout is 2 seconds:
*Mar  6 21:33:26.412: %LINK-3-UPDOWN: Interface BRI0:1, changed state to up
*Mar  6 21:33:26.432: BR0:1 PPP: Treating connection as a callout
*Mar  6 21:33:26.436: BR0:1 PPP: Phase is ESTABLISHING, Active Open [0 sess, 0
  load]
*Mar  6 21:33:26.440: BR0:1 PPP: No remote authentication for call-out

! --- The client will not authenticate the server for an
! --- outgoing call. Remember this is a one-way
! --- authentication example.

*Mar  6 21:33:26.444: BR0:1 LCP: O CONFREQ [Closed] id 82 Len 10
*Mar  6 21:33:26.448: BR0:1 LCP:    MagicNumber 0x2F1A7C63 (0x05062F1A7C63)

! --- Outgoing CONFREQ (CONFigure-REQuest).
! --- Notice that we do not specify an authentication
! --- method, since only the peer will authenticate us.

*Mar  6 21:33:26.475: BR0:1 LCP: I CONFREQ [REQsent] id 13 Len 14
```

Example 4-34 *The Calling Side of a One-Way PAP Authentication Process Has PPP Authentication Debugging*
Enabled (Continued)

```
*Mar  6 21:33:26.479: BR0:1 LCP:    AuthProto PAP (0x0304C023)


! --- Incoming LCP CONFREQ (Configure-Request)
! --- indicating that the peer (server) wishes to use PAP.
*Mar  6 21:33:26.483: BR0:1 LCP:    MagicNumber 0x3DBEE95B (0x05063DBEE95B)
*Mar  6 21:33:26.491: BR0:1 LCP: O CONFACK [REQsent] id 13 Len 14
*Mar  6 21:33:26.495: BR0:1 LCP:    AuthProto PAP (0x0304C023)


! --- This shows the outgoing LCP CONFACK (CONFigure-
! --- ACKnowledge) indicating that the client can do PAP.


*Mar  6 21:33:26.499: BR0:1 LCP:    MagicNumber 0x3DBEE95B (0x05063DBEE95B)
*Mar  6 21:33:26.511: BR0:1 LCP: I CONFACK [ACKsent] id 82 Len 10
*Mar  6 21:33:26.515: BR0:1 LCP:    MagicNumber 0x2F1A7C63 (0x05062F1.A7C63)
*Mar  6 21:33:26.519: BR0:1 LCP: State is Open


! --- This shows LCP negotiation is complete.


*Mar  6 21:33:26.523: BR0:1 PPP: Phase is AUTHENTICATING, by the peer [0 sess, 0
  load]


! --- The PAP authentication (by the peer) begins.


*Mar  6 21:33:26.531: BR0:1 PAP: O AUTH-REQ id 20 Len 18 from "PAPUSER"


! --- The client sends out a PAP AUTH-REQ with username
! --- PAPUSER. This username is configured with the ppp
! --- pap sent-username command.


*Mar  6 21:33:26.555: BR0:1 PAP: I AUTH-ACK id 20 Len 5


! --- The peer responds with a PPP AUTH-ACK, indicating
! --- that it has successfully authenticated the client.
```

Example 4-35 *The Called Side of a One-Way PAP Authentication Process Has PPP Authentication Debugging Enabled*

```
maui-nas-06#show debug
PPP:
  PPP authentication debugging is on
  PPP protocol negotiation debugging is on
maui-nas-06#
*Jan  3 14:07:57.872: %LINK-3-UPDOWN: Interface Serial0:4, changed state to up
*Jan  3 14:07:57.876: Se0:4 PPP: Treating connection as a callin


! --- Since the connection is incoming, we will
! --- authenticate the client.


*Jan  3 14:07:57.876: Se0:4 PPP: Phase is ESTABLISHING,
  Passive Open
*Jan  3 14:07:57.876: Se0:4 LCP: State is Listen
*Jan  3 14:07:58.120: Se0:4 LCP: I CONFREQ [Listen] id
  83 Len 10
*Jan  3 14:07:58.120: Se0:4 LCP:    MagicNumber
  0x2F319828 (0x05062F319828)
*Jan  3 14:07:58.124: Se0:4 LCP: O CONFREQ [Listen] id
  13 Len 14
*Jan  3 14:07:58.124: Se0:4 LCP:    AuthProto PAP
  (0x0304C023)


! --- Outgoing CONFREQ (Configure-Request)
! --- use PAP for the peer authentication.


*Jan  3 14:07:58.124: Se0:4 LCP:    MagicNumber
  0x3DD5D5B9 (0x05063DD5D5B9)
*Jan  3 14:07:58.124: Se0:4 LCP: O CONFACK [Listen] id
  83 Len 10
*Jan  3 14:07:58.124: Se0:4 LCP:    MagicNumber
  0x2F319828 (0x05062F319828)
*Jan  3 14:07:58.172: Se0:4 LCP: I CONFACK [ACKsent] id
  13 Len 14
```

Example 4-35 *The Called Side of a One-Way PAP Authentication Process Has PPP Authentication Debugging Enabled (Continued)*

```
*Jan  3 14:07:58.172: Se0:4 LCP:    AuthProto PAP
  (0x0304C023)
! --- This shows the incoming LCP CONFACK (Configure-
! --- Acknowledge) indicating that the client can do
! --- PAP.


*Jan  3 14:07:58.172: Se0:4 LCP:    MagicNumber
  0x3DD5D5B9 (0x05063DD5D5B9)
*Jan  3 14:07:58.172: Se0:4 LCP: State is Open
*Jan  3 14:07:58.172: Se0:4 PPP: Phase is
  AUTHENTICATING, by this end


! --- The PAP authentication (by this side) begins.


*Jan  3 14:07:58.204: Se0:4 PAP: I AUTH-REQ id 21 Len 18
  from "PAPUSER"


! --- Incoming AUTH-REQ from the peer. This means we
! --- must now verify the identity of the peer.


*Jan  3 14:07:58.204: Se0:4 PPP: Phase is FORWARDING
*Jan  3 14:07:58.204: Se0:4 PPP: Phase is AUTHENTICATING
*Jan  3 14:07:58.204: Se0:4 PAP: Authenticating peer
  PAPUSER


! --- Performing a lookup for the username (PAPUSER) and
! --- password.


*Jan  3 14:07:58.208: Se0:4 PAP: O AUTH-ACK id 21 Len 5


! --- This shows the outgoing AUTH-ACK.
! --- We have verified the username and password and
! --- responded with an AUTH-ACK.
! --- One-way authentication is complete.
```

In certain configurations, it might be observed that the two sides do not agree on PAP as the authentication protocol, or instead agree on CHAP when PAP was desired. Use the following steps to troubleshoot these issues:

Step 1   Verify that the router receiving the call has one of the following authentication commands:

```
ppp authentication pap
ppp authentication pap chap
ppp authentication chap pap
```

Step 2   Verify that the router making the call has **ppp authentication pap callin** configured when unidirectional authentication is desired.

Step 3   Verify that the calling side has the command **ppp pap sent-username** *username* **password** *password* correctly configured. The username and password must match the ones configured on the receiving router.

Use the interface configuration command **ppp chap refuse** on the calling router. By default, Cisco routers accept CHAP as the authentication protocol. If the client wants to do PAP but the access server can do PAP or CHAP, the **ppp chap refuse** command can be used to force the client to accept PAP as the authentication protocol:

```
Router(config)#interface BRI 0/0
Router(config-if)#ppp chap refuse
```

If the two sides agree on PAP as the authentication protocol but the PAP connection fails, it is most likely a username and password issue.

Step 4   Verify that the calling side has the command **ppp pap sent-username** *username* **password** *password* correctly configured, where the username and password match the ones configured on the receiving router.

For two-way authentication, verify that the receiving side has the command **ppp pap sent-username** *username* **password** *password* correctly configured, where the username and password match the ones configured on the calling router.

When doing two-way authentication, if the command **ppp pap sent-username** *username* **password** *password* were not present on the receiving router, and the PPP client attempted to force the server to authenticate remotely, the output of **debug ppp negotiation** or **debug ppp authentication** would indicate the following:

```
*Jan 3 16:47:20.259: Se0:1 PAP: Failed request for PAP credentials.
  Username maui-nas-06
```

This error message indicates a configuration issue, not necessarily a security breach.

Step 5   Verify that the username and password match the ones configured in the command **ppp pap sent-username** *username* **password** *password* on the peer.

If they do not match, the following message is output:

```
*Jan 3 17:18:57.559: Se0:3 PAP: I AUTH-REQ id 25 Len 18 from "PAPUSER"
*Jan 3 17:18:57.559: Se0:3 PPP: Phase is FORWARDING
*Jan 3 17:18:57.559: Se0:3 PPP: Phase is AUTHENTICATING
*Jan 3 17:18:57.559: Se0:3 PAP: Authenticating peer PAPUSER
*Jan 3 17:18:57.559: Se0:3 PAP: O AUTH-NAK id 25 Len 32 msg is "Password
  validation failure"
```

This is an outgoing AUTH-NAK. This means that the mismatch occurred on this router. Verify that the username and password configured locally are identical to that on the peer.

Troubleshooting PPP Authentication CHAP

Debugging CHAP is similar to debugging PAP, as shown in Figure 4-22. Use the **debug ppp authentication** command to determine why an authentication fails.

Figure 4-22 The Same Command Is Used to Debug Both PAP and CHAP Authentication

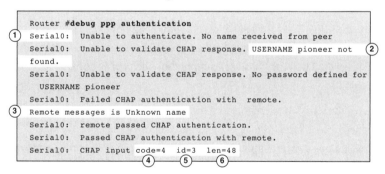

The following is a description of each of the debug fields shown in Figure 4-22 and their possible values:

1. Interface number associated with this debugging information and CHAP access session.

2. The name pioneer in this example is the name received in the CHAP response. The router looks up this name in the list of usernames that are configured for the router.

3. The following messages can appear:

— No name received to authenticate

— Unknown name

— No secret for given name

— Short MD5 response received

— MD compare failed

4. A specific CHAP type packet was detected. Possible values are as follows:

— 1—Challenge

— 2—Response

— 3—Success

— 4—Failure

5. ID number per LCP packet format.

6. Packet length without header.

A common CHAP error is caused by a password mismatch. This can be caused by two things:

- The peer did not supply the password that the local router expected. For example, the router expected (had configured) the password LetmeIn, but the peer used the password letmein. The administrator can either reconfigure the username and password sent by the peer or correct the peer with the right username.

- The local router does not have the password configured correctly. If the administrator has verified that the password supplied by the peer is correct, reconfigure the local router.

NOTE

For TCP/IP, Cisco routers can disable split horizon on all Frame Relay interfaces and multipoint subinterfaces. In fact, they do this by default for most IP routing protocols. However, split horizon cannot be disabled for other routing protocols, such as those used with IPX and AppleTalk. These other protocols must use subinterfaces if dynamic routing is desired.

To remove the existing username and password entry, use the command **no username** *username* where *username* is replaced by the username in the error message. Then configure the username and password using the command **username** *username* **password** *password*. The password must match the password on the remote router.

IP Split Horizon Checking

Split horizon dictates that a routing update received on an interface cannot be retransmitted out the same interface. This rule holds even if the routing update was received on one Frame Relay PVC and was destined for retransmission onto another Frame Relay PVC. In Figure 4-23, this means that Sites B and C can exchange routing information with Site A but cannot exchange routing information with each other. Split horizon does not allow Site A to send routing updates received from Site B to Site C, and vice versa.

Figure 4-23 Split Horizon Is an Issue on Multipoint Interfaces

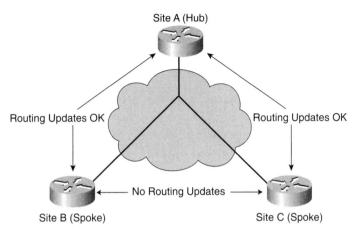

The concept of subinterfaces was created to handle issues caused by split horizon over NBMA networks and distance-vector-based routing protocols. Frame Relay and X.25 are examples of NBMA networks. IPX/SAP, RIP, and AppleTalk RTMP are examples of distance-vector-based routing protocols.

By dividing the partially meshed Frame Relay network into numerous virtual point-to-point networks using subinterfaces, you can overcome the split-horizon problem, as shown in Figure 4-24. Each new point-to-point subnetwork is assigned its own network number. To the routed protocol, each subnetwork now appears to be located on a separate interface. Routing updates received from Site B on one logical point-to-point subinterface can be forwarded to Site C on a separate logical interface without violating split horizon.

Figure 4-24 Point-to-Point Interfaces Ease Routing Between Spoke Routers

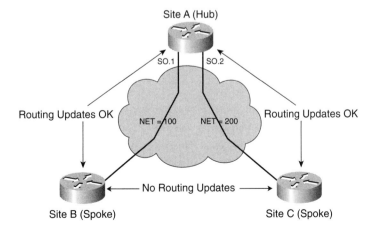

OSPF in an NBMA Environment

Unless special consideration is given to the operation of OSPF in an NBMA environment such as Frame Relay, routing problems will occur. This is because OSPF expects to be able to multicast to all routers within a subnet or broadcast domain. In a Frame Relay hub-and-spoke topology this is not possible. Consequently, some routers and routes are inaccessible.

The problem can be solved by forcing RTB in Figure 4-25 to become the designated router. This is achieved by configuring an OSPF interface priority of 0 on all the spoke routers. Recall that a priority of 0 makes it impossible for a router to be elected as Designated Router (DR) or Backup Designated Router (BDR) for a network. As long as RTB can exchange hellos with RTA and RTC, it can maintain a complete view of the network and pass this routing information to both RTA and RTC.

Figure 4-25 The Hub Router Is the Designated Router

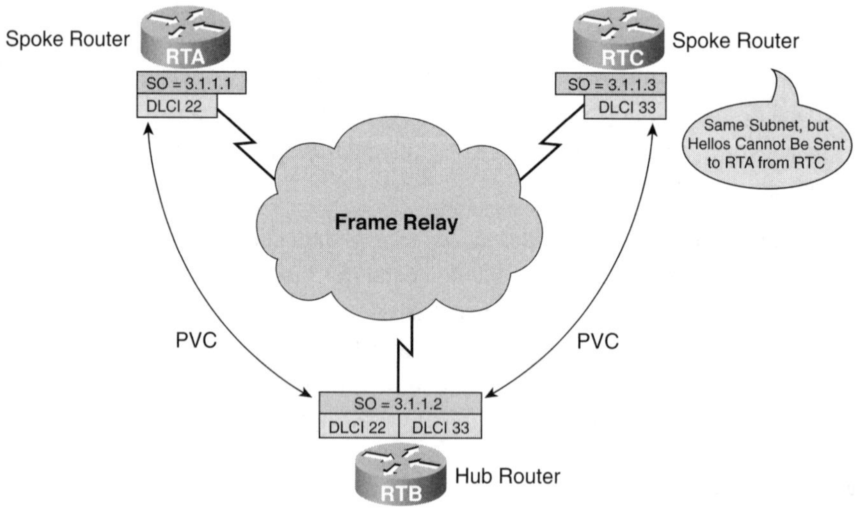

Alternatively, subinterfaces could be used on the hub router, making each link a point-to-point link. Recall that no DR election occurs in a point-to-point configuration. The downside of this technique is the creation of a new subnet or network.

Still another technique to manage OSPF over hub-and-spoke NBMA networks is to explicitly configure OSPF as a point-to-multipoint network. Point-to-multipoint networks have the following properties: Adjacencies are established between all neighboring routers. A point-to-multipoint network has no DR or BDR. When originating a router LSA, the point-to-multipoint interface is reported as a collection of point-to-point links to all the interface's adjacent neighbors, together with a single stub link advertising the interface's IP address with a cost of 0.

A point-to-point OSPF network has no DRs or BDRs.

When flooding out a nonbroadcast interface, the LSU or LSAck packet must be replicated to be sent to each of the interface's neighbors. To configure point-to-multipoint, manually override the detected OSPF network type with the following syntax:

```
Router(config-if)#ip ospf network point-to-multipoint
```

The interface should also be configured with a **frame-relay map ip** command:

```
Router(config-if)#frame-relay map ip address dlci [broadcast]
```

The **broadcast** keyword permits the router to send broadcasts via the specified DLCI to the mapped neighbor or neighbors. If the point-to-multipoint configuration is applied to the sample network, two separate **frame-relay map** statements would have to be configured on the hub router, RTB. See the configurations in Example 4-36.

Example 4-36 *The* **broadcast** *Keyword Permits Broadcasts To Be Propagated to the Neighbors Associated with the Configured DLCI*

```
<Configuration for RTA>
!
interface Serial0
    encapsulation frame-relay
    ip address 3.1.1.1 255.255.255.0
    ip ospf network point-to-multipoint
    frame-relay map ip 3.1.1.2 22 broadcast
!
router ospf 1
    network 3.1.1.0 0.0.0.255 area 0
-------------------------------------------------
<Configuration for RTB>
!
interface Serial0
    encapsulation frame-relay
    ip address 3.1.1.2 255.255.255.0
    ip ospf network point-to-multipoint
    frame-relay map ip 3.1.1.1 200 broadcast
    frame-relay map ip 3.1.1.3 300 broadcast
```

continues

Example 4-36 *The* **broadcast** *Keyword Permits Broadcasts To Be Propagated to the Neighbors Associated with the Configured DLCI (Continued)*

```
!
router ospf 1
    network 3.1.1.0 0.0.0.255 area 0
------------------------------------------------------
<Configuration for RTC>
!
interface Serial0
    encapsulation frame-relay
    ip address 3.1.1.3 255.255.255.0
    ip ospf network point-to-multipoint
    frame-relay map ip 3.1.1.3 33 broadcast
!
router ospf 1
    network 3.1.1.0 0.0.0.255 area 0
```

The Keyword broadcast

NOTE

The OSPF broadcast mechanism assumes that IP Class D addresses are never used for regular traffic over Frame Relay.

The **broadcast** keyword provides two functions. First, it forwards broadcasts and multicasts when multicasting is not enabled. Second, it simplifies the configuration of Open Shortest Path First (OSPF) for nonbroadcast networks that use Frame Relay.

Using the **broadcast** keyword is standard operating procedure for Frame Relay maps.

The **broadcast** keyword might also be required for some routing protocols, such as Apple-Talk. Protocols such as these depend on regular routing table updates, especially when the router at the remote end is waiting for a routing update packet to arrive before adding the route.

By requiring the selection of a designated router, OSPF treats an NBMA network such as Frame Relay in much the same way as it treats a broadcast network. In previous releases, this required manual assignment in the OSPF configuration using the **neighbor** interface mode command. When the **frame-relay map** command is included in the configuration with the **broadcast** keyword, and the **ip ospf network** command with the **broadcast** keyword is configured, there is no need to configure any neighbors manually. OSPF automatically runs over the Frame Relay network as a broadcast network.

The following example maps the destination IP address 172.16.123.1 to DLCI 100:

```
Router(config)#interface serial 0/0
Router(config-if)#frame-relay map IP 172.16.123.1 100 broadcast
```

OSPF uses DLCI 100 to broadcast updates.

Excessive Fragmentation

Fragmentation refers to the reduction of a Layer 3 packet as it is placed in a Layer 2 frame. Each fragment must be less than or equal to the original packet length.

The *maximum transmission unit (MTU)* is the largest Layer 3 packet that can be forwarded out a router or switch interface. Various default MTU settings are shown in Table 4-13. Ethernet and serial interfaces have default MTU values of 1500 bytes.

Table 4-13 The MTU Varies According to the Interface or Media Type

Network Architecture	MTU in Bytes
802.3 Ethernet	1500
4 Mb Token Ring	4464
16 Mb Token Ring	17914
FDDI	4352
X.25	576

When an outbound interface has a smaller MTU than the inbound interface, the packet might have to be fragmented. Consider an Ethernet packet of 1500 bytes that is received on interface fastethernet 0/0 and that must be sent out interface serial 0/0 using X.25 encapsulation. X.25 supports MTU values of 576 bytes.

In this case, the router strips the single Ethernet frame from the Layer 3 packet and reassembles the packet into three X.25 frames. Proper fragment sequencing is maintained in the packet's IP header. The ID value field contains the same value for each fragment. The Offset field value is unique. It defines which part of the original packet is contained in this fragment. Both sequenced and out-of-sequence packets are reassembled at the destination device.

You can use two commands to change the interface MTU size. The interface configuration command **mtu** is used to change the MTU for all Layer 3 protocols. The second interface configuration command, **ip mtu**, is used to set the MTU for the IP protocol.

Although the MTU configuration is relatively straightforward, issues can arise. If both commands are used on an interface, for example, the **ip mtu** value takes precedence for IP. However, if **mtu** is configured after **ip mtu**, the IP MTU value is reset to the same value as the MTU value.

Lab 4.2.1 Troubleshooting Problems at the Physical and Data-Link Layers

In this lab exercise, you define, isolate, and correct the problems outlined in the network support activity log to restore the network to baseline specifications. In this exercise, each workgroup uses a troubleshooting methodology and Cisco commands to start isolating issues.

Summary

This chapter examined troubleshooting techniques and common problems associated with the following Layer 2 protocols and technologies:

- Switches and switched technologies
- PPP
- ISDN
- Frame Relay

The difficulty in troubleshooting these technologies is the inability of common Layer 3 troubleshooting tools, such as ping, to do anything but tell you that the network is down. It is only through a thorough understanding of the protocols and their operation that a network technician can choose the appropriate troubleshooting methodology and IOS commands to solve the problem efficiently.

In the case of switched networks, it is quite possible to design a functional but suboptimal network. With no apparent network failure, only awareness of common problems and the ability to identify Layer 2 traffic paths lets the network technician achieve the full performance a network is capable of.

After completing this chapter, you should be confident that you can recognize common Layer 2 problems, and address them quickly and accurately.

Key Terms

channel service unit (CSU)   A digital interface device that connects end-user equipment to the local digital telephone loop. Often referred to with DSU as CSU/DSU.

cyclic redundancy check (CRC)   An error-checking technique in which the frame recipient calculates a remainder by dividing frame contents by a prime binary divisor and compares the calculated remainder to a value stored in the frame by the sending node.

data service unit (DSU)   A device used in digital transmission that adapts the physical interface on a DTE device to a transmission facility such as T1 or E1. The DSU is also responsible for such functions as signal timing. Often referred to with CSU as CSU/DSU.

Macof   A popular tool for launching a MAC flooding attack. Macof can generate 155,000 MAC entries on a switch per minute. The switch sees this traffic and thinks that the MAC address from the packet the attacker sent is a valid port and adds an entry. The goal is to flood the switch with traffic by filling the CAM table with false entries. After it is flooded, the switch broadcasts traffic without a CAM entry out its local VLAN, allowing the attacker to see traffic he or she wouldn't ordinarily see.

maximum transmission unit (MTU)   The largest Layer 3 packet that can be forwarded out a router or switch interface.

Systems Network Architecture (SNA)   A large, complex, feature-rich network architecture developed in the 1970s by IBM. Similar in some respects to the OSI reference model, but with a number of differences. SNA is essentially composed of seven layers: data flow control, data-link control, path control, physical control, presentation services, transaction services, and transmission control.

Check Your Understanding

Use the following review questions to test your understanding of the concepts covered in this chapter. Answers are listed in Appendix A, "Check Your Understanding Answer Key."

1. What IOS commands let you identify the configured encapsulation on a serial interface? Choose all that apply.

   A. **show controllers**

   B. **show cdp neighbors**

   C. **show interfaces**

   D. **show running-config**

2. What command displays Layer 3 information related to Frame Relay?

    A. **show frame-relay**

    B. **show frame-relay pvc**

    C. **show frame-relay lmi**

    D. **show frame-relay map**

3. What STP issue can result in suboptimal traffic flow?

    A. Misconfigured UplinkFast

    B. PortFast is disabled

    C. Improper root placement

    D. Missing VLAN 1

4. Misconfigured EtherChannel can result in what?

    A. Reset of the VTP configuration revision number

    B. Poor frame distribution

    C. Exaggerated crosstalk

    D. STP loop

5. What technology helps avoid STP loops caused by one-way failure of BPDU flow on a link?

    A. GMRP

    B. STP

    C. UDLD

    D. VTP

6. If a VTP client is added to a switched network, and it has a higher configuration revision number than the other switches in the VTP domain, what is the effect on other VTP clients and servers in the VTP domain?

    A. VLAN 1 is deleted

    B. VLANs configured on the added VTP client are deleted

    C. Nothing

    D. VLANs not configured on the added VTP client are deleted

7. What ISDN command identifies the ISDN switch type?

   A. **debug dialer**

   B. **show isdn status**

   C. **debug isdn events**

   D. **debug isdn q921**

8. A deleted Frame Relay PVC indicates a problem _____.

   A. with the Frame Relay map

   B. with encapsulation type

   C. on the remote end

   D. on the local loop

9. What IOS command identifies the DLCIs advertised by the Frame Relay switch?

   A. **debug frame-relay lmi**

   B. **show frame-relay pvc**

   C. **debug frame-relay events**

   D. **show frame-relay lmi**

10. Detailed LCP negotiation processes can be viewed with what IOS command?

   A. **debug ppp errors**

   B. **debug ppp authentication**

   C. **debug ppp negotiation**

   D. **debug ppp events**

Objectives

After completing this chapter, you will be able to perform tasks related to the following:

- Identify the symptoms of problems occurring at the network layer
- Identify end-system commands and applications used to isolate problems occurring at the network layer
- Analyze Cisco command and application output to isolate problems occurring at the network layer
- Isolate problems occurring at the network layer

Chapter 5

Layer 3 Troubleshooting

Network layer problems include any problem that involves a Layer 3 protocol, whether it be a routed protocol or a routing protocol. This chapter focuses primarily on IP routing protocols. Issues concerning routed protocols, such as IP, and other Layer 3 IP protocols are discussed in the other chapters.

Network layer problems also might include issues at the other layers. Configuring routing over a nonbroadcast multiaccess (NBMA) or dialup network can involve specific configuration and troubleshooting issues. Because these configurations involve a specific Layer 2 technology such as Frame Relay, ISDN, and so on, routing problems involving these technologies are discussed in Chapter 4, "Layer 2 Troubleshooting."

This chapter focuses on the most common troubleshooting issues with both static and dynamic routing protocols. Troubleshooting dynamic routing protocols is separated by common issues pertaining to most routing protocols, such as Layer 1 issues and incorrect network statements, and by specific routing protocols including RIP, IGRP, EIGRP, OSPF, IS-IS, and BGP. Troubleshooting redistribution issues with routing protocols is also discussed in this chapter.

Troubleshooting Network Layer Problems

Network layer problems can appear as a network failure or as a poorly performing network. Routing problems can be complex, with the effect of a problem often appearing far from the source, so the process of isolating the problem is critical. Combinations of static routes, default routes, summary routes, dynamic routes, and redistribution are common in an internetwork. This section addresses the general considerations in troubleshooting at the network layer.

What Are Network Layer Problems?

Network layer problems include any problem that involves a Layer 3 protocol, including both routed and routing protocols, as shown in Figures 5-1 and 5-2. This chapter focuses primarily on IP routing protocols.

Figure 5-1 ARP and ICMP Are Used in Conjunction with IP

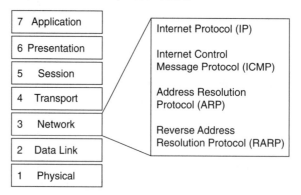

Figure 5-2 Routing Protocols Make Dynamic Routing Possible

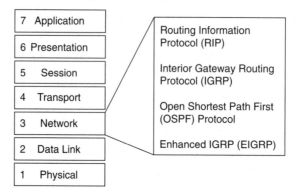

Problems at the network layer can have the following effects on a network:

- Network failure
- Failure to perform optimally

Network failure is when the network is nearly or completely nonfunctional, affecting all users and applications using the network. These failures are usually noticed quickly by users and network administrators and obviously are critical to a company's productivity.

Network optimization problems can be more difficult to discover and sometimes harder to diagnose. These problems usually involve a subset of users, applications, or destinations, or a particular type of traffic. Optimization issues in general can be more difficult to detect and even harder to isolate and diagnose because they usually involve multiple layers or even the host computer itself. Determining that the problem is a network layer problem can take time. Aspects of network optimization are discussed in more detail in Chapter 7, "Layer 1–7 Troubleshooting."

A possible optimization problem on a link at the network layer can be identified because data is transferred in a slow, sporadic, or unexpected manner compared to the data transfer rate documented in the baseline. Symptoms short of a complete failure to route packets might include misrouted packets that are lost or excessive transit delays.

Many of the problems discussed in this chapter can apply to both network failures and optimization problems, depending on the scenario and configuration of the actual network.

Not all the information in this chapter has to do with troubleshooting routing problems. This chapter also contains information on routing optimization, which includes some additional information on how the routing table process operates. Understanding the routing table process is helpful when you're troubleshooting certain situations so that you understand the cause of the problem, not just how to solve it.

Isolating the Problem Methodology

Although this chapter describes many common problems and solutions for troubleshooting various routing protocols, it is important to note that no single template exists for solving these Layer 3 problems. Routing problems are solved with a good methodical process, using a series of commands to isolate and diagnose the problem.

Many of the examples in this chapter are just that—examples. It is important to be able to apply these examples and concepts to other routing protocols and scenarios.

The first step is to isolate the problem. You can do this by identifying and documenting the symptoms.

Here are some areas to explore when diagnosing a possible problem involving routing protocols:

- **General network issues**—Many times a change in the topology, such as a down link, might have effects on other areas of the network that might not be obvious at the time.

These effects can include the installation of new routes, static or dynamic, removal of other routes, and so on.

Here are a couple things to consider:

— Has anything in the network changed recently?

— Is anyone currently working on the network infrastructure?

■ **Connectivity issues**—Check for any equipment and connectivity problems, including the following:

— **Power problems**—Outages, intermittent problems, environmental problems such as overheating, and so on

— **Layer 1 problems**—Cabling problems, bad ports, service provider problems, and so on

Here are some commands you can use to check these and other issues:

— **ping**

— **traceroute**

— **show interface**

— **show ip interface**

■ **Neighbor issues**—If the routing protocol establishes an adjacency with a neighbor, check to see if there are any problems with the routers forming neighbor relationships.

■ **Topology database**—If the routing protocol uses a topology table or database, check the table for anything unexpected, such as missing or unexpected entries.

■ **Routing table**—Check the routing table for anything unexpected, such as missing or unexpected routes. Use **debug** commands to view routing updates and routing table maintenance.

Many troubleshooting issues and solutions are common among different routing protocols. At times, this could depend on whether the routing protocol is distance vector or link-state, whether it uses AS or process ID numbers, whether it forms neighbor relationships, whether it is classful or classless, and whether it has a topology database. For example, split-horizon issues are common with all Interior Gateway Protocol (IGP) distance vector routing protocols, RIP, IGRP, and EIGRP. With IGRP and EIGRP, their AS numbers must be the same for routers to exchange updates, whereas with OSPF the process ID number is local only to that router. In this chapter, some issues described for one routing protocol also might apply to others.

Another issue to always keep in mind is the assignment of IP addresses and masks to interfaces. As often as not, network layer problems involve incorrect IP addressing.

Static Routes, Dynamic Routing, Summarization, Redistribution, and Combinations

Most networks are not configured with only static routes or with only one type of dynamic routing protocol. Most networks are a complex combination of static routes, one or more dynamic routing protocols, manual and automatic route aggregations, redistributions, distribute lists, access lists, and more. Understanding how these protocols and techniques work together and what effect they can have on each other is essential in understanding and troubleshooting networks.

This course examines these issues separately and, at times, in combination. It is impossible to cover every possible scenario and combination. Entire books have been written on each of these topics, so there is no way to cover everything in this chapter or this course. Of course, the number one resource for network engineers is http://www.cisco.com.

It's important that you thoroughly understand the routing protocols and configurations used in many networks. The more time you spend now understanding how the routing protocols function and how they interoperate with other routing protocols, static routes, and the routing table, the less time you'll spend later trying to troubleshoot networks in the field.

Lab 5.1.1   Isolating Network Layer Problems

In this lab, you are given a problem situation that has been escalated to Level 2 Engineering. You analyze user-feedback and end-system data and use Cisco commands and applications to isolate the specific cause of any problems. You use a troubleshooting methodology and Cisco commands to isolate the specific causes of any network problems.

Lab 5.1.2   Correcting Problems at the Network Layer

You complete the laboratory exercise by correcting the problems you isolated in the previous lab, and you practice what you learned in this lesson. In this exercise, you use various Cisco commands to correct network problems.

Troubleshooting Static Routes

It is often a surprise to network engineers that the processing on a router associated with static routes is so involved. Cisco routers must decide when to add or delete a static route to or from the routing table, and this often involves some intricate decision-making. This section describes how routers handle static routes.

Static Routes and Classful Lookups

Routing table maintenance can be more complex for static routes than dynamic routes. Static routes in the routing table can be invalid. In other words, they can reference an inactive exit interface or an intermediate network address that cannot be resolved. The static routing process within the IOS must be able to find invalid static routes and remove them from the routing table, as well as install new static routes that become valid or available.

When the routing table process checks for a resolvable static route using an intermediate address (the IP address referenced in the routing table as the next hop), this check is always done in classful mode. This is regardless of whether the **ip classless** command is used. If the intermediate address cannot be resolved in the routing table in classful mode, the static route is deleted. See the later section "Using Discard Routes" for more details on the effect of **ip classless**.

Example 5-1 shows the output of **show ip route** when all links are up. Example 5-2 shows the output of **debug ip routing** when the 172.16.2.0/24 network goes down. The new routing table is shown in Example 5-3. Because Serial 0/1 is down, the directly connected network 172.16.2.0/24 is deleted from the routing table in Example 5-3.

Example 5-1 *All Links Are Up, and a Default Route Is Included in the Routing Table*

```
RouterB#show ip route
Codes: C-connected,s-static,I-IGRP,R-RIP,M-mobile,B-BGP
  D-EIGRP,EX-EIGRP external,O-OSPF, NSSA external type 2
  N1-OSPF external type 1,B2-OSPF external type 2,E-EGP
  i-IS-IS,L1-IS-IS level-1,L2-IS-IS level-2,ia-IS-IS
inter area
  *-candidate default,U-per-user static route,o-oDR
  P-periodic downloaded static route

Gateway of last resort is 192.168.1.2 to network 0.0.0.0

     172.16.0.0/24 is subnetted, 3 subnets
S    172.16.1.0 [1/0] via 172.16.2.1
C    172.16.2.0 is directly connected, Serial0/1
C    172.16.3.0 is directly connected, FastEthernet0/0
C    192.168.1.0/24 is directly connected, Serial0/0
S*   0.0.0.0/0 [1/0] via 192.168.1.2
RouterB#
```

Example 5-2 *A debug Shows the 172.16.2.0/24 Network Going Down*

```
RouterB#debug ip routing
01:05:28: %LINK-3-UPDOWN: Interface Serial0/1, changed
          state to down
RouterB#
01:05:28: is_up: 0 state: 0 sub state: 1 line:0
01:05:28: RT: interface Serial0/1 removed from routing
          table
01:05:28: RT: del 172.16.2.0/24 via 0.0.0.0, connected
          metric [0/0]
01:05:28: RT: delete subnet route to 172.16.2.0/24
01:05:29: %LINEPRTO-5-UPDOWN: Line protocol on Interface
          Serial0/1, changed state to down
RouterB#
01:05:29: is up: 0 state: 1 line: 0
01:05:29: RT: del 172.16.1.0/24 via 172.16.2.1, static
          metric [1/0]
01:05:29: RT: delete subnet route to 172.16.1.0/24
RouterB#
```

Example 5-3 *The 172.16.3.0/24 Network Is Unaffected by the Network 172.16.2.0/24 Going Down*

```
RouterB#show ip route
Codes: C-connected,s-static,I-IGRP,R-RIP,M-mobile,B-BGP
  D-EIGRP,EX-EIGRP external,O-OSPF, NSSA external type 2
  N1-OSPF external type 1,B2-OSPF external type 2,E-EGP
  i-IS-IS,L1-IS-IS level-1,L2-IS-IS level-2,ia-IS-IS
inter area
  *-candidate default,U-per-user static route,o-oDR
  P-periodic downloaded static route

Gateway of last resort is 192.168.1.2 to network 0.0.0.0

     172.16.0.0/24 is subnetted, 1 subnets
C    172.16.3.0 is directly connected, FastEthernet0/0
C    192.168.1.0/24 is directly connected, Serial0/0
S*   0.0.0.0/0 [1/0] via 192.168.1.2
RouterB#
```

The static route for 172.16.1.0/24 uses the now-deleted 172.16.2.0/24 network to resolve its exit interface of 172.16.2.1. The subnet 172.16.2.0/24 has been removed in the routing table from under the parent classful network of 172.16.0.0. Notice, however, that still another subnet, 172.16.3.0/24, is below that same parent route in Example 5-3. The static route for 172.16.1.0/24 does not use the default route, 0.0.0.0/0 to resolve its next-hop address of 172.16.2.1. Instead, this static route also is removed from the routing table, as shown in Example 5-3. Like the 172.16.2.0/24 subnet, any packets destined for the 172.16.1.0/24 subnet are dropped.

The static route was removed because the routing table uses classful mode to resolve intermediate (next-hop) addresses. There is a reason to use classful mode to resolve intermediate addresses of static routes. If classless mode were used and a default route were present, backup static routes with higher administrative distances would never be installed in the routing table if the primary static route failed. This is because any static route, even one that references a nonexistent intermediate address, could be resolved using the default route.

It is important to remember that the Cisco IOS software stores all static routes, whether or not they are installed in the routing table. The Cisco routing table process invokes a static route function every 60 seconds that checks the routing table to install or remove any static routes according to the dynamically changing routing table.

For example, if an interface has gone down, this function removes any static routes that were resolved using this interface. This might be a static route that includes this interface as its exit interface, or a static route that has an intermediate address, but eventually that intermediate address is ultimately resolved via this downed interface.

In addition, static routes might be installed in the routing table when an interface becomes active or a network is installed in the routing table.

Static Routes and Intermediate Addresses

Static routes can be created by using either an intermediate network address or an exit interface. In most cases, using an exit interface is more efficient during the routing table process for resolving the static route. Figure 5-3 shows a sample network with three routers.

Figure 5-3 Most Routing Issues Can Be Demonstrated with a Few Routers

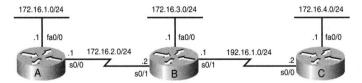

Example 5-4 shows a static route being configured and installed in the routing table.

Example 5-4 *A Static Route Is Configured by Specifying a Destination Network and a Next-Hop IP Address and/or Local Interface*

```
RouterA#show ip route
Codes: C-connected,S-static,I-IGRP,R-RIP,M-moble,B-BGP
<text omitted>


Gateway of last resort is not set


     172.16.0.0/24 is subnetted, z subnets
C     172.16.1.0 is directly connected, FastEthernet0/0
C     172.16.2.0 is directly connected, Serial0/0
RouterA#debug ip routing
RouterA#configure terminal
RouterA(config)#ip route 172.16.3.0 255.255.255.0 172.16.2.2
03:12:45: RT: add 172.16.3.0/24 via 172.16.2.2, static metric [1/0]
RouterA(config)#
```

The static route that was created uses an intermediate IP address of 172.16.2.2. This is sometimes called the next-hop IP address, but the IP address does not have to be the physical next hop. As long as the intermediate IP address can be resolved in the routing table, it does not have to be the actual next-hop router's interface. Ultimately, the static network route (172.16.3.0 in the example) must finally be resolved to a route in the routing table that has an exit interface.

Example 5-5 shows the routing table of Router A after the static route is installed.

Example 5-5 *The Static Route Appears in the Routing Table with the Next-Hop IP Address Displayed. The Local Interface Is Not Specified.*

```
RouterA#show ip route
Codes: C-connected,S-static,I-IGRP,R-RIP,M-moble,B-BGP
<text omitted>
Gateway of last resort is not set


     172.16.0.0/24 is subnetted, 3 subnets
C     172.16.1.0 is directly connected, FastEthernet0/0
C     172.16.2.0 is directly connected, Serial0/0
S     172.16.3.0 [1/0] via 172.16.2.2
RouterA#
```

Notice that the static route that was configured does not contain an exit interface. Instead, the static routing table entry contains the intermediate address that was used when configuring the static route.

Whenever the routing table process needs to use the static route entry for the 172.16.3.0/24 network, it also needs to resolve the intermediate address, 172.16.2.2. This is called a recursive lookup.

Because this routing table entry for the 172.16.3.0/24 route does not contain an exit interface, but instead the intermediate address 172.16.2.2, it cannot use this entry alone to forward the packets. The routing table process uses the intermediate address of 172.16.2.2 and does another lookup (recursive lookup) in the routing table to find a route for this 172.16.2.0 network.

The routing table process finds the directly connected network entry for 172.16.2.0:

```
C 172.16.2.0 is directly connected, Serial0/0
```

Because this entry has an exit interface, Serial0/0, the routing table process can use this route to forward the packets for 172.16.3.0/24. Remember that it takes two routing table lookups to route packets using the static route entry 172.16.3.0/24. The first routing table lookup is for the 172.16.3.0 network, the packet's destination IP address, and the second routing table lookup is for the exit interface of the intermediate address used in the entry. See Figure 5-4.

Figure 5-4 Recursive Route Lookups Are Standard Operating Procedure

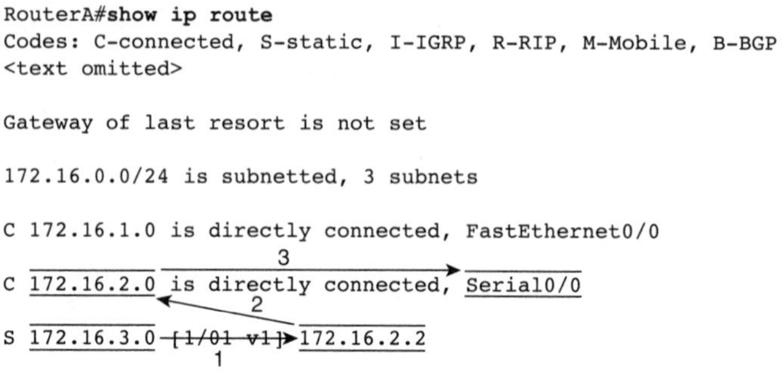

```
RouterA#show ip route
Codes: C-connected, S-static, I-IGRP, R-RIP, M-Mobile, B-BGP
<text omitted>

Gateway of last resort is not set

172.16.0.0/24 is subnetted, 3 subnets

C 172.16.1.0 is directly connected, FastEthernet0/0
                            3
C 172.16.2.0 is directly connected, Serial0/0
                    2
S 172.16.3.0 [1/01 v1] 172.16.2.2
                    1
```

One additional route lookup might not be much of a factor in the performance of the routing process. However, static routes, which take multiple recursive lookups to get resolved, could have an impact.

Static Route Optimization with Serial Networks

There are ways to avoid recursive table lookups, although there might be times when recursive table lookups are preferred and configured by the network administrator.

Most of the time, static routes over serial point-to-point networks can easily avoid recursive route lookups by using an exit interface instead of the intermediate or next-hop address. Example 5-6 shows an example of creating a static route on Router B for the Router A LAN, using an exit interface instead of an intermediate address.

Example 5-6 *A Static Route Is Configured by Specifying a Destination Network and a Next-Hop IP Address and/or a Local Interface*

```
RouterB(config)#ip route 172.16.1.0 255.255.255.0 serial0/0
05:05:30: RT: add 172.16.1.0/24 via 0.0.0.0, static metric [1/0]
RouterB(config)#
```

Examine how this route is installed in the routing table, as shown in Example 5-7.

Example 5-7 *The Static Route Uses a Local Exit Interface Instead of a Next-Hop IP Address*

```
RouterB#show ip route
Codes: C-connected,S-static,I-IGRP,R-RIP,M-moble,B-BGP
<text omitted>

Gateway of last resort is not set

     172.16.0.0/24 is subnetted, 3 subnets
S      172.16.1.0 is directly connected, Serial0/0
C      172.16.2.0 is directly connected, Serial0/0
C      172.16.3.0 is directly connected, FastEthernet0/0
C    192.16.2.0 is directly connected, Serial0/1
RouterB#
```

Instead of using an intermediate address, this route is resolved with the exit interface that was configured with the static **route** command, Serial0/0. The routing process, using this single entry, can forward any packets destined for the 172.16.1.0/24 network. No recursive route lookups are needed. Because only a single routing table lookup is needed, instead of multiple, recursive lookups, this type of static route increases the performance of the routing table process.

Notice that the routing table states that this static route is directly connected:

```
S 172.16.1.0 is directly connected, Serial0/0
```

In the case of a static route, "directly connected" means that the static route is configured with an exit interface. This does not mean that it is a directly connected network of an interface on the router. Like all static routes, the default administrative distance of this static route is still 1. Only directly connected interfaces, which have a code of C in the routing table, can have an administrative distance of 0. Although it is possible to modify the administrative distance of static and dynamic routes, they cannot be given the administrative distance of 0. Likewise, directly connected interfaces can only have an administrative distance of 0.

Static Route Optimization with Ethernet Networks

Configuring static routes without recursive lookups can also be done over multiaccess networks such as Ethernet. In this instance, using only an exit interface instead of an intermediate address causes a problem. Because the network is multiaccess, multiple devices, receivers, and so on probably are sharing this network.

Figure 5-5 shows a network between Router A and Router B that is a multiaccess Fast Ethernet link.

Figure 5-5 Ethernet Networks Are Multiaccess Networks

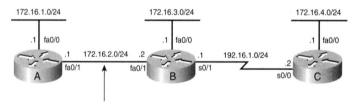

A static route using only an intermediate address could be configured. However, this would cause a recursive routing table lookup. Example 5-8 shows both the static **route** command and its installment in the routing table. When packets need to be routed for 172.16.1.0/14, the recursive route lookup happens first for the 172.16.1.0 network and then for the intermediate address, with a lookup of the 172.16.2.0 network.

Example 5-8 *The Static Route Uses a Next-Hop IP Address Instead of a Local Exit Interface*

```
RouterB(config)#ip route 172.16.1.0 255.255.255.0 172.16.2.1
RouterB(config)#end
RouterB#show ip route
Codes: C-connected,S-static,I-IGRP,R-RIP,M-moble,B-BGP
<text omitted>
```

Example 5-8 *The Static Route Uses a Next-Hop IP Address Instead of a Local Exit Interface (Continued)*

```
Gateway of last resort is not set


     172.16.0.0/24 is subnetted, 3 subnets
S      172.16.1.0 [1/0] via 172.16.2.1
C      172.16.2.0 is directly connected, FastEthernet0/1
C      172.16.3.0 is directly connected, FastEthernet0/0
C    192.16.1.0/24 is directly connected, Serial0/1
RouterB#
```

To avoid the recursive route lookup, the solution is to use both an intermediate address and an exit interface. Example 5-9 shows the recommended way to configure a static route in this case and the routing table entry. When using both the intermediate address and the exit interface, only a single lookup is needed in the routing table lookup process.

Example 5-9 *Ideally, Both the Local Exit Interface and a Next-Hop IP Address Are Used When Configuring a Static Route Via an Ethernet Network*

```
RouterB(config)#ip route 172.16.1.0 255.255.255.0 fastethernet 0/1 172.16.2.1
RouterB(config)#end
RouterB#show ip route
Codes: C-connected,S-static,I-IGRP,R-RIP,M-moble,B-BGP
<text omitted>


Gateway of last resort is not set


     172.16.0.0/24 is subnetted, 3 subnets
S      172.16.1.0 [1/0] via 172.16.2.1 FastEthernet 0/1
C      172.16.2.0 is directly connected, FastEthernet0/1
C      172.16.3.0 is directly connected, FastEthernet0/0
C    192.16.1.0/24 is directly connected, Serial0/1
RouterB#
```

The standard rule of thumb when configuring static routes is to use an exit interface over point-to-point and exit interfaces with the intermediate address over multiaccess networks. This avoids the recursive route lookups caused by static routing entries that contain only an intermediate address.

Recurring Static Route Installation and Deletion

The static routing process checks the routing table every minute to install or remove any static routes. There are circumstances in which this can lead to a recurrence of route installation and deletion.

An interesting but problematic condition can occur when the installation of a new static route affects the resolvability of its own intermediate address, as shown in Example 5-10.

Example 5-10 *A Flapping Route Results When a Static Route Specifies an Unresolvable Next-Hop IP Address*

```
RouterA#show ip route
Codes:C-connected,S-static,I-IGRP,R-RIP,M-moble,B-BGP
  D-EIGRP,EX-EIGRP external,O-OSPF,IA-OSPF interarea
  N1- OSPF NSSA external type 1,N2-OSPF NSSA external
type 2
  E1-OSPF external type 1, E2-OSPF external type 2,E-EGP
  1-IS-IS,L1-IS-IS level-1,L2-IS-IS level-2,ia-IS-IS inter area
  *-candidate default,U-per-user static route,o-ODR
  P-periodic download static route

Gateway of last resort is 0.0.0.0 to network 0.0.0.0

  1 72.16.0.0/24 is subnetted, 2 subnets
C    172.16.1.0 is directly connected, FastEthernet0/0
C    172,16.2.0 is directly connected, Serial0/0
    172.30.0.0/24 is subnetted, 1 subnets
C    172.30.3.0 is directly connected, Loopback2
S* 0.0.0.0/0 is directly connected,serial0/0
RouterA#
RouterA#debug ip routing
IP routing debugging is on
RouterA#configure terminal
Enter configuration commands,one per line.End with CNTL/Z.
RouterA(config)#ip route 20.1.0.0/16 via 20.2..0.2
04:58:32:RT:add 20.1.0.0/16 via 20.2.0.2,Static metric [1/0]
RouterA(config)#end
04:58:35: %SYS-5-CONFIG_I: Configured from console by console
RouterA#
```

Example 5-10 *A Flapping Route Results When a Static Route Specifies an Unresolvable Next-Hop IP Address (Continued)*

```
RouterA#show ip route
Codes:C-connected,S-static,I-IGRP,R-RIP,M-moble,B-BGP
  D-EIGRP,EX-EIGRP external,O-OSPF,IA-OSPF interarea
  N1- OSPF NSSA external type 1,N2-OSPF NSSA external
type 2
  E1-OSPF external type 1, E2-OSPF external type 2,E-EGP
  1-IS-IS,L1-IS-IS level-1,L2-IS-IS level-2,ia-IS-IS inter area
  *-candidate default,U-per-user static route,o-ODR
  P-periodic download static route


Gateway of last resort is 0.0.0.0 to network 0.0.0.0


   20.0.0.0/16 is subnetted, 1 subnets
S     20.1.0.0 [1/0] via 20.2.0.2
   172.30.0.0/24 is subnetted, 2 subnets
C     172.16.1.0 is directly connected, FastEthernet0/0
C     172,16.2.0 is directly connected, Serial0/0
   172.30.3.0/24 is subnetted, 1 subnets
C     172.30.3.0 is directly connected, Loopback2
S* 0.0.0.0/0 is directly connected,serial0/0
RouterA#
```

At first, the 20.1.0.0/16 route is installed in the routing table, and the intermediate address of 20.2.0.2 is resolved using the default route. However, the classful routing table lookup process does not allow a default route to resolve intermediate addresses. After 60 seconds, the next time the static route process is scheduled to run, it removes this route, as shown in Example 5-11. In another 60 seconds, the static route process installs the static route back into the routing table, again using the default route to resolve the intermediate address of 20.2.0.2. This process repeats, causing a flapping route.

Example 5-11 *Every 60 Seconds, the Static Route Is Added to or Removed from the Routing Table*

```
04:59:11:RT del 20.1.0.0/16 via 20.2.0.2, static metric [1/0]
04:59:11:RT delete subnet route to 20.1.0.0/16
04:59:11:RT delete network route to 20.0.0.0
RouterA#
RouterA#show ip route
```

continues

Example 5-11 *Every 60 Seconds, the Static Route Is Added to or Removed from the Routing Table (Continued)*

```
Codes:C-connected,S-static,I-IGRP,R-RIP,M-moble,B-BGP
  D-EIGRP,EX-EIGRP external,O-OSPF,IA-OSPF interarea
  N1- OSPF NSSA external type 1,N2-OSPF NSSA external
type 2
  E1-OSPF external type 1, E2-OSPF external type 2,E-EGP
  1-IS-IS,L1-IS-IS level-1,L2-IS-IS level-2,ia-IS-IS inter area
  *-candidate default,U-per-user static route,o-ODR
  P-periodic download static route


Gateway of last resort is 0.0.0.0 to network 0.0.0.0


   172.16.0.0/24 is subnetted, 2 subnets
C    172.16.1.0 is directly connected, FastEthernet0/0
C    172,16.2.0 is directly connected, Serial0/0
   172.30.0.0/24 is subnetted, 1 subnets
C    172.30.3.0 is directly connected, Loopback2
S* 0.0.0.0/0 is directly connected,serial0/0
RouterA#
RouterA#
05:00:11:RT: add 20.1.0.0/16 via 20.2.0.2, static metric [1/0]
RouterA#show ip route
Codes:C-connected,S-static,I-IGRP,R-RIP,M-moble,B-BGP
  D-EIGRP,EX-EIGRP external,O-OSPF,IA-OSPF interarea
  N1- OSPF NSSA external type 1,N2-OSPF NSSA external
type 2
  E1-OSPF external type 1, E2-OSPF external type 2,E-EGP
  1-IS-IS,L1-IS-IS level-1,L2-IS-IS level-2,ia-IS-IS inter area
  *-candidate default,U-per-user static route,o-ODR
  P-periodic download static route


Gateway of last resort is 0.0.0.0 to network 0.0.0.0


   20.0.0.0/16 is subnetted, 1 subnets
S    20.1.0.0 [1/0] via 20.2.0.2
   172.30.0.0/24 is subnetted, 2 subnets
C    172.16.1.0 is directly connected, FastEthernet0/0
```

Example 5-11 *Every 60 Seconds, the Static Route Is Added to or Removed from the Routing Table (Continued)*

```
C     172,16.2.0 is directly connected, Serial0/0
   172.30.3.0/24 is subnetted, 1 subnets
C     172.30.3.0 is directly connected, Loopback2
S* 0.0.0.0/0 is directly connected,serial0/0
RouterA#
```

This process of adding and deleting this static route is repeated every 60 seconds. Notice the times in the **debug** output shown in Example 5-12. This is also a demonstration of how the static route process is implemented every 60 seconds.

Example 5-12 *The Debug Timers Illustrate the 60-Second Intervals Between Addition and Deletion of the Static Route*

```
RouterA#
05:01:11:RT del 20.1.0.0/16 via 20.2.0.2, static metric [1/0]
05:01:11:RT delete subnet route to 20.1.0.0/16
05:01:11:RT delete network route to 20.0.0.0
RouterA#
05:02:12:RT add 20.1.0.0/16 via 20.2.0.2, static metric [1/0]
RouterA#
05:03:12:RT del 20.1.0.0/16 via 20.2.0.2, static metric [1/0]
05:03:12:RT delete subnet route to 20.1.0.0/16
05:03:12:RT delete network route to 20.0.0.0
RouterA#
05:04:12:RT add 20.1.0.0/16 via 20.2.0.2, static metric [1/0]
RouterA#
05:05:12:RT del 20.1.0.0/16 via 20.2.0.2, static metric [1/0]
05:05:12:RT delete subnet route to 20.1.0.0/16
05:05:12:RT delete network route to 20.0.0.0
RouterA#
05:06:12:RT add 20.1.0.0/16 via 20.2.0.2, static metric [1/0]
RouterA#
05:07:12:RT del 20.1.0.0/16 via 20.2.0.2, static metric [1/0]
05:07:12:RT delete subnet route to 20.1.0.0/16
05:07:12:RT delete network route to 20.0.0.0
```

continues

Example 5-12 *The Debug Timers Illustrate the 60-Second Intervals Between Addition and Deletion of the Static Route (Continued)*

```
RouterA#
05:08:12:RT add 20.1.0.0/16 via 20.2.0.2, static metric [1/0]
RouterA#
05:09:12:RT del 20.1.0.0/16 via 20.2.0.2, static metric [1/0]
05:09:12:RT delete subnet route to 20.1.0.0/16
05:09:12:RT delete network route to 20.0.0.0
RouterA#
05:10:12:RT add 20.1.0.0/16 via 20.2.0.2, static metric [1/0]
RouterA#
```

This situation can create even more instability if this route resolves other static routes. One solution is to always configure static routes to use exit interfaces instead of intermediate addresses wherever possible.

Using Discard Routes

Figure 5-6 shows an example of a typical customer network. The customer network is using a dynamic routing protocol to route the 172.16.0.0/24 and 192.168.1.0/24 traffic within its own network.

Figure 5-6 The Networks to Watch Are the Subnets of 172.16.0.0/16 and 192.168.1.0/24

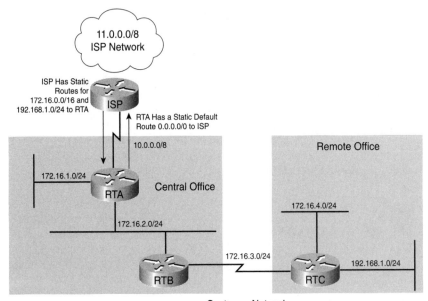

The customer network also includes the remote office with the 172.16.4.0/24 and 192.168.1.0/24 networks.

A 0.0.0.0/0 default route is configured on RTA, sending all default traffic to ISP. RTA propagates this default route to all other routers in the customer network via a dynamic routing protocol.

No dynamic routing protocol is being used between RTA, the customer network entrance router, and the ISP router. The ISP router has two static routes pointing to RTA for 172.16.0.0/16 and 192.168.1.0/24 networks.

All of the networks are up, and there is complete reachability throughout the network and with the ISP. However, the potential for a routing loop problem exists.

Figure 5-7 shows that the network between RTB and RTC fails. The remote office networks of 172.16.4.0/24 and 192.168.1.0/24 can no longer be reached from the central office. After the routing tables are updated, where will RTA or RTB forward packets destined for the 172.16.4.0 network?

Figure 5-7 Network 172.16.3.0/24 Fails

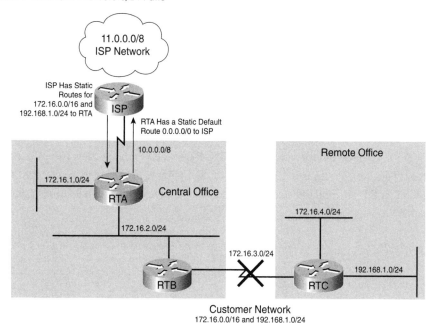

If the routers are configured for classless routing behavior, **ip classless**, RTB forwards all packets destined for 172.16.4.0/24 and 192.168.1.0/24 to RTA using the default 0.0.0.0/0 route. RTA also uses the default route to forward those packets to the ISP router. Example 5-13

shows an example of pings being rerouted from RTA to ISP after RTA has removed the 172.16.4.0/24 network from its routing table.

Example 5-13 *ICMP Packets Are Looping Between ISP and RouterA*

```
RTA#debug ip icmp

(Pings forwarded from RTA to RTB)

06:41:36: IP: s=172.16.2.1 (local),d=172.16.4.1(FastEthernet0/0),len
100,sending


<172.16.4.0/24 deleted from the routing table>


(Pings forwarded from RTA to ISP)

06:42:05: IP: s=10.0.0.2 (local),d=172.16.4.1
(Serial0/0),len 100,sending

06:42:05: IP: s=10.0.0.2 (Serial0/0),d=172.16.4.1
(Serial0/0),len 100,rcvs local pkt.

06:42:07: IP: s=10.0.0.2 (local),d=172.16.4.1
(Serial0/0),len 100,sending

06:42:07: IP: s=10.0.0.2 (Serial0/0),d=172.16.4.1
(Serial0/0),len 100,rcvd local pkt.
```

What does the ISP router do with these packets for 172.16.4.1? Because the ISP router has a static route for the 172.16.0.0/16 network, forwarding traffic to RTA, ISP sends packets destined for the 172.16.4.0/24 network back to RTA. RTA receives the packets from ISP and forwards them back to ISP, still using its default route. Example 5-14 shows the effect of this routing loop on RTA's serial interface as it sends and receives packets on the link it shares with the ISP.

Example 5-14 *The Effect of the Routing Loop Can Be Seen by Periodically Viewing the Counters on the Serial Interface on Router A*

```
RouterA#clear counters serial0/0
Clear "show interface" counters on this interface
[confim]


RouterA#show inter serial0/0
Serial0/0 is up, line protocol is up
  Hardware is PowerQUICC Serial
  Internet address is 10.0.0.2/8
```

Example 5-14 *The Effect of the Routing Loop Can Be Seen by Periodically Viewing the Counters on the Serial Interface on Router A (Continued)*

```
   MTU 1500 bytes, BW 1544 Kbit, DLY 20000 usec,
     reliability 255/255, txload 1/255, rxload 1/255
   Ecapsulation HDLC, loopback not set
   Keepalive set (10 sec)
   Last input 00:00:02,output 00:00:03,output hang never
   Last clearing of "show interface" counters 00:00:05
   Input queue :0/75/0/0 (size/mas/drops/flushes); Total output drops: 0
   Queueing strategy: fifo
   Output queue :0/40 (size/max)
   5 minute input rate 0 bits/sec, 0 packets/sec
   5 minute output rate 0 bits/sec, 0 packets/sec
     1 packets input, 24 bytes, 0 no buffer
     Receives I broadcast, 0 runts, 0 giants, 0 throttles
     O input errors, 0 CRC, 0 frame, 0 overrun, 0 ignored,
     0 abort
     1 packets output, 24 bytes, 0 underruns
     0 output errors, 0 collisions, 0 interface resets
     0 output buffer failers, 0 output buffers swapped out
     0 carrier transitions
     DCD=up DSR=up DTR=up RTS=up CTS=up
RouterA#
<short time later>

RouterA#show inter serial0/0
Serial0/0 is up, Line protocol is up
   Hardware is PowerQUIC Serial
   Internet address is 10.0.0.2/8
   MTU 1500 bytes, BW 1544 Kbit, DLY 20000 useec, reliability 255/255,
       txload 10/255, rxload 10/255
   Encapsulation HDLC, loopback not set
   Keepalive set(10 sec)
   Last input 00:00:06, output 00:00:00, output hang never
   Last clearing of "show interface" counters 00:07:20
   Input queue: 0/75/0/0 (size/max/drops/flushes); Total output drops: 118
```

continues

Example 5-14 *The Effect of the Routing Loop Can Be Seen by Periodically Viewing the Counters on the Serial Interface on Router A (Continued)*

```
   Queuing strategy: fifo
   Output queue: 40/40 (size/max)
   5 minute input rate 62000 bits/sec, 5 packets/sec
   5 minute output rate 63000 bits/sec, 5 packets/sec
      1865 packets input, 2731335 bytes, 0 no buffer
      Received 51 broadcasts, 0 runts, 0 giants, 0 throttles
      1878 packts output, 2755747 bytes, 0 underruns
      0 output errors, 0 collisions, 0 interface resets
      0 output buffer failers, 0 output buffers swapped out
      0 carrier transitions
      DCD=up DSR=up DTR=up RTS=up CTS=up
RouterA#
```

This problem has created a black hole in the network, with a routing loop between RTA and ISP. The packets eventually are dropped as soon as the time-to-live (TTL) field in the IP headers gets decremented to 0.

Solution 1: Classful mode routing (no ip classless)—One solution is to change the routing behavior from classless to classful using the command **no ip classless** on all the customer network routers. Classful routing would cause a router searching its routing table for a best match for 172.16.4.0 to drop the packets if there are routes for other 172.16.0.0/24 subnets but not for 172.16.4.0/24.

With the **no ip classless** command, the router does not use any supernet or default routes when at least one known subnet exists. RTA and RTB drop the packets for 172.16.4.0.

This is usually not the preferred solution, because it changes the routing table lookup behavior for all packets. Packets destined for a discontiguous subnet that rely on a supernet or default route to be forwarded are also dropped, unless that route is specifically in the routing table.

In addition, this does not solve the problem for packets destined for the 192.168.1.0/24 network. Even with using the **no ip classless** command, all packets destined for 192.168.1.0/24 still are caught in a routing loop between RTA and ISP.

In any case, modifying the route lookup process with **no ip classless** is not always an ideal solution, because it might have unforeseen effects on the routing behavior in the network.

Solution 2: Use a discard route—A more elegant and scalable solution is to use a discard route. A *discard route* sends packets to null0, the bit bucket, when the routing table has no specific match and it is undesirable to have those packets forwarded using a supernet or default route.

Example 5-15 shows an example of a discard route for RTA. This route causes RTA to drop all packets for subnets in the 172.16.0.0 network that do not have a specific route in the routing table. Using the failed route example and still using classless routing (**ip classless**), any 172.16.0.0 packets not matching 172.16.1.0/24, 172.16.2.0/24, 172.16.3.0/24, or 172.16.4.0/24 would be routed to null0 using the discard route. RTA would drop these packets instead of forwarding them to ISP.

Example 5-15 *A Discard Route Can Be a Very Useful Tool in Affecting Routing Behavior*

```
Discard Route on RTA:
RouterA(config)#ip route 172.16.0.0 255.255.0.0 null0

RouterA#show ip route
Codes: C-connected,S-static,I-IGRP, R-RIP,M-moble,B-BGP
       D-EIGRP,EX-EIGRP external,O-OSPF,IA-OSPF interarea
       N1- OSPF NSSA external type 1,N2-OSPF NSSA external type 2
       E1-OSPF external type 1, E2-OSPF external type 2,E-EGP
       1-IS-IS,L1-IS-IS level-1,L2-IS-IS level-2,ia-IS-IS inter area
       *-candidate default,U-per-user static route,o-ODR
       P-periodic download static route

Gateway of last resort is 0.0.0.0 to network 0.0.0.0

     172.16.0.0/16 is variably subnetted, 5 subnets, 2 masks
R       172.16.4.0/24 [120/2] via 172.16.2.2, 00:00:19,
        FastEthernet0/0
S       172.16.0.0/16 is directly connected, Null0
C       172.16.1.0/24 is directly connected, Loopback1
C       172.16.2.0/24 is directly connected, FastEthernet0/0
R       172.16.3.0/24 [120/1] via 172.16.2.2, 00:00:19, FastEthernet0/0
C    10.0.0.0/8 is directly connected, Serial0/0
R    192.168.1.0/24 [120/2] via 172.16.2.2, 00:00:00, FastEthernet0/0
S*   0.0.0.0/0 is directly connected, Serial0/0
RouterA#
```

The discard route also keeps traffic with the wrong IP addresses from finding this black hole in the network. Any packets that are incorrectly sent to nonexistent 172.16.0.0/16 subnets, such as the 172.16.5.0/24 subnet, also are dropped by the RTA discard route.

For any packets destined for the 192.168.1.0/24 network from RTA or RTB, using classful mode routing, the **no ip classless** command, would not help. Because this network is not a subnet of a parent network in the routing tables of RTA or RTB, the default route would be used whether or not classful mode routing is used. As soon as 192.168.1.0/24 could no longer be reached, this route would be removed from the routing tables of RTA and RTB. RTA would eventually forward all packets to ISP. Again, the ISP would send these packets back to RTA, causing another black hole.

The solution is to configure another discard route that is used only if the primary route fails, as shown in Example 5-16. This can be done by modifying the default administrative distance of the static route to a value higher than the administrative distance of the dynamic routing protocol being used. It is even better to use an administrative distance value greater than any IGP routing protocol, so it will not matter which routing protocol is used. In many cases, the networks can be summarized within a single supernet covering the entire range of the network without including those routes outside the network:

```
RTA(config)#ip route 192.168.1.0 255.255.255.0 null0 200
```

The discard route enters the routing table only for RTA, when the dynamic route to 192.168.1.0/24 is removed. Example 5-16 shows how the discard route is installed in the routing table, only after the dynamic route is removed because the link between RTB and RTC went down.

Example 5-16 *Sometimes It Is Useful to Specify an Administrative Distance for a Discard Route*

```
RouterA#debug ip routing
IP routing debugging is on
RouterA#configure terminal
Einter configuration command, one per line. End with CNTL/Z.
RouterA(config)#ip route 192.168.1.0 255.255.255.0 null0 200
RouterA(config)#end
RouterA#show ip route
Codes: C-connected,S-static,I-IGRP, R-RIP,M-moble, B-BGP
       D-EIGRP,EX-EIGRP external,O-OSPF,IA-OSPF interarea
       N1- OSPF NSSA external type 1,N2-OSPF NSSA external
       type 2, E1-OSPF external type 1, E2-OSPF external
       type 2, E-EGP, 1-IS-IS,L1-IS-IS level-1,L2-IS-IS
       level-2,ia-IS-IS inter area, *-candidate default,U-
       per-user static route,o-ODR, P-periodic download
       static route
```

Example 5-16 *Sometimes It Is Useful to Specify an Administrative Distance for a Discard Route (Continued)*

```
Gateway of last resort is 0.0.0.0 to network 0.0.0.0


     172.16.0.0/16 is variably subnetted, 5 subnets, 2 masks
R       172.16.4.0/24 [120/2] via 172.16.2.2, 00:00:19, FastEthernet0/0
S       172.16.0.0/16 is directly connected, Null0
C       172.16.1.0/24 is directly connected, Loopback1
C       172.16.2.0/24 is directly connected, FastEthernet0/0
R       172.16.3.0/24 [120/1] via 172.16.2.2, 00:00:19, FastEthernet0/0
C     10.0.0.0/8 is directly connected, Serial0/0
R     192.168.1.0/24 [120/2] via 172.16.2.2, 00:00:00, FastEthernet0/0
S*    0.0.0.0/0 is directly connected, Serial0/0
RouterA#
```

Discard routes can also be useful for blocking packets with private addresses (RFC 1918 address space) from being routed out of the network.

Common IGP Routing Protocol Issues, Causes, and Solutions

This section discusses several possible scenarios that can prevent routes from being installed in the routing table. These are some of the problems that are common to most routing protocols.

Introduction

If routes are not installed in the routing table, the router does not forward the packets to the missing destinations. It is possible that the packets could be incorrectly forwarded using a supernet or default route. This scenario was discussed in the section "Using Discard Routes."

Missing routes in the routing table create reachability problems. Users start complaining that they cannot reach a server or a printer. When you investigate this problem, one of the first things to look for is if the appropriate routers have a route for this destination in their routing tables.

Three possibilities exist for routes not being installed in the routing table:

- **Receiver problem**—The router is receiving the updates, but it is not installing the routes.
- **Intermediate media problem, Layer 2**—The sender sent the updates, but they were lost along the way and the receiver did not receive them.

- **Sender problem**—The sender is not advertising the routes, so the receiving side is not seeing the routes in the routing table.

Some of the common causes for routes not being installed in the routing table are

- Missing or incorrect **network** or **neighbor** statement
- Layer 1 or 2 is down
- Distribute list in/out blocking (sender/receiver)
- Access list blocking
- Advertised network interface is down
- Passive interface

Missing or Incorrect network or neighbor Statement

When you configure or modify a network, it might become apparent that a route is missing from the routing table. There can be many reasons for this. One of the obvious things to check is whether the **network** statement under router configuration has been properly configured.

For IGP routing protocols, the **network** statement does two things:

- It enables the routing protocol on interfaces with IP addresses that match the IP address in the **network** statement, giving the interface the capability to send and receive updates.
- It advertises that network in its own updates to other routers.

Figure 5-8 shows two routers running OSPF between them on an Ethernet LAN.

Figure 5-8 No Ethernet Adjacency Between OSPF Routers

The output of the **show ip ospf neighbor** command shows an empty list. In a normal working scenario, the output would display the OSPF adjacent neighbors.

With some protocols such as OSPF and EIGRP, the routing protocols can be enabled on a per-interface basis using wildcard masks. Careful configuration of the wildcard mask is important so that interfaces are not incorrectly included or incorrectly left out.

An obvious place to begin is by looking at the running configurations on both routers by using the **show running-config** command. Example 5-17 shows the configuration of Router R2. The configuration shows that the **network** statement exists, but a closer look reveals that the wrong wildcard mask is used. The **network** statement is determined in OSPF in exactly the same way that an access list would be defined. The main idea is to include the range of addresses in the area. The **network** statement of 131.108.0.0 with a wildcard mask of 0.0.0.255 does not cover 131.108.1.2. It covers only the range from 131.108.0.0 to 131.108.0.255, as indicated by the wildcard mask.

Example 5-17 *The Inverse Mask Used in the* **network** *Statement Does Not Include the IP Address of Interface E0 on R2*

```
R2#
Interface Loopback0
ip address 131.108.0.1 255.255.255.0
!
interface Ethernet0
!
ip address 131.108.1.2 255.255.255.0
!
router ospf 1
network 131.108.0.0 0.0.0.255 area 0
!
```

Example 5-18 shows the output of the **show ip ospf interface** command. OSPF is not enabled on the Ethernet 0 interface of Router R2.

Example 5-18 *The* **show ip ospf interface** *Command Can Be Used to Determine Whether OSPF Is Enabled on a Particular Interface*

```
R2#show ip ospf interface Ethernet 0
Ethernet0 is up, line protocol is up
  OSPF not enabled on this interface
```

Depending on the routing protocol, several other commands can help you troubleshoot this issue. The **show ip protocols** command shows you which networks originate from this router. The **debug** command can be used to verify whether the routing update is being sent or received, or if there are any mismatched timers, subnet masks, and so on:

- **debug ip rip**
- **debug ip igrp events**

- **debug ip igrp transactions**
- **debug ip eigrp**
- **debug ip ospf events**

The obvious solution is to correctly configure the **network** statements to enable the routing protocol on the appropriate interfaces. In regard to OSPF, there is a rare case in which the configuration shows the correct mask, and the OSPF neighbor list still appears empty. During network configuration under OSPF, a cut and paste of the OSPF configuration might create this problem. Therefore, it is always best to look at the output of **show ip ospf interface** for that specific interface and confirm whether OSPF is enabled on that interface. This specific problem can be corrected by reentering the **network** statement.

Example 5-19 shows the new configuration that fixes the OSPF network problem. In this example, the wildcard mask is 0.0.255.255, which means that it covers the range from 131.108.0.0 to 131.108.255.255.

Example 5-19 *The Wildcard Mask Is Corrected in the OSPF* **network** *Statement*

```
R2(config)#router ospf 1
R2(config)#network 131.108.0.0 0.0.255.255 area 0
```

Example 5-20 shows the output of **show ip ospf neighbor** after the correct network mask is applied. Beginning with Cisco IOS 12.0, the output of **show ip ospf interface** does not display anything if OSPF is not enabled on the interface.

Example 5-20 *The Adjacency Between R1 and R2 Is Active*

```
R2#show ip ospf neighbor

Neighbor     ID  Pri State Dead Time  Address   Interface
131.108.2.1  1   FULL/DR   00:00:38 131.108.1.1 Ethernet0
```

Commands used in this example and some of the commands that can be used for other routing protocols include

- **show ip protocols**
- **show ip interface**
- **show ip interface brief**
- **show ip eigrp interfaces**

- **show ip eigrp neighbors**
- **show ip ospf interface**
- **debug ip routing**
- **debug ip rip**
- **debug ip igrp events**
- **debug ip igrp transactions**
- **debug ip eigrp**
- **debug ip ospf events**
- **debug isis adj packets**
- **debug isis update-packets**

Layer 1 or 2 Is Down

One of the causes of routes not being installed in the routing table is that Layer 1 or Layer 2 is down. If this is the case, it is not a routing protocol problem. Layer 1 or 2 could be down for several reasons. The following is a list of the most common things to check if an interface or line protocol is down:

- Unplugged cable
- Loose cable
- Bad cable
- Bad transceiver
- Bad port
- Bad interface card
- Layer 2 problem at the telco in the case of a WAN link
- Missing **clockrate** statement in the case of a back-to-back serial connection
- Router down at the remote site

Figure 5-9 shows two routers running OSPF between them.

Figure 5-9 *Two OSPF Routers Are Connected Via Ethernet*

Example 5-21 shows the output of the **show ip ospf interface** command for Ethernet 0, which shows that the line protocol is down.

Example 5-21 *The* **show ip ospf interface** *Command Indicates That the Line Protocol Is Down on E0*

```
R2#show ip ospf interface Ethernet 0
Ethernet0 is up, line protocol is down
Internet Address 131.108.1.2/24, Area 0
Process ID 1, Router ID 131.108.1.2, Network Type BROADCAST, Cost: 10
Transmit Delay is 1 sec, State DOWN, Priority 1
No designated router on this network
No backup designated router on this network
Timer intervals configured, Hello 10, Dead 40, Wait 40, Retransmit 5
```

Example 5-22 shows the output of the **debug ip igrp transactions** command. The output shows that the router is not sending or receiving any IGRP updates because Layer 2 is down.

Example 5-22 *A Debug Shows That No IGRP Updates Are Being Sent or Received*

```
R2#debug ip igrp events
IGRP event debugging is on
R2#debug ip igrp transaction
IGRP protocol debugging is on


R2#show debug
IP routing:
IGRP protocol debugging is on
IGRP event debugging is on
```

To correct this problem, you must fix the Layer 2 problem by checking the previously mentioned conditions. The solution could be as simple as plugging in a cable, or it could be as complex as bad hardware, in which case the hardware must be replaced.

Example 5-23 shows the output of the **show ip ospf interface** command for Ethernet 0 after the Layer 2 problem is corrected.

Example 5-23 *The* **show ip ospf interface** *Command Shows That the Line Protocol Is Up on E0 After the Problem Is Corrected*

```
R2#show ip ospf interface Ethernet 0
Ethernet0 is up, line protocol is up
Internet Address 131.108.1.2/24, Area 4
Process ID 1, Router ID 131.108.1.2, Network Type BROADCAST, Cost: 10
Transmit Delay is 1 sec, State BDR, Priority 1
Designated Router (ID) 131.108.2.1, Interface address 131.108.1.1
Backup Designated router(ID) 131.108.1.2, Interface address 131.108.1.2
Timer intervals configured, Hello 10, Dead 40, Wait 40, Retransmit 5
 Hello due in 00:00:07
Neighbor Count is 1, Adjacent neighbor count is 1
 Adjacent with neighbor 131.108.1.1 (Designated Router)
Suppress hello for 0 neighbor(s)
```

Commands used in this example and some of the commands that can be used for other routing protocols include

- **show ip interface**
- **show ip interface brief**
- **show ip eigrp interfaces**
- **show ip ospf interface**
- **debug ip routing**
- **debug ip rip**
- **debug ip igrp transactions**
- **debug ip eigrp**
- **debug isis adj packets**
- **debug isis update-packets**

Distribute List In/Out Blocking

A distribute list is a filtering mechanism for routing updates. Distribute lists are not supported for OSPF or IS-IS. Routers running link-state protocols determine their routes based on information in their link-state database, rather than from the advertised route entries received from their neighbors.

Route filters have no effect on link-state advertisements or the link-state database. This is because a basic requirement of link-state routing protocols is that routers in an area must have identical link-state databases.

In addition, it is important to remember that distribute lists do not permit or deny the actual packets from entering the routers; they only specify which routing updates a router sends or receives. A distribute list calls on an access list and checks which networks are supposed to be permitted. If the access list does not contain the network, it is automatically denied. A distribute list can be applied on incoming or outgoing routing updates.

Figure 5-10 shows two routers running IGRP between them. A **distribute-list 1 in** is configured, as shown in Example 5-24, but because the access list does not contain the **permit** statement for 131.108.0.0, Router R2 does not install this route in the routing table.

Figure 5-10 IGRP Is Running Between the Two Routers

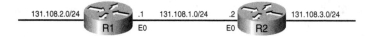

Example 5-24 *R2 Access List Configuration Does Not Permit 131.108.0.0*

```
interface Loopback0
ip address 131.108.3.2 255.255.255.0
!
interface Ethernet0
ip address 131.108.1.2 255.255.255.0
!
router igrp 1
network 131.108.0.0
distribute-list 1 in
!
access-list 1 permit 131.107.0.0 0.0.255.255
```

In the access list configuration, the network 131.108.0.0 is not explicitly permitted (and therefore is denied), so the router does not install any subnets of the 131.108.0.0 network. In this case, the access list was incorrectly configured with the wrong network, 131.107.0.0.

Example 5-25 shows the new configuration of Router R2 with the correct access list.

Example 5-25 *The Access List Associated with the Distribute List Is Corrected*

```
interface Loopback0
ip address 131.108.3.2 255.255.255.0
!
interface Ethernet0
ip address 131.108.1.2 255.255.255.0
!
router igrp 1
network 131.108.0.0
distribute-list 1 in
!
no access-list 1 permit 131.107.0.0 0.0.255.255
access-list 1 permit 131.108.0.0 0.0.255.255
```

Example 5-26 shows that Router R2 is learning IGRP routes after the configuration change.

Example 5-26 *R2 Is Now Learning the IGRP Routes*

```
R2#show ip route 131.108.2.0
Routing entry for 131.108.2.0/24
  Known via "igrp 1", distance 100, metric 8976
  Redistributing via igrp 1
  Advertised by igrp 1 (self originated)
  Last update from 131.108.1.1 on Ethernet0, 00:00:12 ago
  Routing Descriptor Blocks:
  131.108.1.1, from 131.108.1.1, 00:00:12 ago, via Ethernet0
  Route metric is 8976, traffic share count is 1
  Total delay is 25000 microseconds, minimum bandwidth is 1544 Kbit
  Reliability 255/255, minimum MTU 1500 bytes
  Loading 1/255, Hops 0
```

Access List Blocking

Standard access lists are used to filter traffic based on the source address. Extended access lists are used to filter traffic based on the source or destination address. These access lists can be applied on the interface with the interface-level command, **ip access-group** {*access-list number*} {**in** | **out**}, to filter the incoming or outgoing traffic.

When the access list is applied, make sure that it does not block the source address of the routing update. For routing protocols that form adjacencies, make sure that it does not block the Hello packets from being sent or received.

It is very common to implement an access list for security measures at the interface level. In the case of routing protocols such as OSPF that use multicasts to exchange Hellos, be sure to permit the multicast Hello addresses in the access list. Otherwise, the access list might block the OSPF multicast address unknowingly and prevent OSPF from forming neighbors on that interface.

This situation happens only when the access list is blocking Hellos on both routers. If only one side is blocking OSPF Hellos, the output of **show ip ospf neighbor** indicates that the neighbor is stuck in INIT state.

Figure 5-11 shows two routers running OSPF between them.

Figure 5-11 OSPF Is Running Between the Two Routers

Example 5-27 shows the OSPF configuration of routers R1 and R2. The access list permits only incoming TCP and UDP traffic. The inbound access list checks only traffic coming in on that interface. Because there is an implicit **deny** at the end of each access list, this access list blocks the OSPF multicast address of 224.0.0.5. The **access list 101 in** command is defined for debugging purposes only.

Example 5-27 *Incoming TCP and UDP Traffic Is Permitted on Interface E0*

```
R1#
interface Ethernet0
ip address 131.108.1.1 255.255.255.0
ip access-group 100 in
!
access-list 100 permit tcp any any
access-list 100 permit udp any any

access-list 101 permit ip 131.108.1.0 0.0.0.255 host 224.0.0.5

R2#
interface Ethernet0
```

Example 5-27 *Incoming TCP and UDP Traffic Is Permitted on Interface E0 (Continued)*

```
ip address 131.108.1.2 255.255.255.0
ip access-group 100 in
!
access-list 100 permit tcp any any
access-list 100 permit udp any any

access-list 101 permit ip 131.108.1.0 0.0.0.255 host 224.0.0.5
```

Example 5-28 shows the output of the **debug ip packet 101 detail** command. This **debug** tracks down the OSPF Hello packet only on the Ethernet segment. This **debug** shows that the OSPF Hello packet from Router R1 is denied on R2. This is because OSPF packets are carried directly over IP and do not include a TCP or UDP header.

Example 5-28 *OSPF Hello Packets Are Denied Because They Do Not Include TCP or UDP Headers*

```
R2#debug ip packet 101 detail
IP packet debugging is on (detailed) for access list 101
IP: s=131.108.1.2 (Ethernet0), d=244.0.0.5, len 68, access denied, proto=89
```

To correct this problem, the access list must be reconfigured to permit OSPF multicast Hellos. Example 5-29 shows the configuration that fixes this problem. In this configuration, OSPF multicast Hellos are permitted.

Example 5-29 *The Access List Is Patched to Allow OSPF Hello Packets*

```
interface Ethernet0
ip address 131.108.1.2 255.255.255.0
ip access-group 100 in
!
access-list 100 permit tcp any any
access-list 100 permit udp any any
access-list 100 permit ip any host 244.0.0.5
```

Similarly, the access list on the other side needs to be changed, making sure that the OSPF Hellos are permitted in the access list. Example 5-30 shows the OSPF neighbor in FULL state after the configuration is fixed.

Example 5-30 *The OSPF Adjacency Is Now Active*

```
R2#show ip ospf neighbor


Neighbor ID  Pri  State      Dead Time    Address      Interface
131.108.2.1  1    FULL/DR    00:00:37     131.108.1.1  Ethernet0
```

Commands used in this example and some of the commands that can be used for other routing protocols include

- **show ip eigrp neighbors**
- **show ip ospf neighbor**
- **debug ip packet**

Advertised Network Interface Is Down

IGP routing protocols do not advertise any interface network address that is physically down. As soon as the advertised network comes back up, the routing protocol starts advertising it again in its updates.

Figure 5-12 shows two routers running RIP between them.

Figure 5-12 *RIP Is Running Between the Two Routers*

131.108.2.0/24   R1   E0   .1   131.108.1.0/24   .2   E0   R2   131.108.3.0/24

Example 5-31 shows that interface Ethernet 0 is down.

Example 5-31 *The Line Protocol Is Down on Interface Ethernet 0*

```
R2#show interface Ethernet 0
Ethernet0 is up, line protocol is down
Hardware is Lance, address is 0000.0c70.d31e (bia 0000.0c70.d31e)
Internet address is 131.108.1.2/24
```

Example 5-32 shows the output from the **debug ip rip** command. In this **debug**, Router R1 is not sending or receiving any RIP updates, because Layer 2 is down. This **debug** command has no output because of this problem.

Example 5-32 *RIP Updates Are Not Being Sent or Received*

```
R2#debug ip rip
RIP protocol debugging is on
R2#
```

RIP, like other routing protocols, runs above Layer 2. RIP cannot send or receive any routes if Layer 2 is down. To correct this problem, Layer 2 or Layer 1 must be corrected.

Example 5-33 shows the interface Ethernet 0 after the Layer 2 problem is fixed.

Example 5-33 *The Layer 2 Issue Is Resolved, and the Line Protocol on Interface E0 Is Up*

```
R1#show interface Ethernet 0
Ethernet0 is up, line protocol is up
Hardware is Lance, address is 0000.0c70.d31e (bia 0000.0c70.d31e)
Inernet address is 131.108.1.1/24
```

Example 5-34 shows the routing table of Router R2.

Example 5-34 *RIP Updates Are Now Being Sent and Received*

```
R2#show ip route 131.108.2.0
Routing entry for 131.108.2.0/24
  Known via "rip", distance 120, metric 1
  Redistributing via rip
  Last update from 131.108.1.1 on Ethernet0, 00:00:07 ago
  Routing Descriptor Blocks:
  * 131.108.1.1 from 131.108.1.1, 00:00:07 ago, via
Ethernet0
      Route metric is 1, traffic share count is 1
```

Commands used in this example and some of the commands that can be used for other routing protocols include

- **show ip interface**
- **show ip interface brief**
- **show ip eigrp interfaces**
- **show ip ospf interface**
- **debug ip routing**
- **debug ip rip**

- **debug ip igrp transactions**
- **debug ip eigrp**
- **debug isis adj packets**
- **debug isis update-packets**

Passive Interface

The **passive-interface** command works differently with the different IP routing protocols that support it:

- **RIP/IGRP**—With RIP and IGRP, routing updates are received but are not sent.
- **EIGRP**—With EIGRP, the router stops sending Hello packets on passive interfaces. When this happens, EIGRP cannot form neighbor adjacencies on the interface, and routing updates can be neither sent nor received.
- **OSPF**—With OSPF, routing information is neither sent nor received on a passive interface. The network address of the passive interface appears as a stub network in the OSPF domain.

Figure 5-13 shows two routers running IGRP between them.

Figure 5-13 IGRP Is Running Between the Routers

When an interface is defined as passive under IGRP, IGRP receives updates on that interface but does not send any. The **passive-interface** command is used to avoid sending unnecessary updates to a neighbor that does not need to receive any IGRP updates, such as a small router at the edge. A simple default route is enough information for that router to talk to the outside world. It is important to use the **passive-interface** command only where needed. If you don't, undesired results might occur.

Example 5-35 shows the output of the **show ip protocols** command, which shows that the outgoing interface is defined as passive.

Example 5-35 *The* **show ip protocols** *Command Identifies the Passive Interfaces*

```
R1#show ip protocols
Routing Protocol is "IGRP 1"
Sending updates every 30 seconds, next due in 82 seconds
Invalid after 270 seconds, hold down 280, flushed after 630
```

Example 5-35 *The* **show ip protocols** *Command Identifies the Passive Interfaces (Continued)*

```
Outgoing update filter list for all interfaces is
Incoming update filter list for all interfaces is
Default networks flagged in outgoing updates
Default networks accepted from incoming updates
IGRP metric weight K1=1 K2=0, K3=1, K4=0, K5=0
IGRP maximum hopcount 100
IGRP maximum metric variance 1
Redistributing: igrp 1
Routing for Networks:
   131.108.0.0
Passive Interface(s):
   Ethernet0
Routing Information Sources:
   Gateway         Distance         Last Update
   131.108.1.2           100         00:00:09
Distance: (default is 100)
```

Example 5-36 shows the configuration of Router R1, which shows that the outgoing interface is defined as passive.

Example 5-36 *E0 Is Configured as a Passive Interface for IGRP*

```
R1(config)#router igrp 1
R1(config-router)#network 131.108.0.0
R1(config-router)#passive-interface Ethernet 0
```

Examples 5-35 and 5-36 confirm that interface Ethernet 0 is defined as passive, so Router R1 is not sending any updates on Ethernet 0. Sometimes it is desirable for some networks to be advertised and others to be filtered. In this situation, **distribute-list out** would be a better solution.

In this example, the assumption is that the **passive-interface** was configured by mistake, so this command needs to be removed to solve this problem. Example 5-37 shows the new configuration to solve this problem.

Example 5-37 *The Passive Interface Is Removed for Interface E0*

```
R1(config)#router igrp 1
R1(config-router)#network 131.108.0.0
R1(config-router)#no passive-interface Ethernet 0
```

Example 5-38 shows the routing table entry on Router R2 after the problem is fixed.

Example 5-38 *Without the Passive Interface Configured on R1, the Routing Updates Are Received on R2*

```
R2#show ip route 131.108.2.0
Routing entry for 131.108.2.0/24
Known via "igrp 1", distance 100, metric 8976
Redistributing via igrp 1
Advertised by igrp 1 (self originated)
Last update from 131.108.1.1 on Ethernet0, 00:00:12 ago
Routing Descriptor Blocks:
* 131.108.1.1. from 131.108.1.1, 00:00:12 ago, via Ethernet0
Route metric is 8976, traffic share count is 1
Total delay is 25000 microseconds, minimum bandwidth is 1544 Kbit
Reliability 255/255, minimum MTU 1500 bytes
Loading 1/255, Hops 0
```

Commands used in this example and some of the commands that can be used for other routing protocols include

- **show ip protocols**
- **debug ip routing**
- **debug ip rip**
- **debug ip igrp transactions**
- **debug ip eigrp**
- **debug isis adj packets**
- **debug isis update-packets**

Troubleshooting RIP

The next six sections focus on troubleshooting specific routing protocols. This section explores common issues with troubleshooting RIP.

Incompatible RIP Version Types

When RIP is configured on a router, by default the software receives RIP Version 1 (RIPv1) and RIP Version 2 (RIPv2) packets but sends only RIPv1 packets. To send and receive only RIPv1 packets, the router must be configured with the command **version 1** under **router rip**. To send and receive only RIPv2 packets, the router must be configured with the command **version 2** under **router rip**. When the **version** command is used, by default, updates from other routers sending other than the specified version are ignored.

Figure 5-14 shows two routers running RIP between them.

Figure 5-14 RIP Is Running Between the Two Routers

Example 5-39 shows the configuration of Router R2. In this configuration, RIP is configured to send and receive only Version 1 packets. The default RIP configuration, without the **version 1** command, allows the router to receive both Version 1 and 2 packets.

Example 5-39 *RIPv1 Is Configured on R2*

```
R2#
interface Loopback0
ip address 131.108.3.2 255.255.255.0
!
interface Ethernet0
ip address 131.108.1.2 255.255.255.0
!
router rip
version 1
network 131.108.0.0
!
```

Example 5-40 shows the output of the **debug ip rip** command. This command reveals that Router R2 is receiving a RIP packet from Router R1, which is configured to send Version 2 updates.

Example 5-40 *R2 Ignores RIPv2 Packets from R1*

```
R2#debug ip rip
RIP protocol debugging is on
RIP: ignored v2 packet from 131.108.1.1 (illegal version)
```

Example 5-41 shows the output of the **show ip protocols** command, which indicates that the Ethernet 0 interface is sending and receiving RIPv1 packets. This means that if a Version 2 packet is received on Ethernet 0 of R2, it is ignored because the interface can send and receive only Version 1 packets.

Example 5-41 *The **show ip protocols** Command Is Very Useful for Viewing the Versions of RIP Packets Sent and Received on an Interface*

```
R2#show ip protocols

Routing Protocol is "rip"
Sending updates every 30 seconds, next due in 9 seconds
Invalid after 180 seconds, hold down 180, flushed after 240
Outgoing update filter list for all interfaces is
Incoming update filter list for all interfaces is
Redistributing: rip
Default version control: send version 1, receive version 1
Interface       Send  Recv   Key-chain
Ethernet0        1     1
Loopback0        1     1
 Routing for Networks:
131.108.0.0
Routing Information Sources:
Gateway         Distance      Last Update
131.108.1.1          120      00:01:34
Distance:  (default is 120)
R2#
```

Example 5-42 shows the configuration of Router R1. This shows that the sender R1 is configured to send and receive only Version 2 packets.

Example 5-42 *Specifying Version 2 Under RIP Results in Only RIPv2 Packets Being Sent and Received*

```
R1(config)#router rip
R1(config-router)#version 2
R1(config-router)#network 131.108.0.0
```

Example 5-43 shows the output of the **show ip protocols** command, which shows that sender R1 is sending and receiving only Version 2 packets. This is because of the **version 2** command that is configured under router RIP.

Example 5-43 *The* **show ip protocols** *Command Reveals That Only RIPv2 Packets Are Being Sent and Received*

```
R1#show ip protocols
Routing Protocol is "rip"
Sending updates every 30 seconds, next due in 13 seconds
Invalid after 180 seconds, hold down 180, flushed after 240
Outgoing update filter list for all interfaces is
Incoming update filter list for all interfaces is
Redistributing: rip
Default version control: send version 2, receive version 2
Interface        Send  Recv   Key-chain
Ethernet0         2     2
Loopback0         2     2
 Routing for Networks:
131.108.0.0
Routing Information Sources:
Gateway          Distance       Last Update
131.108.1.2          120        00:04:09
Distance:   (default is 120)
```

An obvious solution is to configure all routers to run RIPv2. However, there might be times when this is not possible, and some routers can run only RIPv1. Therefore, another solution is to configure the appropriate interfaces to send and receive the appropriate RIPv1 or RIPv2 packets.

If the receiver, R2, is configured to receive only RIPv1 packets, it ignores the RIPv2 updates. Router R1 must be configured on the sender side so that it will send both Version 1 and Version 2 packets. When R2 receives the Version 1 packet, it installs the routes in the routing table. R2 ignores RIPv2 packets, because it is configured for RIPv1.

Example 5-44 shows the new configuration for R1. In this configuration the sender, the R1 Ethernet 0 interface, is configured to send and receive both RIPv1 and RIPv2 packets.

Example 5-44 *The Particular Versions of RIP Packets That Are Sent and Received Can Be Prescribed at the Interface Level*

```
R1#
interface Loopback0
ip address 131.108.2.1 255.255.255.0
!
interface Ethernet0
ip address 131.108.1.1 255.255.255.0
ip rip send version 1 2
ip rip receive version 1 2
!
router rip
version 2
network 131.108.0.0
```

Example 5-45 shows the output of **show ip protocols**, which indicates that the Ethernet 0 interface is sending and receiving Version 1 and Version 2 packets. The advantage of sending both Version 1 and Version 2 updates is that, if any devices on this Ethernet segment are running Version 1 only or Version 2 only, those devices can communicate with Router R1 on this Ethernet segment.

Example 5-45 *The* **show ip protocols** *Command Reveals What Types of RIP Packets Are Sent and Received on Each Interface*

```
R1#show ip protocols
Routing Protocol is "rip"
Sending updates every 30 seconds, next due in 4 seconds
Invalid after 180 seconds, hold down 180, flushed after 240
Outgoing update filter list for all interfaces is
Incoming update filter list for all interfaces is
Redistributing: rip
Default version control: send version 2, receive version 2
Interface        Send  Recv   Key-chain
Ethernet0         1 2   1 2
Loopback0          2     2
 Routing for Networks:
```

Example 5-45 *The* **show ip protocols** *Command Reveals What Types of RIP Packets Are Sent and Received on Each Interface (Continued)*

```
131.108.0.0
Routing Information Sources:
Gateway           Distance        Last Update
131.108.1.2            120        00:00:07
Distance:  (default is 120)
R1#
```

Example 5-46 shows the Router R2 routing table after the configuration change.

Example 5-46 *R2 Receives an Appropriately Versioned Update for 131.108.2.0/24*

```
R2#show ip route 131.108.2.0
routing entry for 131.108.2.0/24
Known via "rip", distance 120, metric 1
Redistributing via rip
Last update from 131.108.1.1 on Ethernet0, 00:00:07 ago
Routing Descriptor Blocks
* 131.108.1.1, from 131.108.1.1, 00:00:07 ago, via Ethernet0
Route metric is 1, traffic share count is 1
```

Mismatched Authentication Key

One of the options in RIPv2 is that RIPv2 updates can be authenticated for increased security. When authentication is used, a password must be configured on both sides. This password is called the authentication key. If this key does not match the key on the other side, the RIPv2 updates are ignored on both sides.

Figure 5-15 shows two routers running RIP between them.

Figure 5-15 R1 and R2 Are Running RIP Between Them

131.108.2.0/24 — R1 E0 .1 — 131.108.1.0/24 — .2 E0 R2 — 131.108.3.0/24

Example 5-47 shows the configurations of routers R1 and R2. In this configuration, a different RIP authentication key is configured on R1 and R2. The R2 Ethernet interface is configured with the key Cisco1, whereas R1 is configured with the key Cisco. These two keys do not match, so they ignore each other's updates, and the routes are not installed in the routing table.

Example 5-47 *The Configurations for R1 and R2 Include RIP Authentication*

```
R2#
interface Loopback0
ip address 131.108.3.2 255.255.255.0
!
interface Ethernet0
ip address 131.108.1.2 255.255.255.0
ip rip authentication key-chain cisco1
!
router rip
 version 2
 network 131.108.0.0
!
R1#
interface Loopback0
ip address 131.108.2.1 255.255.255.0
!
interface Ethernet0
ip address 131.108.1.1 255.255.255.0
ip rip authentication key-chain cisco
!
Router rip
 version 2
 network 131.108.0.0
!
```

Example 5-48 shows output from the **debug ip rip** command on Router R2 that indicates that
R2 is receiving a RIP packet that has invalid authentication. This means that the authentication
key between sender and receiver does not match.

Example 5-48 *A RIP Debug Reveals Authentication Failure, Which Normally Indicates a Configuration Error*

```
R2#debug ip rip
RIP protocol debugging is on
RIP: ignored v2 packet from 131.108.1.1 (invalid authentication)
```

When using authentication in RIP, make sure that the sender and receiver are configured with
the same authentication key. Sometimes, adding a space at the end of the key can cause the

invalid authentication problems, because a space is interpreted as a literal key entry. As a result, this causes a problem that cannot be corrected just by looking at the configurations.

Debugs show that there is a problem with the authentication key. To solve this problem, configure the same keys on both sender and receiver, or retype the authentication key, making sure that no space is added at the end.

Example 5-49 shows the new configuration to correct this problem. The authentication key is reconfigured on Router R2 to match the key on Router R1.

Example 5-49 *The Authentication Key on R2 Is Corrected*

```
R2#
interface Loopback0
ip address 131.108.3.2 255.255.255.0
!
interface Ethernet0
ip address 131.108.1.2 255.255.255.0
ip rip authentication key-chain cisco

!
router rip
version 2
network 131.108.0.0
!
```

Example 5-50 shows the routing table of R2 after the configuration change.

Example 5-50 *R2 Updates Its Routing Updates After Authentication Is Successful*

```
R2#show ip route 131.108.2.0
Routing entry for 131.108.2.0/24
Known via "rip", distance 120, metric 1
Redistributing via rip
Last update from 131.108.1.1 on Ethernet0, 00:00:07 ago
Routing Descriptor Blocks:
* 131.108.1.1, from 131.108.1.1, 00:00:07 ago, via Ethernet0
Route metric is 1, traffic share count is 1
```

Reaches RIP Hop Count Limit

The RIP metric maximum is 15 hops. If a network has more than 15 hops, RIP is an unsuitable protocol. Figure 5-16 shows a network that produces a RIP hop count limit problem. Router R2 is receiving an update for a RIP route that is more than 15 hops away. R2 does not install that route in the routing table, as shown in Example 5-51.

Figure 5-16 Hop Count Limits Must Be Taken into Account

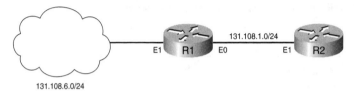

Example 5-51 *131.108.6.0/24 Is Not Installed in the Routing Table Because the Hop Count Limit Is Exceeded*

```
R2#show ip route 131.108.6.0
% subnet not in table
```

The most logical way to start troubleshooting this problem is to look at the routing table of the intermediary routers along the way (R1 in this example) and to determine whether they are receiving a route for the 131.108.6.0/24 network. Example 5-52 shows that Router R1 is receiving RIP routes for the 131.108.6.0/24 network.

Example 5-52 *R1 Is Installing the 131.108.6.0/24 Network Because the Hop Count Limit Is Not Exceeded*

```
R1#show ip route 131.108.6.0
Routing entry for 131.108.6.0/24
Known via "rip", distance 120, metric 15
```

Router R1 is receiving the route in question, but with a metric of 15. R1 adds 1 more to 15 when it advertises this route to R2, which results in an infinite metric, consequently preventing the route from being placed in the routing table.

To verify this, use the output of the **debug ip rip** command on R1, as shown in Example 5-53. The RIP update for the 131.108.6.0/24 network is sent with a metric of 16 out its Ethernet 1 interface toward Router R2.

Example 5-53 *The* **debug ip rip** *Command Reveals Hop Count Violations*

```
R1#debug ip rip
RIP protocol debugging is on
RIP: sending v2 update to 224.0.0.0 via Ethernet1
(131.108.1.1)
          131.108.6.0/24 -> 0.0.0.0, metric 16, tag 0
```

Example 5-54 shows the output of the **debug ip rip** command on Router R2. Router R2 receives this update and discards it, because the metric shows that this network has an infinite distance and, therefore, is unreachable.

Example 5-54 *The 131.108.6.0/24 Network Is Marked Inaccessible*

```
R2#debug ip rip
RIP protocol debugging is on
RIP: received v2 update from 131.108.1.1 on Ethernet1
          131.108.6.0/24 -> 0.0.0.0, in 16 hops (inaccessible)
```

This is a classical RIP problem in which a route passes through more than 15 devices. IP networks these days usually have more than 15 routers. There is no way to overcome this behavior other than to use a routing protocol that does not have a 15-hop limitation. IGRP has a maximum hop count of 255 and EIGRP has a maximum hop count of 224, with both defaulting to 100. IGP routing protocols that do not have this limitation include OSPF, IGRP, EIGRP, and IS-IS.

Discontiguous Networks

When a major network is separated by another major network, this is called a ***discontiguous network***. Figure 5-17 shows an example.

Figure 5-17 Discontiguous Networks Are Problematic with Classful Protocols

Example 5-55 shows the configuration for routers R1 and R2. RIP, with the default of Version 1, is enabled on the Ethernet interfaces of R1 and R2 with the correct **network** statements.

Example 5-55 *Routers R1 and R2 Have a Standard RIP Configuration*

```
R2#
interface Loopback0
ip address 137.99.3.2 255.255.255.0
!
interface Ethernet0
ip address 131.108.1.2 255.255.255.0
!
router rip
 network 131.108.0.0
 network 137.99.0.0
!

R1#
interface Loopback0
ip address 137.99.2.1 255.255.255.0
!
interface Ethernet0
ip address 131.108.1.1 255.255.255.0
!
router rip
 network 131.108.0.0
 network 137.99.0.0
!
```

Example 5-56 shows the **debug ip rip** command output for routers R1 and R2. The debugs show that both routers are sending to the other the summarized major network address for 137.99.0.0 instead of their specific network addresses. As a result, both routers ignore the less specific 137.99.0.0 update because they are already connected to this major network.

Example 5-56 *Consistent with RIPv1 Behavior, the Classful Network 137.99.0.0 Is Advertised by Both R1 and R2*

```
R2#debug ip rip
RIP protocol debugging is on
RIP: received v1 update from 131.108.1.1 on Ethernet0
      137.99.0.0 in 1 hops
RIP: sending v1 update to 255.255.255.255 via Ethernet0 (131.108.1.2)
```

Example 5-56 *Consistent with RIPv1 Behavior, the Classful Network 137.99.0.0 Is Advertised by Both R1 and R2 (Continued)*

```
RIP: build update entries
        network 137.99.0.0 metric 1
R2#


R1#debug ip rip
RIP protocol debugging is on
R1#
RIP: received v1 update from 131.108.1.2 on Ethernet0
     137.99.0.0 in 1 hops
RIP: sending v1 update to 255.255.255.255 via Ethernet0 (131.108.1.1)
RIP: build update entries
        network 137.99.0.0 metric 1
```

RIP does not install the route 137.99.0.0 in the routing table because RIPv1 does not support discontiguous subnets. Several solutions to this problem exist. Example 5-57 shows that a quick solution is to configure each router with a static route to the specific 137.99.0.0 subnet on the other router. Because RIPv1 does not include the subnet information in its routing updates, configuring the static routes is a "patch" to fix this problem. This might be necessary if the routers in question can run only RIPv1.

Example 5-57 *One Solution Is to Use Static Routes to the Subnets of 137.99.0.0*

```
R1#
interface Loopback0
ip address 137.99.2.1 255.255.255.0
!
interface Ethernet0
ip address 131.108.1.1 255.255.255.0
!
router rip
 network 131.108.0.0
 network 137.99.0.0
!
ip route 137.99.3.0 255.255.255.0 131.108.1.2
```

continues

Example 5-57 *One Solution Is to Use Static Routes to the Subnets of 137.99.0.0 (Continued)*

```
R2#
interface Loopback0
ip address 137.99.3.2 255.255.255.0
!
interface Ethernet0
ip address 131.108.1.2 255.255.255.0
!
router rip
 network 131.108.0.0
 network 137.99.0.0
!
ip route 137.99.2.0 255.255.255.0 131.108.1.1
```

Another solution is to change the address on the link between routers R1 and R2 to be part of the 137.99.0.0 network. In other words, assign another subnet on this link, which is part of 137.99.0.0.

Example 5-58 shows a better solution—to enable the classless routing version of RIPv2 with **no auto-summary** configured on both routers. The **no auto-summary** command disables auto summarization of RIPv2 routes when crossing a major network boundary. It is important to disable auto-summarization, or the same unreachability problem will continue. With **no auto-summary**, the specific subnet information is also included in these updates. Example 5-59 shows the routing table of R2 after using this solution.

Example 5-58 *A Better Solution Is to Use RIPv2 with the* **no auto-summary** *Option*

```
router rip
 version 2
 network 131.108.0.0
 network 137.99.0.0
 no auto-summary
```

Example 5-59 *With RIPv2 and the* **no auto-summary** *Option, Routing Tables Are Updated Accurately in Spite of the Discontiguous Networks*

```
R2#show ip route 137.99.2.0
Routing entry for 137.99.2.0/24
Known via "rip", distance 120, metric 1
```

Example 5-59 *With RIPv2 and the* **no auto-summary** *Option, Routing Tables Are Updated Accurately in Spite of the Discontiguous Networks (Continued)*

```
Redistributing via rip
Last update from 131.108.1.1 on Ethernet0, 00:00:07 ago
Routing Descriptor Blocks:
* 131.108.1.1, from 131.108.1.1, 00:00:07 ago, via Ethernet0
Route metric is 1, traffic share count is 1
```

Another solution is to replace the classful RIPv1 routing protocol with a classless routing protocol, such as OSPF, EIGRP, or IS-IS.

Invalid Source Address

When RIP tells the routing table to install the route, it performs a source validity check. If the source is not on the same subnet as the local interface, RIP ignores the update and does not install the routes coming from this source address in the routing table.

In Figure 5-18, the R1 Serial 0 interface is unnumbered to Loopback 0. The Router R2 serial interface is numbered. When Router R2 receives a RIP update from R1, the source address is considered invalid because the source address is not on the same subnet as the R2 serial interface.

NOTE

This same issue exists with IGRP. In the case of EIGRP and OSPF, routers cannot form neighbor relationships if they are not on the same subnet. OSPF performs the subnet number and mask check on all media except point-to-point and virtual links.

Figure 5-18 Unnumbered Interface on R1

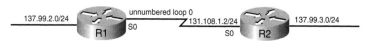

```
137.99.2.0/24          unnumbered loop 0
                   R1  S0      131.108.1.2/24      137.99.3.0/24
                                        S0   R2
```

Example 5-60 shows the configuration of routers R2 and R1. In this configuration, the R1 Serial 0 interface is unnumbered to Loopback 0. The R2 Serial interface is numbered.

Example 5-60 *Configurations for R1 and R2 Include RIPv1*

```
R2#
interface Loopback0
ip address 131.108.3.2 255.255.255.0
!
interface Serial0
ip address 131.108.1.2 255.255.255.0
```

continues

Example 5-60 *Configurations for R1 and R2 Include RIPv1 (Continued)*

```
!
router rip
 network 131.108.0.0
!


R1#
interface Loopback0
ip address 131.108.2.1 255.255.255.0
!
interface Serial0
ip unnumbered Loopback0
!
router rip
 network 131.108.0.0
!
```

The **debug ip rip** output in Example 5-61 shows that R2 is ignoring the RIP update from R1 because of a source validity check. The RIP update coming from R1 is not on the same subnet, so R2 does not install any routes in the routing table from R1.

Example 5-61 *The* **debug ip rip** *Command Reveals a Problem with the Source Validity Check*

```
R2#debug ip rip
RIP protocol debugging is on
RIP: ignored v1 update from bad source 131.108.2.1 on Serial0
R2#
```

When one side is numbered and the other side is unnumbered, this check must be disabled. This is usually the case in a dialup situation when remotes are dialing into an access router. The access router's dialup interface is unnumbered, and all remote routers get an IP address assigned on their dialup interfaces. This same solution can also apply when both sides of the link are unnumbered.

Example 5-62 shows the configuration change on Router R2 to fix this problem.

Example 5-62 *The* **no validate-update-source** *Command Makes It Possible for One End of a Serial Link to Be Unnumbered*

```
R2#
interface Loopback0
ip address 131.108.3.2 255.255.255.0
!
interface Serial0
ip address 131.108.1.2 255.255.255.0
!
router rip
no validate-update-source
network 131.108.0.0
!
```

Example 5-63 shows that after the configuration of R2 is changed, the route gets installed in the routing table.

Example 5-63 *Without the Source Validity Check, the Routing Table Is Updated Successfully on R2*

```
R2#show ip route 131.108.2.0
Routing entry for 131.108.2.0/24
Known via "rip", distance 120, metric 1
Redistributing via rip
Last update from 131.108.1.1 on Ethernet0, 00:00:01 ago
Routing Descriptor Blocks:
* 131.108.1.1, from 131.108.1.1, 00:00:01 ago, via Ethernet0
Route metric is 1, traffic share count is 1
```

Flapping Routes

Running RIP in a complex environment can sometimes cause the flapping of routes. Route flapping refers to the constant deletion and reinsertion of a route within the routing table. To check whether the routes are indeed flapping, check the routing table and look at the age of the routes. If the ages are constantly being reset to 00:00:00, this means that the routes are flapping.

One of the most common reasons is packet loss, which occurs when the packet is dropped on the sender's or receiver's interface. The most common environment this occurs in is Frame Relay, which is used in this scenario.

The existence of packet loss can be verified by using the **show interface** command and examining the interface statistics to determine if the number of packet drops is constantly incrementing. Figure 5-19 shows the Frame Relay scenario used in this example.

Figure 5-19 Routing Over Frame Relay

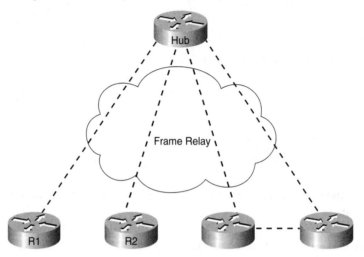

In a large network, especially in a Frame Relay environment, there is a good possibility that when RIP updates are lost, it is occurring in the Frame Relay cloud or that the RIP interface dropped the update. These symptoms can occur in any Layer 2 medium, but this example involves Frame Relay.

By default, if RIP does not receive a route for 180 seconds, the route is put in holddown for 240 seconds, and then it is purged. This situation corrects itself, in time, when a new update is received.

Consider the output shown in Example 5-64, where no RIP updates have been received for 2 minutes and 8 seconds into the fifth update.

Example 5-64 *No RIP Updates Have Been Received for More Than 2 Minutes*

```
Hub#show ip route rip
R    155.155.0.0/16 [120/1] via 131.108.1.1, 00:02:08, Serial0
R    166.166.0.0/16 [120/1] via 131.108.1.1, 00:02:08, Serial0
```

Example 5-65 shows that there are a large number of broadcast drops on the interface.

Example 5-65 *There Are a Large Number of Broadcast Packet Drops on the Serial 0 Interface*

```
Hub#show interface serial 0
Serial 0 is up, line protocol is up
Hardware is MK5025
Description: Charlotte Frame Relay Port DLCI 100
MTU 1500 bytes, BW 1024 Kbit, DLY 20000 usec, rely 255/255, load 44/255
Encapsulation FRAME-RELAY, loopback not set, keepalive set (10 sec)
LMI enq sent 7940, LMI stat recvd 7937, LMI upd recvd 0 , DTE LMI up
LMI enq recvd 0, LMI stat sent 0, LMI upd sent 0
LMI DLCI 1023 LMI type is CISCO frame relay DTE
Broadcast queue 64/64, broadcasts sent/dropped 1769202/1849660,
Interface broadcasts 3579215
```

The **show interfaces serial 0** command further proves that a problem exists at the interface level. Too many drops are occurring at the interface. This is the cause of the route flapping. In the case of Frame Relay, the Frame Relay broadcast queue might have to be tuned. Several white papers on Cisco's Website discuss how to tune the Frame Relay broadcast queue. In a non-Frame Relay situation, the input or output hold queue might need to be increased.

Example 5-66 shows that after the interface drop problem is fixed, the route flapping disappears.

Example 5-66 *The Broadcast Packet Drops Cease After the Frame Relay Broadcast Queue Is Tuned*

```
Hub#show interface serial 0
Serial0 is up, line protocol is up
Hardware is MK5025
Description: Charlotte Frame Relay Port DLCI 100
MTU 1500 bytes, BW 1024 Kbit, DLY 20000 usec, rely 255/255, load 44/255
Encapsulation FRAME-RELAY, loopback not set, keepalive set (10 sec)
LMI enq sent 7940, LMI stat recvd 7937, LMI upd recvd 0, DTE LMI up
LMI enq recvd 0, LMI stat sent 0, LMI upd sent 0
LMI DLCI 1023 LMI type is CISCO frame relay DTE
Broadcast queue 0/256, broadcasts sent/dropped 1769202/0, interface broadcasts
   3579215
```

The output from the **show ip route rip** command in Example 5-67 shows that the routes are stable in the routing table and that the timers are set at a value lower than 30 seconds.

Example 5-67 *RIP Updates Are Now Being Received on the Serial 0 Interface*

```
Hub#show ip route rip
R    155.155.0.0/16 [120/1] via 131.108.1.1, 00:00:07, Serial0
R    166.166.0.0/16 [120/1] via 131.108.1.1, 00:00:07, Serial0
```

Large Routing Tables

Large routing tables can be problematic for a network by increasing the amount of bandwidth required for routing updates, as well as leading to increased memory requirements. Figure 5-20 shows an example of a network that could produce a large routing table. This example has only three routes. In a real network, however, the number of networks could be much higher, and the problem of a large routing table could be much worse.

Figure 5-20 R1 and R2 Are Running RIPv2

R2 is announcing several subnets of the 131.108.0.0 network. Notice that the link between R1 and R2 is also part of the 131.108.0.0 network, so auto-summarization cannot play a role to solve the problem of receiving a subnet route that could be summarized. The auto-summarization feature can work only if the link between R1 and R2 is on a different major network.

Example 5-68 shows that in the configuration of R2, the **ip summary-address** command is not used under the Serial 1 interface to summarize the routes.

Example 5-68 *No Summarization Is Configured on R2*

```
R2#
interface Serial1
 ip address 131.108.4.2 255.255.255.0
!
router rip
 version 2
 network 131.108.0.0
```

Example 5-69 shows the routing table of R1.

Example 5-69 *The Routing Table on R1 Does Not Include Summary Routes*

```
R1#show ip route rip
     131.108.0.0/24 is subnetted, 3 subnets
R       131.108.3.0 [120/1] via 131.108.4.2, 00:00:04, Serial1
R       131.108.2.0 [120/1] via 131.108.4.2, 00:00:04, Serial1
R       131.108.1.0 [120/1] via 131.108.4.2, 00:00:04, Serial1

R1#
```

In this situation, auto-summarization is on but is not helpful, because the whole network is within one major network. Imagine a network with a Class B address space with thousands of subnets. Auto-summarization cannot play a role here, because no major network boundary is crossed. A new feature of summarization was introduced in RIP starting with Cisco IOS Release 12.0.7T. This feature is similar to EIGRP manual summarization.

Example 5-70 shows the new configuration that solves this problem using the **ip summary-address** RIP command. This configuration reduces the size of the routing table. This command can be used with different masks, so if a network has contiguous blocks of a subnet, the router could be configured to summarize subnets into smaller blocks. This would reduce the routes advertised to the RIP network.

Example 5-70 *Summarization Is Configured on R2*

```
R2#
interface Serial1
 ip address 131.108.4.2 255.255.255.0
 ip summary-address rip 131.108.0.0 255.255.252.0
!
Router rip
 version 2
 network 131.108.0.0
```

Based on the preceding configuration, Router R2 summarizes the RIP routes on the Serial 1 interface. Any network subnet that falls in the 131.108.0.0 to 131.108.3.0 range of networks is summarized as a single 131.108.0.0/22 major network. This means that R2 announces only a single summarized route as 131.108.0.0/22 and suppresses the 131.108.1.0/24, 131.108.2.0/24, and 131.108.3.0/24 subnets.

Example 5-71 shows the routing table of Router R1 with a reduced number of entries as a result of the summarization.

Example 5-71 *The Routing Table on R1 Reflects the Summarization Configured on R2*

```
R1#show ip route rip
R    131.108.0.0/22 [120/1] via 131.108.4.2, 00:00:01, Serial1
R1#
```

Troubleshooting IGRP

Although IGRP is not used in production much at all anymore, some legacy implementations still need support. Cisco IOS Release 12.3 and beyond no longer support IGRP (only EIGRP). The following sections describe some typical troubleshooting scenarios for IGRP.

Discontiguous Networks

When a major network is separated by another major network, this is called a discontiguous network. Figure 5-21 shows an example of a discontiguous network in which 137.99.0.0 is a major network. The subnets of this major network are separated by another major network, 131.108.0.0. This situation produces a discontiguous network problem.

Figure 5-21 Discontiguous IGRP Networks

Example 5-72 shows the configuration of routers R1 and R2. IGRP is enabled on the Ethernet interfaces of routers R1 and R2 with the correct **network** statements.

Example 5-72 *R1 and R2 Are Configured with IGRP. Only Classful Networks Can Be Configured with IGRP.*

```
R2#
interface Loopback0
ip address 137.99.3.2 255.255.255.0
!
interface Ethernet0
ip address 131.108.1.2 255.255.255.0
```

Example 5-72 *R1 and R2 Are Configured with IGRP. Only Classful Networks Can Be Configured with IGRP. (Continued)*

```
!
router igrp 1
  network 131.108.0.0
  network 137.99.0.0
!
R1#
interface Loopback0
ip address 137.99.2.1 255.255.255.0
!
interface Ethernet0
ip address 131.108.1.1 255.255.255.0
!
router igrp 1
  network 131.108.0.0
  network 137.99.0.0
!
```

Example 5-73 shows the **debug ip igrp transaction** command output for routers R1 and R2. The debugs show that both routers are sending to each other the summarized major network address for 137.99.0.0 instead of their specific network addresses. As a result, both routers ignore the less specific 137.99.0.0 update, because they are already connected to this major network.

Example 5-73 *The Debugs Show That the Classful Network 137.99.0.0 Is Being Sent by Both R1 and R2*

```
R2#debug ip igrp transaction
IGRP protocol debugging is on
R2#
IGRP: sending update to 255.255.255.255 via Loopback0
     (137.99.3.2)network 131.108.0.0, metric=8476

IGRP: sending update to 255.255.255.255 via Ethernet0
     (131.108.1.2)network 137.99.0.0, metric=501
IGRP: received update from 131.108.1.1 on Ethernet0
     network 137.99.0, metric 8976 (neighbor 501)
R2#
```

continues

Example 5-73 *The Debugs Show That the Classful Network 137.99.0.0 Is Being Sent by Both R1 and R2 (Continued)*

```
R1#debug ip igrp transaction
IGRP protocol debugging is on
R1#
IGRP: sending update to 255.255.255.255 via Loopback0
     (137.99.2.1) network 131.108.0.0, metric=8476
IGRP: sending update to 255.255.255.255 via Ethernet0
     (131.108.1.1)network 137.99.0.0, metric=501

R1#
IGRP: received update from 131.108.1.2 on Ethernet0
     network 137.99.0.0, metric 8976 (neighbor 501)
R1#
```

IGRP does not support discontiguous networks. Several solutions to this problem exist. One solution is to configure a static route on each router to the specific 137.99.0.0 subnet on the other router, as shown in Example 5-74. Because IGRP is a classful routing protocol and does not include the subnet information in its routing updates, configuring the static routes is a "patch" to fix this problem.

Example 5-74 *Static Routes Can Be Configured to Overcome the Discontiguous Network Problem*

```
R1#
interface Loopback0
ip address 137.99.3.2 255.255.255.0
!
interface Ethernet0
ip address 131.108.1.1 255.255.255.0
!
router igrp 1
network 131.108.0.0
network 137.99.0.0
!
ip route 137.99.3.0 255.255.255.0 131.108.1.2
R2#
interface Loopback0
ip address 137.99.2.1 255.255.255.0
```

Example 5-74 *Static Routes Can Be Configured to Overcome the Discontiguous Network Problem (Continued)*

```
!
interface Ethernet0
ip address 131.108.1.2 255.255.255.0
!
router igrp 1
network 131.108.0.0
network 137.99.0.0
!
ip route 137.99.2.0 255.255.255.0 131.108.1.1
```

Another solution is to replace the classful IGRP routing protocol with a classless routing protocol, such as RIPv2, OSPF, EIGRP, or IS-IS. Unlike RIP, no version of IGRP is a classless routing protocol.

If using IGRP is a must, two solutions are possible. The first is to change the address on the link between routers R1 and R2 to be part of the 137.99.0.0 network. In other words, assign another subnet on this link, which is part of 137.99.0.0.

If the addresses cannot be changed, a Generic Routing Encapsulation (GRE) tunnel can be configured between routers R1 and R2. A separate subnet address with the same mask is configured on the tunnel interface, as shown in Example 5-75.

Example 5-75 *A GRE Tunnel Can Be Configured to Overcome the Discontiguous Network Problem*

```
R1#
interface tunnel 0
ip address 137.99.1.1 255.255.255.0
tunnel source Ethernet 0
tunnel destination 131.108.1.2

R2#
interface tunnel 0
ip address 137.99.1.2 255.255.255.0
tunnel source Ethernet 0
tunnel destination 131.108.1.1
```

Discontiguous networks are discouraged and should be avoided even if a protocol supports them, because they limit the summarization capabilities. Example 5-76 shows the routing table entry for R2 after this problem is fixed.

Example 5-76 *R2 Receives Routing Updates Including the 137.99.2.0/24 Network After the GRE Tunnel Is Configured*

```
R2#show ip route 137.99.2.0
Routing entry for 137.99.2.0/24
  Known via "igrp 1", distance 100, metric 8976
  Redistributing via igrp 1
  Advertised by igrp 1 (self originated)
  Last update from 131.108.1.1 on Ethernet0,00:00:12 ago

Routing Descriptor Blocks:
*131.108.1.1, from 131.108.1.1, 00:00:12 ago, via Ethernet0
  Route metric is 8976, traffic share count is 1
  Total delay is 25000 microseconds, minimum bandwidth is 1544 Kbit
  Reliability 255/255, minimum MTU 1500 bytes
  Loading 1/255, Hops 0
```

AS Mismatch

IGRP updates carry their autonomous system (AS) number. When a receiver receives an IGRP update and the sender's AS number does not match its own AS number, IGRP ignores that update. As a result, no IGRP routes are installed in the routing table. Multiple IGRP processes can be run under different AS numbers. These processes are independent of each other.

Example 5-77 shows the configuration of routers R1 and R2. R1 is running IGRP AS 1, and R2 is running IGRP AS 2.

Example 5-77 *R1 and R2 Are Configured with Different AS Numbers*

```
R2#
interface Loopback0
ip address 131.108.3.2 255.255.255.0
!
interface Serial0
ip address 131.108.1.2 255.255.255.0
!
router igrp 2
```

Example 5-77 *R1 and R2 Are Configured with Different AS Numbers (Continued)*

```
  network 131.108.0.0
!
R1#
interface Loopback0
ip address 131.108.2.1 255.255.255.0
!
interface Serial0
  ip address 131.108.1.1 255.255.255.0
!
router igrp 1
network 131.108.0.0
!
```

Example 5-78 shows the output of the **debug ip igrp transaction** and **debug ip packet 100 detail** commands on routers R1 and R2. IGRP is ignoring these updates because of the AS number mismatch. Unfortunately, the **debug** output does not show the mismatch message. However, it does show that IGRP is not displaying the update received message in the debugs.

Example 5-78 *IGRP Updates Do Not Appear in the Debug Displays Because of the AS Mismatch*

```
R1#show debug
Generic IP:
  IP packet debugging is on (detailed)
IP routing:
   IGRP protocol debugging is on
   IGRP event debugging is on
R1#
R1#show access-list 100
access-list 100 permit ip any host 255.255.255.255

R1#debug ip packet 100 detail
IP packet debugging is on (detailed) for access list 100
R1#
R1#debug ip igrp transaction
IGRP protocol debugging is on
```

continues

Example 5-78 *IGRP Updates Do Not Appear in the Debug Displays Because of the AS Mismatch (Continued)*

```
IGRP: sending update to 255.255.255.255 via Serial0 (131.108.1.1)
      subnet 131.108.3.0, metric=501
IP: s=131.108.1.2 (Serial0), d=255.255.255.255, len 64, rcvd 2, proto=9


R2#debug ip packet 100 detailed
IP packet debugging is on (detailed) for access list 100
R2#
R2#debug ip igrp tranaction
IGRP protocol debugging is on
IGRP: sending update to 255.255.255.255 via Serial0 (131.108.1.2)
      subnet 131.108.2.0, metric=501
IP: s=131.108.1.1 (Serial0), d=255.255.255.255, len 64, rcvd 2, proto=9
```

In this example, the sender sends AS 1 in the update. When R2 receives it, it ignores this update because R2 is running IGRP under AS 2. To fix this problem, change the IGRP configurations so that R1 and R2 both agree on one AS number.

Example 5-79 shows the new configuration on R2 that fixes the problem.

Example 5-79 *Changing the AS Number on R2 Fixes the Problem*

```
R2#
interface Loopback0
ip address 131.108.3.2 255.255.255.0
!
interface Serial0
ip address 131.108.1.2 255.255.255.0
!
no router igrp 2
!
router igrp 1
  network 131.108.0.0
!
```

Example 5-80 shows that after the AS mismatch problem is fixed, IGRP routes get installed in the routing table.

Example 5-80 *R2 Is Now Receiving IGRP Routing Updates for the 137.108.2.0/24 Network*

```
R2#show ip route 131.108.2.0
Routing entry for 131.108.2.0/24
  Known via "igrp 1", distance 100, metric 8976
  Redistributing via igrp 1
  Advertised by igrp 1 (self orginated)
  Last update from 131.108.1.1 on Serial0, 00:00:12 ago
  Routing Descriptor Blocks:
  * 131.108.1.1, from 131.108.1.1, 00:00:12 ago, via Serial0
      Route metric is 8976, traffic share count is 1
      Total delay is 25000 microseconds, minimum
      bandwidth is 1544 kbit
      Reliability 255/255, minimum MTU 1500 bytes
      Loading 1/255, Hops 0
```

Misconfigured neighbor Statement

By default, IGRP sends out its updates as a broadcast. IGRP provides a unicast method of
sending IGRP updates using the **neighbor** statement. IGRP will not send the unicast update
to the wrong neighbor or a nonexistent neighbor. Figure 5-22 shows two routers running
IGRP between them.

Figure 5-22 IGRP Over Frame Relay

> **NOTE**
>
> RIPv1 sends updates as
> broadcasts, whereas
> RIPv2, EIGRP, OSPF,
> and IS-IS use multi-
> casts. The same **neigh-
> bor** statement can be
> used with RIPv1.

Example 5-81 shows the IGRP configuration for Router R1. The configuration shows that the
neighbor statement is configured incorrectly. Instead of 131.108.1.2, as shown in Figure 5-22,
the **neighbor** statement points to 131.108.1.3, which does not exist.

Example 5-81 *R1 Is Configured with a **neighbor** Statement*

```
R1#router igrp 1
network 131.108.0.0
neighbor 131.108.1.3
```

IGRP is sending a unicast update to 131.108.1.3, a neighbor that does not exist, as shown in Example 5-81. To resolve this problem, the **neighbor** statement must be configured correctly. Example 5-82 shows the correct configuration on Router R1.

Example 5-82 *The* **neighbor** *Statement Is Corrected*

```
R1#router igrp 1
network 131.108.0.0
no neighbor 131.108.1.3
neighbor 131.108.1.2
```

Example 5-83 shows the IGRP routes installed in the R2 routing table.

Example 5-83 *R2 Is Now Receiving IGRP Routing Updates for the 137.108.2.0/24 Network*

```
R2#show ip route 131.108.2.0
Routing entry for 131.108.2.0/24
  known via "igrp 1", distance 100, metric 8976
  Redistributing via igrp 1
  Advertised by igrp 1 (self originated)
  Last update from 131.108.1.1, on Serial0, 00:00:12 ago
  Routing Descriptor Blocks:
  * 131.108.1.1, from 131.108.1.1, 00:00:12 ago, via Serial0
    Route metric is 8976, traffic share count is 1
    Total delay is 25000 microseconds, minimum bandwidth is 1544 kbit
    Reliability 255/255, minimum MTU 1500 bytes
    Loading 1/255, Hops 0
```

Maximum Paths

By default, for load-balancing purposes, Cisco routers support only four equal paths. The command **maximum-path** can be used for up to six equal-cost paths. If the command is not configured properly, it can cause problems.

Figure 5-23 shows a network setup with multiple equal-cost paths from Router R1 to the 131.108.2.0/24 network.

Figure 5-23 Physical Loop—Multiple Paths

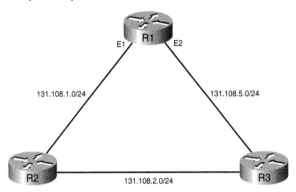

Example 5-84 shows the routing table entry for Router R1, where only one route is being installed in the routing table.

Example 5-84 *R1 Is Installing Only One Route to 137.108.20.0/24*

```
R1#show ip route igrp
131.108.0.0/24 is subnetted, 1 subnets
I 131.108.2.0 [100/8976] via 131.108.5.3, 00:00:09, Ethernet2
```

Example 5-85 shows the output of the **debug ip igrp transactions** command on Router R1, revealing that R1 is receiving two equal-cost path routes. However, the routing table in Example 5-84 shows that only one route is being installed.

Example 5-85 *An IGRP Debug Shows That Information About the Same Route Is Being Received from Two Sources*

```
R1#debug ip igrp transaction
IGRP protocol debugging is on
IGRP: received update from 131.108.5.3 on Ethernet2
      network 137.99.0.0, metric 8976 (neighbor 501)
IGRP:received update from 131.108.1.2 on Ethernet1
      network 137.99.0.0, metric 8976 (neighbor 501)
```

The **maximum-path** command on R1 is configured with the value of 1, which prevents IGRP from installing more than one path in the routing table. By default, the **maximum-path** is set to 4.

If the command **maximum-path 1** is used, it allows only one path to the destination even though more than one path exists. The **maximum-path 1** command should be used only when load balancing is not desired.

By default, the IOS allows up to four equal-cost routes to be installed in the routing table. This can be increased to up to six routes if configured properly. Example 5-86 shows the configuration that installs six equal-cost route paths in the routing table.

Example 5-86 *The Configuration on R1 Is Changed to Allow Up to Six Equal-Cost Paths*

```
R1#router igrp 1
maximum-paths 6
```

This example makes more sense when there are more than four paths and only four are being installed in the routing table. Because four equal-cost routes is the default, the **maximum-paths** command can be configured to accommodate a fifth or possibly sixth route.

Candidate Default

Except for IGRP, the way to set the gateway of last resort for all other routing protocols is to define a static route to 0.0.0.0 with a mask of 0.0.0.0, as shown in Example 5-87. That route can then be propagated within RIP and OSPF with the **default-information originate** command and within EIGRP with the **redistribute static** command. Be aware that commands used to propagate default routes for a given routing protocol are often IOS version-specific.

Example 5-87 *IGRP Does Not Propagate the "Quad-Zero" Default Route*

```
R1(config)#ip route 0.0.0.0 0.0.0.0 131.108.1.1
```

IGRP does not propagate the 0.0.0.0 static route. IGRP has another way to handle this. Figure 5-24 shows a sample network in which Router R1 sends default traffic out the 155.155.155.0/24 network. Router R1 wants to propagate this gateway of last resort to Router R2.

Figure 5-24 155.155.155.0/24 as the Default

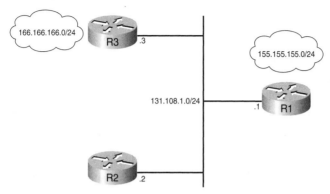

Example 5-88 shows the configuration of Router R1, without a gateway of last resort configured.

Example 5-88 *The Current Configuration on R1 Does Not Include a Default Route*

```
R1#interface Loopback1
  ip address 131.108.2.1 255.255.255.255.0
!
interface Loopback3
  ip address 155.155.155.1 255.255.255.0
!
interface Ethernet0
  ip address 131.108.1.1 255.255.255.0
!
router igrp 1
  network 131.108.0.0
  network 155.155.0.0
```

Example 5-89 shows the routing table in R2, where R2 is receiving 155.155.155.0/24, but it is not a candidate for default.

Example 5-89 *R2 Knows About the 155.155.155.0/24 Network, But It Is Not Tagged as a Default Network*

```
R2#show ip route igrp
I   155.155.0.0/24 [100/8976] via 131.108.1.1, 00:00:22, Ethernet 0
    131.108.0.0/24 is subnetted, 3 subnets
I      131.108.2.0 [100/8976] via 131.108.1.1, 00:00:22, Ethernet 0
```

IGRP is incapable of carrying the 0.0.0.0/0 (also known as a default route). Instead, IGRP uses the **default-network** command to mark a network as a candidate for default.

In this example, R1 is sending 155.155.155.0/24, and it is desirable to make R1 a candidate for default. To do that, the configuration on R1 must be changed to establish 155.155.0.0 as the default network. After this is done, IGRP automatically starts treating 155.155.155.0/24 as the candidate for default and sets the gateway of last resort on Router R2.

Example 5-90 shows the configuration for the default network on R1. This **ip default-network** statement must always point toward a major network, not a subnet. Otherwise, it will not set the gateway of last resort.

Example 5-90 *A Default Network Is Added on R1*

```
R1(config)#ip default-network 155.155.0.0
```

Example 5-91 shows that after the configuration change on R1, the **debug ip igrp transactions** output shows IGRP treating 155.155.0.0 as an exterior route, because it is marked as a candidate for default route.

Example 5-91 *The Network Is Now Being Advertised as an External Route*

```
IGRP: received update from 131.108.1.1 on Serial1
      subnet 131.108.3.0, metric 8976 (neighbor 501)
      subnet 131.108.1.0, metric 10476 (neighbor 8476)
        exterior network 155.155.0.0, metric 8976 (neighbor 501)
```

> **NOTE**
>
> When troubleshooting issues regarding default routes with RIP and OSPF, be sure a static 0.0.0.0/0 route and the **default-information originate** command are configured on the entrance router (or, in the case of OSPF, the ASBR). With EIGRP, the static 0.0.0.0/0 route and the **redistribute static** command must be configured on the entrance router.

Example 5-92 shows that the gateway of last resort is set and that 155.155.155.0/24 is marked as a candidate for default. The * next to the I in the routing table means that this entry is a candidate for default route.

Example 5-92 *R2 Now Sees 155.155.0.0/16 as a Default Route*

```
R2#show ip route
Gateway of last resort is 131.108.1.1 to network 155.155.0.0
```

Example 5-92 *R2 Now Sees 155.155.0.0/16 as a Default Route (Continued)*

```
     137.99.0.0/24 is subnetted, 1 subnets
C    137.99.3.0 is directly connected, Loopback0
I*   155.155.0.0/16 [100/8976] via 131.108.1.1, 00:01:17, Ethernet 0
```

Troubleshooting EIGRP

This section explores the common troubleshooting scenarios for EIGRP. The first priority is to ensure that neighbor relationships are forming between EIGRP neighbors. Particular emphasis is focused on the stuck-in-active issue.

Mismatched K Values

For EIGRP to establish its neighbors, the K constant value to manipulate the EIGRP metric must be the same. In the EIGRP metric calculation, the default for the K value is set so that only the bandwidth and the delay of the interface are used to calculate the EIGRP metric. At times, the network administrator might want other interface values, such as load and reliability, to determine the EIGRP metric. Therefore, the K values must be changed. Because only bandwidth and delay are used in the calculations, the remaining K values are set to a value of 0 by default.

> **NOTE**
>
> Cisco usually recommends that network administrators not modify the default metric of using bandwidth and delay.

However, the K values must be the same for all the routers, or EIGRP will not establish a neighbor relationship. Figure 5-25 shows two routers with mismatched K values.

Figure 5-25 EIGRP K Values Must Match Between Neighbors

Modifying the K values affects how much bandwidth, delay, reliability, and load affect the metric calculation, if at all. Modifying these K values has the following effect:

- K1 for bandwidth
- K2 for load
- K3 for delay
- K4 and K5 for reliability

Example 5-93 shows that the K values on RTR B have been changed to include load and reliability, along with bandwidth and delay. K1, K2, K3, and K4 have all been set to 1. The **metric weights** command shows that these values have been modified. The first value is the type of service (TOS), which is not supported but must be included.

Example 5-93 *The K Values on RTR B Have Been Changed*

```
RTRB(config)#router eigrp 1
RTRB(config-router)#network x.x.x.x
RTRB(config-router)#metric weights 0 1 1 1 1 0
```

RTR A retains the default K values of K1 and K3 set to 1 for bandwidth and delay only, with all other K values set to 0. If a router such as RTR A is using the default, normally the **metric weights** command is not included in the configuration.

The command **show ip eigrp neighbors** on both RTR A and RTB B would show an empty list. Troubleshooting this problem requires careful scrutiny of the router's configuration.

The solution is to configure the same K values on all routers in the EIGRP domain. Example 5-94 shows the modification made to RTR A to match the K values on RTR B. At this point both routers can establish a neighbor relationship and exchange routing information.

Example 5-94 *The K Values on RTR A Are Changed to Match RTR B*

```
RTRA(config)#router eigrp 1
RTRA(config-router)#network x.x.x.x
RTRA(config-router)#metric weights 0 1 1 1 1 0
```

Mismatched AS Number

EIGRP does not form any neighbor relationships with routers that have different autonomous system numbers. If the AS numbers are mismatched, no adjacency is formed. This problem is usually caused by misconfiguration on the routers.

Figure 5-26 shows two routers running EIGRP.

Figure 5-26 EIGRP Is Running Between RTR A and RTR B

Example 5-95 shows the configurations of both routers. Because the two routers have different AS numbers, using the command **show ip eigrp neighbors** on both RTR A and RTB B would show an empty list.

Example 5-95 *The EIGRP Configurations for RTR A and RTR B Use Different AS Numbers*

```
RTR B#show running-config
interface serial 0
IP address 10.1.1.1 255.255.255.0
router eigrp 11
network 10.0.0.0

RTR A#show running-config
Interface serial 0
IP address 10.1.1.2 255.255.255.0
router eigrp 1
network 10.0.0.0
```

The solution is to modify one of the two routers so that the AS numbers are the same. Example 5-96 shows both routers configured with the same AS number, EIGRP AS 1. At this point, both routers can establish a neighbor relationship and exchange routing information.

Example 5-96 *The AS Number Is Changed on RTR B to Match That Configured on RTR A*

```
RTR A#router eigrp 1
network 10.0.0.0

RTR B#router eigrp 1
network 10.0.0.0
```

Stuck in Active—Determining the Problem

When troubleshooting an EIGRP stuck-in-active problem, two questions need to be answered:

- Why is the route active?
- Why is the route stuck?

Determining why the route is active is not necessarily a difficult task. Sometimes, a route that constantly is going active could be caused by a flapping link. Or, if the route is a host route (/32 route), it is possible that it is from a dial-in connection that gets disconnected; in general, a PPP link is advertised as a /32 route. A more important and difficult task is determining why an active route becomes stuck. Usually, an active route gets stuck for one of the following reasons:

- Bad or congested link
- Low router resources, such as low memory or high CPU processing on the router
- Long query range
- Excessive redundancy

By default, the stuck-in-active timer is only 180 seconds. If the EIGRP neighbor does not hear a reply for the query in 180 seconds, neighbors are reset. This adds difficulty in troubleshooting EIGRP routes stuck in active, because when an active route is stuck, there is only 180 seconds to track down the active route query path and find the cause.

The tool that helps troubleshoot the EIGRP stuck-in-active error is the **show ip eigrp topology active** command. Example 5-97 shows sample output from this command. This command shows what routes are currently active, how long the routes have been active, and which neighbors have and have not replied to the query. From the output, you can determine which neighbors have not replied to the query. Track the query path and find the query's status by hopping to the neighbors that have not replied.

Example 5-97 *The* **show ip eigrp topology active** *Command Is Quite Useful When You're Troubleshooting Stuck-in-Active Issues*

```
Router#show ip eigrp topology active
IP-EIGRP Topology Table for AS(1)/ID(10.1.4.2)
A 20.2.1.0/24, 1 succesors, FD is Inaccessible, Q
 1 replies, active 00:01:43, query-origin: Successor
 Origin
 via 10.1.3.1 (Infinity/Infinity), Serial1/0
 via 10.1.4.1 (Infinity/Infinity), Serial1/1, serno 146
Remaining replies:
 Via 10.1.5.2, r, Serial1/2
```

As the output indicates, the route for 20.2.1.0 is in active state and has been active for 1 minute and 43 seconds. The query-origin is Successor Origin, which means that the successor to this route sends the query to this router. At this point, it has received replies from 10.1.3.1 and 10.2.4.1. The reply is Infinity, which means that these two routers also do not know about 20.2.1.0.

The most important output of the **show ip eigrp topology active** command is the Remaining replies section. This router shows that the neighbor 10.1.5.2 from interface Serial 1/2 has not replied to the query.

To proceed further with troubleshooting, the next step is to Telnet to the 10.1.5.2 router to see the status of its EIGRP active routes, again using the **show ip eigrp topology active** command. Sometimes, the router does not list the neighbors that have not replied to the queries in the Remaining replies section.

Example 5-98 shows another example of the **show ip eigrp topology active** command output. The only difference between the two outputs is the list of neighbors that have not replied to the router. However, this does not mean that all the neighbors have replied to the queries. The neighbor 1.1.1.2 has an "r" next to its address. This means that the neighbor has not replied to the queries.

Example 5-98 *The Neighbor at 1.1.1.2 Has an r Next to It, Meaning That It Has Not Replied to Queries*

```
Router#show ip eigrp topology active
IP-EIGRP Topology Table for AS(110)/ID(175.62.8.1)
A 11.11.11.0/24, 1 succesors, FD is Inaccessible
 1 replies, active 00:02:06, query-origin: Successor Origin via 1.1.1.2
 (Infinity/Infinity),r , Serial1/0, serno 171 via 10.1.1.2
 (Infinity/Infinity), Serial1/1, serno 173
```

In other words, the router has two ways of representing neighbors that have not replied to the queries. One way is to list them in the Remaining replies section. The other is to place an r next to the neighbor interface IP address. With the **show ip eigrp topology active** command, the router can use any combination of these methods to represent neighbors that have not yet replied to the queries, as shown in Example 5-99.

Example 5-99 *Neighbors 1.1.1.2 and 10.1.5.2 Have Not Replied to EIGRP Queries*

```
Router#show ip eigrp topology active
IP-EIGRP Topology Table for AS(1)/ID(175.62.8.1)
A 11.11.11.0/24, 1 succesors, FD is Inaccessible
 1 replies, active 00:02:06, query-origin: Successor Origin via 1.1.1.2
 (Infinity/Infinity),r , Serial1/0, serno 171 via 10.1.1.2 (Infinity/Infinity),
 Serial1/1, serno 173\
 Remaining replies:
 Via 10.1.5.2, r, Serial1/2
```

The neighbors that have not replied to the queries are 1.1.1.2 and 10.1.5.2, as shown in Example 5-99. Only one of the nonreplying neighbors, 10.1.5.2, is listed in the Remaining replies section. The other neighbor that has not replied, 1.1.1.2, is listed with the other replying neighbor. To summarize, when you issue the **show ip eigrp topology active** command, the most important part to look for is the neighbors that have not replied to the query. To look for such a neighbor, look for neighbors that have an r next to their interface IP address.

Stuck in Active—Methodology for Troubleshooting

The methods for troubleshooting an EIGRP stuck-in-active problem with the **show ip eigrp topology active** command are useful only when the problem is happening. When the stuck-in-active event is over and the network stabilizes, it is extremely difficult, if not impossible, to backtrack through the problem and find out the cause.

Consider the network shown in Figure 5-27 for an example of troubleshooting the EIGRP stuck-in-active problem. Router A has a FastEthernet interface with network 20.2.1.0/24 that just went away. Router A does not have a feasible successor to go to as a backup route. Router A has no choice but to put the 20.2.1.0/24 route into active state and query its neighbor, Router B. Notice the output of **show ip eigrp topology active** in Router A. The 20.2.1.0/24 route has gone away for 1 minute and 12 seconds, and the neighbor that has not responded is listed as 10.1.1.2 from Serial 0/0, which is Router B. The next step is to Telnet to Router B to see its active route status. You can find out Router B's active route status by issuing the command **show ip eigrp topology active**, as shown in Figure 5-28.

The command **show ip eigrp topology active** on Router B shows that the route 20.2.1.0/24 is also in active status in Router B and that it has gone active for 1 minute and 23 seconds. Most importantly, Router B cannot reply to Router A about 20.2.1.0/24, because Router B is still waiting for the neighbor with IP address 10.1.3.2 (Router D) from Serial 1/2 to reply to the query. The next step is to go to Router D to see the status of the active route 20.2.1.0/24 to see why Router D has not replied to the query. Figure 5-29 shows the output of **show ip eigrp topology active** on Router D.

Router D also put the router 20.2.1.0/24 in active state, where it has been for 1 minute and 43 seconds. Router D cannot answer the query from Router B because Router D is waiting for the router with the IP address of 10.1.5.2 from Serial 1/2 (Router E) to respond to the query. The next step is to go to Router E to see the status of the active route 20.2.1.0/24 and to find out why Router E is not replying to the query. Figure 5-30 shows the status of the active route on Router E.

Figure 5-27 Router A Shows an Active Route for the Five-Router Topology

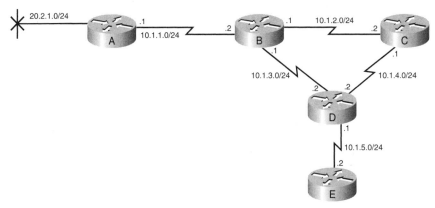

```
RouterA#show ip eigrp topology active
IP-EIGRP Topology Table for AS (1)/ID(20.2.1.1)
A 20.2.1.0/24, 1 successors, FD is Inaccessible
   1 replies, active 00:01:12, query-origin: Local origin
   via Connected (Infinity/Infinity), Ethernet0
   Remaining replies:
   via 10.1.1.2, r, Serial0
```

Figure 5-28 Router B Shows an Active Route

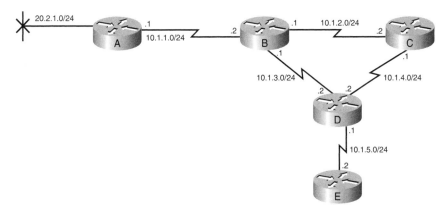

```
RouterB#show ip eigrp topology active
IP-EIGRP Topology Table for AS (1)/ID(10.1.3.1)
A 20.2.1.0/24, 1 successors, FD is Inaccessible
   1 replies, active 00:01:23, query-origin: Successor origin
   via 10.1.1.1 (Infinity/Infinity), Serial1/0
   Remaining replies:
   via 10.1.3.2, r, Serial1/2
```

Figure 5-29 Router D Shows an Active Route

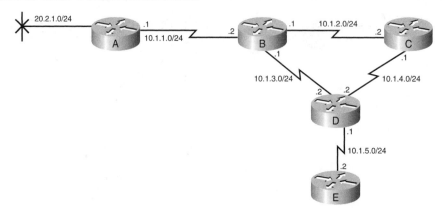

```
RouterD#show ip eigrp topology active
IP-EIGRP Topology Table for AS (1)/ID(10.1.4.1)
A 20.2.1.0/24, 1 successors, FD is Inaccessible, Q
   1 replies, active 00:01:43, query-origin: Successor origin
   via 10.1.3.1 (Infinity/Infinity), Serial1/0
   via 10.1.4.1 (Infinity/Infinity), Serial1/1, serno 146
   Remaining replies:
   via 10.1.5.2, r, Serial1/2
```

Figure 5-30 Router E Shows No Active Routes

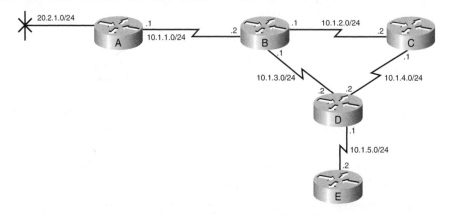

```
RouterE#show ip eigrp topology active
IP-EIGRP Topology Table for AS (1) / ID (10.1.5.2)
```

The output for **show ip eigrp topology active** does not show anything for Router E. This indicates that, as far as Router E is concerned, no routes are in active state. The next step is to Telnet back to Router D to double-check whether the router is still in active state for route 20.2.1.0/24. Telnetting back to Router D shows that Router D is still in active state for route 20.2.1.0/24, but Router E does not have any routes in active state.

Here is a summary of the events so far:

1. Router A went active for route 20.2.1.0/.24 and is waiting for Router B to reply to its query.

2. Router B cannot reply, because it is waiting for the query response from Router D.

3. Router D cannot reply, because it is waiting for Router E to reply to the query.

4. The **show ip eigrp topology active** command in Router E shows that Router E does not think that any routes are active, whereas going back to Router D shows that the route 20.2.1.0/24 is still in active state.

From this sequence of events, you can see that there is clearly a discrepancy between Router D and Router E. More investigation is needed between these two routers.

A look at Router D and Router E CPU utilization and memory usage does not show a problem. The CPU utilization and available memory are normal for both routers. Look at the Router D neighbor list to see if there is a problem with the neighbors. Example 5-100 shows the Router D EIGRP neighbor list.

Example 5-100 *Router D Has Three EIGRP Neighbors*

```
RouterD#show ip eigrp neighbors
IP-EIGRP neighbors for process 1
H   Address   Interface  Hold  Uptime   SRTT RTO   Q    SEQ
                               (sec) (ms)      Cnt  Num
2   10.1.5.2   Se1/2      13    00:00:14  0    5000  1    0
1   10.1.3.1   Se1/0      13    01:22:54  227  1362  0    385
0   10.1.4.1   Se1/1      10    01:24:08  182  1140  0    171
```

Notice that there is a problem in Router D with EIGRP sending a reliable packet to the neighbor with an IP address of 10.1.5.2 (Router E), as shown in Example 5-100. The Q count is 1, and performing the **show ip eigrp neighbors** command a few times in succession shows that the Q count is not decrementing.

The RTO counter is at its maximum value of 5000 ns. This indicates that Router D is trying to send a reliable packet to Router E, but Router E never acknowledges the reliable packet back to Router D. Because Router E does not appear to have a high CPU or memory problem, the link should be tested for reliability between Router D and Router E. Example 5-101 shows the output of a **ping** from Router D to Router E.

Example 5-101 *A Ping from Router D to Router E Fails*

```
RouterD#ping 10.1.5.2


Type escape sequence to abort.
Sending 5, 100-byte ICMP Echos to 10.1.5.2, timeout is 2 seconds:


.....


Success rate is 0 percent (0/5)
```

The ping test shows a success rate of 0 percent. This test shows that a link problem exists between Router D and Router E. The link can pass a multicast packet to establish an EIGRP neighbor relationship, but it is having problems transmitting a unicast packet. This link problem is the root cause of the EIGRP stuck-in-active problem in this example. The way to troubleshoot the EIGRP stuck-in-active problem is to chase the query, hop by hop, and find out the status of the active route at each hop.

This process is typical troubleshooting methodology for combating the EIGRP stuck-in-active problem. Sometimes, chasing the query hop by hop leads to a loop, or too many neighbors did not reply to the query. In this case, simplify and reduce the complexity of the EIGRP topology by cutting down the redundancy. The simpler the EIGRP topology, the easier it is to troubleshoot an EIGRP stuck-in-active problem.

Stuck in Active—The Ultimate Solution

The ultimate solution for preventing the EIGRP stuck-in-active problem is to manually summarize the routes whenever possible and to have a hierarchical network design. The more networks EIGRP summarizes, the less work it has to do when a major convergence takes place. Therefore, this reduces the number of queries being sent and ultimately reduces the occurrence of EIGRP stuck-in-active errors. Figure 5-31 shows a poor network design that does not scale in a large EIGRP network.

Figure 5-31 IP Design Is Critical

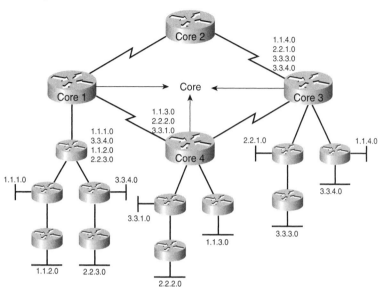

In Figure 5-31, each core router represents a region of the entire network and shows that the IP addressing scheme has no hierarchy. The Core 1 router is injecting routes 1.1.1.0, 3.3.4.0, 1.1.2.0, and 2.2.3.0 into the core network. The addresses are so scattered that no manual summarization is possible.

The other core routers are experiencing the same problem. The Core 3 and Core 4 routers cannot summarize any routes into the core network. As a result of the FastEthernet link of 3.3.3.0 network flapping, the query travels to the Core 3 router. Then the query also is seen in the Core 1 and Core 4 regions. Ultimately, the query travels to all routers in the internetwork. This dramatically increases the likelihood of an EIGRP stuck-in-active problem.

The best practice is to readdress the IP addressing scheme. One region should take only a block of IP addresses. This way, the core routers can summarize the routes into the core, resulting in a reduced routing table in the core. The routers and the query are contained in only one region. Figure 5-32 shows an improved and more scalable EIGRP network design.

Figure 5-32 Good IP Design Is Scalable

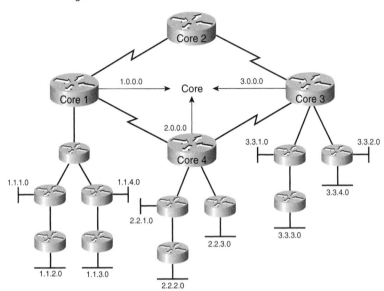

Comparing the sample networks makes it evident that the network presented in the second example is much more structured. The Core 1 router region takes only the 1.0.0.0 block of IP addresses, the Core 4 region takes only the 2.0.0.0 block, and the Core 3 region takes only the 3.0.0.0 block. This allows the three core routers to summarize their routes into the core. If the Fast Ethernet network of 3.3.3.0 flaps in the Core 3 region, the query is bounded only in the Core 3 region and doesn't travel the entire network to affect all the routers in the network. Summarization and hierarchy are the best design practices for a large-scale network.

Duplicate Router IDs

Sometimes EIGRP does not install routes because of a duplicate router ID problem. EIGRP does not use router ID as extensively as OSPF. EIGRP uses the notion of router ID only for external routes to prevent loops. EIGRP chooses the router ID based on the highest IP address of the loopback interfaces on the router. If the router does not have any loopback interface, the highest active IP address of all the interfaces is chosen as the router ID for EIGRP. Figure 5-33 shows the network setup for this example on EIGRP router IDs. Example 5-102 shows the pertinent configurations for the cause of this problem.

Figure 5-33 EIGRP Router IDs Come into Play with External Routes

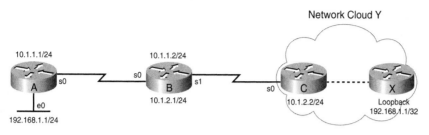

Example 5-102 *The IP Addresses on the EIGRP Routers Affect the Router IDs*

```
RouterA#
interface ethernet 0
ip address 192.168.1.1 255.255.255.0
interface serial 0
ip address 10.1.1.1 255.255.255.0


RouterB#
interface serial 0
ip address 10.1.1.2 255.255.255.0
interface serial 1
ip address 10.1.2.1 255.255.255.0


RouterC#
interface serial 0
ip address 10.1.2.2 255.255.255.0


RouterX#
interface loopback 0
ip address 192.168.1.1 255.255.255.0
```

Router X redistributes a route of 150.150.0.0/16 from OSPF into EIGRP and sends the route
several hops to Router C. Router C receives the route and sends it as an EIGRP external route to
Router B. Router B installs the route in the routing table and sends it to Router A. The **debug**
output in Example 5-103 verifies how Router B sends the route to Router A.

Example 5-103 *A Debug on Router B Shows That 150.150.0.0/16 Is Being Advertised Out Interface Serial 0*

```
RouterB#debug ip eigrp
IP-EIGRP: 150.150.0.0/16 - do advertise out serial 0
```

The problem is that Router A is not installing the 150.150.0.0/16 route in the routing table. As a matter of fact, Router A is not showing the 150.150.0.0/16 route in its topology table. Going back to Router B, the route is in the routing table in Example 5-104, and the topology table appears.

Example 5-104 *The Originating Router for 150.150.0.0/16 Is Indicated in the Output as 192.168.1.1*

```
RouterB#show ip eigrp topology 150.150.0.0 255.255.0.0

IP-EIGRP topology entry for 150.150.0.0/16
State is passive, query origin flag is 1, 1 Successor(s), FD is 3757056
Routing Descriptor Blocks:
10.1.2.2 (Serial1), from 10.1.2.2, Send flag is 0x0
Composite metric is (3757056/3245056), Route is External1

    Vector metric:
    Minimum bandwidth is 1544 Kbit
    Total delay is 82000 microseconds
    Reliability is 255/255
    Load is 1/255
    Minimum MTU is 1500
    Hop count is 7:
    External data:
    Originating router is 192.168.1.1
    AS number or routes is 0
    Administrator tag is 0
```

Router B shows that it is getting the routes from Router C. By looking at the external data section, you see that the originating router is 192.168.1.1, which is seven hops away. The original protocol that originated the route 150.150.0.0/16 is OSPF with a metric of 64. Notice that the originating router is 192.168.1.1. Looking back at the configuration of Router A, notice that Router A also has an IP address of 192.168.1.1 configured on Ethernet 0, and it is the highest IP address on the router.

All this evidence points to a duplicate router ID problem in EIGRP that keeps Router A from installing routes. Because Router X and Router A have the same router ID (192.168.1.1), when Router A receives the route from Router B, it looks at the route's external data section to see who is the originating router. In this case, Router A sees the originating router as 192.168.1.1, which is its own router ID.

Router A does not put the route in its topology table because it thinks that it is the originator of the route and that by receiving the route back from other neighbors, it must be a loop. So, to prevent a routing loop, Router A does not put the route of 150.150.0.0/16 in the topology table. Consequently, the route does not appear in the routing table.

Router A does not install any external routes that originate from Router X because external routes carry the router ID in their EIGRP update packets. Router A installs internal EIGRP routes from Router X without any problem. The duplicate router ID problem happens only for external routes.

The solution to the duplicate router ID problem is to change the IP address of Router X's loopback interface or to change the IP address of Ethernet 0 on Router A. The rule of thumb is to never configure the same IP address on two places in the network. Example 5-105 changes Router X's loopback IP address to 192.168.9.1/32 to fix this problem. The result of the IP address change in Router X is the installation of the 150.150.0.0/16 route in Router A, as shown in Example 5-106.

Example 5-105 *Changing the Loopback Address on Router A Changes Its EIGRP Router ID*

```
RouterX(config)#interface loopback 0
RouterX(config-if)#ip address 192.168.9.1 255.255.255.255
```

Example 5-106 *Router A Installs the 150.150.0.0/16 Network After the Router ID Confusion Is Cleared Up*

```
RouterA#show ip route 150.150.0.0
Routing entry for 150.150.0.0/16
Known via eigrp 1, distance 170, metric 426956, type external
Redistributing via eigrp 1
Last update from 10.1.1.2 on Serial0, 00:06:14 ago
Routing Descriptor Blocks:
*10.1.1.2, from 10.1.1.2, 00:06:14 ago, via Serial0
   Route metric is 4269056, traffic share count is 1
   Total delay is 102000 microseconds,    minimum bandwidth is 1544Kbit
   Reliability 255/255, minimum MTU 1500 bytes
```

continues

Example 5-106 *Router A Installs the 150.150.0.0/16 Network After the Router ID Confusion Is Cleared Up (Continued)*

```
   Loading 1/255, Hops 8


RouterA#show ip eigrp topology 150.150.0.0 255.255.0.0
IP-EIGRP topology entry for 150.150.0.0/16
State is passive, query origin flag is 1,1 Successor(s),
FD is 4269056
Routing Descriptor Blocks:
10.1.1.2 (Serial0), from 10.1.1.2, Send flag is 0x0
Composite metric is (4269056/3757056), Route is External
Vector Metric:
Minimum bandwidth is 1544 kbit
Total delay is 102000 micorseconds
Reliability is 255/255
Load is 1/255
Minimum MTU is 1500
Hop count is 8
External data:
Originating router is 192.168.9.1
AS number or routes is 0
External protocol is OSPF, external metric is 64
Administrator tag is 0
```

EIGRP Error Messages

This section discusses some of the most common EIGRP errors and their meanings:

- The primary route is gone, and no feasible successor exists.

- The neighbor is not on a common subnet.

- EIGRP thinks it knows more routes for a given network than actually exist.

- EIGRP internal error.

- EIGRP attempts to install a route to the destination and fails, most commonly because of the existence of a route with a better administrative distance.

- The interface receives an EIGRP hello packet, and the router attempts to associate the packet with a DUAL descriptor block for that interface, but it does not find one that matches.

■ The router threads a topology table entry as poison in reply to an update, but while the router is building the packet that contains the poison reverse, the router realizes it does not need to send it.

DUAL-3-SIA—This message means that the primary route is gone and no feasible successor is available. The router has sent the queries to its neighbor and has not heard a reply from a particular neighbor for more than 3 minutes. The route state is now stuck in active state.

Neighbor is not on common subnet—This message means that the router has heard a hello packet from a neighbor that is not on the same subnet as the router.

DUAL-3-BADCOUNT—Badcount means that EIGRP believes that it knows of more routes for a given network than actually exist. This message is typically, but not always, seen in conjunction with DUAL-3-SIA, but it is not believed to cause any problems itself.

Unequal, *route*, **dndb =** *metric*, **query =** *metric*—This message indicates that an EIGRP internal error has occurred. However, the router is coded to fully recover from this internal error. The EIGRP internal error is caused by a software problem and should not affect the router's operation. The plan of action is to report this error to the Cisco TAC and have the experts decode the traceback message. At some point the Cisco IOS software should be upgraded accordingly.

IP-EIGRP: Callback: callback_routes—At some point, EIGRP attempted to install routes to the destinations and failed, most commonly because of the existence of a route with a better administrative distance. When this occurs, EIGRP registers its route as a backup route. When the better route disappears from the routing table, EIGRP is called back through callback_routes so that it can attempt to reinstall the routes it is holding in the topology table.

Error: EIGRP: DDB not configured on interface—This message means that when the router's interface receives an EIGRP hello packet and the router attempts to associate the packet with a DUAL descriptor block (DDB) for that interface, it does not find one that matches. This means that the router is receiving a hello packet on the interface that does not have EIGRP configured.

Poison squashed—The router threads a topology table entry as poison in reply to an update (the router is set up for poison reverse). While the router is building the packet that contains the poison reverse, the router realizes that it does not need to send it. For example, if the router receives a query for that route from the neighbor, it is currently threaded to poison.

Troubleshooting OSPF

As with EIGRP, the first order of business with OSPF is to ensure that adjacencies are forming where desired. This section details most of the common troubleshooting issues that come up with OSPF.

Mismatched Parameters

For OSPF to form and maintain neighbor adjacencies, several parameters must match. OSPF neighbors exchange Hello packets periodically (10 seconds by default for LANs) to form neighbor relationships. If specific parameters do not match, the neighbor adjacency is not formed, and the routers do not exchange OSPF updates.

Most mismatch issues can be seen using the **debug ip ospf adj** command.

Hello/dead interval mismatch—Example 5-107 shows the output of R2#**debug ip ospf adj** when the neighbor Hello interval does not match Router R2. The R stands for "received," and the C stands for "configured." Example 5-108 shows the configuration of routers R1 and R2. R2 has a default Hello interval of 10 seconds, whereas R1 has been configured with a Hello interval of 15 seconds. Both the Hello and Dead intervals must match for the routers to form an adjacency. The Dead interval is 4 times the Hello interval.

Example 5-107 *The OSPF Debug Indicates Mismatched Hello Parameters*

```
R2#debug ip ospf adj
OSPF adjacency events debugging is on
R2#
OSPF: Rcv hello from 131.108.2.1 area 4 from Ethernet0
      131.108.1.1
OSPF: Mismatched hello parameters from 131.108.2.1
Dead R 40 C 40, Hello R 15 C 10 Mask R 255.255.255.0
C 255.255.255.0
```

Example 5-108 *The Hello Intervals on R1 and R2 Do Not Match*

```
R2#
interface Ethernet0
ip address 131.108.1.2 255.255.255.0

R1#
interface Ethernet0
ip address 131.108.1.1 255.255.255.0
ip ospf hello-interval 15
```

Example 5-109 shows the corrected R1 configuration. Example 5-110 displays the output of the **show ip ospf neighbor** command. This shows that after the same Hello interval is configured, OSPF forms an adjacency.

Example 5-109 *The Hello Interval on R1 Is Adjusted to Match R2*

```
R1#
interface Ethernet0
ip address 131.108.1.1 255.255.255.0
no ip ospf hello-interval 15
```

Example 5-110 *R1 and R2 Form an OSPF Adjacency After Their Hello Parameters Match*

```
R2#show ip ospf neighbor

Neighbor ID  Pri  State    Dead Time  Address      Interface
131.108.1.2  1    FULL/DR  00:00:32   131.108.1.1  Ethernet0
```

Mismatched authentication type—The output of R2 **debug ip ospf adj** in Example 5-111 indicates that the R2 neighbor is configured for MD5 authentication and that R2 is configured for plain-text authentication. In Example 5-112, the configurations of routers R1 and R2 show that they are using different authentication methods.

Example 5-111 *The OSPF Debug Indicates an Authentication Mismatch*

```
R2#debug ip ospf adj
OSPF adjacency events debugging is on
R2#
OSPF: Rcv pkt from 131.108.1.1, Ethernet0: Mismatch
Authentication type. Input specified type 2, we use type 1.
```

Example 5-112 *R1 and R2 Are Using Different Authentication Methods*

```
R2#
router ospf 1
area 0 authentication
network 131.108.0.0 0.0.255.255 area 0

R1#
router ospf 1
area 0 authentication message-digest
network 131.108.0.0 0.0.255.255 area 0
```

NOTE

Besides the authentication type, the authentication key must also match. Beginning with Cisco IOS Release 12.0.8, RFC 2328 is supported, which allows authentication to be configured on a per-interface basis. Before this release, authentication was supported only on a per-area basis.

To fix this problem, both routers must be configured to use the same type of authentication. You can verify this using the **show ip ospf neighbor** command.

Mismatched area ID—OSPF sends area information in Hello packets. If both sides do not agree that both routers are members of a common area, no OSPF adjacency is formed. The area information is part of the OSPF protocol header.

The output of **debug ip ospf adj** on R1, shown in Example 5-113, indicates that R1 is receiving an OSPF packet from R2 and that the OSPF header has area 0.0.0.1. Looking at the configurations on both routers, you can see that the two routers are configured for different areas, as shown in Example 5-114.

Example 5-113 *R1 and R2 Have a Mismatched Area ID Problem*

```
R1#debug ip ospf adj
OSPF adjacency events debugging is on
R1#
OSPF: Rcv pkt from 131.108.1.2, Ethernet0, area 0.0.0.0
mismatch area 0.0.0.1 in the header
```

Example 5-114 *The Configurations of R1 and R2 Reveal the Error in the Area Assignments*

```
R2#
interface Ethernet0
ip address 131.108.1.2 255.255.255.0
!
router ospf 1
network 131.108.0.0 0.0.255.255 area 1

R1#
interface Ethernet0
ip address 131.108.1.1 255.255.255.0
!
router ospf 1
network 131.108.0.0 0.0.255.255 area 0
```

The solution to this problem is to configure the same area across this common link. To solve this problem, change the area of Router R1 to Area 1. You can use the **show ip ospf neighbor** command to verify that the routers have formed a neighbor relationship.

Mismatched stub/transit/NSSA area options—When OSPF exchanges Hello packets with a neighbor, one of the things it exchanges is an optional capability represented by 8 bits. One of the option fields is for the E bit, which is the OSPF stub flag. When the E bit is set to 0, the area with which the route is associated is a stub area, and no external LSAs are allowed in this area.

If the E bit does not match on both sides, an adjacency is not formed. This is called an optional capabilities mismatch.

The output of **debug ip ospf adj** on R1 in Example 5-115 indicates a stub/transit bit mismatch. Example 5-116 verifies the configuration mismatch.

Example 5-115 *An OSPF Debug Reveals a Stub/Transit Bit Mismatch*

```
R1#debug ip ospf adj
OSPF adjacency events debugging is on
R1#
OSPF: Rcv pkt from 131.108.0.1, Ethernet0 131.108.1.2
OSPF: Hello from 131.108.1.2 with mismatched Stub/Transit area option bit
```

Example 5-116 *The Stub Area Configuration on R1 Is Incomplete*

```
R2#
interface Ethernet0
ip address 131.108.1.2 255.255.255.0
!
router ospf 1
area 1 stub
network 131.108.0.0 0.0.255.255 area 1


R1#
interface Ethernet0
ip address 131.108.1.1 255.255.255.0
!
router ospf 1
network 131.108.0.0 0.0.255.255 area 1
```

The solution is to configure the routers with the appropriate **stub** commands. Example 5-117 shows a configuration change on R1 that fixes the problem. Router R1 is now also a part of the stub area. Using the **show ip ospf neighbor** command verifies that the routers have formed a neighbor relationship.

Example 5-117 *The* **area 1 stub** *Command Is Added to the Configuration of R1*

```
R1#
interface Ethernet0
ip address 131.108.1.1 255.255.255.0
!
router ospf 1
area 1 stub
network 131.108.0.0 0.0.255.255 area 1
```

OSPF State Issues

Routers being neighbors does not guarantee an exchange of link-state updates. Neighbor routers must form adjacencies for this to happen. Interface type plays a major role in how the adjacencies are formed. For example, neighbors on point-to-point links always become adjacent.

As soon as a router decides to form an adjacency with a neighbor, it starts by exchanging a full copy of its link-state database. The neighbor follows suit. After passing through several neighbor states, the routers become adjacent. The following is a list of the different states that OSPF can be stuck in and some of the possible causes.

OSPF stuck in ATTEMPT—This problem is valid only for NBMA networks in which **neighbor** statements have been defined. Stuck in ATTEMPT means that a router is trying to contact a neighbor by sending its Hello, but it has not received a response. The output of **show ip ospf neighbor** in Example 5-118 indicates that this problem exists.

Example 5-118 *R2 Indicates an OSPF Stuck-in-ATTEMPT Issue*

```
R2#show ip ospf neighbor

Neighbor ID  Pri State          Dead Time Address      Interface
N/A           0   ATTEMPT/DROTHER 00:01:57  131.108.1.1 Serial0
```

The most common possible causes of this problem are

- Misconfigured **neighbor** statement.
- Unicast connectivity is broken on the NBMA, which could be caused by a wrong DLCI, an access list, or NAT translating the unicast.

OSPF stuck in INIT—INIT state indicates that a router sees Hello packets from the neighbor, but two-way communication has not been established. A Cisco router includes the router IDs of all neighbors in INIT (or higher) state in the neighbor field of its Hello packets. For two-way communication to be established with a neighbor, a router also must see its own router ID in the neighbor field of the Hello packets coming from the neighbor router. The output of the **show ip ospf neighbor** command in Example 5-119 indicates that the router is stuck in INIT.

Example 5-119 *R2 Indicates a Stuck-in-INIT Issue*

```
R2#show ip ospf neighbor


Neighbor ID  Pri  State    Dead Time  Address      Interface
131.108.2.1  1    INIT/-   00:00:33   131.108.1.1  Ethernet0
```

The most common possible causes of this problem are

- An access list on one side is blocking OSPF Hellos.
- Multicast capabilities are broken on one side (a switch problem).
- Authentication is enabled on only one side.
- The **frame-relay map/dialer map** statement on one side is missing the **broadcast** keyword.
- Hellos are getting lost on one side at Layer 2.

OSPF stuck in 2-WAY—Two-way state indicates that the router has seen its own router ID in the neighbor field of the neighbor Hello packet. The reception of a database descriptor (DBD) packet from a neighbor in INIT state also causes a transition to two-way state. The OSPF neighbor two-way state is not cause for concern.

On networks that require a DR/BDR election to take place, if all routers are configured with priority 0, no election occurs. All routers remain in two-way state, as the **show ip ospf neighbor** command shown in Example 5-120 indicates. The solution is to make sure at least one router has an IP OSPF priority of at least 1.

Example 5-120 *Two-Way State Does Not Necessarily Indicate a Problem*

```
R2#show ip ospf neighbor


Neighbor ID  Pri State         Dead Time  Address      Interface
131.108.2.1  0   2-WAY/DROTHER  00:00:32   131.108.1.1 Ethernet0
```

OSPF stuck in EXSTART/EXCHANGE—OSPF neighbors that are in EXSTART or EXCHANGE state are in the process of trying to exchange DBD packets. The router and its neighbor form a master/slave relationship. The adjacency should continue past this state. If it does not, there is a problem with the DBD exchange, such as a MTU mismatch, or the receipt of an unexpected DBD sequence number.

The most common possible causes of this problem are

- Mismatched interface MTU
- Duplicate router IDs on neighbors
- Inability to ping across with more than certain MTU size
- Broken unicast connectivity, which could be because of a wrong DLCI, an access list, or NAT translating the unicast

The **debug ip ospf adj** command can help diagnose these problems, as shown in Example 5-121, which indicates an MTU interface mismatch.

Example 5-121 *Stuck in EXSTART State Indicates an OSPF DBD Exchange Problem*

```
R1#debug ip ospf adj
OSPF: Retransmitting DBD to 131.108.1.2 on Serial0.1
OSPF: Send DBD to 131.108.1.2 on Serial0.1 seq 0x1E55 opt
      0x2 flag 0x7 len 32
OSPF: Rcv DBD from 131.108.1.2 on Serial0.1 seq 0x22AB opt
      0x2 flag 0x7 len 32 mtu 1500 state EXSTART
OSPF: Nbr 131.108.1.2 has larger interface MTU
```

OSPF stuck in LOADING—In LOADING state, routers send link-state request packets. During the adjacency, if a router receives an outdated or missing link-state advertisement (LSA), it requests that LSA by sending a link-state request packet. Neighbors that do not transition beyond this state are most likely exchanging corrupted LSAs. This problem is usually accompanied by an "%OSPF-4-BADLSA" console message. Because this is not a common problem, it is recommended that the network administrator contact the Cisco TAC.

If a neighbor does not reply or a neighbor reply never reaches the local router, the router also is stuck in LOADING state. The most common possible causes of the problem are

- Mismatched MTU
- Corrupted link-state request packet

The output of the **show ip ospf neighbor** command shown in Example 5-122 indicates that the R2 neighbor is stuck in LOADING. The **debug ip ospf adj** command can help diagnose these problems. Command output can indicate an MTU interface mismatch, as shown in Example 5-123. Command output can also indicate a possible problem caused by packet corruption, as shown in Examples 5-124 and 5-125.

Example 5-122 *Stuck in LOADING State Usually Results from Mismatched MTUs or Corrupted LSR Packets*

```
R2#show ip ospf neighbor


Neighbor ID  Pri State     Dead Time  Address      Interface
131.108.2.1  1   Loading/- 00:00:37   131.108.1.1  Serial0
```

Example 5-123 *The* **debug ip ospf adj** *Command Is Very Useful for OSPF Troubleshooting*

```
R2#debug ip ospf adj
OSPF adjacency events debugging is on
R2#
OSPF: Retransmitting request to 131.108.2.1 on Serial0
OSPF: Database request to 131.108.2.1
OSPF: sent LS REQ packet to 131.108.1.1, length 12
OSPF: Retransmitting request to 131.108.2.1 on Serial0
```

Example 5-124 *The Log Indicates a Problem with Packet Corruption*

```
R2#show log
%OSPF-4-ERRRCV: Received invalid packet: Bad Checksum from 131.108.1.1, Serial0
%OSPF-4-ERRRCV: Received invalid packet: Bad Checksum from 131.108.1.1, Serial0
```

Example 5-125 *The Debug Output Displays Retransmission Requests That Might Indicate Packet Corruption*

```
R1#debug ip ospf adj
OSPF adjacency events debugging is on
R2#
OSPF: Retransmitting request to 131.108.2.1 on Serial0
OSPF: Database request to 131.108.2.1
OSPF: sent LS REQ packet to 131.108.1.1, length 12
OSPF: Retransmitting request to 131.108.2.1 on Serial0
```

One Side of the Point-to-Point Link Is Unnumbered

Figure 5-34 shows a network setup in which the R1 serial link is unnumbered to the loopback interface and the R2 serial link is numbered.

Figure 5-34 Unnumbered Endpoint with OSPF

When OSPF creates a router LSA for point-to-point links, it adheres to the following rule to fill the Link ID and Link Data fields in the router LSA, as described in Table 5-1: The Link Data field for unnumbered point-to-point links should have a MIB-II Index value. Because the link data value of the numbered interface does not match that of the unnumbered interface, this creates a discrepancy in the OSPF database.

Table 5-1 Link ID and Link Data Fields

Type	Description	Link ID	Link Data
1	Point-to-point numbered	Neighbor router ID	Interface IP address
1	Point-to-point unnumbered	Neighbor router ID	MIB-II IfIndex value

Example 5-126 shows the discrepancy in the OSPF database. The R1 router LSA shows the MIB-II IfIndex value in the Link Data field for Serial 0, and the R2 router LSA shows the router serial interface in the Link Data field.

Example 5-126 *There Is a Discrepancy Between the Link Data Field Entries for R1 and R2*

```
R2#show ip ospf database router


OSPF Router with ID (131.108.1.2) (Process ID 1)


Router Link States (Area 0)


Adv Router is not-reachable
LS age: 855
Options: (No TOS-capability, DC)
LS Type: Router Links
Link State ID: 131.108.1.1
Advertising Router: 131.108.1.1
LS Seq Number: 8000000D
```

Example 5-126 *There Is a Discrepancy Between the Link Data Field Entries for R1 and R2 (Continued)*

```
Checksum: 0x55AD

Length: 60

Number of Links: 1


   Link connected to: another Router (point-to-point)

   (Link ID) Neighboring Router ID: 131.108.1.2

   (Link Data) Router Interface address: 0.0.0.4

   Number of TOS metrics: 0

   TOS 0 Metrics: 64


R1#show ip ospf database router


   OSPF Router with ID (131.108.1.1)(Process ID 1)


   Router Link States (Area 0)


Adv Router is not-reachable

LS age: 855

Options: (No TOS-capability, DC)

LS Type: Router Links

Link State ID: 131.108.1.2

Advertising Router: 131.108.1.2

LS Seq Number: 8000000D

Checksum: 0x55AD

Length: 60

Number of Links: 1


   Link connected to: another Router (point-to-point)

   (Link ID) Neighboring Router ID: 131.108.1.1

   (Link Data) Router Interface address: 131.108.1.2

   Number of TOS metrics: 0

   TOS 0 Metrics: 64
```

Example 5-127 shows the configuration on both R1 and R2, with the R1 serial interface unnumbered to a loopback address and the R2 serial interface numbered.

Example 5-127 *The Serial 0 Interface on Router R1 Is Unnumbered*

```
R1#
interface Loopback0
ip address 131.108.1.1 255.255.255.0
!
interface Serial0
ip unnumbered Loopback0
!
router ospf 1
network 131.108.0.0 0.0.255.255 area 0


R2#
interface Serial0
ip address 131.108.1.2 255.255.255.0
!
router ospf 1
network 131.108.0.0 0.0.255.255 area 0
```

To fix this problem, both sides need to be either a numbered point-to-point link or an unnumbered point-to-point link. Example 5-128 shows the new configuration that solves this problem.

Example 5-128 *The Configuration on Interface Serial 0 Is Changed to Remove the Unnumbered Reference*

```
R1#
interface Serial0
ip address 131.108.1.1 255.255.255.0
!
router ospf 1
network 131.108.0.0 0.0.255.255 area 0


R2#
interface Serial0
ip address 131.108.1.2 255.255.255.0
!
router ospf 1
network 131.108.0.0 0.0.255.255 area 0
```

ABR Is Not Generating a Type 4 Summary LSA

One of the functions of a Type 4 summary LSA is to announce the reachability of an ASBR to other areas. The Type 4 LSA is not required if the ASBR exists in the same area.

The ASBR does not generate the Type 4 summary LSA if it is not connected to Area 0. To generate a summary LSA of Type 3 or Type 4, a router must have a connection to Area 0. As a result, the external routes are not installed in the network.

Figure 5-35 shows a network in which R3 redistributes RIP routes into OSPF. Example 5-129 shows that R1 is not installing the external route 200.200.200.0/24 into the routing table.

Figure 5-35 *R3 Redistributes RIP Routes into OSPF*

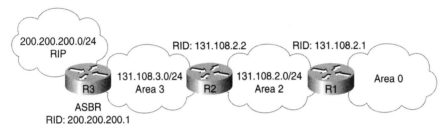

Example 5-129 *R1 Is Not Installing the External Route 200.200.200.0/24*

```
R1#show ip route 200.200.200.0
%Network not in table
R1#
```

The output of the **show ip ospf database external** command in Example 5-130 shows that the route exists in router 1's external OSPF database. However, the output of the **show ip ospf database asbr-summary** command in Example 5-131 shows that this route has no Type 4 LSA.

Example 5-130 *The 200.200.200.0/24 Route Appears in the OSPF Database as an External Route*

```
R1#show ip ospf database external 200.200.200.0


OSPF Router with ID (131.108.2.1) (Process ID 1)


Type-5 AS External Link States
```

continues

Example 5-130 *The 200.200.200.0/24 Route Appears in the OSPF Database as an External Route (Continued)*

```
LS age: 199
Options: (No TOS-capability, DC)
LS Type: AS External Link
Link State ID: 200.200.200.0 (External Network Number)
Advertise Router: 131.108.3.3
LS Seq Number: 80000001
Checksum: 0x4B3A
Length: 36
Network Mask: /24
    Metric Type: 2 (Larger than any link state path)
    TOS: 0
    Metric: 20
    Forward Address: 0.0.0.0
    External Route Tag: 0
```

Example 5-131 *OSPF Router 131.108.3.3 Advertises the 200.200.200.0/24 Route. This ASBR Router Does Not Generate a Type 4 LSA Because It Is Not Connected to Area 0.*

```
R1#show ip ospf database asbr-summary 131.108.3.3


    OSPF Router with ID (131.108.2.1) (Process ID 1)
```

NOTE

All areas in an OSPF autonomous system must be physically or virtually connected to the backbone area (Area 0). For a router to be an ABR, one of its interfaces must be part of Area 0.

The next logical step is to go on the ABR and see if it is indeed an ABR. If it is, it generates a summary LSA of Type 3 or Type 4. If it is not an ABR, it does not generate that summary. The output of the **show ip ospf** command in Example 5-132 shows that Router R2, which is between two areas and might look like an ABR, is not identifying itself as an ABR. If R2 were an ABR, the output would say that is an "Area Border Router."

Example 5-132 *R2 Is Not an ABR Because It Is Not Connected to Area 0*

```
R2#show ip ospf
Routing Process "ospf 1" with ID 131.108.2.2
Supports only single TOS(TOS0) routes
SPF schedule delay 5 secs, Hold time between two SPFs 10 secs
```

In this example, Router R2 does not generate the Type 4 summary LSA because it is not connected to Area 0. To generate a summary LSA of Type 3 or Type 4, a router must have a connection into Area 0.

To solve this problem, Router R2 must be connected to Area 0, either physically or virtually by creating a virtual link, as shown in Example 5-133. When you configure a virtual link on R2, the router becomes virtually connected to Area 0; therefore, it now considers itself an ABR. After R2 gets connected to Area 0, the output of **show ip ospf** shows that it is now an ABR, as shown in Example 5-134.

Example 5-133 *A Virtual Link Is Configured Between R1 and R2 So That Area 3 Is Connected to Area 0*

```
R1#
router ospf 1
area 2 virtual-link 131.108.2.2


R2#
router ospf 1
area 2 virtual-link 131.108.2.1
```

Example 5-134 *With a Virtual Link in Place, R2 Is Connected to Area 0 and Hence Serves as an ABR*

```
R2#show ip ospf
Routing Process "ospf 1" with ID 131.108.2.2
Supports only single TOS(TOS0) routes
It is an area border router
SPF schedule delay 5 secs, Hold time between two SPFs 10 secs
```

After the configuration change on R2, R1 is now generating a Type 4 summary LSA into Area 3, as shown in Example 5-135. Because the Type 4 LSA is now being received, R1 installs the external route 200.200.200.0/24 into its routing table, as shown in Example 5-136.

Example 5-135 *R2 Generates a Type 4 Summary Route After the Virtual Link Is Formed*

```
R1#show ip ospf database asbr-summary


OSPF Router with ID (131.108.2.1) (Process ID 1)


   Summary ASB Link States (Area 2)
```

continues

Example 5-135 *R2 Generates a Type 4 Summary Route After the Virtual Link Is Formed (Continued)*

```
  LS age: 17
  Options: (No TOS-capability, DC)
  LS Type: Summary Links(AS Boundary Router)
  Link State ID: 131.108.3.3 (AS Boundary Router address)
  Advertising Router: 131.108.2.2
  LS Seq Number: 80000001
  Checksum: 0xE269
  Length: 28
  Network Mask: /0
      TOS: 0 Metric: 64
```

Example 5-136 *R1 Is Now Receiving the External Route 200.200.200.0/24*

```
R1#show ip route 200.200.200.0
Routing entry for 200.200.200.0/24
  Known via "ospf 2", distance 110, metric 20, type extern 2, forward metric 128
  Redistributing via ospf 2
  Last update from 131.108.2.2 on Serial0.1, 00:47:24 ago
  Routing Descriptor Blocks:
* 131.108.2.2, from 131.108.3.3, 00:47:24 ago, via Serial0.1
      Route metric is 20, traffic share count is 1
```

Forwarding Address Is Not Known Through the Intra-Area or Interarea Route

When OSPF learns an external LSA, it makes sure that the forwarding address is known through an OSPF intra-area or interarea route before it installs the route in the routing table. In accordance with the RFC 2328 standard, if the forwarding address is not known through an intra-area or interarea route, OSPF does not install the route in the routing table. Figure 5-36 shows OSPF and RIP both running on a common subnet.

Figure 5-36 OSPF and RIP Are Both Running on a Common Subnet

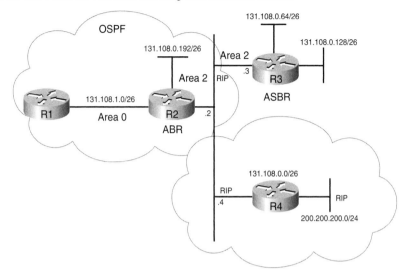

Figure 5-36 shows a network with the following specifications:

- R3 is an ASBR and is redistributing RIP routes into OSPF.
- R4 is running RIP with R3.
- R4 is learning 200.200.200.0/24 through RIP.
- R2 is running OSPF with R3.
- R2 is the ABR.

The network is experiencing a problem of external routes not getting installed in the routing table. Example 5-136 shows the output of **show ip route** for 200.200.200.0/24 on Router R1. This network resides in a RIP domain. Because RIP is being redistributed into OSPF on Router R3, all OSPF routers should see this external OSPF route. However, Router R1 does not see it in its routing table.

Example 5-137 *R1 Is Not Receiving the External Route 200.200.200.0/24*

```
R1#show ip route 200.200.200.0
%Network not in table
R1#
```

Example 5-138 shows the external LSA for 200.200.200.0/24 on R1. The output of the **show ip ospf database external** command shows that the external LSA exists in the OSPF database, but the route is still not being installed in the routing table. Note the forwarding address involved in this external LSA.

Example 5-138 *The External LSA for 200.200.200.0/24 Appears in the OSPF Database*

```
R1#show ip ospf database external 200.200.200.0
    OSPF Router with ID (131.108.1.1) (Process ID 1)
    Type -5 AS External Link States


LS age: 14
Options: (No TOS-capability, DC)
LS Type: AS External Link
Link State ID: 200.200.200.0 (External Network Number)
Advertising Router: 131.108.0.129
LS Seq Number: 80000001
Checksum: 0x88BE
Length: 36
Network Mask: /24
    Metric Type: 2 (Larger than any link state path)
    TOS: 0
    Metric: 20
    Forward Address: 131.108.0.4
    External Route Tag: 0
```

Example 5-139 shows that the route to the forwarding address of 131.108.0.4 is known through an OSPF external route, which explains why R1 is not installing the 200.200.200.0/24 route in the routing table. The ABR is summarizing 131.108.0.0/24 with the **area range** command, so the more specific intra-area routes are summarized into one route, as shown in Example 5-140. This range summarizes all routes under the 131.108.0.0/26 range.

Example 5-139 *The Forwarding Address for 200.200.200.0/24 Is 131.108.0.4 on R4. R1 Learns About 131.108.0.4 Via OSPF*

```
R1#show ip route 131.108.0.4
Routing entry for 131.108.0.0/26
    Known via "ospf 1", distance 110, metric 20, type extern 2, forward metric 70
    Redistributing via ospf 1
    Last update from 131.108.1.2 on Serial0, 00:00:40 ago
```

Example 5-139 *The Forwarding Address for 200.200.200.0/24 Is 131.108.0.4 on R4. R1 Learns About 131.108.0.4 Via OSPF (Continued)*

```
  Routing Descriptor Blocks:
* 131.108.1.2, from 131.108.0.129, 00:00:40 ago, via Serial0
  Route metric is 20, traffic share count is 1
```

Example 5-140 *R2 Is Configured to Advertise the Summary Route 131.108.0.0/24*

```
R2#
router ospf 1
  network 131.108.1.0 0.0.0.255 area 0
  network 131.108.0.0 0.0.0.255 area 2
  area 2 range 131.108.0.0 255.255.255.0
```

Example 5-141 shows that the ASBR is doing the redistribution from RIP into OSPF. This configuration redistributes 131.108.0.0/26, which includes R3's connected interface with IP address 138.108.0.4, the forwarding address that appears in Example 5-138.

Example 5-141 *R3 Redistributes RIP Subnets into OSPF*

```
R3#
router ospf 1
redistribute rip subnets
network 0.0.0.0 255.255.255.255 area 2
!
router rip
network 131.108.0.0
```

R1 sees the forwarding address learned through external OSPF as part of the network 131.108.0.0/26. Also, R2 suppresses the intra-area route for this subnet because R2 is summarizing 131.108.0.0/24. Because the more specific route is always preferred, R1 prefers the more specific external route of 131.108.0.0/26 over the less-specific summarized route of 131.108.0.0/24.

This problem can be solved in one of two ways:

- Do not summarize at the ABR.
- Filter the connected subnet from being redistributed into OSPF at the ASBR.

To implement the first solution, remove the **area range** command on the ABR, as shown in Example 5-142.

Example 5-142 *Removing the Summary Route from R2 Allows the Intra-Area Route 131.108.0.0/26 to Be Advertised to R1*

```
R2#
router ospf 1
   network 131.108.1.0 0.0.0.255 area 0
   network 131.108.0.0 0.0.0.255 area 2
   no area 2 range 131.108.0.0 255.255.255.0
```

To implement the second solution, add a filter to control the redistributed routes on the ASBR. A route map is added to the **redistribute rip** command, as shown in Example 5-143, to prevent the route 131.108.0.0/26 from getting redistributed into OSPF, permitting only the 200.200.200.0/24 route.

Example 5-143 *Restricting R3 to Redistribute Only the 200.200.200.0/24 RIP Network on R3 Prevents R2 from Learning the 131.108.0.0/26 Network as an External Route, so R2 Advertises That Network to R1 as an Internal Route*

```
R3#
router ospf 1
redistribute rip subnets route-map no_connected
network 0.0.0.0 255.255.255.255 area 2
!
router rip
network 131.108.0.0
!
route-map no_connected permit 10
match ip address 1
!
access-list 1 permit 200.200.200.0 0.0.0.255
```

Examples 5-144 and 5-145 show the changes in the R1 routing table for the external 200.200.200.0/24 route. They also show that the forwarding address is now known through OSPF interarea instead of OSPF external.

Example 5-144 *R1 Is Now Receiving the External Route 200.200.200.0/24*

```
R1#show ip route 200.200.200.0
Routing entry for 200.200.200.0/24
Known via "ospf 2", distance 110, metric 20, type extern 2, forward metric 128
Redistributing via ospf 2
Last update from 131.108.1.2 on Serial0.1, 00:47:24 ago
Routing Descriptor Blocks:
* 131.108.1.2, from 131.108.0.29, 00:47:24 ago, via Serial0.1
Route metric is 20, traffic share count is 1
```

Example 5-145 *R1 Is Learning 131.108.0.4 Via Interarea OSPF, Which Explains Why R1 Now Includes 200.200.200.0/24 In Its Routing Table*

```
R1#debug ip route 131.108.0.4
Routing entry for 131.108.0.4/26
Known via "ospf 2", distance 110, metric 64, type inter area
Redistributing via ospf 2
Last update from 131.108.1.2 on Serial0.1, 00:50:25 ago
Routing Descriptor Blocks:
*131.108.1.2 from 131.108.0.193, 00:50:25 ago, via Serial0.1
Route metric is 64, traffic share count is 1
```

Route Summarization Problems

Route summarization allows a group of contiguous networks to be summarized as fewer addresses to help reduce the size of the routing table, thus increasing the performance of OSPF and other routing protocols.

OSPF can use two types of summarization:

- Interarea route summarization that can be done on the ABR
- External route summarization that can be done on the ASBR

Figure 5-37 shows a network in which a router is not summarizing interarea routes.

Figure 5-37 OSPF Can Perform Internal and External Route Summarization

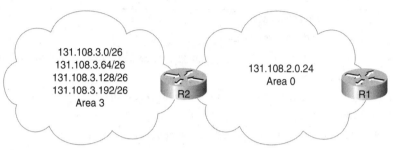

131.108.3.0/26
131.108.3.64/26
131.108.3.128/26
131.108.3.192/26
Area 3

131.108.2.0.24
Area 0

R2

R1

R1 has the **area range** command for summarization of Area 3 routes, as shown in Example 5-146. The syntax of the command is correct, but the problem is that R1 is not an ABR. Router R1 is included in Area 0, but it is not connected to Area 3 and, thus, cannot summarize Area 3 routes.

Example 5-146 *R1 Cannot Summarize Area 3 Routes*

```
R1#
router ospf 1
network 131.108.2.0 0.0.0.255 area 0
area 3 range 131.108.3.0 255.255.255.0
```

A way to check if a router is summarizing the routes properly is to use the **show ip ospf** command. In Example 5-147, the output of **show ip ospf** shows that the area 3 range is passive. Passive means that no addresses within this area fall within this range. In fact, R1 does have the routes in this range; however, because R1 is not connected to area 3, the range appears passive.

Example 5-147 *No Interfaces on R1 Lie in Area 3*

```
R1#show ip ospf

Area 3
    Number of interfaces in this area is 0
    Area has no authentication
    SPF algorithm executed 1 times
    Area ranges are
    131.108.3.0/24
```

Because summarization is not happening, R1 is receiving four routes in the routing table instead of one summarized route, as shown in Example 5-148.

Example 5-148 *R1 Is Not Receiving a Summarized Route for the Subnets of 131.108.3.0/24 Propagated by R2*

```
R1#show ip route
...
O IA   131.108.3.0/26 [110/64] via 131.108.2.2, 00:01:35, Serial0
O IA   131.108.3.64/26 [110/64] via 131.108.2.2, 00:01:35, Serial0
O IA   131.108.3.128/26 [110/64] via 131.108.2.2, 00:01:35, Serial0
O IA   131.108.3.192/26 [110/64] via 131.108.2.2, 00:01:35, Serial0
```

The solution to this problem is to configure the **area range** command on the ABR, which is R2, as shown in Example 5-149. After changing the configuration and removing the **area range** command on R1, verify that the summarization is indeed active by using **show ip ospf** on R2, as shown in Example 5-150. Example 5-151 shows that the summarized route is now being installed in the routing table of R1.

Example 5-149 *Configuring the **area range** Command on R2 Solves the Problem*

```
R2#
router ospf 1
   network 131.108.3.0 0.0.0.255 area 3
   network 131.108.2.0 0.0.0.255 area 0
   area 3 range 131.108.3.0 255.255.255.0
```

Example 5-150 *R2 Has Four Interfaces in Area 3*

```
R2#show ip ospf

   Area 3
      Number of interfaces in this area is 4
      Area has no authentication
      SPF algorithm executed 1 times
      Area ranges are
         131.108.3.0/24 Active (64)
```

NOTE

Similar issues arise with external summarization, which is done on the ASBR. External summarization uses the **summary-address** command only on the ASBR. The **show ip ospf summary-address** command can be used to help troubleshoot external summarization issues. A metric of infinity, as shown in Example 1-152, means that no valid addresses belong to this range of summarization and that there is a problem. (16,777,215 equates to infinity because the external LSA metric is 24 bits long and 2^{24} equals 16,777,216.) Example 1-153 shows the same **show ip ospf summary-address** command, when summarization is configured correctly on the ASBR, with a metric of less than infinity.

Example 5-151 *R1 Is Now Learning the Summary Route 131.108.0.0/24*

```
R1#show ip route

...

O IA   131.108.0.0/24 [110/64] via 131.108.2.2, 00:01:35, Serial0
```

Example 5-152 *R1 Sees the Route 132.108.3.0/24 as Having an "Infinite" Metric*

```
R1#show ip ospf summary-address

OSPF Process 1, Summary-address

132.108.3.0/255.255.255.0 Metric 16777215, Type 0, Tag 0
R1#
```

Example 5-153 *With the Proper* **summary-address** *OSPF Command Configured, R1 Advertises the*
132.108.3.0/24 Network with a Finite Metric

```
R2#show ip ospf summary-address
OSPF Process 1, Summary-address

132.108.3.0/255.255.255.0 Metric 5, Type 0, Tag 0
R2#
```

CPUHOG Problems

When OSPF forms an adjacency, it floods all the link-state update packets to its neighbors.
Sometimes, the flooding process takes a lot of time, depending on the router resources.
CPUHOG messages appear in the log if the router's resources become exhausted because
of flooding.

CPUHOG messages usually appear in two significant stages:

- Neighbor formation process
- LSA refresh process

Neighbor Formation Process

When OSPF forms an adjacency, it floods all its link-state packets to its neighbor. This flooding sometimes takes a lot of CPU processing. Starting with Cisco IOS Release 12.0T, packet
pacing was included to help prevent CPU processing problems from occurring. Before
Release 12.0T, the IOS did not support packet pacing.

During link-state flooding, a router tries to send data as fast as it can over a link. If a link is slow or the router on the other side is slow in responding, the LSA is retransmitted, and eventually it leads to CPUHOG messages. Packet pacing adds a pacing interval between the LS updates. Instead of flooding everything at once, packet pacing sends the packet with a gap of a few milliseconds in between.

Example 5-154 shows the log messages on a router showing CPUHOG during adjacency formation. Packet pacing introduces a delay of 33 ms between packets and 66 ms between retransmissions. This pacing interval reduces the CPUHOG messages, and the adjacency is formed more quickly.

Example 5-154 *CPUHOG Messages Appear During Adjacency Formation and During Each LSA Refresh*

```
R1#show log
%SYS-3-CPUHOG: Task ran for 2424 msec (15/15), process = OSPF Router
%SYS-3-CPUHOG: Task ran for 2340 msec (10/9), process = OSPF Router
%SYS-3-CPUHOG: Task ran for 2264 msec (0/0), process = OSPF Router
```

If a router is experiencing this problem with an IOS prior to Release 12.0T, the solution is to upgrade to 12.0T or higher.

LSA Refresh Process

Starting with Cisco IOS 12.0, the LSA group pacing feature was introduced to eliminate a CPU processing problem that can occur every 30 minutes. Before IOS 12.0, all LSAs were flooded every 30 minutes to refresh the MAXAGE times in the link-state database. Without this flooding, the LSAs would expire after 60 minutes. This flooding is also known as a paranoid update.

This flooding causes CPUHOG messages every 30 minutes, especially in cases where a couple thousand LSAs are all being flooded at the same time. The CPUHOG messages appear in the router log every 30 minutes, as shown in Example 5-154.

LSA group packing looks at the LSA periodic interval (every 4 minutes, by default) and refreshes only LSAs that are past their refresh time. This is an efficient way of reducing a large flood by chopping it down to smaller LSA floods. No extra configuration is required for this feature, but for large numbers of LSAs (generally 10,000 or more), it is recommended that you use small intervals (for example, every 2 minutes); for a few hundred LSAs, use a large interval, such as 20 minutes.

If 10,000 LSAs need to be refreshed, keeping the refresh interval smaller causes the LSA to be checked every 2 or 4 minutes to see how many LSAs have reached the refresh interval, which is 30 minutes. The advantage of checking this frequently is that few LSAs need to be refreshed every 2 or 4 minutes, and this does not cause a huge storm of LSA updates. If the number of LSAs is small, it really doesn't matter whether the refresh occurs every 2 minutes or 20 minutes. This is why it is better to increase the timer so that all the LSAs, which are few in number, can be refreshed at once. Example 5-155 shows how to configure the LSA refresh interval.

Example 5-155 *The* **timer lsa-group pacing** *Command Allows the Engineer to Adjust the Frequency of Periodic LSA Refreshes*

```
R1(config)#router ospf 1
R1(config-router)#timer lsa-group pacing ?
<10-1800> Interval between group of LSA being
refreshed or maxaged
```

SPF Calculation and Route Flapping

Whenever there is a change in topology, OSPF runs the SPF algorithm to compute the Shortest Path First tree again. Unstable links in the OSPF network could cause constant SPF calculations.

Some of the most common reasons for SPF running constantly are

- Interface flaps within the area
- Neighbor interface flaps within the area
- Duplicate router ID

Topology changes in an OSPF network cause SPF calculations within that area. The SPF is not recalculated if the topology change is in another area. Actually, OSPF distributes interarea (between areas) topology information using a distance vector method. The ABRs forward routing information between areas using a distance vector technique similar to that of RIP or IGRP.

The following is an example of SPF running constantly because of an interface flap within the network. This is a common problem in OSPF. Whenever there is a link flap in an area, OSPF runs SPF within that area. So if a network has unstable links, this can cause constant SPF calculations. SPF itself is not a problem because OSPF is just adjusting to the change in the database through calculating SPF. The real problem occurs if small routers are in the area and a constant SPF run might cause a CPU spike in a router.

Because R1 is also included in Area 0, any link flap in Area 0 causes all routers in Area 0 to run SPF, as shown in Figure 5-38.

Figure 5-38 Link Flaps Propagated Within Area 0

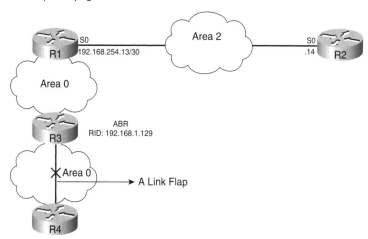

A link flap in an area causes SPF to run. If a link is flapping constantly, this can increase the number of SPF calculations in an area. A constant number of SPF calculations is not a problem, but if the number is incrementing constantly, this indicates a problem.

The output of **show ip ospf** in Example 5-156 shows that there is a huge counter for SPF in Area 0.

Example 5-156 *The* **show ip ospf** *Command Can Be Used to View How Many Times the SPF Algorithm Has Run in a Given Area*

```
R1#show ip ospf
Routing Process "ospf 1" with ID 192.168.254.13
Supports only single TOS(TOS0) routes
It is an area border
SPF schedule delay 5 secs, Hold time between two SPFs 10 secs
Minimum LSA interval 5 secs. Minimum LSA arrival 1 secs
Number of external LSA 8. Checksum Sum 0x48C3E
Number of DCbitless external LSA 0
Number of DoNotAge external LSA 0
Number or areas in this router is 3. 2 normal 1 stub 0 nssa
   Area BACKBONE(0)
   Number of interfaces in this area is 1
   Area has no authentication
   SPF algorithm executed 2668 times
```

The easiest way to find out which LSA is flapping is to turn on **debug ip ospf monitor**. The **debug** command shown in Example 5-157 shows that a router LSA is flapping in Area 0.

Example 5-157 *The* **debug ip ospf monitor** *Command Can Be Used to Isolate a Flapping LSA*

```
R1#debug ip ospf monitor
OSPF: Schedule SPF in area 0.0.0.0
   Change in LS ID 192.168.1.129, LSA type R,
OSPF: Schedule SPF: spf_time 1620348064ms wait_interval 10s
```

The next step is to determine which router LSA is flapping and to check the log for any interface flap. The **show log** command in Example 5-158 shows the log of the router with router ID 192.168.1.129, the ID displayed in the output of the **debug ip ospf monitor** command. The log shows that a serial link keeps going up and down. Whenever an interface flap occurs, it causes SPF to run.

Example 5-158 *The* **show log** *Command Shows That Interface Serial 1 Is Flapping, Causing the LSA Flaps*

```
R3#show log
*Mar 29 01:59:07: %LINEPROTO-5-UPDOWN: Line protocol on Interface Serial1,
   changed state to down
*Mar 29 01:59:09: %LINEPROTO-5-UPDOWN: Line protocol on Interface Serial1,
   changed state to down
*Mar 29 01:59:30: %LINEPROTO-5-UPDOWN: Line protocol on Interface Serial1,
   changed state to down
*Mar 29 02:00:03: %LINEPROTO-5-UPDOWN: Line protocol on Interface Serial1,
   changed state to down
```

This problem has two solutions:

- Fix the link that is flapping.
- Redefine the area boundaries.

Sometimes, the first solution might not be manageable, because the link is flapping as the result of a telco outage that is outside the network boundary. One way to fix this temporarily is to manually shut down the interface.

The second solution requires some redesigning. If the link flap is happening too often, it might be possible to redefine the area, exclude this router from the area, and make it a member of a totally stubby area. Sometimes, this is difficult to implement, depending on this link's physical location.

In short, link flaps are realities; if there are too many, the number of routers in an area should be decreased so that fewer routers are affected.

Troubleshooting IS-IS

IS-IS adjacency troubleshooting is the focus of this section. It is critical that a network engineer ensure that Level 1 and/or Level 2 adjacencies are properly configured for each link. After this section explores adjacency issues, some route advertisement and route flapping problems are considered.

IS-IS Adjacency Problems

IS-IS adjacency-related problems normally are caused by link failures and configuration errors. An IS-IS network is shown in Figure 5-39. On Cisco routers, inspecting the output of the **show interface** command can help you easily identify link failures. Also, because IS-IS routing is not required to establish IP connectivity to directly attached routers, it is easy to discern whether the problem is media-related or specific to the IS-IS configuration.

Figure 5-39 Two IS-IS Areas Are Connected by a Serial Link

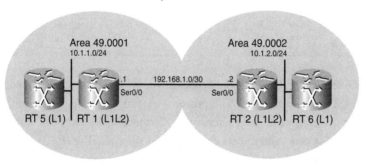

The **show clns neighbors** command is usually the starting point for troubleshooting IS-IS adjacency problems. The output of this command should list all neighbors expected to be adjacent to the router being investigated. The command **show clns is-neighbors** provides similar output, but it is intended to list only neighbor routers or IS-IS adjacencies. **show clns neighbors** lists all types of adjacencies, for both IS-IS and ES-IS.

Using the output from the **show clns neighbors** and **show clns neighbors detail** commands, IS-IS adjacencies can be examined, as shown in Example 5-159. Problems with IS-IS adjacency formation can be registered by the presence of fewer neighbors than expected or a situation in which the status of an expected adjacency is not up. Another symptom could be that the neighbor is known through the ES-IS protocol instead of IS-IS.

Example 5-159 *The* **show clns neighbors** *Command Is Very Useful for Viewing IS-IS Adjacencies*

```
RT1#show clns neighbors

System   Interface   SNPA        State Hold  Type Protocol
Id                                     time
RT2      Se0/0       *HDLC*       Up    27    L2   IS-IS
RT5      Et0/0       00d0.58eb.ff01  Up  27    L1   IS-IS


RT1#show clns neighbors detail

System   Interface   SNPA        State Hold  Type Protocol
Id                                     time
RT2      Se0/0       *HDLC*       Up    24    L2   IS-IS
  Area Address(es):49.0002
  IP Address(es):192.168.1.2*
  Uptime:02:15:11
RT5      Et0/0       00d0.58eb.ff01  Up  23    L1   IS-IS
  Area Address(es):49.0001
  IP Address(es):10.1.1.5*
  Uptime:02:15:11
```

The router RT1 has properly formed adjacencies with its directly connected neighbors, RT2 and RT5. All ISO devices run the ES-IS protocol to facilitate mutual discovery and communication between end systems and routers in the Connectionless Network Service (CLNS) environment. End systems and routers exchange end-system hellos (ESHs) and intermediate-system hellos (ISHs) within the ES-IS framework. Connected routers also receive each other's ISHs and form ES-IS adjacencies. Therefore, it is possible that ES-IS adjacencies might still be formed between two routers even if there are problems with the IS-IS adjacency.

Example 5-160 also shows output from **show clns neighbors**, but it shows problems with the adjacencies formed with RT2 and RT5. In this example, the IS-IS adjacency with RT2 is in INIT state instead of UP. The protocol is correctly shown as IS-IS. The adjacency with RT5 shows UP, but the protocol is ES-IS instead of IS-IS. As explained previously, the ES-IS protocol runs independently of IS-IS; therefore, the ES-IS adjacency formed between RT1 and RT5 has nothing to do with IS-IS.

Example 5-160 *A Problem Is Indicated by the Fact That the Adjacency with RT2 is in INIT State and the Fact That the Neighbor RT5 Is Known Through the ES-IS Protocol*

```
RT1#show clns neighbors

System Interface  SNPA          State  Hold  Type Protocol
Id                                      time
RT2     Se0/0    *HDLC*         Init   27    L2   IS-IS
RT5     Et0/0    00d0.58eb.ff01 Up     27    L1   ES-IS
```

These routers cannot form an IS-IS adjacency with each other, apparently because of a problem in the configuration or the IS-IS environment. Most adjacency problems related to the IS-IS environment can be debugged with the **debug isis adj-packets** command. The output of this command can be daunting if the router under inspection has a lot of neighbors, because the display shows all of the hellos transmitted and received by the local routers.

Some or All of the Adjacencies Are Not Coming Up

The absence of some expected IS-IS adjacencies means that the affected routers cannot exchange routing information, effectively creating reachability problems to certain destinations in the network. Figure 5-39 shows a simple network in which four daisy-chained routers are grouped in twos and placed in separate areas.

Example 5-161 displays different outputs of the **show clns neighbors** command captured on RT1. Example 5-160 displayed two neighbors, but Example 5-160 displays only one neighbor instead of the expected two. RT2 is listed, but RT5 is missing.

Example 5-161 *The* **show clns neighbors** *Command Is Very Useful for Viewing IS-IS Adjacencies*

```
RT1#show clns neighbors

System Interface  SNPA          State  Hold  Type Protocol
Id                                      time
RT2     Se0/0    *HDLC*         Init   27    L2   IS-IS
RT5     Et0/0 00d0.58eb.ff01    Up     25    L1   ES-IS
RT1#show clns neighbors

System Id Interface SNPA    State Holdtime Type Protocol
RT2       Se0/0     *HDLC*  Up    27       L2   IS-IS
```

356 Chapter 5: Layer 3 Troubleshooting

Step 1: Check for link failures—The first step is to check for link failures. On Cisco routers this can be done using the **show ip interface brief** command. If there is a problem, the appropriate interfaces display something other than the up/up state. Shown is an example if there is a link failure problem. The solution is to correct the Layer 1/2 problem.

Step 2: Check for configuration errors—If the link is fine, the next step is to verify the IS-IS configuration, as shown in Example 5-162. Make sure that the IS-IS process is defined and that an network service access point (NSAP) and network entity title (NET) are configured. Unlike other IP routing protocols, the IS-IS configuration does not use **network** statements to enable IS-IS routing on the router interfaces. To enable IS-IS routing for IP on a Cisco router, the **ip router isis** command must be configured on the appropriate interfaces. Make sure that the router-level **passive-interface** command is not being used to disable IS-IS routing on these interfaces. When an interface is made passive, the **ip router isis** command is automatically removed from the interface.

Example 5-162 *The Network Entity Title Is Defined in the IS-IS Router Configuration Mode*

```
router isis
  net 49.0001.0000.0000.0001.00
```

Step 3: Check for mismatched Level 1 and Level 2 interfaces—If the configuration looks correct, the next step is to check for mismatched Level 1 and Level 2 interfaces. IS-IS supports a two-level routing hierarchy in which routing within an area is designated as Level 1 and routing between areas is designated as Level 2. An IS-IS router can be configured to participate in Level 1 routing only (Level 1 router), Level 2 routing only (Level 2 router), or both (Level 1-2 router). Level 1-2 routers act as border routers between IS-IS areas and facilitate interarea communication.

In the default mode of operation, Cisco routers have Level 1-2 capability. Two directly connected routers with a common area ID form a Level 1-2 adjacency by default, even though only a Level 1 adjacency is necessary for them to communicate. Use the **router-level is-type** command to change this behavior.

In Figure 5-39, it is desirable to make RT5 a Level 1-only router while RT1 remains capable of Level 1-2. This requires RT5 to be configured with the **is-type level-1** command, but nothing needs to be done on RT1. If RT1 is made a Level 2-only router with the **is-type level-2-only** command, it cannot form a Level 1 adjacency with RT5. The proper setup is to make RT5 a Level 1 router only if it has limited resources (memory and CPU). RT1 should be a Level 1-2 router for it to communicate with RT5 at Level 1 and with RT2 at Level 2 because RT2 is in another area. Just as with RT5, RT6 can be a Level 1-only router if necessary.

Step 4: Check for area misconfiguration—Two routers in different areas with different area IDs consequently are assigned to different areas; therefore, they form only a Level 2 adjacency. RT5 is configured as Level 1 only, but its area ID is misconfigured to be different from RT1's area ID. These two routers do not form any adjacency. The configuration shown in Example 5-163, even though RT1 is expected to be in area 49.001, has been configured with an area ID of 49.005, placing it in a different area from RT5. Therefore, RT5 must be Level 2-capable to form adjacencies with RT1. However, it has been made a Level-1 router with the command **is-type level-1**. Therefore, no IS-IS adjacency is formed between RT1 and RT5. The solution is to change the area on RT5 to the proper area of 49.0001.

Example 5-163 *RT1 and RT5 Are Configured for Different Areas*

```
hostname RT1
!
interface Ethernet 0/0
  ip address 10.1.1.1 255.255.255.0
  ip router isis
!
router isis
net 49.0001.0000.0000.0001.00


hostname RT5
!
interface Ethernet0/0
ip address 10.1.1.5 255.255.255.0
ip router isis
!
router isis
  net 49.0005.0000.0000.0005.00
is-type level-1
```

Step 5: Check for misconfigured subnets—In recent releases of Cisco IOS software, particularly in the 12.0S, 12.0T, and 12.0T releases, adjacencies are not formed between two neighbors if the directly connected interfaces are not in the same IP subnet. In Example 5-164, RT1's IP address is changed to that of another subnet. In Example 5-165, the output of **debug isis adj-packets** shows that RT1 is rejecting the hello received from RT5 because the interface address 10.1.1.5 advertised by the latter is not on subnet 10.1.8.0/24.

Example 5-164 *The IP Address Is Changed on Interface Ethernet 0/0*

```
RT1#show interface Ethernet 0/0
Ethernet0/0 is up, line protocol is up
  Hardware is AmdP2, address is 00d0.58f7.8941
  (bia 00d0.58f7.8941)
  Internet address is 10.1.1.1/24

RT1#conf t
Enter configuration commands, one per line. End with CNTL/Z.
RT1(config)#int e 0/0
RT1(config-if)#ip address 10.1.8.1 255.255.255.0
RT1(config-if)#^Z
```

Example 5-165 *RT1 Is Rejecting the Hello from RT5*

```
RT1#debug isis adj-packets
IS-IS Adjacency related packets debugging is on

Apr 21 21:55:39: ISIS-Adj: Rec L1 IIH from 00d0.58eb.ff01(Ethernet0/0), cir ty 7
Apr 21 21:55:39: ISIS-Adj: No usable IP interface addresses in LAN IIH from Eth0
Apr 21 21:55:40: ISIS-Adj: Sending L1 IIH on Ethernet0/0, length 1497

Apr 21 21:55:41: ISIS-Adj: Sending serial IIH on Serial0/0, length 1499
Apr 21 21.55:42: ISIS-Adj: Rec L1 IIH from 00d0.58eb.ff01 (Ethernet0/0), cir ty7
Apr 21 21:55:42: ISIS-Adj: No usable IP interface addresses in LAN IIH from Eth0
Apr 21 21:55:43: %CLNS-5-ADJCHANGE: ISIS:Adjacency to RT5 (Ethernet0/0) Down,
Apr 21 21:55:43: ISIS-Adj: L1 adj count 0
```

In earlier Cisco IOS software releases, it didn't matter whether the routers belonged to the different IP subnets, because IS-IS adjacency formation occurs primarily within the CLNP framework, where IP addresses are irrelevant. However, in IP applications, directly connected routers must be on the same subnet, except when IP unnumbered is used. Therefore, the recent behavior provides an extra check for the IP configuration while introducing sanity into IS-IS data structures for tracking IP information.

In summary, it is important to make sure that directly connected routers that need to form IS-IS adjacencies for IP routing are on the same IP subnet.

Step 6: Check for duplicate systems IDs—If the previous steps checked out OK, but a specific neighbor is not in the **show clns neighbors** output, it is possible that adjacency is not being formed because that neighbor has a duplicate system ID with the local router. An IS-IS router does not form an adjacency with a router in the same area that has a duplicate system ID. It also logs duplicate system ID errors, as shown in Example 5-166. Use the **show logging** command to display entries in the log. If duplicate system ID errors are found, the source of the conflict can be determined from the output of **debug adj-packets**, as shown in Example 5-167. This points to the interface where the hellos with the duplicate system ID are coming from.

Example 5-166 *Duplicate System IDs Are Not Allowed in the Same Area*

```
RT1#show logging
Apr 21 16:30:59: %CLNS-3 BADPACKET: ISIS:LAN L1 hello, Duplicate system ID det)
Apr 21 16:31:59: %CLNS-3-BADPACKET: ISIS:LAN L1 hello, Duplicate system ID det)
Apr 21 16:33:00: %CLNS-3-BADPACKET: ISIS:LAN L1 hello, Duplicate system ID det)
```

Example 5-167 *A Duplicate System ID Can Be Isolated with the* **debug isis adj-packets** *Command*

```
RT1#debug isis adj-packets
IS-IS Adjacency related packets debugging is on
RT1#

Apr 21 21:43:08: ISIS-Adj: Sending L2 IIH on Ethernet0/0, length 1497
Apr 21 21:43:09: ISIS-Adj: Sending L1 IIH on Ethernet0/0, length 1497
Apr 21 21:43:09: ISIS-Adj: Rec L1 IIH from 00d0.58eb.ff01
(Ethernet0/0), cir ty 7
Apr 21 21:43:09: ISIS-Adj: Duplicate system id
Apr 21 21:43:12: ISIS-Adj: Sending L1 IIH on Ethernet0/0, length 1497
Apr 21 21:43:12: ISIS-Adj: Sending L2 IIH on Ethernet0/0, length 1497
Apr 21 21:43:12: ISIS-Adj: Rec L1 IIH from 00d0.58eb.ff01 (Ethernet0/0), cir typ7
Apr 21 21:43:08: ISIS-Adj: Duplicate system id
```

Adjacency Is Stuck in INIT State

The most common causes of an adjacency getting stuck in INIT state are mismatched interface MTU and authentication parameters. Figure 5-40 shows two routers running IS-IS. The output from **show clns neighbors** in Example 5-168 shows what an adjacency would look like when stuck in INIT.

Figure 5-40 Connected IS-IS Routers in Distinct Areas

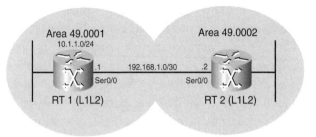

Example 5-168 *The* **show clns neighbors** *Command Can Be Used to Determine Whether Adjacencies Are Forming*

```
RT2#show clns neighbors


System Interface  SNPA      State  Hold  Type Protocol
Id                                 time
RT1     Se0/0     *HDLC*    Init   29    L2   IS-IS
```

Step 1: Check authentication—If IS-IS authentication is configured, the first step in tackling this problem is to address potential issues in this area. The Cisco implementation allows authentication to be configured in three ways: at the domain, area, or interface level. It is important to be sure that the appropriate method is properly configured and that the passwords used are consistent. The output of the **debug isis adj-packets** command in Example 5-169 indicates authentication problems.

Example 5-169 *Authentication Problems Can Be Seen in the Output of the* **debug isis adj-packets** *Command*

```
RT1#debug isis adj-packets
Apr 29 17:09:46: ISIS-Adj: Rec serial IIH from *HDLC* (Serial0/0), cir type L1L9
Apr 29 17:09:46: ISIS-Adj: Authentication failed
Apr 29 17:09:48: ISIS-Adj: Sending serial IIH on Serial0/0, length 1499
Apr 29 17:09:54: ISIS-Adj: Rec serial IIH from *HDLC* (Serial0/0), cir type L1L9
Apr 29 17:09:54: ISIS-Adj: Authentication failed
Apr 29 17:09:56: ISIS-Adj: Sending serial IIH on Serial0/0, length 1499
Apr 29 17.10:03: ISIS-Adj: Rec serial IIH from *HDLC* (Serial0/0), cir type L1L9
Apr 29 17:10:03: ISIS-Adj: Authentication failed
Apr 29 17:10:05: ISIS-Adj: Sending serial IIH on Serial0/0, length 1499
```

Step 2: Check for mismatched MTUs—If there are no authentication issues, the next possibility is mismatched MTUs. The **show clns interface** command in Example 5-170 can quickly verify the MTUs on the other side of the link. The output of **debug isis adj-packets** in Example 5-171 shows when the MTU is changed to produce a mismatch.

Example 5-170 *The MTU on the Opposite End of a Link Can Be Viewed with the* **show clns interface** *Command*

```
RT1#show clns neighbors

System  Interface  SNPA      State Hold  Type Protocol
Id                              time
RT2     Se0/0      *HDLC*     Up    250   IS   IS-IS

RT1#show clns interface s 0/0
Serial0/0 is up, line protocol is up
  Checksums enabled, MTU 1500, Encapsulation HDLC

RT2#show clns int s0/0
Serial0/0 is up, line protocol is up
  Checksums enabled, MTU 1500, Encapsulation HDLC
```

Example 5-171 *The* **debug isis adj-packets** *Command Can Be Used to Identify MTU Mismatches*

```
RT2(config)#interface s 0/0
RT2(config-if)#mtu 2000

RT2#debug isis adj-packets
IS-IS Adjacency related packets debugging is on
RT2#

Apr 20 19:56:23: ISIS-Adj: Sending serial IIH on Serial0/0, length 1999
Apr 20 19:56:23: ISIS-Adj: Rec serial IIH from *HDLC* (Serial0/0), cir type L1L2
Apr 20 19:56:23: ISIS-Adj: rcvd state UP, old state UP, new state UP
Apr 20 19:56:23: ISIS-Adj: Action = ACCEPT
Apr 20 19:56:31: ISIS-Adj: Sending serial IIH on Serial0/0, length 1999
Apr 20 19:56:33: ISIS-Adj: Rec serial IIH from *HDLC* (Serial0/0), cir type L1L2
Apr 20 19:56:33: ISIS-Adj: rcvd state up, old state UP, new state UP
Apr 20 19:56:33: ISIS-Adj: Action = GOING DOWN
```

continues

Example 5-171 *The* **debug isis adj-packets** *Command Can Be Used to Identify MTU Mismatches (Continued)*

```
Apr 20 19:56:39: ISIS-Adj: Rec serial IIH from *HDLC* (Serial0/0), cir type L1L2
Apr 20 19:56:39: ISIS-Adj: rcvd state DOWN, old state UP, new state INIT
Apr 20 19:56:39: ISIS-Adj: Action = GOING DOWN
Apr 20 19:56:39: ISIS-Adj: ADJCHANGE: ISIS: Adjacency to RT1 (Serial0/0) Down, nes
Apr 20 19:56:39: ISIS-Adj: L2 adj count 0
Apr 20 19:56:39: ISIS-Adj: Sending serial IIH on Serial0/0, length 1999
Apr 20 19:56:40: ISIS-Adj: Sending serial IIH on Serial0/0, length 1999
Apr 20 19:56:42: ISIS-Adj: Rec serial IIH from *HDLC* (Serial0/0), cir type L1L2
Apr 20 19:56:42: ISIS-Adj: rcvd state DOWN, old state DOWN, new state INIT
Apr 20 19:56:42: ISIS-Adj: Action = GOING UP, new type=L2
Apr 20 19:56:42: ISIS-Adj: New serial adjacency
Apr 20 19:56:42: ISIS-Adj: Sending serial IIH on Serial0/0, length 1999
Apr 20 19:56:50: ISIS-Adj: Rec serial IIH from *HDLC* (Serial0/0), cir type L1L2
Apr 20 19:56:50: ISIS-Adj: rcvd state DOWN, old state INIT, new state INIT
Apr 20 19:56:50: ISIS-Adj: Action = GOING UP, new type=L2
Apr 20 19:56:51: ISIS-Adj: Sending serial IIH on Serial0/0, length 1999
```

Step 3: Check for disabling of IS-IS hello padding—Cisco IOS software releases starting with 12.0S and 12.0ST allow hello padding to be disabled to reduce significant and unnecessary bandwidth consumption in some network environments. Hello padding is disabled with the assumption that the MTUs match.

This step suggests making sure that hello padding is configured consistently on either side. In general, only suppressing hello padding should not affect the adjacency, as long as the hellos sent out on the transmitting side are smaller than the MTU on the receiving side. Also, disabling hello padding does not disable verification of the maximum acceptable size of received hello packets. The **debug isis adj-packets** command in Example 5-172 can be used to troubleshoot these issues. The **show clns interface** command, shown in Example 5-173, shows the status of hello padding on an interface.

Example 5-172 *The* **debug isis adj-packets** *Command Can Be Used to Troubleshoot IS-IS Hello Padding Issues*

```
RT1#debug isis adj-packets
Apr 29 14:34:22: ISIS-Adj: Rec serial IIH from *HDLC* (Serial0/0), cir type L1L2
Apr 29 14:34:22: ISIS-Adj: rcvd state UP, old state UP, new state UP
Apr 29 14:34:22: ISIS-Adj: Action=ACCEPT
Apr 29 14:34:25: ISIS-Adj: Sending serial IIH on Serial0/0, length 38
```

Example 5-172 *The **debug isis adj-packets** Command Can Be Used to Troubleshoot IS-IS Hello Padding Issues (Continued)*

```
Apr 29 14:34:32: ISIS-Adj: Rec serial IIH from *HDLC* (Serial0/0), cir type L1L2
Apr 29 14:34:32: ISIS-Adj: rcvd state UP, old state UP, new state UP
Apr 29 14:34:22: ISIS-Adj: Action=ACCEPT
Apr 29 14:34:38: ISIS-Adj: Sending serial IIH on Serial0/0, length 38 adding
  issues.
```

Example 5-173 *Use the **show clns interface** Command to View the Status of Hello Padding on an Interface*

```
RT1#show clns interface Serial0/0
Serial0/0 is up, line protocol is up
  Checksums enabled, MTU 1500, Encapsulation HDLC
  ERPDUs enabled, min. interval 10 msec.
  RDPDUs enabled, min. interval 100msec., Addr Mask enabled
  Congestion Experienced bit set at 4 packets
  CLNS fast switching enabled
  CLNS SSE switching disabled
  DEC compatibility mode OFF for this interface
  Next ESH/ISH in 40 seconds
  Routing Protocol: IS-IS
    Circuit Type: level-1-2
    Interface number 0x1, local circuit ID 0x100
    Level-1 Metric: 10, Priority: 64, Circuit ID: RT2.00
    Number of active level-1 adjacencies: 0
    Level-2 Metric: 10, Priority: 64, Circuit ID
    0000.0000.0000.00
    Number of active level-2 adjacencies:1
    Next IS-IS Hello in 3 seconds
  No hello padding
```

ES-IS Adjacency Formed Instead of IS-IS Adjacency Formed

Cisco routers running IS-IS in IP environments still listen to ISHs generated by the ES-IS protocol in conformance with ISO 10589 requirements. When the physical and data-link layers are operational, an ES-IS adjacency can be formed even if appropriate conditions do not exist for establishing an IS-IS adjacency.

Example 5-174 shows what the output for the **show clns neighbors** command looks like when an ES-IS adjacency is formed instead of an IS-IS adjacency. This is usually because IS-IS hellos are not being processed as a result of interface MTU mismatch or misconfigured authentication.

Example 5-174 *An ES-IS Adjacency Can Form Between Intermediate Systems Even When the Conditions for an IS-IS Adjacency Do Not Exist*

```
RT2#show clns neighbors

System Interface  SNPA     State  Hold  Type Protocol
Id                                time
RT2     Se0/0     *HDLC*   Up     250   IS   ES-IS
```

Route Advertisement Problems

Most route advertisement problems can be narrowed down to configuration problems at the source or link-state packet (LSP) propagation issues.

Because IS-IS is a link-state protocol, IS-IS routers depend on LSP flooding to obtain topology and routing information. During stable conditions, each IS-IS router in an area has the same Level 1 link-state database, which contains the LSPs generated by every router in the area.

Dijkstra's algorithm is run over the LS database to obtain the best path to every advertised route. If a route is missing in a section of the area, it is because the routers in that section did not receive the original LSP, or the LSP was received corrupted and, therefore, was purged.

An even simpler reason could be that the route was not even put into the LSP at the source. See Figure 5-41.

Figure 5-41 An IS-IS Network Suffers from an LSP Origination Issue

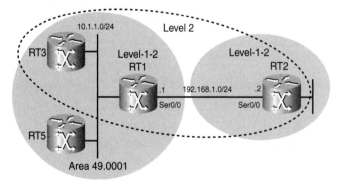

The outputs of **debug isis update-packets** and **debug isis snp-packets** in Example 5-175 can help you decipher this sort of problem as it relates to LSP flooding or issues with link-state database synchronization.

Example 5-175 *Two Debugs Help Troubleshoot LSP Flooding Issues and Link-State Database Synchronization*

```
RT1#debug isis update-packets
Mar  2 23:25:02: %LINEPROTO-5-UPDOWN: Line protocol on Interface Serial0/0, chp
Mar  2 23:25:02: ISIS-Update: Building L2 LSP
Mar  2 23:25:02: ISIS-Update: No change, suppress L2 LSP 0000.0000.0001.00-00,0
Mar  2 23:25:03: %CLNS-5 ADJCHANGE: ISIS: Adjacency to RT2 (Serial0/0) Up, newy
Mar  2 23:25:07: ISIS-Update: Building L2 LSP
Mar  2 23:25:07: ISIS-Update: TLV contents different, code 16
Mar  2 23:25:07: ISIS-Update: Full SPF required
Mar  2 23:25:07: ISIS-Update: Sending L2 LSP 0000.0000.0001.00-00, seq 160, ht0
Mar  2 23:25:07: ISIS-Update: Rec L2 LSP 0000.0000.0002.00-00, seq 1D16, ht 11,
Mar  2 23:25:07: ISIS-Update: from SNPA *HDLC* (Serial0/0)
Mar  2 23:25:07: ISIS-Update: LSP newer than database copy
Mar  2 23:25:07: ISIS-Update: No change
Mar  2 23:25:08: ISIS-SNP: Rec L2 CSNP from 0000.0000.0002 (Serail0/0)
Mar  2 23:25:08: ISIS-SNP: Rec L2 PSNP from 0000.0000.0002 (Serail0/0)
Mar  2 23:25:08: ISIS-SNP: PSNP entry 0000.0000.0001.00-00, seq 160, ht 1197
Mar  2 23:25:08: ISIS-Update: Sending L2 CSNP on Serial0/0
Mar  2 23:25:08: ISIS-Update: Build L2 PSNP entry for 0000.0000.0002.00-00, se6
Mar  2 23:25:08: ISIS-Update: Build L2 PSNP entry for 0000.0000.0006.00-00, se2
Mar  2 23:25:08: ISIS-Update: Sending L2 PSNP on Serial0/0
Mar  2 23:25:09: ISIS-Update: Building L1 LSP
Mar  2 23:25:09: ISIS-Update: Important fields changed
Mar  2 23:25:09: ISIS-Update: Important fields changed
Mar  2 23:25:09: ISIS-Update: Full SPF required
Mar  2 23:25:09: ISIS-Update: Sending L1 LSP 0000.0000.0001.00-00, seq 15A, ht0
Mar  2 23:25:09: ISIS-Update: Sending L1 CSNP on Ethernet0/0


RT5#debug isis snp-packets
IS-IS CSNP/PSNP packets debugging is on
RT5#
Mar  6 20:02:28: ISIS-SNP: Rec L1 CSNP from 0000.0000.0001 (Ethernet0/0)
```

continues

Example 5-175 *Two Debugs Help Troubleshoot LSP Flooding Issues and Link-State Database Synchronization (Continued)*

```
Mar  6 20:02:28: ISIS-SNP: CSNP range 0000.0000.0000.00-00 to FFFF.FFFF.FFFF.FFF
Mar  6 20:02:28: ISIS-SNP: Same entry 0000.0000.0001.00-00, seq 15D
Mar  6 20:02:28: ISIS-SNP: Same entry 0000.0000.0001.01-00, seq 104
Mar  6 20:02:28: ISIS-SNP: Same entry 0000.0000.0005.00-00, seq FEA
```

The output of the **debug isis update-packets** command in Example 5-175 shows RT1 flooding its LSP and also receiving an LSP from RT2. Because the adjacency was brought up, the output also shows the one-time exchange of CSNPs on point-to-point links between RT1 and RT2.

The output of the **debug isis snp-packets** command in Figure 5-174 indicates receipt of CSNP by RT5 from the DIS (RT1). By comparing the contents of the CSNP with the local Level 1 database, RT5 determines that no changes occurred in all known LSPs.

There can be many potential causes of problems in which routes are not reaching remote locations in the network, including adjacency problems, Layer 1/2 problems, IS-IS misconfiguration, and other issues.

Route Flapping Problem

Route flaps normally are caused by unstable links between the source of the route and the location where the flap is being observed. Typically, multiple routes are affected at the same time because of an adjacency change affecting many LSPs, all of which might carry numerous IP prefixes. Also, route flaps could induce consistent running of SPF processes, causing dangerously high CPU utilization on route processors that might crash affected routers. If the advertised LSP changes affect only IP prefixes, only partial route calculation (PRC) is run instead of full SPF calculations. PRC is less costly in terms of CPU cycles than full SPF runs.

Apart from certain destinations not being reachable, obviously implying routing problems, high CPU utilization by the SPF process (the **show process cpu** command) certainly should flag instabilities in the network. High CPU utilization can be observed through the IOS command-line interface, network management applications, or special network performance analysis tools, such as CiscoWorks.

The **show process cpu** command displays CPU utilization information. If high CPU utilization caused by the SPF process is indicated, the **show isis spf-log** command can determine SPF-related events that might cause the high CPU utilization.

The output of the **show isis spf-log** command in Example 5-176 lists SPF process runs by time, trigger, and duration. LSPs are refreshed every 15 minutes, triggering periodic SPF calculations. Such events are labeled PERIODIC in the **show isis spf-log** output. It also shows that at 03:25:25, the process was run over an insignificant period of time because a new LSP was received from RT5. Table 5-2 lists and describes common SPF triggers.

Example 5-176 *The Times, Triggers, and Durations of LSP Process Runs Can Be Displayed*

```
RT1#show isis spf-log


  Level 1 SPF log
When       Duration   Nodes  Count   Last          Triggers
                                     trigger LSP


03:40:08  0          3      1                      PERIODIC
03:25:08  0          3      1                      PERIODIC
03:10:07  0          3      1                      PERIODIC
03:25:07  0          3      1                      PERIODIC
03:25:07  0          3      1                      PERIODIC
03:25:06  0          3      1                      PERIODIC
03:25:06  0          3      1                      PERIODIC
03:25:08  0          3      1                      PERIODIC
03:25:06  0          2      1       RT1.01-00     TLVCONTENT
03:25:06  0          2      1                      PERIODIC
03:25:31  0          2      1                      PERIODIC
03:25:31  0          2      1       RT5.00-00     LSPEXPIRED
03:25:25  0          2      2       RT1.01-00     NEWADJ TLVCONTENT
03:25:06  0          3      1       RT5.00-00     NEWLSP
03:25:06  0          3      1                      PERIODIC
03:25:08  0          3      1                      PERIODIC
```

Table 5-2 Common SPF Triggers

Trigger Code	Description
AREASET	Area change
ATTACHFLAG	Attached bit setting change
CLEAR	Manual change
CONFIG	Configuration change
DELADJ	Adjacency deletion

continues

Table 5-2 Common SPF Triggers (Continued)

Trigger Code	Description
DIS	DIS election
ES	End system information change
HIPPITY LSPDB	Overload bit state change
IP_DEF_ORG	Default information change
IPDOWN	Connected IP prefix down
IP_EXTERNAL	Route redistribution change
IPIA	Interarea route change
IPUP	Connected IP prefix up
NEWADJ	New neighbor adjacency up
NEWLEVEL	IS-IS process level change
NEWMETRIC	New metric assigned to an interface
NEWSYSID	New system ID assigned
PERIODIC	Periodic SPF process (LSPDB refresh interval)
TLVCODE	LSP with a new TLV code field received
TLVCONTENT	LSP with changed TLV contents received

The following IS-IS debugging commands can also be used to narrow down SPF-related problems:

- **debug isis spf-events**
- **debug isis spf-triggers**
- **debug isis spf-statistics**
- **debug isis update-packets**
- **debug isis adj-packets**

Use caution when enabling debugging in a situation in which the route processor CPU already is overtaxed. Example 5-177 shows output of the **debug isis spf-events** command, which displays the events following an interface shutdown to simulate a link flap. The highlighted lines indicate LSPs flagged for recalculation as a result of this event. Events flagging computation of the Level 1 and Level 2 SPF trees also are highlighted.

Example 5-177 *The SPF Events Following an Interface Shutdown Can Be Viewed with the* **debug isis spf-events**
Command

```
RT1#debug isis spf-events

Mar  6 20:17:26: ISIS-SPF: L1 LSP 1 (0000.0000.0001.00-00) flagged for recalculC
Mar  6 20:17:26: ISIS-SPF: L1 LSP 5 (0000.0000.0005.00-00) flagged for recalculC
Mar  6 20:17:28: %LINK-5-CHANGED: Interface Ethernet0/0, changed state to admin
  down
Mar  6 20:17:28: ISIS-SPF: Compute L1 SPT
Mar  6 20:17:28: ISIS-SPF: 3 nodes for level-1
Mar  6 20:17:28: ISIS-SPF: Move 0000.0000.0001.00-00 to PATHS, metric 0
Mar  6 20:17:28: ISIS-SPF: Add 0000.0000.0001.01-00 to TENT, metric 10
Mar  6 20:17:28: ISIS-SPF: Add 0000.0000.0001 to L1 route table, metric 0
Mar  6 20:17:28: ISIS-SPF: Move 0000.0000.0001.01-00 to PATHS, metric 10
Mar  6 20:17:28: ISIS-SPF: Aging L1 LSP 1 (0000.0000.0001.00-00), version 214
Mar  6 20:17:28: ISIS-SPF: Aging L2 LSP 2 (0000.0000.0001.00-00), version 208
Mar  6 20:17:28: ISIS-SPF: Aging L1 LSP 3 (0000.0000.0001.01-00), version 207
Mar  6 20:17:28: ISIS-SPF: Aging L2 LSP 4 (0000.0000.0002.00-00), version 209
Mar  6 20:17:28: ISIS-SPF: Aging L1 LSP 5 (0000.0000.0005.00-00), version 207
Mar  6 20:17:28: ISIS-SPF: Aging L2 LSP 6 (0000.0000.0006.01-00), version 112
Mar  6 20:17:28: ISIS-SPF: Aging L2 LSP 7 (0000.0000.0006.00-00), version 114
Mar  6 20:17:28: ISIS-SPF: Aging L2 LSP 8 (0000.0000.0001.01-00), version 1
Mar  6 20:17:29: %LINEPROTO-5-UPDOWN: Line protocol on Interface Ethernet0/0
Mar  6 20:17:33: ISIS-SPF: Compute L2 SPT
Mar  6 20:17:33: ISIS-SPF: 5 nodes for level-2
```

Most route-flapping problems can be traced to unstable links in the network. In more complicated scenarios, however, the flaps could be caused by LSP corruption storms or even a routing loop. This might be the case when the network has no unstable links but CPU utilization
is high, indicating continuous running of the SPF process.

The **show isis spf-log** command can indicate which LSPs are changing the most frequently
and are triggering the SPF calculations. Similar clues can be gleaned by enabling debugging
of the update process with **debug isis update-packets**. This should be done with care so
that the CPU is not overloaded. The logs also can be observed for LSP error loggings, which
could indicate packet corruption by a culprit device. Zeroing in on any continuously changing
LSPs is critical for determining and addressing the problem.

Troubleshooting BGP

BGP is a complex protocol to troubleshoot in the sense that a network engineer must be able to troubleshoot behavior related to each of the BGP attributes. BGP issues are explored in this section, including neighbor relationship problems, route origination problems, next-hop issues, and dampening.

Troubleshooting BGP Neighbor Relationship Problems

Troubleshooting neighbor relationship issues should follow the OSI reference model. First, Layer 1/2 should be checked, followed by IP connectivity (Layer 3), TCP connections (Layer 4), and finally the BGP configuration. As a rule of thumb, for a BGP neighbor relationship to form between two neighbors, they first must be able to ping each other. The following is a list of problems most commonly seen when forming BGP neighbor relationships:

- Directly connected external BGP neighbors are not initializing
- Nondirectly connected external BGP neighbors are not initializing
- Internal BGP neighbors are not initializing
- BGP neighbors (external and internal) are not initializing

Directly Connected External BGP Neighbors Are Not Initializing

The autonomous system (AS) does not send or receive any IP prefix updates to or from a neighboring AS unless the neighbor relationship reaches Established state, which is the final stage of BGP neighbor establishment. When an AS has a single EBGP connection, no IP connectivity can occur until BGP finalizes its operation of sending and receiving IP prefixes.

Figure 5-42 shows a network in which an external BGP neighbor relationship is configured between AS 109 and AS 110.

Figure 5-42 An External BGP Peering Is Configured Between AS 109 and AS 110

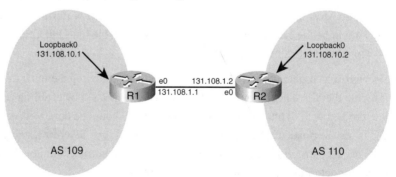

The most common possible causes of directly connected external BGP neighbors not initializing are as follows:

- Layer 2 is down, preventing communication with the directly connected EBGP neighbor.

- An incorrect neighbor IP address is in the BGP configuration.

The BGP neighbor relationship can be verified by using the **show ip bgp summary** and **show ip bgp neighbors** commands, as shown in Example 5-178. These commands show that the BGP neighbor is in Active state. This state indicates that no successful communication between the neighbors has taken place and that the BGP has failed to form a neighbor relationship. The **ping** command can be used to verify the connectivity problem; the output should show the ping failures. The solution to this problem is to correct the Layer 1/2 problem.

Example 5-178 *Either the* **show ip bgp summary** *or* **show ip bgp neighbors** *Command Can Be Used to View the Status of a BGP Neighbor Relationship*

```
R1#show ip bgp summary
BGP router identifier 206.56.89.6 local AS number 109
BGP table version is 1, main routing table version 1
Neighbor  V AS MsgRcvd MsgSent  Tb1Ver Inq QutQ Up/Down State/PfxRcd
131.108.1.2 4 110    3       7      0   0    0 00:03:14 Active


R1#show ip bgp neighbors 131.108.1.2
BGP neighbor is 131.108.1.2, remote AS 110, external link
  BGP Version 4, remote router ID 0.0.0.0
BGP state = Active
Last read 00:04:23, hold time is 180, keepalive interval is 60 seconds
  Received 3 messages, 0 notifications, 0 in queue
  Sent 7 messages, 1 notifications, 0 in queue
  Route refresh request: recieved 0 sent 0
  Minimum time between advertisement runs in 30 seconds.


For address family: IPv4 Unicast
  BGP table verion 1, neighbor version 0
  Index 1, Offset 0, Mask 0x2
  0 acccepted prefixes consume 0 bytes
  Prefix advertised 0, surppressed 0, withdrawn 0
```

continues

Example 5-178 *Either the* **show ip bgp summary** *or* **show ip bgp neighbors** *Command Can Be Used to View the Status of a BGP Neighbor Relationship (Continued)*

```
Connections established 1; dropped 1
Last reset 00:04:44, due to BGP Notification sent, hold time expired
No Active TCP connection
```

Misconfiguration of the neighbor IP address is a fairly common mistake, and it can be caught with a visual inspection of the configuration. However, in a large IP network, this might not be a trivial task. The **debug ip bgp** command can help diagnose this problem, as shown in Example 5-179. Observe that Router R2 is having difficulty communicating with host 131.108.1.11, which has a misconfigured neighbor address on R2, as shown in Example 5-180. The solution is to correct the neighbor address in the configuration of Router R2, as shown in Example 5-181.

Example 5-179 *The* **debug ip bgp** *Command Can Be Used to Troubleshoot a Misconfigured Neighbor IP Address*

```
R2#debug ip bgp
BGP debug is on
R2#
Nov 28 13:25:12: BGP: 131.108.1.11 open active, local address 131.108.1.2
Nov 28 13:25:42: BGP: 131.108.1.11 open failed: Connection timed out;
  remote host not responding
```

Example 5-180 *R2 Has a Misconfigured IP Address in Its* **neighbor** *Statement*

```
R2#router bgp 110
neighbor 131.108.1.11 remote-as 109

 interface Ethernet0
 ip address 131.108.1.2 255.255.255.0
```

Example 5-181 *The* **neighbor** *Statement on R2 Is Corrected*

```
R2#router bgp 110
neighbor 131.108.1.1 remote-as 109
```

Nondirectly Connected External BGP Neighbors Are Not Initializing

In some cases, EBGP neighbors are not directly connected. BGP neighbor relationships can be established between routers trying to make an EBGP neighbor relationship that are separated by one or more routers. Such a neighbor relationship is called EBGP multihop in the IOS.

Peering between loopbacks between EBGP typically is done when multiple interfaces exist between the routers and IP traffic needs to be load-shared among those interfaces. Such a connection is considered nondirectly connected. Figure 5-43 shows an example of a nondirectly connected EBGP session between two loopback interfaces.

Figure 5-43 External BGP Neighbors Can Peer Using Loopbacks

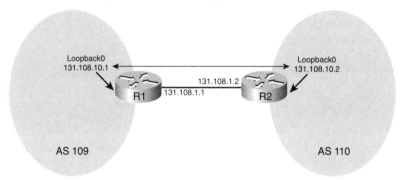

The most common possible causes of nondirectly connected external BGP neighbors not initializing are as follows:

- The route to the nondirectly connected peer address is missing from the routing table.
- The **ebgp-multihop** command is missing in the BGP configuration.
- The **update-source interface** command is missing.

The **show ip bgp summary** and **show ip bgp neighbors** commands can be used to show that the neighbor relationship is in Active state, as shown in Example 5-182. In the case of the **ebgp-multihop** command missing in the BGP configuration, these commands show that the BGP neighbor is in Idle state, because no resources are allocated to the BGP neighbor. This might be because the other side has not received any BGP negotiation.

Example 5-182 *The BGP Neighbor Relationship Is Active*

```
R1#show ip bgp summary
BGP router identifier 131.108.10.1 local AS number 109
BGP table version is 1, main routing table version 1
Neighbor      V  AS MsgRcvd MsgSent    TblVer  Inq OutQ  Up/Down  State/PfxRcd
131.108.1.2   4 110       3       3         0  0     0  00:03:21 Active

R1#show ip bgp neighbors 131.108.1.2
BGP neighbor is 131.108.10.2, remote AS 110, external link
  BGP Version 4, remote router ID 0.0.0.0
BGP state = Active
Last read 00:04:20, hold time is 180, keepalive internal is 60 seconds
  Received 3 messages, 0 notifications, 0 in queue
  Sent 3 messages, 0 notifications, 0 in queue
  Route refresh request: received 0 sent 0
  Minimum time between advertisement runs in 30 seconds.

For address family: IPv4 Unicast
  BGP table version 1, neighbor version 0
  Index 2, Offset 0, Mask 0x4
  0 accepted prefixes consume 0 bytes
  Prefix advertised 0, suppressed 0, withdrawn 0

  Connections established 1; dropped 1
  Last reset 00:04:21, due to User reset
```

The solutions to these possible causes vary and depend on the exact situation. Using the scenario shown in Figure 5-43, the following are some possible solutions.

The solution for a missing route to the nondirectly connected peer address is either to use a static route to the connected peer address (a common practice) or to use an IGP dynamic routing protocol such as OSPF. This is usually an issue when peering is done between peers using loopback addresses.

A possible solution for a missing **ebgp-multihop** command in the BGP configuration is to properly configure this command. Example 5-183 shows an example of configuring this command on Router R1.

Example 5-183 *The* **ebgp-multihop** *Keyword Can Be Used When the Source and Destination of External BGP Peers Lie on Different Subnets*

```
R1#router bgp 109


neighbor 131.108.10.2 remote-as 110
neighbor 131.108.10.2 ebgp-multihop 2
neighbor 131.108.10.2 update-source Loopback0
```

In the case of the missing **update-source** interface command, using the example shown in Figure 5-43, R1 and R2 should be configured with the **update-source** command. This command ensures that the source address is that of Loopback 0, as shown in Example 5-184.

Example 5-184 *The* **update-source** *Keyword Sets the Source of the TCP Session (Port 179) Used by BGP*

```
R1#router bgp 109
neighbor 131.108.10.2 remote-as 110
neighbor 131.108.10.2 ebgp-multihop 2
neighbor 131.108.10.2 update-source Loopback0

R2#router bgp 110
neighbor 131.108.10.1 remote-as 109
neighbor 131.108.10.1 ebgp-multihop 2
neighbor 131.108.10.1 update-source Loopback0
```

Internal BGP Neighbors Are Not Initializing

IBGP can experience issues similar to EBGP in neighbor relationships. IBGP is an important piece of networks that run BGP. The causes of IBGP neighbor relationship issues are identical to those of EBGP:

- The route to the nondirectly connected IBGP neighbor is missing.
- The **update-source interface** command is missing in the BGP configuration.

The same troubleshooting and configuration techniques can be used for IBGP neighbor issues that are used for EBGP neighbor issues.

BGP Neighbors (External and Internal) Are Not Initializing

Interface access list/filters are another common cause of BGP neighbor activation problems. If an interface access list unintentionally blocks TCP packets that carry BGP protocol packets, the BGP neighbor does not come up.

Example 5-185 shows a sample access list 101 that explicitly blocks TCP. Access list 102 has an implicit deny of BGP because of the implicit deny at the end of each access list. Example 5-186 shows the revised access configuration that permits the BGP port (TCP port 179). All BGP packets are permitted because of the second line in access list 101.

Example 5-185 *Blocking TCP Results in Blocking BGP*

```
R1#access-list 101 deny tcp any any
access-list 101 deny udp any any
access-list 101 permit ip any any


interface ethernet 0
ip access-group 101 in

access-list 102 permit udp any any
access-list 102 permit ospf any any

interface ethernet 0
ip access-group 102 in
```

Example 5-186 *Allowing a Destination TCP Port of 179 Enables BGP Peering to Take Place*

```
R1#no access-list 101

access-list 101 deny udp any any
access-list 101 permit tcp any any eq bgp
access-list 102 permit any any
```

Troubleshooting BGP Route Advertisements

Another common problem that BGP operators face occurs in BGP route advertisement/ origination and receiving. BGP originates routes only by configuration. However, it needs no configuration in receiving routes.

Larger ISPs originate new BGP routes for their customers on a daily basis, whereas small-enterprise BGP networks mostly configure BGP route origination upon first setup. Problems in route origination can occur because of either configuration mistakes or a lack of BGP protocol understanding.

It is beyond the scope of this section to discuss all the possible problems that can occur, but here is a list of possible problems that are discussed briefly:

- A BGP route does not get originated
- A problem with propagating/originating a BGP route to IBGP/EBGP neighbors
- A problem with propagating a BGP route to an IBGP neighbor but not to an EBGP neighbor
- A problem with propagating an IBGP route to an IBGP/EBGP neighbor

A BGP Route Does Not Get Originated

BGP originates IP prefixes and announces them to neighboring BGP speakers (IBGP and EBGP) so that the Internet can reach those prefixes. For example, if an IP address associated with www.cisco.com fails to originate because of a BGP configuration mistake or lack of protocol requirements, the Internet will never know about the IP address of www.cisco.com, resulting in no connectivity to this Website. Therefore, it is essential to look at BGP route origination issues in detail.

Several causes of BGP route origination failure exist. The most common are as follows:

- The IP routing table does not have a matching route.
- A configuration error has occurred.
- BGP is auto-summarizing to a classful/network boundary.

BGP requires the IP routing table to have an exact matching entry for the prefix that BGP is trying to advertise using the **network** and **redistribute** commands. The prefix and mask of the network that BGP is trying to advertise must be identical in the IP routing table and in the BGP configurations. Example 5-187 shows a misconfiguration in BGP to advertise 100.100.100.0/24 using the **network** statement. The static route for 100.100.100.0 has a mask of /23, whereas BGP is configured to advertise /24. Therefore, BGP does not consider /24 a valid advertisement, because an exact match does not exist in the routing table.

Example 5-187 *BGP Is Configured to Advertise a Network with the Wrong Mask, So BGP Does Not Originate the Route*

```
router bgp 110
no synchronization
network 100.100.100.0 mask 255.255.255.0
neighbor 131.108.1.2 remote-as 109


ip route 100.100.100.0 255.255.254.0 null 0
```

Another cause to consider is BGP autosummarization of classful networks at major network boundaries. BGP might be trying to redistribute 10.10.10.0/24, but only 10.0.0.0/8 gets advertised. In most cases, it would be desirable to turn off auto-summarization with the **no auto-summary** command so that proper mask routes can be advertised to BGP neighbors.

A Problem with Propagating/Originating a BGP Route to IBGP/EBGP Neighbors

A scenario might arise in which the BGP configuration to originate and propagate routes looks good, but BGP neighbors are not receiving the routes. The originator's BGP table shows all the routes. It's possible that configured distribute-list filters are the cause of the problem or that there's a problem in the policy routing.

A Problem with Propagating a BGP Route to an IBGP Neighbor But Not to an EBGP Neighbor

In some cases, certain routes are not propagated to IBGP neighbors, only to EBGP neighbors.

When IBGP speakers in an AS are not fully meshed and have no route reflector or confederation configuration, any route that is learned from an IBGP neighbor is not given to any other IBGP neighbor. Such routes are advertised only to EBGP neighbors, as shown in Figure 5-44.

Figure 5-44 IBGP Learned Routes Are Advertised to Only EBGP Neighbors

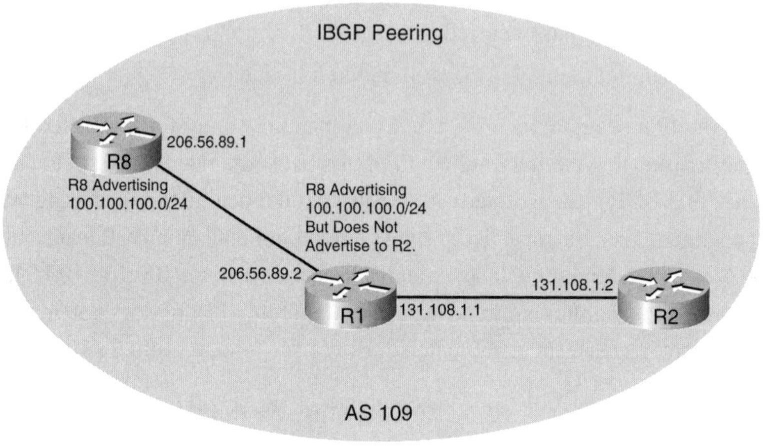

Example 5-188 shows the configuration of the routers R8, R1, and R2. This example shows that the IBGP network is not fully meshed and that the IBGP-learned route is not given to any other IBGP neighbor. Verify this with the **show ip bgp** command. In Example 5-189, "Not

advertised to any peer" in R1 means that even though R2 is the neighbor, it is an IBGP neighbor. Therefore, 100.100.100.0/24 is not advertised.

Example 5-188 *The Configurations of R1, R2, and R8 Do Not Form a Full Mesh*

```
R8#
router bgp 109
no synchronization


network 100.100.100.0 mask 255.255.255.0
neighbor 206.56.89.2 remote-as 109


network 100.100.100.0 255.255.255.0 Null0


R1#
router bgp 109
no synchronization
neighbor 131.108.1.2 remote-as 109
neighbor 206.56.89.1 remote-as 109


R2#
router bgp 109
no synchronization
neighbor 131.108.1.1 remote-as 109
```

Example 5-189 *R1 Is Not Advertising 100.100.100.0/24*

```
R8#show ip bgp 100.100.100.0
BGP routing table entry for 100.100.100.0/24, version 3
Paths: (1 available, best #1, table Default-IP-Routing-Table)
   Advertised to non peer-group peers:
   206.56.89.2
   Local
      0.0.0.0 from 0.0.0.0 (8.8.8.8)
Origin IGP, metric 0, localpref 100, weight 32768, valid, source, local, best


R1#show ip bgp 100.100.100.0
BGP routing table entry for 100.100.100.0/24, version 9
```

continues

Example 5-189 *R1 Is Not Advertising 100.100.100.0/24 (Continued)*

```
Paths: (1 available, best #1, table Default-IP-Routing-Table)
  Not advertised to any peer
  Local
      206.56.89.1 from 206.56.89.1 (8.8.8.8)
        Origin IGP, metric 0, localpref 100, valid, internal, best


R1#show ip bgp summary
BGP router identifier 1.1.1.1, local AS number version 109
BGP table version is 11, main routing table version 11
1 network entries and 1 paths using 133 bytes of memory
1 BGP path attributed entries using 52 bytes of memory
0 BGP route-map cache entries using 0 bytes of memory
0 BGP filter-list cache entries using 0 bytes of memory
BGP activity 24/237 prefixes, 35/34 paths, scan interval 15 secs


Neighbor       V     AS MsgRcvd MsgSent TblVer InQ OutQ Up/Down
131.108.1.2    4    109    4304    4319     11   0    0 1d20h
206.56.89.1    4    109     108     110     11   0    0 01:44:16


State/PfxRcd
        0
        1


R2#show ip bgp 100.100.100.0
% Network not in table
```

It is essential that IBGP-learned routes be propagated to other BGP speakers. BGP operators can use three methods to address this problem:

- Use IBGP full mesh.
- Design a route reflector model, as shown in Figure 5-45 and Example 5-190.
- Design a confederation model, as shown in Figure 5-46 and Example 1-191.

Figure 5-45 R1 Is the Route Reflector

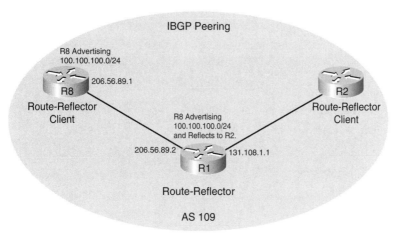

Example 5-190 *R2 and R8 Are Route Reflector Clients*

```
R1#router bgp 109
no synchronization
neighbor 131.108.1.2 remote-as 109
neighbor 131.108.1.2 route-reflector-client
neighbor 206.56.89.1 remote-as 109
neighbor 206.56.89.1 route-reflector-client
```

Figure 5-46 A Confederation Is a Collection of Sub-Autonomous Systems

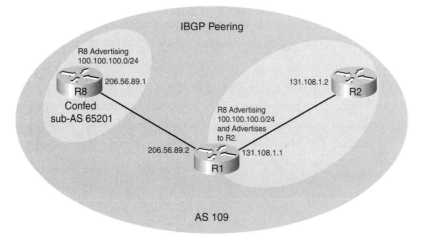

Example 5-191 *Configuring Confederations Involves Configuring the BGP Confederation Identifier and Specifying the BGP Confederation Peers*

```
R8#show ip bgp 100.100.100.0
router bgp 65201
bgp confederation identifier 109
bgp confederation peers 65200
network 100.100.100.0 mask 255.255.255.0
neighbor 205.56.89.2 remote-as 65200


ip route 100.100.100.0 255.255.255.0 Null0


R1#router bgp 65200


bgp confederation identifier 109
bgp confederation peers 65201
neighbor 131.108.1.2 remote-as 65200
neighbor 206.56.89.1 remote-as 65201


R2#router bgp 65200
no synchronization
bgp confederation identifier 109
neighbor 131.108.1.1 remote-as 65200
```

A Problem with Propagating an IBGP Route to an IBGP/EBGP Neighbor

A problem might arise in which an IBGP learned route is not propagated to any BGP neighbor, whether it is an IBGP or EBGP neighbor. One case could be that when an IBGP-learned route is not synchronized, that route is not considered as a candidate to advertise to other BGP neighbors. A BGP route is synchronized only if it was first learned through an IGP or static route.

In Cisco IOS, BGP advertises only what it considers the best path to its neighbors. If an IBGP path is not synchronized, it is not included in the best-path calculation. The output of the **show ip bgp** command shows unsynchronized routes in the BGP table, as shown in Example 5-192. The solution is to either turn off synchronization or make the routes synchronized by redistributing them in the IGP at the router that first introduced this route into the IBGP domain.

Example 5-192 *In Most Cases It Is Safe to Disable Synchronization. With Synchronization Turned Off, It Is Much Easier to Get BGP to Learn and Propagate Routes*

```
R2#show ip bgp 100.100.100.0
BGP routing table entry for 100.100.100.0/24, version 3
Paths: (1 available, no best path)
Flag: 0X208
   Not advertised to any peer
   (65201)
     206.56.89.1 from 131.108.1.1 (1.1.1.1)
Origin IGP, metric 0, localpref 100,  valid, internal, not synchronized
```

Troubleshooting Routes Are Not Being Installed in the IP Routing Table

A common problem is with BGP routes not getting installed into the IP routing table. If a router must forward an IP packet by looking at its IP destination address, the router must have an IP routing table entry for the subnet of the IP destination address.

If the BGP process fails to create an IP routing table entry, all traffic destined for missing IP subnets in the routing table is dropped. This is generic behavior of hop-by-hop IP packet forwarding done by routers.

Problems in this section assume that the BGP table has all the updates for IP prefixes but that BGP is not installing them in the IP routing table, whether or not the prefixes are IBGP-learned or EBGP-learned routes.

The most common causes of IBGP-learned routes not getting installed in the IP routing table are

- IBGP routes are unsynchronized.
- The BGP next hop is unreachable.

The most common causes of EBGP-learned routes not getting installed in the IP routing table are

- The BGP next hop is unreachable in the case of multihop EBGP.
- BGP routes are dampened.
- The multiexit discriminator (MED) value is infinite.

The following sections examine two of these problems in more detail—the BGP next hop is unreachable and BGP routes are dampened.

The BGP Next Hop Is Unreachable

A common problem in BGP occurs when the next hop is unreachable. The cause of this problem (the IBGP-learned route is not getting installed into the IP routing table) is most common in IBGP-learned routes where the BGP next-hop address should have been learned through an IGP. Failure to reach the next hop is an IGP problem; BGP is merely a victim. With BGP, when IP prefixes are advertised to an IBGP neighbor, the prefix's NEXT-HOP attribute does not change. The IBGP receiver must have an IP route to reach this next hop.

Figure 5-47 shows that the next hop of BGP routes advertised to IBGP neighbors is not changed and might result in route installation failure.

Figure 5-47 R2 Needs a Route to 206.56.89.0

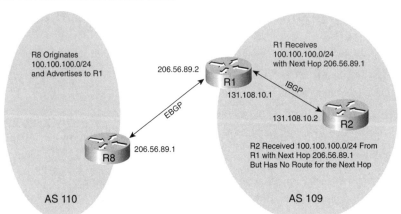

R8 is advertising the 100.100.100.0/24 route to its EBGP peer R1, which advertises this route to R2. However, on R2, the problem of the next hop appears. Example 5-193 shows the configuration of BGP on R8, R1, and R2.

Example 5-193 *R8 Is in AS 110, and R1 and R2 Are in AS 109*

```
R8#router bgp 110
no synchronization
 network 100.100.100.0 mask 255.255.255.0
neighbor 206.56.89.2 remote-as 109


ip route 100.100.100.0 255.255.255.0 Null0


R1#router bgp 109
```

Example 5-193 *R8 Is in AS 110, and R1 and R2 Are in AS 109 (Continued)*

```
 no synchronization
  neighbor 131.108.10.2 remote-as 109
  neighbor 131.108.10.2 update-source Loopback0
  neighbor 206.56.89.1 remote-as 110


R2#router bgp 109
 no synchronization
  neighbor 131.108.10.1 remote-as 109
  neighbor 131.108.10.1 update-source Loopback0
```

R8 is advertising 100.100.100.0/24 to R1, and R1 propagates that to R2 as an IBGP advertisement. R1 receives this route, installs it in its routing table, and propagates it to R2 at
131.108.10.2.

In Example 5-194, R2 is an IBGP peer of R1. R2 receives this BGP route, 100.100.100.0/24
with a next hop of 206.56.89.1, but fails to install it in its IP routing table, as shown in
Example 5-195.

Example 5-194 *R1 and R2 Are IBGP Peers*

```
R1#show ip bgp 100.100.100.0
BGP routing table entry for 100.100.100.0/24, version 2
Paths: (1 availble, best #1, table Default-IP-Routing-Table)
  Advertised to non peer-group peers:
  131.108.10.2
  110
    206.56.89.1 from 206.56.89.1 (100.100.100.8)
      Origin IGP, metric 0, localpref 100, valid, external, best


R1#show ip route 100.100.100.0
Routing entry for 100.100.100.0/24
  Known via "bgp 109", distance 20, metric 0
  Tag 110, type external
  Last update from 206.56.89.1 00:04:50 ago
  Routing Descriptor Blocks:
  * 206.56.89.1, from 206.56.89.1, 00:04:50 ago
      Route metric is 0, traffic share count is 1
      AS Hops 1
```

Example 5-195 *R2 Learns the Route 100.100.100.0/24 Via BGP But Can't Install It in the Routing Table Because the Next Hop Resides on a Network That Is Not in the Routing Table*

```
R2#show ip bgp 100.100.100.0
BGP routing table entry for 100.100.100.0/24, version 0
Paths: (1 available, no best path)
  Not advertised to any peer
  110
    206.56.89.1 (inaccessible) from 131.108.10.1 (131.108.10.1)
      Origin IGP, metric 0, localpref 100, valid, internal

R2#show ip route 100.100.100.0
% Network not in table
```

Remember that for EBGP sessions, the next hop is the IP address of the neighbor that announced the route. For IBGP sessions, routes that originated inside the AS, the next hop is the IP address of the neighbor that announced the route.

For routes injected into the AS via EBGP, the next hop learned from EBGP is carried unaltered into IBGP. The next hop is the IP address of the EBGP neighbor from which the route was learned.

BGP requires the next hop of any BGP route to resolve to a physical interface (the exit interface in the IP routing table). This might or might not require multiple recursive lookups in the IP routing table. Two common solutions exist for addressing this problem:

- Announce the EBGP next hop through an IGP using a static route or redistribution.
- Change the next hop to an internal peering address using the **next-hop-self** command.

Change the configuration of R1 so that the subnet 206.56.89.0/30 is included in its OSPF advertisements of R1 to R2, which would include the address of the next-hop IP address of R8, as shown in Example 5-196. Example 5-197 shows that R2 receives this route through OSPF.

Example 5-196 *Advertising the External Link Via OSPF Is One Way to Ensure That R2 Can Reach the BGP Next Hop for the 100.100.100.0/24 Network*

```
R1#router ospf 1
network 206.56.89.0 0.0.0.3 area 0
```

Example 5-197 *R2 Can Install the 100.100.100.0/24 Network in Its Routing Table Now That the 206.56.89.0/30 Network Is in Its Routing Table*

```
R2#show ip route 206.56.89.0 255.255.255.252
Routing entry for 206.56.89.0/30
  Known via "ospf 1", distance 110, metric 74, type intra area
  Redistributing via ospf 1
  Last update from 131.108.1.1 on Ethernet0, 00:03:17 ago
  Routing Descriptor Blocks:
  * 131.108.1.1, from 1.1.1.1, 00:03:17 ago, via Ethernet0
      Route metric is 74, traffic share count is 1
```

Another solution is to change the BGP next-hop address on R1 to its loopback address when advertising IBGP routes to R2. Example 5-198 shows the configuration on R1 that modifies the BGP next hop to be changed to its own loopback address.

Example 5-198 *The **next-hop-self** Command on R1 Is Another Method of Ensuring That R2 Can Reach the BGP Next Hop for the 100.100.100.0/24 Network*

```
R1#router bgp 109
  neighbor 131.108.10.2 remote-as 109
  neighbor 131.108.10.2 update-source Loopback0
  neighbor 131.108.10.2 next-hop-self
  neighbor 206.56.89.1 remote-as 110
```

The command **neighbor 131.108.10.2 next-hop-self** changes the next hop to its own loopback 0 (131.108.10.1). The **neighbor 131.108.10.2 update-source Loopback0** command makes R1 loopback 0 the source of all BGP packets sent to R2.

The command **show ip bgp** in Example 5-199 shows this change reflected in R2. The exterior next hop changes to the loopback of R1, 131.108.10.1.

Example 5-199 *With **next-hop-self** Configured on R1, R2 Sees the 100.100.100.0/24 Network with Next Hop 131.108.10.1 on R1*

```
R2#show ip bgp 100.100.100.0
BGP routing table entry for 100.100.100.0/24, version 2
Paths: (1 available, best #1, table Default-IP-Routing-Table)
  Not advertised to any peer
```

continues

Example 5-199 *With **next-hop-self** Configured on R1, R2 Sees the 100.100.100.0/24 Network with Next Hop 131.108.10.1 on R1 (Continued)*

```
    110
      131.108.10.1 from 131.108.10.1 (131.108.10.1)
        Orign IGP, metric 0, localpref 100, valid, internal, best
R2#show ip route 100.100.100.0
Routing entry for 100.100.100.0/24
  Known via "bgp 109", distance 200, metric 0
  Tag 110, type internal
  Last update from 131.108.10.1 00:00:25 ago
  Routing Descriptor Blocks:
  * 131.108.10.1, from 131.108.10.1, 00:00:25 ago
      Route metric is 0, traffic share count is 1
      AS Hops 1
```

The second solution is more widely used and is the preferred method of announcing the next hop to IBGP peers. The solution of changing the next hop to an internal peering address allows one less IP subnet to go in the IP routing table. In addition, it helps in troubleshooting because network operators recall their internal loopback addresses quicker than external IP subnets, such as that used in the EBGP connection.

BGP Routes Getting Dampened

Dampening is the way to minimize instability in a local BGP network caused by unstable BGP routes from EBGP neighbors. RFC 2439, *BGP Route Flap Dampening,* describes in detail how dampening works. In short, dampening is the way to assign a penalty for a flapping BGP route.

A withdrawal of a prefix is considered a flap. A penalty of 1000 is assigned for each flap. If the flap penalty reaches the suppress limit because of continued flaps (the default is 2000), the BGP path is suppressed and is taken out of the routing table. This penalty is decayed exponentially based on the half-life time (the default is 15 minutes). When the penalty reaches the reuse value (the default is 750), the path is unsuppressed, is installed in the routing table, and is advertised to other BGP neighbors. Any dampened path can be suppressed only until the maximum suppress time is reached (the default is 60 minutes). Dampening is applied only to EBGP neighbors, not to IBGP neighbors.

BGP dampening is off by default. The following BGP command activates dampening:

```
router bgp 109
bgp dampening
```

Cisco IOS software allows dampening parameters to be changed as follows:

bgp dampening *half-life-time reuse suppress maximum-suppress-time*

The ranges of values for these options are as follows:

- *half-life-time*—1 to 45 minutes. The default is 15 minutes.
- *reuse*—1 to 20,000. The default is 750.
- *suppress*—1 to 20,000. The default is 2,000.
- *maximum-suppress-time*—The maximum duration that a route can be suppressed. The range is 1 to 255. The default is 4 times the *half-life-time*.

Figure 5-48 shows a simple EBGP network between R1 and R2 in AS 109 and AS 110, respectively. R2 has advertised 100.100.100.0/24 to R1. To show how dampening works, R2 is made to flap 100.100.100.0/24 multiple times. Removing the route in the R2 routing table and putting it back again can simulate flapping. R1 receives these flaps and, if it is configured with dampening, assigns penalties per flap.

Figure 5-48 EBGP Joins Autonomous Systems 109 and 110

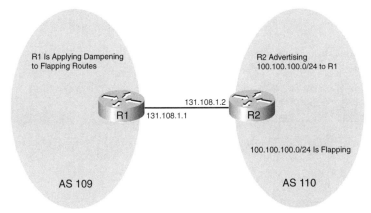

Example 5-200 shows the necessary **debug** commands, **debug ip bgp dampening** and **debug ip bgp updates**, to observe the dampening feature in R1. Most debugs can be run along with an access list to limit the output created by these debugs. Access list 1 permits only the 100.100.100.0 network.

Example 5-200 *Access List 1 Restricts the Debug Output to That Associated with the 100.100.100.0/24 Network*

```
R1#debug ip bgp dampening 1
R1#debug ip bgp updates 1
access-list 1 permit 100.100.100.0 0.0.0.0
```

NOTE

Actually, route damp-
ening can be considered
the solution for ill-
behaved Internet routes,
keeping them in a
stable state.

Example 5-201 shows the debug output and flap statistics in BGP output. The highlighted
debug and **show** command output shows that 100.100.100.0/24 has flapped four times in
3 minutes and 13 seconds. For each flap, a penalty of 1000 is assigned. Because the suppress
limit of 2000 has been exceeded, 100.100.100.0/24 is suppressed and removed from the routing table.

Example 5-201 *The Debug Output Includes Flap Counts and Dampening Penalties*

```
Dec 13 03:33:57.966 MST: BGP(0): 131.108.1.2. rcv UPDATE about 100.100.100.0/24
        -- withdrawn
Dec 13 03:33:57.966 MST: BGP(0): charge penalty for 100.100.100.0/24 path
        110 with halflife-time 15 reuse/suppress 750/2000
Dec 13 03:33:57.966 MST: BGP(0): flapped 4 times since 00:02:58. New penalty is
        3838
R1#show ip bgp 100.100.100.0
 BGP routing table entry for 100.100.100.0/24, version 17
Paths: (1 available, no best path)
Flag: 0x208
 Not advertised to any peer
  110, (suppressed due to dampening)
    131.108.1.2 from 131.108.1.2 (10.0.0.3)
      Origin IGP, metric 0, localpref 100, valid, external
      Dampinfo: penalty 3793, flapped 4 times in 00:03:13, reuse in 00:35:00
```

If R1 wants to reinstall 100.100.100.0/24, it can do the following:

- Wait for the penalty to go below the reuse limit (750).
- Remove dampening altogether from the BGP configuration.
- Clear the flap statistics.

NOTE

Route instabilities in
the Internet affect
everybody. It is every-
one's responsibility to
minimize route oscilla-
tion by being more
aware of the things we
do and why we do
them. Providers are get-
ting tougher on culprits;
there is even talk of
charging an additional
fee per route flap.

Example 5-202 shows how the dampened path can be cleared and immediately get installed
in the routing table. The output in Example 5-202 is from the **debug ip bgp update 1** command, which is on to display the activity in the BGP process. The output in Example 5-203
shows 100.100.100.0/24 going into the IP routing table.

Example 5-202 *A Dampened Path Can Be Cleared and Immediately Installed into the Routing Table*

```
R1#clear ip bgp dampening 100.100.100.0
Dec 13 03:36:56.205 MST: BGP(0): Revise route installing 100.100.100.0/24 ->
        131.108.1.2 to main IP table
```

Example 5-203 *The 100.100.100.0/24 Network Now Resides in the Routing Table*

```
R1#show ip bgp 100.100.100.0
BGP routing table entry for 100.100.100.0/24, version 18
Paths: (1 available, best #1, table Default-IP-Routing-Table)
 Flag: 0x208
  Not advertised to any peer
 110
    131.108.1.2 from 131.108.1.2 (10.0.0.3)
     Origin IGP, metric 0, localpref 100, valid, external, best
R1#show ip route 100.100.100.0
Routing entry for 100.100.100.0/24
  Known via "bgp 109", distance 20, metric 0
 Tag 110, type external
 Last update from 131.108.1.2 00:02:45 ago
 Routing Descriptor Blocks:
 * 131.108.1.2, from 131.108.1.2, 00:02:45 ago
     Route metric is 0, traffic share count is 1
     AS Hops 1, BGP network version 0
```

Troubleshooting Outbound and Inbound BGP Policy Issues

The real power of BGP is in managing IP traffic flows coming into and going out of the AS. BGP in general and Cisco IOS software in particular offer a great deal of flexibility in manipulating the BGP attributes LOCAL_PREFERENCE, MED, and so forth to control BP best-path calculation.

This best-path decision determines how traffic exits the AS. With the large size of BGP networks today, it is crucial that BGP operators understand how BGP attributes should be managed.

Here are some of the most common problems encountered in managing outbound traffic flow:

- Multiple exit points exist, but traffic goes out through one or a few exit routers.
- Traffic takes a different interface from what is shown in the routing table.
- A multiple-BGP connection exists to the same BGP neighbor, but traffic goes out through only one connection.
- Asymmetric routing causes a problem, especially when NAT and time-sensitive applications are used.

Just as in managing outbound IP traffic from an AS, Cisco IOS software offers BGP operators configuration options to manage inbound traffic in an AS. It is important that inbound traffic from other autonomous systems be managed as well. If this does not happen, network capacity will not be fully utilized. This causes congestion in one part of the network while other parts are underutilized. The end result of this mismanagement of inbound traffic flow is sluggish throughput, slow round-trip times, and delays in IP traffic. Therefore, it is essential that all inbound BGP policies be checked and configured correctly.

Here are some of the most common problems in managing inbound IP traffic in an AS using BGP:

- Multiple connections exist to an AS, but all the traffic comes in through one BGP neighbor in the same AS.
- A BGP neighbor in an AS should just be a backup provider, but some traffic from the Internet still comes through that AS.
- Asymmetric routing occurs.
- Traffic to a certain subnet should come through a particular connection, but it is coming from somewhere else.

Each of these problems, both with outbound and inbound policy issues, could require extensive troubleshooting. The next section more thoroughly examines the problem of traffic taking a different interface from what is shown in the routing table. It also gives an example of troubleshooting policy issues.

Traffic Takes a Different Interface Than What Is Shown in the Routing Table

In some scenarios, BGP and the routing table path to a certain destination prefix show Exit A, but the actual traffic leaves through Exit B. Packet forwarding to a destination takes place from the routing table, and network operators expect to see this behavior. However, in most cases, the next hops of prefixes in the routing table are not directly connected, and packet forwarding eventually takes place based on the next-hop path. Figure 5-49 shows that R1 and R2 are two route reflectors, with R6 and R8 as their clients. R6 is advertising 100.100.100.0/24 to R2 and R1, and both reflect this advertisement to R8 with a next hop of 172.16.126.6. Now assume that R8 has a BGP policy that chooses the path for 100.100.100.0/24 from R2 (the upper path) as the best path that it will install in its routing table. However, in the same router, R8, the best IGP path to reach 172.16.126.6 (a next hop of 100.100.100.0/24) is through R1 (the bottom path).

Figure 5-49 R1 and R2 Are Route Reflectors

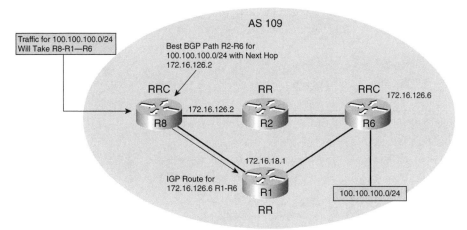

Therefore, the forwarding of IP packets in a router eventually happens by looking at the path for the next hop (172.16.126.6) of the actual path (100.100.100.0/24). In Cisco IOS software, recursive lookup is the term used for finding out the path based on the next hop and the actual prefix. In some cases, more than one recursive lookup must be done to figure out the actual physical path that packets take to reach the destination.

The **show ip bgp** command output shown in Example 5-204 shows the output of 100.100.100.0/24 in R8. The next hop is 172.16.126.6. When traffic is sent to 100.100.100.0/24, it actually is sent to the interface that provides a better route for 172.16.126.6.

Example 5-204 *Traffic Toward 100.100.100.0/24 Takes the R8–R1–R6 Path*

```
R8#show ip bgp 100.100.100.0
BGP routing table entry for 100.100.100.0./24, version 5870
Paths: (1 available, best #1, table Default-IP-Routing_Table)
 Not advertised to any peer
 Local
  172.16.126.6 (metric 20) from 172.16.126.2 (172.16.126.2)
    Origin IGP, metric 0, localpref 100, valid, internal, best
```

In R8, 172.16.126.6 is the next hop for 100.100.100.0/24 advertised by R2 and is considered the best route; therefore, it is installed in the IP routing table. Example 5-204 shows that the best way to reach 172.16.126.6, the next hop of 100.100.100.0/24, is through R1, not through R2.

Example 5-205 *A Static Route Has a Lower Administrative Distance Than a Dynamic Route and Therefore Takes Precedence*

```
R8#show ip route 172.16.126.6
Routing entry for 172.16.126.0/24
  Known via "static", distance 1, metric 0
  Routing Descriptor Blocks:
  * 172.16.18.1
      Route metric is 0, traffic share count is 1
```

The highlighted 172.16.18.1 is the next hop for 172.16.126.6 (a next hop of 100.100.100.0/24).

Therefore, all traffic from or through R8 destined for 100.100.100.0/24 goes through 172.16.18.1 (R1). The output of a traceroute done from R8 to 100.100.100.1 in Example 5-206 shows that traffic flows through 172.16.18.1, which is R1.

Example 5-206 *A* **traceroute** *Verifies the Path of the Traffic to 100.100.100.0/24*

```
R8#traceroute 100.100.100.1

Type escape sequence to abort.
Tracing the route to 100.100.100.1

1 172.16.18.1 4 msec 4 msec 4 msec
2 172.16.126.6 4 msec 8 msec 8 msec
3 172.16.126.6 4 msec 8 msec 8 msec
```

A router might provide a route to a BGP neighbor but might never be in a forwarding path to reach that route. This is because packets are forwarded to the next-hop address of the actual route, which might not be the same router that gave the route in the first place.

If routing and forwarding paths need to match, care must be taken in how next-hop addresses are learned through IGP. To fix the problem shown in Figure 5-49, R8 should have an IGP path for 172.16.126.6 (a next hop of 100.100.100.0/24) through R1.

Lab 5.2.1 Troubleshooting Problems at the Physical, Data-Link, and Network Layers

You complete this laboratory exercise by defining, isolating, and correcting the problems outlined in the scenario to restore the network to baseline specifications. In this exercise, each workgroup uses a troubleshooting methodology and Cisco commands to define, isolate, and correct issues.

Troubleshooting Redistribution

In addition to troubleshooting individual routing protocol behavior, it is critical that you understand how routing protocols, static routes, and connected routes redistribute into RIP, EIGRP, OSPF, IS-IS, and BGP. This section addresses troubleshooting redistribution into each of these routing protocols.

Redistribution Problems with RIP

The most prevalent problem encountered with redistribution is that redistributed routes are not being installed in the routing table of the routers receiving these routes. The most common cause of this is a metric that is not defined during redistribution into RIP.

In RIP, the metric for a route is treated as a hop count that shows the number of routers that exist along this route. The maximum hop count that RIP supports is 15; anything greater than 15 is treated as the infinite metric and is dropped on receipt.

Figure 5-50 shows a network that could produce the problem in which redistributed routes do not get installed in the receiver's routing table. R1 and R3 are running OSPF in Area 0, whereas R1 and R2 are running RIP. R3 is announcing 131.108.6.0/24 through OSPF to R1. In R1, OSPF routes are being redistributed into RIP, but R2 is not receiving 131.108.6.0/24 through RIP.

Figure 5-50 Redistribution Is Necessary When RIP and OSPF Are Running in the Same Network

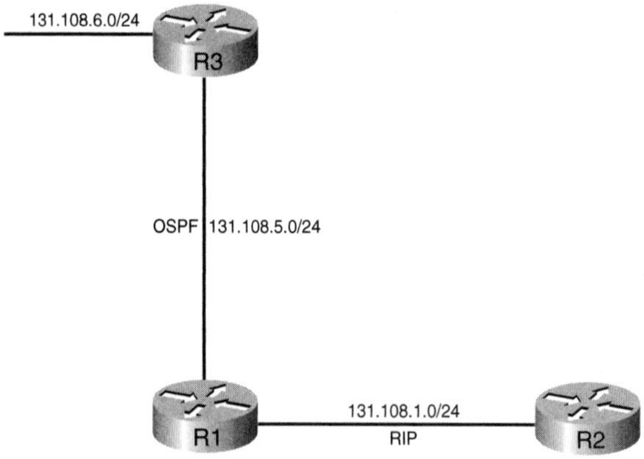

The first step is to investigate whether R1 is receiving 131.108.6.0/24. Example 5-207 shows that R3 is advertising 131.108.6.0/24 through OSPF to R1. Example 5-208 shows that R1 is redistributing OSPF into RIP on R1.

Example 5-207 *R1 Is Learning 131.108.6.0/24 Via OSPF*

```
R1#show ip route 131.108.6.0
Routing entry for 131.108.6.0/24
Known via "ospf 1", distance 110, metric 20, type intra area
```

Example 5-208 *R1 Is Redistributing OSPF into RIP*

```
R1#
router rip
   verison 2
   redistribute ospf 1
   network 131.108.0.0
```

The next step is to check whether R2 is receiving the 131.108.6.0/24 route. Example 5-209 shows that in R2, 131.108.6.0/24 is not present in the routing table.

Example 5-209 *R2 Is Not Receiving the OSPF-to-RIP Redistributed Route*

```
R2#show ip route 131.108.6.0
% Network not in table
```

The output of **debug ip rip** on R2 shows that R2 is receiving the 131.108.6.0/24 route, but with a metric of 16 hops (infinity), as shown in Example 5-210.

Example 5-210 *A Debug Reveals That the Redistributed Route Has an Infinite Metric*

```
R2#debug ip rip


 RIP: received v2 update from 131.108.1.1 on Ethernet1
      131.108.6.0/24 -> 0.0.0.0 in 16 hops (inaccessible)
```

In RIP, 16 is considered an infinite metric. Any update with a metric greater than 15 is not considered for entry into the routing table.

In this example, an OSPF route in R1 for 131.108.6.0/24 has a metric of 20. When OSPF is redistributed into RIP in R1, OSPF advertises 131.108.6.0/24 with a default metric of 20, which exceeds the maximum metric allowed in RIP. OSPF knows only cost as a metric, whereas RIP uses hop count. No metric translation facility exists, so the administrator must configure a metric to be assigned to redistributed routes.

To correct this problem, R1 needs to assign a valid metric when configuring the redistribution. This can be done with either the **metric** option in the **redistribute** command, as shown in Example 5-211, or with the **default-metric** command. In this configuration, all routes redistributed from OSPF into RIP get a metric of 1. R2 treats this metric as hop count.

Example 5-211 *A RIP Metric of 1 Is Assigned to Redistributed OSPF Routes*

```
R1#
router rip
 version 2
 redistribute ospf 1 metric 1
 network 131.108.0.0
```

Example 5-212 shows that R2 is now receiving the correct route with a metric of 1.

Example 5-212 *R2 Is Now Installing 131.108.6.0/24 into the Routing Table*

```
R2#show ip route 131.108.6.0
Routing entry for 131.108.6.0/24
   Known via "rip", distance 120, metric 1
```

Redistribution Problems with IGRP/EIGRP

IGRP has a composite metric made up of bandwidth, delay, reliability, load, and MTU. By default, it uses only bandwidth and delay. Other routing protocols use different metrics. For example, OSPF uses a metric based on interface cost. OSPF cost is derived from the link's bandwidth. Cisco uses 100,100,000/bandwidth to get that cost.

IGRP does not understand the metrics of other protocols (except EIGRP), so you must input a default metric when doing redistribution.

Figure 5-51 shows a network that could produce the problem in which redistributed routes do not get installed in the receiver's routing table. OSPF is redistributed into IGRP at R1, but R2 is not receiving the IGRP routes.

Figure 5-51 IGRP-OSPF Redistribution

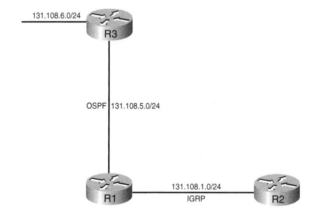

R1 and R3 are running OSPF in Area 0, whereas R1 and R2 are running IGRP. R3 is announcing 131.108.6.0/24 through OSPF to R1. In R1, OSPF routes are being redistributed into IGRP, but R2 is not receiving 131.108.6.0/24 through IGRP.

Example 5-213 shows that R3 is advertising 131.108.6.0/24 through OSPF to R1. Example 5-214 shows that R1 is redistributing OSPF into IGRP. However, examining the routing table in R2, Example 5-215 shows that 131.108.6.0/24 is not being installed in the routing table.

Example 5-213 *R3 Is Advertising 131.108.6.0/24 Via OSPF*

```
R1#show ip route 131.108.6.0
Routing entry for 131.108.6.0/24
  Known via "ospf 1", distance 110, metric 11, type intra area
    Last update from 131.108.5.1 on Ethernet0, 00:04:12 ago
```

Example 5-213 *R3 Is Advertising 131.108.6.0/24 Via OSPF (Continued)*

```
Routing Descriptor Blocks:
* 131.108.5.1, from 131.108.6.1, 00:04:12 ago, via Ethernet0
    Route metric is 11, traffic share count is 1
```

Example 5-214 *R1 Is Redistributing OSPF into IGRP*

```
R1#router igrp 1
 redistribute ospf 1
 redistribute static
  network 131.108.0.0
```

Example 5-215 *R2 Is Not Receiving the Redistributed Route*

```
R2#show ip route 131.108.6.0
%Subnet not in table
```

To solve this problem, R1 needs to include the **metric** option with the **redistribute** statement so that it can convert the OSPF metric properly. Example 5-216 shows the new configuration for R1. OSPF is redistributed into IGRP with metric values of bandwidth, delay, reliability, load, and MTU. Even if reliability and load are not being used in the IGRP metric, these values must be included in the **redistribute** command.

NOTE

MTU is not part of the composite metric for IGRP or EIGRP, but it must be included in the **redistribute** command.

Example 5-216 *The **metric** Keyword and Metric Values Are Added to the **redistribute** Command Under IGRP on R1. This Is Standard Operating Procedure.*

```
R1#router igrp 1
 redistribute ospf 1 metric 1 10000 255 1 1500
 network 131.108.0.0
```

Another solution is to use the **default-metric** command under **router igrp**. Example 5-217 shows the syntax of the **default-metric** command, with the same values for bandwidth, delay, reliability, load, and MTU.

Example 5-217 *The **default-metric** Command Is an Alternative to the **redistribute/metric** Option*

```
R1#router igrp 1
 redistribute ospf 1
 redistribute static
 default-metric 1 10000 255 1 1500
  network 131.108.0.0
```

NOTE

EIGRP uses the same parameters with the **metric** option in the **redistribute** command and with the **default-metric** command. The only significant difference from IGRP is that the metric is multiplied by 256 with EIGRP. Also, if the AS numbers are the same, redistribution happens automatically between IGRP and EIGRP.

The route is now installed in R2's routing table, as shown in Example 5-218.

Example 5-218 *R2 Now Installs 131.108.6.0/24 into the Routing Table*

```
R2#show ip route 131.108.6.0
Routing entry for 131.108.6.0/24
   Known via "igrp", distance 100, metric 8976
```

Redistribution Problems with OSPF

When a router in OSPF does redistribution, it becomes an ASBR. The routes that are redistributed into OSPF could be directly connected routes, static routes, or routes from another routing protocol or another OSPF process.

The two most common problems associated with OSPF and redistribution are as follows:

- OSPF is not installing external routes in the routing table.
- ASBR is not advertising redistributed routes.

OSPF Is Not Installing External Routes in the Routing Table

When OSPF redistributes any routes, whether connected, static, or from a different routing protocol, it generates a Type 5 LSA for those external routes. These Type 5 routes are flooded into every OSPF router, with the exception of those in stub and NSSA areas. Sometimes, the problem is that the external routes are in the OSPF database but are not being installed in the routing table.

The most common causes of this problem are as follows:

- The forwarding address is not known through the intra-area or interarea route.
- The ABR is not generating Type 4 Summary LSAs.

Both of these problems are discussed in the "Troubleshooting OSPF" section.

ASBR Is Not Advertising Redistributed Routes

Whenever a route is known to be connected or static, or when any other routing protocol is redistributed into OSPF, an external LSA is generated for that route. If an OSPF router does not advertise the external route even after the redistribution, this indicates a problem on a router that is doing the redistribution. Mostly, the problem stems from configuration mistakes.

The most common causes of this problem are as follows:

- The **subnets** keyword is missing from the ASBR configuration.
- The **distribute-list out** command is blocking the routes.

Distribute list issues are discussed in the section "Common IGP Routing Protocol Issues, Causes, and Solutions." The following is an example of a problem caused by the missing **subnets** keyword in the ASBR configuration.

When any protocol is redistributed into OSPF, if the networks that are being redistributed are subnets, the **subnets** keyword must be used under the OSPF configuration. If the **subnets** keyword is not added, OSPF ignores all the subnetted routes when generating the external LSA.

This situation could arise when connected or static routes are being redistributed into or out of OSPF. In that case, the same rule applies: The **subnets** keyword must be entered to redistribute subnetted routes.

Figure 5-52 shows a network setup that is redistributing into OSPF.

Figure 5-52 RIP Is Redistributing into OSPF on R1

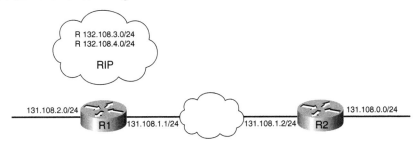

Example 5-219 shows the output of **show ip ospf database external** for 132.108.3.0. The output shows no LSA information, which means that R1 is not even originating the external LSA for 132.108.3.0. Example 5-220 shows the OSPF configuration of R1 and that the **redistribute rip** command under OSPF is missing the **subnets** keyword.

Example 5-219 *R1 Is Not Originating the External LSA for 132.108.3.0/24*

```
R1#show ip ospf database external 132.108.3.0
   OSPF Router with ID (132.108.2.1) (process ID 1)
R1#
```

Example 5-220 *RIP Is Redistributing into OSPF, But Routes Are Not Redistributing*

```
R1#
router ospf 1
 redistribute rip
```

continues

Example 5-220 *RIP Is Redistributing into OSPF, But Routes Are Not Redistributing (Continued)*

```
 network 131.108.1.0 0.0.0.255 area 0
 network 131.108.2.0 0.0.0.255 area 0
 !
router rip
 network 132.108.0.0
 !
```

The solution to this problem is to add the **subnets** keyword to the **subnets** command under OSPF, as shown in Example 5-221. After this option is added, OSPF redistributes all the routes that are subnetted, such as 131.108.3.0 with the /24 mask. Example 5-222 shows that R1 is now generating the external LSA for 132.108.3.0/24 and 132.108.4.0/24.

Example 5-221 *The **subnets** Keyword Is Added to the **redistribute rip** Command*

```
R1#
router ospf 1
redistribute rip subnets
network 132.108.1.0 0.0.0.255 area 0
network 132.108.2.0 0.0.0.255 area 0
```

Example 5-222 *R1 Now Generates the External LSA for 132.108.3.0/24*

```
R1#show ip ospf database external 132.108.3.0
OSPF Router with (ID 131.108.2.1) (process ID 1)


Type-5 AS External Link States


LS age: 1161
Options: (No TOS-capability, DC)
LS Type: AS External Link
Link State ID: 132.108.3.0 (External Network Number)
Advertising Router: 132.108.2.1
LS Seq Number: 80000001
Checksum: 0x550
Lenghth: 36
Network Mask: /24
Metric Type: 2 (Larger than any link state path)
TOS: 0
```

Example 5-222 *R1 Now Generates the External LSA for 132.108.3.0/24 (Continued)*

```
Metric: 1
Forward Address: 0.0.0.0
External Route Tag: 1
R1#


R1#show ip opsf database external 132.108.4.0
OSPF Router with ID (131.108.2.1) (Process ID 1)


Type-5 AS External Link States


LS age: 1161
Options: (No TOS-capability, DC)
LS Type: AS External Link
Link State ID: 132.108.4.0 (External Network Number)
Advertising Router: 132.108.2.1
LS Seq Number: 80000001
Checksum: 0x550
Lenghth: 36
Network Mask: /24
Metric Type: 2 (Larger than any link state path)
TOS: 0
Metric: 1
Forward Address: 0.0.0.0
External Route Tag: 1


R1#
```

Redistribution Problems with IS-IS

Cisco IOS allows IP routes to be imported into IS-IS. Examples of the external sources are static routes and other dynamic routing protocols such as RIP and OSPF. The IP external reachability TLV is used to add external routes to the IS-IS domain. Even though RFC 1195 specifies IP external reachability for only Level 2 LSPs, Cisco IOS provides a special capability for using them in Level 1 LSPs, which allows external routes into a Level 1 area.

Most service provider networks use IS-IS as the IGP in large single-area Level 1-only or Level 2-only domains. For those with Level 1-only backbones, the capability to redistribute into Level 1 provides flexibility to import external routes into the IS-IS domain. Even though this behavior is not standardized, it should not pose interoperability issues with other vendors' routers, because both existing IS-IS standards, ISO 10589 and RFC 1195, require IS-IS implementations to ignore unsupported or unknown optional TLVs encountered while parsing IS-IS packets.

The IOS router-level command **redistribute** enables redistribution. This command takes on other options, such as metric value, metric type, route map, and so on. In the Cisco implementation of IS-IS, CLNS static routes are automatically distributed into IS-IS. However, IP static routes are redistributed only by manual configuration.

When static IP routes need to be redistributed, the **redistribute** command requires the keyword **ip** to go with it, in addition to the other arguments previously mentioned. The metric type for external routes can be either internal or external. Internal metrics are comparable to metrics used for internal routes. External metrics require the I/E bit (bit 7) of the metric field to be set in addition to the actual metric, resulting in higher metric values. In current Cisco IOS software releases, when using narrow metrics, bit 8 of the default metric field is set for external metrics, resulting in an increase of the metric value by 128.

By default, the internal metric type is assigned if nothing is specified in the configuration. Also, the external routes are added to Level 2 unless Level 1 is explicitly stated in the configuration. Figure 5-53 illustrates basic examples of redistribution in IS-IS.

Figure 5-53 Two IS-IS Areas Are Connected by Routers RT1 and RT2

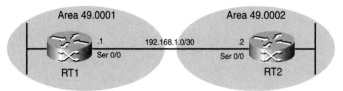

In Example 5-223, only the **ip** keyword is used with the **redistribute** command.

Example 5-223 *Static Routes Are Being Redistributed into IS-IS*

```
RT1#conf t
Enter configuation commands, one per line. End with CNTL/Z.
RT1(config)#router isis
RT1(config-router)#redistribute static ip
RT1(config-router)#^Z

RT1#show running-config
```

Example 5-223 *Static Routes Are Being Redistributed into IS-IS (Continued)*

```
<output omitted>
router isis
 redistribute static ip metric 0 metric-type internal level-2
 net 49.0001.0000.0000.0001.00
 !
ip route 172.16.1.0 255.255.255.0 Null0
<output omitted>
```

Note that below **show running-config**, the internal metric type has been assigned by default; the metric applied is 0. In Example 5-224, the output of **show isis database** on RT1 shows that the external static route has been added to only the Level 2 LSP.

Example 5-224 *The External Static Route 172.16.1.0/24 Was Added as an L2 IS-IS LSP*

```
RT1#show isis database RT1.00-00 detail
IS-IS   Level-1   LSP  RT1.00-00
LSPID          LSP          Seq     Num  LSP   Checksum  LSP  Holdtime  ATT/P/OL
RT1.00-00    *0x00000DB0   0xEB25              979                 1/0/0

  Area Address: 49.0001
  NLPID:            0xcc
  Hostname: RT1
  IP Address:   10.0.0.1
  Metric: 10     IP 10.1.1.0 255.255.255.0
  Metric: 10     IP 10.0.0.1 255.255.255.255
  Metric: 10     IP 192.168.1.0 255.255.255.252
  Metric: 10     IS RT1 .02
  Metric: 10     IS RT1 .01
  Metric: 0      ES RT1
IS-IS level-2 LSP RT1.00-00
LSPID          LSP          Seq     Num  LSP   Checksum  LSP  Holdtime  ATT/P/OL
RT1.00-00    *0x00000E3D   0x6F45                        977          0/0/0
  Area Address: 49.0001
  NLPID:        0xcc
  Hostname: RT1
  IP Address: 10.0.0.1
```

continues

Example 5-224 *The External Static Route 172.16.1.0/24 Was Added as an L2 IS-IS LSP (Continued)*

```
  Metric: 10    IS RT1 .02
  Metric: 10    IS RT1 .01
  Metric: 10    IS RT2 .00
  Metric: 0     IP-External 172.16.1.0 255.255.255.0
  Metric: 10    IP 10.1.1.0 255.255.255.0
  Metric: 0     IP 10.0.0.1 255.255.255.255
```

The metric type is explicitly set to external in this configuration, but no metric value is applied, as shown in Example 5-225. As explained previously, the I/E bit then needs to be set for the external metric type, effectively increasing the metric value by 64. However, Cisco IOS sets bit 8 of the narrow metric instead of bit 7, consequently adding 128 instead to the original value of 0. The Level 2 LSP displayed shows 128 as the metric value for the external route, 172.16.1.0/24.

Example 5-225 *The **metric-type external** Option Is Added to the **redistribute static ip** Command*

```
RT1#conf t
Enter configuration commands, one per line. End with CNTL/Z.
RT1(config)#router isis
RT1(config-config)#redistribute static ip metric-type external
RT1(config-router)#^Z

RT1#show running-config
<output omitted>
router isis
 redistribute static ip metric 0metric-type external level-2
 net 49.0001.0000.0001.00
!
iproute 172.16.1.0 255.255.255.0 null 0
<output omitted>

RT1#show isis database level-2 RT1.00-00 detail

IS-IS Level-2 LSP RT1.00-00
LSPID       LSP Seq Num LSP Checksum LSP Holdtime ATT/P/OL
RT1.00-00   *0x00000E44 0x7FAD          703          0/0/0
Area Address: 49.0001
```

Example 5-225 *The* **metric-type external** *Option Is Added to the* **redistribute static ip** *Command (Continued)*

```
NLPID:        0xcc
Hostname: RT1
IP Address:   10.0.0.1
Metric: 10        IS RT1 .02
Metric: 10        IS RT1 .01
Metric: 10        IS RT1 .00
Metric: 128       IP-External 172.16.1.0 255.255.255.0
Metric: 10        Ip 10.1.1.0 255.255.255.0
Metric: 10        Ip 10.0.0.1 255.255.255.255
Metric: 10        Ip 192.168.1.0 255.255.255.252
```

The IP routing table output from RT2 in Example 5-226 shows the external route, 172.16.1.0/24, which was redistributed from a static source into IS-IS on router RT1. The metric entered for this route, 138, is the total of the metric on the outgoing interface from RT2 to RT1 (10) plus the metric of 128 advertised by RT1. Other routes received from RT1 (10.0.0.1/32 and 10.1.1.0/24) are registered with a metric of 20 (10 advertised by RT1 and an additional 10 for the metric from RT2 to RT1).

Example 5-226 *The Routing Table on RT2 Installs the External Route 172.16.1.0/24*

```
RT2#show ip route
     172.16.0.0/24 is subnetted, 2 subnets
i L2    172.16.1.0 [115/138] via 192.168.1.1 serial0/0
     10.0.0.0/8 is variably subnetted, 4 subnets, 2 masks
C       10.0.0.2/32 is directly connected, loopback0
i L2    10.1.1.0/24 [115/20] via 192.168.1.1, Serial0/0
C       10.2.2.0/24 is directly connected, Ethernet0/0
i L2    10.0.0.1/32 [115/20] via 192.168.1.1, Serial0/0
     192.168.1.0/30 is subnetted, 1 subnets
C       192.168.1.0 is directly connected, serial0/0
```

The **route-map** option of the **redistribute** command provides more flexibility for configuring redistribution, such as selective importation of external routes into the IS-IS environment, applying special tags, and even setting the metric of redistributed routes. When used for selective importation of routes into IS-IS, route maps provide a filtering effect by controlling which elements from an external source are allowed or denied entry into IS-IS.

In Example 5-227, static routes are redistributed into IS-IS while filtering through the route map TEST. Route map TEST matches the static routes against access list 1, which permits only 172.16.2.0/24 into the IS-IS environment. RT1 LSP is shown from RT2. Also shown is the routing table of RT2.

Example 5-227 route-map TEST *Permits Only the 172.16.2.0/24 Network to Be Redistributed*

```
RT1#show running-config
!
router isis
 redistribute static ip metric 0 route-map TEST metric-type external level-2
 net 49.0001.0000.0000.0001.00
!

ip route 172.16.1.0 255.255.255.0 Null0
ip route 172.16.2.0 255.255.255.0 Null0
!
access-list 1 permit 172.16.2.0
!
route-map TEST permit 10
 match ip address 1


RT2#show isis database level-2 RT1.00-00 detail


IS-IS Level-2 LSP RT1.00-00
LSPID       LSP Seq Num LSP Checksum LSP Holdtime ATT/P/OL
RT1.00-00  *0x00000E62 0x8588         1026         0/0/0
Area Address: 49.0001
NLPID:       0xcc
Hostname: RT1
IP Address:   10.0.0.1
Metric: 10       IS RT1 .02
Metric: 10       IS RT1 .01
Metric: 10       IS RT2 .00
Metric: 128      IP-External 172.16.2.0 255.255.255.0
Metric: 10       IP 10.1.1.0 255.255.255.0
Metric: 10       IP 10.0.0.1 255.255.255.255
Metric: 10       IP 192.168.1.0 255.255.255.252
```

Example 5-227 route-map **TEST** *Permits Only the 172.16.2.0/24 Network to Be Redistributed (Continued)*

```
RT2#show ip route
     172.16.0.0/24 is subnetted, 1 subnets
i L2    172.16.2.0 [115/138] via 192.168.1.1. serial0/0
     10.0.0.0/8 is variably subnetted, 4 subnets, 2 masks
C       10.0.0.2/32 is directly connected, loopback0
i L2    10.1.1.0/24 [115/20] via 192.168.1.1, Serial0/0
C       10.2.2.0/24 is directly connected, Ethernet0/0
i L2    10.0.0.1/32 [115/20] via 192.168.1.1, Serial0/0
     192.168.1.0/30 is subnetted, 1 subnets
C       192.168.1.0 is directly connected, serial0/0
```

In Example 5-228, the route map approach is used to set the metric for routes imported into IS-IS.

Example 5-228 route-map **SETMETRIC** *Sets the Metric for the Routes Redistributed into IS-IS*

```
RT1#show running-config
!
router isis
 redistribute static ip route-map SETMETRIC
 net 49.0001.0000.0000.0001.00
 is-type level-1
 metric-style wide
!

route-map SETMETRIC permit 10
 set metric 1000
 set level level-1

RT1#show isis database detail RT1.00-00 level-1
IS-IS Level-1 LSP RT1.00-00
LSPID       LSP Seq Num LSP Checksum LSP Holdtime ATT/P/OL
RT1.00-00   *0x00000E56 0x0A4C        1128        0/0/0
Area Address: 49
NLPID:       0xcc
Hostname: RT1
```

continues

Example 5-228 route-map SETMETRIC *Sets the Metric for the Routes Redistributed into IS-IS (Continued)*

```
IP Address:    10.0.0.1
Metric: 10          IS-Extended RT1 .02
Metric: 10          IS-Extended RT1 .01
Metric: 10          IS-Extended RT2 .00
Metric: 1000           IP 10.1.1.0 255.255.255.0
Metric: 1000           IP 10.0.0.1 255.255.255.255
Metric: 1000           IP 192.168.1.0 255.255.255.252
```

Redistribution Problems with BGP

In this example of redistribution with BGP, the discussion focuses more on design and configuration issues than on troubleshooting problems.

On an AS border router, outgoing route advertisements affect incoming traffic, and incoming route advertisements affect outgoing traffic. As a result, outgoing and incoming advertisements should be considered separately. The example in this section discusses injecting BGP routes into an IGP, because this is the situation for most enterprise networks.

Prefixes that are learned from an EBGP neighbor are automatically added to the routing table. In Figure 5-54, for instance, AS 300 advertises two routes: 192.168.250.0/24 and 192.168.1.212/30. The IGP for AS 300 and the configuration of router Tahoe are unimportant in this example.

Figure 5-54 AS 300 Originates Two BGP Routes

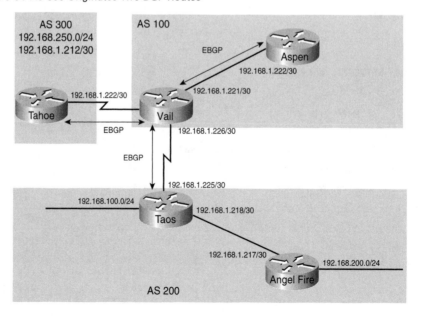

The important observations are that the prefixes advertised by Tahoe to its external BGP peer are displayed in the Taos routing table as reachable and that pings to a destination in AS 300 are successful, as shown in Example 5-229. An extended ping is used because the subnet of the Taos serial interface, 192.168.1.224/30, is not advertised. The BGP-learned routes are tagged in the routing table with a B.

Example 5-229 *Taos Can Successfully Ping from 192.168.100.1 to 192.168.250.1*

```
Taos#show ip route
Codes: C - connected, S - static, I - IGRP, R - RIP, M - Mobile, B - BGP,
D - EIGRP, EX - EIGRP external, O - OSPF, IA - OSPF inter area,
N1 - OSPF NSSA external type 1, N2 - OSPF NSSA external type 2,
E1 - OSPF external type 1, E2 - OSPF external type 2, E - EGP, i - IS-IS,
L1 - IS-IS level-1, L2 IS-IS level-2, * - candidate default,
U - per-user static route, O -  ODR, T - traffic engineered route
Gateway of last resort is not set
D    192.168.200.0/24 [90/409600] via 192.168.1.217,   00:25:37, ethernet0
B    192.168.250.0/24 [20/0] via 192.168.1.226, 16:18:12
     192.168.1.0/24 is variably subnetted, 4 subnets, 2 masks
D       192.168.1.0/24 is a summary, 00:25:43 Null0
C       192.168.1.224/30 is directly connected, Serial0/0
C       192.168.1.216/30 is directly connected, Ethernet0/0
B       192.168.1.212 [20/0] via 192.168.1.226 16:18:12
C    192.168.100.0/24 is directly connected, Ethernet1


Taos#ping
Protocol [ip]:
Target IP address: 192.168.250.1
Repeat count [5]:
Datagram size [100]:
Timeout in seconds [2]:
Extended commands [n]: y
Source address or interface: 192.168.100.1
Type of service [0]:
Set DF bit in IP header? [no]:
Validate reply data? [no]:
Data pattern [0xABCD]:
Loose, Strict, Record, Timestamp, Verbose[none]:
```

continues

Example 5-229 *Taos Can Successfully Ping from 192.168.100.1 to 192.168.250.1 (Continued)*

```
Sweep range of sizes [n]:
Type escape sequence to abort.
Sending 5, 100-byte ICMP Echos to 192.168.250.1. timeout is 2 seconds:
!!!!!
Success rate is 100 percent (5/5), round-trip min/avg/max = 8/64/112 ms
Taos#
```

Although the networks of AS 300 can be reached from Taos, the BGP routes must be advertised into EIGRP before the networks can be reached from AS 200 interior routers. One way to accomplish this is with the redistribution at Taos, as demonstrated by the configuration shown in Example 5-230.

Example 5-230 *Taos Redistributes BGP into EIGRP*

```
router eigrp 200
 redistribute bgp 200 metric 10000 100 255 1 1500 passive-interface serial0
 network 192.168.1.0
 network 192.168.100.0
!
router bgp 200
 network 192.168.1.216 mask 255.255.255.252
 network 192.168.100.0
 network 192.168.200.0
 neighbor 192.168.1.226 remote-as 100
```

Example 5-231 shows that AS 300 prefixes are advertised to AngelFire and that the destinations can be reached. Redistribution picks up every BGP route, but the administrator might want only a subset of the BGP routes to be redistributed. In such a case, route filters are required to suppress the unwanted routes.

Example 5-231 *AngelFire Receives the Redistributed BGP Routes*

```
AngelFire#show ip route
Codes: C - connected, S - static, I - IGRP, R - RIP, M - Mobile, B - BGP,
D - EIGRP, EX - EIGRP external, O - OSPF, IA - OSPF inter area,
N1 - OSPF NSSA external type 1, N2 - OSPF NSSA external type 2,
E1 - OSPF external type 1, E2 - OSPF external type 2, E - EGP, i - IS-IS,
L1 - IS-IS level-1, L2 IS-IS level-2, * - candidate default,
```

Example 5-231 *AngelFire Receives the Redistributed BGP Routes (Continued)*

```
U - per-user static route, O -  ODR


Gateway of last resort is not set


D   192.168.100.0/24 [90/409600] via 192.168.1.218,   01:14:22, ethernet0/0
    192.168.1.0/24 is variably subnetted, 4 subnets, 2 masks
D     192.168.1.224/30 [90/2195456] via 192.168.1.218,   01:16:44, ethernet0/0
C     192.168.1.216/30 is directly connected, Ethernet0/0
D EX  192.168.1.212/30 [170/307200] via 192.168.1.218,   00:03:55, ethernet0/0
D EX 192.168.250.0/24 [170/307200] via 192.168.1.218,   00:03:55, ethernet0/0
C     192.168.1.216/30 is directly connected, Ethernet0/1


AngelFire#ping 192.168.250.1


Type escape sequence to abort.
Sending 5, 100-byte ICMP Echos to 192.168.2550.1, timeout is 2 seconds:
!!!!!
Success rate is 100 percent (5/5), round-trip min/avg/max = 4/8/12 ms
AngelFire#
```

Another vitally important reason exists for not redistributing BGP routes into an IGP. A full Internet routing table consists of more than 100,000 prefixes, and an IGP process will "choke" trying to process so many routes. Redistributing a full Internet table, or even a large partial table, would inevitably cause a major network crash. Never use a BGP-to-IGP redistribution on an Internet-facing router.

For more control over which routes are advertised into AS 200, you can use static routes, as shown in Example 5-232. In this configuration, only 192.168.250.0/24 is advertised into the AS. As shown in Example 5-233, AngelFire has no knowledge of subnet 192.168.1.212/30. Using static routes in configuration has the added benefit of protecting AS 200 from instabilities. If network 192.168.250.0 flaps in AS 300, the changes are not advertised any further into AS 200 than Taos.

Example 5-232 *A Static Route to 192.168.250.0/24 Can Be Used in Lieu of the BGP-Learned Route*

```
router eigrp 200
 redistribute bgp 200 metric 10000 100 255 1 1500 passive-interface serial0
 network 192.168.1.0
 network 192.168.100.0
!
router bgp 200
 network 192.168.1.216 mask 255.255.255.252
 network 192.168.100.0
 network 192.168.200.0
 neighbor 192.168.1.226 remote-as 100
!
ip route 192.168.250.0 255.255.255.0 Serial0
```

Example 5-233 *AngelFire Is Not Learning the 192.168.1.212/30 Route*

```
AngelFire#show ip route
Codes: C - connected, S - static, I - IGRP, R - RIP, M - Mobile, B - BGP,
D - EIGRP, EX - EIGRP external, O - OSPF, IA - OSPF inter area,
N1 - OSPF NSSA external type 1, N2 - OSPF NSSA external type 2,
E1 - OSPF external type 1, E2 - OSPF external type 2, E - EGP, i - IS-IS,
L1 - IS-IS level-1, L2 IS-IS level-2, * - candidate default,
U - per-user static route, O -  ODR

Gateway of last resort is not set

D    192.168.100.0/24 [90/409600] via 192.168.1.218,   00:14:33, ethernet0/0
     192.168.1.0/24 is variably subnetted, 3 subnets, 2 masks
D       192.168.1.224/30 [90/2195456] via 192.168.1.218,   00:14:33, ethernet0/0
C       192.168.1.216/30 is directly connected, Ethernet0/0
D EX 192.168.250.0/24 [170/307200] via 192.168.1.218,   00:11:17, ethernet0/0
C       192.168.200.0/24 is directly connected, Ethernet0/1

AngelFire#ping 192.168.250.1

Type escape sequence to abort.
Sending 5, 100-byte ICMP Echos to 192.168.2550.1, timeout is 2 seconds:
```

Example 5-233 *AngelFire Is Not Learning the 192.168.1.212/30 Route (Continued)*

```
!!!!!
Success rate is 100 percent (5/5), round-trip min/avg/max = 4/7/8 ms
AngelFire#
```

Of course, in a single-homed AS, such as AS 200 in Figure 5-54, little reason exists to advertise any external routes into the AS. Unless you need to advertise specific routes into the AS,
a default route suffices, as shown in Example 5-234. In this configuration, Taos generates a
default route and advertises it to all EIGRP speakers; however, BGP can also be configured to
generate a default route. To advertise a default from Vail to its BGP neighbors, you could use
the configuration shown in Example 5-235.

Example 5-234 *Taos Can Also Simply Advertise a Default Route to AngelFire Via EIGRP*

```
router eigrp 200
 redistribute bgp 200 metric 10000 100 255 1 1500 passive-interface serial0
 network 192.168.1.0
 network 192.168.100.0
!
router bgp 200
 network 192.168.1.216 mask 255.255.255.252
 network 192.168.100.0
 network 192.168.200.0
 neighbor 192.168.1.226 remote-as 100
!
ip classless
ip route 0.0.0.0 0.0.0.0 Serial0
```

Example 5-235 *Another Option Is for Vail to Use BGP to Advertise a Default Route by Advertising the 0.0.0.0*
Network and a Discard Quad-Zero Route

```
router bgp 100
 network 0.0.0.0
 neighbor 192.168.1.210 remote-as 300
 neighbor 192.168.1.222 remote-as 100
 neighbor 192.168.1.225 remote-as 200
!
ip classless
ip route 0.0.0.0 0.0.0.0 Null0
```

A default route to the Null0 interface is created statically, and the route is advertised with the **network** command. The assumption with the configuration is that Vail has full routing information. All packets are forwarded to Vail; any destination address that cannot be matched to a more specific route matches the static route and is dropped.

In some design cases, a default should be sent to some neighbors but not to others. To send a default from Vail to Taos, but not to any of Vail's other neighbors, use the configuration shown in Example 5-236.

Example 5-236 *Another Option Is for Vail to Send a Default Route Strictly to Taos*

```
router bgp 100
 network 0.0.0.0
 neighbor 192.168.1.210 remote-as 300
 neighbor 192.168.1.222 remote-as 100
 neighbor 192.168.1.225 remote-as 200
 neighbor 192.168.1.225 default-originate
```

The BGP **neighbor default-originate** command is similar to the OSPF **default information-originate always** command in that a default is advertised whether or not the router actually has a default route. Notice in the configuration that the static route from the preceding configuration is no longer present; however, a route to 0.0.0.0/0 is still advertised to Taos. Example 5-237 shows Tahoe's routing table. Unlike Taos, Tahoe does not have an entry for 0.0.0.0/0.

Example 5-237 *Taos Learns a Default Route from Vail*

```
Taos#show ip route
Codes: C - connected, S - static, I - IGRP, R - RIP, M - Mobile, B - BGP,
D - EIGRP, EX - EIGRP external, O - OSPF, IA - OSPF inter area,
N1 - OSPF NSSA external type 1, N2 - OSPF NSSA external type 2,
E1 - OSPF external type 1, E2 - OSPF external type 2, E - EGP, i - IS-IS,
L1 - IS-IS level-1, L2 IS-IS level-2, * - candidate default,
U - per-user static route, O -  ODR, T - traffic engineered route

Gateway of last resort is 192.168.1.226 to network 0.0.0.0

D    192.168.200.0/24 [90/409600] via 192.168.1.217,   02:06:34, ethernet0
B    192.168.250.0/24 [20/0] via 192.168.1.226, 00:46:03
     192.168.1.0/24 is variably subnetted, 4 subnets, 2 masks
D       192.168.1.0/24 is a summary, 02:06:34 Null0
```

Example 5-237 *Taos Learns a Default Route from Vail (Continued)*

```
C      192.168.1.224/30 is directly connected, Serial0/0
C      192.168.1.216/30 is directly connected, Ethernet0/0
B      192.168.1.212/30 [20/0] via 192.168.1.226 00:46:04
C    192.168.100.0/24 is directly connected, Ethernet1
B*   0.0.0.0/0 [20/0] via 192.168.1.226, 00:47:03
taos#


Tahoe#show ip route
Codes: C - connected, S - static, I - IGRP, R - RIP, M - Mobile, B - BGP,
D - EIGRP, EX - EIGRP external, O - OSPF, IA - OSPF inter area,
N1 - OSPF NSSA external type 1, N2 - OSPF NSSA external type 2,
E1 - OSPF external type 1, E2 - OSPF external type 2, E - EGP, i - IS-IS,
L1 - IS-IS level-1, L2 IS-IS level-2, * - candidate default


Gateway of last resort is not set

B    192.168.100.0/24 [20/0] via 192.168.1.209, 00:48:26
     192.168.1.0/24 is variably subnetted, 3 subnets
B       192.168.1.216 [20/0] via 192.168.1.209 00:48:26
C       192.168.1.208 is directly connected, Serial0
C       192.168.1.212 is directly connected, Serial1
C    192.168.250.0 is directly connected, Ethernet0
B    192.168.200.0 [20/0] via 192.168.1.209 00:48:27
Tahoe#
```

The advertisement of a default route to a BGP neighbor does not suppress the more specific routes. The routes from AS 300 are still present in the Taos routing table. In some cases, this can be desirable. For example, an ISP might send a customer the routes to all its other customers (a partial Internet table), as well as a default to the rest of the Internet. Such a case is useful when multihomed to the same ISP. The customer network can then make best-path choices to the ISP's customers and use the default route for all other external destinations.

If only the default is to be sent, a router must use a filter to suppress all more specific routers. The configuration shown in Example 5-238, using the **neighbor distribute-list** command, is just one way to filter BGP routes.

Example 5-238 *A Filter Should Be Added to the Vail Configuration So That Only the Default Route Is Advertised Via BGP*

```
router bgp 100
 network 0.0.0.0
 neighbor 192.168.1.210 remote-as 300
 neighbor 192.168.1.222 remote-as 100
 neighbor 192.168.1.225 remote-as 200
 neighbor 192.168.1.225 default-originate
 neighbor 192.168.1.225 distribute-list 1 out
!
access-list 1 permit 0.0.0.0
access-list 1 deny any
```

 Lab 5.3.1   Troubleshooting Problems at the Physical, Data-Link, and Network Layers

You complete this laboratory exercise by defining, isolating, and correcting the problems outlined in the scenario to restore the network to baseline specifications. In this exercise, each workgroup uses a troubleshooting methodology and Cisco commands to define, isolate, and correct issues.

Summary

The following concepts were covered in this chapter:

- Using a methodology for troubleshooting Layer 3 problems is important so that you can isolate and identify the problem as quickly as possible.

- In most networks, static routes are used in combination with dynamic routing protocols. Improper configuration of static routes can lead to less-than-optimal routing and, in some cases, can create routing loops or cause parts of the network to become unreachable.

- Troubleshooting dynamic routing protocols requires a thorough understanding of how the specific routing protocol functions. Some problems are common to all routing protocols, and other problems are particular to the individual routing protocol.

- Troubleshooting redistribution between routing protocols requires an understanding of how the particular routing protocols function and how to redistribute their different metrics.

Key Terms

discard route   A route that sends packets to null0, the bit bucket, when there is no specific match in the routing table and it is undesirable to have those packets forwarded using a supernet or default route.

discontiguous network   A subnet of a major network separated by a subnet of another major network.

Check Your Understanding

Use the following review questions to test your understanding of the concepts covered in this chapter. Answers are listed in Appendix A, "Check Your Understanding Answer Key."

1. When the routing table process checks for a resolvable static route using an intermediate address, the check is done in what mode?

   A. CEF

   B. Classless

   C. Fast

   D. Classful

2. What type of route is useful for dropping packets when there are no specific matches in the routing table and it is not desirable to have the packets forwarded using a supernet or default route?

   A. Null route

   B. Bit bucket

   C. Discard route

   D. Dead route

3. What is used with distance vector routing protocols to block all outgoing routing updates for a given interface?

   A. Access list

   B. Distribute list

   C. Passive interface

   D. Discard list

4. Which of the following are common RIP issues that keep updates from being installed in the routing table? Choose all that apply.

   A. Stub area

   B. Mismatched authentication key

   C. Unsynchronized database

   D. Incompatible RIP version types

5. Classful routing protocols cannot accurately handle what type of network?

   A. Discontiguous

   B. NBMA

   C. Variable-length

   D. Intermediary

6. EIGRP neighbor adjacencies require which of the following?

   A. Matching AS numbers

   B. Properly defined **network** statements

   C. Matching K values

   D. Duplicate router IDs

7. Type 4 summary LSAs are not advertised by an OSPF router in what case?

   A. The router is an ABR

   B. The router is an ASBR

   C. The router is not connected to Area 0

   D. The router is not connected to a stub area

8. What are some possible causes of an IS-IS adjacency's being stuck in INIT state?

   A. The attached bit is set

   B. MTU mismatch

   C. Hello padding is disabled

   D. Authentication mismatch

9. In the command **bgp dampening** *half-life-time reuse suppress maximum-suppress-time,* what are the respective default values (in seconds) for *half-life-time, reuse, suppress,* and *maximum-suppress-time?*

    A. 15, 750, 1000, 30

    B. 10, 500, 1000, 30

    C. 15, 750, 2000, 60

    D. 10, 300, 1000, 40

10. When redistributing OSPF into IGRP, what keyword is normally required to ensure proper redistribution?

    A. static

    B. subnets ppp authentication

    C. metric

    D. metric-type

Objectives

After completing this chapter, you will be able to perform tasks related to the following:

- Be familiar with the usual sources of transport layer problems, including TCP, UDP, NAT, access lists, and NetBIOS and NetBEUI
- Identify the symptoms of a problem at the transport layer
- Isolate a problem at the transport layer
- Correct a problem at the transport layer

Chapter 6

Layer 4 Troubleshooting

This chapter covers the operation of various transport layer networking technologies used on routers and hosts, including

- Transport Control Protocol
- User Datagram Protocol
- NetBIOS
- Network Address Translation
- Extended access lists

This chapter also discusses tools and methodologies you can use to troubleshoot transport layer networking issues.

Characteristics of Transport Layer Technologies

The transport layer provides end-to-end traffic accountability. Layer 4 technologies ensure reliable data delivery using acknowledgments, sequence numbers, and flow control mechanisms. The transport layer is the first layer that provides end-user functions. This section explores general characteristics of transport layer technologies.

Common Transport Layer Technologies

Problems at the transport layer can present symptoms ranging from suboptimal network operation to complete network communications failure. There are at least 35 recognized transport layer protocols. Some of the more common are

- User Datagram Protocol (UDP)
- Transport Control Protocol (TCP)

- Sequenced Packet Exchange (SPX)
- AppleTalk Transaction Protocol (ATP)
- NetBIOS

This section discusses the characteristics of these protocols and related transport layer technologies.

A specific network protocol can communicate with another network protocol at the layer above or below it, as shown in Figure 6-1. Within the TCP/IP protocol suite, Layer 4 operations are primarily handled by UDP and TCP.

Figure 6-1 Network Protocols Communicate with Adjacent Layers

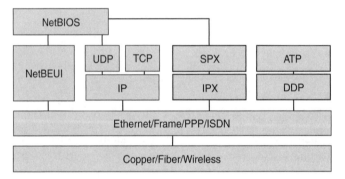

UDP and TCP rely on IP at the network layer and use port numbers to identify what higher-layer application traffic is contained in the packet, as shown in Figure 6-2. Internet Control Message Protocol (ICMP) is a protocol from the TCP/IP suite that operates at the network layer, and it too relies on IP. Unlike UDP and TCP, ICMP does not carry user data. ICMP is primarily used by network devices for self-management and self-tuning functions and by network engineers for troubleshooting network problems. UDP, TCP, and ICMP are all used heavily on the Internet, supporting a wide variety of traffic types and applications.

The Network Basic Input/Output System (NetBIOS) was developed for IBM in 1983 by Sytek Corporation. It officially defines a session-level interface and a data transport protocol. IBM extended NetBIOS in 1985 to create the NetBIOS Extended User Interface (NetBEUI) protocol. NetBEUI supports NetBIOS operations at the network layer, as shown in Figure 6-3. NetBEUI and NetBIOS are commonly used in Microsoft and IBM LANs.

Figure 6-2 TCP and UDP at the Transport Layer and ICMP at the Network Layer

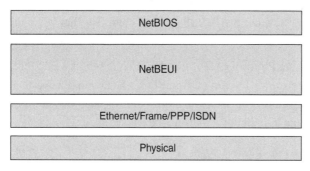

Figure 6-3 NetBEUI and NetBIOS Are Commonly Used in Microsoft and IBM LANs

NetBIOS
NetBEUI
Ethernet/Frame/PPP/ISDN
Physical

NetBEUI operates at the network layer and interfaces directly with the International Organization for Standardization (ISO) Logical Link Control, Type 2 (LLC2) at the data-link layer. NetBIOS interfaces with NetBEUI and with IBM's Server Message Block (SMB) protocol at the application layer. Together, NetBIOS and NetBEUI can be considered to be operating from the network layer through to the presentation layer. Because both NetBIOS and NetBEUI are nonhierarchical broadcast-based protocols, they depend on other hierarchical protocols, such as IP or IPX, to operate in a routed network.

Novell's proprietary protocol suite uses Sequenced Packet Exchange (SPX), shown in Figure 6-4, at the transport layer to implement reliable data delivery. In the early days of local-area networking, Novell's suite of protocols was commonly implemented. Until version 5 of Novell's network operating system, IPX/SPX was the default protocol suite installed for Novell networks.

Figure 6-4 IPX and SPX Were the Default Protocols Used in Novell Networking Until Version 5

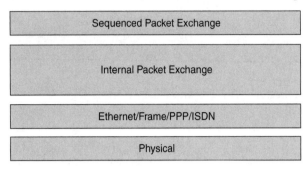

Because IPX is incompatible with IP, networks running the Novell protocols are unable to communicate with the Internet without being translated. Because of the growing need for corporate, academic, and government networks to be connected to the Internet, almost all Novell network installations now use the TCP/IP protocol suite. This has led to the steady decline of the number of new network installations using the IPX/SPX protocol suite.

AppleTalk Transaction Protocol (ATP), shown in Figure 6-5, is used at the transport layer of legacy AppleTalk networks. It relies on AppleTalk's Datagram Delivery Protocol (DDP) at the network layer. Because ATP is incompatible with IP, new Mac networks usually use the TCP/IP protocol suite in preference to using the AppleTalk protocol suite.

Figure 6-5 Macs Now Primarily Use TCP/IP

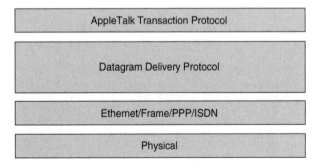

Although legacy networks using IPX/SPX and AppleTalk still exist, troubleshooting these protocol suites is not in the scope of this course and is not discussed further in this curriculum.

User Datagram Protocol

UDP is connectionless and is considered unreliable because it does not guarantee packet delivery. UDP operates on a "best-effort delivery" basis. It does not use packet sequencing, acknowledgment, or retransmission mechanisms for flow control and error detection/correction. Figure 6-6 shows the fields of a UDP segment, and Table 6-1 describes the fields. If flow control and error detection/correction features are required for a UDP-based data flow, these features must be implemented in higher-layer protocols or applications. UDP has a checksum, but checksum failure does not prompt retransmission. UDP has the following features:

- It is connectionless.
- It is unreliable (it provides no software checking for message delivery).
- It transmits messages (called user datagrams).
- It does not reassemble incoming messages.
- It does not use acknowledgments.
- It does not provide flow control.

Figure 6-6 UDP Is One of the Simplest TCP/IP Protocols

16 Bits	16 Bits	16 Bits	16 Bits	16 Bits
Source Port	Destination Port	Length	Checksum	Data...

Table 6-1 UDP Header Fields

Field	Description
Source Port	Number of the calling port
Destination Port	Number of the called port
Length	Length of the segment
Checksum	Calculated checksum of the header and data fields
Data	Upper-layer protocol data

Because UDP does not retransmit lost packets and does not consume bandwidth with acknowledgments, it is relatively lightweight and fast and is suitable for both one-to-one and one-to-many communications. Over congestion-free and error-free networks, UDP is ideal for transferring small amounts of data and for supporting streaming applications such as voice communications and video multicasts. However, using UDP over congested or error-prone networks often results in high degrees of data loss with higher-layer protocols and applications. It also might make users have to initiate data retransmission.

Many higher-layer protocols and applications use UDP:

- Trivial File Transfer Protocol (TFTP)
- Domain Name System (DNS)
- NetBIOS Name Resolution (NetBIOS-NS)
- Windows Internet Name Service (WINS)
- Bootstrap Protocol (BOOTP)
- Dynamic Host Configuration Protocol (DHCP)
- Network Time Protocol (NTP)
- Remote Authentication Dial-In User Service (RADIUS)
- Terminal Access Control Access Control Server (TACACS)
- Real-Time Transport Protocol (RTP)

Transport Control Protocol

Unlike UDP, TCP is connection-oriented. Because TCP implements packet sequencing, acknowledgment, and retransmission mechanisms at the transport layer, it is considered an inherently reliable protocol. These additional features at Layer 4 give TCP a larger operational overhead. It does not carry data payload or consume bandwidth (see Figure 6-7 and Table 6-2). Because of these reliability features, TCP is better suited for one-to-one communications and is rarely used for streaming and one-to-many communications. TCP has the following features:

- It is connection-oriented
- It is reliable
- It divides outgoing messages into segments
- It reassembles messages at the destination station
- It resends anything not received
- It reassembles messages from incoming segments

Figure 6-7 The TCP Header Is Much More Complex Than the UDP Header

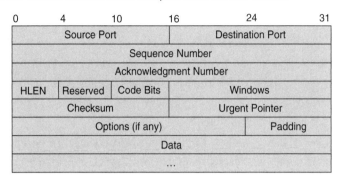

Table 6-2 TCP Header Fields

Field	Description
Source Port	Number of the calling port
Destination Port	Number of the called port
Sequence Number	Number used to ensure correct sequencing of the arriving data
Acknowledgment Number	Next expected TCP octet
HLEN	Number of 32-bit words in the header
Reserved	Set to 0
Code Bits	Control functions (such as setup and termination of a session)
Window	Number of octets the sender is willing to accept
Checksum	Calculated checksum of the header and data fields
Urgent Pointer	Indicates the end of the urgent data
Options (one option)	Maximum TCP segment size
Data	Upper-layer protocol data

TCP implements two main mechanisms for maximizing reliability and efficiency—the three-way handshake and windowing. Understanding these technologies is important to troubleshooting network performance issues and failures.

TCP Three-Way Handshake

The TCP three-way handshake, illustrated in Figure 6-8, occurs during TCP connection establishment and consists of three stages:

1. Session request (TCP SYN)—The initiating host sends a TCP synchronization packet, which has the SYN bit set on. The packet contains the initiating host's own sequence number (seq = x) for the connection. This packet also contains information about the initiating host's TCP receive-window size.

2. Session request acknowledgment (TCP SYN-ACK)—The target host responds to the packet from the initiating host by sending its own synchronization acknowledgment packet. This packet has both the ACK and SYN bits set on. It contains the acknowledgment number generated by incrementing the sequence number from the initiating host by 1 (ack = x + 1) plus the new sequence number from the target host (seq = y). The purpose of this packet is to inform the initiating host that the target host has received and understood the information from the initiating host and to inform the initiating host of the target's TCP receive-window size.

3. Session acknowledgment (TCP ACK)—The initiating hosts receives the TCP SYN/ACK packet from the target host and responds with a session acknowledgment packet. This packet has the SYN bit set off and the ACK bit set on. The acknowledgment number in this packet is generated by incrementing the sequence number from the target host by 1 (ack = y + 1). The purpose of this packet is to inform the target host that the initiating host has received and understood the information sent by the target host. As soon as the target host receives this packet, the TCP session is established, and reliable data exchange can begin.

Figure 6-8 The TCP Three-Way Handshake Makes TCP Connection-Oriented

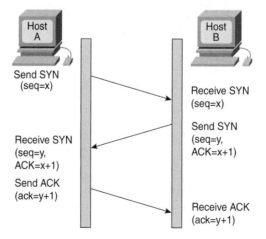

A similar process is followed at TCP connection termination, ensuring full and complete transfer of data and the orderly termination of processes.

TCP Sliding Windows

TCP sliding windows is the mechanism used to implement flow control and packet retransmission. Before we discuss the operation of TCP windows, several terms should be explained:

- **Transmit window**—Where segmented data is sequenced and buffered for transmission on a sending host.
- **Receive window**—Where segments are buffered for resequencing on the receiving host.
- **Segment size**—The maximum size TCP makes each segment (before transmission) when processing data from higher layers.
- **Acknowledgment**—A packet sent from the receiving host to the sending host, acknowledging the receipt of particular packets.
- **Acknowledgment trigger**—An event that triggers the transmission of an acknowledgment packet on the receiving host, such as when two sequential segments are received or when a predefined window threshold is reached.
- **Delayed acknowledgment timer**—How long a receiving host waits for an acknowledgment trigger before sending a delayed acknowledgment.
- **Delayed acknowledgment**—An acknowledgment packet triggered by the delayed acknowledgment timer.
- **Retransmission timer**—How long the sending host waits for an acknowledgment before retransmitting a packet.

Recall that TCP receive-window sizes are exchanged between hosts as part of TCP connection establishment, as shown in Figure 6-9. When hosts in a TCP connection exchange data, they follow this process:

1. The sending host initiates the TCP connection establishment process, during which each host transmits its own receive-window size to the other and sets its own transmit window to the same size as the receive window of the other host.

2. TCP on the sending host processes data from higher-layer protocols into segments (according to the configured segment size) and buffers them for transmission in the transmit window. Segments waiting to be put in the transmit window are buffered in the transmit buffer.

3. Segments in the transmit window are copied, and the copies are passed to the IP process for transmission. At this point, the retransmit timer for each segment is started. When passing the segments to IP, TCP tags each of them with a TCP header containing a sequence number. A copy of each packet remains in the transmit window until an acknowledgment is received, accounting for each segment.

4. The receiving host places the received segments in its receive window in sequence according to the sequence number of each segment and starts a delayed acknowledgment timer for each. When two sequential segments are received or a predefined window threshold is reached, the receiving host sends an acknowledgment packet for the received segments to the sending host. This acknowledgment also contains the current size of the receive window of the receiving host.

5. If an acknowledgment is not triggered on the receiving host before the delayed acknowledgment timer for a segment expires, the receiving host sends a delayed acknowledgment packet for that segment.

6. The sending host receives the acknowledgment (or delayed acknowledgment) from the receiving host and discards the acknowledged segments from its own transmit window. The transmit window now "slides" past the acknowledged segments and accepts new segments waiting for transmission. These new segments are passed to the IP process for transmission (as described in Step 3).

7. If the sending host does not receive the acknowledgment (or delayed acknowledgment) before the retransmit timer expires on a segment (because either the data segment or the acknowledgment was lost in transit), the sending host resends that data segment and resets the appropriate retransmit timer to double its original time.

8. As soon as all segments have been transmitted and acknowledged, the sending host initiates the TCP connection termination process to properly terminate the connection and associated processes on each host.

Figure 6-9 TCP Circuit for DNS Zone File Transfer

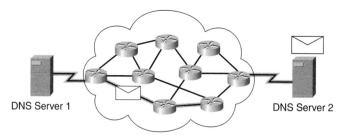

DNS Server 1   DNS Server 2

Because TCP window size is important to the efficient operation of the network, TCP window size can change dynamically during the course of the transmission. In other words, TCP effectively self-tunes its efficiency according to network conditions. This self-tuning mechanism depends on the number of TCP packets successfully received by the receiving host over a percentage of the receive-window size.

If the receiving host receives a large number of sequential data within a short period of time, it exceeds a threshold defined as a percentage of the receive-window size. This causes the receiving host to increase the size of its receive window and informs the sending host of the change by putting this information in one of the outbound acknowledgment packets.

After the sending host receives the acknowledgment packet with the new receive-window size for the receiving host, the sending host increases the size of the transmit window. The receive-window size of the receiving host continues growing until the window's growth threshold is the same as the rate at which the network can support data transfer.

This process continues until the capacity of the slowest network link is saturated and network contention starts to occur. As the gap between the data transfer rate and threshold gets smaller, the rate at which the window grows gets smaller. This explains why, when you download large files from the Internet or across a WAN, the transfer rate initially increases rapidly but plateaus at a fairly constant transfer rate for the remainder of the download.

If the network becomes congested from another source, packets and acknowledgments in existing traffic flows are lost. This causes the same process to operate in reverse, reducing the receive-window size of the receiving host until there is little or no gap between the data transfer rate and the window's threshold.

Standard Access Control Lists

Access control lists (ACLs) can be implemented on routers to permit and deny traffic that matches predefined profiles. Traffic profiles can be configured to match individual hosts, parts of networks, or entire ranges of networks, and they can apply to all IP traffic or to traffic using a specific source or destination port. Access lists can also be used to filter traffic for other operations on the network equipment, particularly network management traffic destined for a network switch or router. Table 6-3 lists common numeric ranges for access lists.

Table 6-3 IP Access List Ranges

	Number Ranges
IP Standard	1 to 99
	1300 to 1999
IP Extended	100 to 199
	2000 to 2699

Standard access lists examine only packets' source addresses. This means they must be implemented at each ingress point for a protected destination. Implementing the standard access list as close as possible to the protected destination reduces the total number of access lists required.

Numbered standard access lists can be used to filter traffic being forwarded to or received by a router or switch. Numbered standard access lists use the number ranges 1 to 99 and 1300 to 1999. Both ranges can be used for standard IP access lists.

Named standard ACLs have the same capabilities and limitations as numbered standard ACLs. The main advantage of a named ACL is better documentation, because the ACL can be named according to its purpose. One significant disadvantage is that other processes, such as Simple Network Management Protocol (SNMP) security, cannot reference named standard ACLs.

Table 6-4 shows the command syntax for creating numbered standard access lists.

Table 6-4 Standard IP Access List Syntax

Command	Description
Router(config)#**access-list** *access-list-number* **remark** *remark*	Indicates the purpose of the **deny** or **permit** statement.
Router(config)#**access-list** *access-list-number* {**deny** I **permit**} *source* [*source-wildcard*] [**log**] or Router(config)#**access-list** *access-list-number* {**deny** I **permit**} **any** [**log**]	Defines a standard IP access list using a source address and wildcard. Defines a standard IP access list using an abbreviation for the source and source mask of 0.0.0.0 255.255.255.255.

Table 6-5 shows the command syntax for creating named standard access lists.

Table 6-5 Named Standard IP Access List Syntax

Command	Description
Router(config)#**access-list standard** *name*	Defines a standard IP access list using a name and enters standard named access list configuration mode.
Router(config-std-nacl)#**remark** *remark*	Allows a comment to be entered about the purpose of the **deny** or **permit** statement in a named access list.
Router(config-std-nacl)#**deny** {*source* [*source-wildcard*] | **any**} [**log**] or Router(config-std-nacl)#**permit** {*source* [*source-wildcard*] | **any**} [**log**]	Specifies one or more conditions allowed or denied, which determines whether the packet is passed or dropped.
Router(config-std-nacl)#**exit**	Exits access list configuration mode.

Extended Access Control Lists

Standard IP access lists can permit or deny packets based only on the packet's source IP address. Extended access lists have more features and can be used to target very specific traffic based on any combination of the following:

- Source address
- Destination address
- Source port
- Destination port

Extended access lists can also be used to filter ICMP traffic based on ICMP type and code. ICMP type and code values and their meanings can be found at http://www.iana.org/ assignments/icmp-parameters.

Because extended access lists can filter on a destination address, they should be implemented as close as possible to the source of the traffic being filtered, typically at the edge of an organization's network. This allows traffic to be examined and filtered before crossing expensive and congested WAN links within the organization.

Numbered extended access lists are used primarily to filter traffic being forwarded through a router. They can be configured to use the number ranges 100 to 199 and 2000 to 2699. The expanded range is available on Cisco IOS Release 12.0 and later.

Named extended access lists are also used primarily to filter traffic being forwarded through a router. They are often used to provide better documentation of the router's configuration.

Table 6-6 shows the command syntax to create a numbered extended access list.

Table 6-6 Extended IP Access List Syntax

Command	Description
Router(config)#**access-list** *access-list-number* **remark** *remark*	Indicates the purpose of the **deny** or **permit** statement.
Router(config)#**access-list** *access-list-number* {**deny**	**permit**} *protocol source source-wildcard destination destination-wildcard* {**precedence** *precedence*} [**tos** *tos*] [**established**] [**log**	**log-input**] [**time-range** *time-range-name*] [**fragments**] or Router(config)#**access-list** *access-list-number* {**deny**	**permit**} *protocol* **any any** [**log**	**log-input**] [**time-range** *time-range-name*] [**fragments**] or Router(config)#**access-list** *access-list-number* {**deny**	**permit**} *protocol* **host** *source* **host** *destination* [**log**	**log-input**] [**time-range** *time-range-name*][**fragments**] or Router(config)#**access-list** *access-list-number* [**dynamic** *dynamic-name* [**timeout** *minutes*]] {**deny**	**permit**} *protocol source source-wildcard destination destination-wildcard* [**precedence** *precedence*] [**tos** *tos*] [**established**] [**log**	**log-input**] [**time-range** *time-range-name*] [**fragments**]	Defines a standard IP access list using a source address and wildcard. Defines a standard IP access list using an abbreviation for the source and source mask of 0.0.0.0 255.255.255.255.

Table 6-7 shows the command syntax to create a named extended access list.

Table 6-7 Named Extended IP Access List Syntax

Command	Description
Router(config)#**ip access-list extended** *name*	Defines an extended IP access list using a name and enters extended named access list configuration mode.
Router(config-ext-nacl)#**remark** *remark*	Allows a comment to be entered about the purpose of the **deny** or **permit** statement in a named access list.
Router(config-ext-nacl)#**deny** | **permit** *protocol source source-wildcard destination destination-wildcard* [**precedence** *precedence*] [**tos** *tos*] [**established**] [**log** | **log-input**] [**time-range** *time-range-name*] [**fragments**] and Router(config-ext-nacl)#**deny** | **permit** *protocol* **any any** [**log** | **log-input**] [**time-range** *time-range-name]* [**fragments**] or Router(config-ext-nacl)#**deny** | **permit** *protocol* **host** *source* **host** *destination* [**log** | **log-input**] [**time-range** *time-range-name*] [**fragments**] or Router(config-ext-nacl)#**dynamic** *dynamic-name* [**timeout** *minutes*] {**deny** | **permit**} *protocol source source-wildcard destination destination-wildcard* [**precedence** *precedence*] [**tos** *tos*] [**established**] [**log** | **log-input**] [**time-range** *time-range-name*] [**fragments**]	In access list configuration mode, specifies the conditions allowed or denied. Specifies a time range to restrict when the **permit** or **deny** statement is in effect. Use the **log** keyword to get access list logging messages, including violations. Use the **log-input** keyword to include the input interface, source Mac address, or Virtual Circuit (VC) in the logging output. or Defines an extended IP access list using an abbreviation for a source and source wildcard of 0.0.0.0 255.255.255.255 and an abbreviation for a destination and destination wildcard of 0.0.0.0 255.255.255.255. or Defines an extended IP access list using an abbreviation for a source and source wildcard of source 0.0.0.0 and an abbreviation for a destination and destination wildcard of destination 0.0.0.0. or Defines a dynamic access list.

Static IP Network Address Translation

IP Network Address Translation (NAT) is a technology defined in RFC 1631 that allows one group of addresses to be represented by another group of addresses. NAT is technically a network layer technology, but it has some features that extend into the transport layer.

As IPv4 started to run out of addresses, several measures were developed to alleviate the pressure. One of these measures was the introduction of reserved private network address spaces in RFC 1918. This RFC reserves three address spaces that the Internet does not recognize or route and that can be reused by networks that do not need to connect to other networks or to the Internet. Internet core routers are configured to drop any packets either sourced from or destined for an address in any of these reserved address spaces. The three address spaces reserved by RFC 1918 are

- **Class A**—10.0.0.0 to 10.255.255.255
- **Class B**—172.16.0.0 to 172.31.255.255
- **Class C**—192.168.0.0 to 192.168.255.255

NAT is a process that allows networks originally configured with one of these reserved address spaces to connect to other privately addressed networks and to the Internet without having to readdress the internal network. NAT is normally an additional process that is run on routers operating on the boundary between two discrete networks.

NAT works, either statically or dynamically, by using a table of IP addresses to rewrite the addressing information in an IP packet header. In its simplest form, the network engineer builds the NAT table manually. The table has addresses used inside the network mapped to addresses used outside the network. Each table entry represents a single host inside the network. See Figure 6-10.

Figure 6-10 Inside NAT Allows Local Host IP Addresses to Be Translated into Global (Public) IP Addresses

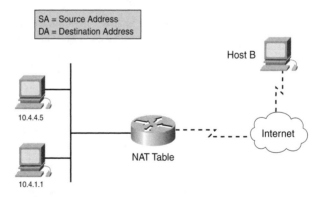

Inside Local IP Address	Global IP Address
10.4.4.5	2.2.2.3
10.4.1.1	2.2.2.2

The following describes the operation of NAT:

- A user at host 10.4.1.1 opens a connection to host B, as shown in Figure 6-10.
- The first packet the router receives from 10.4.1.1 causes the router to check its NAT table. A translation is found because it was statically configured.
- The router replaces the inside local IP address 10.4.1.1 with the selected inside global address (2.2.2.2) and forwards the packet.
- Host B receives the packet and responds to 10.4.1.1 using the inside global IP address 2.2.2.2.
- When the router receives the packet with the inside global IP address of 2.2.2.2, the router performs a NAT table lookup using the inside global address as the reference. The router then translates the address back to 10.4.1.1 and forwards the packet to the host.
- The host with the 10.4.1.1 address receives the packet and continues the conversation.

Dynamic IP Network Address Translation

NAT can be configured in a couple of ways:

- Static table entries
- Dynamic table entries

Static tables are manually defined by a network engineer. They traditionally define a one-to-one mapping between inside and outside IP addresses so that only the IP address portion of the packet header is altered.

Static NAT has the benefit of offering both connectivity and security because hosts on either side of the NAT router cannot communicate if the administrator has not defined an appropriate NAT table entry.

The main disadvantage of static NAT is that it requires one outside address for each inside address that needs to be translated. Because it is unlikely that all the inside hosts will need to communicate through the NAT router at the same time, static NAT wastes precious outside addresses. Another significant disadvantage of static NAT is that it must be manually administered. Manual administration of a NAT table can be difficult for a small network and is likely to be impossible for a large network.

Dynamic NAT has neither of the problems associated with static NAT. Dynamic NAT, illustrated in Example 6-1, creates entries in the NAT table as required and removes them after they have remained idle for a predefined period. Dynamic NAT allows a large number of inside hosts to share a small number of outside addresses. Dynamic NAT also offers greater security than static NAT, because unlike static NAT, entries in a dynamic NAT table are deleted after they have been idle for a short time.

Example 6-1 *Dynamic NAT Translates a Pool of Inside Addresses to a Pool of Outside Addresses*

```
SanJose1(config)#ip nat pool MYNATPOOL 42.0.0.55 42.0.0.62 netmask
  255.255.255.240

SanJose1#show ip nat translations
Pro Inside global   Inside local   Outside local   Outside global
--- 42.0.0.55        192.168.0.20   ---             ---
--- 42.0.0.56        192.168.0.21   ---             ---
```

The main problem with dynamic NAT is that it can be more complex to troubleshoot as the mapping entries in the table change. Sometimes this results in intermittent symptoms and problems. Entries that fail to automatically expire from the NAT table also cause issues with network operation, because they do not release outside addresses that otherwise would have become available.

Dynamic NAT operates by examining the packets as they are processed for forwarding. If a suitable entry already exists in the NAT table, the timer for that entry is reset, the packet's address is updated as appropriate, and the packet is forwarded. If the NAT table does not already have a suitable entry, the NAT process uses an address from the pool of available outside addresses to create a new entry before setting the expiration timer for the entry. It then updates the packet header with the new addressing information and forwards the packet.

If all the outside addresses are currently in use, the NAT process drops the packet and returns an error to the inside host.

NAT with Overload and Port Address Translation

Dynamic NAT also has a feature called overloading, or Port Address Translation (PAT). NAT without overloading operates at the network layer only, and only IP address information is substituted in packet headers. NAT with overloading extends NAT's operation into the transport layer, and UDP and TCP port numbers are included with entries in the NAT table. A significant consideration for implementing NAT with overload is that it can be used only for sessions from network clients. Servers hosting specific applications must listen for session request traffic on specific ports and, therefore, cannot make use of PAT technology.

Recall from previous curricula that UDP and TCP have roughly 65,535 associated ports each. It is highly unlikely that a single client host accessing network resources will legitimately need to use all these ports at the same time. Typically, a single host being used for normal Internet activities maintains about a dozen sessions through a NAT router at any given time. Consider these typical Internet browsing activities:

- How many Web pages are open at the same time?

- Is e-mail or newsgroup software updating messages in the background?
- How many file download sessions are active?
- Are any IM applications running in the background?
- What background processes, such as DNS, are supporting other applications?

Because a single inside host does not require all the ports available on an outside address, NAT overload allows multiple inside hosts to use the unused ports on a common outside address. It does this by including the port numbers for a given session in the translation table. Recall that a single entry in a normal static or dynamic NAT table represents a single host inside the network. In a table for NAT with overload, a single entry now represents a single transport layer session. Example 6-2 shows a translation table with entries for NAT with overload.

Example 6-2 *NAT with Overload Enables Translation of a Single Global IP Address to Multiple Local Addresses*

```
SanJose1(config)#ip nat inside source list 2 pool MYNATPOOL overload


SanJose1#show ip nat translations
Pro Inside global      Inside local      Outside local     Outside global
icmp 42.0.0.55:1536    192.168.0.21:1536 10.0.0.5:1536     10.0.0.5:1536
icmp 42.0.0.55:1536    192.168.0.21:1536 10.0.1.2:1536     10.0.1.2:1536
```

NetBIOS and NetBEUI

NetBIOS and NetBEUI are a pair of protocols that work together to provide easily configured, broadcast-based networking service for computers running the Microsoft Windows family of operating systems. NetBIOS supports the following network services:

- Network name registration and verification
- Session establishment, termination, and management
- Reliable session data transfer (connection-oriented)
- Unreliable datagram data transfer (connectionless)
- Monitoring and management of network interfaces and lower-layer protocols

One of the main advantages of using NetBIOS and NetBEUI is that they are simple to configure. The main failing of NetBIOS is that it uses a broadcast-based nonhierarchical namespace, forcing it to rely on other network layer protocols if used over a routed network. The NetBIOS packet is illustrated in Figure 6-11.

Figure 6-11 NetBIOS Packet Format

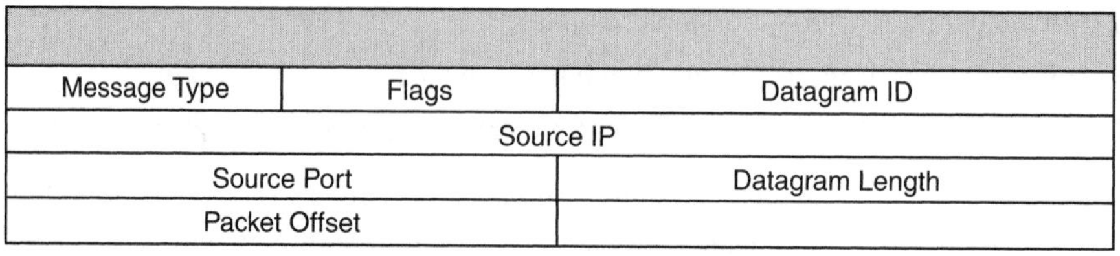

Message Type	Flags	Datagram ID
Source IP		
Source Port		Datagram Length
Packet Offset		

NetBIOS Names

The NetBIOS namespace is 16 bytes long. The first 15 characters are the computer name defined by the user during configuration. The last character is a hexadecimal digit representing the type of data in the NetBIOS name and network service using that data on a given machine. NetBIOS computers advertise this information to show what services they can offer to the remainder of the network. NetBIOS names can also be used to identify a machine as being part of a workgroup or domain. The 16th character is also used to identify a NetBIOS name as being either unique as in a computer name or username, or a group such as a Microsoft Windows workgroup or domain name.

Table 6-8 shows the common suffixes for NetBIOS names and the Microsoft networking services that use them.

Table 6-8 Common NetBIOS Suffixes

Suffix (Hex)	First 15 Characters	Networking Service
00	Computer name	Workstation service
00	Domain name	Domain service
03	Computer name	Messenger service
03	Username	Messenger service
06	Computer name	RAS server service
20	Computer name	File server service
21	Computer name	RAS client service
1B	Domain name	Domain master browser
1C	Domain name	Domain controllers
1D	Domain name	Master browser
1E	Domain name	Browser service elections

NetBIOS in Operation

The operation of NetBIOS has three main stages:

- Name registration
- Name discovery
- Name release

When a Windows NT computer starts up, the various services running on the machine register themselves using the unique NetBIOS name of the machine and the appropriate hexadecimal character at the 16th byte position. This process is called NetBIOS name registration and uses either a broadcast to the local network or a unicast to a local NetBIOS name server if one has been configured for the computer.

When one NetBIOS host needs to communicate with another, it needs the NetBIOS name of the remote machine. This name can be input by the user or can be obtained from a network browse list. The browse list is a list of network names and services available on the network that is maintained by a master browser machine. The browse list is built from the NetBIOS information broadcast during the NetBIOS name registration process during a machine's startup. This list is maintained by the master browser and is sent to one or more backup browsers in the network.

Opening Network Neighborhood in Windows displays the network's browse list. Periodically, the NetBIOS host computer contacts the master browser for a list of backup browsers from which one is selected. The host computer then contacts the backup browser, retrieves the browse list, and displays it to the user.

If the client cannot locate a master browser on the network, it initiates a browser election to ensure that a master browser and at least one backup browser are elected in the network.

The computer browser service only supplies NetBIOS name information. The NetBIOS name discovery process is what occurs when a NetBIOS name needs to be resolved to a lower-level network address. On a local network, this process is completed using either broadcasts to the local network or a unicast message to a NetBIOS name server if present. The NetBIOS name resolution process is discussed next.

When an application or networking service on a host is stopped, the NetBIOS name for the service on that host is available for use by another host. This process, called NetBIOS Name Release, removes services from the network when a network host is shut down.

NetBIOS Name Discovery and Resolution

The operation of NetBIOS-based networks is dependent on resolving NetBIOS names to lower-layer addresses. Because resolving names to addresses is so important, Windows computers use the following process to efficiently check up to six sources of information when attempting to connect to another computer:

1. Check the local NetBIOS name cache

2. Contact a NetBIOS name server

3. Broadcast the name resolution request locally

4. Check the locally stored LMHOSTS file (Windows only)

5. Check the locally stored HOSTS file (Windows only)

6. Contact a DNS server (Windows only)

Windows computers maintain a local cache of recently resolved NetBIOS names. This speeds up resolution of names for computers that are connected to regularly.

A NetBIOS Name Server (NBNS), normally a Microsoft Windows NT server running WINS, maintains name and address information for all computers on the network. Windows computers configured to use an NBNS server do a number of things during startup and shutdown.

During startup, the client computer requests its own name from the name server to check that no other computer on the network has the same computer name. Recall that NetBIOS names must be unique on the network. If the client computer is already registered in the network, the name and address currently being used by the client computer are returned. If the client computer is new to the network, the server returns a message indicating that the requested information is not found, and the client computer registers its own name, address, and services provided in the WINS database. This information remains in the database until the machine is shut down when the client computer requests that its registration be released from the database.

If the NBNS does not contain name resolution information for the requested machine name, the Windows client sends a local broadcast in an attempt to contact the remote host directly. If there is no response, the Windows computer checks locally stored files.

Administrators of Windows computers can configure them with files containing hard-coded name-to-address resolution information. The first of these files is called LMHOSTS (LAN Manager hosts) and is a remnant of older implementations of Windows networking.

If a suitable entry is not found in the LMHOSTS file, another locally stored file called HOSTS is checked. The HOSTS file is similar to the LMHOSTS file and is a remnant of older implementations of TCP/IP networking.

If neither of these local files has been configured with a hard-coded resolution of the desired NetBIOS name and address, and the Windows client is configured to use a DNS server, the DNS server is queried.

NetBIOS and Other Network Layer Protocols

By default, NetBIOS uses the NetBEUI Frame (NBF) protocol at the lower layers of the Open System Interconnection (OSI) model for network communications. NetBEUI has the advantage of being very simple to configure, making it highly suitable for small networks that are unlikely to have a full-time administrator. NetBEUI's main limitation is that it is broadcast-based and cannot operate over routed networks. To work on a larger scale, NetBIOS must replace NetBEUI with either the IPX/SPX or TCP/IP protocol suites at the network layer of the OSI model. The TCP/IP protocol suite is most commonly used.

When NetBIOS interfaces with the TCP/IP protocol stack, it creates the NetBIOS over TCP/IP (NetBT) protocol. This is slightly misleading, because NetBIOS actually interfaces with UDP, not TCP, at the transport layer of the TCP/IP stack, using the NetBIOS data protocol to form NetBT. Recall that NetBIOS provides connection and session management at higher layers in the OSI model. This means that NetBIOS does not need to rely on TCP for these functions and can use the more bandwidth-efficient UDP at the transport layer.

NetBIOS Node Type

Recall that NetBIOS is broadcast-based, but TCP/IP is primarily unicast-based. This means that the behavior of the NetBIOS name resolution process over TCP/IP can be configured depending on the network's size and nature. Misconfiguration of the NetBIOS node type is a common cause of network problems at the transport layer. The behavior of NetBIOS nodes over TCP can be configured as one of four options:

- B-node (broadcast node)
- P-node (peer-to-peer node)
- M-node (mixed node)
- H-node (hybrid node)

NetBIOS hosts configured as NetBIOS broadcast nodes use only UDP datagram broadcasts for NetBIOS name registration and resolution. In large networks, this has the negative impact of increasing the load on the network. By default, routers contain packets generated by Net-BIOS name registration and resolution from broadcast nodes. This means that NetBIOS B-node operation is unsuitable where resources need to be accessed across a router.

Peer-to-peer NetBIOS hosts do not use broadcasts. These hosts rely on having a NetBIOS name server configured to support the operation of NetBIOS name registration and resolution activities. Although this lets NetBIOS computers communicate across routers, it makes the network completely reliant on the operation of the NetBIOS name server. If the NetBIOS name server were to fail, the NetBIOS clients would be unable to communicate with each other because they could not broadcast to locate each other.

Computers with mixed node configuration use both B-node and P-node operation for Net-BIOS name registration and resolution. The default mode of operation for a mixed node host is broadcast. Therefore, if a broadcast fails to return a positive response, the host reverts to peer-to-peer operation. This allows a computer to locate resources on a local network easily and to use a NetBIOS name server if a required resource is not located on the local network segment.

NetBIOS hosts configured as hybrid node clients also use both peer-to-peer and broadcast operation for NetBIOS name registration and resolution. Unlike mixed nodes, hybrid nodes default to using peer-to-peer and revert to using broadcast when peer-to-peer fails to return a positive response.

Troubleshooting Transport Layer Issues on the Router

Network problems can arise from transport layer problems on the router, particularly at the edge of the network where security technologies examine and modify the traffic. This section discusses two of the most commonly implemented transport layer security technologies—ACLs and NAT.

Common Issues with Extended ACLs

Access lists are used to filter all traffic entering and leaving the router. Obviously, the most common issues with extended access lists are the result of misconfiguration by the network engineer. Misconfigurations commonly occur in eight areas:

- Selection of traffic flow
- Order of access control elements
- Implicit **deny any any**
- Addresses and wildcard masks
- Selection of transport layer protocol
- Source and destination port(s)
- Use of the **established** keyword
- Uncommon protocols

Selection of Traffic Flow

Although these points are not listed in any particular order, the most common router miscon-figuration of extended access lists is applying the access list to the incorrect traffic. Traffic is defined by both the router interface through which the traffic is traveling and the direction in which it is traveling. After it is defined, an access list must be applied to the correct interface, and the correct traffic direction must be selected for the access list to function properly.

Order of Access Control Elements

Another common mistake made when configuring ACLs is the order in which access control elements (ACEs) are configured. Although an access list might have an element to specifically permit a particular traffic flow, packets will never match that element if they are being denied by another element earlier in the list.

Recall that the guideline for configuring an access control list is specific to general. This means that the most specific elements are configured at the top of the list and the less specific elements are configured at the end. The more information defined in an element, the more specific that element is. For example, the element **permit tcp 10.0.0.0 0.255.255.255 any eq 110 established** is more specific than the element **permit tcp 10.0.0.0 0.255.255.255 any eq 110** because the first element uses the additional keyword **established**. The element **permit udp host 10.32.96.7 eq 53 any** is more specific than both of these because it matches a more specific (smaller) range of source addresses.

Implicit **deny any any**

Every extended access list has a **deny any any** element implied as the final entry in the list. This serves as a security catchall, ensuring that traffic that does not match any of the administratively configured access control elements is not allowed through. Normally this does not pose an issue when configuring firewall routers, because the guideline for configuring highly secure access lists is to deny everything and specifically permit particular traffic flows. In a situation where high security is not required on the access list, forgetting about this implicit access control element might be the cause of an access list misconfiguration.

Addresses and Wildcard Masks

Although setting a source or destination address might seem like something difficult to get wrong, it still happens quite often. However, a number of things make correctly selecting source and destination addresses more complex:

- Running NAT on the router
- Using complex wildcard masks to select patterns of addresses

The order in which transactions are processed using NAT is based on whether a packet is going from the inside network to the outside network or from the outside network to the inside network.

Inside to outside

1. If IPSec, check the input access list

2. Decryption for Cisco Encryption Technology (CET) or IPSec

3. Check the input access list

4. Check input rate limits

5. Input accounting

6. Policy routing

7. Routing

8. Redirect to the Web cache

9. NAT inside to outside (local-to-global translation)

10. Crypto (check the map and mark it for encryption)

11. Check the output access list

12. Inspect (Context-Based Access Control [CBAC])

13. TCP intercept

14. Encryption

Outside to inside

1. If IPSec, check the input access list

2. Decryption for CET or IPSec

3. Check the input access list

4. Check input rate limits

5. Input accounting

6. NAT outside to inside (global-to-local translation)

7. Policy routing

8. Routing

9. Redirect to the Web cache

10. Crypto (check the map and mark it for encryption)

11. Check the output access list

12. Inspect CBAC

13. TCP intercept

14. Encryption

If the router is running both access lists and NAT, the order in which each of these technologies is applied to a traffic flow is important. The order of operations in the switching path is quite complex, as you can see in the previous lists. The following are the important points to remember.

- Inbound traffic is processed by the inbound access list before being processed by outside-to-inside NAT.
- Outbound traffic is processed by the outbound access list after being processed by inside-to-outside NAT.

Wildcard masks are typically used to select ranges of addresses. For example, the address 198.162.10.0 and wildcard mask 0.0.0.255 could be used to select all hosts in the Class C network address space 198.162.10.0. Generally, these sorts of address and wildcard mask combinations are difficult to get wrong.

More complex wildcard masks can also be used to select patterns of addresses. For example, the address 10.0.32.0 and wildcard mask 0.0.32.15 select the first 15 host addresses in either the 10.0.0.0 network or the 10.0.32.0 network. Complex wildcard masks like this can provide significant improvements in efficiency, especially in large networks with structured and controlled IP addressing schemes. They also require that the network engineer have detailed and thorough knowledge of the network address when designing these complex access list elements.

Selection of Transport Layer Protocol

When configuring ACLs, it is important that only the correct transport layer protocols be specified in the element. Many network engineers, when unsure if a particular traffic flow uses a TCP port or a UDP port, permit both. The first problem with doing this is that it opens additional holes through the firewall, possibly giving intruders an avenue into the network. The other problem is that it introduces an extra element into the ACL. This means that the ACL takes longer to process, introducing more latency into network communications.

Network engineers might also make a mistake and unintentionally configure an ACL to use the incorrect transport layer protocol. For example, an ACL might be intended to permit HTTP traffic but be configured with UDP port 80 (instead of TCP port 80).

Source and Destination Ports

Correctly specifying source and destination ports is usually fairly simple but can be quite complex. In one example of a simple traffic flow, the client end of the connection uses a random high-numbered port to initiate a connection to a specific port at the server end. Defining the correct source and destination ports is not overly complex in this situation.

A more difficult concept is understanding the flow of traffic between two hosts and building the ACLs to properly control the traffic. Simple traffic flows require symmetric access control elements for inbound and outbound access lists. In other words, address and port information for traffic generated by a replying host is the mirror image of address and port information for traffic generated by the initiating host.

Examine this description of a simple e-mail traffic flow traversing a firewall router to understand the relationship for addresses and ports between initiating and responding traffic:

1. A user wants to check his e-mail on a remote ISP mail server.

2. The client PC opens the mail client and initiates a connection to a POP3 mail server.

3. The request for new mail is generated and sent by the client PC.

   - The source address of the request packets is the IP address of the client PC.

   - The source port of the request packets is randomly chosen from above 1024 (for example, TCP port 2113).

   - The destination address of the request packets is the IP address of the mail server.

   - The destination port of the request packets is TCP port 110 (the POP3 mail server).

4. The packets traverse the LAN, get to the firewall router, and are processed by the access list controlling outbound traffic on the external router port.

   - A control element permitting traffic from any port with an internal address to TCP port 110 on the ISP mail server address is configured near the top of the access list.

   - The "request for mail" traffic matches this element and is allowed through the firewall router.

5. Having satisfied an element of the outbound access list, the router forwards the traffic to the next hop on the way to the ISP mail server.

6. The ISP mail server has mail waiting for the user. When the ISP mail server receives the request, it responds with the mail items it has for the user. Because the traffic is now returning to the client PC, the address and port information from the request packets have the source details swapped with the destination details.

   - The source address of the reply packets is the IP address of the ISP mail server.

   - Because the reply is coming from the POP3 mail server, the source port of the reply packets is TCP port 110.

   - The destination address of the reply packets is the IP address of the client PC.

   - The client PC needs to know which process to pass the reply packets to when it receives them. This means the destination port of the reply packets is set as TCP port 2113.

7. The mail server sends the reply packets onto the Internet, and they eventually get back to the firewall router. The traffic must satisfy an element of the access list controlling inbound traffic on the external router port before being forwarded to the LAN.

   - A control element permitting traffic from TCP port 110 from the IP address of the ISP mail server to any port on any internal IP address is configured near the top of the access list.

   - The "reply with mail" traffic matches this element and is allowed through the firewall router.

8. The "reply" traffic reaches the client, where the mail items are displayed by the e-mail client software.

Other traffic flows are quite involved. Network engineers must understand these flows before attempting to control them using access lists. One such complex traffic flow is FTP. It uses TCP at the transport layer and is associated with ports 20 and 21. TCP port 21 is used for FTP control messages, and TCP port 20 is used for FTP data messages.

When an FTP client connects to an FTP server, a control session is established. The port used at the client end is randomly chosen from port numbers above 1023, and the port used to reference the server end is TCP port 21. When the user-based application issues a **get** command to the FTP client, it is requesting a file from the FTP server. This file must be transferred using an FTP data connection so that the user-based application can still control the FTP server and interrupt the file transfer if necessary. The FTP client binds to an additional local port (above 1024) and sends this information to the FTP server through the FTP control connection. The server responds by attempting to open a connection with a source port of TCP port 20 and the destination port supplied by the FTP client.

This process requires that the firewall router controlling this traffic have a single element permitting outbound traffic to TCP port 21 for FTP control data and two elements to allow inbound traffic. The first element needs to allow reply FTP control traffic from TCP port 21 on the FTP server. The other element needs to allow new FTP data traffic from TCP port 20 on the FTP server.

FTP has both passive and active implementations. The active implementation is the one just described. The passive implementation is not discussed here. A good site for more information on passive FTP is http://slacksite.com/other/ftp.html.

Use of the **established** Keyword

In a TCP session, all packets after the first have the ACK bit set. The initiating host sets the SYN bit of the first packet to *on* but does not set the ACK bit. Subsequent packets have both bits set to *on*. Using the **established** keyword means a packet must match the specified source and destination IP addresses. Ports must also have the ACK bit set before a complete match is possible.

An access list can use this characteristic of TCP packets in a connection to control the allowed source of sessions. For example, an access list watching inbound traffic might have an element to permit traffic from a remote Telnet server (source port TCP port 23). By adding the **established** keyword to this element, you can configure the access list to permit traffic from a remote Telnet server, but only if the Telnet connection was initiated from inside the firewall router.

Obviously, the **established** keyword can be used to increase the security provided by an access list. If the **established** keyword is applied to an outbound access list, unexpected results can occur. Again, network engineers need to have a thorough understanding of network traffic flows before implementing the **established** keyword in access lists.

Uncommon Protocols

Extended access lists can be used to control traffic for IP-encapsulated protocols other than TCP, UDP, and ICMP. Misconfigured access lists often cause problems for less-common protocols. One group of uncommon protocols that is gaining popularity is virtual private networking and encryption protocols, including Layer 2 Tunneling Protocol (L2TP), Generic Routing Encapsulation (GRE), Internet Key Exchange (IKE), Internet Security Association and Key Management Protocol (ISAKMP), and Encapsulating Security Payload (ESP).

Because virtual private networks (VPNs) might need to run through firewall routers, network engineers must understand the specifics of the traffic flows required by the VPN. IPSec, for example, uses the ISAKMP protocol for connection setup. ISAKMP requires communications where a packet's source and destination are both UDP port 500. The network engineer must take into account this and other unusual requirements of network traffic for uncommon protocols when configuring the firewall router access lists.

Gathering Information on ACL Operation

One of the most useful commands for viewing access list operation is the **log** keyword on access list entries. This keyword instructs the router to place an entry in the system log whenever that entry condition is matched. The logged event includes details of the packet that matched the access list element.

The **log** keyword can be especially useful for troubleshooting access list operation. It can also provide information on intrusion attempts being blocked by the access list. For example, if the last element in an extended ACL is configured as **deny ip any any log**, the details of any packet not matching a condition higher in the ACL are recorded in the system log. Because this element shows all packets not being matched by a statement earlier in the ACL, it can be useful both for troubleshooting when a certain traffic flow cannot communicate through the firewall router and for showing when an intruder is attempting to access the network.

This log output can be either buffered and viewed on the local system or forwarded to an external syslog server where it can become part of a larger network management system. Use the **show logging** command to view the locally buffered copy of the system log, as shown in Example 6-3.

Example 6-3 *The* **show logging** *Command Displays the Contents of the System Logging*

```
interface ethernet 0
ip address 1.1.1.1 255.0.0.0
ip access-group 1 in
access-list 1 permit 5.6.0.0 0.0.255.255 log
access-list 1 deny 7.9.0.0 0.0.255.255 log


Router#show logging
list 1 permit 5.6.7.7 9 packets
```

The command **show ip access-list** [*number* | *name*] is particularly useful for troubleshooting IP access lists. This command displays the detailed elements of a specific access list in the correct order and the number of packets that have been matched against each element. Alternatively, if no access list number is specified, details of all access lists are shown. Example 6-4 shows typical output from the **show ip access-list** command.

Example 6-4 *The* **show ip access-list** *Command Is Very Useful for Viewing Configured Access Lists and Hits on Each Line of an Access List*

```
Router#show ip access-list
Extended IP access list 101
  deny udp any any eq ntp
  permit tcp any any
  permit udp any any eq tftp
  permit icmp any any
  permit udp any any eq domain
```

When you view the number of access list matches, you should sometimes reset the hit counters using the **clear ip access-list counter** [*number* | *name*] command. This command resets access list counters to 0, making it easier to spot changes in the counters and heavily matched access list elements. Like the **show ip access-list** command, this command can be used to clear the counters for only a specific access list by specifying its name or number. It clears the counters for all IP access lists if no access list name or number is specified. The alternative command **clear access-list counters** [*number | name*] can also be used to clear IP access list statistics. For example, **clear access-list counters 101** clears the counters for access list 101.

The command **show ip interface** shows information about the configuration of interfaces running the IP protocol, including information on any access lists configured for inbound and outbound traffic on the interface. Example 6-5 shows some output from this command.

Example 6-5 *The* **show ip interface** *Command Shows What Access Lists Are Applied to Each Interface*

```
Router#show ip interface fastethernet0/0
FastEthernet0/0 is up, line protocol is up
  Internet address is 1.1.1.2/8
  Broadcast address is 255.255.255.255
  Address determined by setup command
  MTU is 1500 bytes
  Helper address is not set
  Directed broadcast forwarding is disabled
  Outgoing access list is not set
  Inbound access list is not set
  Proxy ARP is enabled
  Security level is default
  Split horizon is enabled
  ICMP redirects are always sent
  ICMP unreachables are always sent
  ICMP mask replies are never sent
  IP fast switching is enabled
  IP fast switching on the same interface is disabled
  IP Flow switching is disabled
  IP Fast switching turbo vector
  IP multicast fast switching is enabled
  IP multicast distributed fast switching is disabled
  IP route-cache flags are Fast
  Router Discovery is disabled
--MORE--
```

Optimizing Access List Operation

Routers handling a lot of traffic and multiple access lists can introduce significant latency into network communications. To minimize the impact that access lists have on network latency, network engineers should optimize existing access lists. The concept is quite simple, although the actual implementation can be a little more complex.

Using the **show ip access-list command**, network administrators can gather information on which access list elements are being used heavily and which ones are not. Using this information, they can rewrite the access list such that the most heavily used elements are nearest to the top. Examples 6-6 and 6-7 show this process for a simple access list.

Example 6-6 *Viewing Access List Counters Makes It Easier to Construct Access Control Lists to Work Efficiently*

```
permit ip host 205.178.18.5 log
permit ip host 205.178.18.10 log


Router#show logging
list 101 permit 205.178.18.5 300 packets
list 101 permit 205.178.18.10 500 packets
```

Example 6-7 *The Most Heavily Used Access Control Entries (ACEs) Should Be Placed Near the Beginning of an Access List*

```
permit ip host 205.178.18.10 log
permit ip host 205.178.18.5 log

Router#show logging
list 101 permit 205.178.18.10 500 packets
list 101 permit 205.178.18.5 300 packets
```

Although this can be achieved fairly easily in simple access lists, using this approach on more complex access lists can be a bit more difficult. Consider an access list that must permit hosts 1 to 5 and 7 to 20 access to remote Web servers but that must block access to that remote service for hosts 6 and 21 to 31. Obviously, changing the order of the access list elements in this access list without regard for the overall reason of the order would "break" the access list.

To optimize complex access lists, the network administrator must identify groups of access list elements by purpose or intention. These groups can then be ordered such that the most heavily used group of elements is nearest to the top.

Common Issues with IP NAT

The biggest problem with all NAT technologies is interoperability with other network technologies, especially those that contain or derive information from host network addressing in the packet. Some of these technologies include the following:

- BOOTP and DHCP
- DNS and WINS
- SNMP
- Tunneling and encryption protocols

BOOTP and DHCP

DHCP was developed from *BOOTP*. Both protocols are used to manage the automatic assignment of IP addresses to clients. Recall that the first packet that a new client sends is a DHCP-Request broadcast IP packet. The DHCP-Request packet has a source IP address of 0.0.0.0, as shown in Figure 6-12. Because NAT requires both a valid destination and source IP address, BOOTP and DHCP can have difficulty operating over a router running either static or dynamic NAT.

Figure 6-12 The DHCP-Request Uses a Source Address of 0.0.0.0, Which NAT Does Not Understand

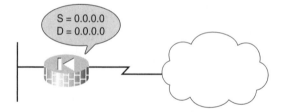

DNS and WINS

DNS and WINS are both name resolution services for networks. It is essential to the correct operation of a network that the information they contain be an accurate representation of the network. Because a router running dynamic NAT changes the relationship between inside and outside addresses regularly (as table entries expire and are re-created as required), a DNS or WINS server outside the NAT router does not have an accurate representation of the network inside the router:

- The outside host requests the IP address for the inside host from the inside NS server.
- The inside NS server returns the inside address of the inside host.

- The NAT router cannot alter the data payload.
- The outside host receives the inside address because the inside host cannot route to the inside host address.

Additionally, DNS and WINS reply packets contain IP address information in the packet's data payload. A DNS or WINS server on the network inside a NAT router resolves the host name to a network address on the inside network. When the NAT router processes the reply packet, the NAT process translates the address in the packet header appropriately but cannot alter the contents of the data payload. The outside host is given the inside address of the inside host. Because the router hides the inside network, the outside network cannot route packets directly to or from it.

SNMP
SNMP traffic often contains the IP address of managed network equipment in the packet's data payload. Similar to DNS packets, NAT cannot alter the addressing information stored in the packet's data payload. Because of this, an SNMP management station on one side of a NAT router might not be able to contact SNMP agents on the other side of the NAT router:

- The SNMP agent inside sends SNMP data to the SNMP management station outside.
- The SNMP management station outside cannot route to the inside address supplied by the SNMP agent inside.

Tunneling and Encryption Protocols
Tunneling and encryption protocols are concerned with both encrypting data to protect packet contents from being intercepted and ensuring that the packet was not interfered with during transit. Not all encryption protocols have problems with NAT. Generally speaking, encryption services operating at the application layer, such as *Pretty Good Privacy (PGP)* and Gnu Privacy Guard (GPG), are unaffected by NAT routers. Encryption and tunneling protocols at OSI model Layers 2 to 4, however, do not usually operate through a NAT router:

- The host inside attempts to establish an ISAKMP connection through the router running NAT with overload.
- The NAT router changes the source port from UDP port 500 to UDP port 62073 (a random high port).
- The receiving ISAKMP host refuses the packet (because it is not from UDP port 500).

Encryption and tunneling protocols often require that traffic be sourced from a specific UDP or TCP port or use a protocol at the transport layer that cannot be processed by NAT. Here are some examples:

- IKE requires that UDP packets be sent to and received from UDP port 500.
- IPSec tunnels use ESP at the transport layer, and GRE tunnels use GRE at the transport layer. Neither ESP nor GRE protocols can be processed by NAT.

If encryption or tunneling protocols must be run through a NAT router, the network administrator can create a static NAT entry for the required port for a single IP address on the inside of the NAT router.

Common NAT Misconfigurations

One of the more common misconfigurations of NAT is forgetting that it affects both inbound and outbound traffic. An inexperienced network administrator might preconfigure a static NAT entry to redirect inbound traffic to a specific inside "backup" host. In the event of a failure on the primary system, traffic could be automatically redirected to the backup system without the administrator's having to do anything. This static NAT statement also changes the source address of traffic from that host, possibly resulting in an undesirable (and unexpected) set of behaviors. At best, this is likely to result in suboptimal operation.

Misconfigured timers can also result in unexpected network behavior and suboptimal operation of dynamic NAT. If NAT timers are too short, entries in the NAT table might expire before replies are received, and packets are discarded, as shown in Figure 6-13. This means that the intended traffic did not get through and the loss of the packets generates retransmissions, consuming more bandwidth. The NAT router log also is filled with errors about closed ports.

Figure 6-13 NAT Timeouts Result in Replies for Requests from Internal Hosts to External Hosts Being Rejected

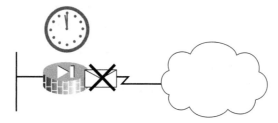

If timers are too long, entries might stay in the NAT table longer than necessary, consuming the available connection pool. In particularly busy networks, this might lead to memory problems on the router, and hosts might be unable to establish connections if the dynamic NAT table is full, as illustrated in Figure 6-14.

Figure 6-14 NAT Tables Consume Memory

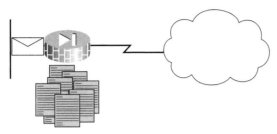

Gathering Information on NAT Configuration and Operation

The **show ip nat** group of commands has two commands. The **show ip nat statistics** command is used to display statistics on static and dynamic translations on the router, as shown in Example 6-8.

Example 6-8 *The* **show ip nat statistics** *Command Displays Statistics on NAT Translations*

```
SanJose1#show ip nat statistics
Total active translations: 3 (3 static, 0 dynamic; 0 extended)
Outside interfaces:
    Serial0/0
Inside interfaces:
    FastEthernet0/0
Hits: 4 Misses: 0
Expired translations: 0
Dynamic mappings:
```

The **show ip nat translations** command displays the NAT table currently in operation on the router, listing both static and dynamic NAT entries (see Example 6-9).

Example 6-9 *The* **show ip nat translations** *Command Conveniently Lists Static and Dynamic Translations*

```
SanJose1(config)#ip nat pool MYNATPOOL 42.0.0.55 42.0.0.62 netmask
    255.255.255.240

SanJose1#show ip nat translations
Pro Inside global    Inside local    Outside local    Outside global
--- 42.0.0.55        192.168.0.20    ---              ---
```

continues

Example 6-9 *The* **show ip nat translations** *Command Conveniently Lists Static and Dynamic Translations (Continued)*

```
--- 42.0.0.56        192.168.0.21   ---           ---

SanJose1(config)#ip nat inside source list 2 pool MYNATPOOL overload

SanJose1#show ip nat translations
Pro Inside global      Inside local      Outside local    Outside global
icmp 42.0.0.55:1536    192.168.0.21:1536  10.0.0.5:1536    10.0.0.5:1536
icmp 42.0.0.55:1536    192.168.0.21:1536  10.0.1.2:1536    10.0.1.2:1536
```

The **show ip nat translations** command has the optional keywords **icmp**, **pptp**, **tcp**, and **udp**, which allow the network engineer to limit the type of entries displayed. The network administrator can also use the **verbose** keyword to display additional information about the entries in the table.

A range of **debug** commands are available for reporting on NAT traffic. A commonly used command is **debug ip nat**, as shown in Example 6-10. This command can also have the information displayed limited to events for specific protocols and processes using the keywords **h323**, **port**, **pptp**, **route**, **skinny**, and **detailed**.

Example 6-10 *The* **debug ip nat** *Command Is Extremely Useful for Troubleshooting NAT— the Debug Output Is Much Easier to Interpret Than Most* **debug** *Command Outputs*

```
SanJose1#debug ip nat detailed
IP NAT detailed debugging is on
07:03:50: NAT:  i: icmp (192.168.0.21, 1536) -> (10.0.0.5, 1536) (101)
07:03:50: NAT:  address not stolen for 192.168.0.21, proto 1 port 1536
07:03:50: NAT:  ipnat_allocation_port: wanted 1536 got 1536
07:03:50: NAT*: o: icmp (10.0.0.5, 1536) -> (42.0.0.55, 1536) (101)
07:03:50: NAT*: i: icmp (192.168.0.21, 1536) -> (10.0.0.5, 1536) (102)
07:03:50: NAT*: o: icmp (10.0.0.5, 1536) -> (42.0.0.55, 1536) (102)
07:03:50: NAT*: i: icmp (192.168.0.21, 1536) -> (10.0.0.5, 1536) (103)
07:03:50: NAT*: o: icmp (10.0.0.5, 1536) -> (42.0.0.55, 1536) (103)
07:03:50: NAT*: i: icmp (192.168.0.21, 1536) -> (10.0.0.5, 1536) (104)
07:03:50: NAT*: o: icmp (10.0.0.5, 1536) -> (42.0.0.55, 1536) (104)
```

Note that the **debug** command can also use a standard access list to limit the information being displayed by the debug process to traffic matching the **permit** statements in the ACL.

When debugging NAT problems, it can be useful to reset NAT statistics or to clear the NAT table of any dynamic entries. Use the command **clear ip nat statistics** to reset the NAT traffic statistics counters. Use the command **clear ip nat translations** * to clear dynamic entries from the NAT table.

Other keywords can be used when clearing the NAT table. The **forced** keyword clears all IP NAT translations even if they are currently in use. The **inside** keyword removes all inside addresses and ports from the table, and the **outside** keyword removes all outside addresses and ports. Using the **tcp** keyword removes only TCP-related entries. Using the **udp** keyword removes only UDP-related NAT entries.

Other Useful Information

A range of other tools can be used to help troubleshoot transport layer problems on network devices:

- Protocol analyzers
- Network device system logs
- Centralized logging system (using Syslog)
- Network management systems

Protocol analyzers, as shown in Figure 6-15, can be used to collect information on network operations from the data-link layer to the application layer. A good protocol analyzer can provide a network engineer with a source of information on network transactions at the transport layer. Protocol analyzers were discussed in Chapter 2, "Troubleshooting Methodologies and Tools."

Configuring buffered local system logging can also provide a rich source of information when troubleshooting network problems. A local system log can also provide historic information on past events. Logging on local systems is highly configurable and can be used to capture general router events as well as other information of interest, such as **debug** messages. The system log buffer uses volatile memory and is cleared by rebooting the router. Because of this, it is recommended that system log events be redirected to an external system.

To configure a router to keep its local log, use the following commands in global configuration mode:

```
Router(config)#logging on
Router(config)#logging buffered [buffer size] [logging level]
```

Figure 6-15 Protocol Analyzers Are an Indispensable Tool for Network Engineers

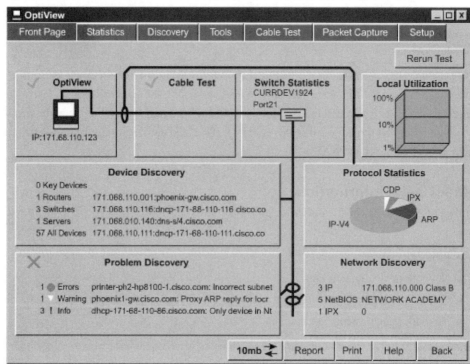

The first step is to ensure that system logging is enabled (note that local system logging is on by default). When configuring the logging buffer, set the size of the log buffer and the level of message to log. There are eight levels of logging, from 0 for emergency messages (indicating that the router is unusable) to 7 for debugging messages generated by engineer-configured **debug** commands. These levels are summarized in Table 6-9.

Table 6-9 System Logging Levels

Level	Keyword	Description	Syslog Definition
0	**emergencies**	System is unusable	LOG_EMERG
1	**alerts**	Immediate action is needed	LOG_ALERT
2	**critical**	Critical conditions exist	LOG_CRIT
3	**errors**	Error conditions exist	LOG_ERR
4	**warnings**	Warning conditions exist	LOG_WARNING

Table 6-9 System Logging Levels (Continued)

Level	Keyword	Description	Syslog Definition
5	**notification**	Normal, but significant, condition	LOG_NOTICE
6	**informational**	Informational messages only	LOG_INFO
7	**debugging**	Debugging messages	LOG_DEBUG

The **show logging** command, as shown in Example 6-11, can be used to display the state of Syslog error and event logging, including host addresses, and whether console logging is enabled. This command also displays SNMP configuration parameters and protocol activity.

Example 6-11 *The* **show logging** *Command Can Be Used in Lieu of a Syslog Server*

```
Router#show logging
Syslog logging: enabled
     Console logging: disabled
     Monitor logging: level debugging, 266 messages logged.
     Trap logging: level informational, 266 messages logged.
     Logging to 192.180.2.238
SNMP logging: disabled, retransmission after 30 seconds 0
messages logged
```

Cisco routers support the Syslog protocol for delivering system log messages to a centralized system. The Syslog protocol uses UDP port 514, making it a lightweight and fast but unreliable delivery mechanism.

Syslog servers are machines that can listen on UDP port 514 and collate information from a number of sources (network devices) simultaneously. This information is stored in a central location, such as a database, from where it can be used to build a report. Such reports can then be used to spot patterns and trends in network traffic, including current and potential problems.

Configuring Syslog for centralized logging is discussed in detail in Chapter 7, "Layer 1–7 Troubleshooting".

To make the logged information more useful, network engineers should set the router's real-time clock and enable date and time stamps for log messages. If messages are logged without setting the device's real-time clock, the date and time stamp uses the router's uptime.

The router's real-time clock can be set manually or can use an NTP source for its information. Using an NTP time source is recommended for a number of reasons:

- The router's real-time clock is reset when the router is rebooted.
- NTP time sources are much more accurate.
- Having all of the devices' real-time clocks synchronized can help trace traffic patterns and trends through the network.

Unlike much of the router configuration, setting the real-time clock is not done from global configuration mode. To manually set the router's real-time clock from privileged mode, use the **clock set** [*hh:mm:ss*] [*day of the month*] [*month*] [*year*] command. Note that the order of *day of the month* and *month* does not matter. For example, the following two commands have the same effect:

```
Router#clock set 15:42:00 12 March 2005
```

```
Router#clock set 15:42:00 March 12 2005
```

NTP servers are available for time queries on the Internet and are arranged in order of importance. A list of NTP servers that are publicly available from the Internet is available at http://www.eecis.udel.edu/~mills/ntp/servers.html. Alternatively, network engineers can build their own internal NTP servers or can purchase and use NT network appliances (often synchronized to geosynchronous satellites) to provide a reliable and accurate time source for network host devices.

To configure the router to query an NTP time source, use these commands in global configuration mode:

```
Router(config)#ntp peer [NTP server IP address]
Router(config)#ntp peer authenticate
```

Note that NTP sends traffic to and from UDP port 123. This needs to be allowed when configuring the firewall router access list.

The network administrator should also set the time zone local to the router so that the router knows how far to adjust the UTC time signal received from the NTP time source. Use this command to configure the router's local time zone:

```
Router(config)#clock timezone [timezone-name] [hours-offset] [minutes-offset]
```

This command can also be used to uniquely identify log messages from the router by specifying a unique time zone name. Note that the *timezone-name* parameter is limited to eight characters.

Example 6-12 shows one way to configure a router with NTP and a local time zone.

Example 6-12 *NTP Is Essential for a Network to Maintain Accurate Documentation*

```
Router(config)#ntp peer 137.189.8.174
Router(config)#clock timezone HongKong +8
Router(config)#
```

To enable date and time stamps for logged messages, use the following command in global configuration mode:

```
Router(config)#service timestamps debug datetime [localtime] [msec] [show-timezone]
```

The keywords **localtime**, **msec**, and **show-timezone** can all be used to add extra information to the logged messages. It is recommended that you include the **msec** keyword, especially on busy routers. Example 6-13 shows messages with the date and time stamp information.

Example 6-13 *The* **service timestamps** *Command Permits Debug Output to Be Displayed with Timestamps*

```
Dec 16 21:43:57: ISDN BR0: TX -> SETUP pd = 8 callref = 0x1E
Dec 16 21:43:57: Bearer Capability i = 0x8890
Dec 16 21:43:57: Channel ID i = 0x83
Dec 16 21:43:57: Keypad Facility i = '18007455790'
Dec 16 21:43:57: ISDN BR0: RX <- SETUP_ACK pd = 8 callref = 0x9E
Dec 16 21:43:57: Channel ID i = 0x89
Dec 16 21:43:58: ISDN BR0: RX <- CALL_PROC pd = 8 callref = 0x9E
Dec 16 21:43:58: Locking Shift to Codeset 5
```

Troubleshooting Transport Layer Issues on Network Hosts

This section explores transport layer issues on end systems. This includes UNIX hosts, OS X hosts, and Windows hosts. Particular emphasis is placed on NetBIOS issues.

Common Transport Layer Issues with IP Networks

TCP window size can dramatically affect the network's performance.

If the TCP window size is too small, the result is additional network overhead from segment acknowledgments. A lot of time is also wasted when the sending host waits for acknowledgments. Increasing the window size allows the sending host to transmit more than one packet at a time, increase network bandwidth utilization, and decrease the time spent waiting for acknowledgments.

Having a TCP window that's too large can also cause problems, especially on a congested network. If the network is dropping a lot of TCP packets and acknowledgments, the sending host wastes a lot of time waiting for retransmit timers to expire. The sending host also adds to the congestion problem by sending large amounts of retransmission traffic. Making the window smaller forces the sending host to send less data at once, reduces its impact on the congestion, and improves the chances of TCP packets and acknowledgments getting through the network successfully.

When operating correctly, TCP self-tunes its behavior according to network conditions. Recall that TCP window sizes are self-tuning. This self-tuning mechanism can be seen in action when you download a large file from the Internet. When the download starts, the rate of transfer is quite slow, because the initial window size is relatively small. As the download proceeds, the rate of download increases rapidly as the window size expands. As the TCP window approaches its optimal size, the increase in the download rate slows until the rate is almost constant. For the remainder of the download, the window size self-tunes to suit prevailing network conditions.

Gathering Transport Layer Information on Windows Machines

Although Telnet normally refers to an application layer protocol and program, it can be a useful tool for troubleshooting problems at other layers, particularly the transport layer. Telnet's usefulness in troubleshooting comes from its ability to connect to a specific destination port on a remote server, allowing it to be used to confirm correct traffic flow from a client to a remote server. Although never intended as a troubleshooting tool, Telnet is particularly useful for transport layer diagnostics. See Figure 6-16.

Telnet can be run as either a command-line utility or with a graphical user interface (GUI). Figure 6-16 shows a command-line Telnet application being used to confirm connectivity to a POP3 server.

Figure 6-16 Telnet Applications Are Becoming Less Common, with SSH Growing in Popularity

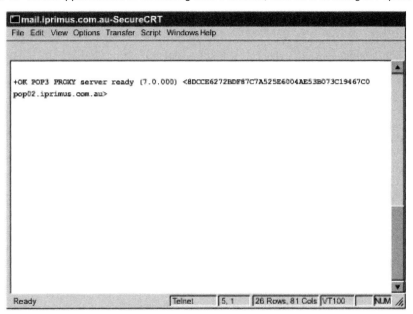

The **ipconfig /all** command, shown in Example 6-14, can provide the network engineer with a lot of information about the configuration of a Windows-based machine. This information covers details of the MAC address at Layer 2, the IP address at Layer 3, NetBIOS information at Layers 4 and 5, and DNS information at Layers 6 and 7.

Example 6-14 *The* **ipconfig** /all *Command Is Used Very Frequently to Troubleshoot Windows Operating System Problems*

```
C:\WINNT>ipconfig /all

Windows 200 IP Configuration

    Host Name.......................:basil

    Primary DNS Suffix..............:

    Node Type.......................:Broadcast

    IP Routing Enabled..............:No

    WINS Proxy Enabled..............:No

    DNS Suffix Search List..........:lan

Ethernet adapter Local Area Connection:

    Connection-specific DNS Suffix...:lan

    Description.....................:Realtek RTL8139/810X Family PCI Fast
```

continues

Example 6-14 *The* **ipconfig /all** *Command Is Used Very Frequently to Troubleshoot Windows Operating System Problems (Continued)*

```
Ethernet NIC
    Physical Address.................:00-20-ED-36-39-0A
    DHCP Enabled.....................:Yes
    Autoconfiguration Enabled........:Yes
    IP Address.......................:192.168.0.100
    Subnet Mask......................:255.255.255.0
    Default Gateway..................:192.168.0.1
    DHCP Server......................:192.168.0.1
    DNS Servers......................:203.134.64.66
            203.134.65.66
            192.189.54.17
            134.115.4.33
    Lease Obtained...................:Wednesday, 12 March 2003 9:31:36 PM
    Lease Expires....................:Saturday, 15 March 2003 9:31:36 PM
C:\WINNT>
```

Gathering Transport Layer Information on UNIX Machines

There are many variants of the UNIX operating system. The most common are SunOS, FreeBSD, SCO, and Linux. All of these operating systems have tools that can be used to troubleshoot network issues. These tools are covered in greater detail elsewhere in this curriculum. They are mentioned here in the context of troubleshooting options for transport layer issues on UNIX hosts.

Note that although these tools often have the same name and purpose, the command-line options required to use them vary greatly from platform to platform. Consult the online manual of the local operating software, using the command **man** [*tool_name*], to get more information about the command-line options of the tool to use.

It is important to note that almost all newer versions of UNIX variants support native packet-filtering firewall features. When troubleshooting transport layer problems with UNIX hosts, network engineers should be aware of the possibility that the problem could be caused by the local machine firewall configuration.

Three common commands are used to configure UNIX firewall features:

- On older UNIX variants using kernel version 2.0, use the **ipfwadm** command.
- On UNIX variants using kernel version 2.2, use the **ipchains** command.
- On newer UNIX variants using kernel version 2.4 or later, use the **iptables** command.

Each new version of the firewall capability has produced a tool with significantly greater features than its predecessor.

The **ifconfig** command is a low-level command used to administer network connections on a UNIX host. This command is used to configure network layer addresses and DHCP operation interface design. **ifconfig** can also be used to configure data-link layer addressing if the network card has a configurable MAC address and is used to enable and disable specific interfaces.

netstat on UNIX hosts operates in much the same way as it does on Windows hosts. On UNIX hosts, **netstat** also provides the network engineer with information on current network connections and sockets and can also filter information displayed.

The **route** command, not surprisingly, is used to add, delete, and manage IP routing information on the UNIX host.

ip is a command available in some newer UNIX variants. This command is a powerful unified network configuration tool that supports some unique configuration capabilities not available in other tools. One important capability of the **ip** tool is its support for multiple protocols, including IPv4, IPv6, and IPX.

This client can be used in the same way for UNIX as for Windows hosts to help troubleshoot transport layer connectivity issues. Another Telnet-like troubleshooting tool is **netcat**.

Common Issues with NetBIOS Networks

There are four common NetBIOS-related issues:

- NetBIOS node-type misconfiguration
- NetBIOS workgroup mismatch
- NetBIOS scope mismatch
- Duplicate NetBIOS names

These issues are usually the result of misconfiguration by a user or network engineer. Note that several of these problems can be caused by DHCP server misconfiguration.

One of the most common misconfigurations on a small NetBIOS network is the NetBIOS node type. Recall that the NetBIOS node type has four possible settings:

- B-node (broadcast node)
- P-node (peer-to-peer node)
- M-node (mixed node)
- H-node (hybrid node)

Obviously, configuring the NetBIOS node type as peer-to-peer in a network that does not have a NetBIOS name server stops the network from functioning. Conversely, using broadcast mode in a routed network stops the hosts from accessing resources across the router.

The NetBIOS node type is usually set using a DHCP server. Recall that DHCP can be used to configure more than just a client IP address. DHCP can be used to set a number of optional settings on the client. The settings are called DHCP options. Common DHCP options are shown in Table 6-10. Because Cisco routers can be configured as DHCP servers, NetBIOS DHCP options need to be taken into account. Use the commands **netbios-name-server** *name-server-address* and **netbios-node-type** *type* from DHCP-configuration mode to implement NetBIOS DHCP options from a Cisco router-based DHCP server.

Table 6-10 DHCP Options

Code	DHCP Option
3	Router address
6	DHCP server address
12	Host name
15	DNS domain name
44	NetBIOS name server address
46	NetBIOS node type
47	NetBIOS scope ID

DHCP options 44 and 46 are commonly used in NetBIOS networks with NetBIOS name servers.

You also can manually set the NetBIOS node type on Windows hosts by editing the Windows Registry. Further information can be found in Knowledge Base article 160177 at http://www.support.microsoft.com.

When two NetBIOS computers have different values defined for the workgroup name, they are unable to communicate. The workgroup name is usually configured during the initial installation of the computer operating system or when networking is added to the computer. The workgroup name is not case-sensitive.

The NetBIOS scope ID is a leftover piece of NetBIOS technology rarely used in modern networking. A NetBIOS scope is a group of computers that can communicate only with each other. Because the NetBIOS Scope ID is blank by default, a single computer misconfigured with a NetBIOS Scope ID cannot communicate with other hosts on the network.

Because this setting is not often used, it can be quite difficult to troubleshoot. Note that like the NetBIOS node type, the NetBIOS scope ID can be controlled centrally from the DHCP server using DHCP option 47. Unlike the node type, however, the Scope ID can also be easily altered on the local machine through the network interface GUI.

When duplicate NetBIOS names exist in a network, the duplicate hosts are unable to connect to the network until they are configured with a unique NetBIOS name. Duplicate NetBIOS names occur most often when the naming scheme in a NetBIOS network has no structure.

In small networks, the lack of a structure poses no real issue. In larger networks, however, a system for ensuring unique NetBIOS naming is strongly recommended.

Note that the host name can be set using DHCP option 12. This option is intended for use when using DHCP reservations (where an IP address is specifically reserved for a given MAC address), because it allows full host-specific network information to be controlled from a single administrative interface. Obviously, using DHCP option 12 with dynamic DHCP clients would cause significant problems on the network.

Gathering NetBIOS Information

Several tools for troubleshooting network problems, such as **ping**, **ipconfig**, and **winipcfg**, are discussed in other chapters. Two additional tools that are useful for gathering TCP and NetBIOS information are **netstat** and **nbtstat**.

netstat is a command-line utility that displays information on protocol statistics and current TCP/IP network connections. **netstat** supports IP, IPv6, ICMP, ICMPv6, TCP, TCPv6, UDP, and UDPv6. It can be used to display information for the following:

- All connections and listening ports running on the host
- Ethernet (Layer 2) statistics for the host, such as number of bytes, number of packets, and errors received and sent for the host
- Port and address information for connections to and from the host
- Which connections the host initiated
- Per-protocol connection information
- Per-protocol statistics
- Routing table entries

netstat can also be configured to requery and redisplay information at a configured interval. By configuring **netstat** to requery at intervals and directing this output to a text file, you can use **netstat** to build a profile of the behavior of the host TCP/IP transport layer operations over time. See Example 6-15.

Example 6-15 *The* **netstat** *Command Is Used to Display Protocol Statistics and TCP/IP Connections*

```
C:\>netstat-?

Displays protocol statistics and current TCP/IP network connections.

NETSTAT [-a][-e][-n][-s][-p proto][-r][interval]

-a          Displays all connections and listening ports.
-e          Displays Ethernet statistics. This may be combined with the
            -s option.
-n          Displays addresses and port numbers in numerical form.
-p proto    Shows connections for the protocol specified by proto: proto
            may be TCP or UDP. If used with the -s options to display
            per-protocol statistics, proto may be ICP, UDP, or IP.
-r          Displays the routing table.
-s          Displays per-protocol statistics. By Default, statistics are
            shown for ICP, UDP and IP; the -p option may be used to
            specify a subset of the default.
interval    Redisplays selected statistics. pausing interval seconds
            between each display. Press CTRL+C to stop redisplaying
            statistics. If omitted, netstat will print the current
            configuration information once.
```

nbtstat is a command-line utility that displays information on protocol statistics and current NetBIOS connections running over TCP/IP. Unlike **netstat**, **nbtstat** also can interrogate remote machines for connection information.

Recall that NetBIOS uses a flat namespace and that accurate NetBIOS name-to-IP address mapping is important for correct operation of a NetBIOS-based network. The functions of **nbtstat** are centered around reporting on and resetting the information in name tables on local machines, remote machines, and central NetBIOS name servers. See Example 6-16.

Example 6-16 *The* **nbtstat** *Command Is Used to Display Protocol Statistics and NetBIOS-Over-TCP/IP Connections*

```
C:\>nbtstat-?

Displays protocol statistics and current TCP/IP connections using NBT.

NBTSTAT [ [-a RemoteName] [-A IP address][-c][-n][-r][-R][-RR][-s][-S]
        [interval]]

-a   <adapter status> Lists the remote machine's name table given its name
-A   <Adapter status> Lists the remote machine's name table given its
                      IP address.
```

Example 6-16 *The* **nbtstat** *Command Is Used to Display Protocol Statistics and NetBIOS-Over-TCP/IP Connections (Continued)*

```
-c   <cache>          Lists NBT's cache or remote [machine] names and
                      their IP addresses.
-n   <names>          Lists local NetBIOS names.
-r   <resolved>       Lists name resolved by broadcast and via WINS
-R   <Reload>         Lists sessions table with the destination IP
                      addresses.
-S   <Sessions>       Lists sessions table with the destination IP
                      addresses.
-s   <sessions>       Lists sessions table converting destination IP
                      addresses to computer NETBIOS names.
-RR  <ReleaseRefresh> Sends Name Release packets to WINs and then, starts
                      Refresh
RemoteName   Remote host machine name.
IP address   Dotted decimal representation of the IP address.
interval     Redisplays selected statistics, pausing interval seconds
             between each display. Press Ctrl+C to stop redisplaying
             statistics.
```

Troubleshooting Complex Network Systems

As a network grows more complex, the chances of network failure and suboptimal performance increase. Problems that might have remained undetected in simpler networks might combine to cause problems in a more complex one. This section explores complex network systems, including issues involving combinations of NAT and ACLs.

Identifying Complex Transport Layer Problems

Complex network problems are usually caused by the combination of smaller problems that by themselves appear to have no immediate impact on the network. To resolve these problems, develop a profile of the symptoms and use this as a starting point for troubleshooting activities. Complex network problems have the following characteristics:

- Interaction of different technologies
- They can be predictable or intermittent
- They can be caused by user behavior

Also keep in mind that some network problems can be triggered by or made more obvious through user behavior. For example, staff at a remote site might need to back up data to a central site every afternoon before going home, causing the WAN link to become congested. This activity is likely to affect other users who are still working over the link. This particular problem can be solved by changing the work process (stop backing up across the WAN link), by provisioning more bandwidth, or possibly by implementing superior routing technologies, such as Link Fragmentation and Interleaving, to better use the link bandwidth. When the symptom is regular and predictable, you can more easily find the cause and solve the problem.

Some network problems are intermittent. These sorts of network problems occur with no obvious pattern and often just go away and reappear at will. Intermittent network problems are significantly more complicated to troubleshoot because the ability to collect solid information becomes increasingly difficult.

Again, intermittent problems might be caused by user behavior. For example, suppose a user is loading a large file across the WAN. This obviously affects the performance of the WAN link, generating a support call to the IT help desk. By the time the IT help desk is made aware of the problem and investigates the issue, the file transfer has finished, and the WAN link performance has returned to normal.

Intermittent problems can also be caused by the interaction of various technologies. Firewalls running dynamic NAT, configuring NAT for load balancing, and running parallel links between systems can all cause intermittent problems in network communications. The key to solving these sorts of issues is understanding the technologies involved.

As shown in Figure 6-17, communication cannot be established between Host A and Host F because of misconfigured ACLs on Routers C and D. Using the traditional problem-solving methodology of reversing changes before trying another possible solution would fail to resolve this problem.

In Figure 6-18, communication between Host B and FTP server D fails intermittently. This time, the problem is caused by dynamic NAT timeouts being too finely tuned. When the Internet is not congested, communications are successful. Because the Internet intermittently gets congested, packets returning from FTP Server D occasionally take too long and the dynamic NAT connection on the router closes, breaking the connection.

In each of these situations, the network engineer would need to be able to recognize the misconfiguration as such, repair the configuration, and, even though the problem is not immediately resolved, be confident that it was a contributing factor.

Figure 6-17 Misconfigured ACLs Are a Common Source of Transport Layer Problems

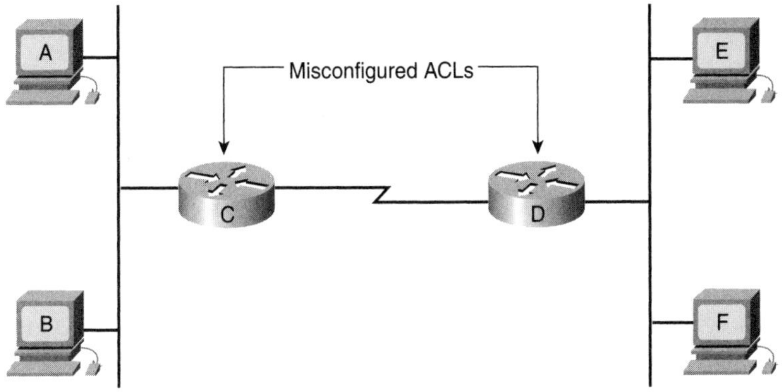

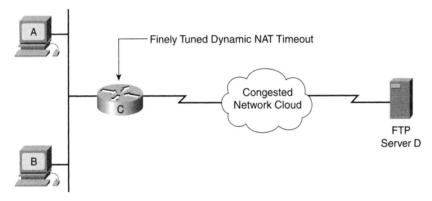

Misconfigured ACLs

Figure 6-18 Communication Between Host B and FTP Server D Fails Intermittently

Finely Tuned Dynamic NAT Timeout

Congested
Network Cloud

FTP
Server D

Disassembling the Problem

A good way to solve a complex problem is one piece at a time. If transport layer connectivity is failing, it might be because of a misconfiguration on more than one device or technology. Following the traffic flow and correcting each problem as it is encountered can be a valid troubleshooting approach. Examining the symptoms and generating a list of possible causes is less likely to be a successful troubleshooting methodology when dealing with more complex issues. The following is a list of suggestions for solving complex network problems:

- Follow the traffic flow.
- Use prior experience and knowledge.

- Gather information at network midpoints.
- Use logged information.
- Document changes.

Even though it is a good practice to reverse changes that have no effect when troubleshooting simple problems, this is unlikely to help solve complex problems. With complex problems, the network engineer has to start relying on his or her own experience and judgment as to what is a probable cause of a problem and what is not.

Mechanisms for disassembling complex problems include gathering information from midpoints in the network communications chain and disabling parts of the system to exclude them as being the cause. This can involve recabling components of the network to insert monitoring hosts or other troubleshooting tools or bypassing suspected equipment. Gathering detailed log information from key points in the communications chain can also help pinpoint specific problem areas.

When resolving complex network problems, the network engineer should always keep a record of changes being made. Keeping a log has the advantage of providing a record in case the configuration changes need to be reversed. A log of activities performed also removes any doubt as to whether a certain activity has been performed, helping the network engineer avoid repeating troubleshooting activities.

Solving the Component Problems

Using the example shown in Figure 6-17, assume that Host A is a Telnet client attempting to access the Telnet server on Host E. In this case, Telnet access fails.

The network engineer can use a protocol analyzer on the Host A network to confirm that the packets are being generated and sent to the router. At this point, the network engineer should notice that the configuration and operation of Host A appear to be correct and that no reply packets are being received. A protocol analyzer running on the remote network is reporting that no Telnet packets are being received. Based on this information, the network engineer can assume that there is a problem with at least one of the routers.

Because the access list on Router C is quite complex, there does not appear to be any problem when the network engineer gives the configuration a visual check using **show ip access-list**. To be sure, however, the **deny ip any any log** statement is configured to highlight any packets not being permitted through the ACL. The messages generated by the ACL logging highlight a misconfiguration that otherwise would have gone unnoticed. The network engineer fixes the misconfiguration. The ACL is updated, and the **show ip access-list** command is used again to confirm that packets are being matched by the new access list element entered for the Telnet traffic.

Because the problem still has not been solved, the network engineer now moves to the configuration of Router D. The ACL filtering inbound traffic on the serial interface is permitting the Telnet traffic, and the packet counter against the appropriate ACE is incrementing with traffic.

Using a protocol analyzer, the network engineer confirms that the Telnet packets are now reaching the network of Host E and that replies are being sent back to Host A. The protocol analyzer on the network of Host A, however, cannot see any of these Telnet packets. It appears as though another problem exists on one of the routers.

The access lists on Router D are not as complex as those on Router C, so the network engineer immediately spots and corrects a configuration error.

The next test works, and the problem is considered resolved. The final activity the network engineer should perform is to remove any unnecessary configuration changes to the network. Using the log of activities generated during troubleshooting, the network administrator identifies that the use of the **deny ip any any log** command only provided diagnostic information and can be removed from the configuration.

Dynamic NAT and Extended ACLs

The interaction of Dynamic NAT and extended access lists can generate complex network problems, particularly with the use of addressing and ports.

Recall that the order of processing inbound traffic on a router is that the inbound traffic is processed by the inbound access list before being processed by outside-to-inside NAT. When designing access lists for implementation on NAT routers, remember that the destination address of inbound traffic is the IP address used by the outbound NAT translation.

When configuring dynamic NAT, you can configure different timeout values for different types of traffic. Table 6-11 shows the commands used to change these values for translations built with and without overloading.

Table 6-11 NAT Timers

Command	Description
Router(config)#**ip nat translation timeout** *seconds*	Changes the timeout value for dynamic address translations that do not use overloading.
Router(config)#**ip nat translation udp-timeout** *seconds*	Changes the UDP timeout value from 5 minutes.
Router(config)#**ip nat translation dns-timeout** *seconds*	Changes the DNS timeout value from 1 minute.

continues

Table 6-11 NAT Timers (Continued)

Command	Description
Router(config)#**ip nat translation tcp-timeout** *seconds*	Changes the TCP timeout value from 24 hours.
Router(config)#**ip nat translation finret-timeout** *seconds*	Changes the Finish and Reset timeout value from 1 minute.

As discussed earlier, highly tuned translation timeouts combined with network congestion can be the cause of intermittent problems in network communications. Different transport layer protocols also have different timeout values by default and can be configured individually. This can mislead network engineers when troubleshooting.

Figure 6-19 shows a router with multiple configuration errors. The symptom presented is that neither Host A nor Host B can establish a reliable connection to download files from Server D using TFTP.

Figure 6-19 Reliable Connection Is Unavailable

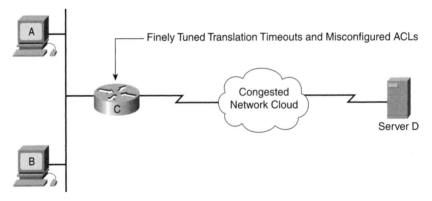

Following the traffic flow, the network engineer checks the local network segment and finds nothing wrong. The access lists filtering outbound traffic are examined, and no faults are found. The NAT process on the router is also building the appropriate translation for the outbound traffic, and the access list filtering inbound traffic has an entry to permit traffic from UDP port 69 on the TFTP server to any UDP port on the private IP addresses allocated to Hosts A and B. The engineer can ping Server D from both Hosts A and B and from Router C.

At this stage, the network engineer configures the **deny ip any any log** command to find out if the traffic is returning from the TFTP server but is being blocked by the access list. The logged messages indicate that TFTP traffic from Server D is getting back to the router but is addressed to the IP address of the router serial interface being used as the NAT overload outside address. The network engineer corrects the problems with the ACL and tries another TFTP download.

Host A can now establish a connection with Server D but loses the connection when doing a large file transfer. There is no pattern as to the point during the transfer at which the connection is lost. The network engineer suspects that this might be a problem with UDP packets being lost in transit, but he uses a protocol analyzer on the WAN link to make sure. (Installing the WAN protocol analyzer interrupts network communications, so the engineer waits until everyone has gone to lunch.)

Results from the protocol analyzer show that the router is receiving more TFTP packets than it should. This means that there is a problem with the router. Examining the router system log in greater detail, the network engineer finds some error messages stating that the router has "received packets for which no translation exists." The network engineer examines the router's configuration and notices the following block in the configuration script:

```
ip nat translation udp-timeout 18
ip nat translation dns-timeout 120
ip nat translation tcp-timeout 3600
```

Assuming that the first statement is an error, the network engineer replaces it with **ip nat translation udp-timeout 180** and tests the file transfer again. The large file is transferred successfully, and the problem is considered solved. After updating the appropriate documentation, the network engineer removes the unnecessary additions to the network configuration, such as the WAN protocol analyzer and the **deny ip any any log** statement in the inbound ACL.

TCP Load Distribution with NAT

NAT on Cisco routers allows network engineers to provide TCP load distribution among hosts. Figure 6-20 shows TCP load distribution. The steps to configure TCP load distribution with NAT are described in Table 6-12.

Figure 6-20 TCP Load Distribution

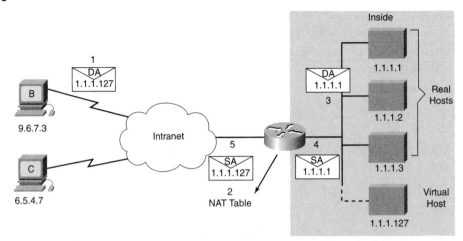

Protocol	Inside Local IP Address: Port	Inside Global IP Address: Port	Outside Global IP Address: Port
TCP	1.1.1.1:23	1.1.1.127:23	9.6.7.5:3058
TCP	1.1.1.2:23	1.1.1.127:23	6.5.4.7:4371
TCP	1.1.1.3:23	1.1.1.127:23	9.6.7.3:3062

Table 6-12 TCP Load Distribution

Command	Description
Router(config)#**ip nat pool** *name start-ip end-ip* {**netmask** *netmask*	*prefix-length*} **type rotary**	Defines a pool of addresses containing the addresses of the real hosts.
Router(config)#**access-list** *access-list-number* **permit source** [*source-wildcard*]	Defines an access list permitting the address of the virtual host.
Router(config)#**ip nat inside destination list** *access-list-number* **pool** *name*	Establishes dynamic inside destination translation, specifying the access list defined in the prior step.
Router(config)#**interface** *type number*	Specifies the inside interface.
Router(config-if)#**ip nat inside**	Marks the interface as connected to the inside.
Router(config)#**interface** *type number*	Specifies the outside interface.
Router(config-if)#**ip nat outside**	Marks the interface as connected to the outside.

Although TCP load distribution can improve the performance of some types of network transactions (such as accessing a corporate intranet Web service), it can also be a source of network complexity, resulting in intermittent fault behaviors when something goes wrong.

Example 1—Host Fault

Assume that the network is configured as shown in Figure 6-20. The router is distributing TCP connections evenly among the hosts, as it should. Overnight, power to Host 1.1.1.2 fails, and the device is no longer on the network. Because the router does not know this, it continues to forward TCP connection requests to the failed host. The result of this is that one in three connection attempts fails, presenting a seemingly intermittent fault.

After a little investigation, the network engineer realizes that every third connection attempt is failing and immediately suspects that one of the hosts might have failed. Power is restored to Host 1.1.1.2, and network performance returns to normal.

Example 2—Host Misconfiguration

Using the network configuration shown in Figure 6-20, assume that a new network engineer is instructed to build a new server. Because the new network engineer does not understand how the TCP load distribution system works, the new server is configured with the IP address assigned to the virtual host on the NAT router. When the new server is powered up, it detects an IP address conflict and cannot establish a connection to the network. The new engineer examines the interface configuration on the router to locate and confirm the duplicate IP address but cannot find it in the interface configuration.

After discussing the problem with a more experienced engineer, the new engineer reconfigures the new server with correct IP settings, reboots, and connects to the network.

Summary

You should understand the operation of various transport layer networking technologies on routers and hosts. These technologies include

- TCP
- UDP
- NetBIOS
- NAT
- Extended access lists

You should also have gained an appreciation of the various tools and methodologies that can help you troubleshoot transport layer issues.

Key Terms

Bootstrap Protocol (BOOTP)   A protocol that lets a network user automatically receive an IP address and have an operating system booted without user involvement. The BOOTP server automatically assigns the IP address from a pool of addresses for a certain duration of time. BOOTP is the basis for the more advanced protocol DHCP.

NetBIOS Extended User Interface (NetBEUI)   An extended version of NetBIOS. NetBEUI formalizes the frame format that was not specified as part of NetBIOS. NetBEUI was developed by IBM for its LAN Manager product and has been adopted by Microsoft for its Windows NT, LAN Manager, and Windows for Workgroups products.

Network Basic Input/Output System (NetBIOS)   A program that allows applications on different computers to communicate within a LAN. It was created by IBM for its early PC Network, was adopted by Microsoft, and has since become a de facto industry standard.

Pretty Good Privacy (PGP)   A program used to encrypt and decrypt e-mail over the Internet. It can also be used to send an encrypted digital signature that lets the receiver verify the sender's identity and know that the message was not changed en route.

Check Your Understanding

Use the following review questions to test your understanding of the concepts covered in this chapter. Answers are listed in Appendix A, "Check Your Understanding Answer Key."

1. Which of the following protocols are connectionless and unreliable?

   A. TFTP

   B. DNS

   C. DHCP

   D. RADIUS

2. Which of the following protocols are connection-oriented and reliable?

   A. HTTP

   B. FTP

   C. SMTP

   D. SNMP

3. Which of the following are configurable ranges for numbered standard access control lists?

    A. 1 to 99

    B. 100 to 199

    C. 1300 to 1999

    D. 2000 to 2699

4. Named extended ACLs can filter traffic based on which of the following?

    A. Source IP address

    B. Destination IP address

    C. Source port

    D. Destination port

5. The reserved private address space includes which of the following networks?

    A. 10.0.0.0/8

    B. 172.17.0.0/16

    C. 172.16.0.0/12

    D. 192.168.0.0/24

6. What type of NAT allows Internet hosts to access an inside local IP address?

    A. Inside dynamic NAT

    B. Outside dynamic NAT

    C. Inside static NAT

    D. Outside static NAT

7. What command clears NAT translations on the IOS?

    A. **nat -d ***

    B. **clear ip nat translations**

    C. **clear ip nat**

    D. **clear ip nat translations ***

8. PAT makes it possible to deploy NAT with which of the following options (as opposed to NAT without PAT)?

   A. Many-to-one IP translations

   B. Many-to-many IP translations

   C. One-to-one IP translations

   D. None of the above

9. What command displays the NIC MAC address on a Windows 2000 server?

   A. nbtstat

   B. netstat

   C. ipconfig /all

   D. tracert

10. What UNIX command configures firewall features?

   A. ifconfig

   B. nslookup

   C. ipconfig

   D. iptables

Objectives

After completing this chapter, you will be able to perform tasks related to the following:

- Be familiar with the usual sources of application layer problems, including TCP, UDP, NAT, access lists, NetBIOS, and NetBEUI
- Identify the symptoms of a problem at the application layer
- Isolate a problem at the application layer
- Correct a problem at the application layer

Chapter 7

Layer 1–7 Troubleshooting

Troubleshooting at the Application Layer

The application layer is the top layer in the TCP/IP reference model, as shown in Figure 7-1. When the International Organization for Standardization (ISO) developed the Open System Interconnection (OSI) reference model, the application layer functions were divided into three separate, more detailed layers. Although the OSI version is more detailed, it is more common to refer to the application layer of TCP/IP, because it is more encompassing.

Figure 7-1 Several Common Protocols, Such as FTP, Can Be Classified as Application Layer Protocols, But They Also Have Functions That Overlap with the Transport Layer

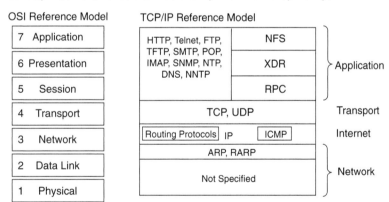

Overview

The application layer is the interface that separates application software from the transport layer. It deals with high-level protocols rather than segments, bytes, packets, or bits.

It provides network services for users and their programs and is the layer in which user-access network processes reside. These processes include the ones users interact with directly, as well as other processes of which the users are unaware.

This layer includes all application layer protocols that use the host-to-host transport protocols to deliver data (see Table 7-1). Other functions that process user data, such as data encryption, decryption, compression, and decompression, can also reside at the application layer.

Most of the application layer protocols provide user services. Application layer protocols typically are used for network management, file transfer, distributed file services, terminal emulation, and e-mail, as shown in Tables 7-1 and 7-2. However, new user services are often added (such as Virtual Private Networks [VPNs], Voice over IP [VoIP], and so on).

Table 7-1 Common Application Layer Protocols

Application	Protocol/Port	Description
WWW browser	HTTP (TCP port 80)	Web browsers and servers use HTTP to transfer the files that make up Web pages.
File transfer	FTP (TCP ports 20 and 21)	FTP provides a way to move files between computer systems.
Terminal emulation	Telnet (TCP port 23)	The Telnet protocol provides terminal emulation services over a reliable TCP stream.
E-mail	SMTP (TCP port 25) IMAP4 (TCP port 143) POP3 (TCP port 110)	Simple Mail Transfer Protocol (SMTP) is used to transfer e-mail between mail servers. Mail clients use it to send mail. Mail clients use either Post Office Protocol version 3 (POP3) or *Internet Message Access Protocol (IMAP)* to receive mail.

Table 7-2 SNMP and X Window System

Application	Protocol/Port	Description
Network management	SNMP (UDP port 161)	Simple Network Management Protocol (SNMP)
Distributed File Service	X Window System (UDP ports 6000 to 6063) NFS, XDR, RPC (UDP port 111)	*X Window System* is a popular protocol that permits intelligent terminals to communicate with remote computers as if they were directly attached. Network File System (NFS), External Data Representation (XDR), and *remote-procedure call (RPC)* combine to allow transparent access to remote network resources.

The most widely known and implemented TCP/IP application layer protocols are as follows:

- Telnet lets users establish terminal session connections with remote hosts.
- HTTP supports the exchange of text, graphic images, sound, video, and other multimedia files on the World Wide Web.
- FTP performs interactive file transfers between hosts.
- TFTP performs basic interactive file transfers typically between hosts and networking devices (such as routers, switches, and so on).
- SMTP supports basic message delivery services.
- POP is used to connect to mail servers and download e-mail.
- SNMP is used to collect management information from network devices.
- Domain Name System (DNS) maps IP addresses to the names assigned to network devices—commonly called the name service.
- *Network File System (NFS)* lets computers mount drives on remote hosts and operate them as if they were local drives. Originally developed by Sun Microsystems, it combines with two other application layer protocols, External Data Representation (XDR) and Remote-Procedure Call (RPC), to allow transparent access to remote network resources.

Other application layer protocols include the following:

- **Finger**—User Information Protocol
- **IMAP4**—Internet Message Access Protocol version 4
- **IPDC**—IP Device Control
- **ISAKMP**—Internet Security Association and Key Management Protocol
- **LDAP**—Lightweight Directory Access Protocol
- **NTP**—Network Time Protocol
- **POP3**—Post Office Protocol version 3
- **RLOGIN**—Remote Login
- **RTSP**—Real-Time Streaming Protocol
- **SCTP**—Stream Control Transmission Protocol
- **S-HTTP**—Secure Hypertext Transfer Protocol
- **SLP**—Service Location Protocol
- **TFTP**—Trivial File Transfer Protocol
- **WCCP**—Web Cache Coordination Protocol
- **X Window System**

These and other network applications use the services of TCP/IP and other lower-layer Internet protocols to provide users with basic network services.

 Lab 7.1.1   Isolating Problems at the Transport and Application Layers

In this lab exercise, you analyze user feedback and end-system data and use Cisco commands and applications to isolate the specific cause of any problems. You use a troubleshooting methodology and Cisco commands to isolate the specific causes of network problems.

Troubleshooting at the Application Layer

The primary responsibility of the upper layers of the OSI model is to provide services such as e-mail, file transfer, and data transport. Application layer problems result when data is not delivered to the destination or when network performance degrades to a level where productivity is affected. Common symptoms of application layer problems are as follows:

- Unreachable or unusable resources when the physical, data link, network, and transport layers are functional
- Operation of a network service or application does not meet a user's normal expectations

You can use the same general troubleshooting process you use to isolate problems at the lower layers to isolate problems at the application layer. The ideas are the same, but the technological focus shifts to involve things such as refused or timed-out connections, access lists, and DNS issues.

Problem isolation is vital to successfully troubleshooting any problem. Merely isolating the problem does not result in the types of changes necessary to return network functions to the documented baseline. To meet the troubleshooting objective of resolving the problem, use the tools and resources that are provided to correctly configure the properties of a properly functioning network.

Overview

Application layer problems prevent services from being provided to application programs. A problem at the application layer can result in unreachable or unusable resources when the physical, data link, network, and transport layers are functional. It is possible to have full network connectivity without the application's being able to provide data.

Another type of problem at the application layer occurs when the physical, data link, network, and transport layers are functional but the data transfer and requests for network services from a single network service or application do not meet the user's normal expectations.

A problem at the application layer might cause users to complain that the network or the particular application that they are working with is sluggish or slower than usual when transferring data or requesting network services. Possible symptoms of application layer problems are as follows:

- Users complain that the network or the particular application they are working with is sluggish or slower than usual
- Error messages from the affected application
- Console messages
- System log file messages
- Management system alarms

Eliminating Layers 1–3

When an application program cannot successfully connect to the destination host, establish at which layer the problem resides. Is it a lower layer problem or a higher layer problem?

For example, assume that the problem is the inability to connect to a remote FTP server. To determine that this is an application layer problem and not a lower layer problem, the first step is to verify Layer 3 connectivity. If successful, Layer 3 and lower can be eliminated as the source of the problem.

To troubleshoot, follow these steps:

Step 1 Ping the default gateway. If it is successful, Layer 1 and Layer 2 services are functioning properly.

Step 2 Verify end-to-end (host-to-host) connectivity. Use an extended ping if you're attempting the ping from a Cisco router.

If these pings are successful, Layer 1 through Layer 3 can be eliminated. Because they are functioning properly, the issue must exist at a higher layer.

 Lab 7.1.2 Correcting Problems at the Transport and Application Layers

In this lab exercise, you correct problems isolated in the previous lab exercise. You use Cisco commands to correct network problems. You follow these steps:

- Implement the plan you developed during the case study
- Verify that the data flow in the network matches the network baseline

Eliminating Layer 4

Layer 4 is the home of UDP and TCP protocols and is not as easy to eliminate.

For example, assume that FTP connection problems exist. To troubleshoot Layer 4, follow these steps:

Step 1 Use the **show access-list** command. Could any access lists be stopping traffic? Notice which access lists have matches.

Step 2 Clear the access list counters with the **clear access-list counters** command, and try to establish an FTP connection again.

Step 3 Verify the access list counters. Have any increased? Should they increase?

Improperly configured access lists are common problem areas. Be sure you understand the implications of each access list statement. This might sound strange, but sometimes it helps to think like the packet.

For example, does the following extended access list permit FTP file transfer?

```
access-list 101 permit udp any any eq 21
```

Although this looks correct, it does not permit FTP file transfers because it references UDP and not TCP. The correct access list is

```
access-list 101 permit tcp any any eq 21
```

However, if the access lists are functioning as expected, the problem must lie in a higher layer.

Isolating Application Layer Problems

Even though there might be IP connectivity between a source and a destination, problems might still exist for a specific upper-layer protocol such as FTP, HTTP, or Telnet. These protocols ride on top of the basic IP transport but are subject to protocol-specific problems relating to packet filters and firewalls. It is possible that everything except mail works between a given source and destination. Figure 7-2 illustrates a problem in which basic connectivity is established between a client and a Web server, but HTTP access fails.

Before troubleshooting at this level, it is important to establish whether IP connectivity exists between the source and the destination. If IP connectivity exists, the issue must be at the application layer.

The following list outlines possible issues:

- A packet filter/firewall issue might have arisen for the specific protocol, data connection, or return traffic.
- The specific service could be down on the server.
- An authentication problem might have occurred on the server for the source or source network.
- There could be a version mismatch or incompatibility with the client and server software.
- The standard application port numbers have been changed.

Figure 7-2 Success with a Ping Does Not Imply Success with Application Layer Protocols

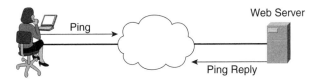

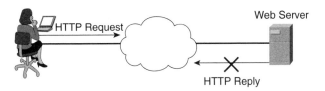

Troubleshooting an upper-layer protocol connectivity problem requires understanding the protocol's process. This information is usually found in the latest Request for Comments (RFC) for the protocol or on the developer Web page. Figure 7-3 shows several protocols and their corresponding OSI layers.

Figure 7-3 Protocols Are Conveniently Associated with Their Corresponding OSI Layers

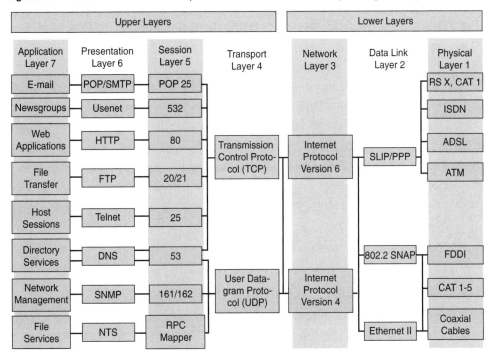

Here are some questions you should answer to make certain that you understand the protocol's functions:

- What IP protocols does the protocol use (TCP, UDP, ICMP, or IGMP)?
- What TCP or UDP port numbers does the protocol use?
- Does the protocol require any inbound TCP connections or inbound UDP packets?
- Does the protocol embed IP addresses in the data portion of the packet?
- Are the protocols being used on a client or a server?

If the protocol embeds IP addresses in the data portion of the packet and NAT has been configured anywhere along the packet's path, the NAT gateway needs to know how to deal with that particular protocol, or the connection will fail. NAT gateways typically change information in the data portion of a packet only when they have been specifically coded to do so. Some examples of protocols that embed IP addresses in the data portion of the packet are FTP, Structured Query Language Network (SQLNet), and Microsoft Windows Internet Name Service (WINS).

If there is a question about whether a firewall or router is interfering with the flow of data for a particular application or protocol, you can take several steps to see exactly what is happening. These steps might not all be possible in every situation.

- Move the client outside the firewall or address translation device.
- Verify whether the client can connect to a server on the same subnet as the client.
- Capture a network trace at the client LAN and on the LAN closest to the server or, preferably, on the server LAN.
- If the service is ASCII-based, Telnet to the port of the service from the router closest to the server, and then work backward into the network toward the client.

Identifying Support Resources

You can resolve some application problems by reading technical documentation at the software vendor or developer's Web site. These sites also have patches and version updates you can download to repair bugs or incompatibilities.

When troubleshooting network problems, network administrators must know where to find information. The following sites can help:

- **Internet Engineering Task Force (IETF)**—http://www.ietf.org
- **International Telecommunication Union (ITU)**—http://www.itu.int/home
- **Frame Relay Forum**—http://www.frforum.com
- **ATM Forum**—http://www.atmforum.com

Here are some other good sources of information:

- Standards organizations
- Technical forums
- Cisco Technical Assistance Center (TAC)
- Discussion groups

Accessing Support Resources

In most cases, you can resolve network problems without receiving outside technical support. However, the solutions to some problems might be elusive, requiring you to seek professional help. This is when you should use the Cisco Systems TAC.

It is suggested that you do the following before calling the TAC:

- Have an up-to-date SMARTnet agreement.
- Have the service contract number ready. The TAC will ask for it.
- Have a diagram of the network or the affected portion of the network. Make sure that it lists all of the IP addresses and associated network masks or prefix lengths.
- List the steps you've already taken and their results for the TAC engineer.
- If the problem appears to be with only a few routers (fewer than four), capture the output from these routers using the **show tech** command.

Dial-in or Telnet access also helps considerably in effective problem resolution.

Correcting Application Layer Problems

To correct application layer problems, follow these steps:

Step 1 Make a backup. Before proceeding, ensure that you have saved a valid configuration for any device on which the configuration might be modified. This will let you recover to a known initial state.

Step 2 Make initial hardware and software configuration changes. If the correction requires more than one change, make only one change at a time.

Step 3 Evaluate and document each change and its results. If the results of any problem-solving steps are unsuccessful, immediately undo the changes. If the problem is intermittent, wait to see if the problem occurs again before evaluating the effect of any change.

Step 4 Verify that the change actually fixed the problem without introducing any new problems. The network should be returned to baseline operation, and no new or old symptoms should be present. If the problem is not solved, undo all the changes. If new or additional problems are discovered, modify the correction plan.

Stop making changes when the original problem appears to be solved.

If necessary, get input from an outside resource. This might be a coworker, a consultant, or the TAC. On rare occasions a core dump might be necessary, which creates output that a specialist at Cisco Systems can analyze.

When the problem is resolved, document the solution.

Gathering Information on Application Layer Problems

To make quick and accurate troubleshooting decisions, a network administrator must be able to get the right information at the right time. This section explores IOS and end-system commands for troubleshooting application layer problems. It also discusses interpreting error messages and using Syslog, protocol analyzers, and network management systems.

Overview

Several tools are available to help in this troubleshooting process. However, the best time to explore and learn about these tools is not when you encounter a problem. The best time is when the network is functioning correctly. This way, you can establish and record network baselines. When problems occur, administrators should refer to the normal baseline to identify inconsistencies more quickly.

In short, an administrator not only must know about the tools, but also must be able to recognize and decipher the pertinent information provided by the various tools.

An administrator should be fluent with all the following tools:

- Command line (UNIX, DOS, Cisco IOS)
- Windows, UNIX, IOS utilities
- Protocol analyzers
- Network management systems
- System logs

The following section highlights some of the tools available and their typical use. It is assumed that you are somewhat proficient with most of these tools.

Lab 7.2.1   Troubleshooting Problems at All Logical Layers

In this lab exercise, you define, isolate, and correct problems to restore the network to baseline specifications. You follow these steps:

- Define the problem by questioning users and using end-system tools.
- Isolate the problem by analyzing documented symptoms and using Cisco tools.
- Consider options for solving the problem.
- Develop a troubleshooting implementation plan for correcting the problems you've identified.
- Execute a troubleshooting implementation plan.
- Verify that the network is restored to baseline specifications and that new problems have not been introduced into the network.

Common TCP/IP Commands

The TCP/IP protocol suite offers several commands to help troubleshoot application layer problems. Most of these commands should be very familiar, whereas others might be new. Take the time to fully understand and appreciate the value of the commands listed in Table 7-3.

Table 7-3 TCP/IP Tools

Tool	Windows Platform	UNIX Platform	Cisco IOS
ping	ping	ping	ping extended ping
traceroute	tracert pathping	traceroute	traceroute extended traceroute
netstat	netstat	netstat	netstat
nslookup	nslookup	nslookup	—

ping is the most frequently used network monitoring and troubleshooting tool. Although it basically tests Layer 3 connectivity, it can be used to help solve application layer problems.

For example, you can use **ping** to identify a DNS application layer problem, as shown in Table 7-4.

Table 7-4 Using **ping**

Step	Specific ping	Description
1	**ping www.cisco.com**	Pings, by name, a remote computer connected to the router. If this works, name resolution is working, and the network is OK.
2	**ping 127.0.0.1**	If Step 1 does not work, ping the loopback adapter (**ping 127.0.0.1**). This should be successful unless TCP/IP is not installed and configured correctly on the local machine.
3	**ping** *myhost*	This step pings the local PC named *myhost*. If this fails, TCP/IP is probably misconfigured or is not installed.
4	**ping** *gateway*	Pings the default gateway. If an error is received, check the TCP/IP configuration. Also check to see if you have the proper gateway for your subnet.
5	**ping** *ip_address*	Pings a computer on the other side of the gateway by IP address (if you know it). If successful, basic connectivity is confirmed. If the ping using the computer's name does not work, name resolution is not working.

If high latency occurs because of congestion, application layer problems might occur because of timeout issues. In a WAN setting, latency between packets should be expected. However, in a LAN setting, excessive latency between packets could indicate network problems. **ping** is an excellent tool for identifying latency issues.

traceroute can be used to pinpoint a network problem. It identifies each intermediate router on the way from Host A to Host B. As shown in Figure 7-4, **traceroute** sends the first packet with a TTL value of 1. The first router decrements it. Because the value drops to 0, the router discards the packet and sends an ICMP Time-to-live Exceeded message back to the sender. **traceroute** then sends a packet with a TTL value of 2, which the first router decrements and routes. But the second router decrements it to 0 and sends back an ICMP error message. Ultimately, the TTL gets high enough for the packet to reach the destination host, and **traceroute** finishes, or some maximum value (usually 30) is reached and **traceroute** ends the trace.

Most **traceroute** programs send a UDP datagram to a randomly selected high UDP port. Microsoft's **tracert** uses an ICMP echo request message (a **ping** packet) instead, which might explain why some trace results do not match those of other users.

Figure 7-4 traceroute Relies on ICMP and the TTL in IP Headers

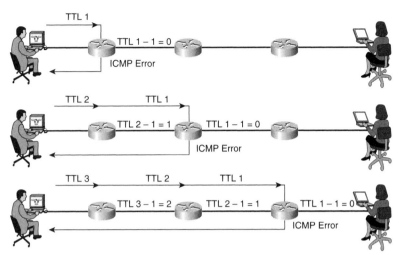

pathping is a Windows NT/2000/XP feature that combines the features of the **ping** and **tracert** commands with additional information-gathering features. The **pathping** command sends packets to each router on the way to a final destination over a period of time and then computes results based on the packets returned from each hop. **pathping** displays the degree of packet loss at any given router or link. This makes it easier to determine which routers or links might be causing network problems.

netstat is used to report on the system's routing table, TCP and UDP protocols, open connections (ports), and the remote system's ports. It gets this networking information by reading the routing tables in the memory, and then it provides an ASCII format at the terminal.

Every machine connected to an IP network has an IP routing table. How this information is displayed depends on the platform. Example 7-1 shows the output of **netstat -n** and **netstat -r** on a Windows platform. (**netstat -r** produces the same output as **route print**.)

Example 7-1 netstat *Is Useful for Viewing the State of TCP and UDP Connections*

```
C:\>netstat -n


Active Connections
  Proto   Local Address         Foreign Address        State
  TCP     192.168.2.33:1600     64.12.24.154:5190      ESTABLISHED
  TCP     192.168.2.33:1066     64.12.200.151:5190     ESTABLISHED
  TCP     192.168.2.33:1270     192.168.2.1:80         CLOSE_WAIT
```

continues

Example 7-1 netstat *Is Useful for Viewing the State of TCP and UDP Connections (Continued)*

```
TCP       192.168.2.33:1344       216.223.88.231:443       ESTABLISHED
TCP       192.168.2.33:2466       192.168.2.1:80           TIME_WAIT


C:\>netstat -r


Route Table
===================================================================
Interface List
0x1 ........................ MS TCP Loopback interface
0x2 ...00 08 74 e2 1a 28 .... 3Com 3c920 Integrated Fast Ethernet Controller
   (3C905C-TX Compatible) - Packet Scheduler Miniport
0x3 ...00 50 f2 7a c5 0e .... Microsoft Broadband Networking Wireless Notebook
   Adapter - Packet Scheduler Miniport
===================================================================

===================================================================
Active Routes:
Network Destination        Netmask          Gateway    Interface  Metric
          0.0.0.0          0.0.0.0      192.168.2.1  192.168.2.33      30
        127.0.0.0        255.0.0.0        127.0.0.1    127.0.0.1       1
      192.168.2.0    255.255.255.0    192.168.2.33  192.168.2.33      30
     192.168.2.33  255.255.255.255        127.0.0.1    127.0.0.1      30
    192.168.2.255  255.255.255.255    192.168.2.33  192.168.2.33      30
        224.0.0.0        224.0.0.0    192.168.2.33  192.168.2.33      30
  255.255.255.255  255.255.255.255    192.168.2.33            2       1
  255.255.255.255  255.255.255.255    192.168.2.33  192.168.2.33       1
Default Gateway:       192.168.2.1
===================================================================
Persistent Routes:
  None
```

Other useful **netstat** commands include **netstat -a**, which displays all connections, and **netstat -e**, which displays Ethernet statistics.

The most useful tool for troubleshooting DNS problems is **nslookup**. It lets a user enter a host name (such as cisco.com) and find out the corresponding IP address. It also does reverse name lookup and finds the host name for a specified IP address.

nslookup sends a domain name query packet to a designated (or default) DNS server. Depending on the system being used, the default might be the local DNS name server at the service provider, some intermediate name server, or the root server system for the entire domain name system hierarchy.

Platform-Specific TCP/IP Utilities

The traffic requirements of various platforms influence how network devices are configured. Table 7-5 shows five situations in which traffic requirements affect router setup.

Table 7-5 General Windows Troubleshooting Considerations

Traffic Requirement	Router Setup
NetBEUI traffic	Transparent bridging or source-route bridging (SRB)
Transparent bridging or SRB	Data-link switching (DLSw) or remote SRB (RSRB)
Novell Type 20 NetBIOS traffic	**ipx type-20-propagation**
A Microsoft WINS server is configured on the segment	Resolves NetBIOS names to IP addresses
UDP encapsulated NetBIOS broadcasts through IP	**ip helper-address** and **ip forward-protocol udp**

TCP/IP troubleshooting combines facts gathered from network devices such as routers and switches and facts gathered from a client or server.

To check the local host configuration on a Windows NT/2000/XP system, open a DOS command window on the host and enter the **ipconfig /all** command, as shown in Figure 7-5. The resulting output displays the TCP/IP address configuration, default gateway, DHCP server, and DNS server addresses. If any IP addresses are incorrect or if no IP address is displayed, determine the correct IP address, and edit it or enter it for the local host.

The Windows NT/2000/XP platform logs most incorrect IP address or subnet mask errors in the Event Viewer. Examine the Event Viewer system log and look for any entry with TCP/IP or DHCP as the source, as shown in Figure 7-6. Read the appropriate entries by double-clicking them, as shown in Figure 7-7. Because DHCP configures TCP/IP remotely, DHCP errors cannot be corrected from the local computer.

Figure 7-5 DNS Servers for a Windows Host Can Be Viewed with the **ipconfig /all** Command

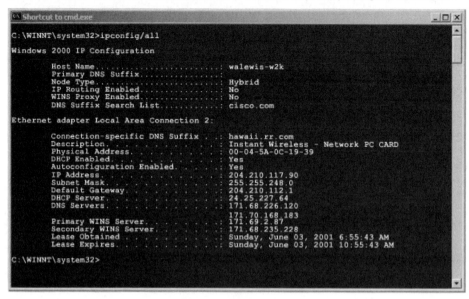

Figure 7-6 Windows 2000 and XP Users Can Use the Event Viewer to View IP Addressing Problems

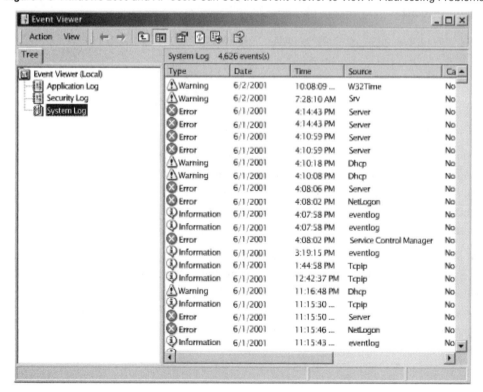

Figure 7-7 Specific Information on Each Event Viewer Entry Is Available

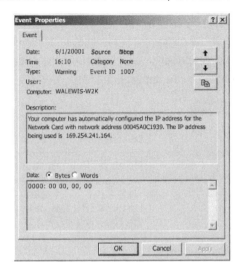

Also check the configurations on the NT/2000/XP server. If a connection using an IP address is possible but it cannot be made using Microsoft networking (for example, Network Neighborhood), try to isolate a problem with the Windows NT/2000/XP server configuration. Problem areas with Microsoft networking relate to NetBIOS support and associated mechanisms used to resolve non-IP entities with IP addresses. Non-IP problems can be checked using the **nbtstat** command, as shown in Figure 7-8.

Figure 7-8 The **nbtstat** Command Displays NetBIOS Information

```
Shortcut to cmd.exe                                                    _ □ x

C:\WINNT\system32>nbtstat -n

Local Area COnnection 2:
Node IpAddress: [204.210.117.90] Scope Id: []

                NetBIOS Local Name Table

       Name              Type           Status
    ---------------------------------------------------
    WALEWIS-W2K      <20>  UNIQUE     Registered
    WALEWIS-W2K      <00>  UNIQUE     Registered
    WALEWIS-W2K      <03>  UNIQUE     Registered
    CISCO_IS         <00>  GROUP      Registered

C:\WINNT\system32>nbtstat  c

Local Area COnnection 2:
Node IpAddress: [204.210.117.90] Scope Id: []

                NetBIOS Remote Cache Name Table

       Name              Type      Host Address    Life [sec]
    ----------------------------------------------------------
    CISCO_IS         <IC>  GROUP        64.102.2.74      467

C:\WINNT\system32>
```

As a last resort, try rebooting the Windows system. Although this practice is not encouraged, it frequently repairs the problem.

Table 7-6 shows some general commands used to isolate application layer problems. Although many of these commands display lower-layer information, the commands are still useful because they highlight problems in the application layer.

Table 7-6 Windows Troubleshooting Commands

Command	Description
winipcfg	Displays IP information for hosts running Windows 9x and Me.
ipconfig /all	Displays IP information for hosts running Windows NT/2000/XP.
pathping {*ip-address* | *domain-name*}	Windows NT/2000/XP route-tracing tool.
nbtstat	Resolves NetBIOS names to IP addresses.
ifconfig -a	Displays IP information for UNIX and Mac OS X hosts.
nslookup {*ip-address* | *domain-name*}	Displays the identity of the name server being used.
cat /etc/resolv.conf	Displays the identity of the name server from hosts running UNIX.

Example 7-2 shows the output of the **ifconfig** command.

Example 7-2 *The* **ifconfig** *UNIX Command Is Used to Configure a Network Interface and to Display the Status of Currently Active Interfaces*

```
Bobweb:~/home#ifconfig
eth0      Link encap:Ethernet  HWaddr 00:05:5D:08:1D:D2
          inet addr:192.168.1.13  Bcast:192.168.1.255  Mask:255.255.255.0
          UP BROADCAST RUNNING MULTICAST  MTU:1500  Metric:1
          RX packets:368357 errors:227 dropped:0 overruns:0 frame:280
          TX packets:472047 errors:0 dropped:0 overruns:0 carrier:0
          collisions:3 txqueuelen:100
          RX bytes:52377780 (49.9 MiB)  TX bytes:87648477 (83.5 MiB)
          Interrupt:10 Base address:0xd000
```

Example 7-2 *The* **ifconfig** *UNIX Command Is Used to Configure a Network Interface and to Display the Status of Currently Active Interfaces (Continued)*

```
lo        Link encap:Local Loopback
          inet addr:127.0.0.1  Mask:255.0.0.0
          UP LOOPBACK RUNNING  MTU:16436  Metric:1
          RX packets:105360 errors:0 dropped:0 overruns:0 frame:0
          TX packets:105360 errors:0 dropped:0 overruns:0 carrier:0
          collisions:0 txqueuelen:0
          RX bytes:11138446 (10.6 MiB)  TX bytes:11138446 (10.6 MiB)

Bobweb:~/home#
```

Cisco IOS Commands

The Cisco IOS software offers powerful commands to help you monitor and troubleshoot network problems. This section describes some of the most common and useful commands.

- The **show** commands help you monitor installation behavior and normal network behavior, as well as isolate problem areas, as shown in Example 7-3.

- The **debug** commands help you isolate protocol and configuration problems, as shown in Example 7-4.

Example 7-3 *IOS* **show** *Commands Are Helpful in Isolating Problems*

```
Router#show ?
  access-expression  List access expression
  access-lists       List access lists
  accounting         Accounting data for active sessions
  adjacency          Adjacent nodes
  aliases            Display alias commands
  alps               Alps information
  appletalk          AppleTalk information
  arap               Show Appletalk Remote Access statistics
  arp                ARP table
  async              Information on terminal lines used as router interfaces
  backup             Backup status
  bridge             Bridge Forwarding/Filtering Database [verbose]
  bsc                BSC interface information
  bstun              BSTUN interface information
```

continues

Example 7-3 *IOS* **show** *Commands Are Helpful in Isolating Problems (Continued)*

```
buffers            Buffer pool statistics
c2600              Show c2600 information
call               Show Calls
cdp                CDP information
cef                Cisco Express Forwarding
class-map          Show QoS Class Map
clock              Display the system clock
cls                DLC user information
compress           Show compression statistics
configuration      Contents of Non-Volatile memory
context            Show context information
controllers        Interface controller status
debugging          State of each debugging option
decnet             DECnet information
dhcp               Dynamic Host Configuration Protocol status
diag               Show diagnostic information for port adapters/modules
dial-peer          Dial Plan Mapping Table for, e.g. VoIP Peers
dialer             Dialer parameters and statistics
dialplan           Voice telephony dial plan
dlsw               Data Link Switching information
dnsix              Shows Dnsix/DMDP information
drip               DRiP DB
dspu               Display DSPU information
dxi                atm-dxi information
entry              Queued terminal entries
environment        Environmental monitor statistics
exception          exception informations
fax                Show calls stored in the history table for fax
file               Show filesystem information
flash:             display information about flash: file system
frame-relay        Frame-Relay information
fras               FRAS Information
fras-host          FRAS Host Information
gateway            Show status of gateway
history            Display the session command history
hosts              IP domain-name, lookup style, nameservers, and host table
```

Example 7-3 *IOS* **show** *Commands Are Helpful in Isolating Problems (Continued)*

```
interfaces       Interface status and configuration
ip               IP information
ipx              Novell IPX information
isdn             ISDN information
key              Key information
line             TTY line information
llc2             IBM LLC2 circuit information
lnm              IBM LAN manager
local-ack        Local Acknowledgement virtual circuits
location         Display the system location
logging          Show the contents of logging buffers
memory           Memory statistics
modemcap         Show Modem Capabilities database
mpoa             MPOA show commands
ncia             Native Client Interface Architecture
netbios-cache    NetBIOS name cache contents
ntp              Network time protocol
num-exp          Number Expansion (Speed Dial) information
pas              Port Adaptor Information
pci              PCI Information
policy-map       Show QoS Policy Map
ppp              PPP parameters and statistics
printers         Show LPD printer information
privilege        Show current privilege level
processes        Active process statistics
protocols        Active network routing protocols
qllc             Display qllc-llc2 and qllc-sdlc conversion information
queue            Show queue contents
queueing         Show queueing configuration
registry         Function registry information
reload           Scheduled reload information
rhosts           Remote-host+user equivalences
rif              RIF cache entries
rmon             rmon statistics
route-map        route-map information
```

continues

Example 7-3 *IOS* **show** *Commands Are Helpful in Isolating Problems (Continued)*

```
rtpspi                RTP Service Provider Interface
rtr                   Response Time Reporter (RTR)
running-config        Current operating configuration
sdllc                 Display sdlc - llc2 conversion information
sessions              Information about Telnet connections
sgbp                  SGBP group information
smds                  SMDS information
smf                   Software MAC filter
smrp                  Simple Multicast Routing Protocol (SMRP) information
sna                   Display SNA host information
snapshot              Snapshot parameters and statistics
snmp                  snmp statistics
source-bridge         Source-bridge parameters and statistics
spanning-tree         Spanning tree topology
sscop                 SSCOP
stacks                Process stack utilization
standby               Hot standby protocol information
startup-config        Contents of startup configuration
stun                  STUN status and configuration
subscriber-policy     Subscriber policy
subsys                Show subsystem information
tacacs                Shows tacacs+ server statistics
tcp                   Status of TCP connections
tech-support          Show system information for Tech-Support
terminal              Display terminal configuration parameters
time-range            Time range
traffic-shape         traffic rate shaping configuration
users                 Display information about terminal lines
version               System hardware and software status
vlans                 Virtual LANs Information
voice                 Voice port configuration & stats
vpdn                  VPDN information
whoami                Info on current tty line
x25                   X.25 information
x29                   X.29 information
```

Example 7-4 *IOS* **debug** *Commands Are Used When* **show** *Commands Are Insufficient for Isolating Problems*

```
Router#debug ?
  aaa                AAA Authentication, Authorization and Accounting
  access-expression  Boolean access expression
  adjacency          adjacency
  all                Enable all debugging
  alps               ALPS debug information
  apple              Appletalk information
  arap               Appletalk Remote Access
  arp                IP ARP and HP Probe transactions
  aspp               ASPP information
  async              Async interface information
  backup             Backup events
  bri-interface      bri network interface events
  bsc                BSC information
  bstun              BSTUN information
  callback           Callback activity
  ccfrf11            CCFRF11 information
  cch323             CCH323 information
  ccswvoice          ccswvoice information
  cdp                CDP information
  chat               Chat scripts activity
  cls                CLS Information
  compress           COMPRESS traffic
  condition          Condition
  confmodem          Modem configuration database
  cpp                Cpp information
  custom-queue       Custom output queueing
  decnet             DECnet information
  dhcp               DHCP client activity
  dialer             Dial on Demand
  dlsw               Data Link Switching (DLSw) events
  dnsix              Dnsix information
  domain             Domain Name System
  drip               DRiP debug information
  dspu               DSPU Information
```

continues

Example 7-4 *IOS* **debug** *Commands Are Used When* **show** *Commands Are Insufficient for Isolating Problems (Continued)*

```
dxi                   atm-dxi information
eigrp                 EIGRP Protocol information
entry                 Incoming queue entries
ethernet-interface    Ethernet network interface events
fastethernet          Fast Ethernet interface information
frame-relay           Frame Relay
fras                  FRAS Debug
fras-host             FRAS Host Debug
h225                  H.225 Library Debugging
h245                  H.245 Library Debugging
interface             interface
ip                    IP information
ipx                   Novell/IPX information
isdn                  ISDN information
lane                  LAN Emulation
lapb                  LAPB protocol transactions
lex                   LAN Extender protocol
list                  Set interface or/and access list for the next debug command
llc2                  LLC2 type II Information
lnm                   Lan Network Manager information
lnx                   generic qllc/llc2 conversion activity
local-ack             Local ACKnowledgement information
modem                 Modem control/process activation
mop                   DECnet MOP server events
mpoa                  MPOA debug options
ncia                  Native Client Interface Architecture (NCIA) events
netbios-name-cache    NetBIOS name cache tracing
nhrp                  NHRP protocol
ntp                   NTP information
nvram                 Debug NVRAM behavior
packet                Log unknown packets
pad                   X25 PAD protocol
ppp                   PPP (Point to Point Protocol) information
printer               LPD printer protocol
priority              Priority output queueing
probe                 HP Probe Proxy Requests
```

Example 7-4 *IOS* **debug** *Commands Are Used When* **show** *Commands Are Insufficient for Isolating*
            Problems (Continued)

```
qllc              qllc debug information
radius            RADIUS protocol
ras               H.323 RAS Library
rif               RIF cache transactions
rtpspi            RTP Service Provider Interface.
rtr               RTR Monitor Information
sdlc              SDLC information
sdllc             SDLLC media translation
serial            Serial interface information
sgbp              SGBP debugging
smf               Software MAC filter
smrp              SMRP information
sna               SNA Information
snapshot          Snapshot activity
snmp              SNMP information
source            Source bridging information
spantree          Spanning tree information
sscop             SSCOP
standby           Hot standby protocol
stun              STUN information
tacacs            TACACS authentication and authorization
tbridge           Transparent Bridging
telnet            Incoming telnet connections
tftp              TFTP debugging
token             Token Ring information
tunnel            Generic Tunnel Interface
udptn             UDPtn async data transport
v120              V120 information
vlan              vLAN information
voip              RTP information
voip              VOIP  information
voip              VOIP information
voip              VOIP ivr information
vpdn              VPDN information
vpm               Voice Port Module SPI information
```

continues

Example 7-4 *IOS* **debug** *Commands Are Used When* **show** *Commands Are Insufficient for Isolating Problems (Continued)*

vprofile	Virtual Profile information
vtemplate	Virtual Template information
vtsp	Voice Telephony Call Control information
x25	X.25, CMNS and XOT information
x28	X28 mode

The router **show** commands are among the most important tools for understanding a router's status, detecting neighboring routers, monitoring the network in general, and isolating problems in the network.

These commands are essential in almost any troubleshooting and monitoring situation. Use **show** commands for the following activities:

- Monitoring router behavior during initial installation
- Monitoring normal network operation
- Isolating problem interfaces, nodes, media, or applications
- Determining when a network is congested
- Determining the status of servers, clients, or other neighbors

The **debug** EXEC commands can provide a wealth of information about the traffic being seen (or not seen) on an interface, error messages generated by nodes on the network, protocol-specific diagnostic packets, and other useful troubleshooting data. Be conservative with **debug** commands, because they often generate quite a bit of extraneous data.

Use **debug** commands to isolate problems, not to monitor normal network operation. Use **debug** commands to look for specific types of traffic or problems after you narrow the problem to a likely subset of causes.

Table 7-7 shows examples of IOS troubleshooting commands.

Table 7-7 IOS Troubleshooting Commands

Command	Description
show stack	Shows stack dump information for the last crash.
show log	Shows the log information for the current run of the software if logging is buffered. You need to configure logging of router information. It is not set up by default.
show tech-support	Shows all the information that Cisco technical support needs.

System Logs

Logging lets the router or switch keep track of events that occur. Logging can help you find trends, system error messages, outages, and a variety of other network events.

How you choose to implement system logging and manage logging data might affect your ability to manage your networks and effectively troubleshoot problems. Take the time to develop a logging strategy that will provide reliable data when required.

Monitoring activity in the log files is an important aspect of network management that should be conducted regularly. Monitoring the log files allows you to carry out appropriate and timely action when you detect problems, such as breaches of security or events that are likely to lead to a potential security breach.

The logging facility does the following:

- It provides logging information for monitoring and troubleshooting.
- It lets you select the types of logging information captured.
- It lets you select the destination of captured logging information.

Several types of events can be monitored, as shown in Figure 7-9. Messages are classified in terms of severity. Level 0 is the highest level (most severe), and level 7 is the lowest (least severe). System messages can be saved based on the type of facility and the severity level.

Figure 7-9 Syslog Error Message Levels Determine the Type of Logging Output

Highest Level

Level	Keyword	Description	Syslog Definition
0	emergencies	System Is Unusable.	LOG_EMERG
1	alerts	Immediate Action Is Needed.	LOG_ALERT
2	critical	Critical Conditions Exist.	LOG_CRIT
3	errors	Error Conditons Exist.	LOG_ERR
4	warnings	Warning Conditions Exist.	LOG_WARNING
5	notification	Normal but Significant Condition.	LOG_NOTICE
6	informational	Informational Messages Only.	LOG_INFO
7	debugging	Debugging Messages.	LOG_DEBUG

Lowest Level

Syslog messages can be categorized as follows:

- Warning, errors, critical, alerts, and emergencies are error-level messages generated by software or hardware malfunctions.
- Notification-level messages are generated by interface up/down transitions and system restart messages.

- Informational-level messages are generated by reload requests and low-process stack messages.

- Debugging-level messages are generated by output from the **debug** commands.

Which event an administrator decides to capture depends largely on the information he or she is seeking. For example, logs can be invaluable in characterizing and responding to security incidents. To do so, the most important events to log include change of interface status, changes to the system configuration, access list matches, and events detected by the optional firewall and intrusion detection features.

The logging facility can also be configured to send captured logging information to select destinations. By default, switches and routers normally log significant system messages to their internal buffer and the system console.

The four destinations to which Syslog messages can be forwarded are described in Figure 7-10:

- Console terminal
- Virtual terminals
- Syslog server
- Internal buffer

Figure 7-10 Different Types of Logging Require Different Amounts of System Overhead

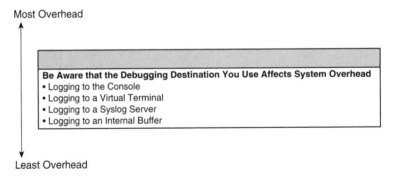

Be aware that the debugging destination that is used affects system overhead. Logging to the console produces very high overhead, whereas logging to a virtual terminal produces less overhead. Logging to a Syslog server produces even less, and logging to an internal buffer produces the least overhead of any method.

Time, specifically the time stamp, is a valuable piece of information used to determine when a problem arose. The idea is that many network problems can often be correlated to system configuration changes, modifications to the network topology (both intentional and unintentional), and so on. For this reason, Syslog messages should be time-stamped to enhance real-time debugging and management, as shown in Example 7-5.

Example 7-5 *The* **service timestamps debug datetime** *Command Causes All Debug Output to Be Timestamped*

```
Router(config)#service timestamps debug ?
  datetime  Timestamp with the date and time
  uptime    Timestamp with the system uptime
  <cr>


Router(config)#service timestamps debug datetime
Router#
*Mar 19 19:30:33: RIP: sending V1 update to 255.255.255.255
via Loopback0 (192.168.1.1)
*Mar 19 19:30:33: RIP: build update entries - suppressing null update
```

Syslog Destinations

Message logging is enabled by default. However, it could have been disabled with the **no logging on** command.

To enable message logging to all supported destinations other than the console (the default), enter the following:

```
Router(config)#logging on
```

The logging process controls the distribution of logging messages to the various destinations, such as the logging buffer, terminal lines, and Syslog server. To turn logging on and off for these destinations individually, use the **logging buffered**, **logging monitor**, and **logging** global configuration commands, as shown in Figure 7-11.

If the **no logging on** command has been configured, no messages are sent to these destinations. Only the console receives messages.

However, disabling the **logging on** command substantially slows down the router. Any process that is generating debug or error messages waits until the messages have been displayed on the console before continuing.

Additionally, the logging process logs messages to the console and the various destinations after the processes that generated them have completed. When the logging process is disabled, messages are displayed on the console as soon as they are produced, often appearing in the middle of command output.

The **logging synchronous** line configuration command also affects the display of messages to the console. When it is configured, messages appear only after the user presses Enter.

Figure 7-11 The **logging on** Command Is a Default Setting

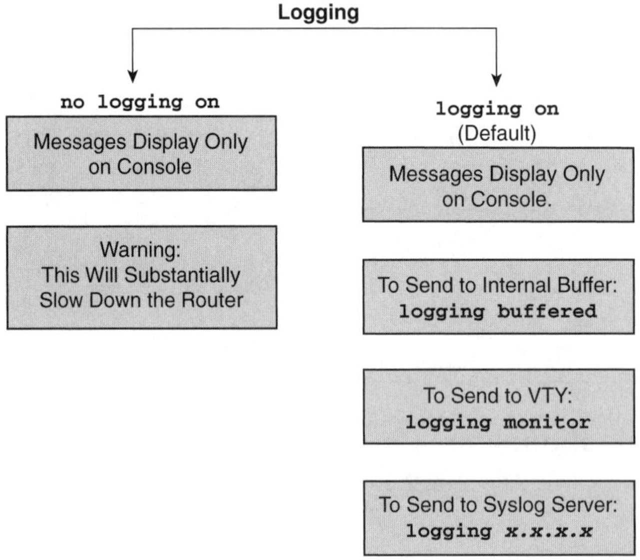

Logging

no logging on

| Messages Display Only on Console |

| Warning: This Will Substantially Slow Down the Router |

logging on (Default)

| Messages Display Only on Console. |

| To Send to Internal Buffer: **logging buffered** |

| To Send to VTY: **logging monitor** |

| To Send to Syslog Server: **logging x.x.x.x** |

Different logging levels and corresponding keywords can be used when setting logging levels. The highest-level message is Level 0, emergencies. The lowest level is 7, debugging, which also displays the largest number of messages.

To limit the types of messages that are logged to the console, use the **logging console** command:

```
Router(config)#logging console level
```

The **logging console** command limits the logging of messages displayed on the console terminal to the specified level and (numerically) lower levels. You can enter the level number or level name. For example, the following set the console logging to the warnings level:

```
Router(config)#logging console warnings
```

or

```
Router(config)#logging console 4
```

These lines display all warnings (4), as well as error (3), critical (2), alert (1), and emergency (0) messages.

The **no logging console** command disables logging to the console terminal.

To log messages to an internal buffer, use the **logging buffered** router configuration command:

```
Router(config)#logging buffered
```

The **logging buffered** command, shown in Example 7-6, copies logging messages to an internal buffer instead of writing them to the console terminal. The buffer is circular in nature. Therefore, newer messages overwrite older ones.

Example 7-6 *The* **logging buffered** *Command Copies Messages to an Internal Buffer*

```
Router(config)#logging buffered debugging
Router(config)#exit
Router#debug ip rip
RIP protocol debugging is on
Router#show logging
Syslog logging: enbabled (1 message dropped, 0 flushes, 0 overruns)
   Console logging: disabled
   Monitor logging: level debugging, 0 messages logged
   Buffer logging: level debugging, 7 messages logged
   Trap logging: level informational, 26 message lines logged


Log Buffer (4096 bytes):

2w4d: %SYS-5-CONFIG_I: Configured from console by console
*Mar 19 20:29:03: RIP: sending V1 update to 255.255.255.255
via Loopback0 (192.168.1.1)
*Mar 19 20:29:03: RIP: build update entries - suppressing null update
*Mar 19 20:29:29: RIP: sending V1 update to 255.255.255.255
via Loopback0 (192.168.1.1)
*Mar 19 20:29:03: RIP: build update entries - suppressing null update
```

To limit the types of messages that are logged to the buffer, use the **logging buffered** *level* command:

```
Router(config)#logging buffered level
```

The *level* argument is one of the keywords listed in Figure 7-9. To display the messages that are logged in the buffer, use the privileged EXEC command **show logging**. Use the **clear logging** command to reset the logging buffer. The **no logging buffered** command cancels the use of the buffer and writes messages to the console terminal (the default).

To log messages logged to the terminal lines (VTY), use the **logging monitor** router configuration command:

```
Router(config)#logging monitor level
```

The **logging monitor** command limits the logging messages displayed on terminal lines other than the console line to messages with a level up to and including the specified *level* argument. The *level* argument is one of the keywords listed in Figure 7-9.

To display logging messages on a terminal (virtual console), use the privileged EXEC command **terminal monitor**.

Messages can also be logged to a Syslog server. The host is required to run a Syslog server application such as UNIX Syslog server (native in most UNIX implementations) or Kiwi Syslog Daemon (Windows 9x, Me, XP, NT 4, and 2000). Commands to set up a UNIX Syslog server are covered later in this chapter.

To log messages to the Syslog server host, use the **logging** *ip-address* configuration command:

```
Router(config)#logging ip-address
```

The **logging** command identifies a Syslog server host to receive logging messages. The *ip-address* argument is the host's IP address. By issuing this command more than once, you create a list of Syslog servers to receive logging messages.

The **no logging** command deletes the Syslog server with the specified address from the list of Syslogs.

To limit the number of messages sent to the Syslog servers, use the **logging trap** router configuration command:

```
Router(config)#logging trap level
```

The **logging trap** command limits the logging messages sent to Syslog servers to messages with a level up to and including the specified *level* argument. The *level* argument is one of the keywords listed in Figure 7-9. The default trap level is **informational**. The **no logging trap** command disables logging to Syslog servers.

Deciphering Syslog Messages

All messages begin with a percent sign and are displayed in the following format:

```
%FACILITY-SEVERITY-MNEMONIC: Message-text
```

FACILITY is a code, consisting of two to five uppercase letters, indicating the facility to which the message refers. A facility might be a hardware device, a protocol, or a module of the system software, as shown in Table 7-8. The IOS has more than 500 service identifiers.

Table 7-8 FACILITY Codes

Code	Facility
AT	AppleTalk
BGP	Border Gateway Protocol
EGP	Exterior Gateway Protocol
HELLO	HELLO Protocol
IGRP	Interior Gateway Routing Protocol
IP	Internet Protocol
IPRT	IP Routing
TCP	Transmission Control Protocol

SEVERITY is a single-digit code from 0 to 7 that reflects the condition's severity. A lower number indicates a more serious situation, as shown in Table 7-9. *MNEMONIC* is a code consisting of uppercase letters that uniquely identify the message.

Table 7-9 Severity Levels

Level	Description
0	The system is unusable.
1	Immediate action is needed.
2	Critical conditions exist.
3	Error conditions exist.
4	Warning conditions exist.
5	A normal but significant condition.
6	Informational messages only.
7	Debugging messages.

Message-text is a text string describing the condition. This portion of the message sometimes contains detailed information about the event being reported, including terminal port numbers, network addresses, or addresses that correspond to locations in the system memory address space. Because the information in these variable fields changes from message to message (see Table 7-10), it is represented here by short strings enclosed in square brackets ([ ]). For example, a decimal number is represented as [dec].

Table 7-10 Variable Fields

Representation	Type of Information
[dec]	Decimal number
[hex]	Hexadecimal number
[char]	Single character
[chars]	Character string
[enet]	Ethernet address (such as 0000.DEAD.00C0)
[inet]	Internet address (such as 12.128.2.16)
[t-line]	Terminal line number in octal (or decimal if the decimal-tty service is enabled)

Here's a sample error message:

```
%HELLO-2-NORDB: Redistributed IGRP without rdb
```

In this message, **HELLO** is the facility, **2** is the severity, and **NORDB** is the mnemonic. This message indicates that an internal software error has occurred and that technical support should be contacted for assistance.

Here's another error message:

```
%IP-4-DUPADDR Duplicate address [inet] on [chars], sourced by [enet]
```

This indicates that another system on the network segment is using this IP address and that the IP address on one of the two systems should be changed.

If one or more error messages reoccur after the recommended action has been taken, contact Cisco or a local field service organization.

Protocol Analyzers

Network management involves using network and protocol analysis tools to establish a network system baseline and to monitor and optimize performance. Figure 7-12 shows some of these tools and the corresponding OSI layers at which they work.

Figure 7-12 Protocol Analyzers Work at Layers 2 to 7

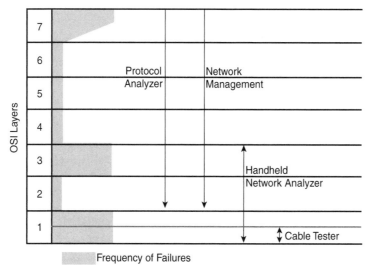

NOTE

Some devices come equipped with traffic monitoring capabilities. For example, the Cisco Catalyst 6500 series switch can be equipped with a Network Analysis Module (NAM). The NAM is an integrated and powerful traffic monitoring system. It comes with an embedded Web-based traffic analyzer that provides full-scale remote monitoring and troubleshooting capabilities accessible through a Web browser.

Protocol analyzers are almost always software-based. They are used to gather information about traffic flows and are very useful for establishing a network baseline. Although they do not decode the contents of frames, protocol analyzers are often used to solve Layer 2 and higher problems.

They can be used to assist in locating traffic overloads, planning for network expansion, detecting intruders, establishing baseline performance, and distributing traffic more efficiently.

Using these tools effectively is not easy. Administrators must be able to decipher and interpret the information generated.

Examples of protocol analyzers include Fluke's Protocol Inspector and Sniffer Pro Protocol Analyzer.

Network Management Systems

Network management systems (NMSs) are always software-based tools. They continually monitor the network. There are various types of NMSs, and not all are equal. Some are better at status monitoring and fault management tracking, and others are better at service-level reporting. The choice is sometimes confusing because features overlap.

NMS functions can be categorized into three main categories:

- Operations management
- Device management
- Service management

Operations management tools are used for active monitoring of day-to-day network administration. The software provides features such as network topology discovery, status monitoring, fault management, and basic real-time performance data. Major vendors include HP OpenView (the current market leader), Computer Associates, and IBM Tivoli.

Device management tools are typically vendor-specific. They are used to manage a vendor's network components to make configuration changes to network devices and to apply rules and policies. Most provide graphical tools to interact with actual devices. Examples of device management tools include Cisco Systems' CiscoWorks (Cisco), Navis iEngineer (Lucent), HP OpenView, and Optivity (Nortel).

Service management tools focus on quality of service (QoS) and service-level guarantee issues. They collect performance data over time that is then used to establish a baseline, trend analysis, historical usage analysis, and service-level reporting. The tools focus on comparing the expected quality of network resources with actual results. Major vendors include HP, Lucent, and NetScout Systems.

Network management tools use SNMP to capture and communicate device data. NMS periodically polls the devices it manages, sending queries about their current status. The monitored devices respond by transmitting the requested data and by sending traps (called *notifications* in SNMPv2).

A *trap* is an unsolicited message to the NMS, generated when a monitored parameter reaches unacceptable levels. For example, an environmental monitoring device might send a trap when the temperature level is too low or too high. Traps are useful because they provide a method for a device to signal that something unexpected has occurred.

In SNMP, the term *manager* refers both to the monitoring software running on the NMS and the actual device running the software. Similarly, the term *agent* refers to the device being monitored and to the software used by the monitored devices to generate and transmit their status data.

SNMP is a client/server protocol that normally communicates on TCP and UDP ports 161. SNMP traps use TCP and UDP ports 162. Some vendors use nonstandard ports for traps. (For example, Cisco uses TCP and UDP ports 1993.)

Troubleshooting TCP/IP Application Layer Protocols

Application layer protocols can be very difficult to isolate. Test and eliminate any problems in the lower layers before attempting to isolate upper-layer problems.

This section focuses on how to isolate the following problems with various application layer protocols:

- Telnet
- HTTP
- SMTP, POP, and IMAP
- FTP and TFTP
- DNS
- SNMP
- NTP
- DHCP

Overview

Client/server systems, terminal and consoles, Web traffic, e-mail, file transfer, SNMP and NTP, DNS, and DHCP are the TCP/IP application protocols discussed in this section. Each of these TCP/IP application protocols is explored, addressing the common issues associated with them.

Client/Server Systems

A client/server model is a network architecture in which a computer (client) requests access to services offered on another remote host (server), as shown in Figure 7-13. The model provides a convenient way to remotely interconnect programs located in different locations. Computer transactions using the client/server model are very common.

Figure 7-13 The Client/Server Model Is Illustrated Every Day by Internet Users Connecting to Web Servers

Clients are PCs or workstations on which users run applications. Clients rely on servers for resources, such as files, devices, and even processing power.

A client is defined as a requester of services, and a server is defined as a provider of services. A single machine can be both a client and a server, depending on the software configuration.

Servers are powerful computers dedicated to managing disk drives (file servers), printers (print servers), or network traffic (network servers). A server receives a request and, after any necessary processing, the requested file is returned to the client. Typically, multiple client programs share the services of a common server.

Terminals and Consoles

Telnet is the standard terminal emulation protocol in the TCP/IP protocol stack. Telnet is defined in RFC 854 and operates over TCP port 23. Telnet and FTP were the first two services available on ARPANET.

To understand how Telnet works, first you must understand the difference between a console and a terminal. A console is a keyboard and monitor that are directly connected to the computer system. In mainframe computing, a console was also called a dumb terminal because it operated only by using the resources of the remote server. A microcomputer is now more commonly used as a console.

All consoles require a terminal connection to enable users to log in to remote systems and use resources (such as CPU, applications, and storage) as if they were connected to a local system. A terminal is a console that artificially emulates the console's physical hookup. The destination host assumes it has a direct connection to the client because the terminal just provides a communication channel for the user's input and output. A terminal program is commonly used to connect to a central server over the network.

The term *terminal emulator* refers to a terminal application that is implemented in software. Clients can use the Telnet program to establish a terminal connection. Other software such as HyperTerminal or TeraTerm can also be used. They typically offer more advanced features.

Network administrators often overlook Telnet as a troubleshooting tool. However, Telnetting to a host allows better verification of network status than just using ping. Telnet runs on top of the TCP protocol, so it establishes a more reliable indication of accessibility than ICMP echo requests can. It also tests higher-level functions of the destination host system. A server might be inaccessible for application layer functions, but it still answers pings because those are handled by the lower-layer protocols.

Telnet also has an additional feature that makes it valuable for troubleshooting application layer protocols. Telnet client applications allow the user to select the destination port number to be used. You can use this feature to connect to other TCP ports on destination hosts to test other functions. This means that Telnet can contact network application programs other than a Telnet server. This can be useful as a substitute for a client application program.

For example, Telnetting to port 25 (SMTP) verifies that the e-mail server is answering. You Telnet to port 80 (HTTP) to verify that the Web server is answering.

Finally, a useful IOS command to use when testing an access list is **ip telnet source-interface**. This specifies the IP address of an interface as the source address for Telnet connections. To reset the source address to the default for each connection, use the **no** form of this command.

By default, Telnet uses the IP address of the closest interface to the destination as the source address. However, sometimes another interface might be preferred as the source. Conceptually, this is similar to specifying another source IP address when using an extended **ping** command.

The following example forces the IP address for FastEthernet interface 0/1 as the source address for Telnet connections:

```
Router(config)#ip telnet source-interface FastEthernet 0/1
```

Table 7-11 shows a couple of IOS commands used to isolate Telnet problems.

Table 7-11 Troubleshooting Telnet with IOS

Command	Description
telnet {*ip-address* | *hostname*}	Tests the functionality of the Telnet application.
debug telnet	Displays events during the negotiation process of a Telnet connection.

Web Traffic

HTTP is the protocol used to transfer the files that make up Web pages. Although the HTTP specification allows data to be transferred on port 80 using either TCP or UDP, most implementations use TCP.

HTTPS is a secure version of the HTTP protocol. Aside from the initial connection and setup, HTTPS and HTTP are basically the same. The difference lies in the initial setup between client and server. HTTPS uses the Secure Socket Layer (SSL) protocol. SSL was created to secure credit card purchases over the Internet. It requires that both sides of a connection be authenticated and that data be encrypted and decrypted. It uses port 443 to initiate a secure connection.

HTTP connectivity can be tested using any Telnet application that allows a port number to be specified by Telnetting to the IP address of the destination server using port 80.

- If the connection failed, a message states that the Telnet application could not open a connection to the host on port 80.

NOTE

By default, characters are not echoed in Microsoft Telnet upon successful connection to a Web server unless local echo is enabled in the preferences

- If the connection was successful, a hello message might be displayed or a Telnet window opens, but there will be no response. This indicates HTTP connectivity to the server. To have the Web server respond, enter **GET / HTTP/1.0** and press the Enter key twice.

Electronic Mail

SMTP is used to transport e-mail messages in ASCII format using TCP between clients and servers. Other protocols such as POP and IMAP are used to retrieve e-mails from mail servers.

For example, assume that User-A wants to send e-mail to User-B. When User-A clicks the Send button, e-mail is sent to the local e-mail server using the SMTP protocol. The e-mail server then sends the e-mail using SMTP to User-B's e-mail server. It remains stored there until User-B collects it. Later, User-B connects to the local e-mail server and downloads the e-mail using either POP3 or IMAP4. This process is illustrated in Figure 7-14.

Figure 7-14 E-mail Is Commonly Sent with SMTP and Is Received Using POP3

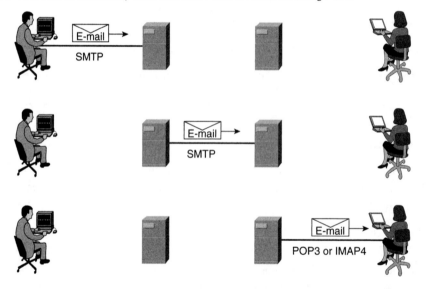

POP3 is the current version of the protocol. It is incompatible with earlier versions. POP3 downloads user e-mails to the local computer. For this reason, POP3 is best suited in situations in which users retrieve their e-mail from the same computer. If users use different computers, their e-mails likely will be spread around several computers.

IMAP4 is another alternative that lets users download their e-mail at any time to any computer.

Because these different protocols are used to send and receive mail, it is possible that mail clients can perform one task but not the other. Therefore, when verifying the configuration of a mail client, both the mail relay (SMTP) server and mail (POP or IMAP) servers should be verified.

SMTP, IMAP, and POP connectivity can be tested using any Telnet application that allows a port number to be specified. Telnet to the IP address of the destination server using ports 25, 143, and 110, respectively.

The commands shown in Table 7-12 can be used to isolate application layer problems related to e-mail and the POP3, SMTP, and IMAP protocols.

Table 7-12 Commands That Isolate E-Mail Problems

Command	Description
telnet {*ip-address* | *host*} **25**	Tests SMTP protocol functionality.
telnet {*ip-address* | *host*} **110**	Tests POP protocol functionality.
telnet {*ip-address* | *host*} **143**	Tests IMAP protocol functionality.

If there is a problem with the receiving system, the user should see a text error message. If the connection was successful, a hello message appears, or an unresponsive Telnet window opens. This indicates connectivity to the server. At this point, the user can use POP3 or SMTP text-based commands to perform basic e-mail procedures such as authenticating, reading, deleting, or sending messages. For example, basic POP commands include **user**, **pass**, **stat**, **list**, **top**, **uidl**, **retr**, **dele**, **noop**, **rset**, and **quit**.

File Transfer

FTP is used to upload and download files between remote computer systems on a network. Servers run FTP services or FTP daemons, and clients connect by way of the TCP/IP FTP client command-line interface or with a third-party commercial program that offers a graphical user interface (such as WS_FTP Pro, UNIX NcFTP Client, or Linux IglooFTP PRO). A Web browser can also make FTP requests to download programs selected from a Web page.

FTP uses two or more TCP connections to accomplish data transfers. To start a session, the FTP client opens a TCP connection to port 21 on the FTP server. This connection, called the control connection, is used to pass commands and results between the client and the server. No data, such as file transfers or directory listings, is passed over the control connection. Instead, data is transferred over a separate TCP connection called the data connection.

This data connection can be opened in several different ways:

- **Traditional (or active)**—The FTP server opens a TCP connection back to the client's port 20. This method doesn't work on a multiuser system because many users might make simultaneous FTP requests, and the system can't match incoming FTP data connections to the appropriate user.

- **Multiuser traditional (or active)**—The FTP client instructs the FTP server to open a connection on a random port in the range 1024 to 65,535. This method creates a rather large security hole because it requires system administrators to permit inbound TCP connections to all ports greater than 1023. Although firewalls that monitor FTP traffic and dynamically allow inbound connections help close this security hole, many corporate networks do not permit this type of traffic. Most command-line FTP clients default to this method of transfer and offer a passive command (or something similar) to switch to passive mode.

- **Passive mode**—The FTP client instructs the FTP server that it wants a passive connection, and the server replies with an IP address and port number to which the FTP client can open a TCP data connection. This method is by far the most secure, because it requires no inbound TCP connections to the FTP client. Many corporate networks permit only this type of FTP transfer. Most Web browsers default to this method of FTP transfer.

Consider a typical FTP connection process that connects to an FTP server and downloads a file called README, as shown in Example 7-7. After logging in to an FTP server, the user could enter **help** to get a listing of acceptable commands. Some of the more popular FTP commands are **ascii**, **binary**, **cd**, **dir**, **get**, **help**, **ls**, **mkdir**, **put**, **pwd**, and **quit**.

Example 7-7 *Command-Line FTP Preceded All the GUI-Based FTP Utilities Commonly Used Today*

```
C:\>ftp ftp.cisco.com

Connected to ftp.cisco.com.

User (ftp.cisco.com:(none)): myname

331 Password required for myname

Password: ********

230 User myname logged in
```

Example 7-7 *Command-Line FTP Preceded All the GUI-Based FTP Utilities Commonly Used Today (Continued)*

```
ftp>ls

200 PORT: Command successful

150 Opening ASCII mode data connection for file list

.

..

README

226 Transfer complete.

ftp: 47 bytes received in 0.00Seconds
47000.00Kbytes/sec.



ftp>get README

200 PORT: Command successful

150 Opening ASCII mode data connection for README

226 Transfer complete.

ftp: 2278 bytes received in 0.01Seconds
227.80Kbytes/sec.



ftp>quit

221 Goodbye.
```

An FTP connection can be tested using any Telnet application that allows a port number to be specified. Telnet to the IP address of the destination server using port 21. If the connection is successful, a hello message is displayed, or an unresponsive Telnet window opens. This indicates connectivity to the server. At this point you might want to enter **help** to see which commands are available. Because the connection to the FTP server is by way of Telnet, the choice of commands varies.

In some instances, a router can be configured to act as an FTP server. FTP clients can copy files to and from certain directories on the router. For example, the FTP server allows retrieval of files, such as Syslog files, from the disk file system on the router.

When the router receives a request for an FTP connection, the FTP Server process is started. At this point, the user typically is prompted for a username and password. After supplying a valid username and password, the user can enter various commands.

TFTP is a simplified version of FTP. Unlike FTP, which uses the TCP transport protocol, TFTP operates over port 69 and uses UDP. UDP makes TFTP faster at uploading and downloading files.

A client can only read or write a file to a TFTP server. Unlike FTP, TFTP does not support directory browsing, file renaming, logging in, or statistics. For this reason, a user must know the filename of the file he or she wants to download.

A common TFTP application is to back up and restore router configuration files and IOS images.

The commands shown in Table 7-13 display information about files with FTP and TFTP. A troubleshooter uses the information from these commands to isolate problems at the application layer that are related to the FTP and TFTP protocols.

Table 7-13 TFTP Troubleshooting

Command	Description
copy tftp	Tests functionality by invoking the TFTP application.
telnet {*ip-address*	*host*} **21**	Tests FTP protocol functionality.
debug tftp	Displays activity related to the operation of TFTP.

Network Management and Time Protocols

Logging time is very important in determining when a problem started. Most network problems can be narrowed down to a configuration change or modifications to the network topology. A synchronized time lets you correlate Syslog and Cisco IOS debug output to specific events. Although the primary goal of problem resolution is to fix the problem, it is also quite helpful to know when the problem originated so that the problem can be resolved and avoided in the future.

NTP synchronizes timekeeping among a set of distributed time servers and clients. This synchronization allows events to be correlated when system logs are created and other time-specific events occur. For timestamps to be of use, it is a good idea for all the routers and switches in the network to derive time from a common network time source.

Configuring time services on routers requires EXEC and configuration commands, as shown in Example 7-8. To configure the time zone properties on the router, the configuration commands **clock timezone** and **clock summer-time** are used. The commands **ntp server** *ip-addr* and **ntp source** *interface* define the NTP server(s) and the source IP address of the NTP requests.

Example 7-8 *Configuring NTP Makes It Easy to Synchronize the Clocks on the Devices in a Network*

```
Configuring NTP Settings:


Router(config)#clock timezone EST -5
Router(config)#clock summer-time EDT recurring
Router(config)#ntp server 192.168.1.10
Router(config)#ntp source loopback 0


Configuring the system clock:


Router#clock set 11:15:05 11 March 2004
```

The router's internal clock is set using the EXEC command **clock set**. To view NTP peer status information, use the **show ntp associations** and **show ntp status** commands.

SNMP is an application-layer protocol that facilitates the exchange of management information between network devices. It is part of the TCP/IP protocol suite.

Although troubleshooting is necessary to recover from problems, the network administrator's ultimate goal is to avoid problems. That is also the goal of network management software. The network management software used on TCP/IP networks is based on SNMP.

SNMP is a client/server protocol. In SNMP terminology, it is described as a manager/agent protocol. The agent (the server) runs on the device being managed, which is called the managed network entity. The agent monitors the status of the device and reports that status to the manager.

The manager (the client) runs on the NMS. The NMS collects information from all the different devices that are being managed, consolidates it, and presents it to the network administrator. This design places all of the data manipulation tools and most of the human interaction on the NMS. Concentrating the bulk of the work on the manager means that the agent software is small and easy to implement. This is why most TCP/IP network equipment comes with an SNMP management agent.

SNMP is a request/response protocol. UDP port 161 is its well-known port. SNMP uses UDP as its transport protocol because it has no need for the overhead of TCP. Reliability is not required because each request generates a response. If the SNMP application does not receive a response, it simply reissues the request. Sequencing is not needed because each request and each response travels as a single datagram.

The NMS periodically requests the status of each managed device (GetRequest), and each agent responds with the status of its device (GetResponse). Making periodic requests is called *polling*. Polling reduces the burden on the agent because the NMS decides when polls are needed, and the agent simply responds. Polling also reduces the burden on the network because the polls originate from a single system at a predictable rate. The shortcoming of polling is that it does not allow for real-time updates. If a problem occurs on a managed device, the manager does not find out until the agent is polled. To handle this, SNMP uses a modified polling system called *trap-directed polling*.

A *trap* is an interrupt signaled by a predefined event. When a trap event occurs, the SNMP agent does not wait for the manager to poll. Instead, it immediately sends information to the manager. Traps allow the agent to inform the manager of unusual events while allowing the manager to maintain control of polling. SNMP traps are sent on UDP port 162. The manager sends polls on port 161 and listens for traps on port 162.

The commands shown in Table 7-14 display information about SNMP and NTP. A troubleshooter uses the information from these commands to isolate problems at the application layer that are related to the SNMP and NTP protocols.

Table 7-14 SNMP and NTP Troubleshooting

Command	Description
debug snmp packets	Displays packet activity related to the operation of SNMP.
debug ntp events	Displays events related to the operation of NTP.
debug ntp packets	Displays packet activity related to the operation of NTP.
show ntp associations	Shows the status of NTP associations configured for the system.
show ntp status	Displays current NTP settings.

Table 7-15 lists commands that make configuration changes that troubleshooters can use to correct problems with network management protocols at the application layer.

Table 7-15 Configure SNMP and NTP

Command	Description
snmp-server enable {traps | informs}	Enables SNMP traps or informs.
snmp-server community	Configures a community string to act like a password to regulate access to the agent on the router.
snmp-server host	Configures the recipient of an SNMP trap operation.
ntp server	Configures the NTP server.
set ntp client enable	Enables NTP client mode.
ntp peer	Configures the NTP peer.
ntp source	Configures the interface for the NTP source address.
no snmp-server	Disables SNMP agent operation.
set ntp {broadcastclient | client} disable	Disables NTP broadcast-client or client mode.
show ntp	Displays NTP settings.

Name Resolution

DNS is the service that translates computer and server names to IP addresses. These names are called fully qualified domain names (FQDNs).

Before DNS, network servers were identified using the IP addresses. However, this became very cumbersome. Eventually, individuals started writing HOSTS files, which contained names of servers and IP addresses assigned to them. This way, users would FTP or Telnet to a system by using their names instead of the IP addresses. This worked well, so the HOSTS file was placed on every system on the Internet.

Because administrators of each system maintained the files independently, this created new problems. First, if the text database changed, there was no way to update it automatically on every system. Essentially, the response was to create a centralized HOSTS file that would be the definitive HOSTS file on the Internet. Routinely, administrators checked this central file for any changes and updated the HOSTS files on their local systems when there were changes.

This system had many problems. For example, with only one HOSTS file on the whole Internet, if that site went down, nobody knew what any of the DNS names were. Also, as more and more systems were added, the HOSTS file started to get very big. Finally, the HOSTS names did not provide for any kind of hierarchy. Therefore, if somebody at one site wanted to have a computer named Admin, nobody else in the whole world could have a computer named Admin.

The answer to these problems was DNS. It allows computer systems to resolve FQDN to IP addresses.

The Internet has many DNS servers. However, each DNS server stores only a portion of the entire Internet namespace. A DNS hierarchy lets DNS servers find their neighbors and ask each other for information about a specific host.

A domain is a label in the DNS hierarchy, as shown in Figure 7-15. Each node in the DNS hierarchy represents a domain. Domains under the top-level domains represent individual organizations or entities. These domains can be further divided into subdomains to ease administration of an organization's host computers. Domains, starting with the top-level domains and branching out below, divide the total DNS namespace. The top-level domain names are closely controlled by the Internet Network Information Center (InterNIC), a division of the Internet Assigned Numbers Authority (IANA), which is responsible for assigning these names.

Figure 7-15 DNS Is a Hierarchical Service

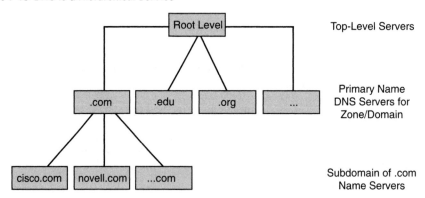

Top-level domain names are part of most URLs. For example, .com, .edu, .net, .gov, and .org are top-level domain names. These top-level domains contain the basis for the rest of the domain naming structure. Individual organizations are granted second-level domain names within one or more of these top-level domains. Because names have to be unique in a domain, they must be registered.

When an organization wants to acquire a second-level domain name, it must submit a request to the InterNIC. If the domain name is available and the InterNIC does not have a problem with it, it is assigned to the organization in exchange for a small biannual fee. The organization itself is responsible for assigning third-level and lower domains.

In Figure 7-16, the client makes a request to the corporate DNS server. The DNS server checks its cache to see if the query has already been resolved. In this situation, the corporate DNS server has no record of this query. Therefore, the corporate DNS server switches roles and now acts as a client and issues an iterative query to the local ISP.

Figure 7-16 DNS Queries and Responses Are Used to Resolve IP Addresses to Fully Qualified Domain Names

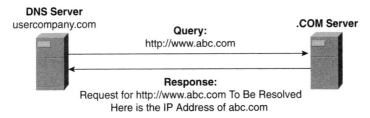

The ISP name server has no record of this resolved request. The ISP server replies with a hint to query the root domain server.

The DNS server issues an iterative query at the top of the DNS hierarchy to the root-level server. After each query and response, the server goes down the DNS tree until it finally finds the correct resolved name.

The most effective command for testing and resolving DNS issues is the **nslookup** command, which has the following uses:

- **nslookup** *FQDN*—Resolves IP addresses from fully qualified domain names (FQDNs).
- **nslookup 193.133.219.25**—Reverse DNS. Resolves an FQDN from an IP address.

If the lookup request fails, **nslookup** prints an error message. Table 7-16 lists the possible error messages.

Table 7-16 nslookup Error Messages

Error Message	Description
Timed out	A request timed out. This might happen if the DNS service was not running on the DNS server that is authoritative for the name.
No response from server	The server is not receiving requests on UDP port 53. No DNS name server is running on the server computer.
No records	The DNS name server does not have resource records of the current query type for the computer, although the computer name is valid.
Nonexistent domain	The computer or DNS domain name does not exist.
Connection refused or Network is unreachable	The connection to the DNS name server could not be made.
Server failed	The DNS server is running but is not working properly. The DNS name server found an internal inconsistency in its database and could not return a valid answer.
Refused	The DNS name server refused to service the request.
Format error	The DNS name server found that the request packet was not in the proper format. This might indicate an error in **nslookup**.

A router can be configured to use DNS lookups so that **ping** or **traceroute** commands can be used with a host name rather than an IP address. Use the commands shown in Table 7-17 to do so.

Table 7-17 DNS Troubleshooting

Command	Description
ip domain-lookup	Enables DNS-based host name-to-address translation.
ip name-server	Specifies the address of one or more name servers.

Table 7-17 DNS Troubleshooting (Continued)

Command	Description
ip domain-list	Defines a list of domains, each to be tried in turn. If no domain list exists, the domain name specified with the **ip domain-name** global configuration command is used. If a domain list exists, the default domain name is not used.
ip domain-name	Defines a default domain name that the Cisco IOS software uses to complete unqualified host names (names without a dotted-decimal domain name). Do not include the initial period that separates the unqualified name from the domain name.

Dynamic Host Configuration Protocol (DHCP)

DHCP is used to dynamically assign IP addresses to hosts. Although it is not a true TCP/IP application program, it is important to cover it in some detail.

DHCP uses a client/server structure to provide configuration parameters to hosts. It consists of a protocol that provides host-specific configuration parameters from a DHCP server (or a collection of DHCP servers) to a host and a mechanism to allocate network addresses to a host.

The **service dhcp** and **ip helper-address** commands display information about the DHCP application. A troubleshooter uses the information from the commands shown in Table 7-18 to isolate problems with DHCP.

Table 7-18 DHCP Troubleshooting

Command	Description
show ip dhcp binding	Displays address bindings on a DHCP server.
show dhcp lease	Shows DHCP addresses leased from a server.
debug dhcp [detail]	Displays DHCP client activities and monitors the status of DHCP packets.
debug ip dhcp server events	Reports DHCP server events, such as address assignments and database updates.

Troubleshooting TCP/IP Application Layer Problems

Telnet, HTTP, e-mail, FTP, and DNS applications are explored in this section. This time the applications themselves, rather than the underlying protocols, are the focus. Troubleshooting these applications is the final topic of this book.

Troubleshooting Telnet Problems

The following section discusses common application layer problems and the suggested steps required to solve these problems. The focus of this section is to develop an awareness of steps required to logically solve problems.

Many problems can stop a Telnet session from being established. The steps to troubleshoot particular problems change depending on the specific problem. However, a good trouble-shooter can solve these problems by methodically eliminating potential issues.

Telnet Troubleshooting Example

The second-level network engineer for a company in Toronto wants to remotely manage a router in Calgary. However, she is unable to establish a Telnet connection to it from her office computer. This is odd, because Telnet to the router was possible the day before.

The computer has IP connectivity to a switch named Toronto_SW, and the switch is connected to a router named Toronto. The engineer also has console access to both devices. Her division supports the 172.22.0.0/16 subnet. Therefore, the engineer consoles into Toronto_SW to see if she can ping the Calgary router, as shown in Example 7-9.

Example 7-9 *The Ping to Calgary Is Successful*

```
Toronto_SW>ping Calgary

Type escape sequence to abort.

Sending 5, 100-byte ICMP Echos to 172.22.128.1, timeout is 2 seconds:

!!!!!

Success rate is 100 percent (5/5), round-trip min/avg/max
= 16/18/20 ms

Toronto_SW>
```

Toronto_SW can ping Calgary. Therefore, it appears that the lower OSI layers between these devices are working.

Next, the engineer tries to Telnet from the Toronto switch to the Calgary router, but this attempt is unsuccessful. It is possible that Telnet has been disabled, has been moved to a port other than 23 on the Calgary router, or is being blocked by an inbound access list. By consoling into the Toronto router and opening a Telnet session to Calgary, as shown in Example 7-10, you eliminate these possibilities.

Example 7-10 *A Successful Telnet to Calgary Verifies Layer 7 Connectivity*

```
Toronto>telnet Calgary

Trying Calgary (172.22.128.1)... Open
  BaseBaseBaseBaseBaseBaseBaseBaseBaseBaseBaseBaseBaseBase


    Calgary


  an ACME Distribution Workgroup Router


    -- Baseline --


BaseBaseBaseBaseBaseBaseBaseBaseBaseBaseBaseBaseBaseBase


User Access Verification


Password:


Calgary>
```

While Telnetted into the Calgary router, you can check for signs of recent configuration changes using the **show logging** and **show clock** commands, as shown in Example 7-11. No configuration changes have been made on Calgary for several days, so the engineer returns to the console session on Toronto.

Example 7-11 *The* **show logging** *Command on Calgary Shows EIGRP Neighbor Adjacencies Forming*

```
Calgary>show logging

Syslog logging: enabled (0 messages dropped, 1 messages rate-limited, 0 flushes,
  0 overruns)

    Console logging: level debugging, 40 messages logged

    Monitor logging: level debugging, 0 messages logged

    Buffer logging: level debugging, 19 messages logged

    Logging Exception size (4096 bytes)

    Count and timestamp logging messages: disabled

    Trap logging: level informational, 46 message lines logged

        Logging to 172.27.227.9, 5 message lines logged



Log Buffer (65536 bytes):



Dec 13 06:02:25: %CONTROLLER-5-UPDOWN: Controller T1 0/1, changed state to
  administratively down

Dec 13 06:02:27: %LINK-3-UPDOWN: Interface Serial0/0:0, changed state to up

Dec 13 06:02:27: %LINK-3-UPDOWN: Interface Serial0/0:1, changed state to up

Dec 13 06:02:28: %LINEPROTO-5-UPDOWN: Line protocol on Interface Serial0/0:0,
  changed state to up
```

Example 7-11 *The* **show logging** *Command on Calgary Shows EIGRP Neighbor Adjacencies Forming (Continued)*

```
Dec 13 06:02:28: %LINEPROTO-5-UPDOWN: Line protocol on Interface Serial0/0:1,
  changed state to up

Dec 13 06:02:56: %LINEPROTO-5-UPDOWN: Line protocol on Interface Serial0/0:0,
  changed state to down

Dec 13 06:02:56: %LINEPROTO-5-UPDOWN: Line protocol on Interface Serial0/0:1,
  changed state to down

 .


 .


 .


Dec 13 06:02:56: %LINK-3-UPDOWN: Interface FastEthernet0/0, changed state to up

Dec 13 06:02:56: %LINK-3-UPDOWN: Interface Serial1/0, changed state to up

Dec 13 06:02:56: %DUAL-5-NBRCHANGE: IP-EIGRP 202:
Neighbor 172.22.128.130 (FastEthernet0/0) is up: new adjacency

Dec 13 06:02:56: %LINK-3-UPDOWN: Interface Serial1/1, changed state to up

Dec 13 06:02:57: %LINEPROTO-5-UPDOWN: Line protocol on Interface FastEthernet0/0,
  changed state to up

Dec 13 06:02:57: %LINEPROTO-5-UPDOWN: Line protocol on Interface Serial1/0,
  changed state to up

Dec 13 06:03:07: %LINEPROTO-5-UPDOWN: Line protocol on Interface Serial1/1,
  changed state to up

Dec 13 06:04:34: %SYS-5-CONFIG_I: Configured from console by console
```

continues

Example 7-11 *The* **show logging** *Command on Calgary Shows EIGRP Neighbor Adjacencies Forming (Continued)*

```
Dec 13 15:50:44: %LINEPROTO-5-UPDOWN: Line protocol on Interface Serial0/0:0,
  changed state to up

Dec 13 15:50:44: %LINEPROTO-5-UPDOWN: Line protocol on Interface Serial0/0:1,
  changed state to up

Dec 13 15:51:34: %DUAL-5-NBRCHANGE: IP-EIGRP 202:
Neighbor 172.22.126.1 (Serial0/0:0) is up: new adjacency

Dec 13 15:51:34: %DUAL-5-NBRCHANGE: IP-EIGRP 202:
Neighbor 172.22.126.129 (Serial0/0:1) is up: new adjacency


Calgary>

Calgary>show clock

14:55:24.159 EST Thu Dec 19 2002

Calgary>
```

The engineer looks for signs of recent configuration changes on Toronto with the **show logging** and **show clock** commands, as shown in Example 7-12. Although changes made to the running configuration cannot be confirmed, the fact that someone else was in configuration mode on Toronto in the last few hours *can* be confirmed.

Example 7-12 *Toronto's Buffer Indicates Some Recent Configuration Changes*

```
Calgary>exit

[Connection to Calgary closed by foreign host]

Toronto>

Toronto>show logging
```

Example 7-12 *Toronto's Buffer Indicates Some Recent Configuration Changes (Continued)*

```
Syslog logging: enabled (0 messages dropped, 1 messages rate-limited, 0 flushes,
   0 overruns)

   Console logging: level debugging, 115 messages logged

   Monitor logging: level debugging, 0 messages logged

   Buffer logging: level debugging, 155 messages logged

   Logging Exception size (4096 bytes)

   Count and timestamp logging messages: disabled

   Trap logging: level informational, 186 message lines logged

       Logging to 172.27.227.9, 139 message lines logged

Log Buffer (65536 bytes):

Dec 19 12:19:15: %SYS-5-CONFIG_I: Configured from console by vty0 (172.22.126.2)

Dec 19 13:03:06: %SYS-5-CONFIG_I: Configured from console by vty0 (172.22.126.2)

Dec 19 13:21:07: %SYS-5-CONFIG_I: Configured from console by vty0 (172.22.126.2)

Toronto>

Toronto>show clock

15:53:22.258 EST Thu Dec 19 2002
Toronto>
```

So far you know that pings to Calgary from Toronto_SW are successful, but Telnet sessions are not. Telnet sessions are possible from the Toronto router. Another administrator could possibly have made configuration changes on the Toronto router.

Because of the facts, you suspect that the problem is probably with an extended access list filtering too much traffic. To confirm this suspicion, use the **show access-lists** command on the Toronto router to review the current access lists that are configured, as shown in Example 7-13.

Example 7-13 *The* **show access-lists** *Command Indicates Matches with Individual Access Control Entries*

```
Toronto>show access-lists
Standard IP access list 21
    permit 172.28.128.7
    permit 172.28.128.8
    permit 172.27.227.7
    permit 172.27.227.8
    permit 172.22.0.0, wildcard bits 0.0.255.255 (18 matches)

Standard IP access list Admin
    permit 172.22.121.0, wildcard bits 0.0.0.255 (95 matches)
    permit 172.22.125.0, wildcard bits 0.0.0.255

Standard IP access list END_USERS
    permit 172.22.124.0, wildcard bits 0.0.0.255
    permit 172.22.122.0, wildcard bits 0.0.1.255

Extended IP access list Traffic
    permit icmp any any (15 matches)
    permit tcp 172.22.0.0 0.0.255.255 any eq ftp-data
    permit tcp 172.22.0.0 0.0.255.255 any eq ftp
    permit tcp 172.22.0.0 0.0.255.255 any eq www
    permit udp 172.22.0.0 0.0.255.255 any eq tftp
Toronto>
```

The only extended access list configured is called Traffic. Notice that it explicitly permits ICMP, FTP, WWW, and TFTP traffic. However, the implicit deny at the end of the list blocks Telnet traffic that comes from Toronto_SW.

To determine which interface on Toronto is being used to forward traffic to Calgary, use the
show ip route command, as shown in Example 7-14. This reveals that traffic for Calgary is
sent across the interface named Serial0/0:0.

Example 7-14 *Traffic for Calgary Is Sent Out Interface Serial 0/0*

```
Toronto>show ip route


Gateway of last resort is 172.22.126.2 to network 0.0.0.0

D EX 172.21.0.0/16 [170/3873280] via 172.22.126.2, 2d00h, Serial0/0:0

D EX 172.23.0.0/16 [170/3873280] via 172.22.126.2, 2d00h, Serial0/0:0

     172.22.0.0/16 is variably subnetted, 13 subnets, 2 masks

D       172.22.128.0/26 [90/3973120] via 172.22.126.2, 6d00h, Serial0/0:0

D       172.22.129.0/26 [90/3975680] via 172.22.126.2, 6d00h, Serial0/0:0

C       172.22.126.128/26 is directly connected, Serial0/0:1

C       172.22.127.128/26 is directly connected, Serial1/1

D EX    172.22.0.0/16 [170/3873280] via 172.22.126.2, 2d02h, Serial0/0:0

D       172.22.128.128/26 [90/3847680] via 172.22.126.2, 6d00h, Serial0/0:0

C       172.22.122.0/26 is directly connected, FastEthernet0/0.2

C       172.22.123.0/26 is directly connected, FastEthernet0/0.3

C       172.22.121.0/26 is directly connected, FastEthernet0/0.1

C       172.22.126.0/26 is directly connected, Serial0/0:0
```

continues

Example 7-14 *Traffic for Calgary Is Sent Out Interface Serial 0/0 (Continued)*

```
C       172.22.127.0/26 is directly connected, Serial1/0

C       172.22.124.0/26 is directly connected, FastEthernet0/0.4

C       172.22.125.0/26 is directly connected, Loopback0

D EX 172.25.0.0/16 [170/3873280] via 172.22.126.2, 2d00h, Serial0/0:0

D EX 172.24.0.0/16 [170/3873280] via 172.22.126.2, 2d00h, Serial0/0:0

D EX 172.26.0.0/16 [170/3873280] via 172.22.126.2, 2d00h, Serial0/0:0

D EX 198.133.219.0/24 [170/3873280] via 172.22.126.2, 2d00h, Serial0/0:0

D*EX 0.0.0.0/0 [170/3847936] via 172.22.126.2, 6d00h, Serial0/0:0

Toronto>
```

Finally, verify that the access list named Traffic is applied to Serial0/0:0 of Toronto using the
show ip interface serial 0/0:0 command, as shown in Example 7-15.

Example 7-15 *The Traffic Access List Is Applied to Interface Serial 0/0:0*

```
Toronto>show ip interface serial 0/0:0

Serial0/0:0 is up, line protocol is up

  Internet address is 172.22.126.1/26

  Broadcast address is 255.255.255.255

  Address determined by setup command

  MTU is 1500 bytes

  Helper address is not set
```

Example 7-15 *The Traffic Access List Is Applied to Interface Serial 0/0:0 (Continued)*

```
  Directed broadcast forwarding is disabled


  Multicast reserved groups joined: 224.0.0.10


  Outgoing access list is Traffic


  Inbound  access list is not set


 .

Toronto>enable
```

To see how Traffic is configured, review the access list in the running configuration, as shown
in Example 7-16.

Example 7-16 *The* **show run** *Command Reveals the Configuration of the Traffic Access List*

```
Toronto#show running-config | begin ip access-list extended Traffic

ip access-list extended Traffic

 remark Allow ICMP, Telnet outbound, FTP & WWW

 permit icmp any any

 permit tcp 172.22.0.0 0.0.255.255 any eq ftp-data

 permit tcp 172.22.0.0 0.0.255.255 any eq ftp

 permit tcp 172.22.0.0 0.0.255.255 any eq www

 permit udp 172.22.0.0 0.0.255.255 any eq tftp

!

logging source-interface Loopback0
```

continues

Example 7-16 *The* **show run** *Command Reveals the Configuration of the Traffic Access List (Continued)*

```
logging 172.27.227.9

access-list 21 permit 172.28.128.7

access-list 21 permit 172.28.128.8

access-list 21 remark Also allow Lenexa and Elmhurst to Telnet in

access-list 21 permit 172.27.227.7

access-list 21 permit 172.27.227.8

access-list 21 remark Allow this workgroup to Telnet in

access-list 21 permit 172.22.0.0 0.0.255.255

!

route-map USE_FAST permit 10

 match ip address Admin

 set interface Serial0/0:1

!

. . .

Toronto#
```

The issue is now isolated. The outbound access list named Traffic does not include a **permit** statement for Telnet. All Telnet traffic from the LAN traffic connected to the Toronto switch is being filtered. The **remark** statement for the access list Traffic states that it should support outbound TCP Telnet connections.

The engineer corrects the extended access list named Traffic and adds a line to support Telnet traffic from Toronto's clients, as shown in Example 7-17.

Example 7-17 *The Traffic Access List Is Adjusted to Allow Telnet Traffic from Toronto_SW's Attached Clients*

```
Toronto>enable

Toronto#conf terminal

Enter configuration commands, one per line.  End with CNTL/Z.

Toronto(config)#ip access-list extended Traffic

Toronto(config-ext-nacl)#permit tcp 172.22.0.0 0.0.255.255 any eq telnet

Toronto(config-ext-nacl)#exit

Toronto#

Dec 19 16:16:02: %SYS-5-CONFIG_I: Configured from console by console

Toronto#show access-lists Traffic

Extended IP access list Traffic

    permit icmp any any (15 matches)

    permit tcp 172.22.0.0 0.0.255.255 any eq ftp-data

    permit tcp 172.22.0.0 0.0.255.255 any eq ftp

    permit tcp 172.22.0.0 0.0.255.255 any eq www

    permit udp 172.22.0.0 0.0.255.255 any eq tftp

    permit tcp 172.22.0.0 0.0.255.255 any eq telnet

Toronto#
```

Finally, you verify the configuration change by consoling into Toronto_SW and Telnetting to Calgary, as shown in Example 7-18.

Example 7-18 *Telnet Now Succeeds, as Verified by a Telnet to Calgary from Tornoto_SW*

```
Toronto_SW>telnet Calgary

Trying Calgary (172.22.128.1)... Open

BaseBaseBaseBaseBaseBaseBaseBaseBaseBaseBaseBaseBaseBase

  Calgary

  an ACME Distribution Workgroup Router

  -- Baseline --

BaseBaseBaseBaseBaseBaseBaseBaseBaseBaseBaseBaseBaseBase



User Access Verification

Password:

Calgary>
```

The incomplete extended access list has been updated to support Telnet. The application problem has been resolved by correcting the transport layer problem. The baseline configuration has been restored.

Troubleshooting HTTP Problems

Problems with HTTP connectivity can be hard to narrow down. Although Web browsers are not the greatest utilities for detailed troubleshooting of the HTTP protocol, they are nonetheless useful for determining whether clients on the Internet might connect to a specific Web server. Even if a Web server responds correctly to HTTP commands using the Telnet utility, this fact does not guarantee that the Web server will accomplish its goal of serving Web pages to the Internet public. The only choice is to connect to the Web server by using a popular Web browser.

When managing Web servers, it is a good idea to keep a variety of Web browsers on hand. You should test all Web servers and Web pages with both Netscape Navigator and Microsoft Internet Explorer.

Be sure to try accessing the Web server from various hosts to eliminate individual computer browser problems.

The commands shown in Table 7-19 make router configuration changes that troubleshooters can use to correct problems with Web protocols at the application layer.

Table 7-19 HTTP Commands

Command	Description
ip http authentication	Specifies a particular authentication method for HTTP server users.
ip http port	Specifies the port to be used by the Cisco Web browser interface.
ip http server	Enables the Cisco Web browser interface on a router or access server.

Troubleshooting E-Mail Problems

Troubleshooting e-mail problems can be easy. However, sometimes other factors can keep users from properly retrieving or sending e-mail. A mistyped setting can cause a lot of problems. Careful configuration is key to the success of using an e-mail server.

E-Mail Troubleshooting Example

In a fairly short period of time, a large number of network users call to report that they cannot send e-mail, but they can receive it. The network has separate servers for sending and receiving e-mail. An SMTP server is used to send e-mail, and a POP3 server is used to receive and save e-mail.

Because the users are receiving e-mail, it is doubtful that the POP3 server is malfunctioning. The problem of sending e-mail could be isolated to the server running the SMTP protocol.

Testing the physical, data link, and network layers reveals no problems.

To test the transport layer, attempt to Telnet into the SMTP server through the port number for the SMTP protocol (25). A hello message is not received from the server. This indicates problems at either the transport or application layer.

Check the following:

- Is the router denying access to port 25?
- Is the e-mail client properly configured?
- Is the address being used to Telnet the SMTP server?

Troubleshooting FTP Problems

Generally, if a client has connectivity by way of the control connection but cannot retrieve directory listings or transfer files, there is an issue with opening the data connection. Try specifying passive mode, because this is permitted by most firewalls.

Another common problem with FTP is being able to transfer small files but not large files, with the transfer generally failing at the same place or time in every file. Remember that the data connection (and the transfer) will be closed if the control connection closes. This is because the control connection is typically dormant during large file transfers. It is possible for the connection to close in NAT/PAT environments in which there is a timeout on TCP connections. Increasing the timeout on dormant TCP connections might resolve this problem. If an FTP client is not properly coded, this problem might occur.

Because FTP file transfers generally create packets of maximum size, an MTU mismatch problem almost always causes file transfers to fail in a single direction (**get**s might fail, but **put**s might work). A server located on a LAN medium that supports larger MTUs (such as Token Ring, which can have an MTU of 4096 or larger) can be the cause of this problem. Normally this problem is resolved automatically by fragmentation, but misconfigurations or having the IP Don't Fragment option set in the IP datagrams can prevent automatic resolution of these types of problems.

TFTP Troubleshooting Example

The second-level network engineer for Orlando has console access to the distribution router named Orlando and IP connectivity to all other devices in his division. The division supports the 172.21.0.0/16 subnet.

Biff from Network Operations stops by the office. He reports that somehow the Cisco IOS has been erased from the Orlando router. He says that he was trying to retrieve it from Baltimore but he cannot get TFTP to work.

The engineer knows from the base configuration information that there is at least a 100-MB FastEthernet link between Orlando and Baltimore, so this would be a good source to use for downloading the IOS image. He connects to the console port on Orlando to assess the situation.

First, he reviews the available commands from within ROMMON mode, as shown in Example 7-19. Note that the ROMMON prompt is on 14 and 15, which indicates that several commands have already been issued.

Example 7-19 *ROMMON Has a Very Limited Set of Commands*

```
rommon 14 > ?

alias          set and display aliases command

boot           boot up an external process

break          set/show/clear the breakpoint

confreg        configuration register utility

cont           continue executing a downloaded image

context        display the context of a loaded image

cookie         display contents of cookie PROM in hex

dev            list the device table

dir            list files in file system

dis            display instruction stream

dnld           serial download a program module

frame          print out a selected stack frame

help           monitor built in command help

history        monitor command history

meminfo        main memory information
```

continues

Example 7-19 *ROMMON Has a Very Limited Set of Commands (Continued)*

```
repeat           repeat a monitor command

reset            system reset

set              display the monitor variables

stack            produce a stack trace

sync             write monitor environment to NVRAM

sysret           print out info from last system return

tftpdnld         tftp image download

unalias          unset an alias

unset            unset a monitor variable

xmodem           x/ymodem image download

rommon 15 >
```

Next, he enters the ROMMON **boot** command, as shown in Example 7-20, to try to boot the router in case the Cisco IOS image is not really missing.

Example 7-20 *The ROMMON* **boot** *Command Fails*

```
rommon 15 > boot

loadprog: bad file magic number:      0x0

boot: cannot load "flash:"

rommon 16 >
```

Entering the **boot** command doesn't work, so the engineer attempts to **reset** the router, as shown in Example 7-21, to see if that restores the IOS image.

Example 7-21 *The ROMMON* **reset** *Command Also Fails*

```
rommon 16 > reset

System Bootstrap, Version 12.2(4r)XL, RELEASE SOFTWARE  (fc1)

TAC Support: http://www.cisco.com/tac

Copyright (c) 2001 by cisco Systems, Inc.

C1700 platform with 65536 Kbytes of main memory

loadprog: bad file magic number:      0x0

boot: cannot load "flash:"

System Bootstrap, Version 12.2(4r)XL, RELEASE SOFTWARE (fc1)

TAC Support: http://www.cisco.com/tac

Copyright (c) 2001 by cisco Systems, Inc.

C1700 platform with 65536 Kbytes of main memory

loadprog: bad file magic number:      0x0

boot: cannot load "flash:"

System Bootstrap, Version 12.2(4r)XL, RELEASE SOFTWARE (fc1)

TAC Support: http://www.cisco.com/tac

Copyright (c) 2001 by cisco Systems, Inc.

C1700 platform with 65536 Kbytes of main memory

rommon 1 >
```

Entering the **reset** command does not restore the image, so the engineer decides to look for the IOS image in the file system, as shown in Example 7-22.

Example 7-22 *The IOS Image Is Missing from Flash*

```
rommon 1 > dir

usage: dir <device>

rommon 2 > dir flash:

        File size           Checksum    File name

      5858 bytes (0x16e2)     0x699a     base.cfg

rommon 2 >
```

Biff is correct. There is no IOS image in Flash memory. At 5858 bytes, base.cfg is not big enough to be an IOS image. The engineer learns from Biff that the image was erased while someone was saving a backup configuration file.

The engineer decides to use TFTP to recover the image. He reviews the commands available from ROMMON level, as shown in Example 7-23.

Example 7-23 *You Can Review the Available ROMMON Commands Using* ?

```
rommon 2 > ?

alias              set and display aliases command

boot               boot up an external process

break              set/show/clear the breakpoint

confreg            configuration register utility

cont               continue executing a downloaded image

context            display the context of a loaded image
```

Example 7-23 *You Can Review the Available ROMMON Commands Using* **?** *(Continued)*

```
cookie          display contents of cookie PROM in hex

dev             list the device table

dir             list files in file system

dis             display instruction stream

dnld            serial download a program module

frame           print out a selected stack frame

help            monitor builtin command help

history         monitor command history

meminfo         main memory information

repeat          repeat a monitor command

reset           system reset

set             display the monitor variables

stack           produce a stack trace

sync            write monitor environment to NVRAM

sysret          print out info from last system return

tftpdnld        tftp image download

unalias         unset an alias

unset           unset a monitor variable
```

continues

Example 7-23 *You Can Review the Available ROMMON Commands Using* **?** *(Continued)*

```
xmodem                 x/ymodem image download


rommon 3 >
```

The engineer decides that **tftpdnld** is the command necessary to download the image from Baltimore. Baltimore is running a TFTP server that is offering an image with the filename flash:c1700-sv8y-mz.122-8.YL.bin.

The engineer enters the **tftpdnld** command, as shown in Example 7-24.

Example 7-24 *The* **tftpdnld** *Command Can Be Used to Recover the IOS Image*

```
rommon 3 > tftpdnld

Missing or illegal ip address for variable IP_ADDRESS

Illegal IP address.

usage: tftpdnld [-r]

  Use this command for disaster recovery only to recover an image via TFTP.

   Monitor variables are used to set up parameters for the transfer.(Syntax:

   "VARIABLE_NAME=value" and use "set" to show current variables.) "ctrl-c" or

   "break" stops the transfer before flash erase begins. The following variables

  are REQUIRED to be set for tftpdnld:

        IP_ADDRESS: The IP address for this unit

        IP_SUBNET_MASK: The subnet mask for this unit

        DEFAULT_GATEWAY: The default gateway for this unit
```

Example 7-24 *The* **tftpdnld** *Command Can Be Used to Recover the IOS Image (Continued)*

```
          TFTP_SERVER: The IP address of the server to fetch from


            TFTP_FILE: The filename to fetch

    The following variables are OPTIONAL:

          TFTP_VERBOSE: Print setting. 0=quiet, 1=progress(default), 2=verbose

     TFTP_RETRY_COUNT: Retry count for ARP and TFTP (default=7)

          TFTP_TIMEOUT: Overall timeout of operation in seconds (default=7200)

        TFTP_CHECKSUM: Perform checksum test on image, 0=no, 1=yes (default=1)

  Command line options:

   -r: do not write flash, load to DRAM only and launch image


rommon 4 >
```

The attempt fails. The command output displays messages that are symptoms of an issue with the TFTP application layer protocol.

The engineer has isolated the TFTP issues to the **tftpdnld** ROMMON command. He needs the IP address and mask for the local router, the default gateway for the local router, the IP address of the TFTP server, and the name of the file to be transferred:

> Local IP address—172.21.128.129
>
> Local mask—255.255.255.128
>
> Local default gateway—172.21.128.130
>
> TFTP server—172.22.128.129
>
> File—c1700-sv8y-mz.122-8.YL.bin

By reviewing the relevant information on http://www.cisco.com, the engineer realizes he needs to enter **variable_name=variable** to set these variables.

The engineer configures the TFTP variables on the Orlando router, as shown in Example 7-25. This step is case-sensitive. He removes a space in the **DEFAULT_GATEWAY=** line and continues.

Example 7-25 *Several Parameters Must Be Entered with the* **tftpdnld** *Command*

```
rommon 5 > IP_ADDRESS=11.171.178.129


rommon 6 > IP_SUBNET_MASK=255.255.255.128


rommon 7 > DEFAULT_GATEWAY= 11.171.178.130


monitor: command "DEFAULT_GATEWAY=" not found


rommon 8 > DEFAULT_GATEWAY=11.171.178.130


rommon 9 > TFTP_SERVER=21.121.128.129


rommon 10 > TFTP_FILE=c1700-sv8y-mz.122-8.YL.bin


rommon 11 >
```

The engineer now invokes the TFTP program, as shown in Example 7-26. Because he has configured the parameters to support TFTP, the TFTP download process seems to work. It appears that the application layer issue of missing TFTP parameters has been resolved.

Example 7-26 *TFTP Is Invoked with Another Instance of the* **tftpdnld** *Command*

```
rommon 11 > tftpdnld


         IP_ADDRESS: 172.21.178.129


      IP_SUBNET_MASK: 255.255.255.128


     DEFAULT_GATEWAY: 172.21.178.130


         TFTP_SERVER: 172.22.128.129


          TFTP_FILE: flash:/c1700-sv8y-mz.122-8.YL.BIN
```

Example 7-26 *TFTP Is Invoked with Another Instance of the* **tftpdnld** *Command (Continued)*

```
Invoke this command for disaster recovery only.


WARNING: all existing data in all partitions on flash will be lost!


Do you wish to continue? y/n:  [n]:  y


Receiving c1700-sv8y-mz.122-8.YL.BIN from 172.22.128.129
!!!!!!!!!!!!!!!!!!!!!!!!!!!!!!!!!!!!!!!!!!!!!!!!!!!!!!!!!!!!!!!!!!!!!!!!!!!!!!!!!!!
!!!!!!!!!!!!!!!!!!!!!!!!!!!!!!!!!!!!!!!!!!!!!!!!!!!!!!!!!!!!!!!!!!!!!!!!!!!!!!!!!!!.
.
.
!!!!!!!!!!!!!!!!!!!!!!!!!!!!!!!!!!!!!!!!!!!!!!!!!!!!!!!!!!!!!!!!!!!!!!!!!!!!!!!!!!!!
!!!!!!!!!!!!!!!!!!!!!!!!!!!!!!!!!!!!!!!!!!!!!!!!!!!!!!!!!!!!!!!!!!


File reception completed.


Copying file c1700-sv8y-mz.122-8.YL.BIN to flash.


Erasing flash at 0x62fe0000


Programming location 61980000


rommon 12 >
```

The engineer now needs to boot the router using the new image, as shown in Example 7-27.

Example 7-27 *Now the* **boot** *Command Is Successful*

```
rommon 12 > boot


program load complete, entry point: 0x80008000, size: 0x98d494


Self decompressing the image :
```

continues

Example 7-27 *Now the* **boot** *Command Is Successful (Continued)*

```
#################################################################
#################################################################
####################### [OK]
.
.
.


Cisco Internetwork Operating System Software

IOS (tm) C1700 Software (C1700-SV8Y-M), Version 12.2(8)YL, EARLY DEPLOYMENT
  RELEASE SOFTWARE (fc1)

Synched to technology version 12.2(10.3)T1

TAC Support: http://www.cisco.com/tac

Copyright (c) 1986-2002 by cisco Systems, Inc.

Compiled Wed 17-Jul-02 14:04 by ealyon

Image text-base: 0x80008124, data-base: 0x8122D408
.
.
.

Press RETURN to get started!
```

The IOS image has been restored. He finishes the task by restoring the baseline configuration files.

Troubleshooting DNS Problems

DNS name resolution can fail even when IP connectivity works properly. To troubleshoot this problem, use one of the following methods to determine if DNS is resolving the destination's name:

Step 1   Ping the destination by name, and look for an error message indicating that the name could not be resolved.

Step 2   If you're working on a UNIX machine, use **nslookup** *fully-qualified domain name* to perform a DNS lookup on the destination. If it is successful, the host's address should be displayed:

unix% nslookup www.somedomain.com
Server: localhost
Address: 127.0.0.1

Non-authoritative answer:
Name: www.somedomain.com
Address: 10.1.1.1

If **nslookup** fails, the output should be similar to the following:

unix% nslookup www.somedomain.com
Server: localhost
Address: 127.0.0.1

*** localhost cannot find www.notvalid.com: Non-existent host/domain

Step 3   Verify the name of the DNS server that should be used to help resolve the name. This can be found in different places on each operating system. If you're unsure how to find it, consult the device manual. The following are the instructions for several common platforms:

- On a Cisco router, enter **show run** and look for the name server.
- On Windows 9x and Windows Me, enter **winipcfg.exe**.
- On Windows XP, 2000, or NT, enter **ipconfig.exe**.
- On a UNIX platform, enter **cat /etc/resolv.conf** at a command prompt.

Step 4   Verify that the name server can be pinged using its IP address. If the ping fails, the problem is at a lower layer.

Step 5   Verify that names can be resolved within the local domain. For example, if a host is host1.test.com, the names of other hosts in the test.com domain, such as host2.test.com, should resolve to an IP address.

Step 6   Verify that one or more domain names outside the local domain can be resolved. If names from all domains except that of the destination can be resolved, it is possible that there is a problem with the DNS for the destination host. Contact the administrator of the destination device.

If names within the local domain or a large number of external domains cannot be resolved, contact the DNS administrator, because there might be a problem with the local DNS (or the local host could be using the wrong domain server).

Summary

This chapter described the importance of troubleshooting and went into some detail about troubleshooting application layer problems. It examined the most helpful troubleshooting tools and provided sample scenarios to illustrate the troubleshooting process at work. You learned what IOS, UNIX, and Windows commands are used to troubleshoot application layer protocols as well as applications. At this point you have explored troubleshooting all seven layers of the OSI model. You have learned the appropriate tools and commands to use when troubleshooting problems at each layer of the OSI model. In each case, a systematic troubleshooting methodology was used.

Key Terms

Network File System (NFS)   Allows computers to mount drives on remote hosts and operate them as if they were local drives.

Internet Message Access Protocol (IMAP)   The standard protocol for accessing e-mail from your local server. IMAP is a client/server protocol in which your Internet server receives and holds e-mail for you. You can view just the heading and the sender of the letter and then decide whether to download the mail. You can also create and manipulate multiple folders or mailboxes on the server, delete messages, and search for certain parts or an entire note. IMAP requires continual access to the server during the time you are working with your mail.

Remote Procedure Call (RPC)   A protocol that one program can use to request a service from a program located in another computer in a network without having to understand network details. The requesting program is a client, and the service-providing program is the server. Like a regular or local procedure call, an RPC is a synchronous operation that requires the requesting program to be suspended until the results of the remote procedure are returned.

X Window System   A popular protocol that permits intelligent terminals to communicate with remote computers as if they were directly attached.

Check Your Understanding

Use the following review questions to test your understanding of the concepts covered in this chapter. Answers are listed in Appendix A, "Check Your Understanding Answer Key."

1. What OSI layer should you troubleshoot when **ping** is successful, but HTTP fails to a given destination?

   A. Physical

   B. Data link

   C. Network

   D. Application

2. What command output is commonly requested by the Cisco TAC?

   A. **show run**

   B. **show interface**

   C. **show ip route**

   D. **show tech-support**

3. What is recommended as an initial step in troubleshooting an application layer problem?

    A. Document changes

    B. Evaluate results

    C. Back up pertinent files

    D. Make initial software and hardware configuration changes

4. Which of the following are two common TCP/IP troubleshooting commands?

    A. cat

    B. netstat

    C. nslookup

    D. nbtstat

5. What Windows 2000 utility do network administrators use to view possible IP address problems?

    A. IIS

    B. Services

    C. Task Manager

    D. Event Viewer

6. What UNIX command displays the status of active interfaces?

    A. ifconfig

    B. ipconfig

    C. winipcfg

    D. intf

7. What Syslog error message level is associated with level 7?

    A. Emergencies

    B. Alerts

    C. Debugging

    D. Warnings

8. Which logging destination requires the greatest system overhead?

    A. Buffer

    B. Console

    C. Virtual terminal

    D. Syslog server

9. What IOS command ensures that debug messages are time-stamped?

    A. **timestamp debug**

    B. **timestamp service**

    C. **service timestamp debug**

    D. **debug timestamp**

10. IOS error messages have what form of output?

    A. *%MNEMONIC-FACILITY-SEVERITY*: *Message-text*

    B. *%SEVERITY-MNEMONIC-FACILITY*: *Message-text*

    C. *%SEVERITY-FACILITY-MNEMONIC*: *Message-text*

    D. *%FACILITY-SEVERITY-MNEMONIC*: *Message-text*

Check Your Understanding Answer Key

Chapter 1

1. _____ allows for discovery of the true performance and operation of the network in terms of the policies that have been defined. It also allows for a snapshot of the current state of variables throughout the network.

   A. Performance monitoring

   B. Fault isolation

   C. Baselining

   D. Troubleshooting

   Answer: C

2. How often should baseline analysis of the network be conducted?

   A. Once

   B. Weekly

   C. Monthly

   D. On a regular basis

   Answer: D

3. In planning a baseline, which of the following should be identified? Choose all that apply.

   A. QoS

   B. Boundaries

   C. Devices

   D. Ports of interest

   Answer: C, D

4. Which of the following are two qualifications for the duration of the baseline?

   A. 1 day

   B. No more than 6 weeks

   C. 1 year

   D. At least 7 days

   Answer: B, D

5. Baseline information is recorded in what types of documentation? Choose all that apply.

   A. Network management databases

   B. QoS databases

   C. Network configuration tables

   D. Topology diagrams

   Answer: A, C, D

6. What is normally included in a network configuration table? Choose all that apply.

   A. Device name

   B. Data link layer addresses

   C. Network layer addresses

   D. Applications

   Answer: A, B, C

7. What is normally included in a topology diagram? Choose all that apply.

   A. Device names

   B. Routing protocols

   C. IP addresses

   D. Media types

   Answer: A, B, C, D

8. Guidelines for creating network documentation include which of the following? Choose all that apply.

   A. Knowing the objective

   B. Being consistent

   C. Keeping the documents accessible

   D. Maintaining the documentation

   Answer: A, B, C, D

9. What is normally included in an end-system configuration table? Choose all that apply.

   A. DNS server

   B. IP address

   C. Operating system

   D. Device name

   Answer: A, B, C, D

10. What is normally included in an end-system topology diagram? Choose all that apply.

    A. Port speed

    B. How devices are connected to the network

    C. IP address

    D. Device name and function

    Answer: B, C, D

Chapter 2

1. Encapsulation at the transport layer involves what?

   A. Bits

   B. Packets

   C. Segments

   D. Frames

   Answer: C

2. What are the three stages of the general troubleshooting process? Choose all that apply.

   A. Documenting the problem

   B. Correcting the problem

   C. Gathering symptoms

   D. Isolating the problem

   Answer: B, C, D

3. What is the correct order for the three stages from Question 2?

   A. D, A, B

   B. C, D, B

   C. C, D, A

   D. C, A, B

   Answer: B

4. What troubleshooting approach is recommended for complicated problems?

   A. Top-down

   B. Replacement

   C. Bottom-up

   D. Divide-and-conquer

   Answer: C

5. What might be a suspected problem when using the top-down troubleshooting approach?

   A. Connectivity problem

   B. Hardware issue

   C. Software issue

   D. Physical fault

Answer: C

6. What troubleshooting approach is generally recommended for a new problem?

   A. Replacement

   B. Divide-and-conquer

   C. Bottom-up

   D. Top-down

Answer: C

7. What is often helpful when employing the divide-and-conquer approach to troubleshooting?

   A. Network configuration diagram

   B. Sophisticated network management tool

   C. Past troubleshooting experience

   D. Topology diagram

Answer: C

8. What are the five stages of gathering symptoms for a network problem, in order?

   A. Analyze existing symptoms, determine ownership, narrow the scope, determine symptoms, document symptoms

   B. Narrow the scope, analyze existing symptoms, determine ownership, determine symptoms, document symptoms

   C. Analyze existing symptoms, narrow the scope, determine ownership, determine symptoms, document symptoms

   D. Determine ownership, analyze existing symptoms, narrow the scope, determine symptoms, document symptoms

Answer: A

9. What are the five stages of gathering end-system symptoms, in order?

   A. Determine symptoms, document symptoms, analyze symptoms, interview the user

   B. Determine symptoms, interview the user, analyze symptoms, document symptoms

   C. Analyze symptoms, interview the user, determine symptoms, document symptoms

   D. Interview the user, analyze symptoms, determine symptoms, document symptoms

   Answer: D

10. Which type of network management has the goal of detecting, logging, and notifying users of network problems to keep the network running effectively?

    A. Performance management

    B. Configuration management

    C. Accounting management

    D. Fault management

    Answer: D

Chapter 3

1. Failure at the physical layer translates into failure at which of the following OSI layers? Choose all that apply.

   A. Network

   B. Transport

   C. Data link

   D. Application

   Answer: A, B, C, D

2. Power fluctuations are manifested in which of the following ways? Choose all that apply.

   A. Power failure

   B. Power spike

   C. Brownout

   D. Dirty power

   Answer: A, B, C, D

3. If **show interfaces** output indicates "interface is up, line protocol is down" on a serial link, what are some possible causes? Choose all that apply.

   A. Encapsulation mismatch

   B. Layer 1 connectivity to the telco, but no Layer 2 connectivity to the remote router

   C. The interface does not have Layer 1 connectivity to the telco

   D. PPP authentication was unsuccessful

   Answer: A, B, D

4. Which of the following might be factors in decreasing the rate at which data is transmitted across the medium? Choose all that apply.

   A. Faulty medium or hardware

   B. Large collision domains

   C. EMI effects

   D. Exceeding the medium's design limits

   Answer: A, B, C, D

5. What issue arises from exceeding the design limits of a particular medium?

   A. NEXT

   B. Return loss

   C. Attenuation

   D. FEXT

   Answer: C

6. What term represents a measure of all reflections caused by impedance mismatches along a physical path?

   A. Return loss

   B. Noise quotient

   C. Cumulative impedance

   D. Attenuation

   Answer: A

7. A late collision occurs when a collision is detected by a device after it has sent the _____ bit of its frame.

   A. 1st

   B. 128th

   C. 512th

   D. 1512th

   Answer: C

8. Shared Ethernet networks are believed to suffer from throughput problems when average traffic loads approach a maximum average capacity of _____ percent.

   A. 40

   B. 50

   C. 60

   D. 70

   Answer: A

9. Error messages with Cisco IOS are displayed as what?

   A. *#FACILITY-MNEMONIC-SEVERITY: Message-text*

   B. *&FACILITY-MNEMONIC-SEVERITY: Message-text*

   C. *$FACILITY-SEVERITY-MNEMONIC: Message-text*

   D. *%FACILITY-SEVERITY-MNEMONIC: Message-text*

   Answer: D

10. Which IOS command is used to determine if high CPU utilization is a problem on a router?

    A. **show interfaces**

    B. **show controllers**

    C. **show buffers**

    D. **show processes cpu**

    Answer: D

Chapter 4

1. What IOS commands let you identify the configured encapsulation on a serial interface? Choose all that apply.

   A. **show controllers**

   B. **show cdp neighbor**

   C. **show interfaces**

   D. **show running-config**

   Answer: C, D

2. What command displays Layer 3 information related to Frame Relay?

   A. **show frame-relay**

   B. **show frame-relay pvc**

   C. **show frame-relay lmi**

   D. **show frame-relay map**

   Answer: D

3. What STP issue can result in suboptimal traffic flow?

   A. Misconfigured UplinkFast

   B. PortFast is disabled

   C. Improper root placement

   D. Missing VLAN 1

   Answer: C

4. Misconfigured EtherChannel can result in what?

   A. Reset of the VTP configuration revision number

   B. Poor frame distribution

   C. Exaggerated crosstalk

   D. STP loop

   Answer: B, D

5. What technology helps avoid STP loops caused by one-way failure of BPDU flow on a link?

   A. GMRP

   B. STP

   C. UDLD

   D. VTP

   Answer: C

6. If a VTP client is added to a switched network, and it has a higher configuration revision number than the other switches in the VTP domain, what is the effect on other VTP clients and servers in the VTP domain?

   A. VLAN 1 is deleted

   B. VLANs configured on the added VTP client are deleted

   C. Nothing

   D. VLANs not configured on the added VTP client are deleted

   Answer: D

7. What ISDN command identifies the ISDN switch type?

   A. **debug dialer**

   B. **show isdn status**

   C. **debug isdn events**

   D. **debug isdn q921**

   Answer: B

8. A deleted Frame Relay PVC indicates a problem _____.

   A. with the Frame Relay map

   B. with encapsulation type

   C. on the remote end

   D. on the local loop

   Answer: D

9. What IOS command identifies the DLCIs advertised by the Frame Relay switch?

   A. debug frame-relay lmi

   B. show frame-relay pvc

   C. debug frame-relay events

   D. show frame-relay lmi

   Answer: A

10. Detailed LCP negotiation processes can be viewed with what IOS command?

   A. debug ppp errors

   B. debug ppp authentication

   C. debug ppp negotiation

   D. debug ppp events

   Answer: C

Chapter 5

1. When the routing table process checks for a resolvable static route using an intermediate address, the check is done in what mode?

   A. CEF

   B. Classless

   C. Fast

   D. Classful

   Answer: D

2. What type of route is useful for dropping packets when there are no specific matches in the routing table and it is not desirable to have the packets forwarded using a supernet or default route?

   A. Null route

   B. Bit bucket

   C. Discard route

   D. Dead route

   Answer: C

3. What is used with distance vector routing protocols to block all outgoing routing updates for a given interface?

   A. Access list

   B. Distribute list

   C. Passive interface

   D. Discard list

   Answer: C

4. Which of the following are common RIP issues that keep updates from being installed in the routing table? Choose all that apply.

   A. Stub area

   B. Mismatched authentication key

   C. Unsynchronized database

   D. Incompatible RIP version types

   Answer: B, D

5. Classful routing protocols cannot accurately handle what type of network?

   A. Discontiguous

   B. NBMA

   C. Variable-length

   D. Intermediary

   Answer: A

6. EIGRP neighbor adjacencies require which of the following?

   A. Matching AS numbers

   B. Properly defined **network** statements

   C. Matching K values

   D. Duplicate router IDs

   Answer:

7. Type 4 summary LSAs are not advertised by an OSPF router in what case?

    A. The router is an ABR

    B. The router is an ASBR

    C. The router is not connected to area 0

    D. The router is not connected to a stub area

Answer: C

8. What are some possible causes of an IS-IS adjacency's being stuck in INIT state?

    A. The attached bit is set

    B. MTU mismatch

    C. Hello padding is disabled

    D. Authentication mismatch

Answer: B, C, D

9. In the command **bgp dampening** *half-life-time reuse suppress maximum-supress-time,* what are the respective default values (in seconds) for *half-life-time, reuse, suppress,* and *maximum-suppress-time?*

    A. 15, 750, 1000, 30

    B. 10, 500, 1000, 30

    C. 15, 750, 2000, 60

    D. 10, 300, 1000, 40

Answer: C

10. When redistributing OSPF into IGRP, what keyword is normally required to ensure proper redistribution?

    A. **static**

    B. **subnets ppp authentication**

    C. **metric**

    D. **metric-type**

Answer: C

Chapter 6

1. Which of the following protocols are connectionless and unreliable?

    A. TFTP

    B. DNS

    C. DHCP

    D. RADIUS

    Answer: A, B, C, D

2. Which of the following protocols are connection-oriented and reliable?

    A. HTTP

    B. FTP

    C. SMTP

    D. SNMP

    Answer: A, B, C

3. Which of the following are configurable ranges for numbered standard access control lists?

    A. 1 to 99

    B. 100 to 199

    C. 1300 to 1999

    D. 2000 to 2699

    Answer: A, C

4. Named extended ACLs can filter traffic based on which of the following?

    A. Source IP address

    B. Destination IP address

    C. Source port

    D. Destination port

    Answer: A, B, C, D

5. The reserved private address space includes which of the following networks?

   A. 10.0.0.0/8

   B. 172.17.0.0/16

   C. 172.16.0.0/12

   D. 192.168.0.0/24

   Answer: A, C, D

6. What type of NAT allows Internet hosts to access an inside local IP address?

   A. Inside dynamic NAT

   B. Outside dynamic NAT

   C. Inside static NAT

   D. Outside static NAT

   Answer: C

7. What command clears NAT translations on the IOS?

   A. nat -d *

   B. clear ip nat translations

   C. clear ip nat

   D. clear ip nat translations *

   Answer: D

8. PAT makes it possible to deploy NAT with which of the following options (as opposed to NAT without PAT)?

   A. Many-to-one IP translations

   B. Many-to-many IP translations

   C. One-to-one IP translations

   D. None of the above

   Answer: A, B

9. What command displays the NIC MAC address on a Windows 2000 server?

A. nbtstat

B. netstat

C. ipconfig /all

D. tracert

Answer: C

10. What UNIX command configures firewall features?

A. ifconfig

B. nslookup

C. ipconfig

D. iptables

Answer: D

Chapter 7

1. What OSI layer should you troubleshoot when **ping** is successful but HTTP fails to a given destination?

A. Physical

B. Data link

C. Network

D. Application

Answer: D

2. What command output is commonly requested by the Cisco TAC?

A. show run

B. show interface

C. show ip route

D. show tech-support

Answer: D

3. What is recommended as an initial step in troubleshooting an application layer problem?

    A. Document changes

    B. Evaluate results

    C. Back up pertinent files

    D. Make initial software and hardware configuration changes

Answer: C

4. Which of the following are two common TCP/IP troubleshooting commands?

    A. cat

    B. netstat

    C. nslookup

    D. nbtstat

Answer: B, C

5. What Windows 2000 utility do network administrators use to view possible IP address problems?

    A. IIS

    B. Services

    C. Task Manager

    D. Event Viewer

Answer: D

6. What UNIX command displays the status of active interfaces?

    A. ifconfig

    B. ipconfig

    C. winipcfg

    D. intf

Answer: A

7. What syslog error message level is associated with Level 7?

    A. Emergencies

    B. Alerts

    C. Debugging

    D. Warnings

    Answer: C

8. Which logging destination requires the greatest system overhead?

    A. Buffer

    B. Console

    C. Virtual terminal

    D. Syslog server

    Answer: B

9. What IOS command ensures that debug messages are time-stamped?

    A. timestamp debug

    B. timestamp service

    C. service timestamp debug

    D. debug timestamp

    Answer: C

10. IOS error messages have what form of output?

    A. *%MNEMONIC-FACILITY-SEVERITY: Message-text*

    B. *%SEVERITY-MNEMONIC-FACILITY: Message-text*

    C. *%SEVERITY-FACILITY-MNEMONIC: Message-text*

    D. *%FACILITY-SEVERITY-MNEMONIC: Message-text*

    Answer: D

Objectives

After completing this appendix, you will be able to perform tasks related to the following:

- Port/connectivity problems
- Troubleshooting unicast IP routing with Cisco Express Forwarding

Appendix B

Catalyst OS Troubleshooting

This appendix provides information on troubleshooting common issues with the Catalyst 6000/6500 series switches running hybrid mode CatOS on the Supervisor Engine and IOS on the Multilayer Switch Feature Card (MSFC). Following an orderly troubleshooting process of collecting specific diagnostics ensures that information necessary to resolve the problem is not lost. Refining the scope of the problem saves valuable time in finding a solution.

Port/Connectivity Problems

Working with CatOS often requires a significant amount of time troubleshooting port errors. Here some common problems related to port conditions, and solutions are detailed.

Catalyst Switch to NIC Compatibility Issues

This section provides possible solutions if your switch port is connected to a workstation/server using a Network Interface Card (NIC), and you find network issues such as slow performance on the workstation/server, intermittent connectivity problems, or Catalyst switch issues dealing with physical connectivity and data-link errors.

Verifying the Physical Connection and Link

When you troubleshoot NIC issues, the first step is to verify physical connectivity. Visual inspection of the switch should show a LINK light indicator when connected to a link partner. In addition, the NIC also might have a LINK light indicator. You should check the switch's command-line interface (CLI) to verify physical connectivity. The port in question should show connected for CatOS software, as opposed to the output shown in Example B-1.

Example B-1 *Verifying Physical Connectivity on CatOS*

```
Switch> (enable) show port 3/1
Port Name       Status       VLAN     Level     Duplex    Speed      Type

----------    --------     -------   -------   -------   ------   ----------------

3/1           notconnect     1       normal    half       100     100BaseFX MM
```

States other than connected indicate a physical connectivity issue. The steps for troubleshooting physical connectivity are as follows:

Step 1 Set the speed and duplex of both the NIC and the switch to 10 Mbps, full duplex. Is there physical connectivity? If you want to, repeat this step and set the speed to 100 Mbps, full duplex. Setting the speed and duplex manually should not be required to establish physical connectivity.

Step 2 Replace the cable with a known-good Category 5 10/100 Mbps Ethernet cable, and update the NIC drivers.

Step 3 Attempt physical connectivity across multiple switch ports. Verify that the problem is consistent across multiple switch ports. Also try multiple switches if applicable.

Step 4 Replace the NIC. Is the problem consistent with the same brand and model of NIC?

Step 5 Open a case with the Cisco Technical Assistance Center (TAC) and/or with the NIC vendor.

Maintaining Link (Link Up/Down Situations)

Under certain circumstances, interoperability issues between Cisco switches and various NICs might result in continuous or intermittent link up/down situations. These link up/down situations are usually a result of power management features or jitter tolerance issues associated with the NIC.

The messages displayed for link up/down situations are detailed in Example B-2. All of these messages are normal for link up/down situations.

Example B-2 *Link Up/Down Situations Can Be a Result of Power Management Features*

```
%PAGP-5-PORTFROMSTP:Port 3/3 left bridge port 3/3
%PAGP-5-PORTTOSTP:Port 3/3 joined bridge port 3/3
```

Here are some common resolutions for these issues:

- **Disable Windows 2000 and Windows Millennium Edition (Me) power management functions**—Windows 2000 and Windows Me employ a power management capability that can disable the NIC. When the NIC is disabled for power management, it drops the link to the switch. If you're concerned about the link's going up and down on NICs using Windows 2000 or Windows Me, disable the power management feature as a first means of troubleshooting link up/down situations.

- **Disable NIC power management functionality**—Many NICs support their own power management capability. When troubleshooting link up/down issues, disable this feature as another means of troubleshooting. For information on disabling power management, refer to the NIC documentation.

- **Adjust switch jitter tolerance**—Jitter tolerance, according to IEEE 802.33u-1995, shall not exceed 1.4 nanoseconds. However, there have been situations in which NICs operating out-of-spec with respect to excessive jitter can cause link up/down situations on Catalyst 6500 10/100 ports. The workaround for this issue is to increase the jitter tolerance on the Catalyst 6500 switches for 10/100 ports to 3.1 seconds. The command to enable this feature is **set option debounce enable**. The ultimate solution is to replace the out-of-spec NICs instead of using the debounce option.

Understanding Data Link Errors

Many performance issues with NICs can be related to data-link errors. Excessive errors usually indicate a problem. When operating at a half-duplex setting, some data-link errors such as Frame Check Sequence (FCS), alignment, runts, and collisions are normal. Generally, a 1 percent ratio of errors to total traffic is acceptable for half-duplex connections. If the ratio of errors to input packets is greater than 2 or 3 percent, you might notice performance degradation.

In half-duplex environments, it is possible for both the switch and the connected device to sense the wire and transmit at exactly the same time. This would result in a collision. Collisions can cause runts, FCS, and alignment errors because the frame isn't completely copied to the wire. This results in fragmented frames.

When operating at full duplex, FCS, Cyclic Redundancy Checks (CRCs), alignment errors, and runt counters should be minimal. If the link is operating at full duplex, the collision counter is inactive. If the FCS, CRC, alignment, or runt counters are incrementing, check for a duplex mismatch. Duplex mismatch is a situation in which the switch is operating at full duplex and the connected device is operating at half duplex, or the other way around. The result of a duplex mismatch is extremely slow performance, intermittent connectivity, and loss of connection. Duplex mismatch is a common problem. Other possible causes of data link errors at full duplex are bad cables, a faulty switch port, and NIC software or hardware issues.

When troubleshooting NIC performance issues, view the output of the **show port** *mod#/port#* command and the **show mac** *mod#/port#* command, and note the counter information. See Tables B-1 to B-4. Table B-1 describes counters seen in the **show port** command output.

Table B-1 CatOS **show port** Command Counters

Counter	Description
Alignment Errors	Alignment errors are a count of the number of frames received that do not end with an even number of octets and that have a bad CRC.
FCS	FCS error count is the number of frames that were transmitted or received with a bad checksum (CRC value) in the Ethernet frame. These frames are dropped and are not propagated onto other ports.
Xmit-Err	This indicates that the internal transmit buffer is full.
Rcv-Err	This indicates that the receive buffer is full.
UnderSize	These are frames that are smaller than 64 bytes (including FCS) and that have a good FCS value.
Single Collisions	Single collisions are the number of times the transmitting port had one collision before successfully transmitting the frame to the medium.
Multiple Collisions	Multiple collisions are the number of times the transmitting port had more than one collision before successfully transmitting the frame to the medium.
Late Collisions	A late collision occurs when two devices transmit at the same time and neither side of the connection detects a collision. The reason for this occurrence is because the time to propagate the signal from one end of the network to the other is longer than the time to put the entire packet on the network. The two devices that cause the late collision never see that the other is sending until after it puts the entire packet on the network. Late collisions are detected by the transmitter after the first slot time of 64-byte times. They are detected only during transmissions of packets longer than 64 bytes. Its detection is exactly the same as for a normal collision; it just happens late when compared to a normal collision.
Excessive Collisions	Excessive collisions are the number of frames that are dropped after 16 attempts to send the packet, resulting in 16 collisions.

Table B-1 CatOS **show port** Command Counters (Continued)

Counter	Description
Carrier Sense	Carrier sense occurs every time an Ethernet controller wants to send data and the counter is incremented when there is an error in the process.
Runts	These are frames smaller than 64 bytes with a bad FCS value.
Giants	These are frames that are greater than 1518 bytes and that have a bad FCS value.

Table B-2 describes possible causes of increasing values for various CatOS counters associated with ports.

Table B-2 Possible Causes of Incrementing CatOS Counters

Counter	Description
Alignment Errors	These are the result of collisions at half duplex, duplex mismatch, bad hardware (NIC, cable, or port), or connected device generating frames that do not end with an octet and that have a bad FCS.
FCS	These are the result of collisions at half duplex, duplex mismatch, bad hardware (NIC, cable, or port), or a connected device generating frames with a bad FCS.
Xmit-Err	This counter indicates excessive input rates of traffic. It also indicates that the transmit buffer is full. This counter should increment only when the switch is unable to forward out the port at a desired rate. Situations such as excessive collisions and 10 Mb ports cause the transmit buffer to become full. Increasing the speed and moving the link partner to full duplex should minimize this occurrence.
Rcv-Err	This counter indicates excessive output rates of traffic. It also indicates that the receive buffer is full. This counter should be 0 unless there is excessive traffic through the switch. In some switches, the outlost counter has a direct correlation to Rcv-Err.
UnderSize	This counter indicates a bad frame generated by the connected device.
Single Collisions	This counter indicates a half-duplex configuration.
Multiple Collisions	This counter indicates a half-duplex configuration.

continues

Table B-2 Possible Causes of Incrementing CatOS Counters (Continued)

Counter	Description
Late Collisions	This counter indicates faulty hardware (NIC, cable, or switch port) or duplex mismatch.
Excessive Collisions	This counter indicates overutilization of the switch port at half duplex or a duplex mismatch.
Carrier Sense	This counter indicates faulty hardware (NIC, cable, or switch port).
Runts	This counter is a result of collisions, duplex mismatch, dot1q, or an Inter-Switch Link (ISL) configuration issue.
Giants	On older hardware, this counter indicates faulty hardware, dot1q, or an ISL configuration issue. Newer devices can support giant (or jumbo) frames. Jumbo frames permit enhanced performance on Gigabit and 10 Gigabit Ethernet links.

Table B-3 explains the counters displayed in the **show mac** CatOS command.

Table B-3 CatOS **show mac** Command Counters

Counter	Description
Rcv-Unicast	This counter indicates the number of unicast packets received.
Rcv-Multicast	This counter indicates the number of multicast packets received.
Rcv-Broadcast	This counter indicates the number of broadcast packets received.
Xmit-Unicast	This counter indicates the number of unicast packets transmitted.
Xmit-Multicast	This counter indicates the number of multicast packets transmitted.
Xmit-Broadcast	This counter indicates the number of broadcast packets transmitted.
Delay Exceeded	This counter indicates the number of frames discarded because of excessive delay in the switching process.
MTU-Exced	This counter indicates that one of the devices on the port or segment is transmitting more than the allowed frame size.
In-Discard	This counter is a count of valid frames received that were discarded or filtered by the forwarding process.
Lrn-Discard	This counter indicates packets that are forwarded that should not be forwarded.

Table B-3 CatOS **show mac** Command Counters (Continued)

Counter	Description
In-Lost	This counter indicates packets that could not be received because the input buffers are full.
Out-Lost	This counter indicates packets that could not be transmitted because the output buffers are full.

Table B-4 lists common causes of increasing values for certain CatOS counters.

Table B-4 Possible Causes of Incrementing CatOS Counters

Counter	Possible Cause
Delay Exced	A severe problem with the switch. Open a case with the TAC.
MTU-Exced	Verify ISL and dot1q configurations. Verify that another switch or router is not injecting frame over MTU into the switch network.
Lrn-Discard	Increments when the switch receives traffic on a trunk for a specific VLAN while the switch does not have any other ports on that VLAN. This counter also increments when the packet's destination address is learned on the port on which the packet is received.
In-Lost	Excessive input rate of traffic.
Out-Lost	Excessive output rate of traffic. Increments in this counter are more likely to occur when connected to low-speed devices. The first step in troubleshooting Out-Lost increments is to verify that the link partner is running 100 Mbps full duplex without any errors.

You can see additional counter information by issuing the command **show counter** *mod#/ port#*. You must issue this command for a single port at a time.

Gigabit Auto-Negotiation (No Link to the Connected Device)

Gigabit Ethernet has an auto-negotiation procedure that is more extensive than what is used for 10/100 Mbps Ethernet (Gigabit auto-negotiation spec IEEE Std 802.3z-1998). Gigabit auto-negotiation negotiates flow control, duplex mode, and remote fault information. You must either enable or disable link negotiation on both ends of the link. Both ends of the link must be set to the same value, or the link will not connect.

If either device does not support Gigabit auto-negotiation, disabling Gigabit auto-negotiation forces the link up. The default configuration on all Cisco switches is for auto-negotiation to be enabled. Disabling auto-negotiation hides link drops and other physical layer problems. Only disable auto-negotiation to end devices such as older Gigabit NICs that do not support Gigabit auto-negotiation. Do not disable auto-negotiation between switches unless absolutely required, because physical layer problems might go undetected and result in spanning tree loops. The alternative to disabling auto-negotiation is contacting the vendor for a software or hardware upgrade for IEEE 802.3z Gigabit auto-negotiation support.

Issue the following command for Gigabit auto-negotiation configuration:

```
set port negotiation mod#/port# enable | disable
```

Port Shown in errDisable State by show port Command

A port might be errDisabled (error-disabled) for many reasons. Some of the error conditions are as follows:

- Duplex mismatch
- Port-channel misconfiguration
- Bridge Protocol Data Unit (BPDU) guard violation
- Unidirectional Link Detection (UDLD) condition
- Broadcast suppression
- Address Resolution Protocol (ARP) inspection
- Crossbar fallback
- Security options, such as port security

When a port is errDisabled, it is effectively shut down; no traffic is sent or received on that port. The port light emitting diode (LED) is set to the color amber, and when you issue the **show port** command, the port status shows errDisable. Example B-3 shows what an errDisabled port looks like from the switch's command-line interface (CLI).

Example B-3 *Verifying errDisable State with CatOS*

```
Console> (enable) show port 11/1
Port  Name              Status     Vlan       Level  Duplex Speed Type
----- ----------------- ---------- ---------- ------ ------ ----- ------------
11/1                    errDisable 1          normal  auto   auto 10/100BaseTX


---- output omitted ----
```

To recover from errDisable state, you have to disable and reenable the port by issuing the **set port disable** *mod/port* and **set port enable** *mod/port* commands.

For further information on the errDisable state, see the article "Recovering From errDisable Port State on the CatOS Platforms" at the following site. It explains the causes of ports going into an errDisable state and provides further troubleshooting steps to avoid the condition.

www.cisco.com/en/US/tech/tk389/tk214/technologies_tech_note09186a0080093dcb.shtml

Troubleshooting Unicast IP Routing with Cisco Express Forwarding

If connectivity issues are occurring between workstations in different VLANs, you might need to troubleshoot the Cisco Express Forwarding (CEF) feature on the Catalyst 6500 Supervisor 2-based systems to ensure that proper entries are available in the hardware forwarding tables. This section discusses troubleshooting IP routing on a Catalyst 6500 with a Supervisor Engine 2 (Sup 2), Policy Feature Card 2 (PFC 2), and Multilayer Switch Feature Card 2 (MSFC 2). First, we'll briefly review CEF.

CEF was originally an IOS switching technique designed to route packets faster. CEF is much more scalable than fast switching (there is no need to send the first packet to process switching). The Catalyst 6500 with Sup 2 uses a hardware-based CEF forwarding mechanism implemented on the PFC 2. CEF mainly uses two tables to store the information needed for routing: the Forwarding Information Base (FIB) and the adjacency table.

CEF uses a FIB to make IP destination prefix-based switching decisions (longest match first). The FIB is conceptually similar to a routing table or information base. It maintains a mirror image of the forwarding information contained in the IP routing table. When routing or topology changes occur in the network, the IP routing table is updated, and those changes are reflected in the FIB. The FIB maintains the next-hop address information based on the information in the IP routing table. Because of a one-to-one correlation between FIB entries and routing table entries, the FIB contains all known routes and eliminates the need for route cache maintenance that is associated with switching paths, such as fast switching and optimum switching. There will always be a match in the FIB, whether default or wildcard.

Nodes in the network are said to be adjacent if they can reach each other with a single hop across a link layer. In addition to the FIB, CEF uses adjacency tables to prepend Layer 2 (L2) addressing information. The adjacency table maintains L2 next-hop addresses for all FIB entries. This means that a complete FIB entry contains a pointer to a location in the adjacency table that holds the L2 rewrite information for the next hop to reach the final IP destination. For the hardware CEF to work on the Catalyst 6500/Sup 2 system, IP CEF needs to run on the MSFC 2.

How to Read the FIB and Adjacency Table on PFC 2

The FIB table of the PFC 2 should be exactly the same as the FIB table on the MSFC 2. On the PFC 2, all IP prefixes in the FIB are stored in Ternary Content Addressable Memory (TCAM) and are sorted by mask length starting with the longest mask. This means that first you find all the entries with a mask of 32 (host entry), and then all entries with a mask length of 31, and so on until you reach an entry with a mask length of 0. This is the default entry. The FIB is read sequentially, and the first hit is used as a match. Consider the FIB table on the PFC 2 displayed in Example B-4.

Example B-4 *Viewing the CEF FIB Table on the PFC 2 on a Catalyst 6500*

```
Cat6k> (enable) show mls entry cef

Mod FIB-Type Destination-IP  Destination-Mask NextHop-IP      Weight

--- --------- --------------- ---------------- --------------- ------

15 receive   0.0.0.0         255.255.255.255

!--- First entry with mask length 32.

15 receive   255.255.255.255 255.255.255.255

15 receive   192.168.254.254 255.255.255.255

15 receive   10.48.72.237    255.255.255.255

15 receive   10.48.72.0      255.255.255.255

15 receive   10.48.72.255    255.255.255.255

15 receive   192.168.222.7   255.255.255.255

15 receive   192.168.100.254 255.255.255.255

15 receive   192.168.10.254  255.255.255.255

15 resolved  192.168.199.3   255.255.255.255  192.168.199.3      1

15 resolved  192.168.222.2   255.255.255.255  192.168.222.2      1

15 resolved  192.168.199.2   255.255.255.255  192.168.199.2      1

15 resolved  192.168.254.252 255.255.255.255  192.168.199.3      1

!--- Last entry with mask length 32.

15 connected 192.168.222.0   255.255.255.252

!--- Only entry with mask length 30.

15 receive   224.0.0.0       255.255.255.0

!--- First entry with mask length 24.

15 connected 10.48.72.0      255.255.255.0

15 connected 192.168.10.0    255.255.255.0

15 connected 192.168.11.0    255.255.255.0

15 connected 192.168.100.0   255.255.255.0
```

Example B-4 *Viewing the CEF FIB Table on the PFC 2 on a Catalyst 6500 (Continued)*

```
15 connected 192.168.101.0   255.255.255.0
15 connected 192.168.199.0   255.255.255.0
!--- Last entry with mask length 24.
15 connected 127.0.0.0        255.0.0. 0
!--- Entry with mask length 8.
15 wildcard  0.0.0.0          0.0.0. 0
!--- Entry with mask length 0.
```

Each entry consists of the following fields:

- **Mod**—The MSFC 2 that installs the entry is either 15 or 16, depending on which is the designated MSFC 2.
- **FIB-Type**—The type associated with this specific entry. The possible FIB-Types are as follows:
  - **receive**—The prefix associated with MSFC interfaces. It contains a prefix with a mask of 32 corresponding to the IP address of the MSFC interfaces and an IP address of the broadcast subnet.
  - **resolved**—The prefix associated with a valid next-hop address. It contains any prefix with a resolved adjacency for the next hop.
  - **connected**—The prefix associated with a connected network.
  - **wildcard**—Matches all entries (drop or MSFC redirect). This entry is present only if no default entry exists, and it is present with a mask length of 0.
  - **default**—The default route. As the wildcard entry, it matches all subnets and is present with a mask length of 0. It points to the next hop. This default CEF entry is present only if a default route is present in the routing table.
  - **drop**—All packets matching an entry with a drop are dropped.
- **Destination-IP**—The destination IP address or IP subnet concerned.
- **Destination-Mask**—The mask associated with the entry. As you can see, the FIB is ranked starting with the longest mask (255.255.255.255) and ends with the shortest possible mask (0.0.0.0).
- **Next-Hop IP**—Displays the next-hop IP if it exists.
- **Weight**—Next hop loadsharing weight.

You can view the complete adjacency table by entering the command shown in Example B-5.

Example B-5 *Viewing the CEF Adjacency Table*

```
Cat6k> (enable) show mls entry cef adjacency
Mod:15
Destination-IP : 192.168.98.2 Destination-Mask : 255.255.255.255
FIB-Type :resolved
AdjType NextHop-IP      NextHop-Mac        VLAN Encp Tx-Packets   Tx-Octets
------- --------------- ------------------ ---- ---- ------------ ----------
connect  192.168.98.2    00-90-21-41-c5-57   98 ARPA          0            0
```

Troubleshooting Method

Before going into some examples and details of troubleshooting, this section summarizes the methods used to troubleshoot connectivity or reachability to a specific IP address. Keep in mind that the CEF table on the PFC 2 is a mirror of the CEF table on the MSFC 2. Therefore, the PFC 2 holds the correct information to reach an IP address only if the information known by the MSFC 2 is also correct. As such, you always need to verify the following information:

From the MSFC 2:

Step 1   Verify that the information held in the IP routing on the MSFC 2 table is correct by issuing the **sh ip route** command (or **sh ip route** *x.x.x.x* to avoid browsing the complete routing table), and verify that the output contains the expected next hop. If it doesn't, you need to check the routing protocol, configuration, routing protocol neighbor, and any other troubleshooting that is relevant to the routing protocol you are running.

Step 2   Verify that the next hop (or the final destination for the connected network) has a correct resolved ARP entry on the MSFC 2 by issuing the **sh ip arp** **next_hop_ip_address** command to verify that the ARP is resolved and contains the correct Media Access Control (MAC) address. If the MAC address is incorrect, you need to verify whether another device owns that IP address. Eventually, you need to track the switch level on the port that connects the device that owns that MAC address. If the ARP entry is incomplete, this means that you did not get any replies from that host. You need to verify that the host is up and running. A sniffer might be used on the host to see if it gets the ARP reply and if it answers correctly.

Step 3   Verify that the CEF table on the MSFC 2 contains the correct information and that adjacency is resolved by performing the following steps:

a. Issue the **sh ip cef destination_network** command to verify that the next hop in the CEF table matches the next hop in the IP routing table (from Step 1).

b. Verify that the adjacency is correct by issuing the **sh adjacency detail | begin next_hop_ip_address** command. This should contain the same MAC address of the ARP seen in Step 2.

If Steps 1 and 2 provide correct results, but Step 3a or 3b fails, you are facing an IOS CEF issue that is likely unrelated to the Catalyst 6000. You must try to clear the ARP table and the IP route table.

From the PFC 2:

Step 1   Verify that the FIB information stored on the PFC 2 is correct and matches the information stored in the CEF table on the MSFC 2 (as seen previously in Step 3) by issuing the **show mls entry cef ip destination_ip_network/destination_ subnet_mask** command and verifying that the next-hop IP address is the one you expect. If this information does not match the results in Step 3, this points to a communication problem between the MSFC 2 and the PFC 2 (internal to the Catalyst 6000). Verify that there is not a known bug for the CatOS of the PFC 2 or the IOS of the MSFC 2 that you are running. You can restore the correct entry by issuing the **clear ip route** command on the MSFC 2.

Step 2   Verify the adjacency table on the PFC 2 by issuing the **show mls entry cef ip next_hop_ip_address/32 adjacency** command to verify that it contains the same MAC address as the one seen previously in Steps 2 and 3b. If the adjacency in the PFC 2 does not match the adjacency for the next hop in Step 3b, you are probably facing an issue of internal communication between the MSFC 2 and PFC 2. You can try clearing the adjacency to restore the correct information.

Step 3   Call the TAC if problems persist after you follow the suggested guidelines for the MSFC 2 and PFC 2.

Glossary

attenuation   Loss of communication signal energy.

baseline   A collection of data used to determine where opportunities exist for optimizing the network environment. A network baseline is used to decide whether to make recommendations to add bandwidth or introduce quality of service to enhance services.

baseline analysis   The interpretation of the data collected in a baseline.

baselining   The process of collecting data to be used as a reference for future decision-making and troubleshooting.

Bootstrap Protocol (BootP)   A protocol that lets a network user automatically receive an IP address and have an operating system booted without user involvement. The BOOTP server automatically assigns the IP address from a pool of addresses for a certain duration of time. BOOTP is the basis for the more advanced protocol DHCP.

channel service unit (CSU)   A digital interface device that connects end-user equipment to the local digital telephone loop. Often referred to with DSU as CSU/DSU.

crosstalk   Interfering energy transferred from one circuit to another.

cyclic redundancy check (CRC)   An error-checking technique in which the frame recipient calculates a remainder by dividing frame contents by a prime binary divisor and compares the calculated remainder to a value stored in the frame by the sending node.

data service unit (DSU)   A device used in digital transmission that adapts the physical interface on a DTE device to a transmission facility such as T1 or E1. The DSU is also responsible for such functions as signal timing. Often referred to with CSU as CSU/DSU.

discard route   A route that sends packets to null0, the bit bucket, when there is no specific match in the routing table and it is undesirable to have those packets forwarded using a supernet or default route.

discontiguous network   A subnet of a major network separated by a subnet of another major network.

electromagnetic interference (EMI)   Interference by electromagnetic signals that can cause reduced data integrity and increased error rates on transmission channels.

end-system network configuration table   Baseline documentation that shows accurate records of the hardware and software used in end systems.

end-system topology diagram   A graphical representation of selected tabular data gathered in the end-system network configuration table.

expert system   A system that uses a set of rules, combined with information about network configuration and operation, to diagnose, solve, or offer potential solutions to network problems.

Internet Message Access Protocol (IMAP)   The standard protocol for accessing e-mail from your local server. IMAP is a client/server protocol in which your Internet server receives and holds e-mail for you. You can view just the heading and the sender of the letter, and then decide whether to download the mail. You can also create and manipulate multiple folders or mailboxes on the server, delete messages, and search for certain parts or an entire note. IMAP requires continual access to the server during the time you are working with your mail.

jabber   A condition in which a network device continually transmits random, meaningless data onto the network.

knowledge base   A database collection of empirical information on a specific technical area. It includes real solutions to common problems encountered.

Macof   A popular tool for launching a MAC flooding attack. Macof can generate 155,000 MAC entries on a switch per minute. The switch sees this traffic and thinks that the MAC address from the packet the attacker sent is a valid port and adds an entry. The goal is to flood the switch with traffic by filling the CAM table with false entries. After it is flooded, the switch broadcasts traffic without a CAM entry out its local VLAN, allowing the attacker to see traffic he or she wouldn't ordinarily see.

maximum transmission unit (MTU)   The largest Layer 3 packet that can be forwarded out a router or switch interface.

NetBEUI (NetBIOS Extended User Interface)   An extended version of NetBIOS. NetBEUI formalizes the frame format that was not specified as part of NetBIOS. NetBEUI was developed by IBM for its LAN Manager product and has been adopted by Microsoft for its Windows NT, LAN Manager, and Windows for Workgroups products.

NetBIOS (Network Basic Input/Output System)   A program that allows applications on different computers to communicate within a LAN. It was created by IBM for its early PC Network, was adopted by Microsoft, and has since become a de facto industry standard.

network configuration table   A table including accurate, up-to-date records of the hardware and software used in a network. The network configuration table should provide the trouble-shooter with all of the information necessary to identify and correct the network fault.

Network File System (NFS)   Allows computers to mount drives on remote hosts and operate them as if they were local drives.

noise   Undesirable communications channel signals. Random noise can be generated by many sources, including wireless communications such as FM radio stations, police radio, building security, avionics for automated landing, and many more.

nonbroadcast multiaccess (NBMA) network   A multiaccess network that does not support broadcasting (such as Frame Relay) or in which broadcasting is not feasible (for example, an SMDS broadcast group).

Pretty Good Privacy (PGP)   A program used to encrypt and decrypt e-mail over the Internet. It can also be used to send an encrypted digital signature that lets the receiver verify the sender's identity and know that the message was not changed en route.

Remote Procedure Call (RPC)   A protocol that one program can use to request a service from a program located in another computer in a network without having to understand net-work details. The requesting program is a client, and the service-providing program is the server. Like a regular or local procedure call, an RPC is a synchronous operation that requires the requesting program to be suspended until the results of the remote procedure are returned.

return loss   A measure of all reflections that are caused by the impedance mismatches at all locations along the link. It indicates how well the characteristic impedance of the cable matches its rated impedance over a range of frequencies.

Systems Network Architecture (SNA)   A large, complex, feature-rich network architecture developed in the 1970s by IBM. Similar in some respects to the OSI reference model, but with a number of differences. SNA is essentially composed of seven layers: data flow control, data link control, path control, physical control, presentation services, transaction services, and transmission control.

threshold   A measure that indicates a warning level, such as collisions and errors.

topology diagram   A graphical representation of a network. A topology diagram illustrates how each device in a network is connected, while also detailing the aspects of its logical architecture.

X Window System   A popular protocol that permits intelligent terminals to communicate with remote computers as if they were directly attached.

Index

OSPF, 400–403
RIP, 395–397
RIP, 276
   discontiguous networks, 285–289
   flapping routes, 291–294
   incompatible version types, 277–281
   invalid source addresses, 289–291
   large routing tables, 294–296
   metric maximums, 284–285
   mismatched authentication keys, 281–284
static routes, 241
   classful lookups, 242–244
   intermediate addresses, 244–246
   optimization, 246–249
   recurring, 250–254

Layer 4
ACLs, 433–435
complex network systems, troubleshooting, 473–481
eliminating, 491–492
extended ACLs, 435–437
hosts, troubleshooting, 465
NAT, 438–441
NetBEUI, 441–446
NetBIOS, 441–446
TCP, 428–433
technologies, 423–426
tools, troubleshooting, 461–465
troubleshooting, 446
   gathering ACL information, 452–454
   misconfiguring extended ACLs, 446–452
   NAT interoperability, 456–461
   optimizing ACLs, 455
UDP, 427–428

Layer 4 transport layer, 487
layers
application. *See* application layer, 487
eliminating, 491–492
frames, loss of, 159

modular, 46
   control information, 50
   data encapsulation, 46–48
   decapsulation, 51
   device locations, 52–53
   OSI/TCP/IP comparisons, 51
   physical medium bits, 49–50
physical, 84
   attenuation, 91–92
   cabling faults, 109–112
   collisions, 93–95, 114–116
   configuration script errors, 117
   connectivity, 84
   console messages, 88–90
   CPU overload, 118–121
   EMI, 116–117
   end-system commands, 102–106
   equipment indicators, 86
   error messages, 99–102
   failing cables, 123–126
   ghosts, 97
   hardware failures, 113
   interrface configurations, 126–127
   isolation, 121–122
   jabber, 96
   noise, 92–93
   operational statistics, 128–131
   optimizaton, 90
   performance lower than baselines, 90
   power failures, 87–88, 107–109
   redundancy, 136
   resources, 97–98
   return loss, 92
   short frames, 96
   solutions, 131–135
   support, 137
   transmissons, 96–97
   upper layer component operations, 84
   utilization, 98–99
protocol analyzers, 521